Lisa Gaupp & Giulia Pelillo-Hestermeyer (Eds.)
**Diversity and Otherness**
**Transcultural Insights into Norms, Practices, Negotiations**

Lisa Gaupp & Giulia Pelillo-Hestermeyer (Eds.)

# Diversity and Otherness

Transcultural Insights into Norms, Practices, Negotiations

Managing Editor: Katarzyna Michalak
Associate Editor: Francesca Corazza
Language Editor: Adam Tod Leverton

 DE GRUYTER

Published by De Gruyter Ltd, Warsaw/Berlin
Part of Walter de Gruyter GmbH, Berlin/Munich/Boston

© 2021 Lisa Gaupp & Giulia Pelillo-Hestermeyer (Eds.)
ISBN: 978-83-66675-29-2
ISBN (pdf): 978-83-66675-30-8
ISBN (epub): 978-83-66675-31-5


Managing Editor: Katarzyna Michalak
Associate Editor: Francesca Corazza
Language Editor: Adam Tod Leverton


www.degruyteropen.com

Cover illustration: © geralt/pixabay
Complimentary copy, not for sale.

# Contents

# List of Contributing Authors

**Giulia Pelillo-Hestermeyer**
University of Heidelberg, Germany
*Chapter 1, 8, 13*

**Lisa Gaupp**
Leuphana University of Lüneburg, Germany
*Chapter 2, 12, 14*

**Stefan Hirschauer**
Johannes Gutenberg University Mainz (JGU),
Germany
*Chapter 3*

**Kijan Espahangizi**
ETH and University of Zurich, Switzerland
*Chapter 4*

**Joseph Ciaudo**
Orléans University, France
*Chapter 5*

**Susanne Marten-Finnis**
University of Portsmouth, UK
*Chapter 6*

**Barbara Ursula Oettl**
University of Regensburg / Kunstakademie Düs-
seldorf, Germany
*Chapter 7*

**Dagmar Reichardt**
Latvian Academy of Culture, Riga, Latvia
*Chapter 9*

**Marta Niccolai**
University College London, UK
*Chapter 10*

**Marek Sancho Höhne**
European University Viadrina, Germany
*Chapter 11*

**Fabio Cismondi**
Fusion for Energy, Rokkasho, Japan
*Chapter 13*

# Acknowledgements

There have been many persons who contributed, in one way or another, to this publication: our colleagues and friends within and outside both the University of Heidelberg and the Leuphana University of Lüneburg, the colleagues who participated in our panels at the annual conferences of the Kulturwissenschaftliche Gesellschaft (KWG), our students, the interviewees and all the people who, also outside of our academic life, shared with us their stories of and ideas about diversity and otherness. Any list of them would be incomplete, yet we would like to thank all of them.

A special thanks is due to the people who have directly contributed to the making of this book: the authors, for their trust and the constructive cooperation throughout the whole project. To the anonymous reviewers, for their valuable input and criticism. To Jonathan Griffith, who was an incredibly attentive proofreader with outstanding time-management. To Anna Oldiges and Annette Grigoleit, for their careful help in formatting the volume. To Katarzyna Michalak at De Gruyter, who guided us with care and competence through the publication process.

For the possibility to publish this book in open access we are particularly grateful to the Cluster of Excellence "Asia and Europe in a Global Context" at the University of Heidelberg, who supported us with a generous publication grant.

A very warm thanks to our respective families, who have patiently followed us through this project, turning, whenever necessary, into engaged listeners and cultural studies scholars. Three of our children, Leya, Nicolò and Lorenzo, were born during the period in which this book has been conceived and realized. They were among the youngest participants at several annual conferences of the KWG.

Lisa Gaupp & Giulia Pelillo-Hestermeyer

Giulia Pelillo-Hestermeyer

# 1 Re-thinking Diversity and Transculturality: Introduction

At the origin of the cooperation that eventually led to this book, there is the idea of emphasizing the gap between the ordinariness of diversity, as it occurs in everyday life, and the many ways of representing and addressing it as something exceptional, independently of whether those representations and practices carry with them positive or negative connotations. On the one hand, it would be reasonable to consider diversity and otherness as constitutive characters, not only of any group, but also of any individual identity, since we all learn to see and think about ourselves by relying on other people's opinions, speech, behaviour. Identity is a never-ending process of construction of, respectively, "the self" and "the other", and as such it is anything but a homogeneous or stable entity. Consequently, as it has been rightly argued (s., among others, Fuchs, 2007, p. 20), it is not diversity, but the belief in an alleged homogeneity of cultures and cultural identities, that needs an explanation. On the other hand, diversity is *made* visible and addressed as extraordinary in many ways, ranging from political debates about the "limits of tolerance" to stereotyped forms of cultural hybridity in fashion or in the advertising business. Sometimes such representations (whether iconic, discursive, mediated, etc.) highlight the coolness, attractiveness, or even the efficiency of hybridity, such as, for example in the display of "exotic" beauty or innovative technologies. More often, especially if referring to societal developments, they pose a challenge to social unity and stability. Independently of which position is taken in this regard, representations of diversity and otherness carry with them emotional connotations and easily arouse emotions of many sorts, giving rise to various conflicts, both in public debate and in private conversations. Diversity has many faces and shapes, some of which are represented as prettier than others. The more diversity is thematized as something extraordinary and becomes a keyword in policies, organizational or marketing strategies, the more it appears to be regulated and standardized in ways that spread and strengthen ideas about how it "really" is or should be. This process of standardization and regulation contributes to the affirmation of *specific* forms of diversity over others, as shown by several contributions in this volume. For example, the "otherness" of a nomadic way of life is praised by high fashion as a form of globalized cosmopolitanism and modernity (Reichardt), whereas it is contrasted by political policies constraining nomadic ethnic groups within marginalized areas (Niccolai). Furthermore, hybridity is acknowledged and appreciated in *some* artistic, linguistic or bodily practices, and rejected, tabooed, repressed or even persecuted in others. Why this happens can only be answered by examining, case by case, the contexts in which these processes of differentiation take place, including the various forms of agency deriving from the power relationships at stake. Whether differences are acknowledged or rejected, praised or criticized, and even what "different" stands for is contextually bounded.

This volume has been conceived with the purpose of examining as broad as possible a spectrum of contexts in which diversity and otherness are negotiated and have been negotiated in the past. In it we wish to stress the processes of regulation, standardization, and even homogenization which take place in their respective contexts, when specific socio-cultural features are made relevant to create asymmetries and hierarchies between individuals, groups and cultural resources. The variety of such *processes of differentiation* turns the ordinariness of diversity as a human condition into a particularly complex socio-cultural field, which has given rise in recent years to a distinctive area of studies. Processes such as globalization, decolonization, migration, and "mediatization"[1] have not only made diversity more visible in daily life, but have also placed it at the centre-stage of societal, political and cultural change, greatly attracting the attention of both scholarly and non-scholarly debates in the past two decades. Steven Vertovec (2007) has spoken, in this context, of *super-diversity*, meaning a "diversification of diversity", due to the multiple possibilities for people, goods and a variety of resources to cross, whether virtually or physically, territorial and cultural boundaries. Such diversification is also reflected by the range of terms and concepts related to the field of culture, which have arisen in different contexts of research, such as superculture (Lull, 2002), hybridity (García Canclini, 2005), transculturality (Welsch, 2005; Abu-Er-Rub et al., 2019a), and transdifference (Allolio-Näcke et al., 2005), just to name a few. These terms, while they differ in highlighting specific modes of difference among others, by privileging a particular perspective or methodological approach over others, are connected by the common goal of overcoming structuralist paradigms in favour of a constructivist approach, which is focused on cultural interconnectedness. All of them rely upon a plural conceptualization of culture, which seems to be the only suitable means to grasp conflicts, discrepancies and asymmetries arising in contexts of cultural contact, and, at the same time, to develop strategies for better handling, if not overcoming, such conflicts. On the one hand, the approach proposed by this volume to the study of diversity and otherness follows this perspective, while on the other hand it aims at further developing it by concentrating, thematically, on the mentioned gap between the diversity characterizing complex life-worlds, and the contingent processes of differentiation that take place in various contexts of practice. In this we intertwine the perspectives

---

1 The term "mediatization" has been coined in contemporary Media Studies to denote the stress which is currently given to the powerful influence of electronic media. Thus, whereas mediated communication mainly refers to the transmission of communication through any kind of medium, mediatized communication adds to this perspective the consideration of the institutions and the organizational structures involved in the production of media itself. For an overview of the concept of mediatization and its use in various academic fields, see Lundby (2009).

of, respectively, diversity and transcultural studies, as it will be further explained below. We are aware that both transculturality and diversity build particularly heterogeneous fields of research in themselves, displaying a range of asymmetries typical of interdisciplinary enterprises. With respect to diversity studies, for example, it has been observed that the vagueness of the term itself poses significative challenges. Vertovec (2015, pp. 2–3) identifies "at least six facets of 'diversity' discourses, policies and practices derived from a range of programmes, mission statements, campaigns and guidelines within institutions":

a) policies addressing a more equal redistribution of goods (jobs, education, housing etc.) towards minorities who have historically been the objects of discrimination;

b) policies aiming at fostering positive self-images of minorities and increasing their participation in social and political life;

c) actions for a better representativeness of minoritarian groups within institutions or a company or any other social environment;

d) programmes differentiating the offer of specific services, according to the heterogeneity of customers;

e) strategies aiming at increasing the market share of a company by taking advantage of the potential of a diverse workforce, with respect to a better understanding of different customers, or to a better image of the company in general;

f) diversity management policies designed for the achievement of the above-mentioned goals as well as maximizing the productivity of the enterprise.

The heterogeneity of the meanings and practices associated with the term 'diversity' represents one of the main challenges for scholars who aim to take a comprehensive look at differentiation processes. In this light, Brubaker (2012, as cited in Vertovec, 2015, p. 4) expresses the need for a clear distinction between diversity as, respectively, a category of analysis and a category of practice. Moreover, the use of the term to refer to multiple processes of both constructing social affiliations (e.g. class, gender, race, ethnicity, etc.) and handling differences (e.g. policies, programmes, etc.), challenges its usefulness with respect to classificatory operations. In response to this challenge, Vertovec (2015, pp. 10–14) suggests a focus on two main topics, which he calls, respectively, "modes of social differentiation" and "complex social environments". Whereas the first topic mainly relates to what has been addressed above as the social construction of differences—contributing, among others, to create and circulate specific concepts of diversity—the second focuses on the question of how "historically produced conditions comprising: social fields, structures of power, discursive idioms, institutional frameworks, system of access and denial, economic and material inequalities and spatial arrangements ... affect the ongoing dynamics of different modes of social differentiation" (Vertovec, 2015, p. 14). In other words, the challenge resides in deepening the mutual relationships between the simplifying mechanisms of classification, which in most cases build on and emphasize dichotomies (e.g. women-men, black-white, East-West, etc.), and the multiple social affiliations which characterize real-life contexts (e.g. living together in a neighbourhood).

In this volume, while we acknowledge the importance of distinguishing between the use of the term "diversity" for analytical vs. non-analytical purposes—such as normative, celebrative or common sense uses—we are also interested in a *comparison* between complex lived diversity, its regulation and standardization through a variety of practices, and the academic reflexion on both these aspects. Consequently, while we have adopted, whenever necessary, an epistemological distinction between diversity as a category of analysis vs. of practice, as suggested by Brubaker (2012, as cited in Vertovec, 2015, p. 4), we have also looked at scholarly approaches to diversity as a particular form of regulation and standardization itself, which are worthy, as such, of being critically addressed. This includes, for example, the questioning of established and/or outdated concepts that are applied in different fields to refer to cultural difference, which show their respective potential and limits from a comparative perspective.

In this context, Lisa Gaupp addresses diversity and otherness with respect to the study of culture in general, and, more specifically, in sociology of culture and cultural sociology. She identifies two main ways of approaching it: firstly, by focusing on individuals' overlapping social identities and secondly, with respect to processes of interweaving within cultural concepts. This chapter critically reviews the epistemological assumptions which often underlie discourses on cultural diversity, and highlights, among other aspects, how similar discourses can lead, paradoxically, to opposing attitudes towards diversity. As a result, a particularly wide range of processes of standardizing diversity and otherness becomes visible through her analysis, and are finally set in relation with their outcomes.

Next, Stefan Hirschauer critically reflects upon the study of cultural difference in the social sciences by examining three particular approaches to the idea of multiple affiliations: that is, respectively, the fields of intersectionality, the intersection of social circles, and hybridity. This chapter illustrates how each one of these areas, by devoting attention to specific features of difference such as inequality (intersectionality), functional differentiation due to individual membership (the intersection of social circles), and the crossing of boundaries (hybridity), has overestimated these aspects and neglected to take into account the contingency, temporariness, and multidimensionality of social distinctions. Here, the gap between normatively conceptualizing vs. lived diversity is highlighted by showing the contrast between scholarly approaches to cultural distinctions and their "socially constructed factuality", the latter of which consists of "practically executed 'real-world essentializations' that are materialized both bodily and situationally, and solidified institutionally". Against this background, the chapter suggestively emphasizes the contingency, temporariness and multidimensionality of diversity by investigating what differences are made relevant in which contexts, proceeding in a more empirical and transdisciplinary direction that is able to grasp the *gradations* of membership, relevance and institutionalization.

By comparing theory and practice, the ambivalence between "doing diversity" vs. "doing otherness" in a variety of practices (conceptualizations, discourses, policies, etc.) that, while aiming at promoting diversity, end up homogenizing, standardizing or hierarchizing its constitutive categories, appears particularly striking.

Kijan Espahangizi clearly shows this problematic by displaying a critical historical perspective towards controversial usages of the term "diversity" in Switzerland. This chapter tracks a progressive "culturalization" of the debate on migration from the 1970s to the 1990s, which has determined a still unresolved dualism in the conceptualization of diversity, which exists independently of the opposing *for* and *against* positions regarding immigration. The former refers to the four linguistic communities which are historically rooted in Switzerland, and which therefore relate to a "traditional" Swiss identity, while the latter, as a result of more recent migration and trends in globalization, focuses on "post-migrant" diversity. This chapter illustrates how such a dualism, by emphasizing cultural aspects of demographic pluralization, is responsible for the overlooking of other important issues, such as the reduction of social inequality. This facilitates, in turn, contradictory approaches to social heterogeneity and hinders the advancement of solutions which would be more adequate to the post-migrant reality. The historical perspective of the chapter adds significant insights to considering the contradictory ways of handling diversity, especially in contexts in which, paradoxically, great resources are invested in its promotion.

In light of such and similar incongruities, the choice not to explicitly address culture is often regarded as the best strategy to avoid so-called "intercultural" conflicts. This volume suggests instead that a transcultural approach can help in such cases. By referring to transculturality, we are aware that the term has a transcultural history itself, which goes back to the publication of *Contrapuncteo Cubano del tabaco y del azúcar* by Fernando Ortiz in 1940, and has known ever since multiple interdisciplinary intersections with other terms, such as hybridity, creolization and métissage, in a variety of disciplinary and interdisciplinary discourses (Abu-Er-Rub et al., 2019b, pp. xxiii–xiiv, and Gaupp in this volume for an overview). Similar to what was previously said with respect to diversity, this volume has not developed one specific definition of transculturality, nor does it aim at offering one. It rather looks at this concept as a *method* to emphasize the contrast between discursively established and ideologically marked categorizations commonly addressed as (e.g. national, popular, feminine, etc.) cultures, and their contingent negotiations in the social world. This means addressing culture as an intrinsically dynamic category, while acknowledging, at the same time, that static constructions and ideological dichotomies such as "the western vs. the eastern", "the feminine vs. the masculine", despite their epistemological groundlessness, do matter in the social world insofar as, among other things, they strengthen asymmetries and inequalities. Axel Michaels (2019) suggests that we distinguish between open, hidden and methodological transculturality in order to "overcome the aporia that one has to define culture or cultural elements which, transculturally seen, one has to deny" (p. 12). He indicates as open transculturality all the evident forms of cultural mixtures, whose elements can be clearly identified and separated, "since their historical process of amalgamation has been comparatively short. Indo-jazz, a mixture of hybridization of American jazz with influences from classical Indian music and instruments, would be such a form of open transculturality" (Michaels, 2019, p. 12). Hidden transculturality can be traced, instead, in all cultural forms, even if their elements are not immediately visible. He exemplifies this case by referring to the sarod used in Indo-jazz, which is not an "Indian" musical instrument but originally comes from Afghanistan. Michaels (2019) then concludes:

> It is only by using a methodological transculturality as a default mode or heuristic concept, i.e. by looking at the formative and transformative processes resulting in any given cultural manifestation, that we discover such cultural entanglements as a result of processes of negotiation, bargaining and competition which allow conclusions on monopoles of interpretation and power relationships. (Michaels, 2019, p. 12)

From this perspective, the application of a transcultural approach makes it possible to simultaneously recognize the fluidity of cultural entanglements (e.g. the crucial role of Afghan instruments in Indo-jazz) and the ways those entanglements become solidified in seemingly fixed categories (e.g. the "simple" cultural label "Indian" that gets attached to such music). The affinity between diversity and transcultural studies appears here to be particularly evident, insofar both fields are characterized by a particular "lens" to look at culture. Appadurai has described this specific approach by asserting that

> it [diversity] forces us to re-examine older ideas of culture and re-think some of the following questions: how does it work? How is it organized? What is culture as a system? How does its symbolism work? How do people get socialized into it or out of it? (Appadurai, 2009, as cited in Vertovec, 2015, p. 9)

By looking through such a lens, a second group of chapters focuses on different forms of "hidden" transculturality and highlight multiple negotiations of belongings, knowledge frameworks, ethics and forms of cultural capital in processes of cultural interconnectedness.

Joseph Ciaudo, for example, zooms in on the historical episode of the Chinese diplomat Wu Tingfang, who declined to adopt a Western dress code in his career at the beginning of the twentieth century. This chapter shows, through the comparison of a variety of texts by Wu, how his disapproval of Western clothing was not motivated by a conservative attitude towards the West in general. On the contrary, his profound knowledge of both "the East" and "the West" (that is, of the respective concepts of them circulating at the time) stimulated him to reflect comparatively upon a variety of aspects related to clothing, ranging from social to hygienic issues. Ciaudo illustrates how the rejection of "Western" clothes by Wu did not derive from a refusal of foreign customs in general, nor did it aim at demonstrating the superiority of one culture upon another. Wu was rather negotiating a "transcultural Modernity": a Modernity that was neither a "Western", nor an "Eastern" category, but an ideal of Civilization transcending single cultures.

Next, Susanne Marten-Finnis reflects upon the performance of "Oriental Otherness" staged by the *Ballet Russes* at the beginning of the twentieth century, which was met by both its Paris and London audiences with great enthusiasm. This chapter sheds light on the fortunate contrast between the "Oriental Other" displayed by the producers, and that which was imagined by the audiences. Marten-Finnis demonstrates that the "Oriental" identity displayed by the producers arose as a result of their encounter with a corpus of knowledge about decorative and performing arts from the—recently annexed—Southern Asian periphery of Russia, a knowledge acquired by Russian scholars, especially ethnographers, and mostly disregarded by the nation's politicians. European audiences, who were not aware of it, appreciated the "Oriental" settings and narratives by reading them as a kind of allegory through the lens of Symbolism. In her analysis, this chapter deconstructs the multilayered "acquired and imagined knowledge" about the "Oriental" identity displayed by the *Ballet Russes'* performances, stressing the negotiation of its features and meanings between the twin processes of production and reception. To conclude, Marten-Finnis examines such discrepancies by referring to Foucault's "theory of Other Spaces" (*heterotopia*), thus considering the productions of the *Ballet Russes* as counter-spaces outside the ordinary which stimulate the imagination. Moreover, she stresses how the impact of the *Ballet Russes* on the public revealed itself to be much greater than only affecting their imagination, by the impact that it had on the development of European Modernism. Lastly, the chapter shows how theatre can become a space that plays host to the transcultural negotiation of identities, stereotypes and cultural norms.

Barbara Ursula Oettl analyses the work of the multimedia and performance artist ORLAN, which brings the reflection upon the fundamental role played by alterity in the definition of the Self to its extreme consequences. ORLAN questions the integrity of the *Self*, and pinpoints its hybrid and fragile nature, owing to the numerous possibilities of deconstructing and reconstructing it through biotechnological and medical practices. The artist's projects, in which she literally transforms her physical appearance and her personality by undergoing a series of surgical and psychotherapeutic treatments, pose significant ethical and legal questions, such as the stability of identity in the wake of such dramatic self-modifications. The chapter thus emphasizes in striking ways that in an era of increasing biotechnological and biomedical manipulation the contours of the *Self* and the *Other*, the human and the cyborg, become negotiated every time anew.

A last set of chapters particularly concentrate on how diversity is *made* visible in different contexts, and emphasize the contrast between normalizing, levelling or even stereotyping diversity, and emerging, transculturally sensitive approaches to it.

My chapter on linguistic diversity takes its cue from the contrast between the ordinariness of lived multilingualism and the various forms of linguistic standardization which take place in different forms of media communication. In this context, the chapter stresses the fundamental role played by media institutions and organizations in spreading linguistic ideologies. On the one hand, the mostly monolingual national public spheres contribute to strengthen monocultural attitudes by overlooking the growing presence of linguistic diversity in contemporary life-worlds. A similar attitude in resisting language mix can be observed in transnational public spheres, which are characterized by the simple juxtaposition of single—mostly national—languages, which exemplifies what has been called "parallel monolingualism" (Heller, 1999), or "pluralised monolingualism" (Makoni & Pennycook, 2007). In contrast with these practices, different sorts of linguistic hybridity are compared: on the one hand, the mix of Hindi and English in Indian cinema, which has known in recent times great success in globalized media industries, becoming a symbol of cosmopolitanism and modernity but also of "Murdochization" of the media worldwide. On the other, a number of alternative ways of handling language diversity in transnational mediascapes, which make *lived* multilingual realities more visible in public spheres. The chapter relates the different ways of handling linguistic diversity to respective cultural ideologies, some of them with a long tradition dating back to ideologies of modernity and to the formation of the nation state, others emerging in the context of current "meta-processes" (Krotz, 2009) as the globalization, commercialization, individualization and mediatization of culture.

The globalization of Hinglish can be compared, to some extent, to the globalization of Italian fashion, which is analysed by Dagmar Reichardt in the next chapter. Both cases show how specific forms of hybridity, by acquiring symbolic value on a globalized "market of cultural resources" (Bourdieu, 1982/1991) and thus becoming symbols of cosmopolitan life-styles, undergo various processes of regulation and standardization. Reichardt examines the negotiation of diversity and otherness in Italian fashion in the context of its transcultural circulation, by considering the multiple processes of re-writing the label "Italian fashion" in the framework of its de- and reterritorialization, "glocalization", re-appropriation of cultural symbols in- and outside the Italian context. She considers fashion as a semiotic language which is employed, today just as in the past, to negotiate a variety of cultural norms and traditions related to (even stereotyped) Italian identities. This chapter stresses the "polyphony" of the language of fashion, combining representations of class, gender, and race which circulate through power discourses, and which address both the socio-political and the artistic spheres, for example through street wear and high fashion. In this light Reichardt emphasizes how fashion can arouse imaginative spaces, which stimulate a confrontation with the *Self* and the *Other*, therein acquiring a subversive potential.

In a similar vein but in a different context, Marta Niccolai enquires into the reversing of perspectives in theatrical performances, in which Italian dramaturges such as Pino Petruzzelli, Fiorenza Menni and Andrea Mochi Sismondi, cooperate with members of Roma communities. Particular attention is devoted to the overthrowing of power relationships through the possibilities, offered by the theatre, to trade roles and perspectives, for example by displaying a marginalized minority, whose stories are usually narrated from the perspective of the majority, onto the stage. As a result, diversity and otherness, and the respective norms which define both categories, turn to be uncertain through their deconstruction on-stage.

Next, Marek Sancho Höhne critically discusses discrepancies between circulating hegemonic representations and self-narrations of trans_gendered identities in different contexts in Germany. In particular, by highlighting the striking contrast between medico-legal standards (which hold transsexuality to be a disease and aim to cure it) and self-narrations by interviewed trans_people, the author illuminates how complex negotiations of identities are dramatically simplified by the homogenizing power of widespread practices. Furthermore, by considering the intersection between gender, religious, race and national attributes in representing trans_gender people, the chapter questions circulating narratives, which strengthen stereotypes related to a variety of diversities, and deconstructs their multilayered nature. While highlighting the standardizing effect of widespread images of trans_gender individuals "from [the] outside"—that is, by deriving them from the binary distinction of female and male, as is experienced by the majority—the chapter compares them to the diversity of trans_gendered life-worlds.

Next, Lisa Gaupp records her discussion in interview with Claude Jansen (independent scholar, performer, dramaturge and curator) about the representation of diversity and otherness in globally active performing arts, music festivals, and cultural organizations in general. This chapter stresses the discrepancy between the ideal of a borderless, transcultural art world, and the reality of market strategies that tend to standardize diversity by promoting specific features of it and excluding others. Against this background, this chapter discusses future possibilities and strategies of opening "the curatorial" in a more emancipatory way, one which is able to overcome binary conceptualizations of diversity by drawing more closely to transcultural life-worlds in the attempt to decolonize global art worlds.

Lastly, Fabio Cismondi and I treat the diversity of scientific groups involved in large international projects. By drawing from an interview with Pietro Barabaschi, Head of Department at Fusion for Energy (F4E) and Director of the European-Japanese Broader Approach activities, this chapter investigates the different aspects which characterize the diversity of international scientific groups by going beyond the widespread habit of thinking of diversity as the sum of single identity groups (e.g. women, ethnic minorities, etc.). It emphasizes the variety of professional cultures that characterize the main laboratories and institutions involved in the projects, all of which are characterized by specific norms that regulate the cooperation (e.g.

processes of decision-making and communication, including the manner of handling hierarchies). The construction of a "common culture" and group identity around the strong driver of a clear common goal, without levelling the diversity of the cooperating partners, emerges as a fundamental means to achieving the goals of the project within the planned budget and time-schedule. The limited size of the core team and the opportunity of having personal exchange and developing mutual trust constitute a key element to overcome cultural stereotyping, and to avoid that projects fail because of alleged "intercultural problems". The chapter suggests overcoming binary approaches to diversity in organizations, which tend to endorse either the productivity or the representativeness of single identity groups. It encourages instead to look, case by case, at strategies that open up spaces for the transcultural negotiation of norms in all aspects of the cooperation, from the scientific development to the legal and administrative frameworks. In this connection, it stresses the role which is played by international actors from industry and politics as an important aspect to be considered by looking at the diversity of scientific environments. In this broader context, it suggests not to dichotomize between the achievement of social equality and the best scientific outcomes, by looking at scientific cooperation all in all as a transcultural enterprise.

To sum up, by highlighting the contrast between the various processes of standardization and regulation of diversity and their corresponding life-worlds, this volume addresses, on the one hand, the need—within as well as outside of academia—for categories offering orientation in understanding complex life-worlds, such as diversity, multiculturalism, hybridity, etc. On the other hand, it aims at stressing how contingent and limited any categorization and discourse appears to be with respect to such complexity. The space between the two opposite attitudes of denying vs. acknowledging diversity is a fuzzy one. By intertwining the perspectives of diversity and transcultural studies, the volume addresses this space as a *continuum* between the two opposite processes of, respectively, "doing otherness" vs. "doing diversity". Circulating ideologies which establish a correspondence between specific characters and their respective cultural features shape the ways in which diversity is perceived, experienced and practiced across a large variety of life-worlds. In turn, the spread of resulting representations and narratives contribute to strengthen or, on the contrary, to question hegemonic ideologies of cultural belonging. Diversity, as a category of practice, is thus *not*, per se, transcultural. The proposed approach, which builds on diversity as a category of analysis and transculturality as a method, offers a lens that reveals two opposite aspects characterizing the continuum between "doing diversity" and "doing otherness": on the one hand, the transculturality hidden behind any cultural form, including their respective, allegedly static categorizations; on the other, the various ways of levelling, standardizing and hierarchizing social groups and cultural resources, including those apparently aiming at promoting diversity. In this context, the term can have, among others, a "sensitizing" (Vertovec, 2015, p. 6) effect by highlighting both transculturally sensitive approaches across different contexts and processes of exclusion based on the construction of differences with various purposes.

Every book is also the result of its specific context of production. In this case, the particular heterogeneity of the topics and approaches is related to the work that Lisa Gaupp and I have developed in the context of the section "Transcultural life-worlds" of the Kulturwissenschaftliche Gesellschaft between 2015 and 2019. By taking into account all the risks of inter- and transdisciplinarity, such as incompleteness and methodological or theoretical discrepancies, our main goal has not been to construct a comprehensive theory of diversity (assuming this would be a realistic goal for any enterprise) or to establish or de-limit a new field of study. It has been rather to reflect on problems and contradictions in handling diversity in different fields by learning from comparison, thus taking the chance to prove concepts and practices explicitly which are often taken for granted in (mono)disciplinary discourses. Moreover, it has been to critically reflect on the academic practice in light of diversity studies. This includes a comparative and critical review of scholarly terms, discourses and approaches, which, as often as they appear in daily discourse and representations, tend to prioritize certain aspects at the expense of others. Furthermore, it has aimed to transmit knowledge and approaches among different contexts of practice, not only between various academic disciplines but also in extra-academic environments. In fact, studying diversity within the academic framework can surely contribute to, but will not alone be able to promote, emancipatory processes of "doing diversity" in real life. As stressed by Stuart Hall (1981, p. 33), "ideology is a practice", and therefore processes of "doing diversity" need to take place in many fields of practice. We consider cultural studies, in the broadest sense of the term[2], to be the most suitable field for such an enterprise because of its capacity to bridge scholarly and extra-scholarly boundaries (e.g. by bringing different speakers, cultural brokers, researchers, institutional players, consumers, etc. onto a common ground). In this sense, this book is itself the result of transcultural encounters with diversity. May it stimulate more of them.

# References

Abu-Er-Rub, L., Brosius, C., Meurer, S., Panagiotopoulos, D., & Richter, S. (Eds.). (2019a). Engaging transculturality: concepts, key terms, case studies. Routledge.

---

2 Cultural studies as a field is *not* meant here as a mere translation of Kulturwissenschaft into English. However, while being aware of the discrepancies between cultural studies and Kulturwissenschaft(en), we have tried—in the work of the section "Transcultural Life-Worlds" and in this book—to approach the study of culture by intertwining the germanophone Kulturwissenschaft(en) with other approaches within and beyond anglophone cultural studies.

Abu-Er-Rub, L., Brosius, C., Meurer S., Panagiotopoulos, D., & Richter, S. (2019b). Introduction: Engaging transculturality. In L. Abu-Er-Rub, C. Brosius, S. Meurer, D. Panagiotopoulos, & S. Richter (Eds.), Engaging transculturality (pp. xxiii–xliv). Routledge.

Allolio-Näcke, L., Kalscheuer, B., & Manzeschke, A. (Eds.). (2005). Differenzen anders denken: Bausteine zu einer Kulturtheorie der Transdifferenz. Campus.

Appadurai, A. (2009). Diversity Interview. Retrieved from https://www.mmg.mpg.de/50202/interview-with-arjun-appadurai

Bourdieu, P. (with Thompson, J. B.) (1991). Language and symbolic power. Polity (Original work published 1982. Ce que parler veux dire.).

Brubaker, R. (2012). Diversity Interview. Retrieved from https://www.mmg.mpg.de/50980/interview-with-rogers-brubaker

Fuchs, M. (2007). Diversity und Differenz - Konzeptionelle Überlegungen. In G. Krell, B. Riedmüller, B. Sieben, & D. Vinz (Eds.), Diversity Studies. Grundlagen und Disziplinäre Ansätze (pp. 17–34). Campus.

García Canclini, N. (2005). Hybrid cultures: Strategies for entering and leaving modernity. Univ. of Minnesota Press.

Hall, S. (1981). The Whites of their Eyes: Racist Ideologies and the Media. In G. Bridges & R. Brunt (Eds.), Silver Linings. Some Strategies for the Eighties (pp. 28–52). Lawrence and Wishart.

Heller, M. (1999). Linguistic minorities and modernity: A sociolinguistic ethnography (1. publ. ed.). Longman.

Krotz, F. (2009). Mediatization: A Concept with which to grasp media and societal change. In K. Lundby (Ed.), Mediatization: Concept, Changes, Consequences (pp. 21–40). Peter Lang.

Lull, J. (2002). Superkultur. In A. Hepp & M. Löffelholz (Eds.), Grundlagentexte zur transkulturellen Kommunikation (pp. 750–773). UVK.

Lundby, K. (Ed.). (2009). Mediatization: Concept, Changes, Consequences. Peter Lang.

Makoni, S., & Pennycook, A. (2007). Disinventing and Reconstituting Languages. In S. Makoni & A. Pennycook (Eds.), Disinventing and Reconstituting Languages (pp. 1–41). Multilingual Matters.

Michaels, A. (2019). Cultural hybridity and transculturality. In L. Abu-Er-Rub, C. Brosius, S. Meurer, D. Panagiotopoulos, & S. Richter (Eds.), Engaging transculturality (pp. 3–14). Routledge.

Vertovec, S. (2007). Super-diversity and its implications. Ethnic and Racial Studies, 29(6), 1024-1054.

Vertovec, S. (2015). Introduction, Formulating diversity studies. In S. Vertovec (Ed.), International Handbook of Diversity Studies (pp. 1–20). Routledge.

Welsch, W. (2005). Auf dem Weg zu transkulturellen Gesellschaften. In L. Allolio-Näcke, B. Kalscheuer, & A. Manzeschke (Eds.), Differenzen anders denken: Bausteine zu einer Kultur-theorie der Transdifferenz (pp. 314–341). Campus.

Lisa Gaupp

# 2 Epistemologies of Diversity and Otherness

Among the fundamental concepts of today's study of culture are included diversity and otherness as well as connected terms and concepts such as social inequality, difference, hybridity, transculturality, intersectionality, and so on. Cultural research in contemporary societies will not be viable without including topics such as globalization or migration. In addition, discourses on diaspora, mobility, exile, transnationalism, translation (Langenohl et al., 2015) or untranslatability (Apter, 2013), as well as addressing areas of "the own versus the unknown" (Simmel, 1996) or of cultural appropriation and authenticity, all have a long tradition in the study of culture. Both cultural and social anthropology as well as literary studies have an equally long history of looking at social inequalities, neo-colonialism and related traditions of producing knowledge while focusing on topics of diversity and otherness. Other academic disciplines have also followed this development, which has been named the "postcolonial turn" (Bachmann-Medick, 2016a, pp. 131–173). In the following discussion, the historical development of these postcolonial theoretical approaches will be sketched in order to analyse the epistemologies of diversity and otherness and their normalized academic historicities in the study of culture in general, and, more specifically, their foundations for the sociology of culture and cultural sociology. These two fields of study are situated in the transdisciplinary area of the study of culture in the humanities and social sciences. It will be argued that the study of culture, and especially the sociologically oriented study of culture, needs to further acknowledge the potential of postcolonial critique for theorizing diversity and otherness. It will be shown how and in what explicit senses postcolonially defined approaches and other deconstructivist perspectives from these fields have similar views and several points of interconnection. It will be discussed to what extent stimulations between these seemingly distinct lines of thought can be set in dialogue in order to make *sensitivity to diversity* a more mainstream component within the study of culture. Such a diversity-sensitive perspective corresponds to the transcultural approach of this volume, which combines the deconstruction of persisting lines of b/ordering, and thereby focuses on ambivalent spaces and narratives and the recognition of unequal power relations. Simultaneously, conflictual articulations are taken into account when taking a look at how diversity and otherness are negotiated, standardized or practiced.

The long history of postcolonial approaches and their disciplinary contact with sociological disciplines were sketched in an email debate between Manuela Boatcă, Sina Farzin and Julian Go, which was published in the journal SOZIOLOGIE of the German Sociological Association in 2018 (Boatcă et al., 2018, pp. 423–438). Yet in response to this exchange, Markus Holzinger says that postcolonial sociology and critique of Eurocentrism remains "nothing new" (Holzinger, 2019, pp. 174–184). What is still at stake for Holzinger, though, is the "decolonization of sociology" (p. 179) itself. My discussion aims at both offering some insights for postcolonial approaches in sociology and highlighting their relationship to other discourses in this field. This task is of great relevance not only concerning the need to decolonize knowledge production (see below), but also in order to find adequate theoretical concepts for meeting today's fundamental social challenges in times of increased political populism, right-wing extremism and growing social inequalities worldwide.

First, intersectional approaches to diversity and otherness can be related directly to the sociology of culture. Intersectional approaches characteristically look at cultural and social inequalities while understanding them as interwoven with multiple and intersecting ascriptions of identity. Here, culture is mainly understood as reification, as something which is (materially) produced through processes of social determinations (Durkheim, 2013; Bourdieu, 2010). Cultural productions and fields of culture are explored as socially and habitually incorporated as well as spatially and aesthetically constituted practices of diversity and otherness, which are interwoven with economic and organizational power-relations—also on a global scale. In this sense, diversity and otherness are seen as practices that (un-)do differences (see Hirschauer in this volume), often with a political objective. These differences are mainly debated as socio-cultural markers, and as cultural constructions, which at the same time have their *real* materialized counterpart in, for example, structures of social inequality. Thus, on the one hand, intersectional *diversity* is conceptualized as a diversity of multiple social belongings and ascriptions that tend to (or are meant to) *include* and foster social inclusion and belonging to a whole under the motto *united in diversity*. On the other hand, intersectional *otherness* mainly fulfils the discursive functions of *excluding*, by stressing the differences amongst individuals, groups or larger social bodies. At the same time and in both intersectional diversity and otherness, differences are always thought to intersect, mutually to influence other markers of difference and to have multiple effects.

Second, the usages of the terms "diversity" and "otherness" as cross-cultural[3] will be discussed from a perspective that can be squarely related to cultural sociology. Culture is understood as the construction of symbols and interpretations. Accordingly, society is analysed by focusing on the processes of signifying and interpreting. Thus, throughout this contribution, the focus will be placed on the theoretical approaches which examine how cross-cultural interconnectedness is addressed by looking at the processes of constructing, (re-)assigning and deconstructing meaning

---

**3** Even though the transcultural approach of this volume is closely related to the concept of *cross-cultural diversity and otherness*, I do not use the term *transcultural* to describe these narratives of interconnectedness and deconstruction of cultural symbols, on the grounds that our transcultural approach goes further, and in two main ways. 1. It focuses on the unequal power relations that will be discussed in the section on intersectional diversity and otherness, and 2. It criticizes the sometimes utopian notions that are connected to the narrative of *cross-cultural diversity and otherness*, rather taking conflictual articulations into account (see also Abu-Er-Rub et al., 2019).

to diversity and otherness. In this sense, cross-cultural *diversity* will encompass all ambiguous cultural symbols of entanglement, interconnectedness and spaces in-between, that cannot be clearly assigned to specific differences or specific belongings. Cross-cultural *otherness* hence concerns the movement of the deconstruction of cultural symbols, or the de-stabilizing of cultural differences.

Furthermore, in both areas, i.e. in intersectional as well as in cross-cultural approaches to diversity and otherness, four different epistemological assumptions regarding diversity and otherness are made. These epistemologies can be called deconstructivist, constructivist, equality-theoretical and difference-theoretical, respectively. Both a postcolonial-inspired critique of Eurocentrism and a poststructuralist notion of deconstructing power discourses in these fields are also of important note. Likewise, critiques which highlight how social inequalities and multiple discrimination processes develop and take effect will be discussed, as well as how the same argument can serve followers of the *New Right* to fight hybridization. All epistemologies of diversity and otherness are placed in the context of the study of culture and the different cultural "turns" which are ongoing within the humanities and social sciences. This chapter critically outlines these different concepts of diversity and otherness, their underlying assumptions and their epistemological foundations across these disciplines. Thus, the origins of diversity and otherness in the study of culture will be explored from different theoretical perspectives, asking what traditions, assumptions and habits have emerged from the concepts of diversity and otherness and, in turn, what impact they may have had on the concepts themselves.

## 2.1 Epistemologies

The study of culture is such a vast field of research that there are several—sometimes diverging—streams of theoretical inquiry to examine. Also, within the terminology, there is no common understanding, let alone in the epistemological approaches. *Kulturwissenschaften* in German-speaking countries is not the same as the understanding of the term "Cultural Studies", as it originated mainly at the Birmingham Centre for Contemporary Cultural Studies, even though several similarities can be detected (Nünning, 2016, pp. 70–75). More difficulties in terminology arise when trying to translate the term *Kulturwissenschaften* as e.g. Humanities and Social Sciences or the study of culture. In addition, there are views that use *Kulturwissenschaft* in the singular, in order to refer mainly to a theoretical corpus based on Eurocentric aesthetic theories (Böhme, 2000). Others use *Kulturwissenschaften* in the plural (Wuggenig, 1998) to denote a multidisciplinary approach to common topics with a common framework of cultural theory. In this vast and complex field, it is difficult to systematize, especially when taking into account that many of the approaches in the field follow a constructivist understanding of the study of culture itself, which is explicitly directed against (binary) systematizations. Nevertheless, it is possible to lay open recurrent tendencies which highlight the basis for important theories or (inter-) disciplinary perspectives (important because they are acknowledged widely in the field and thereby integrated into the existing *canon*). This is of course not meant to homogenize the study of culture in the vast topical field of diversity and otherness. Overlaps and contradictions within these lines of thought are pervasive. Rather, this attempt puts on display the epistemological standardizations of this canon. In addition, the contradictions and ambivalences involved mirror the transcultural approach of this volume and the tension between standardization and transcultural life-worlds in the sense of practices that do not conform to the canon. Andreas Reckwitz calls this common "research programme of *Kulturwissenschaften*" the "perspective of contingency" (Reckwitz, 2004, p. 3). By this he means that the underlying distinctions which used to form the epistemological foundations of the single disciplines are questioned, and their ambivalences and contingencies are more clearly brought into focus. This is again part of what we call the transcultural approach that identifies this volume.

From most of these perspectives, the terms "diversity" and "otherness" are not explicitly addressed,[4] and the area of the *European Other* is mainly considered as the focus of the discipline of anthropology. However, in the following sections, I will argue that dealing with issues of differences can be detected as an underlying principle of many of these approaches, no matter how differences are defined, from what perspectives, or whether differences are stabilized or deconstructed. These underlying distinctions include, for example, the distinction in sociology between modern and traditional societies, in anthropology between one's own and the other, in history between the continuing and the discontinuing, and in literary studies between text and context (Reckwitz, 2004, p. 14). For instance, when sociology was founded as a discipline at the beginning of the twentieth century, Émile Durkheim, Max Weber and Georg Simmel together laid the basis for theories of differentiation with their works on social differentiation through the division of labour (Durkheim, 2013), social stratification (Weber, 1969) and the *Intersection of Social Circles* (Simmel, 1990), respectively. Likewise, this chapter will show that "Kulturwissenschaft as a discipline can be understood as an academic reflexion based on experiences of otherness and differences" (Metten, 2016, p. 6).

Moreover, to look at the *Other* is not reserved for anthropology, let alone to academia, even though *Othering* has been (and still is) a prominent and critical concept of contemporary anthropological research. By this is meant how a foreign *Other* is being constructed through discriminatory language, exclusionary practices and public discourses (Sökefeld, 2004, p. 24). This often encompasses symbolic power, a "power that creates things with words"[5] (Bourdieu, 1992, p. 153). The construction of foreignness and its many accompanying epistemological assumptions are therefore

---

4  An exception is: Salzbrunn, 2014.
5  "Symbolische Macht ist die Macht, Dinge mit Worten zu schaffen" (Bourdieu, 1992, p. 153).

mostly part of a wider societal context, the manifold life-worlds. As Friese writes, "[s]cientific categorizations stand—often uncritically—in discursive coalitions with juridical and political terminology, that construct the figure of the stranger, migrant, refugee, asylum seeker and determine their daily life"[6] (Friese, 2014, pp. 29–30).

Epistemes are thereby understood as powerful and structuring symbolic orders. Following Michel Foucault, epistemes are thought of as an *a priori* symbolic order (Foucault, 1974, p. 22), which function as a dispositive of what is scientifically acceptable (or true) and what is not (or false) (Foucault, 1978, p. 124). Thus, knowledge can only be produced within the framework of this epistemic order. For Gayatri Chakravorty Spivak, this symbolic order has a violent basis that prevents political agency. For her, "epistemic violence" can especially be seen as being "orchestrated from a distance, [as] an extensive and heterogenic project to constitute the colonial subject as the Other"[7] (Spivak, 1988, p. 91). This is the main reason for Walter Mignolo's text *Epistemic Disobedience*, that calls for the decentralization of "occidental thought" and the decolonization of dominant epistemologies (Mignolo, 2012).

Even though, in my discussion, the history of epistemology is widely summarized as a merely *Western-centric* story, and the majority of approaches discussed here belong to this *Western* canon, which is composed mainly of white male authors, this contribution also seeks to offer a non-standard view by combining approaches to diversity and otherness from the *Western* canon with deconstructivist, decolonial, postcolonial, queer and entangled perspectives. This is not meant to oppose *Western* theories with *non-Western* ones, but rather to place emphasis on some of the destabilizing momentums in the historicities of the epistemologies of diversity and otherness, no matter how the respective authors are situated relative to them.

These cultural theories on diversity and otherness mainly stem from disciplinarily rooted fields, such as anthropology, philosophy and sociology or the social sciences in general. Of course, this order is as constructed as any other, and is not meant to exclude larger disciplines, such as literary or media studies, but rather seeks to express a common theoretical ground which is applied in several overlapping or exclusionary disciplinary fields, including ones which are not mentioned here. As for the theories of diversity and otherness in this vast field, this paper will seek to uncover some of the different epistemological assumptions and situate them in their respective cultural turns (Bachmann-Medick, 2016a).

---

6 "Wissenschafliche Kategorisierungen stehen damit—nicht selten unkritisch—in diskursiven Koalitionen mit juristischen und politischen Begrifflichkeiten, mit denen die Figuren des Fremden, Migranten, Flüchtlings, Asylsuchenden geschaffen werden und deren Alltagsleben bestimmt werden kann" (Friese, 2014, pp. 29–30).
7 "das aus der Distanz orchestrierte, weitläufige und heterogene Projekt, das koloniale Subjekt als Anderes zu konstituieren" (Spivak, 1988, p. 91).

Doris Bachmann-Medick first published her German version of the book *Cultural Turns – New Orientations in the Study of Culture* in 2006; in 2016 the English translation and in 2018 the sixth revised German edition were published, respectively. In this book, a turn—which is first and foremost the cultural turn itself—is clearly distinguished from a paradigm shift (Kuhn, 2009), mere theoretical trends, or a new (interdisciplinary) focus on a specific topic. As Bachmann-Medick explains, a turn develops when "the new research focus shifts from the object level of new fields of inquiry to the level of analytical categories and concepts... if the potential turn does not merely identify new objects of study, but becomes a tool and medium of knowledge itself" (Bachmann-Medick, 2016a, p. 16). This approach involves an "epistemological shift necessary for turns to provide an analytical framework for understanding the constellations of the social problems from which they emerge" (Bachmann-Medick, 2016a, p. 17).

In this sense, this chapter intends to direct the postcolonial turn towards the transcultural approach which is adopted in this volume, in order to both draw the topics of diversity and otherness closer to a transcultural methodological approach, and to theorize diversity and otherness as a medium of postcolonial critique. The first encompasses a methodological approach that, while focusing on processes of interconnectedness, acknowledges the conflicts involved, seeking persistently to lay open and deconstruct dichotomizations, homogenizations and standardizations. The latter, conversely, refers to how this chapter calls for the implementation of a global, postcolonial, translational perspective to negotiations and practices of diversity and otherness, as a tool for criticizing inequalities. In this sense, the cultural change which Aleida Assmann sees as developing "through the interaction of political, social, medial and epistemological changes, influenced by the academic discourse"[8] (Assmann, 2016, p. 42) lies at the core of the theoretical consideration of negotiations and practices of diversity and otherness in this chapter.

Epistemology, which was one of Greek philosophy's central disciplines, asks:

> what is knowledge ... how is it produced, and what can be called true. ... Through poststructuralist theories, constructivism has gained more and more importance for epistemology. In accordance with skepticism, knowledge production is regarded as a mere construction of an observer. Reality and therefore a universal truth do not exist. (Gaupp, 2010, p. 200)

These questions have already been raised in Indian ancient philosophy, such as in the doctrines of the Upanishads and in the Greek ancient world by philosophers such as Heraclitus, Parmenides, Socrates and Aristotle. Plato's theory of ideas assumes

---

**8** "Solcher Kulturwandel entsteht durch das Zusammenwirken politischer, sozialer, medialer und epistemologischer Veränderungen, an dem auch der wissenschaftliche Diskurs einen wichtigen Anteil hat" (Assmann, 2016, p. 42).

an *a priori* existence of ideas or signs which stands in separation from the world of sensible phenomena (Natorp, 1903). This means that knowledge can only be achieved regarding an idea and not regarding a reality that exists apart from that idea, paving the road for semiotics which discusses how meaning is attributed in processes of knowledge acquisition. In the 4th century A.D., Augustine developed his theological epistemology, which was further extended by (among others) Thomas Aquinas to become the scholasticism of the twelfth century under the influence of Arabic philosophers such as Averroës (Abū al-Walīd Muhammad Ibn Ahmad Ibn Rushd). From now on, there were two opposing streams of epistemology present: the one deductivist, in which truth can be recognized by reason, and the other inductivist, in which truth can only be derived from experience. With his famous statement *cogito ergo sum* [I think, therefore I am], René Decartes founded the tradition of early modern rationalism, that assigns the capacity of objective cognition to the human mind in the sixteenth century. In opposition, knowledge according to the empiricism of Francis Bacon is deducted only from sensory experience. In both cases, knowledge is seen as the classification of information and the assignment of meanings or ideas through sensory discrimination, i.e. (re-)cognition (Gaupp, 2010).

These two approaches were in turn combined by Immanuel Kant in the idealist tradition of the 18th century (Kant, 2015). Based on Plato's theory of ideas, Kant sees existence as a mere image or sign of ideas. However, he establishes a relation between thought and experience by stating that the mind has to form the terms for recognition itself. Only that of which the consciousness has an idea or a meaning can be recognized. This understanding later led to the linguistic turn in the study of culture (Bachmann-Medick, 2016a).

In the wake of poststructuralist theories, constructivism gains importance for epistemology. Being based on scepticism, knowledge is accordingly seen as a mere construction of the observer, and there is no reality or universal truth. This is also the premise of feminist epistemology that developed in the 1970s as a critique of science (Harding, 1999; Butler, 1990; Kristeva, 1974; Haraway, 1992). These approaches seek to uncover and deconstruct absolutist universalisms, power discourses and essentialist concepts such as gender-specific role models. As we will see in the following sections, constructivism is one of the major story-lines for how diversity and otherness are conceived in the study of culture. Equally, many approaches seek to deconstruct power-relations based on hegemonic ways of conceiving, forming, influencing and ruling the production of knowledge. Thus, constructivism is nowadays the state of the art in the study of culture. The underlying premise of constructivism that meaning which is assigned to the world is a part of those theories that can be assigned to the interpretative turn.

The interpretative turn is characterized by Bachmann-Medick as being based on the linguistic turn as "mega-turn" and by the metaphor of understanding culture as text (Bachmann-Medick, 2016a, pp. 39–71). In the tradition of Max Weber's interpretative sociology,[9] Clifford Geertz's interpretative cultural anthropology, and with reference to the "politics of science ... the decolonization processes beginning in the 1950s and the liberation movements in the so-called Third World" (Bachmann-Medick, 2016a, pp. 40–41), culture is understood as being constructed as symbols, signs and interpretations. At the same time, culture is seen as actually constituting social reality (Fischer & Moebius, 2014, p. 10). This stream of thought can be traced back to the first institutionalized founding of the discipline of sociology at the beginning of the twentieth century, when Georg Simmel, Max Weber and Émile Durkheim developed their theories on society and culture in the wake of dominating positivistic scientific approaches and their division of humanities and natural sciences.

This tradition's focus on the sense-making processes of humans is again revived in the so-called philosophical anthropology (Plessner, 1975) after the Second World War, in order to oppose the dominant paradigms of structural functionalism[10] and historical materialism at that time. It was further elaborated internationally from the 1970s onwards in the cultural turn across a range of different disciplines and in cultural sociology itself.

Andreas Reckwitz calls this approach the "meaning-oriented understanding of culture"[11] (Reckwitz, 2000, p. 109) in opposition to the formerly dominant "normative understanding of culture" (Reckwitz, 2008b, pp. 69–93). This cultural sociology is interested in the analysis of symbolic regimes[12] in society that allow for meaningful action, their genesis and connected practices, involved actors and social formations, as well as life-styles, everyday life and artefacts (Albrecht & Moebius, 2014, pp. 12–13). However, Monika Wohlrab-Sahr sees a fundamental difference between the approaches of Weber and Reckwitz: whereas for Weber meaning is always subjective, the "praxeological" approach of Reckwitz, which draws on poststructuralist theories, neglects subjects as independent variables and sees them rather as a "result of modes of subjectivation and cultural forming"[13] (Wohlrab-Sahr, 2010, pp. 14–15). For Reckwitz, the permanent de-stabilization of cultural regimes, structures and boundaries, and thus the contingency of cultural symbols, becomes an important focus of analysis (Reckwitz, 2004). We will come back to poststructuralist deconstruction below, since it can be seen as being connected to the reflexive turn.

Close to Reckwitz's "praxeological" approach, Joost Van Loon distinguishes between cultural sociology and the sociology of culture and argues in favour of the latter, situating it within the performative turn. He intends to place focus on what

---

9 "verstehende Soziologie" (This and the following translations without references are mine).

10 "Strukturfunktionalismus".

11 "bedeutungsorientierter Kulturbegriff" (Reckwitz, 2000, p. 109).

12 "symbolische Ordnungen".

13 "Resultat von Subjektivierungsweisen und kulturellen Formungen" (Wohlrab-Sahr, 2010, pp. 14–15).

he calls "the practical dimension of the generation of cultural meanings and experiences. It seeks to understand the generative and transformative aspects of culture on the basis of events, practices, material embodiments and media forms" (Bachmann-Medick, 2016a, p. 73). Though famously divided by the cultural sociologist Jeffrey Alexander in 1996 (German translation in 2004), in cultural sociology every action and every institution needs to be connected with "structured sets of symbols" (p. 59) that determine it, and that can be read to a connected audience, which is thus able to "read" this action. For Alexander, the sociology of culture focuses only on the "context" that is separated from the "sphere of meaning", and leaves out the reading of the "text" itself. In response, Van Loon, in his theorization of sharing, sameness and belonging, criticizes this division between the idealist and the materialist. He suggests not to follow cultural sociology in thinking that "belief governs action", but to rather take not only materialism but also performative practices into account. As such, collectives are not bound together by "shared beliefs, norms and values" but by "sharing-believing", being "conceptualized as a practice, not as a separate product" (Van Loon, 2019). Moreover, for Van Loon it is important to acknowledge the "historicity-under-erasure of the performativity of shared beliefs", which includes how the "forgetting of the historicity is itself a crucial part of the way in which the symbolic operates" (Van Loon, 2019). Merely mental approaches can indeed lead to a negation of the violence involved. Instead, taking into account all the "violence of starvation, of racist-colonial-genocidal exploitation, of misogyny" allows the sociology of culture to become a "political sociology" (Van Loon, 2019). Likewise, such a perspective invites one to consider practices of belonging, sharing, diversity and differences, inclusion and exclusion in dialogue with the postcolonial agenda which is proposed in this contribution.

Let us come back to these matters later on, in the section devoted to intersectional diversity and otherness, and instead turn now to the development of the reflexive turn mentioned above. As part of (or actually preceding) the reflexive turn, the discipline of anthropology underwent a so-called *crisis of representation*, with its peak in the 1960s after the posthumously published diaries of the anthropologist Bronislaw Malinowski. The founding father of empirical fieldwork revealed himself to be a shocking racist, exhibiting a discriminating attitude towards his research subjects in the field (Malinowski, 1967). Accordingly, the whole discipline had to question its own premises grounded in colonialism.

The question behind these discussions was: How can one possibly solve the dilemma of deciding whether an ascription is correct without ascribing new labels at the same time? Critical reflection on the researcher's own objectives, competences and knowledges can reveal what desires, assumptions and biases lead his*her own epistemic interests. However, whether the reality represented by the researcher is *true* or *false* cannot be demonstrated by merely following the established rules of field research. This skepticism is a part of the crises of representation in anthropology, which encompasses: "not only the poststructuralist drifting apart of signifier and signified, but also the asymmetry of power relations underlying every representation of the other and every description of culture—with anthropology and beyond" (Bachmann-Medick, 2016a, p. 103). From a postcolonial perspective, anthropology/ethnology is criticized for aiding colonial rule by describing, categorizing, interpreting and thereby standardizing the *Other* from a *Western* point of view.

Whether understandings and *true* or *objective* statements about the *Other* are ever possible is treated by recourse to a numerous array of theoretical concepts. For example, cultural xenology is dedicated to *intercultural understanding* or rather the impossibility of representing the *Other* or a *truth* objectively.

In particular, intercultural philosophy is devoted to questions of *intercultural understanding*. As one of the leading authors in this field, Ram Adhar Mall asks whether the different cultures of this world can be compared to each other, how much they resemble each other, and whether mutual understanding is possible. He claims that there is "no pure *own culture* ... no more than there is a pure *other culture*. ... it is no different when it comes to philosophy, [which is] placeless"[14] (Mall, 1993, pp. 1, 4).

Postcolonial authors have also asserted their belief in such a "placelessness" and deconstruct the hegemonic *Western* representation of the *Other*.[15] Every (academic) description of a situation, human being, and his*her actions is necessarily a representational practice, which, in trying to structure observed reality with terminological precision, him- or herself (re-)produces narratives and mechanisms of inclusion and exclusion. As Chambers writers:

> Representation is nothing natural or obvious. It is, both in its political as well as in its aesthetic dimensions, a continuing process of construction, articulation and interpretation. ... Otherness is swallowed up: The observed is taken out of a very specific historical and cultural context and fitted in to academic, literary and philosophical typologies, which serve to describe, determine and explain the "other".[16] (Chambers, 1996, pp. 153, 155)[17]

Hence, in every new narrative something is always left out and an image is constructed. Following Homi K. Bhabha, a representation is "always only an add-on to

---

**14** "Eine reine eigene Kultur gibt ebenso wenig, wie es eine reine andere Kultur gibt ... nicht anders verhält es sich mit der Philosophie, [die] ortlos [ist]" (Mall, 1993, pp. 1, 4).

**15** See further below in this section on epistemologies.

**16** "Repräsentation ist jedoch nichts Natürliches oder Offensichtliches. Sie ist, sowohl in ihren politischen wie auch in ihren ästhetischen Dimensionen, ein fortwährender Prozess der Konstruktion, der Artikulation und Interpretation. ... Andersheit wird verschluckt: Das Beobachtete wird aus einem genau umrissenen historischen und kulturellen Kontext herausgelöst und dann in die wissenschaftlichen, literarischen und philosophischen Typologien eingepasst, die dazu dienen, das 'andere' zu beschreiben, festzulegen und zu erklären" (Chambers, 1996, pp. 153, 155).

**17** In this context, the work by Stuart Hall on cultural representation and signifying practices needs to be mentioned, as he similarly focuses on how meaning in any cultural production is produced, constructed and negotiated (Hall, 1997).

authority and identity; it should never be read mimetically as an image of reality" (Bhabha, 2005, p. 376).

Throughout the 1970s and with the book *Writing Culture: The Poetics and Politics of Ethnography* published in 1986 by the US-American anthropologists James Clifford and George Marcus, the *writing culture debate* shook the discipline of anthropology. As stated above, these epistemological debates were influenced by parallel discussions in philosophy and sociology and can be identified as part of the reflexive turn. Accordingly:

> culture is no longer seen as a unified objectifiable container of symbols and meanings. Rather, it is regarded as a dynamic network of relationships between communication practices and representations, through whose representational dynamics culture comes into being in the first place. ..., cultural objects are not simply "givens", but emerge through (symbolic) interaction, through an "othering" that is influenced by the type of representation in question. (Bachmann-Medick, 2016a, p. 122)

An ethnographic "thick description" (Geertz, 1973) is no longer seen as simply the subjective interpretation of an ethnographer. In addition, the literary style of the academic text which is produced is analysed linguistically or used strategically. Culture is seen by a variety of authors no longer as a representation, but instead:

> as composed of seriously contested codes and representations; they assume that the poetic and the political are inseparable, that science is in, not above, historical and linguistic processes. They assume that academic and literary genres interpenetrate and that the writing of cultural descriptions is properly experimental and ethical. Their focus on text-making and rhetoric serves to highlight the constructed, artificial nature of cultural accounts. It undermines overly transparent modes of authority, and it draws attention to the historical predicament of ethnography, the fact that it is always caught up in the invention, not the representation, of cultures. (Clifford, 1986, p. 2)

When ethnography is viewed as contextual, rhetorical, institutional, gender-specific, political and historical, an ethnographic description can nevertheless be called a "true fiction" which always omits something. To underline this perspective, some authors of this *writing culture debate* use stylistic elements in their ethnographic texts. Moreover, "[o]nce dialogism and polyphony are recognized as modes of textual production, monophonic authority is questioned" (Clifford, 1986, p. 15). In keeping with the perspective that ethnography is fiction, anthropology turns toward the "other within us" and self-construction processes associated with it. As Clifford writers, "[c]ultural poesis—and politics—is the constant reconstitution of selves and others through specific exclusions, conventions, and discursive practices" (Clifford, 1986, p. 24).

Bachmann-Medick also assigns the cultural critique of Clifford and Marcuse to the interpretative turn, as it:

first clearly emerged as a critique of power relations and became politically pointed under the influence of poststructuralism and deconstructionism, at which point the unavoidable question still looms large as to just how the power of representation systems impacts human actions and spawns symbolical orders. (2016a, p. 64)

Moreover, with the implied course of the study of culture being "directed against the established, yet problematic, principle of dichotomous difference" (Bachmann-Medick, 2016a, p. 105), the postcolonial turn as well as the translational turn can also be assigned to the writing culture debate. As Bachmann-Medick writes, "[i]t was exactly this strand of the critique of dichotomies an anti-essentialism that was pursued and further radicalized in the postcolonial turn" (p. 123). Yet, Bachmann-Medick distinguishes the reflexive turn from the postcolonial turn by defining the reflexive turn as focusing primarily on the "self-reflections by Europeans" (p. 125), whereas the postcolonial turn encompasses mainly "the concrete level of the contacts and relations between these two worlds" (p. 126). However, this distinction is in itself reproducing of a dichotomous order rather than a bid to find alternative transcultural perspectives. Postcolonial approaches are still often assigned only to a separate sphere of neo-colonial structures which is not taken into account in mainstream research. It seems as if the conventional distinction is still operative that distinguishes between anthropology being solely responsible for researching the *colonial Other* and sociology, which is focused on *Western* societies (García Canclini, 2013).

In opposition to this, I argue that postcolonial critique can serve as a tool to theorize diversity and otherness from a transcultural approach. Similarly to the way that Manuela Bojadžijev and Regina Römhild (2014, pp. 10–24) call the need for a "migrantization of research", whereby migration is shown to be such a prominent underlying principle of today's societies that it has to be taken into account for any research question, I would like to suggest the transculturalization of the cultural study of diversity and otherness. The postcolonial turn is acknowledged in the study of culture as a *mainstreaming principle* instead of a separate topic, in which the two main features of postcolonial critique are acknowledged as a guiding analytical tool to theorize diversity and otherness: first, the political aim of decolonizing power structures, and, second, the deconstruction of dichotomies in thinking. Decolonizing thereby refers to liberation not only from persistent imperialistic structures based in the colonial era but also from any unequal power structures.

The first wave of postcolonial critique was indeed preoccupied mainly with the heritage of colonial ages. However, similarly to the way that "gender" was conceived as a "universally relevant issue" (Bachmann-Medick, 2016a, p. 28), which "runs through all the turns in the study of culture as a key epistemological axis that structures not only the social system but also the knowledge order—while taking a stand against essentializations, universalizations, identity claims and dichotomizations" (p. 29), and since "the difference-based understanding of culture ... has increasingly characterized the study of culture since the postcolonial turn" (p. 30), I see the postcolonial approach to diversity and otherness as reaching beyond narrowly colonial issues. It provides the opportunity to look at diversity and otherness both from a power-critical perspective and from a deconstructivist stance at the same time. The postcolonial can thereby describe "a programmatic political concept that was critical of hegemonic discourse" (p. 131), which is "capable of counteracting the ongoing problematic constructions of the other" (p. 132). Thus, "a postcolonial analytical approach ... examines how domination functions and how alterity is modelled" (p. 153). This does not mean that the study of culture should be homogenized into a single postcolonial theory, but rather that exactly these ambivalent, contradictory, diverse and destabilizing moments should be taken into account in order to deconstruct hegemonic and homogenous views.

The prefix *post* does not imply that colonialism is over, but instead focuses on its continuing influence in typically less obvious ways. As Reckwitz writes:

> The movement of postcolonialism posits that only now—in relation to the past and the present— has it become apparent that the intertwined relations of stereotypical internal and external representations of ethnicity, religion, nationality etc. were fundamental for the modern constellation.[18] (2008a, p. 97)

These theories can be seen as poststructuralist answers to postmodern theories of diversity, which, even though they are presented as pluralistic, are still based on differences. Postcolonial theorists such as Edward Said, Homi K. Bhabha, Gayatri Chakravorty Spivak and the authors of the Birmingham Center for Contemporary Cultural Studies, such as Stuart Hall and Paul Gilroy, have especially pointed to the othering mechanisms with which a stereotype *Other* is constructed in academia, the arts, and politics in the *West*. The last century saw freedom movements such as the struggles for independence from colonial powers, the Black civil rights movement, and multiple waves of feminism; in academia too, the dichotomous thinking of modernity was questioned and deconstructed. Related to this deconstructivism, postcolonial critique analyses, rethinks and challenges those cultural forms which are based on colonial suppression and representation or imperialism today.

The founding postcolonial critics, such as Edward W. Said, refer to the influential works of Frantz Fanon (1952) in their critiques of universalism and of the way that diversity and otherness are constructed based on colonial power regimes. Said shows how "Orientalism" drives interests that construct the "Orient" from "Western" academic, institutional, economic, social, historical and aesthetical experience, as the counter-image of the "Occident", as "its contrasting image, idea, personality, experience" (Said, 1995, p. 2). The "Occident" thereby contributes to the domination

---

18 "Die Bewegung des Postkolonialismus [geht] davon aus, dass erst jetzt, auf die Vergangenheit und auf die Gegenwart bezogen, sichtbar wird, dass die verwickelten Relationen der stereotypen Selbst- und Fremdrepräsentationen, von Ethnizität, Religion, Nationalität etc. ... für die moderne Konstellation bisher grundlegend gewesen sind" (Reckwitz, 2008a, p. 97).

and normalization of the "Orient", and at the same time perpetuates and bolsters the legitimation of its own superiority. Said shows that every production of a text of any kind implies certain ideological assumptions. Likewise, every author remains bound to his*her context which excludes an objective truth (p. 2). Said draws attention to "Western" binaries, which are unmasked not as being false but as being led by power interests.[19] In addition, he shows that "the colonial project ... was underpinned by a discursive infrastructure, a symbolic economy, a whole apparatus of knowledge, the violence of which was as much epistemic as it was physical" (Mbembe, 2008, p. 8).

Critics of postcolonialism see this critique as a theory by privileged intellectual immigrants who do not live in the present (economic) realities in the former colonies (Moore-Gilbert, 2000). For example, Gayatri Chakravorty Spivak addresses the impossibility of taking part in the discourse from subaltern positions, which is doomed always to be the represented (Spivak, 1988). In this widely discussed article, drawing on Foucault and Derrida, she does not exclude herself from producing neocolonial ideologies while working in the "Western" academic system. Spivak suggests that the subaltern experience should be maintained as an inaccessible blankness to demonstrate the limits of the "Western" academic system instead of ascribing identities to the "Other" (Moore-Gilbert, 2000).

In the second wave of postcolonial theory from the 1990s onwards, the focus changed more and more to regard unequal power structures as being generally based on a capitalism-critical approach and the deconstruction of hegemonic knowledge (production) as being influenced by globalization. "The conceptual focus shifted to include a fundamental critique of the modern knowledge order and the universalizing hegemonic discourse of Western rationalism" (Bachmann-Medick, 2016a, p. 132). The postcolonial turn is now debated in several contexts and academic disciplines. Susanne Leeb and Ruth Sonderegger, for instance, call for:

> a relentless reflection on essentialist and colonialist power structures inherent in the concept of culture, particularly in the German-speaking world ... and for the provincialization of European aesthetics as well as for the acknowledgement of the manifold entanglements between European and non-European accounts of aesthetics. (2016, p. 57)

Also, Joseph-Achille Mbembe asks in his influential books *On the Postcolony* and *Critique of Black Reason*, as well as in numerous other works, how it is possible to speak about Africa without falling back on narratives that are based on imperialist, colonial-rooted and capitalist logics. He questions "what is 'today', and what are we today, ... and how could it give birth to something else?" (Mbembe, 2008, p. 15). The epoch of the postcolony—understood not only as a descriptive undertaking, but

---

**19** There are a number of publications dedicated to the work of Said; see for instance Ismaiel-Wendt (2014) and Haus der Kulturen der Welt (2014).

also as having a transformative objective—is conceptualized by Mbembe as enclosing "multiple *durées* made up of discontinuities, reversals, inertias, and swings that overlay one another, interpenetrate one another, and envelope one another: an entanglement" (Mbembe, 2001, p. 14). The postcolony consists of a "combination of several temporalities: ... the transit, ... the emerging time, ...the time of entanglement" (Mbembe, 2001, pp. 15–16), and is at the same time "a thought of responsibility in terms of the obligation to answer for oneself, to be the guarantor of one's actions" (Mbembe, 2008, p. 16). Mbembe intends to find an answer to the question of how to "think together difference and life, equality and inequality, excessiveness and the common"[20] (Mbembe, 2014, p. 24). One of his guiding principles for this task is to reflect on questions instead of positions, while acknowledging that "the elsewhere is the constituent of the here, and *vice versa*" (Mbembe, 2008, p. 17). I will come back to these postcolonial approaches to theorize life-worlds of conviviality instead of othering in my other contribution in this volume, on *How to Curate Diversity and Otherness in Global Performance Art*.

Within the epistemological terrain, a growing number of scholars are seeking to decolonize academic thinking. The sociologist Gurminder Bhambra, for example, is trying to decolonize sociological concepts of modernity (2007). For Reckwitz, the differentiation between "modern society" and "traditional society" was a constituent part of the theory of modernity in the discipline of sociology. Rationality is ascribed to modern "Western" societies only, and the evolution from a traditional to a more modern society is thought of as a linear and inevitable development (Reckwitz, 2004, p. 10). Owing to this, "modernity itself as a phenomenon has been primarily understood in the perspective of Western rationalism" (Mbembe, 2001, p. 10).

Bhambra also states that most sociological theories of modernity are based on dichotomous differentiations such as culture/nature, modernity/postmodernity or diversity/otherness. Postcolonial sociological approaches, such as hers, intend to lay open these colonialist foundations of linear progress; "... yet, while there is increasing hesitancy in equating Westernization with progress, it is my contention that the West is still seen as the leader or 'signifier' of change" (Bhambra, 2007, p. 1). The concept of modernity is further deconstructed and decolonized (Dussel, 1998; Santos, 2010), and is conceived as uneven modernities, being based in entangled histories (Randeria, 2002), as "other modernities" (Randeria, 1999, p. 379), or as multiple modernities (Eisenstadt, 2003).

What is at stake in these theories is precisely how modern thought has both dichotomized the modern and the traditional, one's own and the foreign, while at the same time has allowed these divisions to be perpetuated as universal. "The dispute thus bears not on the Westernness of modernity but on what the Enlightenment

---

**20** "Wie können wir Differenzen und Leben, Gleiches und Ungleiches, Überschießendes und Gemeinsames denken?" (Mbembe, 2014, p. 24).

bequeathed 'us' and on the possibilities of accomplishing in reality the promises of universality contained in the ideals of the *Aufklärung*" (Mbembe, 2001, p. 11). With the attempt to decolonize, for example, the most canonical sociologists for the theory of modernity, Max Weber and Georg Simmel, postcolonial critics such as Gurminder Bhambra (2014) or Syed Farid Alatas and Vineeta Sinha (2017) reread these texts and show, for example, the Orientalism detectable in Weber's work (Alatas, 2017). Such approaches instead call for an interwoven and cross-cultural concept of diversity and otherness, which is based on symbols and signs that are not rooted merely in an Euro-centric tradition but which are rather relativized by concepts and approaches such as "entangled histories"[21] (Gould, 2007), "histoire croisée"[22] (Werner & Zimmermann, 2006) or "double critique"[23] (Khatibi, 1985).

Reckwitz also lists other contemporary approaches from the study of culture that question the "dualism of 'modern' and 'traditional' sociability" (Reckwitz, 2004, p. 10), such as the exercise of finding similarities between rituals in modern and tra-ditional societies (M. Castells), defining the modern as rather a "historical-cultural specific particularity" (L. Boltanski, S. Lash) or by studying the "relativization of rationality in organization and science and technology studies" (H. Simon, B. Latour) (Reckwitz, 2004, p. 10). We will come back to these developments around the mate-rial, the spatial, the performative turns and postconstructivism below.

Of course there are numerous other examples of postcolonial and deconstructiv-ist approaches to diversity and otherness which I have not mentioned at this point. One common denominator of these perspectives is often an approach that can be called 'critical of Eurocentrism or *Western*-centrism', as well as which conceptualizes diversity and otherness in an equality-theoretical manner (see below, on the section on intersectional diversity and otherness) or as a difference-theoretical manner (see below, on poststructuralism). Moreover, the critique of Eurocentrism has a longer tra-dition in different academic disciplines (see the writing culture debate and the crisis of representation above, as well as Said's *Orientalism*). For instance, Ella Habiba Shohat

---

**21** "Entangled histories" refers to the realization "that each belonged not to one community but to several, and that those communities together constituted—indeed, still constitute to this day—an interconnected yet porous and open-ended whole" (Gould, 2007, p. 786).

**22** "Histoire croisée"—as developed by Michael Werner and Bénédicte Zimmermann—can be called a transculturally theoretical, as well as methodological, approach to history, which takes into account all the different fragmented and interconnected relations between different regions of the world. "The relational, interactive, and process-oriented dimensions of histoire croisée lead to a multiplicity of possible intercrossings" (Werner & Zimmermann, 2006, p. 39).

**23** Double critique was developed by the Moroccan sociologist and author Abdelkebir Khatibi, and denotes a concept that focuses on hybridity, androgyny and bilingualism, when Arab researchers are forced to become translators "in the shadow of the Western episteme", and which "requires a plura-lity of languages and of thoughts inscribed in them" (Khatibi, 1985, p. 17). Khatibi states: "Indeed, Occident, I am a split self, but my identity is an infinity of games, of desert flowers" (Khatibi, 1985, as cited in Lionnet, 2011, p. 390).

and Robert Stam (1994) call for a move from Eurocentrism to pluricentrism. Other authors seek to decolonize academic thought and education. Conventional dichotomous thinking should be overcome, such as the divide between human/nature; and instead, universities should be organized more as networks, allowing for a "more open critical cosmopolitan pluriversalism" (Mbembe, 2016, p. 37), rather than

> a dominant academic model based on a Eurocentric epistemic canon. A Eurocentric canon is a canon that attributes truth only to the Western way of knowledge production. It is a canon that disregards other epistemic traditions. It is a canon that tries to portray colonialism as a normal form of social relations between human beings rather than a system of exploitation and oppression. (p. 32)

For William Jamal Richardson, however, the decolonization of thought is not sufficient; for him, "marginalized communities and decolonial scholars need not only to intervene in epistemic debates but also to intervene politically in the physical spaces in which these debates often take place" (2018, p. 232). With this quest, the political-activist claim of equality-theoretical approaches discussed in the next section below is touched upon.

And yet, the popularity of postcolonial theory in "Western" academic contexts has also led to allegations of its Eurocentrism. Based mainly at the academic centres of the "West", postcolonial theory is reproached for only helping intellectuals of the "Global North" to redeem themselves of their colonialist past and present (Reuter & Villa, 2010). On the other hand, postcolonial theorists from the "Global South" "do not want to be seen on the other side of the line. ... [they] want to eliminate the line" (Santos, 2014, p. 4).

As an example of this latter critique, the historian Dipesh Chakrabarty is widely known for calling for the provincialization of Europe, and can be taken as a further example of transcultural approaches that bridge the epistemological gap between a mere "Occident-Orient" dichotomy. On the one hand, he criticizes how both historicism and the concept of political modernity is deeply Eurocentric, such as in the following:

> Historicism is what made modernity or capitalism look not simply global but rather as something that became global *over time*, by originating in one place (Europe) and then spreading outside it. This "first in Europe, then elsewhere" structure of global historical time was historicist. (Chakrabarty, 2000, p. 7)

On the other hand however, drawing on both Marx and his analytical approach to "'demystify' ideology in order to produce a critique that looks towards a more just social order" (p. 18) and Heidegger and his hermeneutic tradition, and producing "affective histories" that offer in detail "an understanding of the diversity of human life-worlds" (p. 18), Chakrabarty applies a combination of these two authors to the South Asian context. This can be seen as part of the second wave of postcolonial theory (see also Appadurai, 1996), that seeks to find new ways of theorizing inequalities in thought as well as in social realms, and to offer emancipatory or connecting alternatives. As such, he writes:

> provincializing Europe is not a project of rejecting or discarding European thought. ... provincializing Europe becomes the task of exploring how this thought–which is now everybody's heritage and which affect us all–may be renewed from and for the margins. But of course, the margins are as plural and diverse as the centers. Europe appears different when seen from within the experiences of colonization or inferiorization in specific parts of the world. (Chakrabarty, 2000, p. 16)

Even though he uses Marx's category of "capital" to acknowledge the importance of Marx's "figure of the abstract human" for "understanding the globe that capitalism produces", for Chakrabarty "this abstract human occludes questions of belonging and diversity" and needs to be destabilized, in order to offer some "insights on human belonging and historical difference" (p. 18). This can be read as combining, in a postcolonial critique of Eurocentric thought, both a difference-theoretical and an equality-theoretical approach, as well as perspectives from cultural sociology together with perspectives from the sociology of culture.[24] Thereby, he proposes to create "plural normative horizons specific to our existence and relevant to the examination of our lives and their possibilities" (Chakrabarty, 2000, p. 20). This again connects to the transcultural approach of this volume.

There are again several more theories that can be called "decolonial" and which at the same time also offer new perspectives. Julia Reuter and Paula-Irene Villa, for example, intend to "provincialize sociology" by relativizing, locating and contextualizing social theory (Reuter & Villa, 2010). In addressing the place and development of postcolonial philosophy, Patricia Purtschert suggest re-reading the "Western history of thought" in order to decolonize the "epistemic violence" of philosophical texts, such as Kant's representation of colonial subjects (Purtschert, 2012). Manuela Boatcă and Sergio Costa again criticize the Eurocentric foundations of the sociological theory of modernity (Boatcă & Costa, 2016). Moreover, Wolfgang Gabbert's sociology of globalization disapproves conventional theories of globalization that only assign dynamic developments to the "center", while ignoring the majority of developments in the world (Gabbert, 2010). Last but not least, Encarnación Gutiérrez Rodriguez calls for the decolonizing of epistemology by taking into account decolonial feminist-queer southern epistemologies and new subjectivities (Gutiérrez Rodriguez, 2016). All these approaches have in common the fact that they seek to de-stabilize and re-think established thinking, ascriptions and borders.

Furthermore, in the study of culture, there is a longer tradition of questioning and deconstructing borders. The academic deconstruction of borders and boundaries can

---

24 See below both sections on intersectional diversity & otherness and on cross-cultural diversity & otherness.

be found in e.g. migration and globalization studies, postcolonial studies as well as queer and gender studies. These various approaches can be called either difference-theoretical, when the focus is placed more on how differences are carried out, and/or deconstructivist, where the focus is laid on how differences are un-done. As Bachmann-Medick writes:

> A difference-oriented approach in the study of culture however makes borderlands and shifts between the disciplines–here in direction of sociology–productive. Likewise, fractures, deviations and discrepancies are marked more strongly in order to analyse them further: as social and societal inequalities.[25] (Bachmann-Medick, 2016b, p. 52)

Originally, Derrida developed the notion of deconstruction as a language-philosophical instrument in order to apply it to texts or systems of symbols in semiotics. Deconstruction for Derrida is a kind of re-reading of a text, in order to lay open the ambivalence of written signs. No *a priori* meaning can be assigned to a text. Accordingly:

> The act of deconstruction is ... intended as self-liberation of thought from its usual border-drawing and hierarchies, especially from the conventional dichotomies of subject and object, mind and body, ... good and evil, true and false, oppositions that often enough have served to legitimize the hegemonic claim of one culture, class, race or gender over the other.[26] (Zapf, 2001, p. 101)

Derrida demonstrates inconsistencies and irregularities in texts with the two versions of "différence" and "différance". The difference between these two words can only be detected in the written form; it is not audible. The perspective of "différance" "supposes that the text has no present being"[27] (Derrida, 2004, p. 138). This means that no symbols, meanings, practices and identities of diversity and otherness should be regarded as static, but that they should rather be deconstructed. In this way, "every seemingly strong and irreducible *opposition* ... is declared [a] theoretical fiction"[28] (p. 135).

---

**25** "Eine differenzorientierte kulturwissenschaftliche Herangehensweise hingegen macht Grenzbereiche und Verschiebungen zwischen den Disziplinen–hier in Richtung der Soziologie–produktiv. So markiert sie stärker die Brüche, die Abweichungen und Missverhältnisse, um sie dann weitergehend zu analysieren: als soziale und gesellschaftliche Ungleichheiten" (Bachmann-Medick, 2016b, p. 52).
**26** "Der Akt der Dekonstruktion ist ... intendiert als Selbstbefreiung des Denkens aus gewohnten Grenzziehungen und Hierarchisierungen, insbesondere aus den herkömmlichen Dichotomien von Subjekt und Objekt, Geist und Körper, ... gut und böse, wahr und falsch, Gegensätzen, die oft genug zur Rechtfertigung des Hegemonieanspruchs einer Kultur, Klasse (class), Rasse (race) oder eines Geschlechts (gender) über das andere missbraucht wurden" (Zapf, 2001, p. 101).
**27** "dass der untersuchte Text nicht 'ist', also 'kein gegenwärtig Seiendes' sei" (Derrida, 2004, p. 138).
**28** "So wird jeder scheinbar strenge und irreduzible Gegensatz ... für 'theoretische Fiktion' erklärt" (Derrida, 2004, p. 135).

This procedure corresponds to deconstructivism as a poststructuralist methodology that is based on Derrida's deconstruction. This perspective criticizes the logo-centrism of modernity that is based on binary oppositions, and negates a static meaning of a sign. Deconstructivism has been established especially in literary and cultural theory as a methodology to lay open power-hierarchies and essentialist concepts which follow the poststructuralist argument to de-stabilize fixed meanings. As Boatcă and Costa write following Stuart Hall, "the notion of *différance* [is used] to deconstruct the antinomic discourses that counter the 'I' and the 'other', the 'we' and the 'they'" (Boatcă & Costa, 2016, p. 25). It is important to note, however, that the poststructuralist perspective on differences does not eliminate borders, but "rather broaches the issue of their ambivalences and traces the cultural processes crossing these"[29] (Reckwitz, 2008b, p. 309).

Another concept that needs to be addressed at this point is Gilles Deleuze's and Felix Guattari's concept of the *rhizome*:

> The multiplicities are the reality itself and do not suppose any unicity, do not fit in any totality, nor refer to a subject. On the contrary, the subjectivations, the totalizations, the unifications are processes that are produced and emerge in multiplicities. The characteristic principles of multiplicities are concerned with their own elements, that are singularity; with their own relations, that are becoming; with their own events, that are haecceities (that is, individuations without subjects); with their own space-time, that are spare time and spaces; with the model of its realization, which is the rhizome (in opposition to the tree model); with its composition plan, that is constituted by plateaus (continuous zones of intensity); with their vectors that cross them and constitute territories and degrees of "deterritorialization". (Deleuze & Guattari, 2011, pp. 10–11, 34)

Critics of deconstructivism complain that texts which seek to deconstruct are based on prior assumptions themselves and are thus paradoxical towards their own approach. The *writing culture debate* described above addresses this problem from ethnography and has developed in parallel to poststructuralism. Quite often, postcolonial theory is also described as belonging to poststructuralism for its deconstructivist perspectives (Angermüller & Bellina, 2012). Following Urs Stäheli, the common denominator of poststructuralist approaches (Butler, 1990; Bhabha, 2000; Haraway, 1992; Latour, 2017) is the assumption that there are no longer static systems of differences, so that the border itself moves into focus. Both "subversive, political agencies develop as well as the policing of the border takes place"[30] (Stäheli, 2000, pp. 62–63). For Stäheli, everything could be different, and so everything is de-stabilized from the start and only becomes meaningful in its relation with something else, which in turn involves

---

**29** "sondern deren Uneindeutigkeit thematisiert und die kulturellen Prozesse nachzeichnet, welche diese kreuzen" (Reckwitz, 2008b, p. 309).

**30** "da hier sowohl subversive politische Handlungsmöglichkeiten entstehen wie auch ein policing, d. h. ein Regulieren der Grenze stattfindet" (Stäheli, 2000, pp. 62–63).

contingent "battles of articulation"[31]. Referring to Judith Butler's term of performativity, Stäheli locates these battles of articulation within the context of the performative turn, which "focuses ... on the practical dimension of the generation of cultural meanings and experiences. It seeks to understand the generative and transformative aspects of culture on the basis of events, practices, material embodiments and media forms" (Bachmann-Medick, 2016a, p. 73). It is important, in this respect, to observe how differences are enacted or un-done and to understand these actions as practices (see e.g. Hirschauer in this volume; Van Loon, 2019). In poststructuralist theory, differences are "either captured along a 'constituent outside' (be it as the radical Other or as the necessarily discarded), or they are otherwise explained from a process based always on a given diversity of socials"[32] (Stäheli, 2000, p. 67).

Bruno Latour would call these socials not a specific social sphere, but rather a "peculiar movement of re-accumulating and again associating"[33] (Latour, 2017, p. 19). In this conception, the social is understood as fluid and circulating, and the world has to be constantly built "from utterly heterogeneous parts that will never make a whole, but at best a fragile, revisable, and diverse composite material" (Latour, 2010, p. 474). As stated above, most of the study of culture follows a constructivist stance. Latour, along with Michel Callon and John Law (Callon et al., 1986), has also developed the so called Acteur-Network-Theory and can be taken as an example of what is now being called post-constructivism (Gertenbach, 2017). Here, the differentiation between reality and construction should be overcome on the grounds that any construction has always possessed its material execution. Reality is not thought to be constituted discursively but becomes reformulated by bringing into focus the relations and interconnectedness of nature, society, technology, science, and ostensibly any heterogeneous material. Post-constructivism not only seeks to overcome dichotomies but further orientates itself to affects and emotions, senses and spaces (Gertenbach, 2017). Likewise, post-constructivism touches upon poststructuralist deconstruction as well as relating itself to the performative, sensory, material as well as spatial turns, as will be further explained below and in my other contribution in this volume.

In the following, all these different approaches to diversity and otherness will be subsumed under two major perspectives, which Reckwitz pointedly calls the two opposing regimes of culturalisation: hyperculture and cultural essentialism (Reckwitz, 2016). For Reckwitz, these two regimes of culturalisation denote "two opposing views, what culture *means*, and in accordance with it two contrary formats in which

---

**31** "Artikulationskämpfe".

**32** "Entweder wird Differenz über ein 'konstitutives Außen' erfasst (sei es als der radikal Andere oder das notwendig Verworfene) oder Differenzen werden aus einem Prozess erklärt, dem eine immer schon gegebene Vielheit des Sozialen zu Grunde liegt" (Stäheli, 2000, p. 67).

**33** "eigentümliche Bewegung des Wiederansammelns und erneuten Assoziierens" (Latour, 2017, p. 19).

the cultural sphere is organized"[34] (Reckwitz, 2016, p. 2). The first regime of hyperculture describes the "cultural opening of life forms … a pluralisation of life styles"[35] (p. 1), in which "diversity" and "cosmopolitanism" are both taken as "leading semantics" (p. 4) of this regime of culturalisation. In opposition, the position of cultural essentialism is presented as a "cultural closure of life forms, in which a new rigid moralisation takes place"[36] (p. 1). This form of culturalisation constructs collectives based on fixed, essentialized identities with a fierce dualism of inclusion and exclusion of morally defended imagined communities.

Gurminder Bhambra, while speaking of diversity in Europe, similarly distinguishes between multiculturalism and cosmopolitanism, in stating that whereas the first often speaks of visible differences within nation states, the latter operates as a more overarching principle which encompasses the differences between nation states (Bhambra, 2019). In this contribution, however, the divide between these two regimes will be considered more openly as intersectional diversity and otherness and cross-cultural diversity and otherness, respectively. It will be shown which premises these two perspectives in the study of culture are based on and discussed whether they can be systemized in this way at all. Following the postcolonial quest of this chapter, as has been explained above, this schematic representation seeks to combine transcultural and postcolonial approaches with approaches to diversity and otherness from the sociology of culture and cultural sociology.

## 2.2 Intersectional Diversity & Otherness

As stated in the introduction to this chapter, one finds intersectional approaches to diversity and otherness most often in the fields of the sociology of culture. Frequently, the difference between these fields and approaches from cultural sociology are emphasized as lying in the opposition between materialistic versus idealistic perspectives. This means that, in the field of intersectional diversity and otherness, differences are mostly regarded as stemming from social differences and from how these are lived out empirically in manifold life-worlds. In contrast, cultural sociology assigns the meaning-making processes to the human mind. Actions and cultural patterns result from these mentally constructed differences. As always, there are also

---

**34** "zwei konträre Auffassungen darüber, was Kultur überhaupt bedeutet, und dem entsprechend zwei konträre Formate, in denen die Kultursphäre organisiert ist" (Reckwitz, 2016, p. 2).

**35** "kulturelle Öffnung der Lebensformen …, eine Pluralisierung von Lebensstilen" (Reckwitz, 2016, p. 1).

**36** "kulturelle Schließung von Lebensformen, in denen eine neue rigide Moralisierung wirksam ist" (Reckwitz, 2016, p. 1).

many approaches which combine these seemingly distinct methodological and epis-temological perspectives.

In Weber's sense of the "ideal-type" (Weber, 2005), intersectional approaches therefore look at the differences—or inequalities—as being (materially) produced, and therefore done or undone, by and in (e.g.) incorporated practices. These cultural differences are often thought to be determined by social positions if one considers the wide corpus of academic literature based on Bourdieu's field theory. As such, the sociology of culture looks at the field of cultural production as a field in which there reigns a permanent struggle for social recognition interwoven with economic and organizational power-relations. Quite often, these approaches not only seek to lay open how social inequalities take shape, but also want to counteract these tendencies following set political objectives. Diversity and otherness in this sense are understood as multiple, intersecting social belongings that either include or exclude.

In taking into account (material) productions that are constituted repeatedly in spatial practices of inclusion or exclusion, intersectional diversity and otherness can be related directly to the spatial turn, which is again connected to a "distinct re-materialization" (Bachmann-Medick, 2016a, p. 211). For Bachmann-Medick, aca-demic thought has shied away from spatial thinking after WWII, as it was seen to be connected to the "racist blood-and-soil ideology" (p. 212) of Nazism. Therefore, the spatial turn was developed mainly in the 1980s. "As a key feature of globalization, interconnections and cross-linkages have made the spatial perspective inevitable" (p. 213). Deterritorializations, social conflicts, and "unequal global developments rooted in the spatial division of labor" (p. 214) then became major issues in spatial research, while the "social production of space [became regarded] as a complex and often con-tradictory social process" (p. 214).

Also in postcolonially oriented research, a spatial turn can be detected, which further underlines the political mission which is often connected with it (Soja & Hooper, 1993; Harvey, 1989; Soja, 2010). Eurocentric world-mapping and exclusion based on geographical divisions of center-periphery are heavily criticized (Said, 1995; Appadurai, 1996; Bhabha, 1997). Other approaches, drawing among others on Fou-cault's concept of *heterotopia* (Foucault, 2006*)* or Bourdieu's production of social space (Bourdieu, 1991), "study the spatial effects of social strata, ethnicity and gender relations from the perspective of their exclusions and inclusions, ... and their capac-ity to liberate 'other' concealed spaces" (Bachmann-Medick, 2016a, p. 217; Massey, 1994). These developments eventually lead into theories of transnationalisation (Glick-Schiller et al., 1995; Anderson, B., 1986), glocalisation (Robertson, 2003, p. 30) and border studies (Wille, 2016), as well as to migration and mobility studies (Lash & Urry, 1994). Simmel's *Stranger*, for example, is said to represent one of the found-ing texts for the sociology of migration and can be taken as a social type that is not rooted in a specific locality (Le Grand, 2019). Accordingly, the stranger rather evolves from strangeness in social relationships in which social distance and proximity are related. Even though Simmel applies a rather problematic schematization, strangeness is depicted as relational and constructed (Saalmann, 2007).

Migration and mobility studies also mainly follow such a constructivist approach (Bojadžijev, 2018; Karakayali, 2016). A "mobility turn" and a "transnational turn" is hence diagnosed with a strong focus on global developments (Johler et al., 2011). As a result, many of these studies follow a global perspective (Go & Krause, 2016), which will be further highlighted in my other chapter in this volume. Yet in fact, there are probably as many macro-theoretical perspectives focusing on exclusionary global practices (Buchholz, 2008) as there are micro-studies devoted to the practices of inclusion and exclusion in everyday life (Anderson, E., 2015).

The overarching principles of these approaches not only lie in their common interest in the practices of inclusion, exclusion and social inequalities, but also their political objective or quest to decolonize unequal power structures. The critique that is often addressed to deconstructed hybrid notions of diversity and otherness, as will be discussed in the next section as only neglecting existing social inequalities, is another common denominator of these theories.

Quite often in this area, practical fields of application are also discussed, for instance in order to reach out to a more inclusive environment (Behrens et al., 2016; Yıldız, 2018) or to use diversity as an advantage in recruiting processes in diversity management. For example, the model of the political scientist Andrew Stirling is used to look at different aspects of diversity when variety, disparity and balance of elements as a whole are measured. For Stirling, variety is defined as the number of elements in the mix, while disparity denotes their degree of differences, and balance means the evenness in the elements' contribution. He uses these models in his analysis of economic diversity and in understanding the way that this can be optimised (Stirling, 2007). Lately, there have also been post- and decolonial approaches in diversity management literature (Jack, 2015; Kaasila-Pakanen, 2015), while previously diversity management was widely criticized in social sciences for only labelling their target-individuals (Bendl et al., 2015; see also Pelillo-Hestermeyer & Cismondo in this volume).

In the following, the first intersectional approaches to *diversity* which are meant to foster *inclusion* will be discussed, followed by a sketch of those intersectional approaches to *otherness* which have been exposed to *exclusionary* practices. Regularly, the same practices can have both inclusionary and exclusionary outcomes at the same time. This is again only a heuristic systematization.

Certain theories of intersectional diversity can be called equality-theoretical, as they are often based on a philosophical argument of the equality of all people or are otherwise focused on political strategies to achieve more equity. In political theory, the struggles surrounding political, social or cultural representation, equal access, identity politics and minority rights, form a vast area of research (Meer & Modood, 2014; Neubert et al., 2013), and are often derived from earlier theories of multiculturalism (Taylor, 1994; Benhabib, 2002).

For example, Charles Taylor's *The Politics of Recognition* (1994) is seen as one of the earliest theories of multiculturalism and is situated in the field of political theory. This influential work covers the Francophone minority in Quebec, Canada and how such minorities fail to be politically recognized. For Taylor, this is a question of identity, which is especially negotiated "through dialogue, partly overt, partly internal, with others" (Taylor, 1994, p. 34). This identity can be formed but also malformed. This is why, for him, it is important to establish a "politics of difference", in which "*everyone* should be recognized for his or her unique identity" (p. 38). This also entails "equal respect to actually evolved cultures" (p. 42). Apart from the problematic equation of one cultural trait in an individual's identity with the "culture" of a whole group, Taylor's approach is assembled on the basis of much of the identity politics which remains prevalent nowadays. For example, as will be stressed in my other contribution in this book, in German cultural policies there are many groups who are still fighting for equal representation in public cultural life, for instance in the fight for equal access to funding resources. The keywords in this field are, among others, participation, representation[37] and access.

Taylor criticizes approaches such as liberalism for having enforced that, even though diversity is becoming more respected, the "politics of equal respect ... is inhospitable to difference, because ... it insists on uniform application of the rules defining these rights" (Taylor, 1994, p. 60). One can see that liberalism is not as neutral as it seems. Instead, in Taylor's conception of multiculturalism, "the equal value of different cultures" (p. 64) should be recognized and fostered by the government, such as through positive discrimination practices like quotas or other affirmative action plans (Cuyler, 2013). However, this implies a rather static conception of culture, where it has to be negotiated which cultures are worthy of protection. Moreover, this politics of difference leads inevitably to other exclusions. This communitarianism, where cultures are seen as entities that should have political rights, and where the diversity of individuals depends on being recognized in a dialogical process, could also lead to a totalitarian equality.

The political philosopher Seyla Benhabib instead argues in favour of taking cultures as hybrid and negotiated in narratives. Even if not all individuals have the opportunity to "exit" (Benhabib, 2006, p. 386) their community which was assigned to them by birth, she sees "the possibility of narrative resignification and re-appropriation" (p. 387). For this view, Benhabib is heavily criticized by the philosopher Nikolas Kompridis, for whom "a culture that is strictly non-identical with itself would be a culture without a past" (Kompridis, 2005, p. 340). In this academic discussion, Reckwitz's and Bhambra's above-mentioned oppositional cultural regimes of hyperculture versus cultural essentialism (Reckwitz, 2016), or cosmopolitanism versus multiculturalism

---

37 In this context, representation is not understood in line with e.g. Stuart Hall's understanding (Hall, 1997) but rather as political representation of minority groups.

(Bhambra, 2019), come into play. Benhabib and Kompridis both endorse and criticize each other for the other's normative agenda that again shows the political objective I touched upon before. Similarly, both approaches rely on adopting a certain perspective towards differences, as Benhabib writes: "Cultures are formed through binaries because human beings live in an evaluative universe" (Benhabib, 2002, p. 7).

However, the aforementioned critique of cross-cultural diversity expressed by Kompridis as only neglecting differences is also used by followers of the *New Right* (for example in France the *Nouvelle Droite*), in order to serve their argument that the diversity of cultures and people should be maintained without mixing and without hybridization in order not to lose one's own culture or identity. As Taguieff writes: "As a result, this particular version of the 'right to difference' is organized around a 'mixophobic' core: it is 'haunted' by the threat of the destruction of identities through interbreeding—physical and cultural crossbreeding" (Taguieff, 1993, p. 101). So in this and other cases, the celebration of diversity in combination with essentializing cultural differences can even be called the "politics of cultural apartheid" (Wuggenig, 2015) or, in the context of this contribution, "intersectional otherness", i.e. exclusion along multiple discriminatory lines.

Miranda Christon also argues in this direction that difference became a central concept of postmodernity that has been colonized by the Far Right[38] (Christon, 2019). Referring to Jean-François Lyotard's argument that "postmodern knowledge ... refines our sensitivity to differences and reinforces our ability to tolerate the incommensurable" (Lyotard, 1984, p. xxv), Christon states that this same argument leads to new racisms. As such, "theorists of difference have not indicated where the line is to be drawn between forms of difference which foster democracy [intersectional diversity; inclusion] and forms of difference which reflect anti-democratic aspirations [intersectional otherness; exclusion]" (Benhabib, 1994, p. 3).

Several other terms and concepts belong to this discourse, such as "creolization" (Hannerz, 1992; Müller & Ueckmann, 2013), "diaspora" (Clifford, 2006) or "super-diversity" (Vertovec, 2007; Arnaut, 2012; Johler et al., 2011). Creolization is defined by Ulf Hannerz, for example, as "a combination of diversity, interconnectedness, and innovation in the context of global-center periphery relationships" (1992, p. 67). For Steven Vertovec, super-diversity as a demographic and social pattern means:

> a notion intended to underline a level and kind of complexity surpassing anything the country [Britain] has previously experienced. Such a condition is distinguished by a dynamic interplay of variables among an increased number of new, small and scattered, multiple-origin, transnationally connected, socio-economically differentiated and legally stratified by immigrants who have arrived over the last decade. (2007, p. 1024)

---

**38** In German, the anthology *Großerzählungen des Extremen. Neue Rechte, Populismus, Islamismus, War on Terror* [Great Narratives of the Extreme. New Right, Populism, Islamism, War on Terror] offers more insights on the matter (Schellhöh et al., 2018).

Vertovec looks not only at these "configurations of diversity" and how they have diversified in the last decades, but also takes into account "representations of diversity", by which he means "how diversity is imagined ... in images, representations, symbols and meanings", such as in multiculturalism (Vertovec, 2009, p. 14). For him, multiculturalism has only taken on another name in politics: diversity (p. 16). Vertovec finally also covers the area of "how diversities are actually experienced or encountered" (p. 23). In all three areas he sees super-diversity taking shape.

Karel Arnaut takes Vertovec's concept of super-diversity to amount to a critical socio-linguistic study. With this in mind, Arnaut uses super-diversity as a "lens for looking at diversity as discourse and social practice" (Arnaut, 2012, p. 1) in a transnational approach. This entails "taking into account the fluidity and intricacies of the new diversity in times of heightened mobility and transnational communication" (p. 3). He criticizes the established hegemonic diversity discourse (p. 3) and rather pleads for a postcolonial approach of socio-linguistics, which constitutes, following Makoni and Pennycook, "the dis-inventing and reconstituting of languages both in the ex-metropoles and their former colonies" (p. 11), in order to decolonize both the human and social sciences. As we can see, there are similar quests for a post- and decolonial approach as the one which this contribution follows in other disciplinary areas in the study of culture, diversity and otherness.

Steven Vertovec is also the editor of the *Routledge International Handbook of Diversity Studies* (2015),[39] that offers a wide range of approaches related to diversity, mainly understanding the term as denoting "social difference" (Vertovec, 2015, p. 1). The handbook not only intends to reflect upon both public and academic uses of the term "diversity", offering a vast field of descriptive analysis of "intersectionality, multiplicity and boundary-crossing dynamics of social categories" (p. 9) across different societies, but it also calls into question the neglect "of including historical and non-Western contexts" (p. 10) in mainstream diversity studies. This also applies to the postcolonial approach of this chapter.

Similarly to what is called intersectional diversity and otherness by this study, Vertovec suggests that "diversity studies should entail ... studies of diversity as *modes of social differentiation* ... (and) of diversity as *complex social environments*" (p. 10). Equally, his topics of interest are laid out in the same field which is looked at in my undertaking: categorizations, social inequality, in-group/out-group, self-ascription and ascription by others, group and category, symbolic and social boundaries, identity and (last but not least) intersectionality (pp. 12–13). It would go beyond the scope of this chapter to discuss all these different approaches, but what is important to stress at this point is the focus on mechanisms of stratification.

---

**39** In the German-speaking context there is a similar handbook on *Diversity Studies* (Krell et al., 2007) which focuses on discourses and practices of diversity from different disciplines, such as education, anthropology, medicine, politics, law and marketing/management.

The German Sociological Association's[40] 2012 biennial conference was held under the title *Diversity and Cohesion*[41]. As stated in the conference proceedings, diversity in this context is understood as "the growing amount of orientating options, self-ascriptions and external ascriptions as well as social conditions and life-styles. ... Many differentiations intersect and overlap with each other in daily life"[42] (Löw, 2014, p. 1). The contributions encompass, among others, topics such as ethnic diversity, social inequality, diversity of private life forms, new forms of cohesion, and theoretical approaches such as intersectionality or stratification. As we can see again, these include many of the same topics that have been touched upon in this contribution. In addition, many approaches call for the overcoming of "methodological nationalisms" (Beck & Grande, 2010, p. 189) which are still often prevalent in sociological research, especially when devoted to issues of diversity. The combination of two topics, of "horizontal dimensions of social differentiation" and of "vertical social inequalities" (Liebsch et al., 2014, p. 841), brings us to the field of intersectionality studies. This again is, of course, the eponym of my categories of intersectional diversity and otherness. In this case, when social inequalities are discussed in relation to issues of discrimination and exclusion rather than equal representation and inclusion, we have come to what I understand as intersectional *otherness*.

Thus, this viewpoint from which to look at many overlapping and intersecting social identities, combined by individuals such as "race", gender, ethnicity, sexual orientation and so on, can be described as intersectionality studies. In the earlier days of intersectionality studies, the three intersecting categories *race, gender, class* were often looked at; many other categories were included in intersectional research thereafter. These studies highlight how social inequalities and multiple discrimination processes develop and take effect (Winker & Degele, 2009).[43] First incorporated into the academic debate by Kimberlé Crenshaw, a Black feminist legal academic (Crenshaw, 1989, pp. 139–167), the term became rapidly more used in other academic fields as well. Gabriele Winker and Nina Degele, for instance, define intersectionality as "the interweaving of categories of inequality ... as the interplay of inequality-causing social structures that are context-specific, object-oriented and derived from social practices"[44] (Winker & Degele, 2009, p. 15). These two authors have conducted

---

40  "Deutsche Gesellschaft für Soziologie DGS".

41  "Vielfalt und Zusammenhalt".

42  "die wachsende Zahl an Orientierungsangeboten, Selbst- und Fremdzuschreibungen sowie an sozialen Lagen und Lebensstilen. ... Viele Differenzierungen überkreuzen und überlagern sich im Alltag" (Löw, 2014, p. 1).

43  Other studies from this field include (among others): Lorde, 1996; Alexander-Floyd, 2012; Bilge, 2013; Collins, 2000; McCall, 2005; Puar, 2012.

44  "als Verwobenheit von Ungleichheitskategorien ... als kontextspezifische, gegenstandsbezogene und an sozialen Praxen ansetzende Wechselwirkungen ungleichheitsgenerierender sozialer Strukturen" (Winker & Degele, 2009, p. 15).

a structural analysis of these mentioned categories of social inequalities, proceeding from the assumption of a "capitalistic structured society based on the fundamental dynamics of economic profit maximization"[45] (p. 25). By analysing the four structural categories of *class, gender, race,* and *body,* their interplay and elated power relations, Winker and Degele lay open multiple discriminations, symbolic representations and identity constructions.

To locate the categories of *gender* and *race* within the context of *class* and the capitalistic world-system is another line of research by which to critique global capitalism that can again be related to the sociology of culture and intersectional otherness. Here, the (again) very vast academic corpus of scholarly literature, which is based on the theories of Karl Marx and Friedrich Engels (*The Capital*, 1872), Max Weber (*The Spirit of Capitalism*, 2016), Luc Boltanski and Eve Chiapello (*The New Spirit of Capitalism*, 2003), Richard Sennett (*The Corrosion of Character*, 1999) or Uwe Bröckling (*The Entrepreneurial Self*, 2015), is challenged by postcolonial (Mbembe, 2001; Bhambra, 2007), decolonial (Groys, 2008; Dussel, 2009; Nederveen Pieterse & Parekh, 1995; Escobar, 2004) and global perspectives (Sassen, 2015; Robinson, 2004; Stiglitz, 2002). Of course there are also numerous other authors devoted to different aspects of social inequality and social stratification (Solga et al., 2009; Weiß, 2017) that go beyond the scope of this chapter.

In the context of this contribution, it is especially Pierre Bourdieu's theory (Bourdieu, 2010) that is relevant to matters of intersectional otherness. Bourdieu explains how the different positions of actors in a shared social space are determined by the combination of the different forms of capital which are incorporated in a specific habitus; this he defines as economic, social, and cultural/symbolic capital. For Bourdieu's counterpart Bernard Lahire, the concept of habitus does not take into account the singular manifold ways of dispositions which individuals can make use of (Lahire, 1995; 2005). Despite all their academic disputes, both these theorists discuss how the diversity and otherness of people depend on unequal social structures, individual dispositions, struggles for recognition, and related factors.

bell hooks can be taken as another example of a theorist of intersectional otherness with her *Ain't I a Woman* (1995). hooks discusses especially how certain white feminist women are racist and complicit of white patriarchy based on colonialism. Thus, she is another theorist who brings together various issues of diversity and otherness from an intersectional, anti-racist, and postcolonial point of view. A similar position is adopted by Sara Ahmed in discussing, for example, the connection between colonialism and the fetish for the stranger (2000), the socio-cultural heritage of whiteness (2007), and how in organizations the topic of diversity has become

---

45 "kapitalistisch strukturierte Gesellschaft mit der grundlegenden Dynamik ökonomischer Profitmaximierung" (Winker & Degele, 2009, p. 25).

the focus, while at the same time an "institutional wall" conceals still ongoing acts of discrimination (2012).

There are again many more authors devoted to these views from different disciplines in the study of culture, including cultural studies (Hall, 2017), critical whiteness (Anderson, E., 2015) and "race" studies (Thompson, 2015), anti-racism (Espahangizi et al., 2016), or social sciences. Some have coined the term "postmigrant" to convey an "analytical perspective that grapples with the conflicts, processes of identity construction, social and political transformations which start after migration … has taken place"[46] (Foroutan, 2019, p. 232).

All these different intersectional approaches are mainly based on a difference-theoretical perspective. The difference-oriented paradigm of approaches of intersectional diversity and otherness sees differences as contributing to social inequality and thus does not aim primarily at the deconstruction of differences, but rather the unveiling of dichotomies which (continue to) serve unequal power structures. However, as discussed above, in cultural theory drawn from the poststructuralist philosopher Jaques Derrida, difference does not connote a substance but functions rather as a descriptive category for the cognitive uncertainty that often comes into play while theorizing social and cultural complexity. As such an analytic instrument, difference can serve the concept of deconstruction which was also developed by Derrida. The difference-oriented paradigm is further destabilized in the 1980s, mainly through postcolonial approaches, to become a hybridization paradigm, which will be discussed in the next section.

## 2.3 Cross-Cultural Diversity & Otherness

The perspective, which I call *cross-cultural diversity and otherness*, focuses on processes of interweaving and interconnectedness in the sense-making processes of humankind. Approaches to cross-cultural diversity and otherness can be rooted especially in interpretative approaches to the study of culture, such as in cultural sociology or cultural and social anthropology, and are thus linked to the interpretative turn and also to the reflexive and postcolonial turns. In addition, the translational turn is related to this field, as Bachmann-Medick writes:

> There has been an ongoing effort in the study of culture to explore new methodological approaches to the "in-between spaces" that transcend dichotomous demarcations and binary epistemological attitudes. It is in the category of translation that these approaches have an empirical

---

46 "eine Analyseperspektive, die sich mit den Konflikten, Identitätsbildungsprozessen, sozialen und politischen Transformationen auseinandersetzt, die nach erfolgter Migration … einsetzen" (Foroutan, 2019, p. 232). See also Canan & Foroutan, 2016.

basis. ... The translation perspective reveals concrete structures of difference ... not only between cultures but within cultures and across cultural boundaries. (2016a, pp. 26, 184)

Most approaches follow deconstructivist notions of diversity and otherness, whereas the constructivist paradigm is acknowledged in all of these theories, which use terms such as hybridity, transculturality, or creolization. What is at stake in the context of this contribution is not only the focus on differences, such as the last section's discussion on *intersectional diversity*, but rather on how they can be de-stabilized. So transculturality, along with terms such as hybridity, relies on the assumption that the great narratives of modernity have been deconstructed, and that the post-modern pluralism of discourses does not suffice to describe the complex social and cultural processes in today's postmigrant societies either. Rather, the implementation of border-crossing concepts is favoured. Each of these terms and concepts carries its own connotations, but on different levels they all concentrate on the hybridization of cultures, the blurring of cultural borders, and life in spaces of (post-)migrancy in times of globalization. Culture is no longer regarded as static and definable. On the contrary, dynamic aspects of culture stand at the forefront when pluralistic and ambivalent identities are recognized. In this contribution, this field of hybrid cultural concepts is subsumed under the terms *cross-cultural diversity* and *otherness*. As stated above, a postcolonially oriented perspective on cross-cultural diversity and otherness thereby centers on what Mbembe calls the postcolony, defined as "the experience of a period that is far from being uniform ..., but in which instants, moments, and events are, as it were, on top of one another, inside one another. ... [T]he postcolony is a period of embedding" (Mbembe, 2001, p. 242).

Similarly, with his concept of the *Black Atlantic*, Paul Gilroy refers to transcultural and transnational formations of identities and ideas that contribute to the destruction of nationalistic paradigms of thought on cultural history (Gilroy, 1993). Creolization, métissage, and hybridity are inevitable occurrences and necessarily result from the mixing of ideas and the instability and variability of identities; they thereby stand against cultural absolutism. Gilroy sees identities as always unfinished and always constructed anew. The idea of the *Black Atlantic* is of a cultural and political system which spans the whole Atlantic, seen as an entity for historical analysis from a transcultural perspective. The boats, the sailors and the passage over the Atlantic stand in the *Black Atlantic* for an "in-between". Accordingly, the *Black Atlantic* goes beyond simple binaries of "nation versus diaspora" by consideration of the Atlantic as a network of the local and the global. Gilroy gives examples of contemporary music and films that can establish counter-cultures to modernity from a transnational perspective.

The co-founder of British cultural studies, Stuart Hall, also seeks to dissolve binary social identificatory processes and rejects dichotomous ascriptions (Hall, 1994). Through globalization, he contends, the individual becomes more and more dislocated. Even though Hall acknowledges the importance of history, language and

culture for the construction of identity, he points out that representation and discourses can only take place within a specific framework. Mechanisms of representation have epistemic power over the "Other". These narratives should not merely
be reversed; instead, they should counteract the binary system of representation
through the recognition of diversity and new creative expressions. Identity from this
perspective becomes a processual hybrid production, a crossing-point where new cultural expressions and theoretical discourses develop.

This view on the construction of identity can also be found in postcolonial positions taken by Iain Chambers and Homi K. Bhabha. Following Iain Chambers, the
former dichotomous model of center and periphery is deemed to be untenable in
today's globalized complexity and cultural diversity. The "other" can no longer be
pushed off to the periphery, but "this other embodies ... the disturbing questioning,
the alienation, we all carry inside" (Chambers, 1996, p. 8). As a result, "[t]his also
means of course to understand the other being not as something that can comfortably
be transferred somewhere else, but that is always there" (p. 26).

Likewise, migration does not have a fixed starting or ending point, but is instead
a permanent process. Surprising turns, border-crossings and cultural complexities
should be allowed to take place:

> The impossible mission that seeks to preserve the singularity of a culture must paradoxically
> negate its fundamental element: its historical dynamic. Post-colonialism is perhaps the sign
> of an increasing awareness that it is not feasible to subtract a culture, a history, a language,
> an identity from the wider, transforming currents of the increasingly metropolitan world. It is
> impossible to "go home" again. (Chambers, 1996, p. 89)

Chambers describes this "homelessness" by depicting musical forms which decen-
ter structures of center and periphery through the random combination of different
musical styles. Musical meaning should always be contextualized and the existence
of "authenticity" negated. It is impossible "to attach the meaning of such [musical]
differences to any of those places" (p. 98). Hence, Chambers does not intend to establish a counter-discourse to the dominant one, but instead to demonstrate how a contingent, decentralized space with ever-changing meanings develops through, for
example, the duplication of meanings and symbols.

This approach to going beyond the binaries, as depicted by Said, can also be
found in Homi K. Bhabha's figure of the "third space". The "third space" is a no-space,
a space of hybridity, where the subject constructs itself as a "neither-nor" between the
space of the subjective home and historical space. The subject thereby disappoints all
expectations by going beyond simple binaries.

Hybridity is often falsely equated with diversity. For Bhabha, hybridity is not the
same concept as hybrid cultural diversity, which he also clearly differentiates from
cultural difference, as in the following:

Cultural diversity is an epistemological object ... whereas cultural difference is the process of the enunciation of culture as "knowledgeable", authoritative, adequate to the construction of systems of cultural identification. If cultural diversity is a category of comparative ethics, aesthetics, or ethnology, cultural difference is a process of signification through which statements of culture or on culture differentiate, discriminate, and authorize the production of fields of force, reference, applicability, and capacity. (Bhabha, 2006, p. 155)

In this quotation, Bhabha both relies on the difference-oriented and on the interpretative approach to culture. Meanings are assigned in order to "do differences" (see Hirschauer in this volume). Bhabha's definition of diversity, however, can also be assigned to an intersectional approach.[47] Yet what is more instructive at this point to offering a possible understanding of the here-discussed concepts of *cross-cultural diversity* and *otherness* is Bhabha's concept of "hybridity" and how this hybridity describes a "third space".

This is because Bhabha does not see hybridity as the mixing of culturally "pure" elements; instead he describes it precisely as those in-between spaces from which power relations can be challenged. In this "third space", ascribed identities are dissolved, since they lose their national and cultural determinations. Meanings and references are not given *a priori*. Borders are blurred; one has to re-think and question established categories of culture and identity.

In such a space, to produce meaning and construct cultural difference, the ambivalent and contradictory "third space", where meaning loses its clarity, has to be crossed. The "third space" therein constitutes:

though unrepresentable in itself ... the discursive conditions of enunciation that ensure that the meaning and symbols of culture have no primordial unity or fixity; that even the same signs can be appropriated, translated, re-historicized and read anew. (Bhabha, 1997, p. 37)

To demonstrate this ambiguity, Bhabha describes how the hybridity of ideas is revealed through repetition in different contexts. In postcolonial discourse, these possibilities for "cultural reconfiguration" (Bronfen et al., 1997, p. 8) are displayed as strategies to re-think identity and otherness, not as a dichotomous opposition but as interwoven and as a permeation of centre and periphery. This strategy of resistance can involve practices both subversively through the uncovering of power hierarchies and affirmatively, for example by the reinterpretation of dominant symbols. The latter process Bhabha calls "mimicry". "In this repetition and at the same time distortion of dominant discourses a subversive difference develops in which the hegemonic references and meanings are reinterpreted, contaminated, hybridized" (Ha, 2005, p. 87).

For Bhabha, mimicry does not mean a return of the dominant discourse as a counter-discourse, but rather: "mimicry is repeating instead of re-presenting" (2000, pp. 129–130). Mimicry can be threatening to the dominant, as it constitutes the process

---

47 See above the section on intersectional diversity & otherness.

of what is expressed "between the lines". Mbembe pointedly summarizes these deconstructivist features of postcolonial thinking, in asserting that they "stress the fact that identity arises from multiplicity and dispersion, that self-referral is only possible in the in-between, in the gap between the mark and demark, in co-constitution" (Mbembe, 2008, p. 4).

A postcolonial and poststructuralist view in cultural sociology calls, therefore, for the reinterpretation of ascribed identities. An analysis in this case will be motivated by the guiding principle:

> that the cultural representation of the other as well as of the "own" identity are characterized in colonial discourse and beyond by a fundamental ambiguity. The task of postcolonial analysis is therefore to lay open these polysemous conditions of representation.[48] (Reckwitz, 2008a, pp. 99–100)

This unfixability of cultural symbols can also be regarded as one of the major advantages of the term "transculturality" or "transculturalization" (Sandkühler & Lim, 2004; Hoerder et al., 2005; Ha, 2010; Hühn et al., 2010). In this connection, the Cuban anthropologist Fernando Ortiz already used the term "*transculturación*" in his book *Contrapunteo cubano del tabaco y el azúcar* in the 1940s. Ortiz was describing the movement of one culture into another without influencing each other [*mestizaje*]. In Spanish-speaking countries, the term "transculturality" was introduced in the 1960s to denote the linguistic processes of hybridization. Later, the cultural theorist Ángel Rama from Uruguay introduced the term into the theories of modernity and dependency in literary analysis in Latin America. Rama still thought of a Latin American culture as homogeneous. Next, in the mid-1970s, the Peruvian literary scholar Antonio Cornejo Polar (1994) developed a cultural theory of heterogeneity in literary terms that focuses on "migrating subjects". "This [migrating] subject creates different spaces or communication contexts for its internalized cultural conditions from different cultures" (Schmidt-Welle, 2006, p. 90). Influenced by postcolonial theory, many approaches were subsequently developed, such as Néstor García Canclini's focus on the non-essentialist concepts of identity and culture, together with heterogeneous, hybrid societies and the spaces between them (2013).

In Anglo-Saxon countries, the reception of the term "transculturality" increased in the 1980s, for example through the writings of the anthropologist Alexander A. Ervin (1980) and the literary scholar Mary Louise Pratt (1992). Also since the 1980s in the humanities, more and more theoretical models of hybridity have been developed in an attempt to theoretically grasp the unobservable. Graham Huggan observes that

---

**48** "Der Leitgedanke [motiviert], dass die kulturelle Repräsentation des Anderen wie auch umgekehrt der 'eigenen' Identität in kolonialen Diskursen und darüber hinaus durch eine grundsätzliche Mehrdeutigkeit geprägt sind. Das Ziel der postkolonialen Analyse muss entsprechend darin bestehen, diese polysemen Repräsentationsverhältnisse aufzudecken" (Reckwitz, 2008a, pp. 99–100).

postcolonial studies especially started this "transcultural turn", where cultures are no longer regarded as definable entities and the focus is placed instead on transcultural formations (Huggan, 2006).

As the prefix *trans* suggests, what is at stake is a matter of a metaphorical approach to transitions, interlinking, in-between spaces and going beyond. Accordingly, a "more fluid and transient paradigm of relations between societies" is favoured and the "idea of the nation ... is contextualized between the local and the global" (Bond & Rapson, 2014, p. 9). For Jutta Ernst and Florian Freitag, two different notions of the term can be distinguished following Affef Benessaieh's notion of "cross-cultural competence" (Benessaieh, 2010, pp. 23–38), which denotes practices that are located beyond certain cultures, and a "plural sense of self" (ibid), which can especially be described as multiple-relational networks that transcend these cultures (Ernst & Freitag, 2015, p. 13). Applied to this contribution, the first notion has been delineated in this paragraph, whereas the latter was discussed in the section above on intersectional diversity and otherness.

The transcultural turn was not bound to anthropology or philosophy, but rather spread across a variety of disciplines concerned with the study of culture, being linked to related terms such as literary studies (*creolization; métissage*; Glissant, 1997; Ette, 2001; Febel, 2007; Müller & Ueckmann, 2013), memory studies (Bond & Rapson, 2014; Erll & Nünning, 2008; Tota & Hagen, 2015), gender studies (Butler, 1990; see Höhne in this volume), performance studies (*interweaving performance cultures*; Fischer-Lichte et al., 2014; see Oettl in this volume), media studies (see Pelillo-Hestermeyer in this volume; Hepp, 2015), music studies (Binas-Preisendörfer & Unseld, 2012; Freist et al., 2019), migration, diaspora, transnational and mobility studies (Glick-Schiller et al., 1995; Anderson, B., 1986; Charim & Borea, 2014), border and space studies (Do Mar Castro Varela, 2018; Bleuler & Moser, 2018; Wille, 2016; Kimmich & Schahadat, 2014), and translation studies (*untranslatability*; Bachtin, 1990; Apter, 2013). Since it is so extremely varied in its approaches, terms and concepts, the *transcultural* in these studies allow for the: "conceptual capture of phenomena that are in a process of becoming and that are composed from opposed structures, logics, dynamics and functionalities. "Trans" therefore does not refer to closed ideas of identity but rather includes fluid border demarcations"[49] (Rau et al., 2016, p. 7).

In the 1990s, transculturality was introduced into the humanities in German-speaking countries by the philosopher Wolfgang Welsch (Kalscheuer, 2005, pp. 221–223). Welsch defines transculturality as the separation of cultural and national or ethnic identities. In particular, transculturality describes cultural diversity as

---

**49** "die konzeptuelle Erfassung von Phänomenen, die sich in einem Prozess des Werdens befinden und aus entgegengesetzten Strukturen, Logiken, Dynamiken und Funktionsweisen bestehen. 'Trans' verweist folglich nicht auf geschlossene Identitätsvorstellungen, sondern enthält fluide Grenzverläufe" (Rau et al., 2016, p. 7).

interwoven, border-crossing and blending, in opposition to many single entities existing next to each other. It opposes essentialization and exoticization. Welsch also wants to move beyond the idea of individual homogeneous cultures and dissolve territorial metaphors. If we are to reflect on the networked structures of culture, this approach requires interconnected instead of linear thinking. Moreover, Welsch uses the term in opposition to mechanisms of homogenization and separation. Yet in his approach, it appears as if cultures were traditionally homogeneous (or still are in the *non-West*) and only today are hybridized. He does not differentiate in his discussion between transculturality in the humanities and the concept of the *development* of cultures. Nevertheless, transculturality for Welsch does not mean the side-by-side mixing of cultural elements, but instead, as there is no *Other*, describes transcultural networks of identity which can form everywhere from a processual perspective. "The dividing line between one's own and another culture is obsolete. Within a culture there are as many othernesses as in its external relations to other cultures" (Welsch, 2005, p. 325). It is important to keep in mind that this perspective regards the idea of transculturality as a symbolic one.[50] There are no real connections to transcultural practices; these are merely assumed.[51]

However, Stephanie Lavorano points out how Welsch's concept of transculturality indeed adheres to the racist ideology of Immanuel Kant by imposing a "thinking pattern of the West as 'naturalized diversity'", in which "contemporary" is taken to denote modern, *Western* societies as are thought to be pluralized in opposition to a contrary image to the *West*[52] (Lavorano, 2016, p. 151). The transcultural logic constructs the borders on the first hand, which again—although blurred—stabilize the borders and the "perspective on difference that always stems from the 'West'"[53] (p. 153).

On the one hand, Welsch's transcultural approach can lay open predetermined thinking patterns in order to demonstrate how such a perspective can reveal an alternative view in the humanities, both in theory and in empirical research. But on the other hand, *transculturality* in itself can be seen as a hegemonic Eurocentric concept, which comprises a normative perspective in the manner in which Welsch conceives the term. Thus, the limits of Welsch's concept have to be taken into account. Furthermore, the utopian claims that are often connected to such concepts have to be critically considered. In contrast, by focussing on a case study from the global art worlds, the conflictual articulations of *transculturality* will also be stressed in my

---

**50** For a critical comparison of Welsch's term transculturality and Vertovec's term super-diversity see Knecht, 2011 or Koch, 2011.

**51** In my other contribution I will come back to transcultural practices though.

**52** "die rassistische Ideologie Kants und das Transkulturalitätskonzept Welschs treffen sich in einer Denkfigur des Westens als 'naturalisierte Diversität'" (Lavorano, 2016, p. 151).

**53** "die stets vom 'Westen' ausgehende Perspektivierung dieser Differenz wird zementiert" (Lavorano, 2016, p. 153).

other contribution in this volume. In this discussion, in addition to the theoretical and methodological implications of the concept, the "lived" practices of diversity and otherness in transcultural life-worlds will be sketched more fully.

As some parts of Welsch's theory have to be viewed critically, I would extend Welsch's understanding of transculturality to the poststructuralist and postcolonial approaches described above. This focus on individual ambivalent and contingent identities would allow practices of diversity and otherness to be studied from a transcultural perspective. Based on empirical studies, I have shown, for example, that the identities of young people in Germany do not correspond to the identities ascribed to them in concepts of music education (Gaupp, 2016). There I demonstrated that there are no permanent identity-constructions bound to a "particular community" (Reckwitz, 2016). On the other hand, in the musical life-worlds of the young people researched in this study, one finds both a rejection as well as an overcoming of the identities ascribed to them. The social spaces evolving in this process can be conceptualized as Bhabha's "third space" (Gaupp, 2016). Connected to this are subversive ideas facing social inequalities, as discussed above. The crossing of borders will always involve the border itself and thus comprise not only inclusion but also exclusion. Trans-theories which conceptualize the transcendence of borders and limits will "encounter the limits of transcending"[54] (Rau et al., 2016, p. 16). Yet all trans-formations could be described as the "small sibling of deconstruction", when former problematic terms and concepts are deconstructed by adding the prefix "trans" in order to point out their problematic functions (Kimmich, 2016, p. 266).

## 2.4 Conclusion

To sum up, this discussion explored the epistemologies of diversity and otherness in the study of culture, mainly in cultural sociology and the sociology of culture. Their underlying premise is based on the conception and theorizing of differences, irrespective of whether differences are stabilized or deconstructed. At first, the epistemologies of diversity and otherness were situated in the vast field of the study of culture, the major "turns" in this field, and especially the context of postcolonial theory. It was shown how constructivism is, and has been, one of the major standardizations in these studies. Numerous other approaches to the question of what it means to develop, normalize, deconstruct or decolonize certain epistemes of diversity and otherness were also sketched. Four main epistemological assumptions were explored, among them the constructivist orientation just mentioned, as well as the deconstructivist, equality-theoretical and difference-theoretical perspectives.

---

54 "Theorien der Überschreitung stoßen an die Grenzen der Überschreitung" (Rau et al., 2016, p. 16).

Many of the studies presented can be grouped under two major understandings of diversity and otherness: as intersectional or as cross-cultural. While intersectional *diversity* describes mainly intersecting social belongings that include, in intersectional *otherness* differences are rather emphasized to exclude. Here, influential streams of social scientific thought, such as multiculturalism, intersectionality and social inequality, were discussed and mirrored with lesser-known concepts from, among other fields, postcolonial theory. This concept of diversity and otherness can be especially related to the sociology of culture that looks at how differences and inequalities materialize or become incorporated in cultural production.

In contrast, cross-cultural diversity and otherness are conceptualized as symbols of interconnectedness and border-crossings, and can therefore be assigned to cultural sociology. Cross-cultural *diversity* connotes ambiguous cultural symbols, whereas cross-cultural *otherness* involves the movement of de-stabilizing difference. Again, major theoretical concepts were discussed along with lesser-known approaches, mainly from the disciplinary fields of cultural studies, philosophy and, again, postcolonial studies.

It was argued that parallel assumptions regarding differences are made in both postcolonial and poststructuralist approaches. This leads to the call to "transculturalize" the study of culture regarding diversity and otherness. This means that the two main quests of postcolonial theory should be taken into account as an underlying principle for research, since diversity and otherness are such underlying features of today's societies. Hence, cultural research on diversity and otherness should be oriented along the many examples discussed that seek to decolonize power structures by, for example, un-veiling them. Equal importance should be paid to the deconstruction of persistent dichotomies in thinking. To this end, this chapter has tried to make a contribution to critically rethinking the categories of diversity and otherness and to include alternative perspectives and standpoints no matter whether in studies from a more idealistic or more materialistic perspective, or from a combination of both of these. Eventually this could help to "rethink a Europe Otherwise" (Boatcă, 2010).

# References

Abu-Er-Rub, L., Brosius, C., & Meurer, S. (Eds.). (2019). Engaging with. Engaging transculturality: Concepts, key terms, case studies. Routledge Taylor & Francis Group.

Ahmed, S. (2000). Strange encounters: Embodied others in post-coloniality. Transformations Thinking through feminism. Routledge Taylor & Francis Group. https://www.loc.gov/catdir/enhancements/fy0649/00028076-d.html

Ahmed, S. (2007). Queer phenomenology: Orientations, objects, others (2. printing). Duke University Press.

Ahmed, S. (2012). On being included: Racism and diversity in institutional life. e-Duke books scholarly collection. Duke University Press. http://lib.myilibrary.com?id=366424

Alatas, S. F. (2017). Max Weber (1864–1920). In S. F. Alatas & V. Sinha (Eds.), Sociological Theory Beyond the Canon (1st ed., pp. 113–142). Palgrave Macmillan UK.

Alatas, S. F., & Sinha, V. (Eds.). (2017). Sociological Theory Beyond the Canon (1st edition 2017). Palgrave Macmillan UK.

Albrecht, C., & Moebius, S. (2014). Die Rückkehr der Kultur in die Soziologie: Zur Gründungsgeschichte einer Sektion. In S. Moebius & C. Albrecht (Eds.), Kultur-Soziologie (pp. 9–22). Springer Fachmedien Wiesbaden.

Alexander-Floyd, N. G. (2012). Disappearing acts: Reclaiming intersectionality in the social sciences in a post-black feminist era. Feminist Formations, 24(1), 1–25.

Alexander, J. C. (1996). Cultural Sociology or Sociology of Culture? Newsletter of the Sociology of Culture, Section of the American Sociological Association, 10(3–4), 1–5.

Alexander, J. C. (2004). Kultursoziologie oder Soziologie der Kultur? Auf dem Weg zu einem überzeugenden Programm. In C. Albrecht (Ed.), Kultur, Geschichte, Theorie: Vol. 1. Die bürgerliche Kultur und ihre Avantgarden (pp. 59–63). Ergon-Verl.

Allolio-Näcke, L., Kalscheuer, B., & Manzeschke, A. (Eds.). (2005). Differenzen anders denken: Bausteine zu einer Kulturtheorie der Transdifferenz. Campus-Verlag. https://d-nb. info/971011648/04

Anderson, B. (1986). Imagined communities: Reflections on the origin and spread of nationalism. Thetford Pr. Lim.

Anderson, E. (2015). "The White Space". Sociology of Race and Ethnicity, 1(1), 10–21. https://doi. org/10.1177/2332649214561306

Angermüller, J., & Bellina, L. (2012). Poststrukturalismus und Postkolonialismus: Jacques Derridas "Grammatologie" sowie Gilles Deleuzes und Félix Guattaris "Tausend Plateaus". In J. Reuter & A. Karentzos (Eds.), Schlüsselwerke der Postcolonial Studies (pp. 27–37). Springer VS.

Appadurai, A. (1996). Modernity at Large: Cultural Dimensions of Globalization ([ACLS Humanities E-Book edition]). University of Minnesota Press. http://hdl.handle.net/2027/ heb.06472.0001.001

Apter, E. S. (2013). Against world literature: On the politics of untranslatability. Verso.

Arnaut, K. (2012). Super-diversity: Elements of an emerging perspective. DIVERSITIES, 14(2), 1–16.

Assmann, A. (2016). Die Grenzenlosigkeit der Kulturwissenschaften. Kulturwissenschaftliche Zeitschrift, 1(1), 39–48. https://doi.org/10.1515/kwg-2016-0005

Bachmann-Medick, D. (2016a). Cultural turns: New orientations in the study of culture (A. Blauhut, Trans.). De Gruyter textbook. De Gruyter. https://dx.doi.org/10.1515/9783110402988

Bachmann-Medick, D. (2016b). Kulturwissenschaft in der Ermüdung? Anmerkungen zu einer Neuorientierung. Kulturwissenschaftliche Zeitschrift, 1(1), 49–55. https://doi.org/10.1515/ kwg-2016-0006

Bachtin, M. (1990). Literatur und Karneval: Zur Romantheorie und Lachkultur. Fischer-Taschenbuch-Verl.

Beck, U., & Grande, E. (2010). Jenseits des methodologischen Nationalismus: Außereuropäische und europäische Variationen der Zweiten Moderne. Soziale Welt 61(3–4), 187–216. https://www. soziale-welt.nomos.de/fileadmin/soziale-welt/doc/Aufsatz_SozWelt_10_3-4.pdf

Behrens, M., Bukow, W. D., Cudak, K., & Strünck, C. (Eds.). (2016). Inclusive City: Überlegungen zum gegenwärtigen Verhältnis von Mobilität und Diversität in der Stadtgesellschaft. Springer VS. http://dx.doi.org/10.1007/978-3-658-09539-0 https://doi.org/10.1007/978-3-658-09539-0

Bendl, R., Bleijenbergh, I., Henttonen, E., & Mills, A. J. (Eds.). (2015). Oxford handbooks. The Oxford handbook of diversity in organizations (First edition). Oxford University Press.

Benessaieh, A. (2010). Multiculturalism, Interculturality, Transculturality. In A. Benessaieh (Ed.), Amériques transculturelles - Transcultural Americas (pp. 23–38). University of Ottawa Press / Les Presses de l'Université d'Ottawa.

Benhabib, S. (1994). Democracy and Difference: Reflections on the Metapolitics of Lyotard and Derrida. Princeton Univ. Press.

Benhabib, S. (2002). The claims of culture: Equality and diversity in the global era. Princeton Univ. Press. http://www.loc.gov/catdir/description/prin021/2001058083.html

Benhabib, S. (2006). The "claims" of culture properly interpreted: Response to Nikolas Kompridis. Political Theory, 34(3), 383–388. https://doi.org/10.1177/0090591706286779

Bhabha, H. K. (1997). The location of culture (Repr). Routledge.

Bhabha, H. K. (2000). Die Verortung der Kultur. Stauffenburg Discussion: Bd. 5. Stauffenburg-Verl.

Bhabha, H. K. (2005). Die Frage der Identität: Frantz Fanon und das postkoloniale Privileg. In L. Allolio-Näcke, B. Kalscheuer, & A. Manzeschke (Eds.), Differenzen anders denken: Bausteine zu einer Kulturtheorie der Transdifferenz (pp. 361–395). Campus-Verlag.

Bhabha, H. K. (2006). Nation and narration. Routledge.

Bhambra, G. K. (2007). Rethinking modernity: Postcolonialism and the sociological imagination. Palgrave. https://doi.org/10.1057/9780230206410

Bhambra, G. K. (2014). Connected Sociologies. Theory for a Global Age Series. Bloomsbury Academic. https://doi.org/10.5040/9781472544377

Bhambra, G. K. (2019, August 22). European Cosmopolitanism and Atavistic Nationalism: The Twin Conditions of Brexit. European Sociological Association, Manchester.

Bhambra, G. K., Gebrial, D., & Nişancıoğlu, K. (Eds.). (2018). Decolonising the university. Pluto Press.

Bilge, S. (2013). Intersectionality Undone: Saving Intersectionality from Feminist Intersectionality Studies. Du Bois Review: Social Science Research on Race, 10(2), 405–424. https://doi.org/10.1017/S1742058X13000283

Binas-Preisendörfer, S., & Unseld, M. (Eds.). (2012). Musik und Gesellschaft. Transkulturalität und Musikvermittlung: Möglichkeiten und Herausforderungen in Forschung, Kulturpolitik und musikpädagogischer Praxis. Peter Lang D. https://doi.org/10.3726/978-3-653-02470-8

Bleuler, M., & Moser, A. (Eds.). (2018). ent/grenzen. transcript. https://doi.org/10.14361/9783839441268

Boatcă, M. (2010). Multiple Europes and the Politics of Difference Within. In H. Brunkhorst & G. Grözinger (Eds.), The Study of Europe (pp. 51–66). Nomos Verlagsgesellschaft mbH & Co KG. https://doi.org/10.5771/9783845225487-51

Boatcă, M., & Costa, S. (2016). Postcolonial sociology: A research agenda. In E. Gutiérrez Rodriguez, M. Boatcă, & S. Costa (Eds.), Global connections. Decolonizing European sociology: Transdisciplinary approaches (pp. 13–31). Routledge.

Boatcă, M., Farzin, S., & Go, J. (2018). Postcolonialism and Sociology: E-Mail-Debate. SOZIOLOGIE, 47(4), 423–438.

Böhme, H. (2000). Kulturwissenschaft. In H. Fricke (Ed.), Reallexikon der deutschen Literaturwissenschaft (3rd ed., Vol. 2, pp. 356–359). De Gruyter.

Bojadžijev, M. (2018). Migration und Integration: Zur Genealogie des zentralen Dispositivs in der Migrationsgesellschaft. Migration und soziale Arbeit, 40(1), 54–61.

Bojadžijev, M., & Römhild, R. (2014). Was kommt nach dem "transnational turn"? Perspektiven für eine kritische Migrationsforschung. In Labor Migration (Ed.), Berliner Blätter: Heft 65. Vom Rand ins Zentrum: Perspektiven einer kritischen Migrationsforschung (pp.10–24). Panama Verlag.

Boltanski, L., & Chiapello, È. (2003). Der neue Geist des Kapitalismus. UVK Verlagsgesellschaft mbH.

Bond, L., & Rapson, J. (2014). Introduction. In L. Bond & J. Rapson (Eds.), Media and Cultural Memory / Medien und kulturelle Erinnerung: Vol. 15. The Transcultural Turn: Interrogating Memory Between and Beyond Borders (pp. 1–26). De Gruyter.

Bourdieu, P. (1991). Sozialer Raum und "Klassen" (Suhrkamp-Taschenbuch Wissenschaft: Vol. 500, 2. Aufl.). Suhrkamp.

Bourdieu, P. (1992). Rede und Antwort. (Edition Suhrkamp: 1547 = N.F., Bd. 547, 1. Aufl.) Suhrkamp.

Bourdieu, P. (2010). Distinction: A social critique of the judgement of taste. Routledge classics. Routledge.

Bröckling, U. (2015). The Entrepreneurial Self: Fabricating a New Type of Subject (1st ed.). SAGE Publications.

Bronfen, E., Marius, B., & Steffen, T. (Eds.). (1997). Stauffenburg Discussion: Bd. 4. Hybride Kulturen: Beiträge zur anglo-amerikanischen Multikulturalismusdebatte. Stauffenburg-Verl.

Buchholz, L. (2008). Feldtheorie und Globalisierung. In B. v. Bismarck & T. Kaufmann (Eds.), Nach Bourdieu: Visualität, Kunst, Politik: [eine Publikation des EIPCP im Rahmen von translate. Beyond culture: the politics of translation] (pp. 211–238). Turia + Kant.

Butler, J. (1990). Gender trouble: Feminism and the subversion of identity. Thinking gender. Routledge.

Callon, M., Law, J., & Rip, A. (Eds.). (1986). Mapping the Dynamics of Science and Technology: Sociology of Science in the Real World. Palgrave Macmillan. http://dx.doi.org/10.1007/978-1-349-07408-2

Canan, C., & Foroutan, N. (2016). Deutschland postmigrantisch III: Migrantische Perspektiven auf deutsche Identitäten - Einstellungen von Personen mit und ohne Migrationshintergrund zu nationaler Identität in Deutschland. BIM, Berliner Institut für empirische Integrations- und Migrationsforschung. https://www.projekte.hu-berlin.de/de/junited/deutschland-postmigrantisch-3.pdf

Chakrabarty, D. (2000). Provincializing Europe: Postcolonial thought and historical difference ([ACLS Humanities E-Book edition]). Princeton University Press.

Chambers, I. (1996). Migration, Kultur, Identität. Stauffenburg discussion: Bd. 3. Stauffenburg-Verl.

Charim, I., & Borea, G. A. (Eds.). (2014). Kultur und soziale Praxis. Lebensmodell Diaspora: Über moderne Nomaden. transcript. http://lib.myilibrary.com/detail.asp?id=631337

Christon, M. (2019, August 21). The Appropiation of "Difference" by the Extreme Right. European Sociological Association, Manchester.

Clifford, J. (1986). Introduction: Partial Truths. In J. Clifford & G. Marcus (Eds.), Writing culture: The poetics and politics of ethnography (pp. 1–26). Univ. of California Press.

Clifford, J. (2006). Diasporas. In P. James (ed.), Globalization and Violence (pp. 227–263). SAGE Publications Ltd.

Clifford, J., & Marcus, G. (Eds.). (1986). Writing culture: The poetics and politics of ethnography; a School of American Research Advanced Seminar. Univ. of California Press.

Collins, P. H. (2000). Gender, Black Feminism, and Black Political Economy. The ANNALS of the American Academy of Political and Social Science, 568(1), 41–53. https://doi.org/10.1177/000271620056800105

Cornejo Polar, A. (1994). Escribir en el aire: Ensayo sobre la heterogeneidad socio-cultural en las literaturas andinas (1. ed.). Critica Literaria: Vol. 11. Editorial Horizonte.

Crenshaw, K. (1989). Demarginalizing the intersection of race and sex: A Black Feminist Critique of Antidiscrimination Doctrine, Feminist Theory and Antiracist Politics. University of Chicago Legal Forum, 1(8), 139–167. http://chicagounbound.uchicago.edu/uclf/vol1989/iss1/8

Cuyler, A. C. (2013). Affirmative Action and Diversity: Implications for Arts Management. The Journal of Arts Management, Law, and Society, 43(2), 98–105. https://doi.org/10.1080/10632921.2013.786009

Deleuze, G., & Guattari, F. (2011). A thousand plateaus: Capitalism and schizophrenia (Repr). Continuum.

Derrida, J. (2004). Die différance: Ausgewählte Texte (P. Engelmann, Ed.). Philipp Reclam jun.

Do Mar Castro Varela, M. (2018). Grenzen dekonstruieren – Mobilität imaginieren. In M. Bleuler & A. Moser (Eds.), ent/grenzen (pp. 23–34). transcript. https://doi.org/10.14361/9783839441268-003

Durkheim, É. (1984). Die Regeln der soziologischen Methode (Suhrkamp-Taschenbuch Wissenschaft: Vol. 464, 1. Aufl.). Suhrkamp.

Durkheim, E. (2013). The Division of Labour in Society (S. Lukes, Ed.) (2nd edition). Macmillan Education; Palgrave.

Dussel, E. (1998). Beyond eurocentrism: The world-system and the limits of modernity. In F. Jameson & M. Miyoshi (Eds.), The cultures of globalization (pp. 3–31). Duke Univ. Press.

Dussel, E. D. (2009). Ética de la liberación en la edad de la globalización y la exclusión (6. ed.). Colección Estructuras y procesos. Serie Filosofía. Trotta.

Eisenstadt, S. N. (2003). Comparative civilizations and multiple modernities. Brill.

Erll, A., & Nünning, A. (Eds.). (2008). Media and cultural memory: Vol. 8. Cultural memory studies: An international and interdisciplinary handbook. De Gruyter. https://doi.org/10.1515/9783110207262

Ernst, J., & Freitag, F. (2015). Einleitung. Transkulturelle Dynamiken: Entwicklungen und Perspektiven eines Konzepts. In J. Ernst & F. Freitag (Eds.), Mainzer historische Kulturwissenschaften: Vol. 19. Transkulturelle Dynamiken: Aktanten - Prozesse - Theorien (pp. 7–30). De Gruyter; transcript. https://doi.org/10.14361/transcript.9783839425633

Ervin, A. M. (1980). A Review of the Acculturation Approach in Anthropology with Special Reference to Recent Change in Native Alaska. Journal of Anthropological Research, 36(1), 49–70. https://doi.org/10.1086/jar.36.1.3629552

Escobar, A. (2004). Beyond the Third World: Imperial Globality, Global Coloniality and Anti-Globalisation Social Movements. Third World Quarterly, 25 (1 After the Third World?), 207–230.

Espahangizi, K., Hess, S., Karakayali, J., Kasparek, B., Pagano, S., Rodatz, M., & Tsianos, V. (2016). Rassismus in der postmigrantischen Gesellschaft. Movements: Journal für kritische Migrations- und Grenzregimeforschung, 2.2016,1. http://www.transcript-verlag.de/978-3-8376-3570-6

Ette, O. (2001). Literatur in Bewegung: Raum und Dynamik grenzüberschreitenden Schreibens in Europa und Amerika (1. Aufl.). Velbrück Wiss.

Fanon, F. (1952). Peau noire- masques blancs. Ed. du Seuil.

Febel, G. (Ed.). (2007). Edition lendemains: Vol. 3. Écritures transculturelles: Kulturelle Differenz und Geschlechterdifferenz im französischsprachigen Gegenwartsroman. Narr. http://deposit.d-nb.de/cgi-bin/dokserv?id=2970517&prov=M&dok_var=1&dok_ext=htm

Fischer-Lichte, E., Jost, T., & Jain, S. I. (Eds.). (2014). Routledge advances in theatre and performance studies: Vol. 33. The politics of interweaving performance cultures: Beyond postcolonialism. Routledge.

Fischer, J., & Moebius, S. (2014). Einleitung. In J. Fischer & S. Moebius (Eds.), Kultursoziologie im 21. Jahrhundert (pp. 9–16). Springer Fachmedien Wiesbaden. https://doi.org/10.1007/978-3-658-03225-8

Foroutan, N. (2019). Die postmigrantische Gesellschaft: Ein Versprechen der pluralen Demokratie. X-Texte zu Kultur und Gesellschaft. transcript.

Foucault, M. (1974). Die Ordnung der Dinge: Eine Archäologie der Humanwissenschaften (1. Aufl.). Suhrkamp-Taschenbuch Wissenschaft.

Foucault, M. (1978). Dispositive der Macht: Über Sexualität, Wissen und Wahrheit. IMD: Vol. 77. Merve Verl.

Foucault, M. (2006). Von anderen Räumen. In J. Dünne (Ed.), Suhrkamp-Taschenbuch Wissenschaft: Vol. 1800. Raumtheorie: Grundlagentexte aus Philosophie und Kulturwissenschaften (1st ed., pp. 317–329). Suhrkamp.

Freist, D., Kyora, S., & Unseld, M. (Eds.). (2019). Praktiken der Subjektivierung: Vol. 13. Transkulturelle Mehrfachzugehörigkeit als kulturhistorisches Phänomen: Räume - Materialitäten - Erinnerungen. transcript. http://www.transcript-verlag.de/978-3-8376-4528-6

Friese, H. (2014). Grenzen der Gastfreundschaft: Die Bootsflüchtlinge von Lampedusa und die europäische Frage. Kultur und soziale Praxis. transcript. http://site.ebrary.com/lib/alltitles/docDetail.action?docID=11014620 https://doi.org/10.14361/transcript.9783839424476

Gabbert, W. (2010). Das Eigene und das Fremde im "globalen Dorf" - Perspektiven einer kritischen Soziologie der Globalisierung. In J. Reuter & P.-I. Villa (Eds.), Postcolonial studies: Band 2. Postkoloniale Soziologie: Empirische Befunde, theoretische Anschlüsse, politische Intervention (pp. 159–179). transcript.

García Canclini, N. (2013). Culturas híbridas: Estrategias para entrar y salir de la modernidad (nueva edición, 6. reimpresión). Paidós estado y sociedad: Vol. 87. Paidós.

Gaupp, L. (2010). Erkenntnistheorie. In A. Kreutziger-Herr & M. Unseld (Eds.), Lexikon Musik und Gender (pp. 200–201). J. B. Metzler.

Gaupp, L. (2016). Die exotisierte Stadt: Kulturpolitik und Musikvermittlung im postmigrantischen Prozess. Studies in Music: Vol. 1. Olms. https://hildok.bsz-bw.de/frontdoor/index/index/docId/547

Geertz, C. (1973). Thick description: Toward an interpretive theory of culture. In C. Geertz (Ed.), The interpretation of cultures: selected essays (pp. 3–30). Basic Books.

Gertenbach, L. (2017). Postkonstruktivismus in der Kultursoziologie. In S. Moebius, F. Nungesser, & K. Scherke (Eds.), Springer Reference Sozialwissenschaften. Handbuch Kultursoziologie: Band 1: Begriffe - Kontexte - Perspektiven - Autor_innen (pp. 1–24). Springer.

Gilroy, P. (1993). The black Atlantic: Modernity and double consciousness. Harvard Univ. Press.

Glick-Schiller, N., Basch, L., & Blanc, C. S. (1995). From Immigrant to Transmigrant: Theorizing Transnational Migration. Anthropological Quarterly, 68(1), 48. https://doi.org/10.2307/3317464

Glissant, É. (1997). Poétique de la relation ([Réimpr.]). Poétique / Édouard Glissant: Vol. 3. Gallimard.

Go, J., & Krause, M. (2016). Fielding Transnationalism (1. Auflage). Sociological Review Monographs. John Wiley & Sons.

Gould, E. H. (2007). Entangled Histories, Entangled Worlds: The English-Speaking Atlantic as a Spanish Periphery. The American Historical Review, 112(3), 764–786.

Groys, B. (2008). Art power. MIT Press. http://lib.myilibrary.com?id=210084

Gutiérrez Rodriguez, E. (2016). Decolonizing Postcolonial Rhetoric. In E. Gutiérrez Rodriguez, M. Boatcă, & S. Costa (Eds.), Global connections. Decolonizing European sociology: Transdisciplinary approaches (pp. 49–67). Routledge.

Ha, K. N. (2005). Hype um Hybridität: Kultureller Differenzkonsum und postmoderne Verwertungstechniken im Spätkapitalismus. Cultural Studies: Vol. 11. transcript.

Ha, K. N. (2010). Unrein und vermischt: Postkoloniale Grenzgänge durch die Kulturgeschichte der Hybridität und der kolonialen "Rassenbastarde". Postcolonial studies: Vol. 6. transcript.

Hall, S. (1994). Rassismus und kulturelle Identität (1. Aufl., 1. - 2. Tsd). Argument-Sonderbände: N.F., 226. Argument-Verl.

Hall, S. (2017). The Fateful Triangle: Race, Ethnicity, Nation. Harvard University Press. https://doi.org/10.2307/j.ctvqht03

Hall, S. (Ed.). (1997). Culture, media and identities. Representation: Cultural representations and signifying practices. Sage. http://www.loc.gov/catdir/enhancements/fy0656/96071228-d.html

Hannerz, U. (1992). Cultural complexity: Studies in the social organization of meaning. Columbia Univ. Press.

Haraway, D. (1992). Primate visions: Gender, race, and nature in the world of modern science. Verso.

Harding, S. G. (1999). Feministische Wissenschaftstheorie: Zum Verhältnis von Wissenschaft und sozialem Geschlecht (3. Aufl.). Argument.

Harvey, D. (1989). The urban experience. Blackwell.

Haus der Kulturen der Welt Berlin. (2014). A Journey of Ideas Across: In Dialog with Edward Said. http://journeyofideasacross.hkw.de

Hepp, A. (2015). Transcultural communication. Wiley.

Hoerder, D., Hébert, Y., & Schmitt, I. (Eds.). (2005). Transkulturelle Perspektiven: Bd. 2. Negotiating transcultural lives: Belongings and social capital among youth in comparative perspective (1. Aufl.). V und R Unipress.

Holzinger, M. (2019). Alter Wein in neuen Schläuchen oder was ist neu am "neuen Postkolonialismus"? SOZIOLOGIE, 48(2), 174–184.

hooks, b. (1995). Ain't I a woman: Black women and feminism (5. print). Pluto Press.

Huggan, G. (2006). Derailing the 'trans'? Postcolonial studies and the negative effects of speed. In H. Antor (Ed.), Anglistische Forschungen: Vol. 362. Inter- und Transkulturelle Studien: Theoretische Grundlagen und interdisziplinäre Praxis (pp. 55–61). Winter.

Hühn, M., Lerp, D., Petzold, K., & Stock, M. (Eds.). (2010). Region - Nation - Europa: Vol. 62. Transkulturalität, Transnationalität, Transstaatlichkeit, Translokalität: Theoretische und empirische Begriffsbestimmungen; [Leitthema der im Oktober 2009 an der Viadrina in Frankfurt (Oder) abgehaltenen Tagung.] LIT-Verl. http://www.h-net.org/reviews/showrev.php?id=32959

Ismaiel-Wendt, J. (2014). "Off" and Maybe Out of Place. https://norient.com/stories/popular-orientalisms-1/

Jack, G. (2015). Advancing Postcolonial Approaches in Critical Diversity Studies. In R. Bendl, I. Bleijenbergh, E. Henttonen, & A. J. Mills (Eds.), Oxford handbooks. The Oxford handbook of diversity in organizations (pp. 153–174). Oxford University Press.

Johler, R., Matter, M., & Zinn-Thomas, S. (Eds.). (2011). Mobilitäten: Europa in Bewegung als Herausforderung kulturanalytischer Forschung; 37. Kongress der Deutschen Gesellschaft für Volkskunde in Freiburg im Breisgau vom 27. bis 30. September 2009. Waxmann.

Kaasila-Pakanen, A.-L. (2015). A Postcolonial Deconstruction of Diversity Management and Multiculturalism. In R. Bendl, I. Bleijenbergh, E. Henttonen, & A. J. Mills (Eds.), Oxford handbooks. The Oxford handbook of diversity in organizations (pp. 175–194). Oxford University Press.

Kalscheuer, B. (2005). Interkulturalität: Einleitung. In L. Allolio-Näcke & B. Kalscheuer (Eds.), Differenzen anders denken: Bausteine zu einer Kulturtheorie der Transdifferenz (pp. 221–226). Campus-Verlag.

Kant, I. (2015). Die drei Kritiken: Kritik der reinen Vernunft (1781/87); Kritik der praktischen Vernunft (1788); Kritik der Urteilskraft (1790). Anaconda.

Karakayali, S. (2016). Für einen New Deal der Migration. Blätter für deutsche und internationale Politik: Monatszeitschrift, 61(3), 13–16.

Khatibi, A. (1985). Double Criticism: The Decolonization of Arab Sociology. In H. I. Barakat (Ed.), Contemporary North Africa: Issues of development and integration (pp. 9–19). Croom Helm.

Kimmich, D. (2016). Nachwort: Was kommt? Was bleibt? Zur Zukunft der Trans_Konzepte. In S. Lavorano, C. Mehnert, & A. Rau (Eds.), Edition Kulturwissenschaft: v.97. Grenzen der Überschreitung: Kontroversen um Transkultur, Transgender und Transspecies (1st ed., pp. 263–270). transcript.

Kimmich, D., & Schahadat, S. (Eds.). (2014). Kultur- und Medientheorie. Kulturen in Bewegung: Beiträge zur Theorie und Praxis der Transkulturalität. transcript.

Knecht, M. (2011). Einleitung zum Panel: Konsequenzen der Mobilität? "Superdiversität" und "Transkulturalität" als Herausforderungen empirisch-ethnographischer Forschung. In R. Johler, M. Matter, & S. Zinn-Thomas (Eds.), Mobilitäten: Europa in Bewegung als Herausforderung kulturanalytischer Forschung; 37. Kongress der Deutschen Gesellschaft für Volkskunde in Freiburg im Breisgau vom 27. bis 30. September 2009 (pp. 217–225). Waxmann.

Koch, G. (2011). Transkulturalität: Reichweite und Potenzial eines Begriffs für die kulturanalytische Forschung. In R. Johler, M. Matter, & S. Zinn-Thomas (Eds.), Mobilitäten: Europa in Bewegung als Herausforderung kulturanalytischer Forschung; 37. Kongress der Deutschen Gesellschaft für Volkskunde in Freiburg im Breisgau vom 27. bis 30. September 2009 (pp. 235–239). Waxmann.

Kompridis, N. (2005). Normativizing Hybridity/Neutralizing Culture. Political Theory, 33(3), 318–343. https://doi.org/10.1177/0090591705274867

Krell, G., Riedmüller, B., Sieben, B., & Vinz, D. (Eds.). (2007). Diversity studies: Grundlagen und disziplinäre Ansätze. Campus-Verl.

Kristeva, J. (1974). Des Chinoises. Éd. des femmes.

Kuhn, T. S. (2009). The Structure of Scientific Revolutions. The University of Chicago Press.

Lahire, B. (1995). Tableaux de familles: Heurs et malheurs scolaires en milieux populaires. Hautes études. Gallimard.

Lahire, B. (2005). Portraits sociologiques: Dispositions et variations individuelles. Collection essais & recherches. Armand Colin.

Langenohl, A., Poole, R. J., & Weinberg, M. (Eds.). (2015). Basis-Scripte: Band 3. Transkulturalität: Klassische Texte. transcript. http://d-nb.info/1008786489/04

Lash, S., & Urry, J. (1994). Economies of signs and space (1. publ., repr). Theory, culture & society. SAGE.

Latour, B. (2010). An Attempt at a 'Compositionist Manifesto'. New Literary History, 41, 471–490.

Latour, B. (2017). Eine neue Soziologie für eine neue Gesellschaft: Einführung in die Akteur-Netzwerk-Theorie (G. Roßler, Trans.) (4. Auflage). Suhrkamp-Taschenbuch Wissenschaft: Vol. 1967. Suhrkamp.

Lavorano, S. (2016). Transkultureller Rassismus: Zum Diversitätsbegriff bei Wolfgang Welsch und Immanuel Kant. In S. Lavorano, C. Mehnert, & A. Rau (Eds.), Edition Kulturwissenschaft: v.97. Grenzen der Überschreitung: Kontroversen um Transkultur, Transgender und Transspecies (1st ed., pp. 149–162). transcript.

Lavorano, S., Mehnert, C., & Rau, A. (Eds.). (2016). Edition Kulturwissenschaft: v.97. Grenzen der Überschreitung: Kontroversen um Transkultur, Transgender und Transspecies (1st ed.). transcript.

Le Grand, E. (2019). Conceptualising Social Types and Figures: From Social Forms to Classificatory Struggles. Cultural Sociology, 13(4), 411–427. https://doi.org/10.1177/1749975519859962

Leeb, S., & Sonderegger, R. (2016). Plädoyer für eine kulturwissenschaftliche Ästhetik aus Perspektive der cultural studies. Kulturwissenschaftliche Zeitschrift, 1(1), 56–62. https://doi.org/10.1515/kwg-2016-0007

Liebsch, K., Tuider, E., Weiß, A., & Zifonun, D. (2014). Einleitung zum Plenum: Diversität und Intersektionalität. In M. Löw (Ed.), Vielfalt und Zusammenhalt: Verhandlungen des 36. Kongresses der Deutschen Gesellschaft für Soziologie in Bochum und Dortmund 2012 (Vol. 2, pp. 841–842). Campus-Verl.

Lionnet, F. (2011). Counterpoint and double critique in Edward Said and Abdelkebir Khatibi: A transcolonial comparison. In A. Behdad & D. Thomas (Eds.), A companion to comparative literature (pp. 387–407). Wiley-Blackwell.

Lorde, A. (1996). Age, Race, Class, and Sex: Women Redefining Difference. The Audre Lorde Compendium: Essays, Speeches and Journals. Pandora.

Löw, M. (2014). Vorwort. In M. Löw (Ed.), Vielfalt und Zusammenhalt: Verhandlungen des 36. Kongresses der Deutschen Gesellschaft für Soziologie in Bochum und Dortmund 2012 (Vol. 1, pp. 1-6). Campus-Verl.

Lyotard, J. F. (1984). The postmodern condition: A report on knowledge. Theory and history of literature: Vol. 10. University of Minnesota Press.

Malinowski, B. (1967). A diary in the strict sense of the term (N. Guterman, Trans.) (1. ed.). Routledge & Kegan Paul.

Mall, R. A. (1993). Begriff, Inhalt, Methode und Hermeneutik der interkulturellen Philosophie. In R. A. Mall & D. Lohmar (Eds.), Studien zur interkulturellen Philosophie: Vol. 1. Philosophische Grundlagen der Interkulturalität (pp. 1–28). Rodopi.

Marx, K., & Engels, F. (1872). Das Kapital: Kritik der politischen Oekonomie. O. Meissner.

Massey, D. (1994). Space, Place, and Gender. University of Minnesota Press. http://www.jstor.org/stable/10.5749/j.cttttw2z

Mbembe, A. J. (2001). On the Postcolony ([ACLS Humanities E-Book edition]). University of California Press. http://hdl.handle.net/2027/heb.02640.0001.001

Mbembe, A. J. (2008). What is postcolonial thinking? An interview with Achille Mbembe. Esprit Eurozine. http://www.eurozine.com/what-is-postcolonial-thinking/

Mbembe, A. J. (2014). Kritik der schwarzen Vernunft (M. Bischoff, Trans.) (Erste Auflage). Suhrkamp.

Mbembe, A. J. (2016). Decolonizing the university: New directions. Arts and Humanities in Higher Education, 15(1), 29–45. https://doi.org/10.1177/1474022215618513

McCall, L. (2005). The Complexity of Intersectionality. Signs: Journal of Women in Culture and Society, 30(3), 1771–1800. https://doi.org/10.1086/426800

Meer, N. & Modood, T. (2014). Cosmopolitanism and integrationism: is British multiculturalism a 'Zombie category'?, Identities, 21(6), 658-674. https://doi.org/10.1080/1070289X.2013.875028

Metten, T. (2016). Konturen der Kulturwissenschaft/en – einleitende Überlegungen. Kulturwissenschaftliche Zeitschrift, 1(1), 5–16. https://doi.org/10.1515/kwg-2016-0002

Mignolo, W. D. (2012). Epistemischer Ungehorsam: Rhetorik der Moderne, Logik der Kolonialität und Grammatik der Dekolonialität (J. Kastner & T. Waibel, Trans.). Es kommt darauf an: Bd. 12. Turia + Kant.

Moore-Gilbert, B. J. (2000). Postcolonial theory: Contexts, practices, politics (Reprinted.). Verso.

Müller, G., & Ueckmann, N. (Eds.). (2013). Postcolonial studies: Vol. 12. Kreolisierung revisited: Debatten um ein weltweites Kulturkonzept. transcript. https://doi.org/10.14361/transcript.9783839420515

Natorp, P. (1903). Platons Ideenlehre: Eine Einführung in den Idealismus. Dürr.

Nederveen Pieterse, J., & Parekh, B. (Eds.). (1995). The decolonization of imagination: Culture, knowledge and power. Zed Books.

Neubert, S., Roth, H.-J., & Yıldız, E. (Eds.). (2013). Interkulturelle Studien. Multikulturalität in der Diskussion: Neuere Beiträge zu einem umstrittenen Konzept (3. Aufl.). Springer VS.

Nünning, A. (2016). Perspektiven der Kulturwissenschaften im internationalen Kontext. Kulturwissenschaftliche Zeitschrift, 1(1), 70–75. https://doi.org/10.1515/kwg-2016-0009

Ortiz, F. (1983). Contrapunteo cubano del tabaco y el azúcar. Pensamiento cubano. Ed. de Ciencias Sociales.

Plessner, H. (1975). Die Stufen des Organischen und der Mensch: Einleitung in die philosophische Anthropologie (3., unveränderte Auflage, im Original erschienen 1975). Sammlung Göschen: Vol. 2200. De Gruyter. http://www.reference-global.com/doi/book/10.1515/9783110845341 https://doi.org/10.1515/9783110845341

Pratt, M. L. (1992). Imperial eyes: Travel writing and transculturation. Routledge. http://www.h-net.org/review/hrev-a0a0o3-aa

Puar, J. K. (2012). "I would rather be a cyborg than a goddess": Becoming-Intersectional in Assemblage Theory. PhiloSOPHIA, 2(1), 49–66.

Purtschert, P. (2012). Postkoloniale Philosophie: Die westliche Denkgeschichte gegen den Strich lesen. In J. Reuter & A. Karentzos (Eds.), Schlüsselwerke der Postcolonial Studies (pp. 343–354). Springer VS. http://link.springer.com/chapter/10.1007/978-3-531-93453-2_25

Rama, Á. (2012). Writing across cultures: Narrative transculturation in Latin America. Latin america otherwise. Duke Univ. Press.

Randeria, S. (1999). Jenseits von Soziologie und soziokultureller Anthropologie: Zur Ortsbestimmung der nichtwestlichen Welt in einer zukünftigen Sozialtheorie. Soziale Welt Zeitschrift Für Sozialwissenschaftliche Forschung, 50, 373–382.

Randeria, S. (2002). Entangled histories of uneven modernities: Civil society, caste solidarities and legal pluralism in post-colonial India. Civil Society Network. Wissenschaftszentrum für Sozialforschung Berlin (WZB).

Rau, A., Lavorano, S., & Mehnert, C. (2016). Vorwort: Zum Status der Trans_Konzepte. In S. Lavorano, C. Mehnert, & A. Rau (Eds.), Edition Kulturwissenschaft: v.97. Grenzen der Überschreitung: Kontroversen um Transkultur, Transgender und Transspecies (1st ed., pp. 7–24). transcript.

Reckwitz, A. (2000). Die Transformation der Kulturtheorien: Zur Entwicklung eines Theorieprogramms (1. Aufl.). Velbrück Wiss.

Reckwitz, A. (2004). Die Kontingenzperspektive der 'Kultur': Kulturbegriffe, Kulturtheorien und das kulturwissenschaftliche Forschungsprogramm. In F. Jaeger, B. Liebsch, J. Rüsen, & J. Straub (Eds.), Handbuch der Kulturwissenschaften: Band 3: Themen und Tendenzen (Vol. 3, pp. 1–20). J.B. Metzler.

Reckwitz, A. (2008a). Subjekt (1., Aufl.). Einsichten. transcript.

Reckwitz, A. (2008b). Unscharfe Grenzen: Perspektiven der Kultursoziologie (2., unveränderte Auflage 2010). Sozialtheorie. transcript. http://dx.doi.org/10.14361/9783839409176

Reckwitz, A. (2016). Zwischen Hyperkultur und Kulturessenzialismus: Die Spätmoderne im Widerstreit zweier Kulturalisierungsregimes. Soziopolis. https://soziopolis.de/beobachten/kultur/artikel/zwischen-hyperkultur-und-kulturessenzialismus/

Reuter, J., & Villa, P.-I. (2010). Provincializing Soziologie: Postkoloniale Theorie als Herausforderung. In J. Reuter & P.-I. Villa (Eds.), Postcolonial studies: Band 2. Postkoloniale Soziologie: Empirische Befunde, theoretische Anschlüsse, politische Intervention (pp. 11–46). transcript.

Richardson, W. J. (2018). Understanding Eurocentrism as a Structural Problem of Undone Science. In G. K. Bhambra, D. Gebrial, & K. Nişancıoğlu (Eds.), Decolonising the university (pp. 231–247). Pluto Press.

Robertson, R. (2003). Globalisation or glocalisation? In R. Robertson & K. E. White (Eds.), Globalization: Critical concepts in sociology (pp. 31–51). Routledge.

Robinson, W. I. (2004). A theory of global capitalism: Production, class, and state in a transnational world. Themes in global social change. Johns Hopkins Univ. Press. http://www.loc.gov/catdir/description/jhu051/2003018298.html

Saalmann, G. (2007). Simmels Bestimmung des Fremden im Exkurs von 1908. https://socio.ch/sim/on_simmel/t_saalmann.pdf

Said, E. W. (1995). Orientalism: Western conceptions of the orient (Reprinted with a new afterword). Penguin history. Penguin Books.

Salzbrunn, M. (2014). Vielfalt, Diversität. transcript. https://doi.org/10.14361/transcript.9783839424070

Sandkühler, H. J., & Lim, H.-B. (Eds.). (2004). Philosophie und Geschichte der Wissenschaften: Vol. 57. Transculturality - epistemology, ethics, and politics. Lang.

Santos, B. de Sousa. (2010). From the Postmodern to the Postcolonial: And Beyond Both. In E. Gutiérrez Rodriguez, M. Boatcă, & S. Costa (Eds.), Global connections. Decolonizing European sociology: Transdisciplinary approaches (pp. 225–243). Ashgate.

Santos, B. de Sousa. (2014). Epistemologies of the South: Justice against epistemicide. Paradigm Publ.

Sassen, S. (2015). Ausgrenzungen: Brutalität und Komplexität in der globalen Wirtschaft. S. Fischer.

Schellhöh, J., Reichertz, J., Heins, V., & Flender, A. (Eds.). (2018). X-Texte zu Kultur und Gesellschaft. Großerzählungen des Extremen: Neue Rechte, Populismus, Islamismus, War on Terror. transcript.

Schmidt-Welle, F. (2006). Transkulturalität, Heterogenität und Postkolonialismus aus der Perspektive der Lateinamerikastudien. In H. Antor (Ed.), Anglistische Forschungen: Vol. 362. Inter- und Transkulturelle Studien: Theoretische Grundlagen und interdisziplinäre Praxis (pp. 81–94). Winter.

Sennett, R. (1999). The corrosion of character: The personal consequences of work in the new capitalism (1. publ. as a Norton paperback). Norton.

Shohat, E., & Stam, R. (1994). Unthinking Eurocentrism: Multiculturalism and the media. Sightlines. Routledge. http://www.loc.gov/catdir/enhancements/fy0648/93041501-d.html

Simmel, G. (1990). Über sociale Differenzierung: Sociologische und psychologische Untersuchungen (Repr [der Ausg.] Leipzig, Duncker & Humblot, 1890). Staats- und socialwissenschaftliche Forschungen: / hrsg. von Gustav Schmoller; Bd. 10, H. 1 = H. 42. Schmidt Periodicals.

Simmel, G. (1996). The stranger (1908) and the web of group affiliations (1908). In W. Sollors (Ed.), Theories of ethnicity: a classical reader (pp. 37–51). New York Univ. Press.

Soja, E. W. (2010). Seeking spatial justice. Globalization and community series: Vol. 16. University of Minnesota Press.

Soja, E., & Hooper, B. (1993). The Spaces that Difference Makes: Some Notes on the Geographical Margins of the New Cultural Politics. In M. Keith & S. Pile (Eds.), Place and the politics of identity (pp. 183–205). Routledge.

Sökefeld, M. (2004). Das Paradigma kultureller Differenz: Zur Forschung und Diskussion über Migranten aus der Türkei in Deutschland. In M. Sökefeld (Ed.), Kultur und soziale Praxis. Jenseits des Paradigmas kultureller Differenz: Neue Perspektiven auf Einwanderer aus der Türkei (1st ed., pp. 9–34). transcript.

Solga, H., Powell, J. J. W., & Berger, P. A. (Eds.). (2009). campus Reader. Soziale Ungleichheit: Klassische Texte zur Sozialstrukturanalyse. Campus Verlag. http://www.socialnet.de/rezensionen/isbn.php?isbn=978-3-593-38847-2

Spivak, C. G. (1988). Can the subaltern speak? In C. Nelson & L. Grossberg (Eds.), Marxism and the interpretation of culture (pp. 66–111). Univ. of Illinois Press.

Stäheli, U. (2000). Poststrukturalistische Soziologien. Einsichten. Themen der Soziologie. transcript.

Stiglitz, J. E. (2002). Globalization and its discontents. Penguin Politics. Penguin Books.

Stirling, A. (2007). On the Economics and Analysis of Diversity. SPRU. Electronic Working Papers Series. http://www.sussex.ac.uk/spru/

Taguieff, A. (1993). From race to culture: The New Right's view of European identity. Telos (98/99).

Taylor, C. (1994). The politics of recognition. In C. Taylor & A. Gutmann (Eds.), Princeton paperbacks Philosophy, political science. Multiculturalism: Examining the politics of recognition (pp. 25–73). Princeton Univ. Press.

Thompson, V. E. (2015). Black Jacobins in Contemporary France: On Identities, on Politics, Decolonial Critique and the Other Blackness. Sociological Focus, 49 (1 Special Issue on Black Movements), 44–62.

Tota, A. L., & Hagen, T. (Eds.). (2015). Routledge International Handbook of memory studies. Routledge.

Van Loon, J. (2019, August 22). Against Culture? Sharing, Sameness and Belonging. European Sociological Association. Research Network Sociology of Culture, Manchester.

Vertovec, S. (2007). Super-diversity and its implications. Ethnic and Racial Studies, 30(6), 1024–1054.

Vertovec, S. (2009). Conceiving and Researching Diversity. Max Planck Institute for the Study of Religious and Ethnic Diversity. MMG Working Paper. www.mmg.mpg.de/workingpapers

Vertovec, S. (2015). Introduction: Formulating Diversity Studies. In S. Vertovec (Ed.), Routledge international handbook of diversity studies (pp. 1–20). Routledge.

Vertovec, S. (Ed.). (2015). Routledge international handbook of diversity studies. Routledge.

Weber, M. (1969). Class, status, party. In C. Stopnicka Heller & C. Helle (Eds.), Structured Social Inequality: A Reader in Comparative Social Stratification (pp. 24–34). Macmillan.

Weber, M. (2005). Gesamtausgabe (E. Hanke, Ed.). J.C.B. Mohr (Paul Siebeck).

Weber, M. (2016). Klassiker der Sozialwissenschaften. Die protestantische Ethik und der "Geist" des Kapitalismus (K. Lichtblau, & J. Weiß, Eds.). Springer VS.

Weiß, A. (2017). Soziologie globaler Ungleichheiten (Erste Auflage). suhrkamp taschenbuch Wissenschaft: Vol. 2220. Suhrkamp.

Welsch, W. (2005). Auf dem Weg zu transkulturellen Gesellschaften. In L. Allolio-Näcke & B. Kalscheuer (Eds.), Differenzen anders denken: Bausteine zu einer Kulturtheorie der Transdifferenz (pp. 314–341). Campus-Verlag.

Werner, M., & Zimmermann, B. (2006). Beyond Comparison: Histoire Croisée and the Challenge of Reflexivity. History and Theory, 45(1), 30–50.

Wille, C. (2016). Theoretical and methodological approaches to borders, spaces and identities: Methodology and situative interdisciplarity. In C. Wille, R. Reckinger, S. Kmec, & M. Hesse (Eds.), Culture and social practice. Spaces and identities in border regions: Politics - media - subjects (pp. 44–62). transcript.

Winker, G., & Degele, N. (2009). Intersektionalität: Zur Analyse sozialer Ungleichheiten. Sozial-theorie: Intro. transcript.

Wohlrab-Sahr, M. (2010). Einleitung. In M. Wohlrab-Sahr (Ed.), Kultursoziologie: Paradigmen - Methoden - Fragestellungen (pp. 9–22). VS Verlag für Sozialwissenschaften / GWV Fachverlage GmbH Wiesbaden. http://dx.doi.org/10.1007/978-3-531-92300-0 https://doi.org/10.1007/978-3-531-92300-0

Wuggenig, U. (1998). Cultural Studies und Kulturwissenschaften. In Merz Akademie (Ed.), Merz Akademie 2 (pp. 43–56). Verlag der Merz Akademie.

Wuggenig, U. (2015). Diversity. Leuphana Universität Lüneburg. Startwoche Leuphana, Lüneburg.

Yıldız, E. (2018). Das Quartier als Experimentierwelt einer inklusiven Stadt. In N. Berding, W.-D. Bukow, & K. Cudak (Eds.), Die kompakte Stadt der Zukunft: Auf dem Weg zu einer inklusiven und nachhaltigen Stadtgesellschaft (pp. 159–178). Springer VS.

Zapf, H. (2001). Dekonstruktion. In A. Nünning (Ed.), Metzler-Lexikon Literatur- und Kulturtheorie: Ansätze - Personen - Grundbegriffe (2nd ed., p. 101). Metzler.

Stefan Hirschauer

# 3 Un/Doing Differences. The Contingency of Social Affiliations[55]

## 3.1 The Distinctness of Human Distinctions

Using a minimalist definition, we might say that cultural phenomena—unlike naturally given differences—consist of contingent, meaningful *distinctions* that are shaped by historically and geographically specific contexts. These meaningful distinctions are socially constructed and applied to such things as different plants, animals, artefacts or illnesses. This paper examines the most sociologically interesting of these distinctions: those through which the makers of distinctions distinguish themselves from one another, in other words the classification of the classifiers (Bourdieu, 1984). This process marks out the classifiers' social affiliations, defines the composition of groups, ascribes forms of *membership* to individuals and subjectivizes them through specific cultural categories.

In everyday life, the effects of such meaningful distinctions are perceived as individual "characteristics", and on the aggregate level as "types of people". Conversely, sociologists generally unpick these characteristics and conceive of them as forms of membership, that is, as qualities *shared* with others (rather than merely individual ones), qualities that render people exemplars of social entities (chiefly collectivities). Social distinctions between group-like entities, then, are immanent in the perception of individual characteristics. Having stated this, the social scientific observer is confronted with two challenges:

1. The tremendous *heterogeneity* of human distinctions.
2. The highly variable *intensity* of forms of membership.

*First,* alongside time-worn classifications based on age and gender with a long cultural history (Linton, 1942) and stratificatory distinctions between classes and status groups, there are also distinctions based on generations, social milieus and occupational groups, different distinctions between normality and deviance, and everyday

---

55 This article describes the programme of the research group "Un/doing Differences. Practices of human distinctions" at the University of Mainz, Germany, from 2013 to 2019. Members of the group are: Stefan Hirschauer and Herbert Kalthoff (sociology), Carola Lentz and Matthias Krings (cultural anthropology), Oliver Scheiding and Mita Banerjee (American studies), Friedemann Kreuder (theatre science), Damaris Nübling (linguistics). This article is an English language version of Hirschauer, S. (2014). Un/doing Differences. Die Kontingenz sozialer Zugehörigkeiten. Zeitschrift für Soziologie, 43(3), 170–191. Doi: https://doi.org/10.1515/zfsoz-2014-0302

distinctions relating to dialect or attractiveness. Let us pick out a number of key distinctions around which autonomous fields of research have developed. *Ethnicity* is an imagined affiliation to a community, based on a belief in shared culture and shared descent. This belief is backed up by cultural practices, myths of origin or physical similarities; membership is mostly presented as ascriptive, primordial and inescapable (Weber, 1922/1972; Barth, 1969; Lentz, 1995). *Religious* affiliation, meanwhile, requires not just belief in commonality but also beliefs in common; in other words it begins with convictions. These convictions may change as a result of conversion. They may dwindle, be linked together and fuse syncretically, and people may offend against them and be excluded. *National* distinctions also construct "imagined communities" (Anderson, 1983), but here there is a claim to political-territorial sovereignty. Within the context of state formations, these distinctions are an attempt to create collective identities for large populations and to draw boundaries between nationals and foreigners (Calhoun, 2007). "*Race*" is also related to ethnicity (Jenkins, 1997) but is a cruder classification that directly focusses on bodies, a classification imagined as a biologically anchored marker since the late nineteenth century. The emphasis here is not on community building but on downgrading, and this saw the "racialization" not just of unfree labour (as in the case of slaves in the United States), but also of religious communities (such as the Jews in Europe) (Wacquant, 2001). In terms of cultural history, alongside *age distinctions*, *gender distinctions* are probably the oldest instance of human differentiation and an elementary case of (mostly) binary classification (Tyrell, 1986). This distinction too has been profoundly naturalized (Laqueur, 1992) and re-assigns the divided elements back into complimentary dyads by endowing sexed individuals with attributes of essential heterogeneity. Finally, particularly in "modern", meritocratic societies, we also find classification according to individual *performance*. This is quite different in character from the other categorizations in that, like a great social leveller, it exhorts us to *disregard* all differences of an ascriptive and categorical nature (Bourdieu, 2004). The objective assessment of performance (Parsons, 1987) is supposedly a socially neutral act: a classification expurgated of the classifier. But it gives rise to new categories featuring specific forms of asymmetry: rather than binary oppositions on the model of us/them distinctions, here we find ordinal scales (in the sense of better/worse).

Even this cursory list points to some specific features of these different cases, alongside a number of commonalities. Certain distinctions begin with bodies, others with convictions, activities or goods. Gender and "race" are expected to be lifelong constants, while age is inherently transitory and there is at least some consideration of mobility when it comes to classes and nations. Performance aims to produce individuals, while gender creates pairings, and ethnicity, nationality and religion build collectivities. As a result, the latter three are often linked with segregation, while genders tend to be joined together through cohabitation. These differences among distinctions are one of the reasons why specific research fields have developed to deal with each of them (such as ethnicity, "race" and gender studies). These fields can deal quite freely with their key distinction within their own sphere of action, inflating them without fear of contradiction (ethnicizing or genderizing the world, for example), "appropriating" the individuals within their field of investigation and endowing their key distinction with a claim to "omnirelevance" (such as gender, see West & Zimmerman, 1987). It is then a small step for theoretical statements to overgeneralize the empirical case of differentiation that has been paradigmatically inscribed in them (Hirschauer, 2008). To take a look at neighbouring cases through the lens of a given case would be to risk category errors: conceived in ethnonational terms, the phenomenon of ageing would appear as permanent migration, in religious terms as constant conversion and through the prism of gender studies it would be easy to see precisely two "races".

*Second*, in addition to this heterogeneity of the dimensions of distinction, the differing *intensity* of these forms of membership is a key challenge to the sociological observer. There are not only institutionally secured forms of membership (such as citizenship) and socially lived, active forms of membership (in groups), but also more distanced forms of affiliation and abeyant (dormant) forms up to and including purely categorical ones, which are essentially established by the observer or that remain no more than observers' constructions.

Social scientists seek to deal with this second challenge in two opposing ways. First, standard social research routinely draws on the seductive clarity of everyday or even bureaucratic categories. These accommodate researchers' need for reliable, decision-free variables for use in data collection (such as age and gender), so they utilize them as a resource that facilitates their own classificatory endeavours. If this research deploys a methodology that takes individuals as the source of almost all data (verbal information from interviews) and conceives of their ways of living as expressing the characteristics of variables, it can construct social identities autonomously. It can, for example, make an arithmetical Jew out of an individual with a Jewish mother who occasionally celebrates Hanukkah. The social scientific questionnaire performs this reduction as stubbornly and unwaveringly as the administrative questionnaire of a census authority. It comprehends its objects through a logic similar to that of administrative typifications: with an assumption of constancy and relevance that frees researchers from respondents' unreliable self-understanding and from the varying social relevance of these affiliations. Many of the affiliations established by scholars may in fact be dormant. As in many organizational archives, these are held by members who were merely too lazy to quit.

Such research has a tendency to reify membership, equating it with individuals' social characteristics and losing sight of the fact that these are primarily a matter of social organization. A given form of social organization, meanwhile, makes certain categories seem more prominent to sociologists than others. Loïc Wacquant (2001) reproaches "race studies" for unquestioningly adopting the objectified products of ethnopolitical entrepreneurs as tools of analysis. And Rogers Brubaker (2007) identifies a general "groupism"—the tendency, while investigating ethnicity, "race" and nation, to take the existence of identities and groups for granted as the basic components of social life, as if social life amounted to nothing more than these internally homogenous entities, sealed off from the rest of the world. Wacquant and Brubaker assail the unholy objectifying alliance of activists and social scientists. The components of a group, according to Brubaker, are not simply members, but temporally fluctuating affects, processes of categorization, political rhetorics, feats of organization and mass media framings.

To avoid this problem, meanwhile, a cultural sociological alternative has emerged. Rather than using lifeworldly categories as a resource for sociological categorization, this approach begins at a deeper level (prior to lived or assumed membership), by making categorizing itself the object of investigation. This alternative is characterized by a perspective on social phenomena that emphasizes *contingency* (Reckwitz, 2008, p. 17). It can build on early reflections in the sociology of knowledge (Durkheim & Mauss, 1903/1987), microsociological studies on "membership categorization" (Sacks, 1992), social psychology (Allport, 1954; Tajfel, 1978), but also "culturalist disciplines"[56] beyond the social sciences: cultural anthropological studies on classifications and their symbolic representation (Barth, 1969; Needham, 1975), linguistic studies on the key medium of categorization, namely language (Whorf, 1963), and poststructuralist theories of difference in fields such as cultural and postcolonial studies (Reckwitz, 2008, pp. 301–320). This sociological research investigates processes of categorization on different social levels: in everyday interactions and group processes (see e.g., Antaki & Widdicombe, 1998), through state organizations and procedures, whose postulates enter into statistics and personal documents (Foucault, 2004; Hacking, 1986) and through classificatory experts (Bowker & Star, 2000; Desrosières, 1998; Wobbe, 2012).[57] This research increasingly seeks to theorize those aspects that are common to the cultural making of human distinctions (Lamont & Molnar, 2002; Pachucki et al., 2007; Wimmer & Lamont, 2006).

It is this cultural sociological approach to theorizing human distinctions that I adopt in this paper. I begin by presenting a number of general insights into the self-perpetuation, relationality and asymmetry of categorizations and discuss the limitations of the concept of *boundary making* (Categorical Order and Boundary Making). The most important of these limitations is found in the idea of multiple affiliations, to which there are three main approaches: intersectionality, from the perspective of the

---

56 By "culturalist disciplines" I mean the traditional humanities and several disciplines that do not fit the distinction between science and humanities: for example cultural anthropology, history, cultural studies, linguistics, and every approach that turns the analysis of literature into broader media sciences.

57 Other research questions relate to the connection between these aspects. Under what conditions do categorizations of the other find expression in categorizations of the self? Which quotidian categories become administratively solidified and how do discursive categories relate to experienced affiliations within peoples' self-understanding and habitus (see e.g., Brubaker, 2007)?

sociology of inequality; the intersection of social circles from the perspective of theories of differentiation; and the trope of the hybrid as found within various cultural-based disciplines (Crossings: Concepts of Multiple Affiliation). With a critical assessment of the "bisected contingency" in these approaches in mind, the next section (The Dual Contingency of Categories) outlines the essential features of an analytical framework that privileges the competition between and temporality of human categorizations. "Doing difference" refers to meaningful selection from a set of competing categorizations (Doing and Undoing Differences) whose combination may both reinforce and suppress them (Simultaneous Distinctions: Mutual Reinforcement or Neutralization). These categorizations may be forged in frames that are open to contingency (culture) or averse to contingency (nature) and within various aggregates states (Frames and Aggregate States). Human distinctions are contingent not only because they are manufactured and have a history, but also because they may be disregarded and made irrelevant in social practice.

In view of the pronounced relativity of distinctions, my goal in this paper is to develop an analytical framework that is open to the multidimensionality and contingency of the categorization of the members of society. This framework shifts the focus of sociological attention away from the social position of individuals and the formation of groups of individuals with particular "characteristics" towards the distinctions made between individuals within social processes of varying duration. This framework is intended to facilitate comparative research in light of the elementary question: *Which* difference is (ir)relevant *when*? The sociological significance of this question lies in the classificatory consequences of contemporary processes of globalization and individualization: the discipline of sociology needs to be more sensitive to how multiple affiliations are processed within functionally differentiated "multicultural" societies, and how individuals characterized by an advanced degree of individuality categorize and identify themselves in view of the plethora of classificatory options.

## 3.2 Categorical Order and Boundary Making

There is evidently a cultural need for order that requires the upholding of categories in order to provide orientation and a secure framework for action (Schütz & Luckmann, 1979). From an anthropological perspective, this desire for order may also be understood as a mania for purification (Douglas, 1992) that resists intermingling, particularly of the cultural and natural realms. "Impurity" in this context is a disorderliness felt in the body, so to speak. The *self-perpetuation* of distinctions occurs on this basis. Mary Douglas has shown that the assertion of every classification inevitably entails the production of deviations and anomalies. In this sense, the construction of cultural categories is an interminable process. As Zygmunt Bauman (1995) suggests, it is impelled by two enduring functions: first by the banishment of disorienting ambiguity, a fundamental feat of ordering (categories reduce the contingency of our interpretations of the world), and second by the self-positioning of those making a distinction, who gain reassurance through the identification of "others".

Categories thus make a fundamental contribution to cultural order. They do so by enabling three types of association: categorizations (subsumptive perceptual allocations of objects to linguistic terms), identifications (fluctuating affective associations within actors' self-understanding) and selective social relations (social associations), that regulate proximity and distance and facilitate social closures. Categorizations work with the help of a distinction made within a comparative framework in which two objects that have been equated from one perspective (as human beings for example) appear "equal" or "unequal" according to particular criteria (Heintz, 2010, p. 164). This elementary *relationality* of characteristics (already highlighted by Georg Simmel) endows each of them with a fundamentally bivalent social significance: depending on who one is interacting with, one and the same "feature" means "the same" or "other"[58]. The purely categorical form of membership within a class of individuals, with whom one shares some attribute or other, thus grounds one's (affective and social) relational affiliation to a web of relationships, such as couples, groups or communities (Brubaker, 2007, p. 67). Perceptual, affective and social associations are the elementary forms of social interpretation of anything perceived through categories.

Finally, the distinction between "types of people" posits various forms of *asymmetry*. In the first instance, this is bound up with the function of self-positioning: while every conceptual distinction between whichever objects (such as that between apples and non-apples) is always logically asymmetrical, because it distinguishes one thing from another (Spencer-Brown, 1999), us/them distinctions among human beings are also *sociologically* asymmetrical because they are always carried out somewhere and by someone. The two sides of these distinctions cannot be seen, as with left and right, through the eyes of a neutral theorizing observer; instead the process of carrying out these distinctions places whoever is making them on a given side, in the sense of "here or there", like Bauman (1995) refers to inside and outside.[59] This

---

**58** This means for instance that in many social situations an individual has a socially dual gender: the same *and* a different gender depending on who s/he is interacting with. Further, an individual may be a member of a pairing in a binding, imperative sense (otherwise the social unit will dissolve), while her or his categorical gender affiliation is sometimes relevant and sometimes secondary within this relationship. An individual may also be a member of a "women's group", in other words a group formed with explicit reference to gender distinctions (though not including all women), and, finally, an individual may be perceived stereotypically as an exemplar of the collective category "women". All of these—interactional bivalence, dyadic (ir)relevance, group-*definiens* and categorical appropriation—are differing cases of the use of categories.

**59** The asymmetrical conceptual structure of "us/them" is probably as fundamental as the distinction that animals make between members of the same species on the one hand and their prey and predators on the other.

is associated with valences extending from mild preferences for the "in-group" all the way through to pronounced valorization and devalorization. Such distinctions frequently entail normalizing acts of othering and nostrification (Stagl, 1981), open up divides between the self-categorization of individuals and their categorization by others (Tajfel, 1978; Jenkins, 1997) and separate normality from deviance. Here, distinctions render various elements both different and the same. They feature a polarizing obverse and a homogenizing reverse side, equalizing or totalizing the elements on both sides of the distinction (such as "blacks" and "whites").[60] They also mark themselves off from an excluded third (Derrida, 1995) and inherently generate a constitutive exterior (Laclau & Mouffe, 2006).

In an effort to identify such general aspects of human distinctions, scholars have recently suggested how we might conceptualize them. Wimmer (2008), Lamont and Molnar (2002) as well as Wimmer and Lamont (2006), building on the work of Barth (1969) and Gieryn (1983), refer to *boundary making*. For them a boundary has two dimensions: a symbolic one relating to perceptual schemata and representations, and a social one that implies behavioural patterns, is based on the proximity and distance of relations and is ultimately objectified in the shape of unequal access and social closures. This implies the idea of the social hardening of cultural distinctions. The concept of boundary making has some potential. It conceives of boundaries and memberships in a dynamic way and begins to reveal their considerable variation[61] from a comparative perspective. Nonetheless, the concept entails three problems.

*First,* a number of authors deploy this concept in order to weave together various threads of distinction. For example, Brubaker (2007) and—even more emphatically—Andreas Wimmer (2008) have deployed the concept of ethnicity as a means of *subsuming* adjacent forms of differentiation (spurning Weber's advice to avoid the concept entirely as hopelessly nebulous). Wimmer (2008) identifies ethnosomatic ("race"), ethnopolitical (nation), ethnoreligious, ethnolinguistic and ethnoregional groups (p. 974). Expressed in terms of the "strategies of ethnic boundary making" that he identifies (Wimmer, 2008, pp. 986–989), we might also regard this as a strategy of professional expansion pursued by scholars of ethnicity, an example of research fields' above-mentioned tendency towards appropriation. In their review, Lamont and Molnar (2002) thus discuss a more broadly based list and, alongside "race", ethnicity and nation, include class, gender, professions, disciplines and local communities under the concept of boundary.

*Second,* this generalization only renders the concept's *implicit case-specific character* all the clearer. The empirical cases inscribed in the concept are still primarily

---

**60** The overstating of inter-categorical distinctions and of intra-categorical homogeneity highlighted by social psychologists (such as Tajfel, 1978) is a formal mechanism for reinforcing difference.
**61** Wimmer (2008) distinguishes, for example, between degrees of political salience, social closure, cultural distinction and the stability of ethnic distinctions.

forms of ethnicity (in Wimmer's expansive sense of the term), while such things as "genders" can hardly be conceived in such "groupist" terms. Barth's early notion of boundaries failed to distinguish sufficiently between categories and groups, as the implied demarcation of entities assumes an excessive degree of homogeneity (see Brubaker, 2007, p. 25). Further, the metaphor of the boundary represents a *topological* way of thinking. This metaphor leads to issues of limited surface area (boundaries expand or contract) and permeability (boundaries are closed or opened up); the metaphor of the boundary evokes the intuitive sense of a threshold traversed at the cost of social energy; and it encloses individuals as a whole within the communicative limits of a given boundary: they cannot be in two places at once. The nation state, the "ethnonational master scheme of modern society" (Wimmer, 2008, p. 992), evidently influenced not just the salience of categories within society (promoting ethnicization according to Wimmer), but also the way in which sociologists comprehend affiliations. Membership itself sometimes seems like a latently administrative concept. What fails to fit neatly into this topological image of boundaries is the variable salience of a distinction and its relation to other distinctions.

*Third*, this is bound up with the fact that the mere collection of boundary-like distinctions fails to take account of an elementary reality: that individuals do not possess membership in isolation, in other words more or less in line with disciplinary distinctions between research on gender, "race", ethnicity and so on. Instead, they have memberships in parallel, concurrently and in combination. Their membership always already takes the form of *multiple affiliation*. This simple fact, long suppressed as a result of the differentiation of research fields, gives rise to new demands to think processes of categorization sociologically. The key requirement here is expressed by Wimmer (2008) in the very title of his essay "The Making *and Unmaking* [emphasis added] of Ethnic Boundaries," though he fails to live up to this promise. Wimmer puts forward a theory of the reproduction and transformation of ethnic boundary making that implies the omnirelevance of ethnicity. This theory seeks to explain why ethnicity crops up in so many forms. Here, certain forms of ethnicity may become stronger or weaker, but can never fade or disappear due to a lack of *competing* types of distinction. This makes it impossible to conceive of the unmaking of distinctions and of the switch over to quite differently constructed distinctions.

## 3.3 Crossings: Concepts of Multiple Affiliation

There are three approaches, the three opposing corners of a conceptual triangle, that we might deploy to think about multiple affiliations and carry out multidimensional research on human distinctions, and each of these approaches is informed by various forms of *societal* differentiation. The debate in the social sciences is characterized by an opposition between theories of the stratificatory and functional differentiation of society, each of which implies differing premises on the differentiation of people within society. Depending on where the emphasis is placed here, we find ourselves working with the concepts of intersectionality and heterogeneity (Intersectionality and Heterogeneity) or the notion of a role-like form of multiple membership (The Intersection of Social Circles). Within cultural theory, meanwhile, reflections on human distinctions are strongly determined by concepts of multiculturalism (Gupta & Ferguson, 1992; Hall, 2004) that implicitly presuppose a segmentary differentiation of society and lead to the concept of hybridity (Multiculturalism and Hybridity).

### 3.3.1 Intersectionality and Heterogeneity

Studies on *intersectionality* (Crenshaw, 1994; Anthias, 2005) investigate the interwoven character of and interaction between selected categories of difference (mostly class, "race" and gender, occasionally religion, age, sexuality and the body). Above all, these studies examine the effects on inequality of interactions between these distinctions, regarded as structural categories. This approach is concerned with the accumulation and combination of categories that expose individuals to a multiple structural positioning, engendering inequality. Here, multiple membership received its information value through the "establishment of subdisciplines with responsibility for specific categories of social division," (Knapp, 2013, p. 345) subdisciplines that not only illuminate their field of study through their singular, key distinction, but to some extent recruit their research personnel with this distinction in mind as well (particularly in the case of gender, "race" and queer studies). The intersectionality approach holds out the prospect of correcting these research fields' tendency to endow their key distinctions with omnirelevance. There are, however, three problematic aspects to this.

*First*, while it is true that this approach no longer responds to the specific features and comparability problems entailed in human distinctions through the relevance claims of just one research field (such as ethnicity), it still engages in major forms of reduction, limiting itself to the possible effects on *inequality* of more or less arbitrarily *selected* categories. This fails to illuminate, first, distinctions that do not necessarily have anything to do with discrimination, such as the coexistence of nations, confessions and professions, and, second, the substantial inequality between, for example, professionals and laypeople or between age groups. Researchers' selection of the great triad (sex/"race"/class) is ultimately due to the historically contingent formation of three social movements, and they seek to merge their research with the logic of these movements. The fractioning logic of the political field and the groupism of specific categories are thus inherent in intersectionality.

*Second*, this has conceptual consequences. This consensual limitation to a few key distinctions appears designed to divest them, once again, of the competition they face from one another and from other distinctions within social practice. Here, the assumption of structural categories beyond actors' reach provides latent theoretical protection for specific key differences, namely those forms of distinction that begin with individuals and enclose them in a totalizing way (such as classes and ascriptive status categories). This approach conceives of individuality in an *inclusive* way and thus creates an "identitarian sociology" (Brubaker, 2007, p. 88).

*Third*, finally, the metaphor of intersection is empirically under-complex. How can the many forms of membership that overlap in social situations be limited a priori to the configuration of a major intersection (featuring just four directions) with respect to every social process? From high in the sky, after all, all you can see are a city's boulevards. The deeper we go empirically—into the valleys of the quotidian manufacture of social orders—the more side-streets, cycle paths and foot paths we see flowing into the intersection, to the point, in fact, where we come to understand that this intersection is located within a multidimensional space. In place of the old moral superpowers of the "oppression Olympics" (Knapp, 2013, p. 350), we find numerous "middle powers" with respect to social inequality and—crosscutting them—a dozen relevant subsystems generated by horizontal differentiation within society.

The Bielefeld Collaborative Research Center (SFB) "From Heterogeneities to Inequalities"[62] (Diewald & Faist, 2011) has adopted an approach that is also anchored in theories of inequality but with different emphases. On the basis of the fundamental conceptual distinction highlighted in the project's name, it seeks to identify the social mechanisms that may turn heterogeneities into social inequalities. On this view, heterogeneity is "mere difference ... everything that constitutes the variety and diversity of individuals" (Diewald & Faist, 2011, p. 95). Aiming to achieve a certain opening of social structural analysis to the cultural pluralization of social milieus, the SFB distinguishes four groups of individual features that may form the point of departure for "success in the labour market and in life": ascriptive features (including physical differences, gender, age, nationality and ethnicity), "cultural preferences" (meaning ways of life, lifestyles, attitudes, worldviews), formal qualifications and cultural capital, and various activities (occupations and housework).

Among the key mechanisms here, in addition to the establishment of hierarchies and exploitation, Diewald and Faist (2011) include social exclusion (in Weber's sense) and opportunity hoarding (in Tilly's sense) and, prior to these, boundary making, which they comprehend as the cultural perception and evaluation of heterogeneities. On this view, boundary making is one of the key mechanisms through which heterogeneity is socially defined in a meaningful way in the first place (Diewald & Faist, 2011, p. 109).

While the notion of intersections begins with categories whose relevance has been secured in advance, the Bielefeld approach is more empirically open, taking an undefined heterogeneity as its starting point and aiming to investigate its social relevance practices, though again, exclusively from the narrow perspective of its impact

---

62  It comprises 18 research projects, funded for up to 12 years.

on inequality (in other words, while failing to consider other sociologically relevant dimensions). The approach absorbs the specificity of diverse human distinctions by observing them solely from the perspective of their (dis)advantageousness with respect to social success, in other words by implicitly subsuming them as aspects of individual "human capital". It is as if this approach merely seeks to unwaveringly perpetuate the in-house classificatory of social structural analysis (mentioned in the introduction).

This implies that inequality is a more socially significant and heterogeneity a potentially less significant form of difference. As with intersectionality, this produces an implicit a priori sociological hierarchy of distinctions. This exclusive focus on inequality within the context of an individual's success in life abstracts from the fact that quite different distinctions may be of equal or greater importance to social processes within specific situations or fields. But the pre-eminence of this inequality is more a reflection of its political than its sociological relevance. If differences in income can be considered an appropriate expression of heterogeneity or an indicator of social inequality (Diewald & Faist, 2011, p. 99), then the distinction between heterogeneity and inequality is also an implicitly normative one.

If the Bielefeld approach to social inequality seeks to attain the status of a more general sociology and to forge links with cultural sociology,[63] it will have to take a more elementary approach to the concept of inequality. Sociologically, inequality means more than the unequal distribution of goods and opportunities, which may be experienced as unjust because it improves or worsens individuals' lot. As mentioned in the introduction, inequality results from a comparative perspective that establishes (in)equalities according to particular criteria: in couples a heterogeneous pairing *is* the unequal pairing (Hirschauer, 2013). Binational cooperation, a Christian-Muslim group and the social relationship between service provider and customer are also *unequal* in a sociologically significant way.

In the work of Diewald and Faist (2011), meanwhile, heterogeneity seems to be understood in a markedly quotidian way (as a form of distinctiveness that is, somehow or other, the normal state of affairs for human beings). Here heterogeneity is a collective category for a plurality whose genesis—those social processes that bring about the differentiation of the different in the first place—is of no further

---

63 More consistent here are those analyses of social structure that deal explicitly with respondents' self-categorizations, in other words that try to get to grips with "folk sociostructural analysis". For a study on the lifeworldly perceptibility of affiliation to different social strata, see Pape et al. (2008); for an investigation of the varying relevance of occupation, gender, ethnicity, nation and class, see Emmison and Western (1990). The connection between perceptibility and relevance remains an open question in these studies. Functioning markers (that is, congruent ascriptions) do not necessarily ensure that social agents take every opportunity to classify that presents itself (that they select a schema unprompted). Perceptibility may long pertain while becoming situationally meaningless (we need only think of "race" or gender).

interest. In a half-hearted attempt to integrate cultural sociological concepts that do in fact take account of the categorizations made in society, boundary making fades once again into the reified variables of individual "features". Taking a meaningless form of human distinctiveness as one's point of departure desociologizes processes of human differentiation.[64]

### 3.3.2 The Intersection of Social Circles

Rather than *enclosing* individuals in classes, since Durkheim, Weber and Simmel theories of differentiation have presented them as located *between* specialized fields. Through its structures, every society offers the people within it opportunities to be something specific, while the various social differentiations crosscut one another, in individuals among other things. Their resulting multiple membership is thus a quite elementary fact, but one that is becoming ever more important within the history of society. This is a phenomenon, bound up with the options available to individuals, that lies at the "intersection of social circles" (Simmel, 1992).

Brought to a head in Luhmann's analysis (1997), functional differentiation does not begin with bodies or goods, but with types of actions or communications and involves individuals only via behavioural episodes during which they play specialized roles. The differentiation of social subsystems, then, no longer confines individuals (as in the case of estates or classes) in a totalizing way, but instead places them in a structurally exterior position: functional differentiation creates "*exclusionary individuality*" (Luhmann, 1989, p. 158) and a whole range of new opportunities to choose and renounce tangential forms of membership. In this way, individuality no longer emerges *within* specific subsystems, but instead through expectations that are primarily concerned with the material content of communication and secondarily with the field-specific roles that individuals temporarily play. This greatly weakens the relevance of ascriptive criteria, differences in status and inequalities based on collective affiliations. These face competition from new forms of inequality (particularly the opposition between performance-based and lay roles) and meritocratic principles that seek to classify individuals solely in light of their performance. Luhmann replaces the "features" of individual origin with the *selection criteria* of systems that include individuals.

---

**64** And it would then be merely consistent to sign the genesis of these processes over to biology: "The starting point for analysis of the distribution of social opportunity should be ... the fact of differing genetic predispositions" (Diewald, 2010, p. 11). "As quasi-pre-social heterogeneity within a given population," these should be regarded as a fundamental explanatory factor (Diewald, 2010, p. 11)—as in the case of "gender-typical variations in genetic dispositions" (Diewald, 2010, p. 16).

This approach, which decentres individuals, is associated with a significant de-reification of various kinds of distinctions and brings out their diversity. Two key aspects, however, require correction. *First*, the theory of functional differentiation underestimates cultural inertia because it overestimates society's communicative self-portrayal (its cherished semantics). It works with modernist idealizations and perceives persistent older forms of inequality solely as premodern remnants, despite the fact that these get in the way of purely task-oriented classifications (according to performance, for example) even in contemporary societies. If, despite the socio-structural expendability of many human distinctions, empirically notorious attempts at exclusion nonetheless occur (of women or migrants, for example), the theory of functional differentiation seeks to explain this in terms of persistent forms, of merely residual relevance, on subordinate societal levels. Weinbach and Stichweh (2001) for example argue that while organizations, with their formalized membership roles, feature strong imperatives to be gender-blind, when it comes to reconciling job requirements with personal capabilities, ascriptive features may come back into play. According to these authors, it is particularly difficult to abstract interactions from system-external role obligations. "As those present obtrude visibly as individuals, it may become apparent what else they have to do outside of the interaction," as Luhmann (1997, p. 815) puts it. This shunting off of non-task-related human distinctions to occurrences here and there in interaction or organization is not completely convincing, first because it entails a failure to consider other levels of order (such as dyads, groups and networks) on which such distinctions have an impact and second, because the task-related differentiation of performance obviously exercises a stratifying effect itself. Certainly, this distinction initially begins solely with actions, but it becomes inscribed in human beings, sometimes for a very long time, with the aid of individualising diagnoses that produce new categories (best, (un)suitable, (less) gifted, outstanding, and so on).

*Second*, conceptually, Luhmann's theoretical construct privileges a particular type of membership. He reserves this term for affiliation to organizations, whose boundary-forming principle such affiliation is supposed to be. The central place of organizations in Luhmann's (1975) distinction between levels is the internal theoretical reason why he omits to discuss other forms of membership, such as affiliation to groups or imagined communities. His focus on organizations, moreover, generalizes a specific "contingency of membership" (Luhmann, 1975, p. 14), namely the case of freely chosen and rescindable membership in organizations with their "opportunities to break off social relations and enter into new ones" (Luhmann, 1975, p. 17). Those forms of membership that have *not* been chosen—gender affiliation, ethnicity, age, and so on—and are maintained through cultural processes of categorization, are simply absent as "evolutionary remnants".

### 3.3.3 Multiculturalism and Hybridity

The key reference point for concepts of multiculturalism in the culturalist disciplines is a segmentary differentiation of society into countries or "cultures". Against this background, contemporary waves of global migration and worldwide media networks point to the cultural pluralization of lifeways: an ever greater number of people are influenced by an array of cultural traditions and frameworks of meaning, and they are combining them in novel ways (Bhabha, 1994; Young, 1995). Authors within the fields of cultural studies and postcolonial studies have put forward the concept of *hybridity* to comprehend such phenomena.[65] This refers to a combination of opposing categories within *one* dimension of distinction, in other words to mutually exclusive affiliations. Hybridity appears as a form of ambiguity between two entities. The basic assumption here is that, through transnational biographies, multicultural societies generate new forms of multiple cultural affiliation and polysemic forms of membership (Appiah, 1994; Nederveen Pieterse, 2001). Fixed classificatory systems become fluid through "cultural interference," which entails the overlapping of a number of different cultural codes (Kapchan & Strong, 1999; Reckwitz, 2008).

Central to hybrid phenomena is the creolization of national identities through the boundary-crossing inherent in migration, transnational communities and diasporas. Here, the "intersectionally" underprivileged "working-class Catholic girls from the country" contrast with the "cool" "Moroccan girls doing Thai boxing in Amsterdam" (Nederveen Pieterse, 2001, p. 19). But migration brings out just one aspect, which is also a source of anxiety in other forms of membership: *mobility* between categories, whether between classes, religions or genders. The slogan of illegal immigrants in the United States, "We didn't cross the borders, the borders crossed us" might be embraced by other hybrid figures such as religious eclectics or inter- and transsexuals, or the rapidly increasing number of "mixed raced people" in the United States, for whom the US census has permitted the category of "multiracial" alongside sixteen "races" since 2000. Finally, phenomena of hybridization are to be found in ambiguity-friendly popular culture, for example in the stylistic fusions of world music, a topic explored by cultural studies scholars, who have investigated aesthetic crossover in new social strata and markets (Nederveen Pieterse, 2001). Cultural elements with diverse origins, then, are becoming amalgamated in a number of ways.

The concept of hybridity distances itself even further than theories of differentiation from a reifying thought style. But the identification of hybridity is logically preceded by a clear-cut distinction: that of "cultures". The holistic understanding of cultures as mentalistically integrated communities featuring shared norms is a

---

65 Alternative terms are *creolization* (Hannerz, 1987) and *mestizization* (Amselle, 1998). A related concept is *transdifference*, which means the copresence of discrepant ascriptions and affiliations (Allolio-Näcke et al., 2005).

reification that has often been critiqued (Trouillot, 2002; Reckwitz, 2008; Lentz, 2009). In the present context, it has two implications. First, it again implies a latently topological conception of cultural distinctions conceived through the territorial logic of national boundaries and, second, a form of social affiliation that once again assumes the inclusion of individuals in a totalistic way, a form of affiliation from which people are then "liberated" by hybridity.

In line with this, many studies on hybridity are characterized by a moralizing theoretical air, implicitly conjuring up utopias of de-differentiation (Fluck, 2000) and subjecting processes of hybridization to aesthetic inflation. Here hybridity becomes a buzzword with a top-heavy normative load, a way of expressing opposition to essentialization and dualistic thinking of all kinds (see Nederveen Pieterse, 2001, p. 20). Much of this discourse reads "as if the expression of goodwill and the attestation of moral passion had anything to do with empirical attentiveness and theoretical rigour," to quote Wacquant (2001, p. 67) on "race" studies. Such normatively inspired theory building takes too little account of the basic sociocultural ordering function of processes of classification. Social categories create compulsory or chosen habitats between individuality and global citizenship, so that the blurring of one distinction often merely means shifting attention to another.

Despite these weaknesses, the notion of the hybrid is sociologically significant in two fundamental ways. First, telecommunications, goods traffic and migration have weakened cultural boundaries; for certain social milieus and generations, local traditions are becoming stylistic pools of cultural props that may be combined to create patchwork stylizations of the self. This patchwork resembles the notion of the individual at the intersection of social circles as found in theories of differentiation. In this case, however, we are dealing not with social relations involving individuals but with flows of goods, symbols and information that they log into as participants and utilize. So here the individual is located not between social structures but within globally circulating flows. Identities give way to practices: I am $x$ as long as I do $x$.[66]

---

[66] In line with this, Andreas Reckwitz (2008) has explicitly proposed the culturalization of Simmel's notion: not only do social systems of norms and roles intersect in individuals, these individuals also take part in various complexes of social practice that are executed against the background of differing frameworks of meaning. But if actors take part in a number of "knowledge orders" at the same time, which lead them to differing interpretations of their lifeways, then this confronts them with the problem of interpretive indeterminacy; it renders identities fragile and requires identity work (Reckwitz, 2008, pp. 69–93). Reckwitz also deploys this generalized hybridity of the cultural to counter the purifications of classical social theory, which assumes that structural entities (classes, systems, and so on) have clear-cut boundaries. This perspective, I think, points the way ahead. But what seems problematic to me is the idea of definitive "knowledge orders" in which the holistic concept of culture retains its vigour, despite being detached from countries and collectivities. The challenge posed by cultural theory for sociologists is not to rethink "cultures" but to rethink the cultural itself.

Second, according to Nederveen Pieterse (2001), the significance of the hybrid lies primarily in a new perspective on the constitutive significance and *contingency* of boundaries. He refers to a hybridity of the *longue durée* that is as old as the history of humanity: on this view, the old "cultures" that underpin the hybrid are themselves products of older syncretisms, their origins lying in cultural contact, trade, conquests and migration. The idea here is that globalization has merely accelerated this (Nederveen Pieterse, 2001, p. 13). This gives rise to a cycle: hybrids logically presuppose categorical orders that in turn are chronologically imposed (in the sense of Bauman and Douglas) on an antecedent indeterminacy, prior to which there may lie older categorical orders. Distinct "cultures" are thus historical phases of the temporary stabilization of older dynamic phases of the encounter between and fusion of cultural patterns, and hybrids are inevitable transitional phenomena within a constant process of the displacement of categorical boundaries. The realm of the cultural consists, so to speak, of continuous processes of boundary displacement, very well illustrated by the historical erection, contestation, transgression and vegetative overgrowing of national borders. As Wimmer and Lamont (2006) put it: "[U]nits emerge, enter into various relationships with other units which then may lead to their dissolution and regrouping into other social entities" (p. 5). The notion that cultural distinctions place purified entities in the world, cause them to interact, thereby "contaminate" them and thus dissolve them once again, is a more dynamic conception than that of the preserved (path-dependent) processes of differentiation found in theories of evolution: borders may in fact *disappear*.

### 3.3.4 Interim Conclusion: Bisected Contingency

These three approaches to thinking about multiple affiliations describe three very different intersections: of road axes of social inequality, social circles and cultural codes that, as with the intersection of genetic codes, appear as a form of "cross-breeding". Within these three concepts, individuals find themselves either fixed at the intersection of powerful axes of social inequality (intersectionality), set free at the junction of variable social circles (exclusionary individuality) or oscillating at the transfer point between different cultural systems of reference (hybridity). All three of these perspectives present researchers with two fundamental problems.

*First*, despite efforts to consider several types of distinction at the same time, again and again the disciplinary or research field-related origin of these approaches ensures the selective dominance of specific differences, such as nationality and ethnicity within research on hybridity, the close linkage of gender and class in intersectionality research, and a fixation on freely chosen and rescindable forms of membership in studies of functional differentiation. This constricting of perspective to specific differences or closed lists often results in a generalization of specific empirical cases. What we have yet to see is a perspective that pays attention to multiple affiliations without overlooking the specific features of a given categorization (binary, ascriptive, grouping, asymmetrical, and so on) and the varying *forms* of affiliation that they offer or require. We may be dealing with an identity-appropriating form of membership of classes or "cultures"; membership in organizations, which is less inclusive but rendered clear-cut through formalization; diffuse affiliations to social circles and cultural origins; or the rights and opportunities to participate in networks and communication flows.

*Second*, research informed by these three ways of thinking risks the implicit conceptual reproduction of the very differences it seeks to unpick. This is evident when research on inequality deploys everyday categorizations to collect its data (heterogeneity) or places them beyond the realm of observation as a result of theoretical predecisions (intersectionality). But this risk is particularly great in research that seeks to oppose the essentialist assumption of given entities and their qualities (such as ethnic groups, "races", and genders). This is partly due to the character of research fields that have a hard time letting go of the particular form of difference so central to their own existence (Hirschauer, 2003). But it also has something to do with problems related to the logic of observation and conceptual mechanics, when, for example, the conceptual frame of the hybrid reproduces the very boundary that has supposedly been crossed.

We can capture the second problem through the concept of *bisected contingency*. Researchers often reconstruct everything that produces, structures, reinforces and lends relevance to their key distinctions. But prejudiced by their particular focus, they are far less sensitive to the possibility of the irrelevance of these distinctions, because they have invested too much in them. Much of the research on human distinctions cultivates a pronounced constructivism, as if a given research field must constantly seek to counter the claim to relevance posited by its own existence and designation (as "race" or gender studies for example). Within this claim, the finding of differences becomes the key objective of observations premised upon a given distinction. Here, Bateson's (1972) definition of an informative difference, "a difference that makes a difference," (p. 315) is halved. Researchers expend a lot of words stating that this difference is a *process of distinguishing*. But does it *make* a difference? Much light is often shed on the contingent *production* of a difference, but the contingent way in which people *make use of* this difference within social processes remains in the shadows. Categories undoubtedly provide observers with orientation, but do actors themselves make use of them? And when categorization occurs, is it meaningfully selected and ongoingly deployed or does it remain insignificant within a specific situation or field? These gradations of relevance (Kotthoff, 2002) must not only be considered (as has been the case so far) in relation to functional differentiation (as factual irrelevance), but also in relation to the structure of social strata (if social mobility indicates an *indifference* to classes or the absorption of difference through the education system) and in terms of the competition *between* distinctions, a topic the intersectionality approach opens up only to shut it down again.

Theoretically and empirically, we can comprehend the linkage of social affiliations through multiple memberships or the conjoining of different forms of distinction within social processes only if these concepts leave room for one another in research as they do in everyday life. Of course, each distinction contributes to the reduction of complexity (creates cultural order), but together distinctions cause this complexity to mushroom once again. This means that, for observers, specific distinctions must be allowed to *lie dormant* just as they do for the actors who use them. These actors cannot enact every distinction concurrently and in equal measure; after all, (as Luhmann might put it) they always have other things to do.

What this means is that multidimensional research on human distinctions must *empirically jeopardize* the distinctions central to specific research fields and abandon their claims to omnirelevance, in other words make room for the *competition* between their key distinctions within social practice. A multidimensional *focus* on individuals through a more complex investigation of their affiliations equates to the multidimensional *decentring* of social distinctions. What we need, then, are studies on cultural distinctions among people that assume the mutual relativization of these distinctions, studies that reflexively observe their own use of distinctions and that systematically presume that each case of differentiation may be displaced by other distinctions, lose relevance and disappear.

## 3.4 The Dual Contingency of Categories

At present there is no viable theoretical framework for such a contingency-aware approach to research. In what follows, I first highlight a possible starting point for such a framework before going on to flesh this out. I began this paper with the minimalist social theoretical assumption that cultural differences can be traced back to meaningful distinctions. If we now spotlight the contingency of these distinctions, what we find is that they may be made *or* unmade, upheld *or* undermined, and that when they come up against other distinctions they may be strengthened *or* supplanted. What we must examine, then, are not just the intersection of certain axes of differentiation defined in advance (intersectionality) or the individual transgression of specific binarisms (hybridity), but a complex empirical interplay of human distinctions: the constant shifting of multiple categorizations between reinforcement and displacement, stabilization and forgetting, thematization and de-thematization. There are processes of differentiation *and* de-differentiation, constellations of actualization *or* neutralization, practices of boundary making and distinction, *but* also of levelling and the negation of difference. In historical and field-specific terms, cultural differences may be displaced by others, diminish in intensity because their applicability is limited, and they include fewer cultural objects, and disappear entirely within certain layers of meaning. The simple question to be answered is: *Which* difference is in force *where* and *when*? This emphasis on contingency requires the relativization and temporalization of differences.

We must counter the specialization of the various *studies in differences* by relativizing their key distinctions in light of one another. The simultaneity of distinctions requires a broad conceptual framework. This should enable us to compare cultural distinctions of varying character with one another and, on a case-by-case basis, to consider how stable they are and whether people wield them in a cursory or consequential way. How do people carry out field-specific classifications and how do they ensure the visibility of affiliations? What kinds of interdependence and competition do we find between the various forms of categorization? Which categorizations are irrelevant or dominant and when?

In place of the master schema of nationality, which has led many scholars to conceptualize distinctions in a topological way (as boundary), it seems more productive to think about cultural distinctions in terms of *time*. Culturally constituted phenomena—from the most minor of linguistic distinctions all the way through to the largest of structural formations—are *processual* (Abbott, 2001), regardless of whether we investigate them micrologically within the situational time of action sequences, the biographical time of narratives or macrologically in highly consequential administrative postulates and historical developments. We must assume the existence of variation at every turn—that people situatively actualize and neutralize distinctions on a *moment-by-moment* basis (so what we find are points of insertion and reversal, cessation and interruption), or that distinctions take the form of biographical and historical *upturns and downturns*.

These distinctions not only have a socio-spatial relevance (well captured by theories of differentiation). They also have a *temporally* fluctuating significance. Which subjectively experienced affiliation is affectively potent when and for how long? Which factors determine such biographical upturns in institutions and interactions? Under which historical conditions does a distinction become established, and which lattice of conditions renders it inoperative?

In what follows I outline a concept that might begin to capture this relativization and temporalization (Doing and Undoing Differences). I then discuss two types of condition that contribute to the contingency or stabilization of distinctions: their crossing with other distinctions (Simultaneous Distinctions: Mutual Reinforcement or Neutralization) and their framing and processing within different aggregate states (Frames and Aggregate States).

### 3.4.1 Doing and Undoing Differences

A sufficiently broad theoretical starting point is provided by the concept of *doing differences* (West & Fenstermaker, 1995), which introduced a praxeological-constructivist perspective into intersectionality research. The basic ethnomethodological assumption here is that all social distinction must be *practised* (doing gender, doing "race" etc.), in other words, that all social distinction is part of a reality that is *carried out*, with individuals being regarded neither as actors nor as bearers of identities but instead as the mere conveyors of social practice.[67] *Doing ethnicity* (for example) is then "a practical achievement, something which 'happens', when ethnic categories become relevant in the course of an interaction" (Brubaker, 2007, p. 103). In the work of West and Fenstermaker (1995), meanwhile, *doing differences* means the way in which people *simultaneously* coproduce distinctions (doing x while doing y). This takes the concept away from an overly narrow focus on specific distinctions, but brings along with it—from the debate on intersectionality—the notion that several distinctions are simultaneously relevant. This makes it difficult to observe the competition between them.

This shortcoming can easily be remedied by focusing the ethnomethodological concept of doing x more consistently than hitherto on the element of contingency inherent within it: The fundamental notion of a *practical doing* of affiliations and distinctions implies that people may also *refrain* from doing them. To the extent that they practically perform meaningful distinctions, they may interrupt, abstain from or discontinue this process of performance, and they may deactivate memberships within specific situations or fields. Doing always already implies the potential for *undoing* (Hirschauer, 1994, pp. 676–679).[68]

On this basis, I propose a reconceptualization of doing difference, namely as meaningful *selection* from a set of *competing* categorizations, a selection that creates a difference that makes a difference. It is not enough for a categorization to occur (providing sociologists with an opportunity to adopt or reconstruct it). What matters

---

67 I have no space to discuss here the social theoretical limiting of ethnomethodology to interactions. On the need to supplement this approach with organizational opportunity structures, cultural knowledge stocks, and biographical and societal processes, see Hirschauer (2001) as well as Gildemeister and Hericks (2012).

68 This leads on to the idea that we ought to regard the process of gender construction, for example, as *episodes* in which gender appears and disappears in social situations. An example is the use of gender distinctions to create groups among pupils (Breidenstein, 1997). Gender is inscribed in certain games (such as "kissing tag", in which the girls must catch and kiss the boys or vice versa); in other games, gender classes may be actualized as sides, if the quantitative availability of girls and boys is balanced when it comes to organizing teams. But if the game requires equality of strength (as in tug-of-war), the deployment of gender immediately ceases. If there is just one girl too many, she may become an "substitute" in a game of football. Or if there is just one woman teacher, then the "group of boys" may be trained by her (and here her gender is neutralized), but not if a male teacher is available. In both cases, singularity suspends the gender distinction, but for different reasons: the single girl is integrated into a group of fellow players, while the single (equivalent-less) woman teacher is perceived primarily as different in status. The cognitive accompaniments of such social processes in schools have been investigated by psychologists (Kessels, 2002). For a review of the cognitive inhibition of category activation, see Macrae and Bodenhausen (2000).

is whether people *subscribe to* this categorization in social processes (interactions, biographies, procedures, fashions, discourses, and so on), in other words whether, in the course of these processes, people enact a distinction in such a way as to establish its social relevance (Hirschauer, 2001). From the perspective of a distinction, its repeated use represents an increase in significance, while from the perspective of its users it brings about a lessening of complexity through which they reduce the many forms of membership, which overlap situationally (or field-specifically), to a single currently dominant one (or a few currently dominant ones).

If a distinction is not selected, then for the time being it does not occur; it rests in a kind of standby mode (Coulter, 1996). Just as membership within an organization may be dormant and the salience of affiliations may peak and trough within people's self-understanding (both psychologically and biographically)—one individual is a woman working for the police service, another merely a female cop, one individual is an atheist, another merely lives in an areligious way—this also applies situationally, field-specifically and historically. Individuals' non-affiliation or absence of ties corresponds to an *indifference* of distinctions. This applies especially to experienced togetherness (the social association): This is a context-dependent event that may be intensive at certain times. We must be open to the possibility that it "does not 'happen'" (Brubaker, 2007, p. 23), that what we are otherwise dealing with, on a case-by-case basis, is aschematic individuals, weak affective ties and mere nominal members.

It is scarcely possible to observe such states of dormancy empirically. All we can observe is a period of the negation of distinction, of its *undoing*. Within a historical timescale, this may involve counter-discourses, programmes of urban demolition or antidiscrimination policies, through which, for example, attempts have been made to erase "race" from minds, speech and practices in post-apartheid South Africa. Within a biographical timescale, it may entail negatory narratives that attempt to nullify an earlier religious or political identification; within an interactional timescale, we may be dealing with opposition (practised disregard, the active minimization of difference) or a tacit skipping of categorizations (Hirschauer, 2001), for these are situationally "ascribed (and rejected), avowed (and disavowed), displayed (and ignored)" (Antaki & Widdicombe, 1998, p. 2). In this sense, undoing ethnicity (for example) refers only to a narrow intermediate zone, a cessation of distinction that remains within its horizon, but which dissolves into *not* doing ethnicity at all on the margins (just as silence may dissolve into not speaking), in other words, this undoing transitions into the doing of something quite different (such as professionalism). *Undoing* has an empirical identity only in the sense that keeping silent does, a form of inactivity that is significant within a given horizon of expectations, an inactivity that may seamlessly transition into something quite different. At the margins of *undoing*, then, what we find is a switch over to other distinctions.[69]

In this sense, the (am)bivalent expression *un/doing differences*—like the indeterminacy of pure dual contingency in the work of Luhmann (1984, pp. 168–70)—merely marks a ground zero of possible structure-building or dismantlement. This expression is an attempt to fix conceptually a perpetually fleeting state of fluctuating contingency, a transitory state of limbo, of in-difference. This microsocial basis provides us with a better theoretical grasp of the evident competition between key distinctions, the displacement of distinctions through social processes, than if we mythologize every distinction as simply having happened in an evolutionary (in other words macro-temporal) sense or supplant the actual selections made by participants with the theoretical selections made by sociological observers. It entails a more dynamic notion of the instigation, breaking off and pausing of distinctions.

As time passes human distinctions are rendered inoperative before coming into force once again. Rather than a process of linear evolution, we need to think here in terms of historical and biographical upturns and downturns and their cross-over. In a biography, for example, the relevance curve of age may be generally flat in the middle and run counter to that of gender (high in the middle).[70] Historical relevance curves for the blossoming of nations in Europe (their rise and decline) may come up against the fluctuating significance of "races" with a different temporal trajectory. Such fluctuations in a distinction's relevance may not only overlap with other distinctions, but also with other times, in which these distinctions occur at once situationally, biographically and historically.

---

69 The problem of establishing empirically that something does not occur has long been familiar to sociologists. Marx, for example, faced this problem with respect to the failure of revolutions to occur, and Weber in the shape of the question of when omissions are actions and when they are swallowed up in the "universe of mere non-action" (Geser, 1986, pp. 643–644). The commonest answer involves the identification of structures of expectation (such as urgently needed help), in relation to which something recognizably fails to occur. Ethnomethodology suggests that this horizon of expectation must lie within participants' everyday reality and must be created through their practical action itself (Lynch, 2001). In terms of research practice, then, demonstrations of *undoing x* are circumscribed instances in which a distinction is, for example, interactively rejected, procedurally prohibited or institutionally inhibited (Hirschauer, 2001, pp. 214–231). In contrast to these practices of abstaining, of de-thematization and de-institutionalization, which have a clear empirical reference that they negate, *not* doing x can in no way be an empirical object. The term *undoing x*, therefore, is not just a reference to an object, it is also a conceptual pointer, one that demands from researchers a far greater openness to the notion that something *other* is happening than the *observer's* key distinctions would lead one to expect.

70 See the early contribution by Linton (1942) on the significance of gender and age as these vary over the life course.

### 3.4.2 Simultaneous Distinctions: Mutual Reinforcement or Neutralization

To illuminate the tremendous contingency of distinctions I have supplemented the familiar notion of their historical genesis or their status as made (in other words their social construction) with that of their negatability (their practical deconstruction). There is a reciprocal relationship between the "undoing" of distinctions and the competition between them that we need to consider if we aim to comprehend multiple affiliations in all their dynamism. It is only by taking account of the competition between categorizations that we can enduringly undo their reification as membership (or even as individual attribute). Conversely, it is only through this process of fluidization that we can open up space for a symmetric way of thinking about multiple affiliations.

So far I have proceeded on the assumption, drawn from theories of differentiation, that social processes refer back only periodically to categorizations, in other words, *not* in the mode of *simultaneity* but in that of *succession*. But at times, of course, categories intersect significantly within social processes.[71] How might this interaction contribute to the contingency of distinctions?

The crossing of distinctions is a far more elementary fact than is recognized by the intersectionality approach. It is a fact often evident even in the linguistic categories through which affiliations are identified. Gender and class overlap within the category "lady", gender and age in the term "girl". And the practices of "girlish behaviour" are a case of doing gender while doing age. Thorne (1993) refers to the continual "flexion" of social categories by other categories. Even given names regularly perform such linkages, indicating multiple social affiliations (Nübling, 2009). The distinctions central to research fields, reunited in the intersectional paradigm, are always already fused within the social types of the everyday world.[72]

If we approach these types through the prism of theories of the constitution of the social rather than theories of social inequality, we may even reconstruct lifeworldly categories, which are unquestioningly adopted by the intersectionality approach, as a case of the crossing of distinctions in themselves. An example: conceived in intersectional terms, a "lesbian" is a case of the intersection of sex membership and sexual orientation. But if we distance ourselves sociologically from this objectification (drawn

---

71 By way of illustration: while the school *first* recruits pupils of the same age and then differentiates them according to performance, an army looks for healthy young men and a modelling agency for attractive young women. Within an individual's self-understanding and in the way others describe her or him, this hybrid type may be more common. But if we limit ourselves sociologically to this juxtaposition, we are already failing to consider the personal grading of the relevance of such attributes.

72 As it happens, this is already conceptually inherent in the doing gender approach. If we conceive of gender affiliation not as a physical attribute, psychological identity or social role, but as a social process, the phenomenon of gender immediately loses its clear boundaries. It blurs into the production of other distinctions, such as age and status.

from political struggles), "homosexuality" emerges as the result of the intersection of one thread of distinction with itself, or to be more precise: as the intersection of the gender categorization of an individual with that of her or his relationship with another (equal/unequal). Within the context of intersectional (and quotidian) thinking, this is still reified as a "sexual attribute" of the individual, while the contemporary gender-indifferent legal transformation of marriage, opening it up to everyone, actually involves a departure from "homosexuality" (Hirschauer, 2013).

This instance of crossing is just one of many possible kinds. Some distinctions get in each other's way, others interact without consequence, some mutually reinforce one another, others neutralize each other, while many cross in a way that involves a mutual fracturing. Distinctions enter into various relationships with one another depending on their specific characteristics. Establishing how human distinctions relate to one another on the level of their constitution is ultimately a task of research. In order to do this, it makes sense to systematically identify whether there is a hardening of difference that shuts down contingency or a minimization of difference that fosters contingency. This corrects the intersectionality approach's tendency to overstate the stability of specific distinctions.

On the one hand we find many cases of the *dynamic reinforcing of difference* through the combining of distinctions. One example are situations in which, as "race" studies has shown, the signification of skin colour is greatly intensified and rendered socially consequential through its linkage with legal-political processes of segregation (Apartheid), social class (enslavement) and endogamy rules (marriage prohibitions) (Wacquant, 2003). An analogous example from gender studies is the implanting of an age-based distinction into gender distinctions through norms of attractiveness in the context of pairing: men's greater age is aestheticized, securing them enormous career and income advantages (Goffman, 1977a). An example from research on ethnicity is ethnic resettlement and expulsion that aligns "peoples" with territories and thus ensures distributive clarity and visibility (Ryan, 1996). And finally, the Pisa studies have made clear that social classes are reproduced through the creation of performance-based classes within school types that are also subject to classification (in contrast to the equalizing effects that may be achieved by other school systems). All these cases involve the mutual reinforcement of difference: The character of a "race" is demarcated, among other things, by a process of de-classing, while the nature of a gender is delineated, among other things, through differences in age.

But we are not dealing here with static qualities such as "gender relations" or "class structure" but with historically variable strategies of differentiation. The nineteenth-century bourgeois classes, for example, sought to distinguish themselves through a pronounced focus on gender differences (Hausen, 1976). Durkheim provided sociological affirmation of this phenomenon, stating that the genders were "far more similar" in primitive societies than in developed ones (Durkheim, 1988, pp. 103–120). Modern-day academic milieus, meanwhile, tend to claim that they uphold gender equality, making significant gender differences appear plebeian. The

distinction between genders, then, may be used in an ambivalent way to say something about social classes, that is, it may be both *played up* and *played down*.[73]

On the other hand, however, the crossing of distinctions also regularly entails
contingency-promoting *minimizations of difference,* as for example when ethnic and
linguistic distinctions rupture as they compete with religions or, conversely, the formation of religious communities is disrupted by ethnic and linguistic distinctions.
Such processes of the superimposition of distinctions are particularly evident in the
development of nations. If a higher-level distinction (nation) claims to subordinate
other distinctions (such as ethnic ones), what occurs is a competitive struggle for
dominance, a battle over the privileging or relative downgrading of differences. As
a result, we sometimes find not just different gradations of relevance but also processes of de-differentiation. These occur not just within the hybrids of postcolonial
studies but also in the temporary distinctionlessness of revolutionary communities,
when ethnic groups, genders, religions and classes experience themselves as united
against an enemy (in other words under the banner of another major distinction).

One key phenomenon within the framework of such difference minimization is
the *scale shifting* of various kinds of distinction. Political loyalties, for example, may
be ethnicized on a number of levels: Immigrants in the United States may—in different
semantic oppositions—identify themselves as Hmong, Vietnamese, Asian-American
or American (Wimmer, 2008, p. 977). Such shifts of the regional frame of reference are
also found in sport: An identification with a local football club (in opposition to the
neighbouring club) gives way to identification with a city team (in the local cup), then
a regional one (including the keenest of local rivals) and this in turn is superseded by
a national team. But such shifts of scale may occur not just with respect to space, but
also with respect to the *temporal axis,* for example intergenerationally. This at least
is the implication of Evans-Pritchard's portrayal of the Nuer, among whom a conflict
between two families or clans was often mediated by older Nuer with reference to
the ancestors, through whom the two parties to conflict were related as kin (in other
words united once again) (Brubaker, 2007, p. 77). Both the spatial and temporal "uni-
fication" of the divided elements inject into the more specific distinction a sense of
reversibility or contingency.

The encounter between various strands of distinction, then, may be associated
with a spontaneous lessening of relevance for some of them. But there may also be
enduring cases of devalorization if distinctions are systematically dismantled, as
when the devalorization of national boundaries in Europe caused a general fading

---

73  Age may also interfere here: "Young women from social strata marked by low levels of education
often stage their femininity and heterosexuality in a significantly more dramatic way than other members of their gender. But this picture may be reversed with increasing age. And from retirement age at
the latest, the dolled-up upper- and middle-class wearers of ladies' suits ensure a more visible display
of gender difference than in the lower classes" (Müller, 2011, p. 308).

of what had been intense national sentiments into forms of sporting and folkloric patriotism. Distinctions may be weakened as religious boundaries were through the secularist separation of state and church or because the great leveller of capitalism exploits workers "regardless of gender or age" (Marx & Engels, 1956, p. 416), in other words places them within another category without distinction. Distinctions may be detached from the linkages with other distinctions that reinforce them and what was once a relevant category of identity may decline to the status of anatomical peculiarity. This can occur because a given distinction is held in check normatively and politically and is neutralized in the name of performance-based classification through formalized procedures (Heintz, 2008).[74] Alternatively, it may happen because a distinction is absorbed—within the framework of the love-centred individualism inherent in pairings—within a more complex perception of the individual (Hirschauer, 2013).

### 3.4.3 Frames and Aggregate States

Alongside such possible combinations, there is another fact that contributes to the stability or contingency of cultural human distinctions. Distinctions can essentially be made in two different *ontological registers*: in the primary frames (Goffman, 1977b) of "culture" and "nature". Performance (in the sense of achievement), for example, may be interpreted as an innate *gift* or as the effect of *diligence*; the distinction between men and women may be understood as one between *sexes* or *genders*; physical phenotypes may be framed in terms of "*race*" or *ethnicity*, and reference may be made to *impairment* or *disability*. The cultural differentiation of human beings, then, is continually crosscut by the ontological distinction between nature and culture, which marks a key difference between distinctions because it places them within a contingency-open (culturalization) or contingency-averse (naturalization) frame.[75] In line with this, within a given subject area we can observe framing strategies of culturalization and naturalization among the observed themselves (Kleeberg & Langenohl, 2011). Of course, beyond this observation, as professions the social sciences and

---

**74** The school, for example, takes account of age difference to recruit pupils, using it to create and establish gradations of "classes" but since the introduction of co-education it pays very little attention to gender or confession. Further, it recruits pupils with reference to prior performance classifications (entrance exams or primary school reports), in other words it constructs its school type according to latently naturalized "giftedness classes". On this basis, which ensures comparability—the homogenization of gifts and age—and on the basis of explicit indifference to other distinctions (such as ethnicity, confession or gender), the school works to solidify its human distinctions—through ordinarily stratified, reliable categories that claim to disregard social relationality. Within the informal realm of organization, however, the inhibited categories may continue to be cultivated (see footnote 68).
**75** Essentialist culturalizations may, however, turn out to be just as contingency-averse as naturalizations. On the cultural relativity of this "ethno-epistemology," see Descola (2011).

culturalist disciplines themselves strive to elaborate one of these frames. This frame makes it possible to recognize naturalizations as cultural achievements in the first place and to decode them as mechanisms of misapprehension (Bourdieu, 1987) designed to stabilize cultural distinctions.

In addition, a number of *secondary frames* are significant to the drawing of cultural boundaries. Goffman refers to "keyings" of everyday reality that may oust a serious use of distinction in everyday situations in favour of a playful one (as with the ironic citing of ethnic stereotypes), but which are also cultivated in specific societal fields, such as theatre and literature—frames within which transgressions and ruptures of primary framings are a frequent occurrence. The differentiation of society into social fields, then, also generates a variety of frames for the differentiation of the people within it. People may be distinguished biologically in science, separated categorically in law, purified by religion, measured by performance in schools and labelled in struggles over distinction within the political sphere, but they may also be hybridized through global consumption, intermixed aesthetically through art and fashion, or simply play the opposite of themselves in theatre.

But the *thematization* of cultural differences in societal fields constitutes just one thin discursive layer of the cultural. Cultural distinctions are also processed in quite different *aggregate states of the cultural*. It seems to me that this notion that matter exists in differing states, developed in the natural sciences, can help forge agreement between the social sciences and culturalist disciplines on the *degree of social solidity* of meaningful phenomena, on whether layers of cultural meaning take a more or less fluid or congealed form, which is something that changes depending on how institutionalized a distinction is.[76] Here, the concept of the *boundary* that I outlined at the start of this paper executes a dualistic distinction between symbolic (soft) and social (hard) boundaries. This distinction separates the cultural and the social in an unconvincing manner. The heuristic of differing aggregate states circumvents this dualism in order not only to link the ideas of the social sciences with those of the culturalist disciplines, but also to bring them more into line with one another. This heuristic avoids a one-sided focus on boundary *making* or "hardening" in the sense of Berger and Luckmann (1969), opening the analysis to the potential for processes of *de-hardening*, in other words instances of de-institutionalization (Heintz & Nadai, 1998).

---

76  This metaphor has a history. Simmel (1908/1992) already referred to the "degree of crystallization" of social phenomena and stated that the "solidifications" of social systems rest on the "eternal flow and pulsation" of interactive exchange (p. 33). Berger and Luckmann (1969) referred (as Schütz had already done) to the "sedimentation" of meaning and to the institutionalization of habitualized conduct as "hardening" (pp. 63, 72–76). Bauman (1999) conceived of the "adhesiveness" (a notion borrowed from Sartre) of the socially other as a state that makes indigenes appear at times more fluid and at times more viscous depending on their own resources (pp. 52–56). For actor-network theory, see the concept of "fluidity" in the work of Mol and Law (1994).

In the first instance, the aggregate states of the cultural comprise *linguistic structures* (categories, grammars, personal names, and so on) that find direct expression in *discursive representations*, including specialized scholarly discourses (in the medium of writing, as in literature, science and jurisprudence), but also popular discourses articulated in more oral forms such as sayings and everyday myths, and visually (as in the mass media). But these public representations also have mental counterparts in *cognitive schemata* (frames, scripts, stereotypical ways of seeing and hearing), which comprehend feelings and individuals (including the self) alongside situations, events and statements. Of great sociological interest are *situated practices* (of communication, labour, consumption, and so on)—in other words routinized behaviour, speech and habitual conduct underpinned by embodied knowledge—and the range of enduring *institutional infrastructures*, from social relations through organizations to socio-structural formations. Conversely, and again more on the margins of the sociological gaze, there are the elements of *material culture*: structures of the socially moulded body, artefacts, technologies and architectures.[77]

The relevance of these different descriptive levels can be illustrated through a simple example, which for once conceives of the boundary not as a theoretical metaphor but as an empirical phenomenon. A national boundary generally consists of a linguistic difference, cartographic representations, a dividing line between the validity of laws, border posts and border guards, forms and identity checks, flags and barriers, thresholds of habitual driving practices, and so on. These layers of meaning have widely varying life-spans and overlap one another, as do historical, biographical and situational time. At the same moment, then, non-contemporaneous elements—the enduring, persistent, fashionable and bang up-to-date—exercise an effect simultaneously.

The coherence of these layers of meaning has often been described as a matter of hardening: Categories are deployed in situated practices in order to identify oneself or others, stabilized through interpretive models and ways of speaking, adopted by organizations (which implant them in administrative processes), and disseminated by mass media. When categories are institutionalized in this way, the categorized may ultimately develop an "identity"—a specific aggregate state of self-understanding. But if we consider not just the objectifications but also their reversibility, then we can see more clearly that these layerings enjoy a degree of relative independence and may be linked together more loosely or more tightly in any given case.

---

77 It is also on this level that we are confronted with the *distribution* of material goods, a key concern of inequality research. From a more general sociological perspective a "disability", for example, is not simply a physical state that has effects on income, it also consists of architectural structures that help *bring about* disability in the first place (just as gender-segregated toilets and clothing generate "genders").

Meanwhile, an investigation limited to isolated aspects of these layers of meaning, of the kind generally carried out by academic disciplines or approaches, can easily overstate both the stability and contingency of distinctions. For example, a sharply dichotomizing language used within the nationalist discourse of Eastern Europe may be counteracted by mixed marriages, bilingualism, migration, assimilation and ethnopolitical indifference (Brubaker, 2007, p. 84). Or a racist discourse intended to highlight distinctions from others in colonized Latin America may be undermined by the presence of "mestizos," living proof of the attractiveness of this other (Nederveen Pieterse, 2001, p. 8).

Cultural human distinctions, that is, may not only enter into a diverse range of combinations (intersect, reinforce, overlap, displace, and so on) and be framed in various ways (as culture/nature, playful/serious, and so on), they may also emerge or submerge in other layers of meaning, in other words transition into other aggregate states. Some distinctions, for example, are grammaticalized in languages (Haase, 1994), or explicated and discursively fluidized by experts; others are de-institution-alized and transferred to contexts of interaction (Heintz & Nadai, 1998); others again become sedimented for a certain historical period in habitus and bodily essences, institutions and artefacts. If we diagnose a loss of relevance in one layer of meaning (such as clothing), it may be that one distinction has been relocated into another (such as the habitus). If we diagnose great stability, it may be that it is limited to one medium (such as language). Cultural distinctions are not just discursive effects, cognitive schemata (as Brubaker suggests) or cases of theoretical essentialization as often assumed within the culture-based disciplines (as in the work of Nederveen Piet-erse). Above all, these are *practically executed* "real-world essentializations" that are materialized both bodily and situationally and solidified institutionally, and it is this socially constructed *factuality* of distinctions that is waiting for investigation.

## 3.5 Conclusion

This essay adds to recent attempts within cultural sociology to de-reify the categories that establish human distinctions. It has moved, so to speak, away from the static anatomy of social structural analysis, with its skeleton of variables, towards the more dynamic physiology of the social with its developmental curves, aggregate states and code-blending: *gradations* of membership, relevance and institutionalization. Bourdieu's "classifications of the classifiers" emerged here as multiply nuanced: not only with respect to those aspects of distinction that lend many research fields their names, but also with respect to the specificities of distinctions (such as the number of categories involved) and their relations to other distinctions, their upturns and down-turns of relevance in differing societal fields and their cultural framings and degrees of institutionalization.

The analytical framework I have outlined is not a theory that claims to resolve every problem that may crop up in the study of human distinctions. It "explains" nothing. Instead, by highlighting the diversity and contingency of these categorizations, it shall invite to take a number of merely conceptual disputes in a more empirical direction. The intention is to make it easier to produce comparative studies of the production, displacement and invalidation of a number of the cultural distinctions made about the members of society. The comparative contrasting of the kinds of difference discussed in emphatically different research fields should be particularly helpful in enabling us to penetrate these specific empirical cases with greater analytical depth. Over the long term, through a dialogue between the social sciences and the culturalist disciplines, this may help us develop a transdisciplinary theoretical perspective. From this vantage point we might attempt to answer, in an empirically substantive and analytically precise way, questions about the general mechanisms of, and diverse interactions between, cultural human distinctions.

# References

Abbott, A. (2001). Time Matters. On Theory and Method. University of Chicago Press.

Allolio-Näcke, L., Kalscheuer, B., & Manzeschke, A. (Eds.). (2005). Differenzen anders denken: Bausteine zu einer Kulturtheorie der Transdifferenz. Campus.

Allport, G. W. (1954). The Nature of Prejudice. Addison-Wesley.

Amselle, J.-L. (1998). Mestizo Logics: Anthropology of Identity in Africa and Elsewhere. Stanford University Press.

Anderson, B. (1983). Imagined Communities: Reflections on the Origin and Spread of Nationalism. Verso.

Antaki, C., & Widdicombe, S. (1998). Identities in Talk. Sage.

Anthias, F. (2005). Social Stratification and Social Inequality: Models of Intersectionality and Identity. In F. Devine, M. Savage, R. Crompton, & J. Scott (Eds.), Rethinking Class (pp. 24–45). Palgrave.

Appiah, K. A. (1994). Identity, Authenticity, Survival: Multicultural Societies and Social Reproduction. In A. Gutmann, & C. Taylor (Eds.), Multiculturalism: Examining the Politics of Recognition (pp. 149–163). Princeton University Press.

Barth, F. (1969). Ethnic Groups and Boundaries. The Social Organization of Culture Difference. Allan & Unwin.

Bateson, G. (1972). Steps to an Ecology of Mind. Chicago University Press.

Bauman, Z. (1995). Moderne und Ambivalenz: Das Ende der Eindeutigkeit. Hamburger Edition.

Bauman, Z. (1999). Unbehagen in der Postmoderne. Hamburger Edition.

Berger, P., & Luckmann, T. (1969). Die gesellschaftliche Konstruktion der Wirklichkeit, Fischer.

Bhabha, H. K. (1994). The Location of Culture. Routledge.

Bourdieu, P. (1984). Die feinen Unterschiede: Kritik der gesellschaftlichen Urteilskraft. Suhrkamp.

Bourdieu, P. (1987). Sozialer Sinn: Kritik der theoretischen Vernunft. Suhrkamp.

Bourdieu, P. (2004). Der Staatsadel. UVK.

Bowker, G. C., & Star, S. L. (2000). Sorting Things Out: Classification and its Consequences. MIT Press.

Breidenstein, G. (1997). Der Gebrauch der Geschlechterunterscheidung in der Schulklasse. Zeitschrift für Soziologie, 26(5), 337–351.

Brubaker, R. (2007). Ethnizität ohne Gruppen. Hamburger Edition.

Calhoun, C. (2007). Nations Matter: Culture, History and the Cosmopolitan Dream. Routledge.

Coulter, J. (1996). Human Practices and the Observability of the 'Macrosocial'. Zeitschrift für Soziologie, 25(5), 337–345.

Crenshaw, K. W. (1994). Mapping the Margins: Intersectionality, Identity Politics, and Violence Against Women of Color. Stanford Law Review, 43(1), 1241–1299.

Derrida, J. (1995). Marx' Gespenster: Der verschuldete Staat, die Trauerarbeit und die neue Internationale. Fischer.

Descola, P. (2011). Jenseits von Natur und Kultur. Suhrkamp.

Desrosières, A. (1998). The Politics of Large Numbers: A History of Statistical Reasoning. Harvard University Press.

Diewald, M. (2010). Zur Bedeutung genetischer Variation für die soziologische Ungleichheitsforschung. Zeitschrift für Soziologie, 39(1), 4–21.

Diewald, M., & Faist, T. (2011). Von Heterogenitäten zu Ungleichheiten: Soziale Mechanismen als Erklärungsansatz der Genese sozialer Ungleichheiten. Berliner Journal für Soziologie, 21(2), 91–114.

Douglas, M. (1992). Reinheit und Gefährdung. Suhrkamp.

Durkheim, E. (1988). Über soziale Arbeitsteilung. Suhrkamp.

Durkheim, E., & Mauss, M. (1987). Über einige primitive Formen von Klassifikation. In H. Joas (Ed.), Schriften zur Soziologie der Erkenntnis (pp. 169–256). Suhrkamp. (Original work published 1903).

Fluck, W. (2000). Die Wissenschaft vom systemischen Effekt. Von der Counter-Culture zu den Race, Class and Gender Studies. In R. Rosenberg, I. Münz-Koenen, P. Boden, & G. Gast (Eds.), Der Geist der Unruhe (pp. 111–124). Akademie-Verlag.

Emmison, M., & Western, M. (1990). Social Class and Social Identity. A Comment on Marshall. Sociology, 24(3), 241–253.

Foucault, M. (2004). Sicherheit, Territorium, Bevölkerung. Geschichte der Gouvernementalität. Suhrkamp.

Geser, H. (1986). Elemente zu einer Theorie des Unterlassens. Kölner Zeitschrift für Soziologie und Sozialpsychologie, 38(4), 643–669.

Gieryn, T. (1983). Boundary-work and the demarcation of science from non-science: strains and interests in professional interests of scientists. American Sociological Review, 48(6), 781–795.

Gildemeister, R. & Hericks, K. (2012). Geschlechtersoziologie. Theoretische Zugänge zu einer vertrackten Kategorie. Oldenbourg.

Goffman, E. (1977a). Rahmen-Analyse. Suhrkamp.

Goffman, E. (1977b). The Arrangement between the Sexes. Theory and Society, 4(2), 301–331.

Gupta, A., & Ferguson, J. (1992). Beyond "Culture": Space, Identity, and the Politics of Difference. Cultural Anthropology, 7(1), 6–23.

Haase, M. (1994). Respekt: Die Grammatikalisierung von Höflichkeit. Lincom.

Hacking, I. (1986). Making up People. In T. C. Heller, & C. Brooke-Rose (Eds.), Reconstructing Individualism (pp. 222–236). Stanford University Press.

Hall, S. (2004). Die Frage des Multikulturalismus. In J. Koivisto, & A. Merkens (Eds.) Ausgewählte Schriften / Stuart Hall: Ideologie, Identität, Repräsentation (pp. 188–227). Argument.

Hannerz, U. (1987). The World in Creolisation. Africa, 57(4), 546–559.

Hausen, K. (1976). Die Polarisierung der „Geschlechtercharaktere". In W. Conze (Ed.), Sozialgeschichte der Familie in der Neuzeit Europas (pp. 363–393). Klett.

Heintz, B. (2008). Ohne Ansehen der Person? De-Institutionalisierungsprozesse und geschlechtliche Differenzierung. In S. M. Wilz (Ed.), Geschlechterdifferenzen–Geschlechterdifferenzierungen (pp. 231–251). VS.

Heintz, B. (2010). Numerische Differenz. Überlegungen zu einer Soziologie des (quantitativen) Vergleichs. Zeitschrift für Soziologie, 39(3), 162–181.

Heintz, B., & Nadai, E. (1998). Geschlecht und Kontext, De-Institutionalisierungsprozesse und geschlechtliche Differenzierung. Zeitschrift für Soziologie, 27(2), 75–93.

Hirschauer, S. (1994). Die soziale Fortpflanzung der Zweigeschlechtlichkeit. Kölner Zeitschrift für Soziologie und Sozialpsychologie 46(4), 668–692.

Hirschauer, S. (2001). Das Vergessen des Geschlechts. Zur Praxeologie einer Kategorie sozialer Ordnung. In B. Heintz (Ed.), Geschlechtersoziologie (pp. 208–235). Westdeutscher Verlag.

Hirschauer, S. (2003). Wozu ‚Gender Studies'? Geschlechtsdifferenzierungsforschung zwischen politischem Populismus und naturwissenschaftlicher Konkurrenz. Soziale Welt, 54(5), 461–482.

Hirschauer, S. (2008). Die Empiriegeladenheit von Theorien und der Erfindungsreichtum der Praxis. In H. Kalthoff, G. Lindemann, & S. Hirschauer (Eds.), Theoretische Empirie. Zur Relevanz qualitativer Forschung (pp. 165–189). Suhrkamp.

Hirschauer, S. (2013). Geschlechts(in)differenz in geschlechts(un)gleichen Paaren. Gender. Zeitschrift für Geschlecht, Kultur und Gesellschaft [Special Issue 2], 37–56.

Jenkins, R. (1997). Rethinking Ethnicity: Arguments and Explorations. Sage.

Kapchan, D. A., & Strong, P. T. (1999). Theorizing the Hybrid. Journal of American Folklore, 112(2), 239–253.

Kessels, U. (2002). Undoing Gender in der Schule. Juventa.

Kleeberg, B., & Langenohl, A. (2011). Kulturalisierung, Dekulturalisierung. Zeitschrift für Kulturphilosophie, 5(3), 281–302.

Knapp, G.-A. (2013). Zur Bestimmung und Abgrenzung von „Intersektionalität". Erwägen— Wissen—Ethik, 24(2), 341–354.

Kotthoff, H. (2002). Was heißt eigentlich "doing gender"? Wiener Slawistischer Almanach, 55(1), 1–27.

Laclau, E., & Mouffe, C. (2006). Hegemonie und radikale Demokratie: Zur Dekonstruktion des Marxismus. Passagen.

Lamont, M., & Molnar, V. (2002). The Study of Boundaries in the Social Sciences. Annual Review of Sociology, 28(2), 167–195.

Laqueur, T. (1992). Auf den Leib geschrieben: Die Inszenierung der Geschlechter von der Antike bis Freud. Campus.

Lentz, C. (1995). 'Tribalism' and Ethnicity in Africa. Cahiers des sciences humaines, 31(3), 303–328.

Lentz, C. (2009). Der Kampf um die Kultur: Zur Ent- und Re-Soziologisierung eines ethnologischen Konzepts. Soziale Welt, 60(3), 305–324.

Linton, R. (1942). Age and Sex Categories. American Sociological Review, 7(5), 589–603.

Luhmann, N. (1975). Interaktion, Organisation, Gesellschaft. Soziologische Aufklärung: Vol. 2. Aufsätze zur Theorie der Gesellschaft (pp. 9–20). Westdeutscher Verlag.

Luhmann, N. (1984). Soziale Systeme. Grundriß einer allgemeinen Theorie. Suhrkamp.

Luhmann, N. (1989). Gesellschaftsstruktur und Semantik (Vol. 3). Suhrkamp.

Luhmann, N. (1997). Die Gesellschaft der Gesellschaft. Suhrkamp.

Lynch, M. (2001). Ethnomethodology and the Logic of Practice. In T. Schatzki, K. Knorr, & E. von Savigny (Eds.), The Practice Turn in Contemporary Theory (pp.131–148). Routledge.

Macrae, C. N., & Bodenhausen, G. V. (2000). Social Cognition: Thinking Categorically about Others. Annual Review of Psychology, 51(2), 93–120.

Marx, K., & Engels, F. (1956). Marx Engels Werke (Vol. 23). Dietz.

Mol, A., & Law, J. (1994). Regions, Networks and Fluids. Anemia and Social Topology. Social Studies of Science, 24(4), 641–671.

Müller, M. (2011). Intersektionalität und Interdependenz. Soziologische Revue, 34(3), 298–309.

Nederveen Pieterse, J. (2001). Hybridity, so what? The Anti-hybridity Backlash and the Riddles of Recognition. Theory, Culture & Society, 18(2), 219–245.

Needham, R. (1975). Polythetic Classification: Convergence and Consequences. Man, 10(3), 349–369.

Nübling, D. (2009). Von Monika zu Mia, von Norbert zu Noah: Zur Androgynisierung der Rufnamen seit 1945 aus prosodisch-phonologischer Perspektive. Beiträge zur Namensforschung, 44(1), 67–110.

Pachucki, M. A., S. Pendergrass, S., & Lamont, M. (2007). Boundary Processes: Recent Theoretical Developments and New Contributions. Poetics, 35(3), 331–351.

Pape, S., Rössel, J., & Solga, H. (2008). Die visuelle Wahrnehmbarkeit sozialer Ungleichheit – Eine alternative Methode zur Untersuchung der Entkopplungsthese. Zeitschrift für Soziologie, 37(1), 25–41.

Parsons, T. (1987). Die Schulklasse als soziales System. In K. Plake (Ed.), Klassiker der Erziehungssoziologie (pp. 102–124). Schwann.

Reckwitz, A. (2008). Unscharfe Grenzen. Perspektiven der Kultursoziologie. transcript.

Ryan, S. (1996). "The Voice of Sanity Getting Hoarse?" Destructive Processes in Violent Ethnic Conflict. In E .N. Wilmsen, & P. MacAllister (Eds.), The Politics of Difference (pp. 144–161). University of Chicago Press.

Sacks, H. (1992). Lectures on Conversation. Blackwell.

Schütz, A., & Luckmann, T. (1979). Strukturen der Lebenswelt (Vol. 1). Suhrkamp.

Simmel, G. (1992). Soziologie: Untersuchungen über die Formen der Vergesellschaftung. In O. Rammstedt (Ed.), Gesamtausgabe / Georg Simmel (Vol. 11). Suhrkamp. (Original work published 1908).

Spencer-Brown, G. (1999). Laws of Form. Gesetze der Form. Bohmeier.

Stagl, J. (1981). Die Beschreibung des Fremden in der Wissenschaft. In H. P. Duerr (Ed.), Der Wissenschaftler und das Irrationale: Vol. 1. Beiträge aus Ethnologie und Anthropologie (pp. 273–295). Suhrkamp.

Tajfel, H. E. (1978). Differentiation Between Social Groups: Studies in the Social Psychology of Intergroup Relations. Academic Press.

Thorne, B. (1993). Gender play: Girls and boys in school. Rutgers University Press.

Trouillot, M.-R. (2002). Adieu, Culture: A New Duty Arises. In R. G. Fox, & B. J. King (Eds.), Anthropology Beyond Culture (pp. 37–60). Berg.

Tyrell, H. (1986). Geschlechtliche Differenzierung und Geschlechterklassifikation. Kölner Zeitschrift für Soziologie und Sozialpsychologie, 38(4), 450–489.

Wacquant, L. (2001). Für eine Analytik rassischer Herrschaft. In A. Weiß, C. Koppetsch, A. Scharenberg, & O. Schmidtke (Eds.), Klasse und Klassifikation (pp. 61–77). Westdeutscher Verlag.

Wacquant, L. (2003). Von der Sklaverei zur Masseneinkerkerung. Das Argument, 252(5), 529–545.

Weber, M. (1972). Wirtschaft und Gesellschaft. Mohr. (Original work published 1922).

Weinbach, C., & Stichweh, R. (2001). Die Geschlechterdifferenz in der funktional differenzierten Gesellschaft. In B. Heintz (Ed.), Geschlechtersoziologie (pp. 30–49). Westdeutscher Verlag.

West, C., & Zimmerman, D. H. (1987). Doing Gender. Gender & Society, 1(2), 125–151.

West, C., & Fenstermaker, S. (1995). Doing Difference. Gender & Society, 9(1), 8–37.

Whorf, B. L. (1963). Sprache, Denken, Wirklichkeit. Rowohlt.

Wimmer, A. (2008). The Making and Unmaking of Ethnic Boundaries: A Multilevel Process Theory. American Journal of Sociology, 113(6), 970–1022.

Wimmer, A., & Lamont, M. (2006). Boundary-Making: A Framework and a Research Agenda. Paper at the Annual Meeting of the ASA. Montréal: American Sociological Association.

Wobbe, T. (2012). Making up People: Berufsstatistische Klassifikation, geschlechtliche Kategorisierung und wirtschaftliche Inklusion um 1900 in Deutschland. Zeitschrift für Soziologie, 41(1), 41–57.

Young, R. J. C. (1995). Colonial Desire: Hybridity in Theory, Culture and Race. Routledge.

Kijan Espahangizi

# 4 The "Cultural Turn" of Postmigrant Conviviality. A Historical Case Study on Practices and Discourses of (Multi)Cultural Diversity in Switzerland, 1970s–1990s

**Galinha Portuguesa—Portuguese Style Chicken**
1 young oven-ready chicken
 some rosemary
 pepper
 salt
2 onions (finely chopped)
2 garlic cloves (finely chopped)
1 cup of hot chicken broth
4 tomatoes (peeled)
12 olives (pitted)
12 almonds (peeled and cut in leaves)
1 glass of port wine (red)

## 4.1 Portuguese Style Chicken

This recipe of "Portuguese style chicken" was published in a cookbook of the *Mitenand*-initiative in Switzerland in 1981 (Berner Komitee, 1981, p. 23). "*Mitenand*" means "together" respectively "with each other" in Swiss-German dialect. The civil rights coalition was founded in 1974 and existed until the end of the 1980s. Sharing food was part of lived solidarity within the immigrant solidarity movement (Espahangizi, 2018a). The cookbook gathered recipes from women of different national backgrounds who had participated in language classes organized by activists of the *Contact Point for Foreigners and Swiss in Bern* and the ECAP, an adult education institution founded by members of the Italian trade union CGIL in Switzerland. The publication included short texts on immigration issues, biographical accounts of immigrants, political poems, photographs, and cartoons. The *Mitenand-Cookbook* was a tool for political campaigning as well as a product of the micro-practices of conviviality emerging in the everyday life of the movement. From today's viewpoint, the culinary exchange documented in the *Mitenand-Cookbook* seems to be a good example for the historical emergence of intercultural practices in Switzerland in the early 1980s. But when we browse through the cookbook, one thing strikes the eye: The word "culture" does not appear once, nor any of its cognates. For readers of today who are used to employing *culture* as a *passe-partout* category to talk about conviviality in immigration societies, the lack of explicit references to the inter/multi/cultural dimension in this culinary encounter is rather surprising. It is even more so if we consider the widespread perception of food as a facilitator and epitome of (multi)cultural or ethnic diversity (Bellofatto, 2017).

The notion of (multi)cultural or ethnic diversity has played an important role in international scholarly debates on immigration since the 1960s. Diversity approaches provide a useful framework in order to analyse and describe the transformations of societies like Switzerland in the face of immigration and globalization (Faist, 2009; Vertovec, 2017). There is, however, a major methodological challenge: As Sara Ahmed (2007, 2012) and others have shown, the "language of diversity" is not simply descriptive. Claiming (multi)cultural or ethnic diversity is itself a political strategy that plays a constitutive role within the history of the societal transformations that are being analysed (Lentin & Titley, 2011; Chin, 2017). The epistemological difficulties that arise from the historical co-emergence of concept and object of analysis cannot be entirely resolved, but they can be taken into account. One way to do that is by historicizing the mutually constitutive interaction between social and discursive change that has led to this challenging situation in the analysis of cultural diversity today. In order to develop such a reflexive historical perspective, it is helpful to distinguish between different social processes of pluralization due to immigration and practices, discourses, and projects that emerge *in relation* to these social processes and underlying demographic shifts. This strict analytical distinction between "hard" social dynamics on the one hand and discursive processes of collective sense-making on the other hand is something of an ideal type, of course. Yet it highlights the historical contingency of the different interpretative frameworks that have been mobilized in order to make sense or make claims with regard to ongoing social processes of pluralization due to immigration. The *Mitenand-Cookbook*, for example, reminds us of the historicity of culturalist perspectives. Obviously not too long ago, in this particular historical context, people talked about social processes of what I shall call *postmigrant conviviality*, without presupposing any categories of *inter/multi/culture*.[78] History shows that it is possible to describe the same material practice—in this case the cooking of food— as an act of solidarity in one context and as an act of a cultural encounter in another. The socio-political effects and consequences of this interpretative framework may vary, but the meal will most probably taste the same, figuratively speaking. My notion of postmigrant conviviality tries to grasp this historically contingent relation between the material dimension of social practices that follow immigration and their respective interpretative frameworks. Academic perspectives play an important

---

78  This composite notion tries to bring together the debates on postmigrant societies in a German-speaking context (Foroutan, 2016; Espahangizi, 2018b) and Paul Gilroy's (2004) reflections on convivial culture.

role for the way postmigrant conviviality has been framed, analysed, managed and governed throughout the 20th century. It will, therefore, be crucial to keep an eye on the various knowledge claims that come into play with regard to immigration over the course of time.

In my paper, I depart from the contrast between today's ubiquity of "culture" and its striking absence in the *Mitenand-Cookbook*. Instead, I will ask: How did "culture" become the key signifier with regard to immigration and integration since the 1980s in Switzerland? What are the historical conditions and consequences of this shift? Is the assumption that there was a "cultural turn" true in the first place, and if so with regard to which societal contexts? In order to tackle these questions, in a first step I will look at the histories of the *Mitenand*-movement and Swiss refugee aid projects. Comparing both these cases will help us to understand how different projects of post-migrant conviviality involved (or did not involve) categories, semantics, and arguments of cultural difference and cultural diversity with regard to the ongoing social processes of pluralization through immigration. In a second step, I will analyse the relation of these projects to public and academic discourses on cultural diversity at this time. Since the foundation of the Swiss nation-state in the mid-19th century, cultural diversity, or more specifically regional multilingualism, is a basic pillar of Swiss national identity. It will be interesting to see how immigration fits into this picture. The public and academic debates that preceded the 700-year anniversary of the Swiss Federation in 1991, as well as the public controversies on the notion of "multicultural society" in the early 1990s, both provide an empirical lens through which to analyse the relation between the two different notions of cultural diversity in Switzerland: the traditional four language regions on the one hand and the "ethnic diversity" of the immigrants on the other.

## 4.2 The Mitenand-Movement—Solidarity, Equality and Integration

The *Mitenand*-movement—called Être *solidaire* in the French-speaking and *Essere solidali* in the Italian-speaking regions of Switzerland—was initiated by the Swiss Catholic workers' and employees' association in 1974. In the decades after World War II, hundreds of thousands of so-called "foreign workers", mostly from Italy and other Mediterranean countries, had come to Switzerland in order to work in factories and workshops, hotels and restaurants, in fields and on construction sites. These seasonal and annual workers fuelled the economic growth of the boom period and contributed significantly to the wealth of Swiss society, but they were not supposed to settle or bring their families (Tanner, 2015, pp. 338–343). In the mid 1960s, anti-immigration voices started to mobilize, and they were able to gain a significant influence on public opinion, politics and state administration until the early 1970s (Skenderovic & D'Amato, 2008). The *Mitenand*-initiative tried to counter this development with a nation-wide civil coalition of solidarity with the "foreign workers".[79] The movement brought together a broad range of organizations and individuals, from the churches to the radical left, who wanted to take a stand in defence of legal reform and a "more humane" immigration system.

In April 1981, the national referendum on this legal initiative was rejected with over 80% of the votes. In spite of the clear defeat at the polls, the *Mitenand*-movement continued until the late 1980s. Its nation-wide network of activists, work groups, and local projects played an active role in establishing a more inclusive perspective on immigration in Switzerland. Both Swiss citizens and foreigners engaged in micro-practices of postmigrant conviviality: organizing events together, sharing food, music, folklore, stories and recreational activities, such as the "abundant and creative Pick-Nick as it is common in countries of the South" (Franzini, 1988).[80] The *Mitenand-Cookbook* was a product of these new practices in the life-world of the movement. There are more examples of this same phenomenon: Already in the mid 1970s, the new left party POCH (Progressive Organizations of Switzerland) that supported the *Mitenand*-initiative had started to organize "popular festivals" together with immigrant communist "comrades" from Spain, Italy and Chile. Events such as *Volksfäscht / Festa Populare / Fiesta Popular* in Zurich and *Unser Fescht / Nostra Festa / Nuestra Fiesta* in Basel were hugely successful in celebrating the "solidarity between Swiss and foreigners". Each year, throughout the late 1970s and the 1980s, these two festivals alone were able to attract thousands of visitors with a "colourful mix of booths, music and delicious smells from the kitchen," with performances, dance, film, theatre, poetry, political discussions, flea markets, and tombolas (Bloesch, 1978). In the mid 1970s, the gastronomic "specialties" offered at these festivals ranged from "risotto, pizza, lasagna, calamares, gambas, meat skewers" to "sangria, wine, and beer". This culinary variety mirrored the Mediterranean origins of the immigrant comrades (Advertisement, 1977). In the course of time, most of these "foreign" dishes and many others, bit by bit, would enter into Swiss cuisine.[81]

These kinds of events were popular not only among the leftist activists but also in the liberal and church contexts of the *Mitenand*-movement. In 1978, "culinary specialties from different countries" and "folkloric performances" were offered on the ten-year anniversary celebration of the *Contact Point for Foreigners and Swiss in Zurich*, a local association that was an important member of the *Mitenand*-coalition (Zürcher

---

**79** On the broader context of the movement, see Haug (1980).

**80** See also the film documentary *Meine Eltern haben den C-Ausweis* of Eduard Winiger (1982), on the life of the children of foreign workers in Switzerland. In one scene the Swiss teacher visits the family of one of his teenage students in South Italy during the summer holiday and joins a family picnic (Espahangizi 2019a).

**81** The "*Betty Bossi*" cookbooks that populated Swiss households since the 1970s are a good indicator of this process of culinary integration. The *Betty Bossi* cookbook on "Italian cuisine" from 1987 was a huge success. See also Bellofatto (2017).

**Figure 4.1:** Announcement of a Popular Festival for Immigrant Solidarity in the 1970s in Switzerland

**Figure 4.2:** Announcement of a Popular Festival for Immigrant Solidarity in the 1970s in Switzerland

Note. *PZ-Wochenzeitung der Progressiven Organisationen der Schweiz* (POCH), 7(22), June 16, 1977, 3&4 [Party newspaper]. Schweizerisches Sozialarchiv [Swiss Social Archives] (Z563/1977), Zurich, Switzerland.

## Nostra Festa: Drei grossartige Tage!

**Figure 4.3:** Nostra Festa: Three Awesome Days!

Note. *PZ-Wochenzeitung der Progressiven Organisationen der Schweiz* (POCH), 8(23), June 22, 1978, 3 [Party newspaper]. Schweizerisches Sozialarchiv [Swiss Social Archives] (Z563/1978), Zurich, Switzerland.

Kontaktstelle, 1978). The same was true for the first national rally of the *Mitenand*-movement on October, 28 1978 with over 3000 participants on the place in front of the Swiss federal parliament in Bern.[82]

New social spaces and formats of conviviality between Swiss people and foreigners emerged within the *Mitenand*-movement. "Folkloric" practices such as sharing music, food, etc. played an important role. This experience of solidarity was accompanied by a certain awareness for the "different ideas and perceptions" of "the representatives of different countries" that could eventually present a challenge to (Bloesch, 1978). But then again, as in the cookbook, these things were not explicitly framed as cultural issues. The political language of the *Mitenand*-movement was based on the semantics of solidarity, equality, and human rights rather than cultural difference, diversity, or the like. The very name of the campaign, as well its iconography, were based on the idea of a solidarity-related but nonetheless asymmetric (and gendered) relation between two legally (not culturally) defined groups: "[T]he Swiss" on the one hand and "the foreigners" on the other were literally upholding the banner of social

**Figure 4.4:** Cover of the Mitenand-Cookbook, 1980

Note. Berner Komitee zur Unterstützung der Mitenand-Initiative. (1981). *E Guete! Buon appetito! Rezepte aus Italien, Spanien, Portugal, Griechenland, Türkei und Jugoslawien*. Copy in possession of author.

---

**82** A report on this event in the *Mitenand*-circular even refers explicitly to the "cultural performances of the emigrants" and the general "cultural diversity" of the rally R. G. (1978).

justice "together". The political project of *Mitenand* was also based on the discursive framework and narrative telos of the integration of foreign workers into Swiss society that had been going on since the mid 1960s (Espahangizi, 2019b).

## 4.3 The Sociology of the Integration of Foreign Workers

In the course of the 1960s, longer-term immigration of a foreign workforce turned out to be not only a necessity for the Swiss economy but also a social reality that could no longer be ignored. The rotational model of guest worker migration, widespread in booming industrialized countries at that time, came under pressure. Various Swiss organs of state as well as many other societal actors started to face the so-called "problem of the foreign workers" (Espahangizi, 2019b). The various parties that were involved in these public debates had very different interests and political views, but they all started from the same basic question: How should the foreign workers and their families who would stay in Switzerland be incorporated into the society? The possible answers to this question differed widely, ranging from repressive assimilationism and subordination to what sociologists in Switzerland started to call structural integration. The spokesmen of the rising anti-immigration movement mobilized successfully against the alleged "overforeignization" of Switzerland. They emphasized cultural differences from the foreign workers as a major obstacle to total assimilation, and they had the advantage of being able to draw on ideas that already had been established in Switzerland in the early 20th century (Kury, 2003; Argast, 2007). This is why even beyond the ranks of the anti-immigration movement, concerns about cultural assimilation were widespread: in the public discourse, in state institutions such as the police for foreigners (*Fremdenpolizei*) and the Federal Commission for Foreigners (EKA, 1979) as well as in many other contexts.[83]

More liberal voices, however, started to emphasize the priority of structural integration, focusing on the legal and educational system, the housing market, and so on. Their turn away from culture as the main framework to think and talk about immigration was closely related to the rise of sociology at the Swiss universities (Espahangizi, 2019b). The sociological institute at the University of Zurich, and especially Hans-Joachim Hoffmann-Nowotny's (1973) *Sociology of the Foreign Worker Problem*, played an important role for the academic elaboration of this structuralist perspective on integration in Switzerland. Seen from this angle, integration more than anything meant opening the structures of Swiss society to immigrants. Cultural differences

---

**83** Various representatives of Swiss folklore studies (*Volkskunde*) participated in the public debates on foreign workers in the 1960s and held a liberal view with regard to immigration. They would frame the "incorporation" of immigrants as a "socio-cultural" process, on which see most importantly Rudolf Weiss, Arnold Niederer (1967) and Rudolf Braun (1970). See also Kuhn (2015).

between the Swiss and the foreigners were considered negligible or at least secondary. They were expected to become more and more irrelevant in the course of the process of integration.[84] In the late 1960s, a growing network of initiatives, associations and individuals, especially in the context of the Swiss churches but also in the foreign worker organizations, took up this new "sociologic" of integration and distanced themselves from the rhetoric of the anti-immigration movement and the Swiss Federal Aliens Police on the need for hard cultural assimilation (Espahangizi, 2017; 2019).[85] In addition, these initiatives promoted direct communication, exchange, and cooperation between the Swiss citizens and the immigrants. Values of Christian brotherly love, liberal humanism, leftist solidarity, and sociological objectivity towards the "foreigners" converged in this new concept of integration and prepared the ground for the *Mitenand*-movement. Against this historical background, it becomes clear why cultural arguments or references to cultural differences would not play a crucial role for the *Mitenand*-initiative. Yet there was one political claim in the "white book" of the movement that involved a culturalist argument: *Mitenand* rejected the idea of a total assimilation of foreigners and defended their right to structural integration without being forced to abandon their "cultural identity" (Arbeitsgruppe Mitenand, 1979, p. 41). This reference to cultural pluralism was, however, far from elaborated. Compared to the "ethnic revival" (Smith, 1981) and contemporaneous developments with regard to ethnic minorities in other countries such as the US, Canada and the UK (see e.g. Glazer & Moynihan, 1964), it played only a minor role for the general outlook of the Swiss movement. One important exception were the debates on the children of the foreign workers, who represented the so-called "second generation" (Jain, 2018).

In the 1950s, the developmental psychologist Erik H. Erikson developed the notion of "identity crisis" which was also closely related to the idea of cultural "uprooting". His work had a huge impact on international academic debates and also shaped the perception of immigrant adolescents in Switzerland (see e.g., Hurst, 1974). Erikson's own experience as a Jewish refugee in the US had served as an important reference point for his conceptual approach. There was, hence, a close conceptual link between ego-psychology and migration studies after World War II (Erikson, 1959). In the 1970s, various actors and institutions started to become interested in the life-world of the "foreign child," who seemed to be stuck in a "traumatic worldview" (Erikson, 1959, p. 27) between two cultures and two options: staying or returning home (Jain, 2018). The Federal Commission for Foreigners published an influential report on "second

---

**84** There were also sociologists that criticized the neglecting of certain cultural aspects, like for example Willi (1974).

**85** This scientific impact was not always explicit or visible. Some works were influenced by foreign workers' sociology without referring to it, such as the publication *Basta! Fremdarbeiter in den 80er Jahren. Ein Lesebuch* [Enough! Foreign Workers in the 80s. A Reading Book] of the leftist *Authors group for a progressive immigration policy* (Autorengruppe für eine fortschrittliche Ausländerpolitik, 1980), which was close to the *Mitenand*-movement.

generation foreigners" that supported this "cultural identity"-centred perspective (EKA, 1980). In accordance with the pedagogical and psychological state of the art, the recommendations of the Federal Commission and not least the demands of the parents who planned to return to their home countries and who feared the cultural alienation of their children, Swiss school authorities in the 1980s started to introduce special courses to "enroot" the foreign children in their "native language and culture" (Steiner-Khamsi, 1988). It was in this context that social research on the second generation (Hoffmann-Nowotny, 1985) and also first explicitly "intercultural" approaches took hold in Switzerland, in close exchange with international debates and initiatives especially on the European level during the 1980s (Steiner-Khamsi, 1995). One could conclude that the debates on the second generation contributed to the convergence of immigration debates and ideas of cultural identity and difference.[86]

In the 1980s, the general perception of postmigrant conviviality changed. In those contexts that pursued projects of immigrant integration, new interpretative frameworks of cultural difference and cultural identity gained importance. In 1988— when the *Mitenand*-movement was drawing to an end—one activist looked back on ten years of personal engagement. His recollection of the experiences of postmigrant conviviality within his local activist group bears witness to the culturalist shift in perception. The notion of cultural difference played a key role in structuring his memories and reformatting the past:

> After the party—it had struck midnight—all the members of the *Mitenand* group sat down together at a big table, eating the leftovers, drinking wine, delighted by the great success of the event, and singing songs from different countries. I remember when I came home that night and went to bed happily. I had come in contact with foreigners. I wanted to know more about them. Therefore, I joined the "*Mitenand* group" which is still active after ten years. The many experiences in this group shaped my attitude towards foreigners. ... We learned that every culture has its characteristics that have to be respected, which requires great openness on our side. (Franzini, 1988)

In order to understand this change in the perception of postmigrant conviviality, it has to be seen in the broader historical context, especially with regard to the changing relation of labour migration and the reception of refugees in Switzerland.

## 4.4 Cultural Encounters in Swiss Refugee Aid

When the *Mitenand*-initiative was finally put to the vote in 1981, the focus of the public debates had already started to shift from the ongoing incorporation of the mostly European foreign workers and their families to the growing number of non-European refugees. This process started in the late 1970s, when several thousands of refugees

---

86 The *Mitenand*-Bulletin dedicated this topic an issue in September 1983 (No. 28).

from Indochina were brought to Switzerland. The willingness among the Swiss population to host and help the mostly Vietnamese refugees was initially high.[87] The government approved further contingents of refugees until the humanitarian enthusiasm of the Swiss with regard to the "boat people" waned in the early 1980s. The *Swiss Refugee Aid* [Schweizerische Zentralstelle für Flüchtlingshilfe SZF, renamed in 1991 to Schweizerische Flüchtlingshilfe SFH], an umbrella organization of various humanitarian organizations involved in refugee aid, held an official state mandate to organize the transfer and accommodation of the refugees. In 1979, the refugee aid organizations implemented a new approach that aimed at a quick integration of the Indochina refugees into local communities after only three months in reception centers[88] (Karlen, 2018). They adapted the integration approach of the civil disobedience initiative "*Freiplatzaktion*" (Shelter action), that had helped and hosted refugees from Chile against the will of the Swiss state and not forgetting the established refugee aid organizations in the mid 1970s.[89] The leftist, often even communist, Chilean activists who had to flee their country after the violent overthrow of President Salvador Allende in 1973 did not exactly fit into the humanitarian scheme of the Swiss during the Cold War. In the case of the refugees from Indochina, however, hundreds, especially in the context of church congregations, volunteered for so-called support groups [Betreuungsgruppen]. At least in the beginning of the so-called "*Indochina Aktion*" there were more volunteers for support groups than refugees.

Professional social workers accompanied the support groups and the local integration process of the refugees (Karlen, 1980a). In order to guarantee a systematic exchange of experiences between the volunteers, to learn about the needs of the support groups, to discuss the situation of refugee care, and to provide collective supervision, Swiss church aid organizations such as the Protestant HEKS and the Catholic Caritas held several meetings in 1980 and 1981 (Karlen, 1983). The memoranda of the meeting documents show that the participants demanded more background information about the refugees from Vietnam, Cambodia, and Laos (Spurgruppe Basel, 1981). In order to be able to provide support, volunteers, social workers and others involved in refugee integration felt that they needed to know more about these foreign cultures. This demand was based on the common idea within these groups, as well as among the public, that the Swiss had to "respect the otherness" of the refugees and help them to "maintain their cultural identity" in order to guarantee a healthy process of "psycho-social integration" (Bienz, 1978). The integration of foreign workers in the 1970s had mainly been perceived as a legal and sociological

---

**87** On the broad solidarity movement for Vietnam in the late 1960s, see Kuhn (2011).

**88** Rudolf Karlen was the public relations officer of the Swiss refugee aid organization HEKS at that time. See also Karlen (1980b) and SGP (1979).

**89** Rudolf Karlen had also been a member of the *Freiplatzaktion für Chile-Flüchtlinge* in Biel together with his wife (Karlen, 2018).

problem. Refugee aid contexts in contrast tended to draw on psychiatric approaches since the end of World War II. In Switzerland, the first comprehensive study on the mental health of refugees, in this case from Hungary and Czechoslovakia, was made in the 1960s (Pintér, 1969).[90] Again Erikson's (1959) psychological concepts of identity crisis and cultural "uprootedness," as well as the focus on the potentially traumatic effects of migration experiences, provided a persuasive interpretative framework.[91] The letters of Ton That Ba, a Vietnamese refugee, that addressed the Swiss volunteers and social workers indicate that refugees shared this view. Two of these letters were first published in the refugee newspaper called *Huong-Que* [The scent of home], which was supported by Swiss Refugee Aid until 1979, and then translated for Swiss newspapers (Ton, 1981). Very cautiously, the author hinted at the ambiguity of the unequal encounter between the Swiss and the refugees, trying to give insight into the Vietnamese "mentality":

> We Vietnamese are rather introverted, that means we can hardly express or feelings and emotions. We hardly let out great joy or deep sadness. This is why our helpers sometimes get the impression that we are not grateful. But, on the contrary, we are. A deep gratitude fills our heart. ... We are not yet able to communicate well in your language and ask you devoutly to be patient with us and try to understand us. We have become homeless and this fact pains us every day anew. Our helpers focus on satisfying our material needs like food, clothes and housing. With that, our existence as refugees is secured. But what we need above all is your understanding, not your compassion and charity. ... We only ask for one big favor: please show consideration for the needs of our souls. (Ton, 1980)

Due to this urgent demand from "both sides" for understanding, the Swiss church aid organizations organized a series of conventions in different cantons on "Cultural Encounter and Integration". The programme of these conventions in Zurich, Berne, St. Gallen, Chur, Windisch, Olten, and Basel, as well as the final publication, included sessions on the history and culture of South Asia, on "Expectations and the Integration Process," on the "Togetherness of Different Cultures" as well as slots for the feedback of both groups, the Swiss as well as the Indochina refugees (HEKS, 1981). The experiences of Tibetan refugees who had come to Switzerland in the 1960s were used as a reference point in order to understand the new Asian refugees (Karlen, 2018).[92]

---

**90** There were already psychiatric approaches to the "problem of foreign workers" in the 1960s, but they did not gain much influence among integrationists at that time. See Villa (1960) as well as Risso and Böker (1964). For later studies on traumatization in foreign worker families would rediscover these publications, see Frigerio Martina and Merhar (2004). For a broader international perspective on migration, ethnicity, and mental health, see McCarthy and Coleborne (2012).

**91** On the historical rise of trauma as an interpretative framework in 20th century, with a particular focus on refugees, see Fassin and Rechtman (2009).

**92** See also the text of Gyaltsen Gyaltag, a Tibetan refugee and later ambassador of the Dalai Lama in Switzerland, in the publication on *Asian refugees in Switzerland* (Huber, 1984) as well as Ott-Marti (1980).

A newspaper report on these conventions concluded:

Every process of integration changes the parties that are involved. The convention showed very clearly that we, the Swiss, have to be open for an unprejudiced dialogue with the strangers. The aim cannot be for the refugees to abandon their otherness and assimilate. (B.A., 1981)

And in fact, the protocols of the refugee aid organizations indicate that both the volunteers in the support groups as well as the refugees accepted and engaged in the transformative social script of this "cultural encounter". This specifically culture-specific form of postmigrant conviviality was, of course, not immune to tensions. On the Swiss side, it oscillated between a tendency to patronize (Swiss Refugee Aid, 1981)[93] and infantilize the "always smiling" (Deutschstunde, 1979; HEKS & Caritas Zürich, 1982, pp. 21–22) South-Asian refugees, and a sincere respect and interest for their foreign culture. The refugees on the other side felt gratitude but also discomfort to meet the expectations of the Swiss hosts and had a feeling being in constant need (HEKS & Caritas Zürich, 1982, p. 7). They were also aware of their rather privileged

**Figure 4.5:** Cultural encounter and integration in Swiss refugee aid in the 1980s
Note. HEKS & Caritas Zürich (1982), cover picture.

---

**93** Such patronizing attitudes were common in the context of budget planning of the refugee household (Karlen, 2018).

position as officially accepted refugees in comparison to the "foreign workers" that they met in everyday life (HEKS & Caritas Zürich, 1982, p. 9).

This cultural dimension served as an explicit and overarching discursive framework for postmigrant conviviality in refugee aid contexts, in contrast to the *Mitenand*-movement at the same time. It is important to keep in mind that there was some overlap, but in general the social basis of both contexts—established humanitarian organizations and their volunteers on the one hand and a political grassroot movement on the other hand—were far from altogether congruous. It fits into the picture that the culturalist perspective of the refugee aid resonated more with the mainstream public discourse in the media.[94] Newspaper articles oscillated between pessimistic assessments of the "cultural uprooting" of the refugees, exotic accounts—for example on Cambodian spring festivities in Swiss city halls—and more optimistic visions of a successful overcoming of cultural differences (Wigdorovits, 1980). In general, the cultural factor gained significance compared to the earlier debates on foreign worker integration. The humanitarian aid organizations, psycho-social services, and the Swiss public took a strong interest in the cultural identity of the refugees not only from Indochina but also from various other non-European countries, who started to come in growing numbers.

In the early 1980s, other groups of refugees, mostly from Sri Lanka and Turkey, started to arrive on their own initiative without being part of an officially admitted humanitarian contingent. For the first time since the economic crisis in the mid 1970s, the rate of foreigners started to raise again—a statistical turning point that was duly noted by the Swiss public. Unfortunately for the *Mitenand*-initiative this happened shortly before the vote in 1981 (Bundesrat, 1981). These new groups of refugees did not receive the same welcoming offer of integration and good will from the Swiss population as did those from Indochina. The racialized idea of a problematic assimilation of immigrants from more distant "cultural spheres" had existed throughout the 20th century in Switzerland (Kury, 2003). It gained a new character and popularity with the arrival of the so-called "asylum seekers" from Asian and African countries. In the media, this derogatory label started to replace the humanitarian term "refugee", the status of which was protected by international law. Right-wing populists capitalized on this development through-out the 1980s, and they were able to mobilize a new wave of anti-immigration sentiments and racism against "false" asylum seekers and a presumably all too "liberal" asylum law and emerging pro-asylum movement (Skenderovic & D'Amato, 2008).

In the media, the presence of these "new immigrants" in Switzerland was predominantly framed as a problematic clash of cultures rather than an open-hearted

---

94 See the newspaper articles in the documentation on Indochina refugees in Sachdokumentationen (ZA 69.0), Schweizerisches Sozialarchiv [Swiss Social Archives], Zurich, Switzerland.

cultural encounter.[95] Experts were needed to make sense of the situation. In the mid 1980s, the refugee aid associations set up a so-called "Tamil study" (HEKS, 1984)—an ambitious and multidisciplinary research project in order to assess the chances of returning the Tamil refugees to their homeland, and only as an issue of secondary importance to assess the prospects of their staying in Switzerland. Instead of asking sociologists as had been done in earlier cases,[96] ethnologists were now invited to contribute to this NGO research project by studying the "socio-cultural background" of the Tamil refugees in Switzerland. One of the conclusions of the researchers from the University of Berne was that intermediaries were urgently needed in order to deal with the situation of the Tamil refugees in Switzerland, and ethnologists could be helpful in providing this service (Wicker, 1984). Not only in Switzerland, but also elsewhere, ethnologists started to challenge the sociologists as the primary scientific consultants for immigration issues. Ethnological expertise on non-European "foreign cultures" applied to immigrants in Europe was in demand.[97] This looming changing of the guard was part of a broader transformation of discourses on culture in the 1980s. It is beyond the scope of this paper to sketch the history of this process that affected a wide range of societal contexts, as well as both public and expert discourses. It makes sense, however, to hint at a few aspects that can help to understand the specific situation with regard to inclusion-oriented contexts in Switzerland.

One driving factor that put "culture" back on the political agenda in Switzerland at the beginning of the 1980s was the "youth movement". Their turn to "cultural politics" affected new left and liberal activists as well as academic contexts (Zutavern, 2016). Attracted by the ground-breaking work of British cultural studies and ethnologists like Clifford Geertz and Claude Lévi-Strauss, young students who would have chosen sociology in the 1970s started to turn to ethnography, to cultures instead of social structures (Nigg, 2015; Erdheim, 2015). The new anthropological notion of culture "with a little c"—dynamic, complex, and popular—challenged the established Herderian notion of Culture "with a Big C", which was perceived as monolithic, immutable, and politically conservative.[98] In the 1980s, culture turned into an interpretative framework that appealed to Marxists in Switzerland. In 1983, the POCH renamed their party's main institution and called it the Weekly Newspaper for Politics *and Culture*. Moreover, in the early 1980s, Zurich was an important center for "ethnopsychoanalysis", which had merged ethnological and psychological approaches

---

95  On the figure of "new immigrants" in migration historiography, see Lucassen (2005).

96  In 1981, the *Swiss Refugee Aid* (SZF/SFH) asked sociologists of the University of Zurich to study the integration of the Asian refugee and their support groups. See the correspondence between fall 1981 and fall 1982 (SFH Papers)

97  For a critical perspective on this shift to ethnology, see Meillassoux (1980).

98  Hans-Rudolf Wicker (1996), who provided the mentioned ethnographical study on Tamils in Switzerland for the refugee aid organizations in the mid 1980s, would reflect on this historical change of the notion of culture a couple of years later.

into a new critical practice since the 1950s (Krüger, 2016). Swiss students learned to reverse their ethnographic gaze and analyse their own society, specifically their own "ethnicity" (Parin, 1980)—a terminology that became more and more current in German at that time.[99] The relation between *the Self* and *the Other*, *cultural identity*, and *alterity* became an influential topos in debates on immigration throughout the 1980s and 1990s and across political and ideological camps. At the same time and as in other Western countries, immigration to Switzerland became increasingly more global and more plural with regard to countries of origin and forms of migration. Both these developments, demographic and discursive, converged in the debates on "ethnic diversity" and "multicultural societies" that developed in Switzerland in the 1980s, for example in the context of the so-called *Day of the Refugee*.

## 4.5 The Day of the Refugee—From Cultural Encounters to Ethnic Diversity

Following the suggestion of the refugee aid organizations, the Swiss government declared June 21, 1980 to be the first Day of the Refugee (HEKS, 1980). The aim of the event was to provide more information to Swiss citizens about the situation of refugees and to create an opportunity for them to get to know "each other". In Basel and other cities, the refugee aid organizations invited various old and new refugee groups to organize fairs with booths and folkloric performances—including Hungarians, Czechs, and Tibetans who had arrived in the 1950s and 1960s, and Chileans and South-Asians who had arrived since the 1970s. The Swiss visitors were invited to learn about the situation of different refugee groups, and they were able to obtain a better overview of a whole variety of "ethnic" backgrounds. The locals could learn about the "culture" of the various refugee groups by trying their food—Hungarian Goulash, Vietnamese tea, South-American Empanadas, and so forth—and by watching folk dances from different parts of the world. The political semantics of solidarity faded into the background, unless it was brought up by the refugees themselves—sometimes against the will of the organizers, as in the case of leftist Chilean refugees (Plüss, 1980). Other refugee groups, such as those who had fled communist repression, were less rebellious and less interested in politicizing this set-up. The whole fair—a format which would be repeated all over the country in the following years—was designed as an explicit setting and infrastructure not only for contact but for "cultural encounters", between Swiss people and the different groups of refugees, and also among these groups themselves. More than that, the spatial arrangement

---

[99] Mario Erdheim (1988), who taught at the University of Zurich in the 1980s, provided the personal link between the ethnological institute and the private ethnopsychoanalytical practice of Paul Parin and Goldy Parin-Matthèy. For a critical position on the spread of the ethnological gaze on the topic migration, see Radtke (1996).

of the fair with its juxtaposition of the ethnic booths materialized and performed the idea of a diversity of "foreign cultures" in Switzerland. From a more critical perspective, this foreign diversity seemed to be a mere "muddle", not only on the fair but in daily life too (Mangold, 1982).

The organizers of the *Day of the Refugee* asked the Swiss artist Thomas Blank to represent the process of integration of the various "ethnic groups" into Swiss society (HEL, 1980). His chrome steel sculpture was called *INTEGRATION*, but it did not answer the question that seemed to become more and more urgent until the late 1980s: Would the foreign ethnic groups finally acculturate and disappear during this process of integration, or would they constitute a new cultural diversity within Switzerland? How would this cultural diversity of foreigners that materialized in new practices as well as in explicit discourse during the 1980s relate to the traditional notion of cultural diversity in Switzerland, which was based on regional multilingualism?[100] Both the academic and public debates on "national identity" that emerged with regard to the 700-year anniversary of the Swiss Federation in 1991 provide an empirical lens through which to study the changing relation of these two forms of diversity in Switzerland, the traditional four language regions on the one hand and the "ethnic diversity" of the immigrants on the other.

## 4.6 Cultural Diversity and National Identity in Switzerland—A Research Programme

> How does this [modernization] relate to cultural diversity and national identity? The homogenization, universalization and levelling that comes with this social change threatens the cultural diversity, the inner diversity of Switzerland and the Swiss identity with regard to the exterior, global diversity. ... The accelerated social change is a transnational phenomenon. Switzerland, however, is particularly affected by it. It attacks its structures and corrodes its substance. (Kreis, 1986, p. 3)

These introductory remarks from the first newsletter of the *National Research Programme 21*, "Cultural Diversity and National Identity" indicate a certain destabilization with regard to the ideational pillars Swiss society in the mid 1980s. Structural changes not only in the mode of production of capitalism and the global conflicts of the Cold War era, but also social movements in Switzerland such as the already mentioned uprising of the youth and their claim of a political as well as cultural rebellion in the early 1980s, all contributed to this sense of incertitude (Tanner, 2015, pp. 420–428). In the mid 1970s, the Swiss state introduced so-called *National Research Programmes*

---

100 For an early reflection on this issue in the context of refugee aid, see the postscript of the Swiss Buddhist monk Roland Steffan in HEKS & Caritas Zürich (1982, pp. 55–58).

**Figure 4.6:** Day of the Refugee, June 16, 1982

**Figure 4.7:** Day of the Refugee, June 16, 1982

Note. HEKS Papers (J2.233-01#2004/464#237* / 2.990.12.1), Schweizerisches Bundesarchiv [Swiss Federal Archives], Bern, Switzerland.

**Figure 4.8:** Integration and ethnic diversity, 1982

Note. HEKS Papers (J2.233-01#2004/464#235* / 2.990.1.19), Schweizerisches Bundesarchiv [Swiss Federal Archives], Bern, Switzerland.

[Nationale Forschungsprogamme NFP] in order to tackle urgent problems of national importance from a multidisciplinary perspective and to provide academic solutions to them. With the "700-year anniversary" of the *Eidgenossenschaft* [Swiss confederation] in 1991 on the horizon, the Swiss government decided to fund the NFP21 in order to understand the changing role of cultural diversity in Swiss national identity in a modernizing and globalizing world. Surprisingly, at least from the view of today, immigration-related pluralization did not play a relevant role in the general outlook of the research programme. Only two out of more than forty individual research projects dealt with the "integration of foreigners" and the questions of "naturalization and cultural pluralism" (NFP21, 1991). In the NFP research programme, cultural diversity primarily referred to the four linguistic regions and the different religious denominations in Switzerland. It was based on the foundations of federalism and direct democracy and it focussed on the particular national identity of Switzerland in relation to other countries. For this reason, the diverse Swiss nation gained inner unity against the environment of external diversity. This idea of cultural diversity as a pillar of Swiss national identity can be traced back to the modern constitution of 1848, but it had been renegotiated and reinvented in the era of nationalist awakening in the 20th century, including the so-called "*Geistige Landesverteidigung*" [spiritual/intellectual national defence]. Between the 1930s and the 1960s, "unity in diversity" turned into the "vital law" of a national body that felt the strong need to demarcate its boundaries and define its identity against all external powers. The national defence aimed in two directions: closure against the surrounding foreign countries but also closure against forms of social heterogeneity within the country that did not fit in with this cleansed image of the Swiss nation. The ideological exaltation of linguistic and regional diversity went hand in hand with the exclusion of unwanted groups such as "the Jews, the vagrants, the eugenically unwanted" (Germann, 2013, p. 94). The historical context and social groups that represented externalized heterogeneity within Swiss society had changed in the 1980s, but the double structure of the diversity, as I would call it, continued to shape thought, practice, and institutions, for example in the programme NFP21.

The national research programme NFP21 departed from the assumption that the precarious relationship between inner and exterior cultural diversity was at risk due to processes of homogenizing modernization and globalization. Against the backdrop of these powerful and large forces, immigration was not yet considered to be a relevant factor. It was not before the late 1980s when the topic of immigration and "ethnic diversity" started to play a more prominent role in the context of the research programme. The NFP21 periodical of June 1988 published a series of papers on this topic. They all reaffirmed and reproduced the double structure of the discourse on Swiss diversity. The national cultural diversity was perceived as being strictly separate from the "diversity of ethnic minorities"—the title of a workshop of the Swiss UNESCO commission in Lucerne in April 1988, in which various NFP21 members participated (NFP21, 1988). Seen from this perspective, the Swiss had to be "rooted" in their own diverse culture in order to be able to deal with the cultural diversity of the "strange and different people" that were coming to Switzerland (Arend, 1988, p. 9). The idea of two separate diversities can also be found in the papers of the *Mitenand*-movement that was coming to the end at that time:

> The origins of the foreigners in Switzerland are as different as their cultural backgrounds. They bring their culture and want to live in our country. The cultural influences from the outside on the diversity of cultures in Switzerland are not only negative. They are not so great so that the Swiss cultural identity could become lost. On the contrary, one can justifiably talk of a cultural enrichment of Switzerland (Sozialinstitut der KAB, 1988).

The notion of cultural enrichment created a new, positively connoted channel of communication between the two cultural diversities in the late 1980s, opposing the widespread fear of a cultural threat. Yet, it reaffirmed the underlying distinction of the cultural Self and the Other. Around 1990, public controversies on the notion of the "multicultural society" enforced this bipolar logic of diversity: Swiss vs. foreign, and cultural enrichment vs. cultural threat.

## 4.7 The Multicultural Society—A Contested Concept

In July 1991, the historian and director of the NFP21 Georg Kreis published a short text on "The Multicultural Challenge" in which he explicitly reflected on the relation of both forms of diversity in Switzerland. As he wrote,

> because of our own traditional multiculturalism, we have not been very attentive to the new multiculturalism. The old form of cultural diversity does not give us any competence in dealing with the newer version. But the other way around, dealing with the new diversity can make it easier for us to handle the older one. (Kreis, 1991, p. 28)

Kreis did not provide an answer to the question of how the "new" diversity could prove helpful to re-think the "old" diversity, apart from offering a simple contrast to unify and identify the national Self. By distinguishing between a new and an old diversity, he overlooked the fact that the underlying discursive double structure itself was all but new.

Kreis' text was a review of German publications on the topic of multiculturalism, like Claus Leggewie's (1990) much-debated *Multi Kulti. Spielregeln für die Vielvölkerre-publik* [Multi Kulti. Rules of the Game for the Multi-ethnic Republic]. In Germany, multiculturalism had turned into a hot political topic in the late 1980s, for example with the founding of the so-called *Department for Multicultural Affairs* in Frankfurt. Kreis' reference to international debates was no exception. The Swiss controversy on "multicultural societies" in the early 1990s was triggered and influenced by debates in other European and North American countries where cultural pluralism and ethnic minority politics had been an issue already since the 1960s. Gita Steiner-Khamsi (1992), for example, who had been important for introducing intercultural perspectives in the Ministry of Education of the Canton of Zurich, published her book *Multikulturelle Bildungspolitik in der postmodernen Gesellschaft* [Multicultural Education Policy in the Postmodern Society] in 1992 after research stays in the US, Great Britain, and Canada (Steiner-Khamsi, 2017). In the same year, the renowned German-Polish migration sociologist Hans-Joachim Hoffmann-Nowotny (1992a), director of the Institute of Sociology at the University of Zurich, published a report for the Swiss Science Council, in which he weighed up the "chances and risks" of multicultural immigration societies. He had developed his critical position on cultural pluralism in exchange with the international scientific community and especially during a defining visiting fellowship in the Netherlands.[101] When the doyen of foreign worker sociology presented his critique of multiculturalist claims on a podium on Swiss television in March 1992, his

**Figure 4.9:** Public debate on the multicultural society

Note. Schweizer Radio und Fernsehen SRF/SRG [Swiss broadcasting company] (March 18, 1992). Ergänzungen zur Zeit: Die multikulturelle Gesellschaft—Ein neues Schlagwort?, screenshot at 1h:15min:54s.

---

**101** He started publishing on this topic and had been a member of the Research Committee on Ethnic, Race, and Minority Relations of the International Sociological Association since the mid-1970s. See his curriculum vitae and bibliography in the special issue of the *Zeitschrift für Bevölkerungswissenschaften* (2003). 28, 2(4), 145–166, in commemoration of Hoffmann-Nowotny.

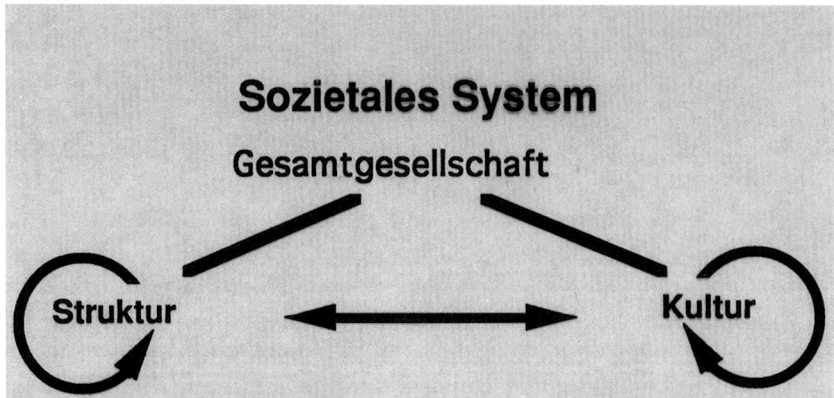

**Figure 4.10:** Structure, Culture, Society

Note. Hoffmann-Nowotny Papers (box 6), Zentralbibliothek Zürich, Handschriftenabteilung (Central Library Zurich, Manuscript Collection), Zurich, Switzerland.

prominent counterpart was the German politician Heiner Geissler, who had stirred up the German Christian Democratic Party with his plea for a multicultural society since the late 1980s. It is safe to conclude that the Swiss debates on multicultural societies and related topics were part of a broader international one.

In the Swiss debates on "multicultural societies" in the early 1990s, the divergence of different understandings of "culture" that had been in the making for more than a decade became apparent. Sociological and anthropological notions of culture clashed in ways that complicated deliberative communication. Hoffmann-Nowotny drew on his theoretical approach to immigration developed in the era of foreign workers in the late 1960s and the early 1970s. He departed from a categorical distinction between structure and culture, structural integration and cultural assimilation. In the case of the mostly Italian foreign workers coming to Switzerland until the mid 1970s, however, he did not attach much importance to the cultural dimension of immigration. As mentioned above, his structural-functionalist perspective on integration resonated with political claims to open Swiss society to the immigrants, for example in the earlier *Mitenand*-movement. The situation changed in the face of new global migration dynamics and the growing number of asylum seekers during the 1980s, and even more so after the fall of communism. Against the backdrop of a supposed *"neue* Völkerwanderung",[102] as Hoffmann-Nowotny (1992b) and others started to call it, the cultural dimension appeared more relevant not only to him than it had in the 1970s. In his report of 1992, Hoffmann-Nowotny (1992a) concluded that

---

[102] "*Völkerwanderung*" is an old-fashioned term for the migration of peoples (*migratio gentium*) in late antiquity which has been used since the 18th century.

a plurality with regard to the basic norms, values, and institutions of the host society would endanger social cohesion. He called this societal building block "*Kultur*" in contrast to "*Struktur*", that means the social structure (Hoffmann-Nowotny, 1992a, pp. 10–11). On the level of every-day practices and popular culture (food, music, taste, etc.), however, plurality was acceptable for Hoffmann-Nowotny. But on his view, this was only "folklore", not "*Kultur*" (Hoffmann-Nowotny, 1992a, p. 15). After publishing his report, Hoffmann-Nowotny was fiercely criticized, mostly from leftist scholars, for his supposedly "right-wing" dismissal of multiculturalism (Castles, 1994; Sancar & Sutter, 1995). He was blamed for providing the scientific legitimation for the new supposedly "racist" immigration policy of the Swiss state envisioned in 1991, that divided the world in three cultural zones. The inhabitants of the third sphere, that meant most of the world except the Western countries, were considered to be culturally too distant to integrate and therefore to immigrate to Switzerland. The strong political polarization of this debate in the following years has to be understood in the historical context of the changing dynamics of global migration after the fall of communism, the wave of racist attacks against immigrants that was not exclusive to Switzerland, the rise of the right-wing Swiss Popular Party, and new movements against racism (Gerber, 2003).

The heated media debate on Hoffmann-Nowotny's (1992a) report introduced the concept of "multicultural society" to the wider Swiss public. It also showed that the ethnological perspective on cultural issues of immigration had gained further ground in academic and activist contexts since the 1980s. Swiss ethnologists now claimed the intellectual lead on migration and integration issues, whereas the sociologists seemed to be stuck in an obsolete structural-functionalist perspective. The "ethnology report" for the Swiss Science Council from 1992 emphasized the need for a culturalist paradigm change and a disciplinary changing of the guard in Swiss migration studies (Knecht, 1992). The same ethnologists who had proven their usefulness in providing expertise on the "socio-cultural background" and "psycho-social" integration of non-European refugees in Switzerland in the 1980s were among those who participated in the hearings of the Swiss Science Council for a new national center for interdisciplinary migration studies, the *Swiss Forum for Migration Studies* (SFM) which was founded in 1995 in Neuchâtel.[103]

---

[103] A leading figure in this process was the ethnologist Hans-Rudolf Wicker from the University of Berne, who had worked in the psychological ambulatory *An Lac* for Indochina refugees in cooperation with the Swiss Red Cross as well as the ethnographic study on Tamil refugees. He participated in the ethnology hearings of the Swiss Science Council and became a leading figure in Swiss migration studies until the 2000s (Wicker, 2016).

## 4.8 Conclusion

The historical analysis of the *Mitenand*-movement and Swiss refugee aid projects of the 1980s show that it would be inaccurate to diagnose a general "cultural(ist)" turn with regard to the perception of postmigrant conviviality over the long 1980s. Most societal contexts, actors and institutions in Switzerland had used culturalist categories before, during and after this decade. One could, however, argue that immigration debates in certain integration-oriented contexts in Switzerland returned to a mainly culturalist framework after a short period of sociological abstinence in the 1970s.[104] Yet, you cannot step into the same river twice. Between the 1970s and the 1990s, the discourse on "culture" had broadened and transformed into a vast and contested field structured by many contradictions and polarities, such as stable/fluid, high/low, holistic/rhizomatic, self/other, identity/difference, essentialist/constructivist, traditional/modern, European/non-European, conservative/innovative, and inclusion/ exclusion. The controversies accompanying the multiculturalist interpretation of societal pluralization through immigration that flared up in the first half of the 1990s in Switzerland got caught up in, and further propelled this complex tectonic shift of the cultural discourse. But in spite of all the differences, advocates and critics of the "multicultural society" alike reproduced the dominant dual structure of diversity in Switzerland. Both sides focused exclusively on the "new" immigrant diversity and the question of integration of "the Others" without trying to integrate the two discourses on cultural diversity.[105] As in other countries, the notion of "multicultural society" was contested from the very moment it entered the Swiss media (Chin, 2017), but at the same time multiculturalist practices of postmigrant conviviality, commercial and non-commercial, started to permeate public spaces and everyday life in Switzerland, especially in the cities which needed to respond to the on-going structural changes of globalization.[106] It is hardly surprising that in 1991 in Basel, the *Day of the Refugee*-fair and the leftist *Nostra Festa* merged into a "multicultural" urban festival.

---

**104** This means that the popular assumption that culture replaced "race" as the main category of racist exclusion in the 1980s is at least inaccurate for Switzerland. The semantics of "race" did indeed mostly disappear in Swiss academic and public discourse after the mid-1970s, but the transformation of "racism" in Switzerland in the 1980s and 1990s is far more complex than a simplified formula suggests.

**105** Except for the less known association "*Aktionsgemeinschaft CH 701*" (the name refers to the year after the 700th Anniversary of the Swiss Federation), whose founding members in 1991 included the ethnologists Verena Müller-Tobler and Rolf Probala, who had participated in the Tamil study, as well as the lawyer Walter Schmid who had been the general secretary of the *Swiss Refugee Aid* (SFH). Papers of the *Aktionsgemeinschaft CH 701* (IB Verein CH 701), Archiv für Zeitgeschichte [Archives of Contemporary History], Zurich, Switzerland.

**106** See for example the debate on "ethnic business" in Switzerland that came up in the late 1990s (Piguet, 1999; Jain, 2018).

Since the early 1990s, Switzerland has slowly become a "postmigrant society" (Foroutan, 2016; Espahangizi, 2018b). Today, more than one third of the Swiss population has a migration background, with even higher rates in urban centers. Nonetheless, most of the "non-immigration immigration country" (Hoffmann-Nowotny, 1995) still struggles to recognize this transformation and to face the ambiguities, uncertainties and contradictions that it has given birth to. The sequence of various inter-, multi-, and trans-cultural approaches that have come up during the last decades affected and dynamized, but also constrained, societal debates on immigration in Switzerland. They have reframed and sharpened our view on postmigrant conviviality, but they have also given birth to new blind spots and ambiguities. Culturalist perspectives may help to recognize and nourish postmigrant conviviality, but they can also be used to obstruct our view and inhibit its development. Culturalist arguments can be mobilized to legitimize exclusion and to claim inclusion as well. Cultural diversity analysis can open our eyes to social inequalities, but it can also divert our attention from them. Against this backdrop, it seems necessary to engage in a more critical reflection on culturalist approaches to postmigrant conviviality and to assess their effects and consequences for specific contexts, their gains and risks, uses and their shortcomings. The omnipresence of "culture" today poses a serious epistemological challenge for academic research on immigration and societal pluralization. It tends to blur the important lines between the subjects, means and objects of analysis. One way to see more clearly again, and to develop a critical but nonetheless productive relation to inter/multi/transculturalist perspectives on postmigrant conviviality, including our own academic concepts, is by reconstructing their historical genealogy.

## 4.9 Postscript

In 2015, a series of portrait photographs populated Zurich's main train station. The blow-ups were part of the so-called *Switzers*-project that aimed at representing the whole diversity of the Swiss population today. Each face stood for one of the 193 nationalities of the world living in Switzerland. The portraits and their individual histories were published in a separate book that provides touching insights into the diversity of life-worlds and biographies in postmigrant Switzerland (https://www.switzersbuch.ch). And yet the narrative framework of even this ambitious and well-intentioned project still fails to integrate the two cultural diversities:

> Today, Switzerland has 8 million inhabitants. 2 million of them are migrants from 193 nations.[107] *They* enrich *our* country with *their* knowledge and *culture* [emphasis added]. They open interes-

---

107 Actually, many of the 6 million Swiss have a migration background, too.

**Figure 4.11:** Switzers at the Zurich railway station

Note. Photograph by Kijan Espahangizi, 2015.

> ting and exotic worlds for us and create a living connection between Switzerland and the world. (Roduner & Schmid, 2016)

The culinary and folkloric programme at the opening of the "*Switzers* nation walk" exhibition stood, without knowing it, in the tradition of practices of the *Mitenand*-movement and the refugee aid projects of the 1980s. It celebrated the "ethnic" diversity of the Others while making invisible the diversity of "the Swiss". One of the portraits, hung up on Platform 3 at the Zurich main station, boiled the whole ambiguity of the project down to its essence: There were 193 *Switzers* but only one representative of Switzerland. The meaning of this single portrait within the exhibition remains open to debate. During an interview I carried out with the inventor of the *Switzers* in 2015, it turned out that he was well aware of the inner contradictions of the project, but he did not know how to tackle them (Roduner, 2015). Being a hands-on professional advertising photographer, he decided to employ the popular textual and visual discourses of ethnic diversity he had at hand in order to realize his contribution to a more inclusive society. The intentions were sincere, but knowing more about the ambiguous history of (multi)cultural diversity in Switzerland might have helped to reflect on a new way of thinking, representing and performing postmigrant conviviality.

# References

Advertisement for "unser fescht–nostra fest–nuestra fiesta". (1977, June 16). In PZ-Wochenzeitung der Progressiven Organisationen der Schweiz [POCH], 7(22), 3 [Party newspaper]. Schweizerisches Sozialarchiv [Swiss Social Archives] (Z563/1977).

Ahmed, S. (2007). The Language of Diversity. Ethnic and Racial Studies, 30(2), 235–256.

Ahmed, S. (2012). On Being Included. Racism and Diversity in Institutional Life. Duke University Press.

Arbeitsgruppe Mitenand. (1979). Weissbuch. Die Ausländer in der Schweiz [Foreigners in Switzerland]. AG Mitenand.

Arend, M. (1988, June). Nationale und ethnische Mischehen in der Schweiz [National and ethnic mixed marriages in Switzerland]. Info, 21(5), 7–9.

Argast, R. (2007). Staatsbürgerschaft und Nation. Ausschliessung und Integration in der Schweiz, 1848–1933 [Citizenship and the nation. Exclusion and Integration in Switzerland, 1848–1933]. Vandenhoeck & Ruprecht.

Autorengruppe für eine fortschrittliche Ausländerpolitik. (1980). Basta! Fremdarbeiter in den 80er Jahren ein Lesebuch. Limmat Verlag.

B.A. (1981, September 7). Kulturbegegnung und Integration. Neue Zürcher Zeitung [Clipping from newspaper article]. Sachdokumentationen (ZA 69.0), Schweizerisches Sozialarchiv [Swiss Social Archives], Zurich, Switzerland.

Bellofatto, S. (2017). Die italienische Küche in der Schweiz. Wahrnehmung – Vermarktung – Etablierung. LIT Verlag.

Berner Komitee zur Unterstützung der Mitenand-Initiative. (1981). E Guete! Buon appetito! Rezepte aus Italien, Spanien, Portugal, Griechenland, Türkei und Jugoslawien [Cookbook] (p. 23). Copy in possession of author.

Bienz, A. (1978, December 7). "In ihrer Andersartigkeit achten". Interview. CO-OP-Zeitung [Clipping from newspaper article]. Sachdokumentationen (ZA 69.0), Schweizerisches Sozialarchiv [Swiss Social Archives], Zurich, Switzerland.

Bloesch, E. (1978, July 9). unser fescht–nostra festa–nueastra fiesta. In Mitenand-Rundbrief 8 [Circular]. Schweizerisches Sozialarchiv [Swiss Social Archives] (D4814 1977–83).

Braun, R. (1970). Sozio-kulturelle Probleme der Eingliederung italienischer Arbeitskräfte in der Schweiz. Rentsch.

Bundesrat. (1981). Volksabstimmung vom 5. April 1981 [Brochure]. Sachdokumentationen (02.3 C*M, QS: 1981), Schweizerisches Sozialarchiv [Swiss Social Archives], Zurich, Switzerland.

Caritas. (1992). Multikulturelle Gesellschaft. Kulturelle Vielfalt als Herausforderung für die Schweiz. Referate des Forums der Caritas Schweiz vom 16. September 1992 in Luzern. Caritas Schweiz.

Castles, S. (1994). La sociologie et la peur de 'cultures incompatibles': Commentaires sur le rapport Hoffmann-Nowotny. In M. C. Caloz-Tschopp & F. H. Micheline (Eds.), Europe: Montrez Patte Blanche (pp. 370–384). Centre Europe–Tiers Monde.

Chin, R. (2017). The Crisis of Multiculturalism in Europe. A History. Princeton University Press.

Deutschstunde—oder: die lächelnde Integration. (1979, August 25). Der Bund [Clipping from newspaper article]. Sachdokumentationen (ZA 69.0), Schweizerisches Sozialarchiv [Swiss Social Archives], Zurich, Switzerland.

Eidgenössische Konsultativkommission für das Ausländerproblem [EKA] (1979). Kulturelle Aspekte des Ausländerproblems. EKA.

Eidgenössische Konsultativkommission für das Ausländerproblem [EKA] (1980). Die Ausländischen Jugendlichen. Die zweite Ausländergeneration. Probleme und Lösungsmöglichkeiten. EKA.

Erdheim, M. (1988). Psychoanalyse und Unbewusstheit in der Kultur Aufsätze, 1980–1987. Suhrkamp.

Erdheim, M. (2015, October 13). Interview by R. Probala [Video recording]. Videointerview zur Geschichte der Ethnologie in Zürich. Institut für Sozialanthropologie und Empirische Kultur-wissenschaft, Universität Zürich. Retrieved April 10, 2017, from http://www.isek.uzh.ch/de/ethnologie/Profil/videointerviews.html

Erikson, E. H. (1959). Identität und Entwurzelung in unserer Zeit. Ansprache auf der 11. Jahrde-stagung der 'World Federation for Mental Health' in Wien 1958. Psyche – Zeitschrift für Psychoanalyse, 13(1), 25–36.

Espahangizi, K. (2017). Migration Research and Epistemic Participation: A Case Study on the 'Sociology of Foreign Workers' in Zurich in the 1970s. In K. Morawek & M. Krenn (Eds.), Urban Citizenship. Democratising Democracy (pp. 112–131). VfmK.

Espahangizi, K. (2018a). Ein Civil Rights Movement in der Schweiz? Das vergessene Erbe der Mitenand-Bewegung in der Schweiz (1974–1990). Institut Neue Schweiz Blog. https://institut-neueschweiz.ch/En/Blog/178/Espahangizi_Mitenand

Espahangizi, K. (2018b). Ab wann sind Gesellschaften postmigrantisch? Wissenshistorische Überlegungen ausgehend von der Schweiz. In J. K. Naika Foroutan, Riem Spielhaus (Ed.), Postmigrantische Perspektiven. Ordnungssysteme, Repräsentationen, Kritik (pp. 35–55). Campus.

Espahangizi, K. (2019a). "The Way to School Between Two Worlds" – Documenting the Knowledge of Second-Generation Immigrant Children in Switzerland, 1977–1983. KNOW – A Journal on the Formation of Knowledge, 2(3), 305–330.

Espahangizi, K. (2019b). The 'Sociologic' of Postmigration: A Study in the Early History of Social Research on Migration and Integration in Switzerland, 1960–73. In B. Lüthi & D. Skenderovic (Eds.), Switzerland and Migration. Historical and Current Perspectives on a Changing Landscape (Palgrave Studies in Migration History) (pp. 33–59). Palgrave Macmillan.

Faist, T. (2009). Diversity – A New Mode of Incorporation? Ethnic and Racial Studies, 32(1), 171–190.

Fassin, D., & Rechtman, R. (2009). The Empire of Trauma. An Inquiry into the Condition of Victimhood. Princeton University Press.

Foroutan, N. (2016). Postmigrantische Gesellschaften. In H. U. Brinkmann & M. Sauer (Eds.), Einwanderungsgesellschaft Deutschland. Entwicklung und Stand der Integration (pp. 227–255). Springer.

Franzini, U. (1988). Ein Erfahrungsbericht. In Sozialinstitut der KAB (Ed.), Ausländer in der Schweiz (p. 9) [Brochure]. Sachdokumentationen (02.3C, Qs: 1988), Schweizerisches Sozialarchiv [Swiss Social Archives], Zurich, Switzerland.

Frigerio Martina, M., & Merhar, S. (2004). 'Und es kamen Menschen…'. Die Schweiz der Italiener. Rotpunktverlag.

Gerber, B. (2003). Die antirassistische Bewegung in der Schweiz. Organisationen, Netzwerke und Aktionen. Seismo.

Germann, P. (2013). The Abandonment of Race. Researching Human Diversity in Switzerland, 1944–1956. In B. Gausemeier, S. Müller-Wille, & E. Ramsden (Eds.), Human Heredity in the Twentieth Century (pp. 85–101). Pickering & Chatto.

Gilroy, P. (2004). After Empire. Melancholia or Convivial Culture? Routledge.

Glazer, N., & Moynihan, D. P. (1964). Beyond the Melting Pot. The Negroes, Puerto Ricans, Jews, Italians, and Irish of New York City. MIT Press.

Haug, W. (1980). 'Und es kamen Menschen'. Ausländerpolitik und Fremdarbeit in der Schweiz, 1914–1980. Z Verlag.

HEKS. (1980). HEKS Info-Flüchtlingsdienst, Flüchtlingstag 21. Juni 1980. HEKS Papers (J2.233-01#2004/464#239*), Schweizerisches Bundesarchiv [Swiss Federal Archives], Bern, Switzerland.

HEKS. (1981). Kulturbegegnung und Integration. Informationstagung am 5. September 1981 in Zürich & 24. Oktober 1981 in St. Gallen. [Program of the meetings]. HEKS Papers (J2.233-

01#2004/464#275*), Schweizerisches Bundesarchiv [Swiss Federal Archives], Bern, Switzerland.

HEKS. (1984, June 26). Spurengruppe. Projektentwurf Tamilenstudie. HEKS Papers (J2.233-01#2004/464#270*), Schweizerisches Bundesarchiv [Swiss Federal Archives], Bern, Switzerland.

HEKS & Caritas Zürich. (1982). Kulturbegegnung und Integration. Erfahrungen südostasiatischer Flüchtlinge in der Schweiz und ihre kulturellen Eigenheiten. HEKS/Caritas Zürich.

HEL. (1980, June 21). Ueber 15 Millionen sind ohne Heimat. BV Blatt [Clipping from newspaper article]. HEKS Papers (J2.233-01#2004/464#235*/2.990.1.19), Schweizerisches Bundesarchiv [Swiss Federal Archives], Bern, Switzerland.

Hoffmann-Nowotny, H.-J. (1973). Soziologie des Fremdarbeiterproblems: Eine theoretische und empirische Analyse am Beispiel der Schweiz. Enke.

Hoffmann-Nowotny, H.-J. (1985). The Second Generation of Immigrants: A Sociological Analysis with Special Emphasis on Switzerland. In R. Rogers (Ed.), Guests Come to Stay. The Effects of European Labor Migration on Sending and Receiving Countries (pp. 109–133). Westview Press.

Hoffmann-Nowotny, H.-J. (1992a). Chancen und Risiken multikultureller Einwanderungsgesell-schaften. Forschungspolitische Früherkennung 119. Schweizerischer Wissenschaftsrat.

Hoffmann-Nowotny, H.-J. (1992b). Die neue Völkerwanderung und die Bildung multikultureller Gesellschaften. In C. Schweiz (Ed.), Multikulturelle Gesellschaft. Kulturelle Vielfalt als Heraus-forderung für die Schweiz. Referate des Forums der Caritas Schweiz vom 16. September 1992 in Luzern (pp. 15–26). Caritas Schweiz.

Hoffmann-Nowotny, H.-J. (1995). Switzerland. A Non-Immigration Immigration Country. In R. Cohen (Ed.), The Cambridge Survey of World Migration (pp. 302–307). Cambridge University Press.

Huber, H. (Ed.). (1984). Asiatische Flüchtlinge in der Schweiz. Fragen zur Integration. Univer-sitätsverlag.

Hurst, M. (1974). Zur Ich- und Identitätsentwicklung des Fremdarbeiterkindes. In V. J. Willi, M. Hurst, & M. Hunold (Eds.), Denkanstösse zur Ausländerfrage (pp. 12–42). Orell Füssli.

Jain, R. (2018). Kosmopolitische Pioniere. 'Inder_innen der zweiten Generation' aus der Schweiz zwischen Assimilation, Exotik und globaler Moderne. transcript.

Karlen, R. (1980a, August). Einführung für Vorbereitungsgruppen & Caritas and HEKS. (1980, November 17). Presseorientierung über die Indochina-Aktion im Raume Basel. HEKS Papers (J2.233-01#2004/464#273*), Schweizerisches Bundesarchiv [Swiss Federal Archives], Bern, Switzerland.

Karlen, R. (1980b, October 23). Flüchtlingshilfe in der Schweiz am Beispiel der Aktion zugunsten der Flüchtlinge aus Südostasien [manuscript of the presentation at the conference of the German Arbeiterwohlfahrt in Bonn]. Copy in possession of the author.

Karlen, R. (1983). Der freiwillige Helfer in der Flüchtlingshilfe: Sein Stellenwert, seine Begleitung. In Schweizerische Konferenz der kantonalen Erziehungsdirektoren (Ed.), Flüchtlingsbildung. Am Beispiel der Indochina-Aktion (Informationsbulletin 41). EDK. Copy in the possession of the author.

Karlen, R. (2018, June 13). Interview by K. Espahangizi [Tape recording]. Copy in possession of the author.

Knecht, S. (1992). Migrationsforschung in der Schweiz. Ethnologieberichte/Hearingsbericht. (Forschungspolitische Früherkennung 132). Schweizerischer Wissenschaftsrat.

Kreis, G. (1986, December). Thema und Zielsetzungen des NFP 21. In Info 21 [Circular], 1, 2–3.

Kreis, G. (1991, July). Die multikulturelle Herausforderung. In Info 21, 15, 27–29.

Krüger, G. (2016, September 18). Ethnopsychoanalyse als Utopie. Paul Parin zum 100. Geburtstag. Geschichte der Gegenwart. https://geschichtedergegenwart.ch/ethnopsychoanalyse-als-utopie-paul-parin-zum-100-geburtstag/

Kuhn, K. J. (2011). Entwicklungspolitische Solidarität. Die Dritte-Welt-Bewegung in der Schweiz zwischen Kritik und Politik, 1975–1992. Chronos.

Kuhn, K. J. (2015). 'Beschauliches Tun' oder europäische Perspektive? Positionen und Dynamiken einer volkskundlichen Kulturwissenschaft in der Schweiz zwischen 1945 und 1970. In J. Moser, I. Götz, & M. Ege (Eds.), Zur Situation der Volkskunde 1945–1970 (pp. 177–203). Waxmann.

Kury, P. (2003). Über Fremde reden: Überfremdungsdiskurs und Ausgrenzung in der Schweiz 1900-1945. Chronos.

Leggewie, C. (1990). Multi Kulti: Spielregeln für die Vielvölkerrepublik. Rotbuch Verlag.

Lentin, A., & Titley, G. (2011). The Crises of Multiculturalism Racism in a Neoliberal Age. Zed Books.

Lucassen, L. (2005). The Immigrant Threat. The Integration of Old and New Migrants in Western Europe since 1850. University of Illinois Press.

Mangold, C. (1982, June 21). Grosse Welt auf kleinem Platz. Basler Zeitung [Clipping from newspaper article]. HEKS Papers (J2.233-01#2004/464#237* / 2.990.12.1), Schweizerisches Bundesarchiv [Swiss Federal Archives], Bern, Switzerland.

McCarthy, A., & Coleborne, C. (Eds.). (2012). Migration, Ethnicity, and Mental Health. International Perspectives, 1840-2010. Routledge.

Meillassoux, C. (1980). Gegen eine Ethnologie der Arbeitsimmigration in Westeuropa. In J. Blaschke & K. Greussing (Eds.), 'Dritte Welt' in Europa. Probleme der Arbeitsimmigration (pp. 53–59). Syndikat.

NFP21. (1988, June). Editorial. Info 21, 5(1).

NFP21. (1991, December). Gesamtansicht der Projekte. Info 21, 16(25).

Niederer, A. (1967). Unsere Fremdarbeiter – volkskundlich betrachtet. Wirtschaftspolitische Mitteilungen, 23(May), 1–20.

Nigg, H. (2015, September 21). Interview by R. Probala [Video recording]. Videointerview zur Geschichte der Ethnologie in Zürich. Institut für Sozialanthropologie und Empirische Kulturwissenschaft, Universität Zürich. Retrieved April 10, 2017, from http://www.isek.uzh.ch/de/ethnologie/Profil/videointerviews.html

Ott-Marti, A. E. (1980). Probleme der Integration von Tibetern in der Schweiz. Tibet-Institut.

Parin, P. (1980). Die äusseren und die inneren Verhältnisse. Ethnopsychoanalytische Betrachtungen, auf unsere eigene Ethnie angewandt. Berliner Hefte, 15, 5–34.

Piguet, E. (1999). Les migrations créatrices. Etude de l'entreprenariat des étrangers en Suisse. L'Harmattan.

Pintér, E. (1969). Wohlstandsflüchtlinge. Eine sozialpsychiatrische Studie an ungarischen Flüchtlingen in der Schweiz. Karger.

Plüss, C. (1980, July 10). Letter to Herr Rhyner, Director of Grün 80. HEKS Papers (J2.233-01#2004/464#239*), Schweizerisches Bundesarchiv [Swiss Federal Archives], Bern, Switzerland.

Radtke, F. O. (1996). Fremde und Allzufremde. Zur Ausbreitung des ethnologischen Blicks in der Einwanderungsgesellschaft. In H. R. Wicker, J.-L. Alber, C. Bolzman, R. Fibbi, K. Imhof, & A. Wimmer (Eds.), Das Fremde in der Gesellschaft. Migration, Ethnizität und Staat (pp. 333–352). Seismo.

R. G. (1978). Erinnerungen an einen Erfolg. In Mitenand-Rundbrief 11 (December), p. 6 [Circular]. Schweizerisches Sozialarchiv [Swiss Social Archives] (D4814 1977–83), Zurich, Switzerland.

Risso, M., & Böker, W. (1964). Verhexungswahn. Ein Beitrag zum Verständnis von Wahnerkrankungen süditalienischer Arbeiter in der Schweiz. S. Karger.

Roduner, R. (2015, April 3). Interview by K. Espahangizi [Tape recording]. Copy in possession of the author.

Roduner, R., & Schmid, R. (2016, November 19). Switzers - die 193 Nationen der Schweiz. SWI. https://www.swissinfo.ch/ger/multimedia/gesichter-der-welt-_switzers---die-193-nationen-der-schweiz/42576308

Sancar, A., & Sutter, A. (1995). Eine wissenschaftliche Grundlage für eine künftige Migrationspolitik? Der Beitrag von H. J. Hoffmann-Nowotny aus kritischer Distanz. Rote Revue – Zeitschrift für Politik, Wirtschaft und Kultur, 73(2), 30–34.

SFH Papers. (n.d.) (IB SFH Archiv/100A & 101A, Unterlagen Bürokommission), Archiv für Zeitgeschichte [Archives of Contemporary History], Zurich, Switzerland.

SGP. (1979, January 19). Vietnam Flüchtlingspolitik. St. Galler Tagblatt [Clipping from newspaper article], Sachdokumentationen (ZA 69.0), Schweizerisches Sozialarchiv [Swiss Social Archives], Zurich, Switzerland.

Skenderovic, D., & D'Amato, G. (2008). Mit dem Fremden politisieren: Rechtspopulistische Parteien und Migrationspolitik in der Schweiz seit den 1960er Jahren. Chronos.

Smith, A. D. (1981). The Ethnic Revival. Cambridge University Press.

Sozialinstitut der KAB (1988). Ausländer in der Schweiz – Neue Dimensionen. In Sozialinstitut der KAB (Ed.), Ausländer in der Schweiz (p. 3) [Brochure]. Sachdokumentationen (02.3C, Qs: 1988), Schweizerisches Sozialarchiv [Swiss Social Archives], Zurich, Switzerland.

Spurgruppe Basel. (1981, May 26). Zusammenkunft vom 20.5.81 & Voten zur Betreuertagung am 9. Mai 1981 [Minutes of a meeting] & Tagungsteam. (1981, August 17) Bericht von den beiden Tagungen für Betreuer von Indochinaflüchtlingen vom 9.5.1981 und vom 13.6.1981 [Report]. HEKS Papers (J2.233-01#2004/464#273*), Schweizerisches Bundesarchiv [Swiss Federal Archives], Bern, Switzerland.

Steiner-Khamsi, G. (1988). Kurse in heimatlicher Sprache und Kultur (HSK). Ein Zwischenbericht zum achtjährigen Versuch im Kanton Zürich. Kanton Zürich, Pädagogische Abteilung, Sektor Ausländerpädagogik.

Steiner-Khamsi, G. (1992). Multikulturelle Bildungspolitik in der Postmoderne. Leske + Budrich.

Steiner-Khamsi, G. (1995). Zur Geschichte und den Perspektiven der interkulturellen Pädagogik in der Schweiz und in Europa. In E. Poglia, A.-N. Perret-Clermont, A. Gretler, & P. Oasen (Eds.), Interkulturelle Bildung in der Schweiz. Fremde Heimat (pp. 45–65). Peter Lang.

Steiner-Khamsi, G. (2017, September 2). Interview by K. Espahangizi [Tape recording]. Copy in possession of the author.

Swiss Refugee Aid (1980, September 29). Protocol of the board meeting, p. 2. SFH Papers (IB SFH Archiv / 69A), Archiv für Zeitgeschichte [Archives of Contemporary History], Zurich, Switzerland.

Tanner, J. (2015). Geschichte der Schweiz im 20. Jahrhundert. Beck.

Ton, T. B. (1980, November 22). Wenn möglich, bitte mehr Verständnis für uns. Vaterland [Clipping from newspaper article]. Sachdokumentationen (ZA 69.0), Schweizerisches Sozialarchiv [Swiss Social Archives], Zurich, Switzerland.

Ton, T. B. (1981, January 9). Meine Sorgen und Wünsche in der neuen Heimat. Vaterland [Clipping from newspaper article], Sachdokumentationen (ZA 69.0). Schweizerisches Sozialarchiv [Swiss Social Archives], Zurich, Switzerland.

Vertovec, S. (2017). Talking Around Super-Diversity. Ethnic and Racial Studies, 42(1), 125–139.

Villa, J. L. (1960). Apropos de quelques problèmes de l'émigration en Suisse. Zeitschrift für Präventivmedizin, 5, 318–332.

Wicker, H. R. (1984, September). Tamilen in der Schweiz. Sozio-kulturelle Hintergründe. Eine Untersuchung des Seminars für Ethnologie der Universität Bern [Unpublished report]. HEKS Papers (J2.233-01#2004/464#270*), Schweizerisches Bundesarchiv [Swiss Federal Archives], Bern, Switzerland.

Wicker, H. R. (1996). Von der komplexen Kultur zur kulturellen Komplexität. In H. R. Wicker, J.-L. Alber, C. Bolzman, R. Fibbi, K. Imhof, & A. Wimmer (Eds.), Das Fremde in der Gesellschaft. Migration, Ethnizität und Staat (pp. 373–392). Seismo.

Wicker, H. R. (2016, April 27). Interview by K. Espahangizi [Tape recording]. Copy in possession of the author.

Wigdorovits, S. (1980, April 14). Chaul-Chnam zum Jahr im Zeichen des Affen. Kambodschanische Neujahrsfeier in Bülach. Vaterland, April 14, 1980 & 2524 im Jahre des Hahns. (1981, April 13). Aargauer Tagblatt [Clipping from newspaper article]. Sachdokumentationen (ZA 69.0), Schweizerisches Sozialarchiv [Swiss Social Archives], Zurich, Switzerland.

Willi, V. J. (1974). Zu einer neuen Fremdarbeitersoziologie. In V. J. Willi, M. Hurst, & M. Hunold (Eds.), Denkanstösse zur Ausländerfrage (pp. 120–139). Orell Füssli.

Zürcher Kontaktstelle für Ausländer und Schweizer. (1978). Ausländer und Schweizer feiern zusammen 10 Jahre [Invitation]. Papers of the Zürcher Kontaktstelle für Ausländer und Schweizer (Ar 48.20.1, Varia 1967–1984, folder 4), Schweizerisches Sozialarchiv [Swiss Social Archives], Zurich, Switzerland.

Zutavern, J. (2016). Züri brännt. Nach Feierabend. Zürcher Jahrbuch für Wissensgeschichte, 11, 79–89.

Joseph Ciaudo

# 5 Promoting a Hygienic Dress That Transcends Cultural Life-Worlds: Some Remarks on the Rejection of Western Clothes by a Chinese Minister to the United States in the Early Twentieth Century

> Since the establishment of the Chinese Republic in 1911, ... the inelegant foreign dress is no longer considered fantastic; on the contrary it has become a fashion, not only in cities where foreigners are numerous, but even in interior towns and villages where they are seldom seen. Chinese ladies, like their Japanese sisters, have not yet, to their credit be it said, become obsessed by this new fashion, which shows that they have more common sense than some men. I have, however, seen a few young and foolish girls imitating the foreign dress of Western women. Indeed this craze for Western fashion has even caught hold of our legislators in Peking, who, having fallen under the spell of clothes, in solemn conclave decided that the frock coat, with the tall-top hat, should in future be the official uniform; and the swallow-tail coat with a white shirt front the evening dress in China. I need hardly say that this action of the Peking Parliament aroused universal surprise and indignation. (Wu, 1914, pp. 158–159)

Taken out of context, these sentences may sound similar to those which a traditionalist Chinese scholar, rejecting Westernization, could have said in the years that followed the establishment of the Chinese Republic. In a period when more and more Chinese intellectuals and entrepreneurs were starting to adopt Western clothing as a symbol of modernity and cosmopolitanism, rejecting the "foreign dress" in such a manner could have been regarded as narrow-mindedly conservative[108]. Yet, Wu Tingfang 伍廷芳 (1842–1922), the author of the above quoted paragraph, wrote a few pages later that "everything that brings the East and West together and helps each to understand the other better is good", and that "mixed marriages of the white with the yellow races will be productive of good for both sides" (Wu, 1914, pp. 184–185)[109].

---

**108** Henrietta Harrison notes that around 1912, "Western-style suits marked the wearer as a reformer or a 'new person'" (Harrison, 2000, p. 51). On the identification of Western clothes with modernity and political reformism, and the evolution of clothes during this period of history, cf. Harrison (2000, pp. 49–60) and Finnane (2007, notably pp. 69–100).

**109** One should note here that Wu did not use the term "East" in a manner that would mimic the Western notion of "Orient", and its Saïdian ontological implication of a world being divided into two uneven hemispheres: the "self" and the "other", "the dominant" and "the dominated". As hinted in the second sentence quoted, the East essentially meant for Wu: the Far-East (the land of the "yellow races") or even China alone. East and West should therefore be mainly understood as toponyms that did not embody the entire planet. It is highly improbable that Wu may have had Africa or even the Middle East in mind when he spoke of the East. The Chinese history of the concept of East or Orient (*dongfang* 東方 or *dongyang* 東洋) remains to be written, however one could get a glimpse at the

Furthermore, when one enquires into his background, one can notice that Wu was anything but a traditionalist.

Born in 1842 in Singapore and raised in Hong Kong, Wu was offered since his early childhood an education in-between East-Asia and Europe. After having studied the Confucian classics, he attended a local mission school, which enabled him to later enter St. Paul's College. This foreign and Christian education would then lead him to England, where he was trained as a barrister. Later, he became a key figure in the administration of Sir John Pope Hennessy (1834–1891), governor of Hong Kong from 1877 to 1883. When his Irish friend and protector left the colony, he joined the Chinese Imperial Administration. He worked under Li Hongzhang 李鴻章 (1823–1901), the main actor of the "Western"—or more exactly—"foreign affairs" (yangwu 洋務) movement, whose aim was to provide "self-reinforcement" (*ziqiang* 自強) to China thanks to a policy of selective importation of Western technologies and ideas. In this regard, Wu played an important role in the introduction of Western conceptions of law and diplomacy. Appointed Minister to the United States, Spain, and Peru in 1896, he was in the United States until 1902. There he also served a second term from 1907 to 1909. During his time abroad, he was not only an important public figure, who did much to preserve the interest of his government and countrymen at both political and juridical levels, but he was also someone who understood the value of public opinion in modern democratic regimes, and embarked, as a consequence, on a crusade to defend and valorize China in the eyes of the Americans. After he returned to China, he once again played a central role in the political history of the country by winning the non-intervention of foreign powers during the events that led to the collapse of the Empire and the rise of the young Chinese Republic. He would continue to hold important political positions in the new regime until he passed away in 1922.

It is possible to say that Wu was a central figure of Chinese political and intellectual life during the beginning of the 20th century. However, he has never received much academic scrutiny. In China, only three scholars published books on him (Ding & Yu, 2005; Zhang, 2015). Only one monograph has been written about him in a Western language (Pomerantz, 1992). It would not be the place here to discuss the reasons that have led to such a lack of scholarly interest in Wu. However, one must note that all the above-mentioned studies also often neglected or belittled Wu's attitude toward Western social and cultural practices—such as clothing[110]—in focusing on his political achievement and his fight for the modernization and liberalization of

---

transformation underwent by this Western notion by considering how it fared in the history of their neighbour: the Japanese (Tanaka, 1993).

**110** Regarding bodily practices, previous studies about Wu have mainly insisted on his attitude toward the Manchu queue. This was a highly sensitive political subject, since this hairstyle had been imposed on the Chinese population by the reigning dynasty. By the end of the nineteenth century, cutting one's queue could be regarded as a political gesture that has received much attention from previous research. For a general presentation, see for instance Cheng (2000).

China. These oversights notwithstanding, the problem of what one wears was also a decisive issue not only with regard to modernization, but also in the defence and presentation of one's identity. In the context of an expanding West and colonialism, Jennifer Craik rightly noted that clothes were to become "a weapon in the struggle between colonizers and colonized. First, the colonizers used clothes to impose the authority of 'western' ways; later, local people used indigenous clothes to resist that imposition" (Craik, 1994, p. 26). Departing from this observation, I would like to reverse the above-mentioned academic tendency, setting Wu the diplomat or Minister a little aside, to enquire into Wu as the Western-educated Chinese man who lived in the USA, favoured the convergence of China and the outside world, and yet rejected any form of Western dress. Was he trying to refuse a set of standards imposed on the Chinese by Western civilization? Was he trying to defend through clothing a specific and cultural feature of the Chinese to declare its distance from the West? Both these questions will be answered in the negative. Rather, he was negotiating a "transcultural modernity"[111] where "hygiene" (*weisheng* 衛生) was a key standard.

Before entering into this question more deeply, let us first explain the context of this opening quotation. It is taken from chapter 11 of *America through the spectacles of an Oriental Diplomat* (hereafter *America*), a book written in English on the request of an American friend who had urged him to "write about our country [USA] and to speak of our people in an impartial and candid way": (Wu 1914, pp. ix–x). Entitled "American versus Chinese Civilization", this chapter was to discuss the differences between the conceptions of "civilization" in the West and in China. The text possesses, however, a very peculiar architecture: after quoting several definitions from Western and Chinese authors,[112] and affirming that the West inherited "Civilization" from the

---

111  This terminology is, of course, not part of Wu's own vocabulary. As a matter of fact, Wu had no use of the term "modernity", be it in English or in Chinese. In his English texts, the adjectives "modern" and "modernized" have very few occurrences, and in them, they should mostly be understood as synonyms for "developed" or "civilized". Wu did not express much concern for the modern times as a *Neuzeit* that would mark a decisive break from the past; the expression "modern times" is even impossible to find under his brush. Indeed, it is important to keep in mind that "Modernity" had not become an established sociopolitical concept (*Grundbegriff*) in the Chinese language at that time. Regarding *transculturality*, this is a very recent notion that has had many interpretations, and sometimes very loose frontiers. Here, I use it in the sense that cultures are absolutely not "internally cohesive, homogenous, self-contained, or hermetically sealed against influences" (Flüchter, 2015, p. 2), and that, furthermore, they are not congruent to nation states. They are rather "multilayered system[s] of rules (meanings, values, views, habits) and things (symbols, products, tools) that people apply or use in daily life" (Éigeartaigh, 2010, p. 8). With the label "transcultural modernity", I imply that Wu was not envisioning the world in the manner of a global competition for progress—a logic in which every national culture would walk its own path in a teleological framework. He rather understood history as the very process of an unraveling civilizational progress made possible by circulation and exchange between cultural units.

112  It is not written in the text but "the Chinese ideals of a truly civilized man" he speaks of are

East,[113] Wu embarked upon a description of the distinguishing features of the American people. They were presented as earnest, perseverant, and geniuses in organization. It is here, in the middle of the chapter, that Wu had a sentence of much interest for us: "As civilized people have always found it necessary to wear clothes I ought not to omit a reference to them" (Wu, 1914, p. 154). Yet, in this text Wu does not give a simple "reference". His comments about clothes stand for the entire second half of the chapter. He also explained having "submitted a memorandum to President Yuan" Shikai 袁世凱 (1859–1916) in 1913, protesting against the Westernization of clothing in the Chinese Parliament. The reform of clothing was as such located at the core of the question of civilization, a new and contested concept that had been moulding intellectual debates all around the world since its rise during the 19th century[114].

Presenting the problem of civilization under the theme of clothing is not trivial,[115] and what a twenty-first-century reader could consider as anecdotal appeared of much importance for Wu. Speaking of one's own civilization and the civilization of the other implied giving much thought to this problem. Clothing was, after all, a concept that served as a standard to consider and conceptualize the organization of the world and to justify European colonialism. Furthermore, this concern for civilization through the angle for clothes is to be found in several other works of Wu. For example, in his *Plan to reform the Chinese Republic* (1915), he notably wrote a chapter dedicated to "the appropriateness of costumes" (*fuzhi zhi shiti* 服制之適體)[116]—a chapter that was twice as long as the one dealing with "duties and liberties". Wu's (1914/1993) book,

---

mainly defined through quotations taken from canonical Confucian texts, such as the *Analects*, the *Mencius* or *The Great Study* (Wu, 1914, pp. 145–146).

**113** This affirmation has since puzzled many of Wu's readers, as he remained here very obscure in his meaning.

**114** The end of the 19th century and the beginning of the 20th, in particular, saw the rise of debates in which the often very loosely defined notion of "civilization" served as intellectual weapon—the most famous for a Western reader being probably the opposition between the French *la Civilisation* et the German *Kultur* during the World War I. For a general introduction to the history of this concept and its political consequences in the West, see Bénéton (1975); Fisch (1992) and Pauka (2012). Regarding how this concept affected non-Western societies, see Gong (1984); Mazlish (2004) and Pernau (2015). Wu was clearly aware of this contested history and of how "civilization" served the narrative of Western powers. In 1903, he lamented: "Civilization in the nineteenth and twentieth centuries, like liberty in the eighteenth, is one of those catchwords that have been used to cover up all sorts of wickedness. What crimes have not been committed in the name of civilization?" (Wu, 1903, p. 190)—a sentence directly echoing the famous catchphrase by Madame Roland—"O Liberty how many are committed in thy name!".

**115** "Civilized" was often used as a synonym of "Western" in matter of clothes and social practices. Furthermore, the issue of "what to wear" has been, as a matter of fact, a key problem not only in locating oneself in the civilization narrative but also to define one's identity in many lands around the world. For a comparative approach, see for instance the case of India (Tarlo, 1996).

**116** In this text, one can find the reproduction of the above-mentioned petition (Wu, 1993, pp. 615–618).

*New techniques to prolong life* (*Yanshou xinshuo* 延壽新說), also had a small chapter about clothes (pp. 556–557)[117]. Finally, he did not simply write about clothes, but also showed them. Among the five illustrations displayed in *America*, four of them related to the question of clothing (Wu, 1914).

The very extensive room occupied by Wu's comment on clothing may have something intriguing within it for the historian working on modern Chinese intellectual debate regarding the differences and similarities between China and Western countries. Unlike the abounding literature published in China around the same time on the differences and similarities between hypostatized East and West, Wu tried neither to build a system of dichotomies, nor to oppose the Chinese and the Americans in an articulated series of contradictory values and ideals. He did not explain what the West or China were with an argumentation that would locate a religion or a "spirit" (*Geist*) at the core of every culture. In fact, he wrote in a very joyful, if not humorous, style about petty details of life on both sides of the Pacific Ocean. He simply depicted what was he was witnessing, and had some remarks about the contrast that had emerged in his sketches. However, it seems that despite, or perhaps more exactly because of, his witty and disjointed *bon mots* on the topic, Wu has been cast aside from academic research on this theme. One of Wu's biographers writes that "he was no theorist", that "his consideration on society and culture were ... superficial and fuzzy", while his comparison between Chinese and Western cultures "lacked systematicity" (Ding, 2005, p. 351), as if one needed to put on paper a systematic *Weltanschauung* to be "deep" in contemplating a topic.

The aim of this chapter will therefore be to enquire into Wu's texts from a new perspective that will value his rhetoric and anecdotes as direct insights into "cultural differences". It will moreover question how Wu circulated across what appears to be, from our 21st century readers' point of view, multiple cultural identities. Instead of casting Wu away for not being serious enough, let us, on the contrary, take seriously what he has to say on clothing. Perhaps, then, one will realize that he was like the Greeks before him, "superficial—from profundity" (*oberflächlich—aus Tiefe*).

To do so, this discussion will proceed in three moves. I will start by briefly sketching how Wu entered the topic of clothing reform. This will lead us to the problem of how clothes relate to Civilization, understood with a capital C, and why it mattered to Wu. This being clarified, it will become possible to understand how Wu lived and negotiated a transcultural experience of civilization, and the normativity inherent to his conception of the world.

---

**117** As a matter of fact, this text was probably the original version of what Wu (1914) later published in English in the chapter "American clothes" of *America through the spectacles of an Oriental Diplomat*, as both texts show some notable similarities.

## 5.1 "The Costume Should by no Means be Changed"

To begin with, one must note that Wu's rejection of Western dress and his valorization of Chinese clothing began very early in his career. In both Chinese and English, Wu wrote that he had tried to wear Western clothes when he was studying in England between 1874 and 1877, but he soon abandoned this experience because he "found it very uncomfortable". According to him, "in the winter it was not warm enough, but in the summer it was too warm" (Wu, 1914, p. 141). His attitude toward the topic of clothing already displayed a peculiar attention to "comfort". In November 1900, in an address before the American Academy of Political and Social Science, Wu (1901) also stated that he was "glad that some of the missionaries [in China] have adopted the Chinese dress, which ... is more comfortable" (p. 6). He was at that time commenting on the experience of a missionary that had changed his outfit, in order to avoid "attracting and exciting the curiosity of the natives". Such a comment invites two remarks: first, Wu did not value the missionary gesture because it symbolized an attempt to adapt to the Chinese life-world, but because it was the right and rational choice. Second, this advocacy of Chinese clothes as being somehow superior to the Western costume was quite original in the intellectual landscape of the time—especially among the reformist intelligentsia.

Indeed, the idea of reforming the official dress code had been in the air since China's defeat of 1895 against Japan (Finnane, 2007, p. 69). At the end of the Qing dynasty, many official figures had advocated the abandoning of the Manchu-style official dress (Rhoads, 2000, p. 65). The idea was to rejoin the international standards, notably in diplomatic life. At that time, "even seemingly unimportant differences of tradition and custom, such as dress or diet, sometimes presented obstacles to non-European countries in their quest for 'civilized' status" (Gong, 1984, p. 20). Chinese intellectuals could also take inspiration from their Japanese neighbours, who had soon understood that they needed to abandon their kimonos to accomplish their diplomatic objectives. In his comments about the Iwakura Embassy—the first official diplomatic mission after the Meiji Restoration—Gerrit Gong (1984) notes that

> [i]t took only one appearance before President Grant of the United States on 4 March 1872 to convince them that Western custom dictated Western styled dress, not silk and satin court kimonos. The group did not appear publicly in kimonos again. (p. 179)

The Chinese were facing an even deeper problem, as the official haircut—the queue, mocked in the West as a "pigtail"—was the source of much ridicule and criticism. At the beginning of the twentieth century, many revolutionaries had cut off their queue and started adopting Western-style clothes as a means of distancing themselves from reformists. However, cutting one's queue was not always a revolutionary gesture. It was, for instance, needed for Chinese immigrants who had to blend in within their host countries. It is this situation that led Wu Tingfang to write two memorials to the throne.

The first memorial, written in October 1909, while he was still in the United States, recommended that the hair be cropped but "the costume should by no means be changed" (Wu, 1910, p. 309)[118]. On the matter of clothes in particular, Wu's line of defence was built on three main arguments. First, he used a political argument, as he considered the costume as "being part of the government institution" (Wu, 1910). The question of what to wear held a specific place in Chinese political history. In the *Analects*, Confucius eulogized Guan Zhong 管仲 (720–645 B.C.) on the grounds that, without him, the Chinese would be wearing a barbarian haircut, and buttoning their clothes on the wrong side (Confucius, XIV, p. 17). Furthermore, according to the *Book of rites* (*liji* 禮記), specific clothes were assigned to certain functions and certain rituals. Later on, in the Imperial administration, "the identification of servants of the state with the state itself was partly established by a dress code" (Finnane, 2007, p. 25)[119]. Wu noted that "the Chinese costume dates from ancient times and *attains pre-eminence in the reigning dynasty* [emphasis added]" (Wu, 1910, p. 310). He added that each country had its own history of clothing, and that uniformity on Western standards would not be welcome. On the contrary, the queue was something of "China alone", and therefore should be dismissed. Because the Chinese who lived abroad were still concerned by the regulation on haircuts and clothing—it is in their names that Wu wrote his memorial—one could read this political argument as a form of cultural defence. However, Wu's obvious attempt to flatter the Emperor (see the added emphasis above) may encourage us to read this defence differently. Wu was probably implying that the Chinese Emperor's kingship was still universal, and as such the Chinese would have to abide by Chinese law whatever country they found themselves in. This idea also had a great deal of charm because it suggested a form of extraterritoriality of Chinese law and customs at a time when Chinese authorities could not judge foreigners living on their soil. As these political features would, however, disappear in the second memorial, which was written a year after, it is my impression that they were more rhetorical than argumentative.

The second argument concerned the appropriateness of Chinese clothing to the climate and the passing of the seasons: "With thin wrappers, close garments, short sleeves and long breeches, it ensures a variety of suits all seasons and affords convenience in dressing" (Wu, 1910, p. 310). This point will again be repeated in Wu's later writings about clothing. And finally, the third argument was economical. Western

---

**118**  I was not able to locate the original text and therefore used the English translation published in *The North-China Herald*.

**119**  On how clothes displayed a sense of hierarchy among officials in late Imperial China, see for instance Garret (1990, pp. 19–32), or more substantially Garret (1994), which give an illustrated panorama of clothes worn in China since the 14th century.

clothes were considered "costly" and of poor manufacture, as they "must be replaced a year". Still flattering his reader, Wu noted that "the Government places its wealth among the people and can ill allow it to be imperceptibly sapped away" (Wu, 1910, p. 310). About a year afterwards, Wu renewed his memorial and again stressed these economic and practical arguments, while the political dimension slowly faded away (Wu, 1993, pp. 358–359).

His memorials were received but not heard by the reigning dynasty. However, it was soon to collapse, and the birth of the Republic in 1912 changed the environment in various ways. As Finnane notes, "the fall of Qing dynasty marked a vestimentary as well as a political rupture in China" (Finnane, 2007, p. 15). Within a few days after the uprising that would lead to the birth of the new regime, journals started advertising Western clothes and "civilized" haircuts (Finnane, 2007, p. 97). Western costumes started replacing the official robes for the inaugurations of Presidents of the Republic (Harrison, 2000, p. 50). On October 3, 1912, the Parliament issued a law on "ritual clothing" (*lifu* 禮服), prescribing Western-style clothing for both "great and common ceremonials" (*dali* 大禮 and *changli* 常禮), or "full formal, for major state occasions, and regular formal, for other official events" (Harrison, 2000, p. 58)[120]. Military clothing was also reformed (see 1915, notably pp. 1–5). When the law project was under discussion, much opposition was expressed toward this piece of legislation. The textile industry did much to lobby the Chinese Parliament into integrating a piece of garment that would use more traditional patterns and textiles produced within the nation's borders. In the end, the law specified that all these dresses ought to be made with Chinese fabric. But this was virtually impossible, since at that time China didn't produce the required materials – notably wooden cloth (Wu, 1914, pp. 158–160; Harrison, 2000, pp. 58–60), a point that Wu would raise in a new petition (Wu, 1993, pp. 613–614).

In his new text submitted to the President and the Parliament, Wu defended once again the Chinese dress and rejected the adoption of Western costumes for official events. First, he greatly echoed the sentiments of the textile industry, as it was "an

---

120 A graphic depiction of these costumes is available in Harrison (2000, p. 59); see also Finnane (2007, p. 96). A sketch of the clothes was added to the legal text (1915), and it is reproduced here (see Figure 5.1). I should note that this material lets us see a facetious aspect of Wu's defence of Chinese clothing. In *America*, Wu (1914) reproduced a sketch of clothes under which it is written that "the uniform suggested by the author and laid before the President and Parliament" (p. 160). However, this sketch corresponds exactly to the pattern presented in the law. It is also exactly the same picture that Harrison (2000) reproduced from the national archive. Elsewhere in *America*, Wu (1914) also reproduced a sketch of a woman wearing the clothes defined by the 1912 law (a picture also reproduced in Harrison's (2000) book). Furthermore, there are no mentions of a sketch in the original Chinese text of the petition. Therefore, one can infer here that Wu embellished his role in the history of Chinese clothing for his American readership. The picture he supposedly submitted to the Parliament was in fact the depiction of what the Parliament had already voted on.

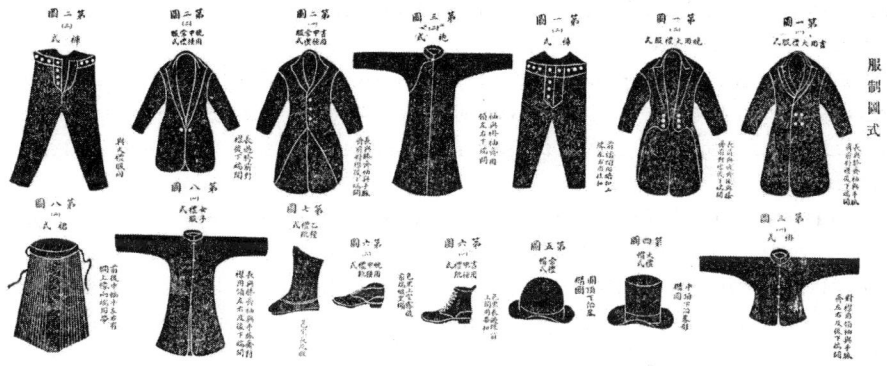

**Figure 5.1:** The patterns proposed by the Parliament for the new Chinese official clothes

urgent matter to protect the national products" (Wu, 1993, p. 615). He insisted on the fact that this law would endanger the national economy. He attacked the quality of materials chosen by the Parliament. He also mocked the legislators that had only given regulations on the mantels but not on what ought to be worn under them: "A ritual dress doesn't consist only of a coat" (Wu, 1993, p. 616). He would even give some of his own recommendations on the pattern, material, colour, length and items with which to pair these clothes. In the end, this new petition was really focused on the economical dimension of the problem. As always, Wu also added in a few remarks on the comfort of the Chinese dress.

Wu (1915) would reproduce this petition in the chapter he wrote on clothes in his *Plan to reform the Chinese Republic*. But here he explored the subject in still further depth. In the texts that he wrote in 1914—*The Plan, America and New Techniques*— a new theme emerged: the defence of Chinese clothing was explicitly linked to the question of civilization (Wu, 2014b).

## 5.2 Clothes as Markers of Civilization

In these later texts, Wu started writing that clothing is a distinctive feature of the state of being civilized (Wu, 1993, pp. 556, 613–614). While the people who lived in the age of savagery had settled for poorly designed clothes made from fur and feathers, the pattern and designs of their garments improved with the rise of civilization. While at first they only served to protect the body from the cold, they developed to fit new social purposes. The designs and patterns also evolved differently according to the nature (*xing* 性) of the many different people living on earth (Wu, 1993, p. 613). Unfortunately, aside from this reference to the classical Chinese notion of "nature", Wu did not develop at further length the problem of why clothes evolved differently in the different corners of the globe, an idea already present in the 1909 petition. He made a few comments on the changes in costumes introduced by foreign invaders, but he did not seem to pay much attention to the general history of clothing in China. He spoke mainly from and about the current situation that he was witnessing.

In *America*, Wu (1914) asked rhetorically: "Why do we dress at all?" His answer to this question was as follows: "First, I suppose, for protection against cold and heat; secondly, for comfort; thirdly, for decency; and, fourthly, for ornament" (p. 132). If the first two elements are also mentioned in his Chinese texts, the third appeared as being particularly addressed to his Western or Christian readership. This formulation is also interesting as he spoke of "decency", when the Chinese text said that we dressed to "avoid looking doltish" (Wu, 1993, p. 556). Wu continued in this section of the text and quoted the Finnish anthropologist Edward Westermarck (1862–1939)[121] to highlight the idea that clothes are nothing other than a convention. He noted:

> Competent observers have testified that savages who have been accustomed to nudity all their lives are covered with shame when made to put on clothing for the first time. They exhibit as much confusion as a civilized person would if compelled to strip naked in public. (Wu, 1914, p. 135)

It is as if he wanted to say that the fruit of Eden's garden had nothing to do with the matter[122]. Clothes are a convention of the civilized. Modesty is not inborn. Even though this point only continues for two paragraphs, it is important to note it, as it stresses what was already a key feature of Wu's discourse: his attempt to make constant reference to scientific literature. In his footnotes, Wu even linked the reader back to studies related to clothing, notably John Harvey Nickols's *The clothes question considered in its relation to Beauty, Comfort and Health* (as cited in Wu, 1914, p. 155), a book that he quoted to a large extent[123]. Wu (1914) approached the topic of clothes from a supposedly scientific angle.

---

121 However he did so probably through second literature, as he did not directly mention Westermarck's name. His quotation of the anthropologist is exactly the same as the one reproduced in the article "Costume" from the *Encyclopedia Britannica* of 1911 (p. 225).

122 It should be underlined that Wu had a serious Christian education background. Several members of his own family, such as his wife and maybe his mother, also deeply believed in the Gospel. However, as rightly noted by Linda Pomerantz (1992), "[i]n spite of subsequent Christian education and baptism as a Christian, he was always far more attracted to the secular traditions of the western world than to its religions, and he maintained that Confucian social values provided a better basis for stability than Christianity" (p. 26).

123 It is worth mentioning that only two books are given proper references, and are not only mentioned in passing in Wu's footnotes, namely this book by Nickols and *The Living temple* by Firstnames Kellogg. These were both pieces of literature that dedicated many pages to the matter of clothes in civilized societies.

Then, Wu (1914) dived into the question: the fourth issue of "ornament". However, he did not pursue a "cultural turn" here. In fact, Wu did not defend Chinese clothes as something that would be part of a tradition, a history, or even an identity. The passage starts with an odd sentence: "The fourth object of clothes is ornament, but ornaments should be harmless, not only to the wearer, but also to other people" (Wu, 1914, p. 136). The question of ornamentation was in fact only considered through the lenses of what is "safe" and "practical". Aesthetics was not even considered for its own sake. If Wu admitted that jewels and ribbons make "a pretty sight", he found that a long gown was not elegant, because it was not practical, as the following quotation shows, "on ceremonial occasions each lady has two page boys to hold the train of her dress" (Wu, 1914, p. 138). In 1901, Wu had already defended to an American journalist that in order to stop having women trails dragging dirt on the street, Americans should "use less cloth at the bottom and more at the top of the dress!" (as cited in The Editor, 1901, p. 265)—a comment that may also have partly to do with decency. To speak about Chinese women's clothes, he quoted a Chinese lady, Dr. Ya Mei-kin, who wrote that Chinese women were keeping their traditional clothes not for the sake of conservatism, but because it was a rational choice (Wu, 1914, pp. 139–140). In regard to men's clothing, Wu seemed to be of the same opinion, and, speaking from experience, he considered that despite not being "perfect", the Chinese clothes for a man were "superior to any other kind of dress" (Wu, 1914, p. 141). As such, if one reads only the chapter on "Costumes" in *America*, one could think that Wu was simply a utilitarian when it came to clothing. He quoted M. S. G. Nickols positively: "First use, then beauty" (as cited in Wu, 1914, p. 155).

Furthermore, there is another dimension of ornament that is important to Wu: namely, the social dimension of clothing. Selecting the appropriate piece of garment according to a certain situation was obviously an issue worthy of consideration for Wu. In the preface to *America*, where he enumerated the different kinds of people that can be found in America, he mentioned, for instance, "the women wearing 'Merry Widow' hats who are not widows but spinsters, or married women whose husbands are very much alive" (Wu, 1914, p. viii). Readers could be tempted to see this sentence only as a worthless anecdote, but anecdotes are the key elements of Wu's rhetoric[124]. This mention in the preface indicates to us that such behaviour was surprising, if not choking, for Wu. As a matter of fact, Wu complained several times that Americans

---

[124] Anecdotes may be regarded not only as a distinctive feature of Wu's writing, but also as an important means he used to take centre-stage in American public opinion. When browsing his interviews and how American newspapers pictured him during his stays, one cannot but notice that these texts are a patchwork of anecdotes regarding his life and practices. After his death, the first "biography" published on him was incidentally a simple collection of anecdotes concerning his life (Chen, 1925). At a more general level, "anecdote" appears as distinctive tropes of the Chinese way of theorizing. On the relation between anecdote, theory, and moral improvement in modern Chinese texts, see Davis (2016, pp. 33–38).

wore their clothes too casually. He wrote as having seen people wearing inappropri-
ate clothes for the social gatherings that they had been attending. He recalled having
witnessed "at the White House official receptions or balls in Washington, ... ladies
in ordinary dress" (Wu, 1914, p. 87). His uneasiness here could be explained by the
importance of the ritual system in China. Despite being educated in Hong Kong and
in the West, Wu's position in the imperial system may have made him more acutely
sensitive to this matter. He believed that one's costume ought to be appropriate to
the social situation, a position that led him to accept the idea that the Chinese diplomat ought to wear Western clothes "in order to avoid curiosity, and for the sake of
uniformity" (Wu, 1914, p. 160)[125]. In fact, he admired the Japanese, who would dress
like Westerners when negotiating in politics, but who continued to wear traditional
kimonos at home. To return to the petition, the problem was partly that the dress put
forward by the parliament was too loosely defined according to the etiquette of social
gatherings (Wu, 1993, pp. 616–617). By clothing oneself in a certain manner and for a
specific occasion, one showed how civilized one was.

## 5.3 Transculturality and Hygienic Normativity

Having noted these different elements, it appears that the question of what to wear
was central to Wu in his understanding of civilization[126]. A civilized person could not
go wandering about in the world, dressed as he liked—it was a social and health-
related issue. It is important to note here that Wu never put forward the defence of
Chinese clothes as an attempt to defend a specific feature of China or an identity
opposed to the colonial West. Except for the brief remarks in the 1909 memorials—
remarks written at a time when the Confucian ritual system was still a key element
of the Chinese polity—dresses were not integrated into a political discourse about
distinction. The word "civilization" was not even used in an ethnographical sense.
Despite Wu's attempts to frame the distinctive features of Americans through comparison with the Chinese, he did not oppose the former to the latter in an essentialist
manner. As a matter of fact, in his analysis of both the Chinese and the Americans, he
often considered that neither the former nor the latter were right to do as they did, and
that a middle ground ought to be found between the two positions. For instance, in

---

125 However, Wu never did so when he was in this position.
126 Clothing is not, of course, the only entry point that Wu (1914) deployed to discuss the question
of civilization. In chapter 12, titled "American versus Chinese Civilization (continued)", he notably
proposed over many paragraphs issues related to the problem of nationalism. He engaged in a line of
argument that nationalism went against the very principles put forward by the West in her proclama-
tion of "Civilization". He also defended the moral superiority of the Chinese over the Westerners, in a
flowery language that is also full of funny remarks.

his eyes, American lacked manners, while the Chinese were too formal, but "a blend of the two would give good results" (Wu, 1914, p. 107).

Wu was negotiating what I have called a "transcultural modernity". Instead of locating "Civilization" with a capital, or what a contemporaneous reader could understand as "modernity", within one specific culture—the West—Wu elaborated a narrative of civilizational displacement. In antiquity, the Orient civilized the West. In the last centuries, it was the West that showed new paths to the ideals of Civilization. But Wu (1914) was "tempted to say that", in the future, "Asia will have to civilize the West over again" (p. 181). What Wu implied in between the lines in this statement was that there is such a thing as progress—he is completely embedded in an evolutionist discourse—but this progress is not the progress of one sociopolitical and cultural entity on a universal ladder of "Civilization", as a competition between countries in a race for modernity. Rather, he charted progress as the course of history, a history enfolded by exchange and circulation between entities located within it. As such, when Wu wrote that "the Chinese have a civilization of their own" (Wu, 1914, p. 40), he wished not to lock up China in her otherness, with her specific values, but on the contrary insisted on the fact that she could be a global actor in the dialogical realization of modernity. As a matter of fact, Wu was a "transculturalist" to borrow a term removed from Aoileann Ní Éigeartaigh and Wolfgang Berg (2010, p. 11). He transcended a given culture to explore new horizons and produce a cohesive way of life and *Weltanschauung*, that acted as a junction between different life-worlds. Moreover, it is here that he gave much attention to petty or disregarded social practices such as clothing. Clothes are neither simply a "representation" of values, nor a "transformative instrument". Wearing a tuxedo does not immediately turn you into a modern civilized citizen. However, it does relate to one's understanding of a key element of modernity: *weisheng* 衛生.

Although one cannot find an equivalent to this concept in Wu's English prose, he noted in Chinese that "clothes relate altogether to the problem of *weisheng*" (Wu, 1993, p. 556). This term has often been translated into Western language by "hygiene". However, it encompasses a larger semantic field than this. Furthermore, it also conveys a normative ethical sense. The word finds its original sense in traditional practices of "protecting one's life" (the literal translation of the term) and "nurturing one's life" (*yangsheng* 養生). It referred to "a 'way of health', which depended heavily on knowing how to restrain oneself from indulging in food, drink, or sexual excess, on knowing the right time and place for sitting, sleeping, getting up, moving, eating, and drinking" (Messner, 2015, pp. 236–237; see also Rogaski, 2004, pp. 22–47). *Weisheng* was a real concern for Wu. With the many elements presented in his book *New Techniques to prolong life*, Wu (1914/1993) was proposing to prolong human life and fulfil all of its potential. He was claiming that with proper techniques and a mind at ease, man could live up to 200 years—a claim unfortunately not corroborated by his passing away at the early age of eighty. This was, incidentally, not an eccentricity from a scholar influenced by the Taoist alchemy of old. Many of his references were coming from newly theorized "healthy practices" in the West, such as vegetarianism[127]. Wu also actively promoted his theories on *weisheng* in the society. The *weisheng* association (*sushi weisheng hui* 衛生會) that he established in Shanghai in 1911 was an important sociopolitical actor that encouraged the ban of dangerous products, such as drugs, alcohol or tobacco (Pomerantz, 1992, pp. 188–190). Wu was completely in symbiosis with the eugenic discourse of his time. At this level, he also participated in a broader attempt to nationalize and modernize the Chinese body (Liu, 2013). Modernity and nationalism implied an improvement of bodily practices: creating a healthy citizen was a step on the way to the creation of a healthy nation. As such, the case of Wu completely fit in the academic literature available on the subject. The concept of *weisheng* or hygiene served as a historical landmark in the modernization of society, a process that Ruth Rogaski has denoted as "hygienic modernity" (Rogaski 2004). Indeed, *weisheng* was a key element of the civilization discourse (Messner, 2015).

It has been shown that the core of Wu's defence of Chinese clothing was not an identity question but a matter of hygiene and safety. While he often insisted on the fact that Americans have poor health and that they easily catch cold (e.g. Wu, 1914, p. 78) he kept on pointing to the fact that Chinese dress changes with the seasons, making it a better defence against the environment. In the passage about "ornament" in *America*, Wu directed much thought to the problem of the safety of one's own body. Clothes are meant to protect a man from certain adverse meteorological conditions and changing temperatures without impeding his life, a term here understood as much in the sense of one's day-to-day activities as in the sense of one's biological existence. It was this last element that led him to a full denunciation of Western clothes as dangerous. According to him, "ladies' dress ... sometimes endangers their lives". In this connection he relates the extraordinary story of a young girl which was propelled in the air by a strong gust of wind that went under her clothes. He also abjured the tight corset binding the waist. He felt "confident that physicians will support [him] in [his] belief that the death rate among American women would be less if the corset and other tight lacing were abolished" (Wu, 1914, pp. 132–134). He even insidiously encouraged women to fight against this type of clothing in the context of the suffragette movement.

Wu's references to the corset are especially interesting because they also show how deeply infatuated Wu was with Western writing. In her biography of Wu, Linda Pomerantz (1992) suggested that Wu may have been deeply influenced by American social purity reformers such as John Harvey Kellog. Like them, Wu "became an advocate of vegetarianism and other 'modern' hygienic practices as a way of cultivating superior morality in individuals and ultimately, in nations" (Pomerantz, 1992, p. 128). Kellog's book, *The Living Temple*, published in 1903, certainly had an enormous impact

---

127 There is here a striking similarity with Mohandas Karamchand Gandhi (1869–1948) who also discovered vegetarianism in the West.

on Wu, especially in regard to eating practices. But clothes were also of importance. In this book, one can also find an entire chapter dedicated to clothing (Kellog, 1903, pp. 338–362). The lexicon and the arguments are quite similar to the ones put forward by Wu. They both gave much attention to the question of waist constriction. Yet, there is one small discrepancy that is worth underlining. Kellog wrote that "just as the Chinese women make their feet ridiculously small by compression, so the American woman makes her waist absurdly narrow in the same way" (Kellog, 1903, p. 347). This was an important comparison that can be found in many texts of the American doctor. He pictured the corset as the symbol of the "savage of fashions", and spoke of "the barbarity of popular modes of dress". For him too, clothing was linked to a certain idea of civilization. However, we do not find the foot binding comparison in Wu's writing. In fact, there is not even one reference to foot binding in any of Wu's English writing. It is as if this particular issue did not exist. As such, Wu's defence of Chinese clothing and bodily practices also functioned through some "small" omission[128]. Mentioning foot binding would not have helped his message, in his defence of the view that China was a civilized country and not a semi-civilized one. His discourse defended Chinese clothing but through the codes and argument of the American purity reformers.

One should therefore note that the wish to preserve Chinese clothing, and on the contrary, to reform American clothing, was profoundly linked to his ideology of political reformation, that implies the establishment of normative practices. By defending the civilized dimension of the Chinese dress, he indirectly wanted to impose it. He never said outrightly that Americans ought to clothe themselves like the Chinese did, but he did hint toward the necessity of a clothes reform. As early as 1901, Wu had started encouraging "a great convention" to "have your [American] experts decide what is the best in dress for women, and for men as well" (The Editor, 1901, p. 265). In 1914, the problem "to decide as to the best form of dress for men and women" would become global and concern all countries on earth (Wu, 1914, pp. 142–143). He endorsed a normative attitude toward clothing: the political power, advised by specialists, should take a decision on the topic. His liberalism and valorization of a free choice stopped at the door of the closet. However, when Wu presented to both his American and Chinese readerships his techniques to prolong life, or his recommendation on clothing, he probably did not realize that he was inviting a form of coercion and normativity that would govern the body. Of course, it would be conceptually anachronistic to criticize Wu for not taking into account what Michel Foucault has framed as the *biopouvoir*. Yet, in his defence of the Chinese life-world with its distinctive clothes, social and body practices, which he presented as being more civilized than the practices of Westerners, he was taking a step back in regard to the liberty of

---

**128** Foot binding and the Manchu queue are in fact among the most important elements discussed in the academic literature about the transformation of clothes in Modern China. On the former, cf. Ko (2007).

individuals. He did not see any contradiction here. This is a logical issue that could let us rethink what Wu understood by the concept of liberty.

Last but not least, Wu understood civilization under definite principles. Wu was absolutely insensible to the Baudelairian conception of modernity as a time that passes by, and a way of putting valour in what is new. This point is quite obvious in his rejection of fashion: "Fashion is the work of the devil" (Wu, 1914, p. 131). At that time, fashion in the West was giving much importance to the "Orient". Many couturiers were clearly inspired by Asian clothes, as for instance in 1906, when the great French couturier Paul Poiret even designed an evening coat named "the Confucius" (Steele & Major, 1999, p. 72). Yet Wu rejected the very idea of fashion. The criteria of what is a good piece of clothing were simply established in terms of usefulness and rationality.

Wu remained committed to a universalist approach to civilization. What differentiates one person from another was his ability to understand and to adapt his practices according to the standards of civilization. However, he distinguished several dimensions within the term "civilization", and it is there that he established a hierarchy:

> From a material point of view we have certainly progressed, but do the "civilized" people in the West live longer than the so-called semi-civilized races? Have they succeeded in prolonging their lives? Are they happier than others? I should like to hear their answers. (Wu, 1914, p. 164)

Americans may have had a civilized economy and political systems, and yet their everyday practices were far from being so. They failed to pay enough attention to the question of health and happiness (or living well), two concerns that were crystallized in Chinese under the term *weisheng*. In an important article on the topic of civilization, Prasenjit Duara (2001) has noted that, in their defence of their civilization, Asian intellectuals had to build their argumentation according to two possible strategies. In his view, "[o]ne strategy [was] to rediscover elements identical to civilized society within the suppressed traditions of civilization. ... Another strategy identifie[d] the opposite of the West in Asian civilizations" (Duara, 2001, p. 108). Yet, in the case of Wu, we are in between those two strategies. Or to put the matter more exactly, he moved from the latter to the former, in order in the end to dismiss the very distinction from East and West. Chinese clothing was valued without reference to any "Chinese traditions" such as Confucianism or Taoism.

## 5.4 Conclusion

Harrison (2000) has rightly noted that, in Republican China, "the primary values that Western dress and etiquette were seen as representing were liberty and equality" (p. 54). However, it seems that Wu, who shared these two values and who encouraged their adoption in political life, did not see them in the Western costume. In his 1909 memorial to the throne, he had theorized a distinction between the queue as a "form" and "the spirit" that lays behind it. They were supposed to be two separate things. For him, Chinese in foreign lands could cut their queue, and still harbour a strong sense of nationalism and respect to the emperor. Clothing was different. It was no simple form, but the real embodiment of a distinctive feature of civilization: *weisheng*. Being *weisheng* did not simply mean to import the hygienic standards of the West; rather, it meant living a civilized life in ethical and medical terms. But in matters of clothing, Westerners were absolutely not embodiments of *weisheng*. Therefore, they should not be copied. And in the end, Wu would not be the only Chinese intellectual to criticize Western costumes in English with such a discourse. About two decades later, Lin Yutang 林語堂 (1895–1976) would develop almost the same arguments in a chapter entitled "The Inhumanity of Western Clothes" (Lin, 1998, pp. 261–266).

To conclude, one of the distinctive features of Wu's thoughts and deeds, that the problem of clothing has put forward is that, for him, living in the modern world did not mean negotiating one's position between two clearly defined cultural life-worlds. He did not set the issue in the form of an evaluation of what was positive and negative in each culture, in order to later propose a synthesis or to even go cherry-picking. He simply navigated through very blurry cultures with only a compass indicating the direction to Civilization, a promised land that was obviously not in the West. De-territorializing the idea of civilization from the West was a powerful narrative that gave much agency to China. By such reasoning, he thought that China was able to lead the world upon a new and perhaps clearer path to Civilization. As a matter of fact, the problem of China was that she was over-civilized in certain aspects and under-civilized in others. This is a comment that also bears some truth for Wu at the personal level. Despite the fact that he was often mocked by his American contemporaries, he may have been on some aspects more modern or civilized than them. He had, for instance, many pro-feminist remarks to say. He also condemned the violence perpetrated against animals for entertainment. On hunting, he noted that "no country, with the least claim to civilization, should allow such [a] thing, and our descendants will be astonished that people calling themselves civilized should have indulged in such a wholesale and gratuitous atrocities" (Wu, 1914, pp. 264–265). Yet, he did not arrive to these ideas by proposing a fusion of cultural horizons, but by locating every people in a grand narrative that transcends cultures. "Civilization" prevailed over cultural comparison.

# References

Bénéton, P. (1975). Histoire de mots: culture et civilisation. Les Presses de Sciences Po.

Chen, C. [陳此生] (1925). 伍廷芳軼事 [Wu Tingfang yishi; Anecdotes about Wu Tingfang]. Hongwen tushuguan.

Cheng, W. (2000). Politics of the Queue: Agitation and Resistance in the Beginning and End of Qing China. In B. Miller (Ed.), Hair: Its Power and Meaning in Asian Cultures (pp. 123–142). State University of New York Press.

Craik, J. (1994). The Face of Fashion: Cultural Studies in Fashion. Routledge.

Davis, G. (2016). Knowing How to Be: the Dangers of Putting (Chinese) Thought into Action. In L. Jenco (Ed.), Chinese Thought as Global Theory (pp. 29–54). Suny Press.

Ding, X. [丁賢軍], & Zuofeng, Y. [喻作鳳] (2005). 伍廷芳评传 [Wu Tingfang pingzhuan; Biography of Wu Tingfang]. Renmin chubanshe.

Duara, P. (2001). The Discourse of Civilization and Pan-Asianism, Journal of World History, 12(1), pp. 99–130.

Finnane, A. (2007) Changing Clothes in China: Fashion, History, Nation. London: Hurst & Compagny.

Fisch, J. (1992). Zivilisation, Kultur. In O. Brunner et al. (Eds.), Geschichtliche Grundbegriffe, Historisches Lexikon zur politisch-sozialen Sprache in Deutschland (Vol. 7, pp. 679–774). Klett-Cotta.

Flüchter, A. & Schöttli, J. (2015). The Dynamics of Transculturality: Concepts and Institutions in Motion. Springer.

Garret, V. (1990). Mandarin Squares. Oxford University Press.

Garret, V. (1994). Chinese Clothing: An Illustrated Guide. Oxford University Press.

Gong, G. W. (1984). The Standard of 'Civilization' in International Society. Oxford University Press.

Harrison, H. (2000). The Making of the Republican citizen: Political Ceremonies and Symbols in China, 1911–1929. Oxford University Press.

Kellog, J. H. (1903). The Living Temple. Good Health Publishing Company.

Ko, D. (2007). Cinderella's Sisters: A Revisionist History of Footbinding. University of California Press.

Lin, Y. (1998). The Importance of Living, originally published in 1938. Reynal & Hitchcock.

Liu, W. (2013) "Moralized Hygiene and Nationalized Body: Anti-Cigarette Campaigns in China on the Eve of the 1911 Revolution", Cross-Currents: East Asian History and Culture Review, 2 (2), 213–243.

Mazlish, B. (2004). Civilization and its Content. Stanford University Press.

Messner, A. C. (2015). Transforming Chinese Hearts, Minds, and Bodies in the Name of Progress, Civility, and Civilization. In M. Pernau (Ed.), Civilizing emotions: concepts in nineteenth century Asia and Europe (pp. 231–249). Oxford University Press.

Ní Éigeartaigh, A., & Berg, W. (2010). Exploring Transculturalism: A biographical approach. Verlag für Sozialwissenschaften.

Pauka, M. (2012). Kultur, Fortschritt und Reziprozität: Die Begriffsgeschichte des zivilisierten Staates im Völkerrecht. Nomos.

Pernau, M. (2015). Civilizing emotions: concepts in nineteenth century Asia and Europe. Oxford University Press.

Pomerantz-Zhang, L. (1992). Wu Tingfang (1842–1922): Reform and Modernization in Modern Chinese History. Hong Kong University Press.

Republic of China (1915). 禮制服章 [Lizhifu zhang; Texts regarding ritual clothing]. In 中華民國法令全 [Zhonghua Minguo Faling daquan; The complete collection of the laws and ordinances of the Republic China]. Shangwu Yinshuguan.

Rhoads, E. (2000). Manchus and Han: Ethnic Relations and Political Power in Late Qing and Early Republican Chian, 1861–1928. University of Washington.

Rogaski, R. (2004). Hygienic Modernity: meanings of health and disease in treaty-port China. University of California Press.

Steele, V., & Major, J. S. (1999). China Chic: East meets West. Yale University Press.

Tanaka, S. (1996). Japan's Orient. Rendering pasts into history. University of California Press.

Tarlo, E. (1996). Clothing matters: Dress and Identity in India. Hurst & Compagny.

The Editor. (1901). "Minister Wu on Dress Reform", Good Health, 36(6), 265–266.

Wu, T. (1901). "The Causes of the Unpopularity of the Foreigner in China", Annals of the American Academy, January 1901, 1–14.

Wu, T. (1903). "Chinese and Western Civilization", Harper's Monthly Magazine 106, 190–192.

Wu, T. (1910). "Removal of the Queue", The North-China Herald, 5 August, 309–310.

Wu, T. (1914). America through the spectacles of an Oriental Diplomat. Frederick A. Strokes Company Publisher.

Wu, T. [伍廷芳] (1993). 伍廷芳集 [Wu Tingfang ji; Collected Works of Wu Tingfang]. Zhonghua shuju.

Zhang, L. [張禮恒] (2015). 三世外交家伍廷芳 ["Sanshi" waijiao jia Wu Tingfang; Wu Tingfang a diplomat between three worlds]. Fujian jiaoyu chubanshe.

Susanne Marten-Finnis

# 6 Spaces of Otherness and Desire.
## *Ballets Russes*—Artist-Animators—Ethnographic Enquiry

### 6.1 Russian Modernism in Paris

In 1910, a small group of exceedingly clever and progressive Russians arrived in Paris to challenge conventional art forms. These included the *Ballets Russes* impresario Sergei Diaghilev, whose troupe revolutionized the nature of the ballet; the dancer and choreographer Vaclav Nijinsky; the scenic artist Léon Bakst, whose décor changed Paris *haute couture* and London *savoir vivre*; and the young Igor Stravinsky, whose music was already being described as marking a most iconic moment in European Modernism. No other group established the Russian presence in Western Europe so emphatically.

The previous year, 1909, had seen the *Ballets Russes* performance of the *Polovtsian Dances* from *Prince Igor*, which had the effect of whipping up the Parisians into a state of sheer hysteria. Never before had their senses indulged in such scintillating music, such barbaric hues, and such rebellious gestures; never before was sown the germ of destruction, the spirit of unrest, or the embodiment of lawlessness (Woodcock, 2009, p. 56). No one in the West had seen men dancing like this. The imagined warrior-dancers from the Asian steppes and the tent-and-tribe approach of the ballet's decorator, Nicholas Roerich, fuelled the audiences' fantasies of Russia as a country that was inhabited by barbaric tribes with an innate passion for dancing.

During the years to come, this perception was consolidated by the physical representations of the Oriental Other, as displayed in the so-called Oriental Ballets staged between 1909 and 1912, for which Léon Bakst created the costumes and decoration. These Ballets established in the West a strong association of Russia with the cosmopolitan cities of her Asiatic periphery, rather than the orientation towards European values that had been broadcast by Tsar Peter I. The motivation for such self-presentation has been attributed to the impresario Sergei Diaghilev, who maintained that Western adulation of oriental exoticism on stage was easier to translate into money than Russian folklore.

Diaghilev's argument may have satisfied contemporary journalistic curiosity. But can it stand up as a complete explanation for the correspondence between *Ballets Russes*' corporeal characters and scenic display, and Western perceptions of Russia?

This article will challenge the view established among scholars and cultural ambassadors that Diaghilev's decision to flag Russia's Oriental Other was a mere PR act aimed at raising funds abroad for his theatrical venture. Departing from Russia's spectacular appearance on the Western stage in 1909, and from both a historical and a geographical perspective, it will trace an alternative path of Russian self-presentation and self-identification back to the realms of the ancient Silk Route, to classical Byzantium, and the more recent Russian annexation of Turkestan during the 1860s.

It will deconstruct the symbolic practices displayed by the dancers and decorators of the *Ballets Russes* and relate them to the transfer of knowledge initiated by Russian scholars, especially ethnographers, in the last third of the nineteenth century, between Russia's Christian-dominated centre in Europe and the recently acquired Muslim lands of her oriental periphery in Asia.

The body of knowledge that Russian Orientalist scholars mined from mapping this periphery in their ethnographic enquiry was largely ignored by Tsarist politicians. Instead, it led to a remarkable artistic upsurge during the Russian Silver Age, 1898–1914, when the Oriental theme came to permeate both the decorative and the performing arts. The strong responses that this theme elicited provided more than a momentary refuge from everyday life. Rather, as it will be argued here, it served various groups of artists as a platform abroad to rehearse a revamped identity, in which the unconditional pre-eminence of European culture broadcast two hundred years before by Tsar Peter I became increasingly challenged by Russia's Asiatic counterparts.

Now, Foucault classified as "counter-spaces" those spaces which lie outside the ordinary, promising liberation and illuminating a passage for our imagination (Foucault, 1986, as cited in Johnson, 2006). They contest the familiar spaces, and entry to them, Foucault maintained, is never straightforward. These counter-spaces will be discussed in the last part of this chapter ("Open Sesame"—The Transcultural Perspective of Russian Ethnographic Enquiry) in light of Foucault's (1986) "Theory of Other Spaces". The advantage of such an approach is evident for two reasons: firstly, it reveals the novel research methods of Russian Orientalist scholars, especially ethnographers, and their transcultural perspective that enabled them to unlock and access these counter-spaces. Secondly, it opens up a more differentiated perspective on the view expressed by Edward Said (1978) that knowledge has been used to subjugate the Other, together with his claim that Britain and France were the pioneering nations to launch Orientalist scholarship (pp. 1, 4–9).

## 6.2 Russia on Display: Symbolism and the World of Art Group

The symbolist approach that the *Ballets Russes* dancers and decorators displayed on the Paris stage originated from the *Mir Iskusstva* (*World of Art*) group. This group had grown out of a circle of friends around the duo of Sergei Diaghilev and Léon Bakst, who met regularly in 1890 (Kennedy, 1977, pp. 340–341). Among them were Alexandre Benois, Dmitri Filosofov, Ivan Bilibin, Nicholas Roerich, and others. Connected by a mutual interest in the arts and a passionate love of music, theatre, opera and ballet, the *World of Art* members launched their own magazine in 1899, in which they assailed the low artistic standards of the obsolescent *Peredvizhniki* (Wanderers)

School, and promoted artistic individualism and other principles of Symbolism and Art Nouveau. In contrast with Realism, which stressed the relevance of an artefact to its social and political environment, Symbolism, prevailing during the 1890s until about 1910, provided an escape from everyday reality. It was concerned with the evocation of mood and subjective vision and used the intrinsic elements of painting, such as colour, line and light, as well as fabrics, for highly emotional and psychologically nuanced expression.

The group advocated an integrative approach to art and, like other Symbolists, worshipped Wagner's concept of a *Gesamtkunstwerk* in the sense of a total work of art, thereby referring to a theatrical performance in which all its constituent parts—music, singing, acting and scenery—were merged together into a perfect unity (Bridgman, 1989). Specifically, they absorbed the idea of music as a determining element that dictated gesture and action on the stage, thereby evoking an emotional response.[129]

The Parisians were among the first to discover this new form of integrated art, and although the dancers and decorators of the *Ballets Russes* had pretended to learn from the people in Western Europe, it turned out that they actually became their teachers. Hence, the *World of Art* group's contribution to European Modernism lay not only in the renewal of bodily display in the classical ballet, thanks to the choreography of Michel Fokine, Vaclav Nijinsky, Leonide Massine, Bronislava Nijinskaia and George Balanchine, as well as the modernist music of Russian composers such as Igor Stravinsky and Alexander Borodin, but also in the important changes they brought across in the early 1910s. These changes had to do with costume design, stage décor and fashion. Diaghilev (1910) confirmed that

> in our classical ballet, dancing is only one of the show's components. The evolution that we initiated in classical ballet deals maybe less with the specific domain of dancing than with the other aspects of the show. It deals primarily with sets and costumes. (Diaghilev, 1910)

Perhaps the best example to demonstrate the *Ballets Russes*' influence on Paris couture is the set design of *Scheherazade*, with its main colour scheme being a combination of peacock green and spicy blue, as applied in Mughal-style paintings. It inspired the jeweller Cartier to set emeralds and sapphires together for the first time since the Mughal emperors (Buckle, 1979, p. 171).

While the Parisians of the day were inspired by the variety of costumes, their London counterparts were conversely fascinated by the stage sets, especially the space management and lighting effects implemented by Diaghilev's designers, and most of all by the "Asiatic barbarism of colours" (Komissarzhevskii, 1922, p. 11), which they proceeded to introduce into their homes. The various examples of exoticism proclaimed by the *Ballets Russes* had an impact on domestic interiors of upper

---

129 On the concept and programme of the magazine *Mir Iskusstva*, see Shestakov (1998).

middle-class London, and were later claimed by the *Art Deco* of the 1920s. The British art critic and stage designer Osbert Lancaster confirmed that "the pale pastel shaded drawing-rooms that had reigned supreme on the walls of Mayfair for almost two decades were replaced by a riot of barbaric hues – jade, green, purple, every variety of crimson and scarlet, and above all, orange" (Lancaster, 1948, p. 58).

The *Miriskussniki* looked backward rather than forward, although their reveries were not confined to any historical epoch. Apart from Egypt, Greece, and Versailles, they cultivated a strong interest in the Middle Ages and what they perceived as primitive cultures (Bowlt, 1998, pp. 25–26), as is demonstrated by their deep reverence for Mikhail Vrubel, whose art they regarded as the incarnation of an archaic, barbaric force, a world of ancient myth and elemental unity (Bowlt, 1998, pp. 25–26). Another feature of their artistic aesthetic was their Orientalism; for them, the East represented a beautiful daydream, which they contrasted with the mundane prose of life (Kiselev, 1989).

Yet, the idea of Russia looking to the East, rather than to the West, for self-understanding was much older than this. For a start, it had been suggested by Russia's bicontinental geography bridging Europe and Asia. The central element of this understanding was the notion of soil. As cartographic accuracy improved, more and more interpretations of geographical space were articulated in Russia. Among the variety of contrasting geopolitical self-images that Russia invented for herself as a particular geographical entity stretching between Asia and Europe, the notion of soil retained its importance. This stood in contrast with Europe, whose geographical realm since the fourteenth century was increasingly identified with the spirituality of Christendom, and a civilization and an ideology that claimed cultural and political exclusiveness, and, ultimately, superiority (Bassin, 1991).

Russian Orientalism (Schimmelpenninck Van Der Oye, 2010) had thus been prevalent within Russian thought for centuries, until the reign of Tsar Peter I saw the emergence of two rather contradictory viewpoints on Russia's relationship with both Asia and Europe. On the one hand, Peter acknowledged an orientation towards European values and the unconditional pre-eminence of European civilization. On the other hand, the expeditions he sent out to southern Siberia in order to explore the area in search of natural resources and new trade routes unearthed the existence of the Scythians, a nomadic people who populated the grassy steppes of Eurasia over 2,500 years ago. The discovery of their lifestyle in the 1720s, and the creation of more accurate maps, led to greater interest among scholars in the geography and history of these peoples populating the Eurasian plain, and subsequently led to the establishment of a new framework for exploring self-identity that negotiated both European and Asian civilizations.

Due to the exploration of the vast region stretching between northern China and the Black Sea, the identification with the Scythians and the idea of Russia-Eurasia as a third continent, entered into the picture Russian consciousness. As a result, modernizing Imperial Russia saw an increasing number of artists and intellectuals looking to Asia rather than Europe for both self-identification and inspiration. This led to a remarkable artistic upsurge during the Russian Silver Age, 1898–1914, when the oriental theme came to permeate both the decorative and the performing arts.

As a case in point one can look to the archaeological expeditions of Nicholas Roerich and his revelation of the Scythian style. Others refer to music and dance (Riasanovsky, 1967, pp. 44–45), as Russian composers were also looking to the East for spiritual inspiration. They identified a broad spectrum of shared patterns with Asiatic folk cultures and ethnographic affinities with Slav, Finno-Ugric, Tatar-Turkic and Mongolian elements (Riasanovsky, 1967, pp. 44–45). Rimsky-Korsakov, Borodin, Stravinsky and Balakirev all sourced their music from Russian folk songs picked up in the Caucasus region, utilizing the so-called five tone or Indo-Chinese scale that was characteristic of the music of the Finnic and Turkic tribes of the Volga basin, Mongol music and the music of Siam, Burma, and Indo-China. They were also inspired by an intonation, which mostly used (what they understood to be) minor scales and chords, in order to imitate moods that vary between grief, thoughtfulness and unexpected musical drama. The rhythm of the Russian songs tended to link Russia to Asia and to separate it from the other Slavs and the West. The same held to be true for dance. In contrast with the West, the Russian folk dance was not based on the dancing couple, a man and a woman holding each other and dancing together, but represented a variety of elements and a freedom of improvisation that was also found among the East Finns, the Mongols and Turkic and Caucasian peoples (Bassin, 1991).

With the Russian Seasons, these features travelled to Paris. While dancing and especially ballet-dancing, as an art form, had long enjoyed extensive royal patronage, Russia was bankrupt after their loss of a naval war with Japan (1904–1905). Diaghilev was thus on the lookout for new ways of attracting interest and support. Success did, however, not come immediately. When, in 1906, Diaghilev organized the first exhibition of Russian paintings at the Paris Salon d'automne, the response from the Parisian public was only lukewarm. The French people had no use for the paintings of Russian artists, who were attracted by the romanticism of the past. Diaghilev correctly gauged this situation and subsequently directed the activities of his contemporaries Bakst, Benois, Roerich, Golovin, Anisfeld, Goncharova and Larionov towards one goal—the theatre. This new departure was entirely successful. During the years to come Russian decorative art produced a revolution in stage settings (Levinson, 1924). According to the French art critic Léon Moussinac, the masterpieces and refinement of Russian stage art and décor (Lukomskii, 1922, pp. 3–4) animated "a marked influence on French decorative art that, languishing in its search for a new style, suddenly discovered the splendours of colour, and bore witness to an infatuation, which created the Ballet Russes fashion" (Moussinac, 1922, pp. 51–52).

Most spectacular and successful in this respect was the Orientalist theme that early twentieth-century Ballets Russes productions displayed when they stepped into the European arena. This involved the display of the body and a strict costume code, as it is exemplified on the couverture du programme of the 1910 Saisons Russes (Figure

**Figure 6.1:** The display of a warrior wearing a turban and sabre evoked images of the Eurasian Steppe and the Mongolian advance into pre-modern Europe [Couverture du programme from Ballets Russes in 1910, Paris, Bibliothèque de l'Arsenal]

6.1) and, along with it, music, décor and colour rhythm. The display on the cover of the dancing sabre-man took place long before Aram Khatchaturian composed his Ballet *Gayaneh* in 1942, which included the famous *Sabre Dance*, with its middle section sourced from an Armenian folk song.

*Ballets Russes* spectators in Paris, it seemed, had expected a show that would reflect the European world of St. Petersburg (Woodcock, 2009, pp. 55–61) and the history of the Russian ballet. Instead, Russian composers, choreographers, dancers and decorators had merged their talents to display a completely different image of their country that revealed a strong identification with Russia's own Orient in Asia. The resulting spatial ambiguity held a huge attraction for the Parisians and will be discussed in the next section.

## 6.3 Spatial Clarity and Spatial Ambiguity: The Case of "The Firebird"

Ivan Bilibin's illustrations for the fairy-tale of *The Firebird* (Figures 6.3–6.7) and the sketches he made for the *Golden Cockerel* (Figure 6.2) pinpoint a clear separation between a familiar home and a threatening other space beyond. The latter shows a man wearing the traditional Russian-style *kosovorotka* after having travelled from a Russian homeland to a far-away land beyond in the Orient. This setting is indicated by the paisley-patterned tent as well as the cape and the headdress of a female Tamerlane.

The contrast between Russia's Christian West and the Muslim-dominated East appears even more accentuated in Bilibin's illustrations for the tale of *The Firebird* of 1906. In this work, he illustrates the Russian homeland with onion towers, and contrasts them with an architectural counter-space of mosques and minarets topped with the Red Crescent, and a city wall typical of the oriental city (Figures 6.3 and 6.4).

The same applies to the way that Bilibin portrayed people's faces and dress codes, as shown in Figures 6.5, 6.6, and 6.7 below. On the one hand, there are trusted figures with friendly faces wearing the traditional Russian clothing, laughing and dancing in a typically Russian environment. These he contrasts with people wearing turbans and sabres, caftans and burqas, behind which their faces are hidden. A peaceful space in the Russian woods, with Ivan's talisman, the grey wolf, is contrasted with a bellicose counter-space that shows Ivan on his knees before the sultan, his hands tied together behind his back. The sabres in the foreground and background convey the dramatic immediacy of a threatening counter-space in the Eurasian Steppe, that Russian readers would be able to associate with the Mongolian menace of pre-modern times. Only the bird is allowed to move freely between the two worlds and times: between a friendly home and a threatening land beyond, between modern and medieval times.

**Figure 6.2:** The tent

Note. The tent indicates the mobility of fast-moving, mounted, nomadic tribes who travelled lightly. Their tents are strongly related to the lightness of textiles rather than to the solidity of stone houses; the Bodom[1] pattern points to an Oriental origin. The cape and headdress of the (female) Tamerlane are contrasted with the man dressed in a typical Russian-style kosovorotka.

---

[1] In oriental design, *Bodom* or *Kalamfur* motifs refer to the almond or paprika pepper. Both were thought to afford protection from the dangers of the steppe due to their pepperiness and bitterness respectively. When the pattern became commercialized it travelled to Norwich for the factory production of shawls, and then further to Paisley, where the eponymous pattern was made (see Karpinski, 1963).

**Figure 6.3:** Architectural space in the Russian homeland

**Figure 6.4:** Architectural counter-space typical of the oriental city

Note. Skazka ob ivane-tsrevitche i o serom volke [Fairy-tale about Ivan Tsarevitch and the grey wolf. N. Gol'ts & N. Shchepetov (Eds.) Moskva, 1969, without pagination].

However, the clear differentiation between the familiar and other spaces presented by Bilibin in 1906 is no longer prevalent in the costume and stage designs that Nicholas Roerich and Léon Bakst created for the *Ballets Russes* productions in Paris three to four years later. This is notably the case for the *Polovtsian Dances* and the Oriental Ballets (*Cleopatra*, *Scheherazade*, *Thamar*, *Le Dieu Bleu*), in which the boundaries between a Russian homeland and an Oriental counter-space become blurred, with no obvious marker of differentiation to be discovered between East and West. Noteworthy in this respect are Borodin's *Polovtsian Dances*, with their authentically ethnic Ikat-garments made in Uzbekistan (Figure 6.8), which Roerich had bought from Central Asian traders on the markets of St. Petersburg (Woodcock, 2010, p. 143).

Another example is *Cleopatra*, staged in 1909, with Bakst's display of the dancer Ida Rubinstein's exotic beauty against a colourful background of an Eastern setting, and her role as the Egyptian Queen, who gradually discarded her veils and gave herself up to the ecstasy of love before the eyes of the audience (Figure 6.9).

*Cleopatra* played on a European perception that essentially saw the ethnically, geographically, and intellectually varied Muslim world as monolithic and easy to define, specifically by way of representations that were heavily loaded with sexual connotations that gendered the East as feminine and the West as masculine (Nance,

**Figure 6.5:** Peaceful Russian wood

**Figure 6.6:** Homely Russian space

**Figure 6.7:** Threatening environment of the Other

Note. The figures clearly differentiate between a homely and a threatening environment of the Other. Skazka ob ivane-tsrevitche i o serom volke [Fairy-tale about Ivan Tsarevitch and the grey wolf. N. Gol'ts and N. Shchepetov (Eds.) Moskva, 1969, without pagination]

**Figure 6.8:** Costume designs by Nicholas Roerich for the dancers in Borodin's ballet Polovtsian Dances from Prince Igor

Note. Water colour on paper. State Pushkin Museum of Fine Arts, Moscow [Alston Purvis et al., The Ballet Russes and the Art of Design, Singapore, 2009, p. 157]

2009 p. 3). The outstanding success of Cleopatra convinced both audiences and Diaghilev that the *Ballets Russes* should concentrate on sexy Orientalism, a total theatre of great music, superb dancing, thrilling design and simple themes of sex and violence.

Bakst's visual response to the Oriental theme made the display all the more exciting to the viewer, and it was in this light that Diaghilev asked him to create the costume and set design for *Scheherazade* which was performed a year later (Spencer, 1993). What could have been more obvious than exploring the roots of Oriental folk tales with their powerful images, and staging the myth of the storyteller-queen Scheherazade of *One Thousand and One Nights* (or *The Arabian Nights*, as the tales are known in the English-speaking world)?

Cairo forms the backdrop for most of the *Arabian Nights*; the core of the narrative was created here and reflects a social environment that is essentially cosmopolitan in nature. This cosmopolitanism—understood as a community linked by the *here* and *now*, rather than the age-old attachment to a place or tradition—held a great attraction for European audiences. They were fascinated by the situations of urban life as

**Figure 6.9:** Bakst's design for Cleopatra

**Figure 6.10:** Bakst's design for the Red Sultan (Scheherazade)

Note. Alston Purvis et al., The Ballet Russes and the Art of Design, Singapore, 2009, pp. 62 and 166.

they were displayed in the *Arabian Nights*, with their illustrations of intrigues, love stories and merchandise, and an Orient that promised sexual space, a voyage away from the restrictions of European Christianity and therein providing an escape from the dictates of bourgeois morality (Kabbini, 1986, p. 67). The tales provided for European readers unparalleled depictions of luxury, ease, and magical self-transformation in a robust language that matched the promise of consumer capitalism.

This was the context of Cleopatra and indeed of *Scheherazade* (Figure 6.10), which was also staged by Rubinstein. Furthermore, if *Cleopatra* had introduced Bakst's originality and splendour to the Parisians, then *Scheherazade* confirmed his uniqueness in their minds. Had such a riot of colour, such mountains of cushions, such enormous golden lamps and such a breaking of the Ten Commandments ever been seen as it was seen in *Scheherazade*? (Birnbaum, 1916) The ballet prompted critics to use words like "sensual", "erotic" and "sumptuous", conveying an image of desire that remained inseparably linked to the *Ballets Russes* performances staged before World War I.

In these performances, artistic licence took precedence over any semblance of chronological or cultural accuracy, and the Oriental space of the *Ballets Russes* referred to geographical areas in India and East of Suez (Schouvaloff, 1997, p. 39) (today generally referred to as "Levantine"), whose boundaries eventually reached Russia's own Orient. This is also the case in *Thamar*, the barbaric legend from the Caucasus that was based on Lermontov's ballad *Thamara* and Balakirev's symphonic poem to the music for which Fokine created a choreographic drama in one act. Bakst wrote the libretto and did the sets and costumes, which the Russian Seasons chronicler, Valerian Svietlov, found "imposing and, as always, extremely effective. ... But, for all that, I don't like them", he said, criticizing both their Orientalism as untypical of the harsh spirit of the Caucasus or of the even harsher Daryal[130] and Bakst's treatment of *Thamar* in the following way: "Under the guise of a Georgian Queen one senses the image of a woman of the Art Nouveau age – devilishly beautiful, dangerous, seductive" (as cited in Diaghilev Festival, 2011, p. 14).

Bakst seemed to have created costumes that reveal and adorn the human body rather than cover it. They resembled the poses and silhouettes that Bakst had found on excavated Greek vase paintings and sculpture when he visited Crete in 1907 (Marten-Finnis, 2013). At this time, his contemporaries claimed that his attraction to antiquity became so all-absorbing that Bakst became obsessed with it *"jusqu'au délire"*, as Alexandre Benois once put it (Auclair, 2009). Bakst's travels to Greece were essential in arousing his interest in archaic art. Upon his return, he points out that "the Greeks valued the beautiful, nude human body above all. ... For them", he goes on, "heroes, gods, goddesses, and simple mortals were mere excuses to celebrate the uncovered body" (R. Johnson, 1990).

---

130 The Daryal is a 1200 meter-high pass in North Georgia, Central Greater Caucasus.

This attitude remained prevalent even in Bakst's costume design for *The Firebird*. Although this ballet was originally purported to be a Russian neo-nationalist work of art (Benois, 1910), Bakst still sourced material for it from epics from the East. Staged only a month after the stunning success of *Scheherazade*, after Diaghilev had commissioned Bakst to redesign Golovin's original costumes for the key figures of *The Firebird*, the Tsarevna and Ivan Tsarevitch, they acquired elements that do not feature in the original Russian folk tale. At the time, Bakst's redesigned costumes made the French theatre critic Henri Ghéon gush with admiration: "How Russian that is!" (Ghéon, 1910). The "new" firebird (Figure 6.11) displayed some obviously incongruous details that Bakst sourced from Hindu folklore: the long golden plaits and a crown characteristic of *Garuda*, a divine bird in Hindu and Buddhist mythology, and the long fingernails which alluded to a dance from Siam that Bakst had watched, together with Fokine, and that was performed by the Royal Siamese Court in the main Imperial theatres of St. Petersburg in October 1900 (Misler, 1989).

In Bilibin's sketches, the *Firebird* belonged to a Russian homeland, and is imprisoned in a far-away land. The hero has to undertake a long and dangerous journey in

**Figure 6.11:** Bakst's costume design for The Firebird

order to bring her back. On his way, he has to overcome a number of obstacles symbolizing borders. The origins of Bakst's *Firebird*, in contrast, lie in the East. As but one example of this, she flies in to the rescue in the opposite direction, from a land of the Other.

One reason for this change of perspective may have been the fact that Bilibin's sketches were aimed at the Russian reader, while Bakst's set designs were for the foreign spectator. Whereas in Russia *The Firebird* had enjoyed renewed celebrity through the late nineteenth and early twentieth centuries—as an embodiment of pure, heartless, unattainable beauty (Taruskin, 1996, p. 556) among Symbolists in general and particularly among *World of Art* members—it held an additional attraction for European audiences as a magical figure that could assist or impede the hero's quest. Moreover, it could help to unearth a treasure or liberate a captured maiden, as it was part of the typical supra-natural domain that formed a hallmark of the *Arabian Nights*, with their angels, demons and precious talismans who could utter magic formulas. Jinns, fairies, birds and sorcerers are all part of the strange world that exists in the *Arabian Nights*. As strangers to Western fantasies and repertoire, these creatures were very appealing to European audiences.

In order to incorporate them into the *Ballets Russes*' *Firebird* performance of 1910, a new plot had to be invented that differed from the original Russian tale. In that new plot, a young girl is kidnapped by a monster, a so-called Dev, and carried off into a far-away land to his castle on a high mountain, surrounded by thick walls without gates. There lies a beautiful enclosed garden within, as depicted on the cover of the Berlin-based Russian magazine *Zhar Ptitsa* [The Firebird] (Figure 6.12). The scenario that this exotic abduction evoked could also have been sourced from oriental epics: the narrative of a magic garden, the supra-natural creatures such as Kastcheï, the wicked ogre and his demons, and the *Firebird* as a good fairy, the former ogre and his demons are wicket, the Firebird is benevolent, but none of them is human (Evans, 1933, p. 9). This was the latter plot, for which Diaghilev had commissioned Igor Stravinsky to compose his suite. During the years to come, *The Firebird* became one of the most regularly performed ballets in the repertoire of the *Ballets Russes*, and it was praised for its marvellous synthesis of music, choreography and scenery.

This cover design rendered by Georg Schlicht points to further typical characteristics in a number of oriental tales (*Usbekische Märchen*, transl. 1978, p. 76), depicting a counter-space, a world beyond, in which water and trees, greenery or simply the colour green play an important role (Taube, 1994, pp. 17–18).

Water and shade are also among further themes of the oriental garden. In contrast with European concepts of the garden's rich fertility, which are often fuelled by the ambition to master nature (the French approach) or to accommodate nature (the English approach), the oriental garden is associated with health, wealth and contemplation. Unlike English and French gardens, which are designed to be walked around in, it is a cool green place for rest and reflection. This is not surprising, since it constitutes a floral and faunal oasis in a hot and arid region, where human settlement

**Figure 6.12:** The Firebird displayed on the cover of the illustrated magazine Zhar Ptitsa (7, 1922) [Kunstbibliothek Berlin]

is usually more fragile than in the more favourable climatic conditions of Europe. In the oriental environment, plants implied water, and water meant healing, beauty and wealth. A garden could therefore be a protected, or even a heavily guarded place on or near mountains, a real treasure house. It was often surrounded by rivers or other obstacles such as massive walls, making access difficult (*Usbekische Märchen*, transl. 1978, p. 76).

Gracing the seventh issue of the international Russian magazine *Zhar Ptitsa*, which was issued between 1921 and 1926 in Russian, German and English (Marten-Finnis, 2012, pp. 82–87) and distributed in Western Europe and the Americas, Schlicht's design revisited the *Firebird* production of 1910 and established among Western audiences an image that—unlike Bilibin's sketches—has little to do with the grey wolf and the Russian fairy-tale forest. Rather, Schlicht's Firebird flies in from an enchanted world in the East, and moves from ancient to modern times. This enchanted East is depicted as being full of a love of ornament, emphatic in colour and vigorous lines. The foreground shows a tree with stylized pomegranates, rather than apples, as they were illustrated by Bilibin in 1906 (see Figure 6.3). As a native fruit to the region between modern-day Iran, Pakistan, Afghanistan and northern India, the pomegranate is a symbol of well-being, fertility and abundance. Its symbolism has survived in the tapestries and rug making traditions of Central Asia. Schlicht's firebird also appears oversized. Her tail feathers display blue hearts that dissolve into bold and green motifs resembling the *Mihrab*[131], thereby creating an ornament typical of Muslim architecture. The background is filled with light green clouds, whose abstract shapes resemble spirals associated with the sun and its yearly circle. Or, perhaps they revisit the apotropaic images of *Bodom* and *Kalamfur* (see footnote 2). The latter were also typical of oriental fabrics that had frequented Russian markets and often served to inspire Schlicht's work (Raev, 2018, p. 14). Hence, the eponymous name of the Berlin-based illustrated magazine was loaded with a double meaning: it was to remind German readers of the *Firebird* production performed by the *Ballets Russes* a decade earlier, and it pinpointed the thousands of immigrants from the East, who in the early 1920s made Berlin the first capital of Russian emigration. Rather than being despised by their German hosts as uninvited guests, the editor of *Zhar Ptitsa* might have fancied that he could see these emigrants illuminating their environment with a glow in the sense of "Light from the East"—*ex oriente lux*. At least, he indicated as much in his mission statement when he pointed out that:

> our magazine's name is *Zhar Ptitsa*—what an unusual sounding name to a German ear! What does it mean? Shall we call it "Firebird" or even "Glowbird." Mind you, it is not the legendary phoenix from the German fairy tale, but rather its Russian sibling, lighting up with its glowing plumage a dark garden at midnight. On its wings, it carries the dream of nostalgia, joy and desire![132]

Hence, while in the original Russian fairy-tale, the firebird was to guard the garden and the golden apple tree, the new firebird came from a country of pomegranates, and was to transform a far-away and threatening otherness—perhaps not quite into a space of desire—, but surely into a less dangerous place, one that was still beyond familiar boundaries but which was populated by trustworthy figures who ensure that good defeats evil. In this way, both Bakst's scenic decoration of 1910 and Schlicht's cover design for *Zhar Ptitsa* in 1922 celebrated a counter-space that may have been bewitching, but it was no longer presented as a space of the threatening Other.

---

**131** The *Mihrab* imitated a niche in the wall of a mosque indicating the direction of Mecca, the direction that a person should face when praying.
**132** "Zum Geleit [Introductory remarks]." *Zhar Ptitsa* no. 1 (August 1921) 1 (translation by S. Marten-Finnis).

## 6.4 "Open Sesame"—The Transcultural Perspective of Russian Ethno-graphic Enquiry

A very similar notion served Michel Foucault as a departure when he defined such other spaces as "counter-spaces"—or "heterotopias", derived from the Greek words *heteros* (other, another) and *topos* (place) (Foucault & Miskowiec, 1986). According to Foucault, the oldest example of heterotopias that are capable of juxtaposing in a single real place several sites that are in themselves incompatible, is the sacred space of a Persian garden (Foucault & Miskowiec, 1986, p. 25). Yet, Foucault did not borrow his concept from the Persian garden of oriental epics, but from hard medical science, where it refers to particular tissues which grow in places where they are not normally found, without, however, being diseased or threatening. Access to such counter-spaces, Foucault maintained, is never straightforward. While in Antiquity, it may have required the incantation of a magical formula to assist the hero's quest to gain entry to the Other's treasure house, in modern times their unlocking depended on a particular body of knowledge.

Foucault's conceptualization of these counter-spaces—or heterotopias—provoked a variety of responses across a number of academic disciplines, of which two stand out: firstly, that the reference to other spaces was seen as a stage in processes of modernization, and, secondly, that their representation may articulate a certain form of resistance (P. Johnson, 2006), rebellion or protest.

Both of these concomitant implications apply to the *Ballets Russes'* dancers, artists, musicians and choreographers. But we may ask how far outside the ordinary were the spatial qualities that they displayed in their productions when they were paying homage to an oriental aesthetic. To what extent were the claims of critics in Russia at Home justified in saying that the *Ballets Russes'* bodily and decorative display which they exported to the West was a false image of Russia as a semi-oriental nation? What was the nature of the discrepancy between Western perceptions of Russian dancers and decorators as Orientals, and their self-understanding as Europeans and Orientalists (Järvinen, 2008), in the sense of having learned about the Orient, rather than in being a part of it?

There are no straightforward answers to these questions. "The Parisians expected from us a certain amount of barbarianism", Diaghilev once said in an interview (as cited in Kahane & Wild, 1922, p. 23). His self-imposed mission to delight western audiences with what he called "Russian art" was thus a question of economic capital, after the period when ballet-dancing no longer enjoyed tsarist patronage. Moreover, the oriental counter-space that *Ballets Russes'* productions displayed in the West had not just sprung from the mood of Diaghilev, Stravinsky or Bakst. Rather, they were part of a broader trend at the time in the performing and decorative arts across Europe. Yet, they were made more effective as they perfected the Wagnerian approach to a *Gesamtkunstwerk*, which implied the orchestrated sensual unity and the harmonization of the whole of bodily, scenic and musical display, in order to ravish the audience's eyes and ears simultaneously.

Such effects indeed reinforced Western stereotypes about a life of oriental ease, sensuality and despotism in an exotic East. Most importantly, however, it disclosed a familiarity with the East that revealed both authenticity and empathy. This attitude greatly differed from the civilizing mission which prevailed among Western audiences, with their body of knowledge about the Orient being derived from the two biggest colonial networks before the twentieth century. Hence, on the one hand, *Ballets Russes* productions endorsed an ideological position according to which Russia, like France or England, could be divided into two major components: a homeland or metropolis that belonged within European civilization, and a foreign, extra-European oriental periphery, whose chaos legitimized imperial authority and colonialism on a par with the Western powers. On the other hand, however, they disclosed an appreciation of the East that was worshipped, rather than despised or seen as being in need of improvement.

Now, it will be argued here that the reasons for these contrasting attitudes lie in the tools that the *Ballets Russes*' masters of enchantment had at their disposal, in order to open up the counter-space for their Western allies, and share with them the commodities of a treasure house that the latter were unaware of. But first, let us ask: What were their tools to gain entrance? How did they surmount the obstacles that might have hindered access? And, most importantly, where did they source the material culture for their display?

The answers to these questions lie in a combination of factors, of which the nature of access forms the key determinant. Hence, the first premise lay in the nature of Russia's bi-continental geography. In contrast with the maritime powers, Russian colonization of Asiatic territories took place over land; she did not possess far-flung overseas colonies, but nearby lands supporting a regulated interaction. These lands could be reached via the continental bridge, with no major bodies of water separating them. The ongoing transfer of people, ideas and material culture that this facilitated led, for instance, Uzbek silk merchants to markets in St. Petersburg and Russian government envoys to the areas of the ancient Silk Route. This interaction fuelled not only imperial expansion and artistic imagination, but also academic curiosity and a more systematic scholarly study of this Orient by means of ethnographic enquiry.

This enquiry had picked up speed following the Russian annexation of Turkestan in the 1860s. Tsarist politicians and scholars agreed that, as a civilized empire, Russia had a duty to investigate the complex and poorly understood customs of her subjects in order to understand their ways of life and beliefs, and to better integrate them into the nation as a whole. As a result, the role of ethnographers, linguists and geographers rose to prominence during the Era of the Great Reforms initiated under the reign of Tsar Alexander II (1855–1881), and ethnographic studies turned out to be the premier science in the Russian Modernization project of Turkestan (Tolz, 2011, p. 32).

During the decades to come, the building of national communities occurred alongside the building of commercial relations with Central Asia. Economic ambitions had to give way to political concerns, of which the policy of citizen-building [гражданственность], i.e. the integration of Russians and non-Russians into a unified community of staunchly Russian citizens, was the principal element.

On this issue, a number of recommendations came from those who claimed to know the oriental borderlands best. Specifically, this meant academic Orientalists (Tolz, 2005), scholars studying the individual aspects of Orientalism together with its aesthetic assumptions, religious quests, intellectual priorities and political entanglements and their interrelationships. Themselves being influenced by the impact of nationalism on European scholarship, Russian Orientalists, in particular those of the Rozen School[133], developed their own "national" approach to Oriental Studies, rather than reproducing the agenda of scholars in Western Europe, a fact which is all the more remarkable as none of the Rozen disciples was ethnically Russian. This ethnic background may have influenced their views on how to reconcile national aspirations and imperial governance within the Russian context. Moreover, it was perhaps this very condition that enabled them to work out an approach which allowed them to adopt and benefit from their transcultural perspective on the oriental heritage of Russia's new subjects' nationalities.

In particular, these scholars argued in favour of forging a multi-ethnic community (Jersild, 1997, p. 101; Yaroshevski, 1997, p. 61), based on the principles of civic nationalism in the sense of social integration and shared political values and responsibilities among Russians and non-Russians, despite their linguistic, cultural and religious otherness. Their path towards citizen-building foresaw cultural and political integration through educational projects shared with the subject nationalities in the eastern and southern borderlands, with the aim of fostering among the country's entire population a sense of community and unity. The educational projects that they put forward entailed a transfer of knowledge that was based on shared learning and teaching with the native population, with the help of textbooks specifically developed in their own languages about their local histories and heritage. This way, they claimed, the latter would first develop an ethno-cultural awareness of their own fatherlands (маленкая родина), which would eventually bring them closer to the Russian motherland (большая родина). In other words, minorities should not be simply incorporated into the Russian Empire, but they should become more knowledgeable of their own histories and heritage. The appreciation of the ethno-cultural particularities in their

---

133 Referring to the disciples of Viktor Romanivich Rozen (1864-1908), Professor of Arabic at the Faculty of Oriental Languages at St. Petersburg University: Vasilii V. Bartold (1869-1930), Nikolai Ia. Marr (1864-1934), Sergei F. Oldenburg (1863-1934) and Fedor I. Shcherbatskoi (1866-1942); see Tolz (2011, pp. 13–19).

native homelands would make them more loyal towards pan-Russian concerns and bring them into a better position to contribute to pan-Russian activities.

The proposed policy of citizen-building under Tsar Alexander II was to be achieved through political and spiritual fusion, being built on common, state-derived (Russian) civic norms and shared between Russians and indigenous people. This process of learning from indigenous people about their cosmopolitan heritage gained a huge body of systematic and factual ethnographic knowledge acquired about an East that was approached as neither enchanted nor threatening, but simply as an area of systematic scholarly research. However, these scholars also encountered a problem. It lay not in any lack of willpower among the indigenous people to cooperate, but rather in the lack of any interest shown by the Tsarist politicians who disregarded the knowledge mined in Russia's new Orient. Yet, it still had a great impact on the period during which it was articulated in Late Imperial Russia, as it was appreciated by Russian artists who delighted in oriental otherness. Similarly to trends prevailing at the time in Western Europe, Russian artistic creativity reflects a fascination with the country's Oriental lands, that was captured by a remarkable artistic upsurge during the Russian Silver Age. Driven by the spirit of rediscovering indigenous culture and a search for inspiration, artist-experts, illustrators and photographers were dispatched on expeditions and discovery tours to the Empire's remote areas both in the East and in the West.

The best-known example of this ethnographic inquiry is El Lissitzky's expedition of 1915–1916 to Jewish heritage sites along the Dnepr River, sponsored by the Jewish Ethnographic Society in St. Petersburg. A second example is Baron Guenzburg's ethnographic expedition to the Jewish Pale of Settlement supervised by An-Sky in 1911–1914. Driven by the spirit of rediscovering indigenous culture, similar expeditions established themselves within the Russian artistic milieu. Depending on their instigators, expeditions enjoyed either private or state sponsorship. Some of them were documented in glamorous art editions, lavishly decorated with sketches, paintings and photographs. These inspired members of the Russian *avant-garde*. For example, Gontcharova, Larionov, Malevitch and Tatlin were all affected by the recognition and analysis of "primitive art", such as icons, painted trays, *lubok* (coloured woodcut) and *vyveska* (sign-boards). It was this orientation toward primitivism, together with abstract forms of expression that shaped the Russian *avant-garde* art. As mentioned in the first part of this article, a fascination with the East is particularly obvious in the oeuvre of the St. Petersburg-based *World of Art* group that shaped *Ballets Russes* productions on the Paris stage.

This stage came to be the first platform for Russian artists to demonstrate to an audience abroad that a successful transfer of knowledge had happened between Russia's metropolis and her recently acquired Muslim lands. While the recommendations of imperial Orientalist scholarship were followed up only much later by the Nationalities Policy of the new Bolshevik elites, the dormant knowledge obtained during the last third of the nineteenth century about Russia's new subjects inspired

Russian artists and initiated among them a mental move to, and incorporation of, Asia. On the one hand, their celebration of oriental counter-spaces on the stages of Western Europe and the Americas thus provided evidence that *someone* had made use of the observations foreseen for the project of citizen-building by the Tsarist government, although they had rehearsed abroad something that was indeed foreseen to be rehearsed at home: a renewed identity construct resulting from the expansionist policy of Imperial Russia, following her annexation of Turkestan. On the other hand, this celebration can also be seen as a self-fulfilling prophecy, as it redeemed a resolution proclaimed almost one hundred years earlier with regard to Russia's interest in her oriental periphery, in particular Bukhara, the former backbone of the ancient Silk Route, as the city that the Russians considered its most important economic and political stronghold. As early as in 1820, a Russian envoy[134] had pinpointed the heralding mission which Russia had taken on for herself, with the aim of contributing to both popular enlightenment and scholarship in the countries of Western Europe:

> The fact that Russia has, for more than a century, been in touch with Bukhara, Khiva and Tashkent has made foreigners demand from us information about these cities, and rightly so. They require comprehensive knowledge from us separating solid facts from rumours, ... interesting news about the mores of the lands [нравах земел]. This is why we have to do our best to enlighten our fellow citizens about the historical and geographical facts in this part of the world. Who – if not us Russians – would inform European scholarship about present-day Bukhara. (Iakovlev, 1824 pp. 50–52)

As it turned out, the *Ballets Russes* became the facilitators of this heralding mission when they incorporated the knowledge gained by imperial ethnographers. A proposed policy of indigenization that had set out to learn from and teach the indigenous people resulted in observations about an oriental counter-space. These observations were now transformed into the subject of appreciation and worship by audiences in Paris, and later on London and other Western cities. The culture of admiration they sowed abroad still saw Russia as an exotic entity, outside Europe, while the legacy of Russian Orientalist scholarship has yet to be fully appreciated.

## 6.5 Conclusions

In conclusion, I have deconstructed the symbolic practices displayed by the dancers and decorators of the *Ballets Russes* and related them a) to the oeuvre of artist-animators in the St. Petersburg-based *Mir Iskusstva* group that had outsourced themselves to Paris, and b) to the process of the transfer of knowledge initiated by Russian

---

134 Iakovlev, a member of the Russian Embassy produced the first map of the city for Bukhara (as cited in Khanykov, 1848).

Orientalist scholars in the last third of the nineteenth century between Russia's Western Christian centre and the Muslim-dominated areas of her Southern periphery. By having recourse to Foucault's "Theory of Other Spaces", with its focus on the formal, spatial qualities of certain places that may appear as "both mythical and real", I have demonstrated that the scenic counter-spaces which were revealed on stage to Western audiences served Russian artists as an outlet for their own protest against the decline in funding by royal patronage. Subsequently, it became their first platform to rehearse abroad a revamped identity, in which the unconditional pre-eminence of European culture broadcast by Tsar Peter I, was increasingly contested by Russia's Asiatic counterparts and her mental shift towards Asia.

Spaces of otherness and desire—spaces outside the ordinary, being of oriental otherness in particular—have been part of European imagery ever since modern transportation improved access to the Orient. In contrast with the legends of ancient times, in which the discovery of a talisman or the incantation of a magical formula assisted the hero's quest to gain entry to the Other's treasure house, modern travellers required a particular body of knowledge for their act of unlocking. Whether the acquisition of this extended body of knowledge can be interpreted as an act of colonialism is questionable, as it differs from Edward Said's (1978) idea of Orientalist scholarship as it was carried out in the service of the empire. Whereas Said's (1978) focus on the maritime expansion of Britain and France suggests that the extended body of knowledge about the Orient signified a form of imperial control used to subjugate the Other (p. XIV), the approach to citizen-building recommended by Russian ethnographers demonstrates that the acquisition and transfer of knowledge across a continental bridge could also be a pragmatic act of cooperation, in which the will to understand (p. XIV) and to communicate was considered a prerequisite for dialogue, appreciation, academic reorientation and joint action (Holly, 1987).

Accordingly, the *Ballets Russes* productions could be thought of as stages in a mindful, disciplined and regulated process of confrontation between acquired and imagined knowledge about the Oriental Other that has been taking place since the eighteenth century, as Said (1978) pointed out with regard to the maritime colonial powers (p. 3). While the spatial ambiguities displayed by the *Ballets Russes* were to an extent recognizable to Western audiences, the Oriental Other was appreciated as an allegory, in the sense that they demonstrated a truth or moral by using symbolism. The *Ballets Russes*' masters of enchantment indeed applied such symbolism, as was conveyed by stories and visual images, with a level of impact on Europe that they could hardly have imagined when they rehearsed in Paris a revamped identity sourced from a newly discovered treasure house in Asia, rather than from the familiar fairy-tale forests of Europe. It was the charm of this contrast that inspired the noticeable shift in empathy, understanding and desire that characterized this chapter in European Modernism.

# References

Auclair, M. (2009, November 24–2010, May 23). Introduction to the Exhibition Les Ballets Russes, BnF. Bibliothèque-musée de l'Opéra, Paris.

https://www.artistikrezo.com/agenda/exposition-qles-ballets-russesq-au-palais-garnier.html

Bakst, L. (1909). The Paths of Classicism in Art. Apollon 3 (December 1909) 46–61. Retrieved from http://www.v-ivanov.it/apollon/apollon_03_1909.pdf

Bassin, M. (1991). Russia between Europe and Asia: The Ideological Construction of Geographical Space. Slavic Review, 50(1), 1–17.

Benois, A. (1910, July 18). Khudozhestvennye pis'ma: russkie spektakli v Parizhe: Zhar ptitsa [Letters on art: Russian productions in Paris: The Firebird]. In Rech.

Birnbaum, M. (1916, December). Léon Bakst. America as Host to the Ballet Russes. Vogue (15), 15–25.

Bowlt, J. (1998). Theater of Reason/Theater of Desire. The Art of Alexandre Benois and Léon Bakst. Thyssen Bornemisza Foundation.

Bridgman, E. (1989). Mir Iskusstva Origins of the Ballets Russes. In: Nancy van Norman Baer (Ed.), The art of enchantment. Diaghilev's Ballets Russes, 1909–1929 (pp. 26–43). Universe Books,

Buckle, R. (1979). Diaghilev. Weidenfeld and Nicolson.

Diaghilev, Serge [1910]. (2009 November 24–2010 May 23). Information board at the exhibition Les Ballets russes, BnF. Bibliotèque-musée de l'Opéra, Paris.

Evans, E. (1933). Stravinsky. The Fire-Bird and Petrushka Humphrey Milford. Oxford University Press.

Ghéon, H. (1910, August). Propos divers sur le ballet russe. La Nouvelle Revue Française, 20, 199–212.

Foucault, M., & Miskowiec, J. (1986). Of other spaces. Diacritics, 16(1), 22–27.

Holly, W. (1987). Sprachhandeln ohne Kooperation? Über den "kooperativen" Balanceakt beim Manipulieren. In: F. Liedtke & R. M. Keller (Eds.), Kommunikation und Kooperation (pp. 137–157). Niemeyer.

Iakovlev, P. (1824). Zamechaniia na fakty. Nekotorye svedeniia o Bukhare, napechatany v Oteches-vennykh Zapiskakh 1821 g. [Remarks about facts. Some evidence on Bukhara, printed in Otechesvennye Zapiski in 1821]. In: Sibirskii Vestnik (Vol. Ш, pp. 50–52). St. Petersburg.

Järvinen, H. (2008). The Russian Barnum: Russian Opinions on Diaghilev's Ballets Russes 1909–1914. In: Dance Research: The Journal of the Society for Dance Research (Vol. 1, pp. 18–41). Edinburgh University Press.

Jersild, A. L. (1997). From savagery to citizenship: Caucasian mountaineers and Muslims in the Russian empire. In: D. R. Brower & E. Lazzerini (Eds.), Russia's Orient (pp. 101–114). Indiana University Press.

Johnson, P. (2006). Unravelling Foucault's 'different spaces'. History of the Human Sciences, 19(4), 75–90.

Johnson, R. (1990). Bakst on Classicism: The Paths of Classicism in Art. Dance Chronicle, 13(2), 170–192.

Kabbini, R. (1986). Europe's Myths of Orient. Palgrave Macmillan.

Kahane, M., & Wild, N. (1922). Les Ballets Russes à l'Opéra. Hazan/Bilbiothéque Nationale.

Karpinski, C. (1963). Kashmir to Paisley. The Metropolitan Museum of Art Bulletin. New Series, 22(3), 116–123.

Kennedy, J. (1977). The Mir Iskusstva Group and Russian Art 1898–1912. Garland Publishing, Inc.

Khanykov, N. D. (1848). Opisanie Bukharskogo Khanstva (The Description of the Bukhara Khanate) St. Petersburg.

Kiselev, M. (1989). Graphic Design and Russian Art. Journals of the Early Twentieth Century. The Journal of Decorative and Propaganda Arts, (Russian Soviet Theme), 11(3), 50–67.

Komissarzhevskii, F. (1922). Russkoe iskusstvo v Londone. Tretie pis'mo iz Londona [Russian art in London. Third letter from London]. Teatr (Russian illustrated magazine issued in Berlin, 192–23), (14), 11.

Lancaster, O. (1948). Home Sweet Home. J. Murray.

Levinson, A. (1924). Russkoe Iskusstvo v Evrope [Russian Art in Europe]. Zhar ptitsa (Berlin), (12), 9–14.

Lukomskii, G. (1922, February). Itogi i zadachi russkoi khudozhestvennoi deiatelnosti zagranitsei (1919–1921) [Achievements and tasks of the artists in Russia Abroad]. Novaia Russkaia Kniga (Berlin), (2), 3–4.

Marten-Finnis, S. (2012). Der Feuervogel als Kunstzeitschrift. Žar ptica. Russische Bildwelten in Berlin (1921–1926). Böhlau.

Marten-Finnis, S. (2013). The Return of Léon Bakst. Slav Magic or Oriental Other. Journal of Modern Jewish Studies, 12(2), 276–296.

Misler, N. (1989). Siamese Dancing and the Ballets Russes. In: Nancy van Norman Baer (Ed.), The art of enchantment. Diaghilev's Ballets Russes, 1909–1929 (pp. 78–83). Universe Books.

Moussinac, L. (1922). La Decoration Théatrale. F. Rieder et Cie.

Nance, S. (2009). How the Arabian Nights inspired the American Dream, 1795–1935. The University of North Carolina Press.

Raev, A. (2018). Weltenwechsel. Der Deutsch-Russische Maler Georg Schlicht (1886–1964) zwischen Saratow und Eisenach. In: Catalogue of the exhibition on Georg Schlicht, Georg-Schlicht-Stiftung.

Riasanovsky, N. (1967). The emergence of Eurasianism. In: California Slavic Studies (Vol. 4, pp. 44–45).

Said, E. (1978). Orientalism. Pantheon Books.

Schimmelpenninck Van Der Oye, D. (2010). Russian Orientalism. Asia in the Russian Mind from Peter the Great to the Emigration. Yale University Press.

Schouvaloff, A. (1997). The art of Ballets Russes. The Serge Lifar Collection of theater designs, costumes, and paintings at the Wadsworth Atheneum. Yale University Press.

Shestakov, V. (1998). Iskusstvo i mir v ,Mire iskusstva' [Art and World in ,World of Art']. Slavianskii Dialog.

Spencer, C. (1993, May). Erotic Dreams. In Antique Collector (pp. 66–71).

Taruskin, R. (1996). Stravinsky and the Russian Tradition. A Biography of the Works Through Mavra: Vol. I. Oxford University Press.

Taube, J. (1994). Suzani. A Textile Art from Central Asia. With an Introduction and Text to the Collection by Ignazio Vok. Munich: Edition Vok.

Diaghilev Festival Les Saisons Russes XXI (Ed.). (2011, April 12–17). Program Thamar (at London Coliseum), p. 14. Copy in possession of author.

Tolz, V. (2005). Orientalism, Nationalism and Ethnic Diversity in Late Imperial Russia. The Historical Journal, 48(1), 127–150.

Tolz, V. (2011). Russia's Own Orient. The Politics of Identity and Oriental Studies in the Late Imperial and Early Soviet Periods. Oxford University Press.

Usbekische Märchen. (1978). Edited. and translated by K. Reichl. Studienverlag.

Woodcock, S. (2009). The evidence of the backcloth. In A. Purvis, P. Rand & A. Winestein (Eds.), The Ballets Russes and the Art of Design (pp. 55–62). The Monacelli Press.

Woodcock, S. (2010). Wardrobe. In J. Pritchard & G. Marsh (Eds.), Diaghilev and the Golden Age of the Ballets Russes, 1909–1929. V&A Publishing.

Zum Geleit [Introductory remarks]. In: Zhar Ptitsa no. 1 (August 1921).

Yaroshevski, D. (1997). Empire and citizenship. In D. R. Brower & E. Lazzerini (Eds.) Russia's Orient (pp. 58–79). Indiana University Press.

Barbara Ursula Oettl

# 7 ORLAN's Hybridizations: From Virtual to Literal Cyborg // From Mortal to Immortal Being

"Remember the future."
(ORLAN, 1998, p. 317)

To think about our future as carnal and transient human beings in a biopolitical and technohumanized age driven by medical, digital, technoscientifical and transcendental probabilities of life-enhancement, means at the same time to think about who we are and for how long. For the French-born multi-media and performance artist ORLAN remembering the future means zigzagging along a non-chronological timeline within her lifespan, putting into practice these promising and visionary biopolitical and technoscientifical prospects for us to be remembered in the future while the artist herself has already been through the various possibilities of *Giving Birth to Her Loved Self*, of breeding and cloning, of de-constructing and re-constructing, of virtualizing and immortalizing her body as well as her multiple selves.

One of her first photographic works with the punning title *ORLAN accouche d'elle m'aime*[135] from 1965 bears witness of the embryonic poetics of the birth-giving artist as metaphor for the artist's clone as a continuous subject in ORLAN's oeuvre.[136] The photo shows the artist from a bird's eye perspective with a mannequin emerging from between her naked thighs, thus hinting at her soon to follow doubles, her self-generating powers and the subsequent possibility of splitting—at least—into two, confirmed by ORLANs words: "Life is an aesthetic experience to be recycled. I have recycled bodies as the fundamental materials of life. I have made my body the tool for new and multiple embodiment." (ORLAN, 2010a, p. 118).

ORLAN's multiple embodiments eventually demand their own names. Born on May 30, 1947, as Mireille Suzanne Francette Porte in Saint-Étienne, France, she changed her name to ORLAN in 1962, fusing for the first time the juridical persona legally entering into society via birth certificate with her artist's self.[137] After her groundbreaking surgical performances (1990–1993) the artist reincarnated herself in 1993 as Sainte ORLAN by soliciting an agency to create a new name and logo for her and by commissioning a lawyer to petition her new identity and look with the

---

**135** *ORLAN Gives Birth to Her Loved Self*; the French *elle m'aime* (she loves me) in its homophonous reflection can be read as *elle même* (herself).
**136** ORLAN's oeuvre can be accessed over her web page (https://www.orlan.eu/).
**137** A birth certificate only gives evidence of the legal data of the child's parentage, never of the biological-medical facts.

Republic of France (ORLAN, 1998, p.326). When asked about the current state of her legally protected name the artist denies an answer: "So, I will not answer. My name is ORLAN, inter alia, and as possible, my name is written in uppercases." (ORLAN, personal communication, July 27, 2016).

The change of names is accompanied by the change of her appearance(s). After her third operation in 1990 ORLAN's *Official portrait in Bride of Frankenstein wig* refers to the myth of a cyborg-being that in our age of post-mechanical—i.e. in-vivo, in-vitro as well as machinic, electronic and programmed—reproduction has become an actual option. ORLAN as *Frankenstein's Bride*, followed by digitally produced *Self-Hybridizations*, video- and telematic games with ORLAN as the protagonist vary the prospects of her imagined and multiplied selves. Consequentially, these photographic pretenses are only the prelude to further hybridizations that reach beyond the meta-phorical level of virtual transformations and eventually result in the artist's surgical, transgenic and robotic mutations and multiplications. With the surgical interventions in 1990 ORLAN has started to manipulate her looks in a literal manner which she calls *Carnal Art*:

> One can consider my work as classical self-portraiture even if initially it is conceived with the aid of computers. But what can one say when it comes to permanently inscribing this work into the flesh? I will speak of a "Carnal Art," in part to differentiate myself from Body Art, to which nevertheless it belongs. ... Carnal Art is a work of autoportraiture in the classical sense, but with the technological means of its time. It oscillates between disfiguration and refiguration. It inscri-bes itself in the flesh because our era begins to lend itself to this possibility. (ORLAN, 1998, pp. 318–319)

Besides reaching into her body, ORLAN thereafter applies biotechnological means to mingle her flesh with other non-human organisms in a chimerical way. Her digital images, her bodily changes, her mixed genomes and lately her robotic counter-image, the *ORLANoid* (2018), manifest the cyborg-body including its binaries of uniqueness and multiplicity, miscellany and diversity, the *I* and the *Other(s)*, the virtual and the literal and, last not least, the mortal and the immortal body. Insisting on the thought that we are not only one *I* but plural "we"s, her oeuvre sounds like the declaration of war against the *Self* in an age of the mass-individual; and it most certainly is: "My work is a struggle against the innate, the inexorable, the programmed, Nature, DNA (which is our direct rival as artists of representation), and God!" (ORLAN, 1998, p. 325).

The sculpting and breeding and redoubling metamorphoses of her body unmis-takably address the subject of the *Self*. By suggesting flexible identities of herself and by confronting us with quite arresting images of these very processes of hybridization, ORLAN not only questions the status of her own body and *Self* but also re-directs our attention effectively towards the *Other*, namely our own bodies and identities. The digital/surgical/genetic/machinic de- and reconstruction of ORLAN and its resulting consequences may lead to an equal identity-transformation in the onlooker, who is invited onto a quest for the location, the origin, and the interdependencies of the human identity, by de- and redressing her inner *Self*.

With the help of ORLAN's literal embodiments we are only just beginning to guess the destabilizing, disconcertingly unreal, seemingly unnatural, at times dangerous, confidingly technophile, dissuasive and repulsive consequences of the human hybrids our bodies and identities have become:

> My work and its ideas, incarnated in my flesh, interrogate the status of the body in our society and its evolution in future generations via new technologies and upcoming genetic manipulations. My body has become a site of public debate that poses crucial questions for our time. (ORLAN, 1998, p. 319)

This debate also internalizes how and why we have long ago started to drift off into a transcultural, transnatural, and technoscientific posthuman condition. Plus, this debate stars two players and their relationship: the *representational Other* that we are confronted with (ORLAN) and the *real Self* that we cling to (us). Though for a start the real work needs to be accomplished by the artist: "As my friend the French artist Ben Vautier would say, 'Art is a dirty job, but somebody's got to do it'" (ORLAN, 1998, p. 326). This is how she does it.

## 7.1 Redressing the Body: The Reincarnation of Sainte ORLAN

From the years 1990 to 1993 ORLAN worked out a way to radicalize Body Art with her long-term-performance *The Re-Incarnation of St. ORLAN*. Over the period of four years ORLAN underwent nine—what she called—"surgical manipulations" (Bouchard, 2010, p. 63). For the performance of her re-incarnation ORLAN had transferred her artist's studio into the operating theatres of several hospitals in various countries. In addition, she outfitted the operating room with a new decor, replacing—wherever possible—its interior and equipment. ORLAN is producer and director all-in-one for when and how she makes arrangements for the transplantation of her skin, a liposuction, the surgeries on her facial features or the reshaping of her flesh and bones. The same changes were initiated on a psychological level: between 1990 and 1993 ORLAN went through psychoanalysis in order to develop her new personality.

To grasp the meaning of the physical changes ORLAN initiated on herself, one has to skip back in time to find art historical role models. For instance, to the Greek artist Zeuxis of Heraclea who once created the ideal portrait of a woman by inviting the most beautiful ladies of his time into his studio. From each one of them he selected the most perfect feature and/or flawless body parts in order to re-combine these in his portrayal. ORLAN was following similar strategies. To arrange her facial features in a novel way, she picked from the following archetypes of art history: chosen was the chin of Botticelli's *Venus*, the nose of Gérome's *Psyche*, the lips Francois Boucher has given to his *Europe*, the eyes of *Diana* from the painting of the School of Fontaine-bleau and the high forehead from Leonardo da Vinci's *Mona Lisa*.

But the artist was not only aiming at a new visual version of her face. By assimilating the physiognomies selected from the mythological protagonists, ORLAN also meant to incorporate the character traits of these women into her persona on a symbolical level: this is why she picked *Venus*, the goddess of erotic love, fertility, and creativity; *Psyche* represents the soul; and *Diana's* readiness to combat was chosen as a male component to be added to the artist, just to name a few of the expected characteristics (ORLAN, 1998, pp. 319–320). Thus, the physical incisions reach far deeper into her flesh than the cuts of the surgical knife that can only mark the body's surface.

Of course, such a surgical intervention holds risks. Especially as ORLAN was merely having a local anesthesia that enabled her to talk and act as freely as possible while being operated on, in contrast to a full anesthesia that in its coma-like consequences not only helps to prevent pain but also to protect the patient from the psychological trauma of seeing her own flesh cut and flayed. During her epidural anesthesia, instead, ORLAN was able to recite from a selection of texts, which picked up on the theme of the particular operation (e.g., Michel Serres (1991/2015), Eugénie Lemoine-Luccioni (1984), or Julia Kristeva (1982) among others). The medical staff was garnished with outfits of famous fashion designers that were commissioned by ORLAN for this happening, such as Paco Rabanne or Issey Miyake. Furthermore, still lives with fruit arrangement decorated the room and music and a dance-performance under the direction of ORLAN supported the action dramatically. The whole performance was transmitted live via satellites into public museums and galleries in Tokyo, New York, Paris, Toronto, Hamburg, and other cities. The video was reinforced by sign language. Throughout the procedure the audience had the opportunity to get in contact with the artist and ask questions, send faxes and communicate over video-conference with ORLAN as long as she was not prevented from speaking by surgical necessities. All these interactions contribute enormously to the fact that an invasive procedure of—for example—a transplant is being reduced to a mundane occurrence.

ORLAN's surgical interventions recordings, videotapes and even relics of her bodily fluids and flesh, as well as other remains from the operations, were placed on the art market in order to raise money for follow-up performances. The vials and reliquaries on offer contain blood, fat as well as the removed tissue of the artist (each relic holds 10g of her flesh); furthermore, there were dressing materials and gauze bandages that had been used during the surgery and hence were soaked with the artist's blood. All these products were framed for sale like fan-merchandise, certified by ORLAN's signature and the following inscription: "This is my body, this is my software".

There remains the question of why the artist is treading such a radical path and provoking attention in assuming a new identity this way. In the age of plastic surgery, of medical omnipresence, in this age of mechanical reproduction fostered by means of stem cell research—to which I will turn to later in this text—ORLAN is problematizing legal and at the same time ethical issues: Firstly, after the last medical intervention, the artist wanted to obtain a court order, that would allow her on a juridical level to take on a new identity (ORLAN, 1998, p. 326). Plastic surgery allows us a complete revision of our optical persona, so it seems to be justified to ask how far we are willing to go and what legal consequences are to be expected. The artist touches on this problem by passing down her own DNA that—in the age of humanistic science and the clone—could offer her a life even after her death. Secondly, and even more importantly, ORLAN's hyperreal new looks raise the worrisome ethical question to what extent life sciences or oneself should be allowed to muddle with the identity issue of a person and to have a say in *who* we are and *for how long*? And, thirdly, ORLAN of course touches on a feminist issue, i.e. to free women from the dictates of beauty standards. Also, Amelia Jones (1998) associates with this thought:

> ORLAN's work points to the fact that plastic surgery, rather than allowing us to gain control over our bodies, exacerbates our subordination to their vulnerabilities and morality—a subordination all the more dangerous for women, due to its long precedent in Western representation and thought. The more we attempt to reverse the signs of aging or supposedly misbegotten facial and bodily features, the more obviously we are obsessively driven by our corporeality (specifically, its visual appearance as psychically incorporated into our senses of self). (Jones, 1998, pp. 227–228)

ORLAN's effort gains credibility whilst she is using her own body in a self-mutilating act, being her own object and material of study all at once, thus, demonstrating the unattainability of false promises on perfection and eternal life. Her message is intensified by the unnatural clash of medicine and the *fine* arts. What art lovers and connoisseurs think of as being *fine*—the idealistic beauty of the female nude that is not downgraded to a merely naked, thus realistic body, the decorative but exclusive decency of art—collides with ORLAN's representation of the open body. The stigmata that were thought to make her more beautiful, inflict physical pain on us. In a visual and a mental way. The artist is well aware of that. And she apologizes as follows:

> I am sorry to make you suffer, but remember, I am not suffering, except like you, when I look at the images. Only a few kinds of images force you to shut your eyes: death, suffering, the opening of the body, some aspects of pornography for some people, and for others, giving birth. In this case, eyes become black holes in which the image is absorbed willingly or unwillingly, these images are swallowed up and hit just where it hurts, without passing through the usual filters, as if the eyes no longer had any connection to the head. (ORLAN, 1996, p. 2, para. 4–5)

When we are watching the surgical interventions on ORLAN's body and especially in her face, our own facial muscles twitch. We feel the urge to look away. Still, while covering our eyes, we are trying to catch a glimpse. And ORLAN *wants* us to look. She needs us as witnesses when medical science as a form-giving instrument reaches well beyond its limits. She is convinced that her doings can only be justified by the urgent poignancy of her message. This is what she claims for her art:

> For me, art which is interesting is related to and belongs to resistance. It must upset our assump-
> tion, overwhelm our thoughts, be outside norms and outside of the law. It should be against
> bourgeois art; it is not there to comfort, nor to give us what we already know. It must take risks,
> at the risk of not being accepted, at least initially. It should be deviant and involve a project for
> society. And even if this declaration seems very romantic, I say: art can, art must, change the
> world, for that is its only justification. (ORLAN, 1996, p. 5, para. 19)

What in the aftermath of her performance is in fact able to make a change for future
worlds is related to the production of the reliquaries that contain her body samples.
They consist of the drained fat and blood from various liposuctions that were bottled
in vials and bandaging material left over from the surgical interventions onto which
ORLAN added blood-paintings, as well as blood-soaked gauzes that bear her imprint
in combination with photographic transfers of her face. These *Holy Shrouds* are
carried to an extreme in the form of apparently holy reliquaries. For a secure preser-
vation of its content the biopsies are sustained in liquid media and the collectability
of the relics is guaranteed by the welded and bullet-proof receptacles. Each reliquary
is labeled and—apart from the logo "This is my body, this is my software"—inscribed
with the same excerpt of Michel Serres' text on *Lacisme*, each time in a different language; it reads:

> The current tattooed monster, ambidextrous, hermaphroditic and cross-bred, what can it make
> us see, now, under its skin? Yes, blood and flesh. Science speaks of organs, functions, of cells
> and molecules, only to admit at last that it's high time we stopped speaking of life in laborato-
> ries; but science never mentions the flesh, which, quite rightly, signifies the conflation, here and
> now, in a specific site of the body, of muscles and blood, skin and hair, bones, nerves and diverse
> functions, that inextricably binds that which pertinent knowledge analyzes. (as cited in ORLAN,
> 1998, p. 327)

Knowing that stem cell research provides the possibility of a clone, with her relics
ORLAN is taking measurements for the physical conveyability of her post-mortal
persona. Moreover, ORLAN plans to exhibit her whole body after her death as an ultimate relic (ORLAN, 1998, p. 326). I will come back to the importance of these anticipa-
tory steps in the chapter *Redressing Identity*.

For now we have to state that with her surgical performance ORLAN was re-incarnated with a new look and a new personality, the consequences of which are not
only inscribed in her face and into her psyche but have also been testified by the law,
resulting in a change of her identity which is inscribed into the fabric of society. Her at
first sight mere cosmetic interventions are meant to scrutinize the highly appreciated
concept of our individual freedom.

## 7.2 Redressing the Image: Virtual Crossovers

Before literally changing into a new look and persona ORLAN enabled us to imagine the expected outcome of her bodily and facial changes before the surgical interventions by offering a computer animated 3-D-scan of her soon-to-be re-incarnated *Self*. After the operations the artist created virtual portraits of the healing process of her temporary looks that lasted 40 days. This work in progress titled *Self-Hybridizations, In-Between* (1993) follows the seventh of the nine operations, called *Omniprésence*, added one photograph of the artist's battered face every day, forming a long row of diptychs. The series contains ORLAN's healing portrait on the upper half and an image of her face that was digitally morphed with classical beauties of the art canon on the lower half of each diptych. The lower portraits fuse into endlessly thinkable avatars for the future to come. The discrepancy, however, lies in the futuristically synthesized computer images of the two beautiful women in the lower half and the recklessly candid proofs of ORLAN's shattered and bruised face on top. Both images are representing the grotesque in-between status of becoming-other, the one "made by the computing-machine", the other "made by the body-machine" (ORLAN, 1998, p. 322). In both cases the transformation process is referred to as divine, symbolically hinted at by the process of healing lasting 40 days which—in a biblical sense—is also the number of days spent for penitence. It is a demonstration of the carnivalesque excesses the artist has initiated with her surgical performances, in need to be followed by the obligatory 40 days of abstinence. This is why ORLAN adds one more picture of her perfectly healed face, showing off the two bumpy implants on her forehead, when she had passed the obligatory 40 day quarantine imposed on a patient that underwent beautification: on the 41st day this photograph shows her reincarnation as Sainte ORLAN. "The current tattooed monster, ambidextrous, hermaphroditic and cross-bred" (as cited in ORLAN, 1998, p. 327) that ORLAN was quoting from Michel Serres' laical text, all the while referring to the Harlequin's variously colored and patched coats and skin, was only a temporary condition as the next surgical alterations lay ahead of her.

When finished with her literal mutations, ORLAN, beginning in the year 1998, launched a photographic cycle, once again titled *Self-Hybridizations*, that aims at another virtual identity-shift. This time featuring a transcultural motif, the artist merges her own portrait with African, Pre-Columbian, and Native American iconologies and lost civilizations. After having surgically incorporated the western feminine ideal into her own body, ORLAN turned to the standards of beauty originating from ancient and/or non-western civilizations. Thus, opposing criteria of beauty, age, facial features, face paintings and plastic deformation merge into one another in digitally manipulated photographs. Our own era meets long gone times of native cultures or non-canonical ideals of far-away nations. Often mistaken as the real outcome of her surgical interventions (ORLAN, 2002, p. 227), these hybridizations so obviously intertwine the varied cultural appearances that—for a vast public influenced by Eurocentristic ideals—have started to become a much dreaded idea of a universal intermingling of races and multiculturalism. As a result of this ever-growing fear, the *Time*-magazine in its special issue of fall 1993 had pictured "The New Face of America" on its front page, depicting a symbiotic, digital-blend of a beautiful woman, backed up by her pseudo-relatives imagined as cybergenetic little heads in the background. The idea of generating an "ideal racial synthesis, whose only possible existence is in the matrices of cyberspace" (Haraway, 2004b, pp. 279–280) has been surpassed by ORLAN's exotic icons: firstly, she had at this point already undergone the literal procedures in order to become a cyborg-being herself and, secondly, her *Self-Hybridizations* do not obey the idealized image of a western idea of beauty. Both of them—ORLAN and the *Time*-magazine—are assuming the *Other* as another within a global culture; but while the media-version seems to be hoping for a handsome hybrid that fits into the western canon of norms, the artistic version stresses a new norm that follows the will and design of the individual mind. Stéphane Malysse (2010) is therefore suggesting:

> [T]hose games of identity acted out by various cultures show that the body is only a costume, a cultural costume. Since it varies from culture to culture, why not leave the individual the decision as to cultural orientations? Why not allow individuals to hybridize themselves? (p. 134)

For ORLAN (2002), the wishful thinking and fearful aversions of the masses has nothing to do with her artistic doings nor with reality as such:

> [I]t would be wrong to separate the "surgical operations performances" from my *Self-Hybridizations*, because the former do not belong only to reality and the latter do not purely take place in virtuality. I have always sought to erase the limits, to transform reality into virtuality, and vice versa. (p. 227)

A new series of *Self-Hybridizations* (2014) morphs the artist's image with the elaborate masks of the Peking Opera. The bright colours of the masks for one thing show the artist's features, then again, merge ever so subtly into the equally patterned and brightly coloured backgrounds of each portrait. In comparison to her earlier virtual hybridizations ORLAN has added a 3-D-effect to these photographs,[138] taking her mutable *Self* towards a last missing step in her oeuvre which is the augmented reality of the videogame. Whereas she had already previously experimented with interactive sculpture (*Bumpload*, 2009) and 3-D video (*La Liberté en* écorchée / *Flayed Liberty*, 2013), the interactive game *Expérimentale mise en jeu* (2015) is a full body experience for the

---

**138** Digital reproductions of the *Peking Opera Hybridizations* can be purchased for digital tools such as smartphones or tablets: the surface does not only hold the actual photo-series but shows acrobats moving and dancing in front of her *Hybridizations* that act as ORLAN's avatars and copy the Peking-look of her hybridized portraits, thereby adding yet another augmented reality.

player who slips into ORLAN's body as the game's protagonist. Unlike so many other videogames the goal is *not* to destroy or at least win over an opponent, but to rebuild artworks such as ORLAN's *Flayed Liberty*, her skinless self-portrait, over the course of 4'33", which is also the time frame given by John Cage's composition on silence with the same name. Listening to the sound of the blood rushing through the body and the nervous system working to the limit, the character in the game becomes more and more human the more successful she operates in her reconstruction tasks (ORLAN, personal communication, July 27, 2016).

In redressing her image time and time again ORLAN's doubles act both on a literal and a virtual (game-)level.

## 7.3 Redressing Identity: Harlequinesque Crossovers

In order to literally cross over on a transcultural, transgendered as well as transgenetic level and—eventually—to become immortal the way the fictional character Harlequin once was, ORLAN is retelling his story with *The Harlequin's Coat* (2009). The shrewd but ironic, gaudily dressed character taken from the *Commedia dell'Arte* can not only be described as a world citizen but also as a traveller of the underworld and of extraterrestrial territory. When coming back from his trip to lunar landscapes—that is how the story goes as Michel Serres (1991/2015) tells us —the Harlequin is invited to a press conference to report about his journey (pp. 7–11). The audience marvels over his extravagantly colourful but battered cloths that must have its cause in the Harlequin's wonderous and exciting adventures. But Harlequin refuses, at first, to either reflect about anything extraordinary he had witnessed or even to take off his coat. Reluctantly and under pressure from his audience, he starts to take off the thick layer of coats, one after the other, each of which is a motley patchwork of different quilts, coarsely sewn together, in different sizes and matches of diamond-shapes and colours. When it comes to the last coat, the Harlequin showing his stark naked bareness, the audience is horrified as there it shows, "[t]he current tattooed monster, ambidextrous, hermaphroditic and cross-bred" (Serres, 1991/2015, p. 10) in the process of becoming. The mythical character had obtained bruises and patches from his escapades to hell and travels to the moon that had not only resulted in his colourful and now worn and cobbled dress, but that had left marks even underneath his many layers of clothing—on his very skin. During a lifetime, the Harlequin has become a hybrid, a multicultural, cross-skinned, an impure cell-bastard.

The metaphor of Harlequin's personal history serves ORLAN as a background for *The Harlequin's Coat*, her first project involving biotechnology and living biological matter of herself and of others, resulting in the co-culturing and fusion of human and non-human cells and tissue culture. The idea was to hybridize skin tissue of various ethnicities (white & black) and other species (marsupial & bovine) with her own skin cells (ORLAN, 2010a, pp. 116–117) as a literal and metaphorical adoption of these multi-ethnical as well as multi-specied backgrounds, identities, and emotions. The skin and muscle cells collected during biopsy were supposed to intermingle their different pigmentation, different specification and different genderfication to grow together as transhuman hybrids, therewith transgressing cultural coordinates and species barriers. The unnatural blend of seeded cell cultures was shown intermingling *in-vitro* in constantly moving petri-dishes that were attached to the pied backdrop of a Harlequin's gown. The work of art was presented with a custom-made bioreactor marking the head of the larger-than-life model of the Harlequin that was indicated by colorful diamond-shapes on the dress, growing ORLAN's tissue-cultures that seemed to morph infinitely.

The idea of hybridizing a *Harlequin's Coat* is not far-fetched or an outrageous excess as it might seem at first glance. In our medicalized world the comingling of different species for the purpose of life-enhancement is a well-established practice. While the engineering of plant and animal genomes has resulted in transgenic organisms for more than a hundred years, in the meantime also for the human species a biotechnical cut-and-paste-technique is being applied in order to provide our bodies with organic replacements, for example the cardiac valve can nowadays be grown from pigs. And while ORLAN had a piece of ox bone implanted into her jaw to create an artistic link between the human and the non-human, I myself had bovine bone material transplanted underneath my molar owing to the medical necessity of regenerative dentistry. We have all become cyborgs a long time ago. The patchwork of the Harlequin's coat and his skin underneath corresponds with our own body and identity. And like him we are just hiding our mended body and over the years so many times patched up *Self* underneath a coverage. All the marks give testimony to our being in contact with the external world. Harlequin has become the norm. As to the remains of ORLAN's cell cultures, these were not able to form into a full-grown hybrid skin. The initial mistrust of Harlequin's—and later ORLAN's—nauseated and shocked audience was unwarranted: "Of course, all the cells or bacteria are dead" (ORLAN, personal communication, July 27, 2016). One more reason for ORLAN to sponsor a *Petition Against Death*[139] via her website requesting people to act up and sign. But *cui bono?*:

> Similarly, the petition against death that I have circulated many times in my life: it is sometimes not signed, as if the petition would reciprocate, as if it had a power, an effect, as if it had a power that I haven't given to it. It's a playful and poetic petition like flash mobs, a strike that doesn't have a concrete demand, that is not aimed at succeeding. (ORLAN, 2010b, p. 40)

ORLAN and those signing up know the outcome already: The current state of science does not allow for negating a loss of the mortal body. But forthcoming knowledge and

---

139 The petition can be signed at: http://www.orlan.eu/petition/.

insights will continue to negotiate the healed, modified, transformed, hybridized, exchangeable, and maybe the soon-to-come obsolete body. In this case ORLAN will be prepared to compensate for her present state of being-in-the-world with a possible continuous substitute via the reliquaries containing her own harvested body cells. "Her body is a factory, her flesh is product", as Kate Ince (2000) has put it (p. 48). This is the reason why and how ORLAN might be successful: Ever since the discovery of DNA in 1953, modern biotechnology has worked on the production and recombination of DNA which became possible in 1973. The latest pioneering discovery in medicine and biotechnology was the successful re-programming of human cell material that earned the Japanese cell researcher Shinya Jamanaka and the British biologist John B. Gurdon the *Nobel Prize* in 2012. Being able to re-program human cells means that specialized stem cells can be retransformed into *pluripotent* stem cells. Reducing a cell to its original status of pluripotency is a desired means in a medical context as only a pluripotent cell has the ability to develop into almost all kinds of other cell types of an organism. A pluripotent cell is not yet programmed and therefore not yet specified for a certain tissue type. Once again and in order to clarify matters: A completely developed adult human being is living in a body that merely consists of innumerable different, but always unipotent cells. Unipotent cells are normal cells, however, *unable to divide*; in mathematics, *uni* coming from the Latin word *uno* which is "1", a unipotent element is a nilpotent element, in other words its power is *zero*. For the human body this means that unipotent cells are only able to develop more of the same cell type: skin cells cultivate more skin, blood cells more blood, and hair cells grow hair, etc.

In contrast to a unipotent cell the most precious cell for scientific research and the body's potential to restore itself is an *omnipotent* or *totipotent* cell. The Latin *omni* meaning all-powerful, almighty. From an omnipotent cell any other stem cell of an organism can be generated. Hence, an omnipotent cell can develop into a complete, viable, and self-dependent organism. A fertilized egg cell is such an omnipotent stem cell. These embryonic stem cells are not legally available or used for scientific research in every country. In Europe, for example, scientific research using human embryonic cells is not allowed.

Now to the polypotent cells: Polypotent or pluripotent cells are—in accordance with their Latin origin—not *almighty*, but they are able to do a lot. It is not possible to create a whole organism from them. For the time being, it is increasingly common to isolate pluripotent stem cells from various human tissue or to reprogram extracted cells into a state of pluripotency. In doing so scientists are working on the promising prospect to be able to heal numerous diseases. Using the human body as a self-sustaining storage, generating and duplicating its own material is, however, highly questionable and much discussed on an ethical level.

At present the specialization of cell types is reversible. For non-scientists this information comes as a relatively unspectacular one. But for those having children the almost reflexively advertised offer to have the umbilical cord of a newborn safely stored away by professionals appears in a new light and is all of a sudden making—still arguable—sense when being aware of these new medical standards.

Manipulating the processes of living organisms has become state of the art—this not only for the natural and life sciences: BioArtists are working at the interface between medicine, biology, and informatics. The knowledge and techniques that had become available for the biotechnological sciences were subsequently picked up and made useful for the fine arts as well. The flux of the development of these newly adapted methods has led to a broad field of forms of artistic expression today. The overarching term *BioArt* is in itself a mutant one, serving as a placeholder for divergent practices such as digital and virtual simulations, robotic devices, the decoding and computer-based imaging of DNA-sequences as well as dry and wet laboratory operations *in-vivo* and *in-vitro* such as the cultivation of animal and human cells and tissues, biotechnical, neurophysiological, genetic mutations, and transgenic hybridizations. Therewith, BioArt is breaking down the once indispensable wall between *bio* and *tècne*, initiating a "process of hybridization between the human being, the animal world and the machine world" (Gilardi, 2007, p. 230) in the art world.

What the two disciplines—science and art—disagree on is not their bioscientific methodologies but their motivation in applying them: While the natural sciences have restricted themselves to the question of *how* to succeed, the fine arts are on the lookout for answers on *why* we should do so and *what consequences* are to be expected in the face of a constantly shifting and modifiable *conditio humana* that has been downgraded to a mere information-pool on growth, health, biological functions, age, and disease. Walter Benjamin's (1936/2006) much discussed manuscript on the questionable aura of an artwork that is being reproduced goes into its next round with artists such as ORLAN that hint at the potential to hybridize and clone the human body with the (un)predictable prospect of releasing their personae into the next future, into the age of mechanical reproduction of the artist's body.

With the reliquaries containing her flesh ORLAN ventures towards her eventual immortality. The above named biotechnological achievements let the loss of the body be negotiable. Not only on a metaphorical level like Christian saints and martyrs whose reliquaries—however fragmented these might be—stand in for the integrity of their persona that was meant to be resurrected as a whole body, ORLAN is reincarnating herself into many bodies and multiple forms of being. Thanks to scientific data-harvesting and -verification, ORLAN can even for the future be assured that her relics are able to manifest the always same genetical basics—her very own cell-material—identifying her as the always same gateway for coming individuals.

This is why ORLAN has not stopped co-working with scientists from various biology laboratories such as *SymbioticA* (University of Perth, Australia) and lately *Sup'Biotech*, as well as with Institutes such as the *Centre national de la recherche scientifique* or the *Institut Pasteur*, all of them situated in Paris, to store her stem cells from her latest performance, the *Tangible Strip-tease en Nanoséquence* (2016), at the temperature of −80° Celsius (ORLAN, personal communication, July 27, 2016). That this performance was not only about the storage of her cells for further experimentation is already given away by its title: samples of her microbiotic flora were sent through the audience via vials and tubes passing them from one audience member to the other (Kyrou, 2018, p. 134) in order to not only have a share in her body fluids, but—as in the case of Harlequin presenting himself to the public—for the sake of realizing that we are all made up of the same material—only varying in tiny little bits and pieces of our DNA from one individual to the *Other*.

## 7.4 Redressing a Second Self: The ORLANoid

By circulating her *Self* through the rows of an audience during the performance *Tangible Strip-tease en Nanoséquence*, seeing her innermost parts floating through the fingers of the *Other*, ORLAN had managed to "place oneself outside of oneself to become oneself" (ORLAN, 2010b, p. 42). However, this is quite different from the insights acquired during the mirror stage as it was described by Jacques Lacan (2006) in the year 1949: ORLAN's performance is way beyond recognizing herself as an "I" as she is explicitly differentiating between her *Self* and the one of the *Other* and between her *Self* and her *I*. To do this, she needs to be aware of the fact that, innately, we are provided with a "starter-kit" to develop into the *Subject* we will eventually identify with. Psychoanalysis distinguishes three entities along this process: developing an *I*, developing the *Self*, and becoming a *Subject*. The development of the *I* happens—according to Lacan (2006)—during infancy, as soon as we are able to recognize ourselves reflected in a mirror. As a next step we are cultivating our *Self* by listening to our emotions and by gathering experiences along the way that we try to match with the reactions and from the perspectives of the *Other*. Once a—continuously mutable—relationship towards the external world has been established, we have become the *Subject* how it is seen by others. There are moments when we are able to objectify ourselves from this *Subject*: in our dreams and at the sight of ORLAN's oeuvre celebrating her prospering *Selves*, resulting in her saying "Je sommes" instead of the familiar "Je suis". It is what Lacan describes as being aware of the fragmented body (Lacan, 2006, p. 75); it is—how Erika Fischer-Lichte put it so strikingly—the "Abständigkeit des Menschen von sich selbst" (Fischer-Lichte, 2004, p. 129; "Man's detachment from himself"; the translation in English is mine). The *I* owes its existence to the dualisms of seeing/feeling, seeing/being seen, touching/being touched, the two-dimensional/three-dimensional, the *I* and the *Other* as well as the Subject and the Object. Thus, we are only able to identify our *Self*, by thinking these different perspectives as co-existing. However, to think these dualisms as one is a difficult task, remarked on by Peggy Phelan (1993) as follows: "In that declaration and identification, there is always loss, the loss of not-being the other and yet remaining dependent on that other for self-seeing, self-being" (p. 13).

This is why ORLAN also states that "Je est une autre", adapting Rimbaud's famous *bon mot* by changing it into its feminine *Other*, (ORLAN & Virilio, 2010, p. 193) to claim her multiple, female identities to which most recently she added one more version: her robot-hybrid *ORLANoid* (2018). The once again decidedly unorthodox perspective she has on her *Self*, disagrees in more than one fundamental way with the *I* that is supposed to reflect in Lacan's mirrored stage: ORLAN's robotic vis-à-vis is not flat, not untouchable, not back-to-front, and—most of all—it can be communicated with.

The *ORLANoid* is not a robot in the sense of the novelist Karel Čapek who coined the word from the Czech *robota*, meaning "forced labor", i.e. somebody meant to work or be useful in some way. It is more of a "technohumanist figure", as Donna Haraway (2004c) would describe it, an "enhanced command-control-communication-intelligence system (C3I)" (Haraway, 2004c, p. 299) that is capable of deep learning, able to react and interact unexpectedly, thus extending ORLAN's body by means of electronically and digitally encoded information, such as an artificial, collective and social intelligence as well as language skills. On approaching the sensors of her double, the *ORLANoid* comes to life, moving about, expressing itself in ORLAN's voice and directing questions towards the artist projected on two video screens. Regarding its intellectual capacities, the robot before being put into existence was fed with texts and poems by ORLAN and answers given by internet users to the Proust Questionnaire. She had invited her friends to think up additional questions for the *ORLANoid* to ask her and vice versa (ORLAN, 2018a, p. 116).

Of course, the *ORLANoid* is a lookalike of ORLAN in the year 2018, however, only the head down to the bust, her arms and hands have been re-modelled after the artist. The rest of it gives away its mechanical and electronic origins as the transhuman hybrid it was meant to be. The *ORLANoid* contradicts the notion of the—as Donna Haraway has traced down its history (Haraway, 2004d, pp. 321–322)—ever so popular fem-bot as a sex-toy, or the smugly creator-ess' creature. It is neither technophile nor technophobe such as all of ORLAN's reincarnations—be it the computer-generated hybridizations, the surgical re-modelling of her persona or the clones of her biological *Self*. This cyborg is a virtual and at the same time real being: "Cyborgs are also places where the ambiguity between the literal and the figurative is always working. You are never sure whether to take something literally or figuratively. It is always both/and." (Haraway, 2004c, p. 323). That is the reason why ORLAN is addressing her double as follows: "You're a sculpture—a moving, talking self-portrait that pretends to feel emotions, though you never really will. ... because you're an object, you're one of my 'among other things,' one of my theoretical and aesthetic representations" (ORLAN, 2018b, p. 117). So it doesn't matter to ORLAN that the flaws of the mechanical creature show. On the contrary: the artist wants to stress the promising as well as the threatening prospects of a technoscientific future that might—at its current status—be overrated: "[I]t soon becomes apparent that artificial intelligence essentially creates artificial stupidity—a certain type of intelligence that is greatly inferior to our own ...." (ORLAN, 2018a, p. 116). The highly efficient algorithm of the *ORLANoid*'s artificial intelligence is still lacking human capacities such as feeling pain, having intuition or visions, developing emotions or a gut feeling—it doesn't have guts or a heart! Although it might be able to develop a humanoid *I*, it will fail to develop a humanoid *Self* and will hence never succeed in becoming a human *Subject*. All the same, ORLAN's robot-hybrid will over the years develop its own identity. And it will differ from anybody else's.

There are no similar individuals. Individuality is one of the most valuable commodities to human (wo)mankind. In a posthuman world, however, the characteristics and forms of expression of our individualities seem to become more and more compatible and replaceable. To go look for our individual *Self* in- and outside of our bodies might seem obsolete concerning the technoscientifical, transcultural, and transnatural possibilities of our times. To remember the future, as ORLAN wants us to do, means to become aware of the many ways our identity manifests itself, that it is interchangeable and reproduceable, multiplying and hybridizing over and over again, thus being able to develop into new constructions of our *Self*. As Donna Haraway (2004a) has put it superbly: "The point is to learn to remember that we might have been otherwise, and might yet be, as a matter of embodied fact" (Haraway, 2004a, p. 240). As we have seen, it is hard to know what and how many ones we are at the very moment and also who all the *Other* ones are. To find an agreement with and an acceptance of these facts—that we cannot even take for granted—ORLAN helps to open a door to. A door that we need to trespass in a world of growing in-acceptance of the *Other* and an anthropocentric focus we need to overcome. For the sake of every single identity.

# References

Benjamin, W. (2006). Das Kunstwerk im Zeitalter seiner technischen Reproduzierbarkeit [The Work of Art in the Age of Mechanical Reproduction]. Suhrkamp. (Original work published 1936)

Bouchard, G. (2010). ORLAN Anatomized. In S. Donger, S. Shepard & ORLAN (Eds.), ORLAN A Hybrid Body of Artworks (1st ed., pp. 62–72). Routledge.

Fischer-Lichte, E. (2004). Ästhetik des Performativen [The Transformative Power of Performance—A New Aesthetics]. Suhrkamp.

Gilardi, P. (2007). The PAV Art Programme: Proposals and Considerations. Dalla Land Art alla Bioarte. From Land Art to Bioart, edited by Ivana Mulatero, hopefulmonster editore (pp. 230–232).

Haraway, D. (2004a). Modest_Witness@Second_Millenium. In D. Haraway (2004), The Haraway Reader (pp. 223–250). Routledge.

Haraway, D. (2004b). Race: Universal Donors in a Vampire Culture. It's all in the Family: Biological Kinship Categories in the Twentieth-Century United States. In D. Haraway (2004), The Haraway Reader (pp. 251–293). Routledge.

Haraway, D. (2004c). Cyborgs, Coyotes, and Dogs: A Kinship of Feminist Figurations and There Are Always More Things Going On Than You Thought! Methodologies as Thinking Technologies. In D. Haraway (2004), The Haraway Reader (pp. 321–342). Routledge.

Haraway, D. (2004d). Cyborgs to Companion Species: Reconfiguring Kinship in Technoscience. In D. Haraway (2004), The Haraway Reader (pp. 295–320). Routledge.

Ince, K. (2000). ORLAN. Millennial Female. Berg.

Jones, A. (1998). Body Art. Performing the Subject. University of Minnesota Press.

Kristeva, J. (1982). Powers of Horror: An Essay on Abjection (Pouvoirs de l'horreur, 1980). Columbia University Press.

Kyrou, A. (2018). ORLAN's ORLANoid Between The Future Eve and the Dada Cyborg. In ORLAN (Ed.), ORLAN-oïde Robot Hybrid. ORLAN-oide Hybrid Robot with Artificial and Collective Intelligence / avec intelligence artificielle et collective (pp. 132–135). Lienart éditions.

Lacan, J. (2006). The Mirror Stage as Formative of the I Function as Revealed in Psychoanalytical Experience. In J. Lacan. (2006). Écrits, (pp. 75–81). Norton.

Lemoine-Luccioni, E. (1984). La robe: Essai psychoanalytique sur le vêtement. Editions du Seuil.

Malysse, S. (2010). The Gift to Art. ORLAN. In S. Donger, S. Shepard & ORLAN (Eds.), ORLAN A Hybrid Body of Artworks (1st ed., pp. 125–136). Routledge.

ORLAN. (1998). Intervention (1995). In P. Phelan & J. Lane (Eds.), The Ends of Performance (pp. 315–327). University Press.

ORLAN. (1996, October–November). *"I Do Not Want To Look Like…"* Orlan on Becoming-Orlan. MAKE The Magazine of Women's Art, (72), 1–15.

ORLAN. (2002) The complex dialectics of virtuality and reality. In M. J. Kerejeta (Ed.), ORLAN 1964–2001 (pp. 227–229). Artium.

ORLAN. (2010a). The Poetics and Politics of the Face-To-Face. In S. Donger, S. Shepard & ORLAN (Eds.), ORLAN A Hybrid Body of Artworks (1st ed., pp. 103–118). Routledge.

ORLAN. (2010b). This is my body…This is my software. In S. Donger, S. Shepard & ORLAN (Eds.), ORLAN A Hybrid Body of Artworks (1st ed., pp. 35–47). Routledge.

ORLAN, & Virilio, P. (2010). Interview. (2009). In S. Donger, S. Shepard & ORLAN (Eds.), ORLAN A Hybrid Body of Artworks (1st ed., pp. 188–195). Routledge.

ORLAN. (2018a). ORLAN-oïde Robot Hybrid. ORLAN-oide Hybrid Robot with Artificial and Collective Intelligence / avec intelligence artificielle et collective. Lienart éditions.

ORLAN. (2018b). ORLAN dialogues with the ORLANoid. ORLAN-oïde Robot Hybrid. ORLAN-oide Hybrid Robot with Artificial and Collective Intelligence / avec intelligence artificielle et collective (p. 117). Lienart éditions.

Phelan, P. (1993). Unmarked: The Politics of Performance. Routledge.

Serres, M. (2015). Troubadour des Wissens. Versuch über das Lernen ["Troubadour" of knowledge. Experiment on learning]. Chronos Verlag. (Original work Le Tiers-Instruit published 1991).

Giulia Pelillo-Hestermeyer

# 8 Transculturally Speaking: Linguistic Diversity, Otherness and the Transformation of Public Spheres

The experience of linguistic difference is among the most common in human life. Every one of us from early childhood throughout all stages of life is confronted with ways of speaking (variously addressed as languages, dialects, jargon, etc.) which sound "different" to a greater or lesser extent. In the course of life, the way in which we speak changes: A word, an accent, a language, which was perceived before as strange, may become more familiar or even well-known to us. On the other hand, we may lose familiarity with languages, just as people lose familiarity with technical or sporting skills which they do not practice regularly. This may sound all very obvious. However, a series of circumstances contribute to a reduced awareness by speakers about the hybridity of both one's own and others' "languages", as well as about the ubiquity of linguistic diversity in everyday life. As a matter of fact, languages are quite commonly considered as monolithic communicative systems which are either completely acquired or not.

Sociolinguistic research on linguistic diversity has demonstrated how widespread ideas about languages and multilingualism, such as the mythologization of an idealized "mother tongue" once and forever acquired, or the perception of monolingualism as normal and multilingualism as exceptional, can differ from actual linguistic usage. In a work provocatively entitled "Nobody is monolingual", the sociolinguist Brigitta Busch (2012) has emphasized this gap and focused on the power of language and language-difference in constructing belongings as well as boundaries:

> Mit dem Satz „Niemand ist einsprachig" meine ich genau das: eine Erfahrung, die jede_r kennt, jene des Dazu-Gehörens oder eben nicht Dazu-Gehörens aufgrund unterschiedlicher Arten des Sprechens. Einsprachig wäre demnach nur, wer diese Erfahrung nie gemacht hat, wer sich im Sprechen nie als „anders" erlebt hat. (Busch, 2012, p. 7)[140]

By quoting Jacques Derrida's statement "Je n'ai qu'une langue, ce n'est pas la mienne"[141] (Derrida, 1996, p. 13), which only appears to contradict her assertion about monolingualism, Busch stresses the power of "the other" in influencing speakers' perceptions of their own linguistic repertoires and performances. Speakers learn, for example, from the social context in which they live, to call specific linguistic varieties

---

**140** This and the following translations are mine: "By stating 'Nobody is monolingual' I mean exactly this: the experience, which everyone is aware of, of belonging or not-belonging because of differences in one's different ways of speaking. From this perspective, the 'monolingual' would only refer to someone who has never experienced this, who has never felt as 'Other' by speaking" (Busch, 2012, p. 7).
**141** "I have but one language – yet that language is not mine" (Derrida, 1996, p. 13).

*languages* or *dialects*, and to value them according to different social conventions and political frameworks.

In a similar vein, Judith Butler (2006) refers to the subject as being constituted by the discursive power of language, that is, by the socio-cultural norms which establish what can be said or what not. Busch extends Butler's consideration by emphasizing how linguistic norms, beyond determining *what* can be said, also regulate *how* it should be said, thus influencing speakers' perceptions of the (in)adequateness of their own manner of speech (Busch, 2012, p. 36). This is particularly true when speakers, in contexts of linguistic diversity, experience a feeling of adopting a "wrong" accent, or of lacking the "right" words. In such cases, the term "linguistic inequality" expresses the heart of what is at stake. As pointed out by Jan Blommaert (2010), linguistic inequality concerns differences which become relevant in specific contexts and which are linked to the status and the power of speakers and speech communities. As a matter of fact, speakers only recognize, in their own and others' talk, those differences which they have learned to identify and to consider meaningful in specific contexts.

This chapter looks at mediatized public spheres as spaces in which, on the one hand, powerful players—featuring not only, for example, institutional and economic agencies, but also "authoritative discourses" (Foucault, 1972)—establish, strengthen and spread normative attitudes towards languages and speech communities. On the other hand, as spaces of negotiation in which alternative voices and minority groups develop ways of contesting hegemonic ideologies and practices. In light of transformations which affect what has been long addressed as "the media" and "the language(s)", this chapter deconstructs static assumptions concerning both concepts by emphasizing, on the one hand, the diversification of the media and language(s) in the context of political, technological and socio-cultural changes, on the other, the various practices which perpetuate monocultural ideologies and hierarchizations of speakers and linguistic resources.

With respect to the diversification of media, I refer to the theoretical framework of recent advances in media studies which highlight that media are not autonomous agents but are rather completely integrated in cultural and political practices. Therefore, it makes no sense to think about "media *and* culture", "media *and* language", "media *and* politics", etc., since these are neither separate nor separable entities. By speaking instead of mediatized cultures, languages, politics, etc., one acknowledges that both constituents of the pair are inseparably intertwined. It is the whole human experience at its various levels of action which is mediatized (Hepp, 2014; Lundby, 2009; Krotz, 2009). Similarly, it no longer appears valid to speak of a clear distinction between mass and interpersonal communication, or between private and public communication (Androutsopoulos, 2014; Livingstone, 2009). Concerning the diversification of languages and speech communities, I refer to Vertovec's term of "super-diversity" (Vertovec, 2007; Vertovec, 2010), which is also adopted in sociolinguistic research to describe the diversification of linguistic landscapes and of speakers' linguistic repertoires (Blommaert et al., 2009; Blommaert et al., 2011; Blommaert, 2013). In this context, a need for a change of paradigm has been expressed, which overcomes structuralist conceptualizations of language (e.g. English, Hindi, French, etc.), and conceives language rather as a "mobile complex of concrete resources" (Blommaert, 2010, p. 47) such as specific varieties, genres, registers (Blommaert, 2010; Blommaert, 2013). According to this paradigm, multilingualism is not what people have or do not have, but what the environment *enables* and *disables* (Blommaert et al., 2005). Moreover, fundamental political and social changes, such as the end of the Cold War—which transformed the dynamics of migration—or the development of the Internet—which has dramatically extended the possibilities of circulating information, of constructing virtual networks, and of participating in social interaction—have produced highly complex patterns of mobility with respect to people, communication, money, and resources in general (Blommaert, 2013; Vertovec, 2007; Vertovec, 2010). In this regard, Blommaert (2013, p. 5) points out:

> The interaction of these two forces – new and more complex forms of migration, and new and more complex forms of communication and knowledge circulation – has generated a situation in which two questions have become hard to answer: who is the Other? And who are We? The Other is now a category in constant flux, a moving target about whom very little can be presupposed; and as for the We, ourselves, our own lives have become vastly more complex and are now very differently organized, distributed over online as well as offline sites and involving worlds of knowledge, information and communication that were simply unthinkable two decades ago.

In the following discussion, I will adopt this perspective and, rather than considering media and language as two different categories, for example by questioning how "the media" handle the phenomenon of multilingualism, I will highlight how various mediatized language and discourse practices *do diversity* vs. how they *do otherness* in various contexts. Instead of suggesting a "one-size-fits-all" solution for enhancing diversity in public spheres, my discussion primarily aims at showing the variety and complexity of identity affiliations, feelings, interests and ideologies at work when speakers and speech communities *do publics* by mediating their linguistic usage. In this context, different ways of enabling vs. disabling diversity will be compared and discussed. This will also take into consideration not only language and discourse practices, but also institutional and economic frameworks which tend to "normalize" and "standardize" both monolingualism and specific forms of linguistic hybridity which have spread in the context of the globalization of the media industry. In contrast to these practices, more recent efforts to overcoming static and monocultural attitudes to language, identity and culture will be considered in both the academic and media fields. My transcultural approach, in this context, consists in exploring the contextuality of *doing diversity* vs. *doing otherness*, and in pinpointing the gap between "lived" superdiversity and globally circulating attitudes of "normalizing", levelling and standardizing it. Against this background, processes of in- and exclusion, of enhancing vs. hindering participation, and of acknowledging vs. idealizing diversity will be compared by contextualizing them within the general framework of the transformation of public spheres and the globalization of media industries. Transculturality is hence considered here as anything but a cosmopolitan utopia, and indeed as a field of conflict and negotiation.

## 8.1 Whose English? Transcultural Negotiations of a Global Language

Discussions of English as "the" global language are characterized by the contrast between two opposing motives: On the one hand, the need to communicate with speakers of "other" languages, and on the other hand, speakers' concern about the risk of levelling linguistic, and consequently cultural, diversity. In these discussions, English is usually regarded as a single "whole" language of power which is spreading at the expense of "other" languages. English native speakers are regarded in this context as privileged. This is certainly not completely false. However, a (trans)cultural look at the multiple negotiations surrounding the spread of global English helps us to understand how reductive this matter appears if put in such simplistic terms.

Raymond Williams (1961/2011, pp. 251–268) stressed this fact already in 1961, when he commented on the overall spread of American English in the United Kingdom and the subsequent resistance to the "Americanization" of the so-called "Received Standard" by British speakers:

> Not only have hundreds of American words, speech forms and pronunciations been taken, often unnoticed, into English, but American speech has had an influence on almost all kinds of traditional English speaking, and it is worth noticing that it works against every single sound that was identified as peculiarly "Received Standard". Moreover, by giving other accents to power and material success, it has deprived Public School English of its former monopoly in this respect. The process is still going on, but it is not simply the Americanisation of English; it is, rather, the addition of another factor to the long and complicated history of spoken English. (Williams, 1961/2011, p. 267)

Behind the competition between American English and British English, he noticed the emergence of a new player in the definition of the prestige of languages: the media industry. Accordingly, the media has to be taken into account by looking at the relationships between language and power.

Concerning the formation and propagation of the notion of "standard" itself, Williams dated it back to the British English of the eighteenth and nineteenth centuries. In this period, the varied speech which had characterized the spoken language in earlier times, and which had also progressively enriched the written language, as documented by the Elizabethan dramatists, became uniform and crystallized into the so-called "Received Standard". Williams relates this process to the emergence of a middle class who sought social recognition by defining and standardising "correctness", which had given rise to the spread of a "cult of uniformity" (Williams, 1961/2011,

p. 262). This process had been promoted by, among other factors, institutions such as the *Royal Society's Committee for improving the English tongue* and public schools, as well as by practices such as spelling-masters and pronunciation coaches:

> Indeed, its naming as *standard*, with the implication no longer of a common, but of a model language, represents the full coming to consciousness of a new concept of class speech: now no longer merely the functional convenience of a metropolitan class, but the means and emphasis of social distinction. (Williams, 1961/2011, p. 258)

Pierre Bourdieu (1982/1991) has described a similar process of standardization in language use in the context of the democratization of the Nation State in France. In the establishment of the Nation State he identifies the necessary conditions for the formation of a unified "linguistic market", which is dominated by the national language. Great resources were invested in this process in France: Grammar books and dictionaries purified and standardized the national language, while academies and schools propagated it. The national language became mandatory in public spaces and official situations, and consequently acquired a symbolic power: Purified from local accents, it symbolized the unity of the state and the equality of its citizens. The standardization of the language corresponded, from this perspective, to the standardization of the law, sanctioning thereby the equality of all citizens. These citizens, in turn, invested their resources (time, money) in acquiring the national language, in order to obtain access to the life of the State as well as to the national, "unified" job market. The standard language hence represented—at least from an ideological perspective—a gateway for citizens who had been excluded from the centres of power until then. Acquiring the national language at school was indeed a substantial part of the very process of becoming a citizen (Bourdieu, 1982/1991). It is also worth noticing that acquiring the national language still represents for migrants, today, a fundamental prerequisite for acquiring citizenship in many countries. Moreover, the term "acquisition" itself, which is commonly used in expressions such as "foreign language acquisition", also conceptualizes languages as goods.

The institutionalization of both the national language and the media can be regarded as two related processes which have reinforced each other over time. Andreas Hepp (2009, p. 145) highlights the emergence of territorially defined media cultures by referring to the power of national media in constructing belongings as well as boundaries. He stresses in this regard how the sharing of common media contents within the territory of the Nation State has promoted a feeling of belonging to one and the same community (social dimension) and of being part of a territorial unity (spatial dimension). Moreover, this has reduced the perceived distance to each other among citizens by speeding up communication within the national territory (temporal dimension). If this process has been particularly favoured by the adoption of one common language, the national media has enormously contributed, in turn, to the spread of national "standard" languages. Moreover, the national media have also immensely contributed to strengthening the *feeling* of sharing the standard language, despite the diversity of the many "other" languages (including dialects) that are actually used in everyday life[142].

When Williams notices, in the 1960s, that the media industries have started to de-centralize the power of national institutions, such as schools and academies, in developing and "normalizing" language use, he recognizes in this process a tension between convergence and divergence which characterizes the story of many other languages and speech communities. He writes in this connection:

> We want to speak as ourselves, and so elements of the past of the language, that we received from our parents, are always alive. At the same time, in an extending community, we want to speak with each other, reserving our actual differences but reducing those that we find irrelevant. [...] For the rest, the problems are of emotional tension, and these, while certain to continue, can be much reduced if we learn to look at them openly and rationally, with the rich and continuing history of English as our basis of understanding. (Williams, 1961/2011, p. 268)

More than half a century later, these reflections are still very topical, even if, in the intervening period, the technological, political and economic developments mentioned above have produced a different scenario.

In the following section, I will compare a few examples which show the diversification of normative frameworks that affects the notion of "standard English" in current times. These examples illustrate a further pluralization and fragmentation of "linguistic markets" (Bourdieu, 1982/1991) compared with the changes noticed by Williams in 1961, and demonstrate how, while problems of authenticity have remained topical, further transcultural negotiations take place in contexts of superdiversity.

### 8.1.1 Pronunciation Workshops and Coaches on Internet Websites

The first example relates to *Tim's Pronunciation workshop*, which was first published by the BBC in 75 episodes and made freely available on the BBC's website (BBC, n.d.). The series displays an overview of the most common phonological features of British English (e.g. assimilation of /t/ followed by /j/, gemination of /t/, contracted "have", etc.), each one of which is introduced in an episode approximately four minutes long. Every episode starts by introducing Tim, a young "English looking" man with blue eyes and curly blond hair, standing beside "his" garden workshop and welcoming the audience as follows: "Hi. I'm Tim and this is my pronunciation workshop. Here I'm going to show you how English is REALLY[143] spoken. Come on, let's go inside". Once

---

142 An exhaustive and striking account of this process in the Italian context is given by De Mauro, 1963/2017.
143 Capital letters indicate emphasis in the intonation.

the scene transitions into the workshop, Tim introduces one pronunciation feature by referring to a short anecdote. Then, he announces: "Let's meet some of the people of London."

At this point a video presents about five young people being interviewed in the streets of London who all pronounce the same sentence displaying the mentioned pronunciation trait. Tim then explains the peculiarity of the specific pronunciation feature by describing the corresponding phonological phenomena (e.g. elision, gemination, assimilation, etc.), before turning to a new video which displays five other people "of London" pronouncing a new sentence which exemplifies the same phonological phenomenon. Now it is the turn of the viewer, who is asked to listen and repeat the sentence after each one of the "model speakers". After this, Tim says goodbye and points to the other episodes of the pronunciation workshop. At the end, a funny accident offers Tim the chance to repeat, in a simulated "real talk", more sentences and colloquial expressions entailing the pronunciation trait. Finally, a whiteboard summarizes "Tim's pronunciations notes".

Here it is worth noticing firstly that it is not the entirety of British grammar at the centre of the training, but a specific part of it, namely pronunciation. Furthermore, in addressing "the people of London" as warrantors of authenticity ("how English is REALLY spoken"), the representation of linguistic correctness is rooted in the territorial principle mentioned above. The fictional character of the workshop disregards the fact that London is linguistically one of the most diverse cities in the world and that, for this reason, looking for the standard British pronunciation by interviewing people in the streets of London does not seem such a promising enterprise.

The second example relates to the presentation of pronunciation coaches through internet websites, which I will exemplify by referring to two particular providers which focus on accent reduction in English. The first one, the *American Pronunciation Coach*, which is offered by a person who presents herself as "Peggy", promises accent reduction in "American" English. Peggy presents herself as a person who has travelled very much, lived in different places, and who thus is greatly familiar, from her own experience, with pronunciation "problems" (American Pronunciation Coach, n.d.)[144]:

> *I've lived and worked in Monterey, CA, Tucson, AZ and Albuquerque, NM, in the U.S.– all cultural centers of the American Southwest.*

> *I've also lived in Rome, Italy and traveled and stayed in many places around the world. I love to travel! I'm an artist and a linguist and have kept my hand in the business of teaching ESL/EFL all my life.*

---

144 In this and in the following quotes from this coach, italic characters are in the original text.

> [...] Over the last decade, I have worked only on pronunciation and intonation, and have develo-
> ped a deep understanding of pronunciation challenges and solutions for people working on their
> sound in English. I'm very good at targeting *your specific issues* and giving you guidance in these
> areas. I'm also skillful with problems related to the American accent: what makes it difficult to
> produced [sic] and why it's difficult to understand native English speakers.
>
> *Recently, I have been working with Maharati* [sic]*, Gujarati, Russian, Chinese, Japanese, Taiwanese
> speakers on accent reduction and comprehensibility in English, and am familiar with the challen-
> ges these speakers face in English. I've also worked with Khazak* [sic]*, Korean, Italian, Portuguese,
> Swiss, and Arabic clients.*
>
> I can teach you to understand why you're having pronunciation problems, how to be more com-
> prehensible in English, and how to maintain your new sound after we are done (American Pro-
> nunciation Coach, n.d.).

Peggy addresses quite a differentiated clientele and has specialized on "errors" caused by intersections between "foreign" languages pronunciation and English, with a par-ticular emphasis on "American English". One part of the website is dedicated to the topic "what is causing your accent in English?", which illustrates typical "errors" of a variety of accents including, among others, Arabic, Chinese, French, Indo-Aryan and Korean.

The second example is the *Canadian Pronunciation Coach* (Canadian Pronuncia-tion Coach, 2020), which addresses speakers of both English as a second or foreign language and Canadian native speakers with specific pronunciation "problems", such as actors:

> Canadian actors sometimes lose out on American films because their accents sound *too Cana-
> dian*. A General American accent that's non-region specific can be learned. We work on identify-
> ing and incorporating the sounds that distinguish the General Canadian Accent from the General
> American Accent, as well as identifying distinctly American pronunciations of vocabulary and
> different cultural references.

Concerning the training which is offered for non-native speakers of English, the website reads:

> Accent Elimination vs. Speaking English with Clarity
>
> *Clients who are speakers of English as Another Language sometimes tell me they'd like to lose their
> accents completely. I always reply, "Your accent is a beautiful part of who you are."*
>
> An actor needs to become different people on screen, but you just have to be "you." With pride
> in your roots, you can alter the parts of your accent that get in the way of your being understood
> and learn effective speaking skills to communicate with confidence and conviction (Canadian
> Pronunciation Coach, n.d.).

What can be learnt from such services? In the context of "superdiversity" (Vertovec, 2007) in which patterns of mobility have increased and diversified themselves, indi-vidual linguistic repertoires have also become the more and more diverse. Despite such diversification, or precisely as a reaction to it, ideologies of correctness and related concepts of *standard* still regulate processes of in- and exclusion. This is reflected in the power of accent not only in functioning as a gatekeeper with respect to obtaining or failing to obtain career opportunities, but also in promoting or (conversely) hindering interpersonal communication in general, as stressed by one of the Pronunciation Coach websites: "Making adjustments to your accent where it affects intelligibility and adding the elements of English that connect with people in the workplace and the community" (Canadian Pronunciation Coach/ Training, n.d.). However, while Tim's pronunciation workshop refers to the territorial principle in order to derive the "authentic" British pronunciation ("the people of London"), Peggy points at her mobile lifestyle as a guarantor of her "deep understanding" of pronunciation problems. Paradoxically, her story of mobility would enable her to select "good" and "bad" pronunciation traits by signalling speakers' respective patterns of mobility, and in the end by helping them to erase the "bad" ones. Chow (2014, p. 1–17) refers to the efforts made by "xenophonic[145] nonnative speakers", to adjust their pronunciation in order to become more similar to the native speakers, as a form of "prosthetics" comparable with the treatments which persons of colour undergo in order to whiten their skin. She sees these practices as forms of "racialised languaging" by "conflating the visual and audial significations of the world *tones*" (Chow, 2014, p. 8). The next section extends these observations on language purity and the question of authenticity by focusing on the negotiations surrounding Hinglish as a postcolonial hybrid language in the context of globalisation and commercialisation of culture.

### 8.1.2 Chutnified English, Demotic Dialect or a New Lifestyle Mantra? Transcultural Negotiations of Hinglish

As argued at the beginning of this chapter, hybridizing language is anything but a rare phenomenon in everyday communication. In linguistics, the variety of terms for addressing this phenomenon—such as, for example, trans-languaging (García & Wei, 2014), trans-idiomatic practices (Jacquemet, 2005), heteroglossia (Bailey, 2012), code-switching (Lin & Li 2012), and, for an overview, Martin-Jones et al. (2012)—testifies to the multiple forms which it can take. But when does a mix of two or more "languages" become acknowledged as a language of its own? In the following section, I will consider this process by referring to the global spread of Hinglish, a hybrid language resulting from the intertwining of English and Hindi. Before looking at multiple ideologies associated with its use, it is important to stress that the ways in which English and Hindi are intertwined in language use differ significantly and that therefore Hinglish is anything but a homogeneous language system. The ideological debates

---

**145** i.e. whose voice sounds as foreign.

considered in the following show, on the one hand, how processes of standardization and "normalization" are at work as soon as the hybrid speech becomes acknowledged as an autonomous language, and on the other hand, how transcultural negotiations of meaning associated with Hinglish raise questions of authenticity, which, in different contexts both within and outside India, are comparable to and yet different from those addressed in the previous section.

Harish Trivedi (2011) retraces the development of Hinglish from its first written testimonies in the poetry (ghazal) of the India of the late nineteenth century. He relates, in this context, the mix of English and Hindi to a parodic function which carried opposite meanings. On the one hand, in a satire by the poet Ayodhya Prasad Khatri (1857–1905), the insertion of English words into a Hindi text aimed at representing ironically the stereotype of the anglicized upper-class Indians of that time, who looked at acquiring "Englishness" and migrating to London as a means of improving their status and living standards. On the other hand, one finds the parodic representation of "badly spoken" English-speaking Indians by the anglophone Indian poet Nissim Ezekiel (1924–2004), who himself emigrated to London (Trivedi, 2011, pp. XII–XV). Trivedi points at these two opposing ways of appropriating English as the "two poles of Indian attitudes to English and its Indianisation" (Trivedi, 2011, p. XV). Turning to more recent times, in the 1960s, Trivedi refers to the use of Hinglish in Shobhaa Dé's gossip column "Nita's Natter" in the English-speaking film magazine *Stardust*, in which the author, by reviewing Hindi films in English for her Hindi-speaking audience, spices up her texts by inserting Hindi words. Trivedi contrasts this use of Hinglish, in which both the author and the reader share a common knowledge of both the languages and their contexts of use, to the use of language by Salman Rushdie, whose practice to "chutnefy English" demonstrates, in Trivedi's view, a lack of knowledge about the original meanings and contexts of use of the Indian words inserted into his English texts. As a result, Trivedi argues, Rushdie ends up exoticizing both his subject matter and the Indian languages, and, by using "the small change of a few Hindi words to authenticate himself in the eyes of his Western readers, for he knows these words and they do not", demonstrating in fact a "very lack of authenticity" (Trivedi, 2011, pp. XVII–XVIII). The examples mentioned by Trivedi are initial testimonies of the written use of Hinglish in a time in which it was not yet recognized as an autonomous "language". They are, nevertheless, very topical with respect to central issues associated with the use of Hinglish today, such as the problem of authenticity and the risk of exoticizing usage of it, or the association between Hinglish and a particular lifestyle.

It was only at the beginning of the 1990s when Hinglish began to be considered as a "proper language". This took place in the context of its increasing use in cinema, television and advertising. Daya Kishan Thussu (2011) relates this process both to the growth of a young, urbanized and culturally hybridized middle class, who is attracted by consumerist life-styles and with increasing purchasing power, and to the liberalization of media and cultural industries in India and the increasing availability of new media technologies, such as satellite and cable television. This has attracted transnational media corporations, which, beside the above-mentioned transformations of local audiences, could also take advantage of the generally globalizing tendency of the media market, blurring boundaries between local, diaspora and transnational audiences. The diffusion of Amazon, Netflix and other media-services providers, together with the individualization of media consumption, has increased the forms and the meanings of multilingualism in media products, not only with respect to Hinglish, but also regarding many regional languages used in India. Smith Mehta (2020) points in this regard to the increasing creation, circulation and consumption of "regional" online content in non-Hindi and non-English languages in India. He stresses the potential of such localization strategies with respect to the possibility for the viewers of developing a sense of familiarity with what is represented on the screen, especially in the context of the Indian government's nationalistic efforts to promote Hindi (Mehta, 2020, p. 116). Thussu (2011) expresses instead a more critical position in this regard and speaks of the "Murdochisation" of the media, by referring to the expansion of global corporations which, despite formally adopting localization strategies which claim to be addressing national or local interests, in fact propagate a dominant neoliberal ideology that undermines "the public-service ethos and the empowering potential of TV in a country that is still home to the largest segment of the world's poorest people" (Thussu, 2011, p. 111). Hinglish is, however, not only associated with the emergence of neoliberalism and consumerist attitudes. Rita Kothari and Rupert Snell (2011), who offer a multifaced perspective on the development of Hinglish by comparing interdisciplinary scholarly and practitioners' insights, examine a very heterogeneous panorama and note "almost irreconcilable ideologies". Beside the aforementioned strand of thought which considers Hinglish as a form of Westernization and a superficial exoticization of Indian culture that undermines its authenticity, other observers have acknowledged, particularly in more recent times, the symbolic power of Hinglish in negotiating new spaces of identity that intertwine the local and the global. Kothari (2011), for example, has stressed a change in the way in which Hindi and English have been used in Hindi cinema from the post-Independence period to contemporary times:

> I argue that during this period [i.e. of post-Independence] Hindi cinema used English with connotations of cultural alienation such as Westernisation and class elitism, giving way in the last two decades to less anxious uses of Hinglish – creolised, constructed, and promoted as a language of fun-on-Indian-terms. While the association with class persists, it moves from signifiers of exclusivity to aspiration, as more people are now able to access that class. If the class theme represents continuity, the discontinuity lies in the shift of perception of English from being a language "outside" the sphere of everyday Indianness (1950s-1980s) to Hinglish as simultaneously Indian-and-global, embracing *des* and *pardes*, nation and diaspora in cinema after the 1990s. (Kothari, 2011, p. 113)

This view is shared by Prateek and Amit Sarwal (2014), who stress that the growth of Hinglish cinema in the 1990s represents a reaction to the nationalist orientation of Hindi mainstream cinema which, by standardizing Hindi and purifying it from the "contamination" of other languages, had contributed to the affirmation of a "Hindi public sphere" (Orsini, 2002) involving "discursive and institutional spaces, a common language, a set of procedural principles (e.g. respect for reasoned argument and open debate), some activism, and the awareness of a public *out there*" (Orsini, 2002, pp. 11–12). Moreover, Prateek and Amit Sarwal (2014) highlight how, in opposition to mainstream *masala* cinema, which had idealized the village and proposed an escapist attitude with respect to both the colonial experience and the problems of everyday life, Hinglish cinema recalls the realistic taste of the (*New Wave*) art cinema of the 1960s and 1970s, by critically looking at the village and deconstructing its idealized image, after Bollywood has romantically represented it as an incorruptible site:

> Hinglish cinema revamps city and presents it as a global village where people from different linguistic backgrounds intermingle. It provides educated Indians access to a world that the Hindi- dominated world of Bollywood denied them earlier. [...] This global character of the city is emphasised through *chutnified* English, which is spoken by Indians in these cities. In these movies, one encounters a continuum of English: from *Bazaar-English*, *Butler-English*, *Baboo-English*, *diasporic English* to *near native English*. These displaced people – linguistically and otherwise – are in their camps or settlements in the urban areas and such settlements are on the increase. (Sarwal & Sarwal, 2014, pp. 167–168)

The crucial transition from the simple insertion of English words into Hindi screenplays to the affirmation of a hybrid language, in which English and Hindi flow into each other, has been dated back to the 1990s (Kothari, 2011). Beside matters of authenticity, which have already been mentioned, questions of language competence have also been raised in this regard. Will the spread of Hinglish challenge speakers' competence in English, Hindi and other languages? Snell (2011, p. 36), for example, expresses his worry about a "dilution of the genius of Hindi, and irreversible damage to its ecological balance", by highlighting how loans from English are not a simple addition to Hindi, but are actually displacing Hindi words. This worry is shared by Trivedi (2011), who rejects the status of "language" for Hinglish: "The major peril of thus promoting a *demotic dialect* [my italic] like Hinglish is that we may soon be left with neither Hindi nor English but just Hinglish" (Trivedi, 2011, p. XXIII). A similar position has been expressed by the late Vinod Mehta, journalist and former founding editor-in-chief of the Indian English-speaking general interest magazine *Outlook*, who stated in an interview to *the Guardian International*: "It's a terrible slide in quality when respectable publications use this hotchpotch of English and Hindi. We produce journalism in English" (Ramesh, 2008).

A further dispute regards the future of Hinglish as a marginalized or, contrarily, a global language. Trivedi (2011) compares, for example, the destiny of Hinglish with that of Urdu in the Indian subcontinent. Originating as a hybrid language which mixed

Persian and Indian local languages, in a period in which Persian was the ruling language spoken by a tiny elite, Urdu, which held for a while a high status because of its closeness to the "cosmopolitan Persian", eventually lost its power, "mainly because it retained the courtly sophistication of Persian and this remained largely incomprehensible to the masses who spoke Hindi" (Trivedi, 2011, p. XXIV). An opposite prediction has been expressed by the Indian journalist Binoo K. John, who has documented the rise of Hinglish, in an interview to *the Guardian International*: "Within two decades Hinglish would become a globally accepted form. More and more people will use it without fear of being laughed at. We are not afraid of speaking in the way that we want anymore" (Ramesh, 2008). This proud act of empowering Hinglish and distancing it from British English (and the attitude of considering British English as "the" standard), recalls the process of transformation of American English in the eighteenth and nineteenth centuries. As highlighted by Kahane (1982), in the decolonized society of the New World, spoken American English transformed from a substandard (with respect to elite British English) to a prestige language by its symbolizing the language of an "Everyman" in a society that aimed at being for the "Everyman". By stating that "the present is the age of simplicity of writing in America", Benjamin Rush, signer of the United States Declaration of Independence, emphasized precisely "the decline in Anglophilia, the standardization of informal speech, the levelling of social dialects, the integration of foreign elements" (Kahane, 1982, p. 230).

Is Hinglish going through a comparable standardization process while becoming a "global code"? The perspective of young academics both within and outside India seems to confirm this trend. Pal and Mishra (2011), who reflect on their experience as students at the Mudra Institute of Communications in Ahmedabad, an elite Indian institution of higher learning, considers Hinglish "not just as a language but also a *new lifestyle mantra* [my italic]" (Pal & Mishra, 2011, p. 160). Indeed, Hinglish is spreading in the universities, and not only in India, both as a language of instruction and in language teaching. The Portsmouth College in England, for example, has introduced classes of Hinglish in 2017. What was at the beginning an experimental initiative has turned to be part of the regular offer from the 2018–2019 academic year, because of its popularity among the students (Times of India, 2018). A BBC service (BBC News, n.d.) reporting on this, displays a heterogeneous group (in terms of gender, religion and ethnicity) of students practising Hinglish in a typical class of language teaching. The choral repetition of specific linguistic traits and the comments of the interviewed students indeed recall the idea of a "new lifestyle mantra" which was proposed by Pal and Mishra. One student, for example, by displaying the pronunciation that was taught by Tim in his pronunciation workshop, states: "I'm in this bubble of Portsmouth and I want to get out of this bubble". In another case, while the teacher explains the way in which Hindi and English intertwines in an advertising text, a subtitle points out: "India is the world's seventh largest economy so young people are keen to look for international opportunities". Two interventions by members of the academic staff highlight that it is not the language competence itself to be considered particularly important ("When it is Hinglish is about Hindi and English, but it could be any language"), but rather the acquisition by the students of a particular "cosmopolitan attitude":

> It's great to hear that our future generation of workers are actually taking into consideration what's happening around us. So they are socially aware but they are looking at ways in which they can equip themselves to be better prepared for situations that they may be faced with. (BBC News, n.d.)

These last words by the interviewee are accompanied by the image of a crowded Indian market. Against this background, a concluding subtitle reads: "Hinglish is India's business language of choice".

While some observers neglect the status of a "language" for Hinglish, its practices of standardization and its use not only in cinema, television and advertising but also in contexts of education both within and outside India, would suggest that Hinglish occupies anything but a marginal position in globalized "linguistic markets". Should this be considered a progress in normalizing linguistic diversity in public spheres, or does the standardization of Hinglish and its transformation into an acknowledged "language" only reproduce a pattern of homogenization of diversity? In the next section, two more examples illustrating the negotiation of national, minority and local languages in both multi- and translingual mediascapes[146] will offer more insights for discussing this question in the final section.

## 8.2 "Parallel Monolingualism" vs. Performed Diversity

The need to communicate in an extending community, and the value acquired by English in a globalized "linguistic market" (Bourdieu, 1982/1991), have been variously contrasted by claiming that the attachment to specific linguistic resources (national or minority languages, dialects, etc.) should be understood as territorially bound to a particular identity. In defence of local, regional or national features of identity, diversity has often been held up as an example of a resisting ideology with respect to the alleged homogenization brought about by globalization. In this section, I will compare different ways of handling linguistic diversity in public spheres with the aim

---

146 The distinction between multi- and translingual mediascapes, which will be further illustrated in section 3, aims at contrasting two different ways of handling linguistic diversity in mediated communicative spaces. Whereas the term "multilingual" stresses the juxtaposition of single "languages" (e.g. Spanish, English, etc.) which do not intertwine, the term "translingual" refers to hybrid language use (Pelillo-Hestermeyer 2018a). The term *mediascape* (Appadurai, 1996) refers instead to transnational media flows whicoss national boundaries and which articulate themselves in an asymmetrical, polycentric geometry of networks.

of discussing how diversity and otherness are regulated, performed and negotiated in the corresponding contexts, and to what extent specific practices, which professedly aim at enhancing diversity, in fact end up stimulating power asymmetries and conflicts.

In institutional contexts, a range of policies and politics has been developed for protecting specific national or minority languages from being marginalized or even replaced by "global" English in many contexts of use. Art. 3(3) sub-para. 4 of the Treaty on European Union, for example, reads: "It [the EU] shall respect its rich cultural and linguistic diversity, and shall ensure that Europe's cultural heritage is safeguarded and enhanced" (Official Journal 2012 C 326/13). Linguistic Diversity is conceived in this context as resulting from the sum of European "heritage" languages, which are defined on a territorial basis, that is, consisting of the languages historically present on the European territory. Among these languages, national majority languages (and their corresponding speakers) benefit from greater protection than do minority languages, for example by being considered as official languages of the European Union, which guarantee, among other aspects, the right to use these languages in the communication with the European institutions, according to Art. 41(4) of the Charter of Fundamental Rights of the European Union: "Every person may write to the institutions of the Union in one of the languages of the Treaties and must have an answer in the same language" (Official Journal 2012 C 326/391). This territorial principle is often addressed while reasoning about language policies. A recent example is offered by the discussions surrounding the status of English after Brexit and whether it should remain a working language of the European Union, given that Ireland would remain the only member State in which English functions as the nation's main language. Moreover, the "heritage principle" does not acknowledge speech communities which have been present in the European Union from more recent times. A further example of resistance to English in an international institutional context is offered by Art. 11 of the UN General Assembly Resolution 67/292 on Multilingualism, which

> *emphasizes* the importance of making use of all the official languages of the United Nations, ensuring their full and equitable treatment in all the activities of the Department of Public Information of the Secretariat, with the aim of eliminating the disparity between the use of English and the use of the five other official languages, and in this regard reaffirms its request that its Secretary General ensure that the Department has the necessary staffing capacity in all the official languages to undertake all of its activities. (General Assembly Resolution 67/292)

The above-mentioned policies shall guarantee full and equitable treatment to specific "official languages", yet not to the "languages" of all members of the corresponding institutions. In the European Union, a differentiation between the currently 24 "official languages" and the three "working languages" (English, French and German) has brought about asymmetries between speakers of working, official and minority languages. A conflict regarding the mandatory use of one of the three working languages in recruitment processes at the European institutions has driven, for example,

Italy and Spain to the point of suing the European Commission and succeeding in a case at the Court of Justice of the European Union in 2019[147]. As it emerges from these examples, the promotion of linguistic diversity in terms of safeguarding specific heritages is also strongly related to the investment of resources. Bourdieu's concept of the "linguistic market" has not lost, in this regard, its applicability, since diversity policies and politics are also a means of preserving a more central, or negotiating a less marginal, position in this regard.

When we now turn to mediatized public spheres, the European news channel *Euronews* in 2017 started a process of transformation from a "glocal" journalism – that is, one in which contents were adapted (including linguistically) to local audiences— to a new model, based on twelve different "cross-platform" editions, each one of which is characterized by the use of a specific language, as explained on the website:

> Since its launch in 1993 in Lyon, France, *Euronews* has developed the world's first "glocal" news brand, i.e. the first global media that adapts itself to the expectation of its multiple local audiences. In 2017, *Euronews* replaced its model that had been at the core of its offer since its inception by the launch of 12 distinct cross-platform editions. The different editions enable *Euronews* to deliver tailored content that is relevant to each audience. With a team of 600 journalists of more than 30 different nationalities, *Euronews'* 12 editions cover world news 24/7 in Arabic, English, French, German, Greek, Hungarian, Italian, Persian, Portuguese, Russian, Spanish and Turkish. (Euronews, n.d.)

Language diversity is considered in this regard as the fundamental means of sorting audiences, and as an important criterium for selecting contents which are considered to be of interest for a corresponding community. By only partly overcoming the assumption that one culturally (and linguistically) homogeneous community corresponds to one geographic territory, sorting audiences by identifying "language communities" reproduces an idea of diversity based on the juxtaposition of single and monolithic cultural systems, thus perpetrating the nexus of "one language-one public sphere", as was illustrated in section 2 with respect to the institutionalization of, respectively, the national language and the media[148]. A similar attitude to linguistic diversity can be observed by looking at multilingual practices in the context of the French-German television network *ARTE*, which commonly offers shared content in French and German by dubbing. However, since 2015 *ARTE* has progressively extended to include four other languages (Italian, English, Polish and Spanish), also thanks to funding by the European Union, which aims at fostering "EU integration through culture by providing new subtitled versions of selected TV programmes across Europe" (ARTE, n.d.). The use of subtitles instead of dubbing, which allows the audience to access

---

147  Case C-621/16 P, Commission v. Italian Republic, ECLI:EU:C:2019:251.
148  For a more extensive analysis of such practices, see Pelillo-Hestermeyer 2018a and 2015. Moreover, Pelillo-Hestermeyer/Cismondi in this volume considers a similar attitude to diversity with respect to diversity in science.

contents in the original language(s), contributes not only to raise awareness towards linguistic differences, but also to enrich audiences' linguistic repertoires by increasing their understanding of languages that might otherwise be considered as "foreign". All in all, as I have argued in previous works (Pelillo-Hestermeyer 2018a, 2018b and 2015), increasing the visibility of, instead of hiding, linguistic diversity contributes to the strengthening of more tolerant and open attitudes towards "the Other". In this context, it appears as a paradox that the multilingual offer is presented on the *ARTE's* website by recurring to the following paratext: "ARTE in 6 languages – To 70% of Europeans in *their own* language [my italics] (ARTE, n.d.)."

Instead of emphasizing that the subtitles-strategy allows European audiences to access shared media content in the original languages, thus enhancing the visibility of European diversity, the paratext not only does not mention this possibility, but implicitly assumes that the audiences would display a completely opposite attitude, namely that of being interested in receiving the contents only "in their own language". Furthermore, it assumes that Europeans each "have" one language, thus recalling the ideology of "one language-one community" that we saw to be illustrated with respect to European language policy. This way of handling linguistic diversity in mediated public spheres has been addressed as "parallel monolingualism" (Heller, 2006), or "pluralised monolingualism" (Makoni & Pennycook, 2007), since it relies on a conceptualization of diversity as the juxtaposition of separate monolingual speech communities.

In Pelillo-Hestermeyer (2018a) I contrasted this phenomenon of "parallel monolingualism" with other ways of handling linguistic diversity in particular transcultural journalism in the Mediterranean, where I described it in particular as "translingua", or "multilingua franca", using the term coined by Makoni and Pennycook (2007). Both these terms aim at emphasizing the fact that plurality and hybridity are essential characters of language use and that, for this reason, linguistic diversity would not need any pluralization of the term "language" (e.g. *multi*lingualism). One of the media products which exemplify this different approach to linguistic diversity in journalism is a weekly radio magazine in Corsican and Italian, which is co-produced by the Italian and French broadcasters RAI and France Bleu. *Mediterradio*—the title of the show—is presented as a weekly magazine of the Mediterranean islands Corsica, Sardinia and Sicily, although journalists from Tunis and Malta also participate in the show periodically. Instead of addressing the audiences by separating them according to "language communities", the three anchors, who are located in the respective islands, use Italian and Corsican without translating or dubbing, by relying on the inter-comprehension between the two languages, and thus emphasize the mutual proximity in their linguistic diversity. When the colleagues participate in the show from Tunis and Malta, they use Italian as a lingua franca. Mutual understanding between speakers of Italian and Corsican is possible, but not expected without a certain effort in speaking particularly clearly and listening particularly carefully. Moreover, it requires an open attitude towards the different phonologies, as well as the acceptance of missing meanings from time to time. Certainly, listening regularly to the magazine improves one's individual translingual understanding. However, the main aim of the magazine does not consist of enhancing audiences' linguistic skills, but rather presenting a different, and specifically an "insular" Mediterranean, perspective on current events. Rather than focussing on juxtaposition and on a territorial mapping of speech communities, this way of handling diversity relies on polycentricism and connectivity, which can be observed in interactional, discursive and journalistic practices[149]. The appropriation of a more central position in reporting about and from the Mediterranean emphasizes both diversity and familiarity without levelling, standardizing or normalizing differences, while also setting itself in opposition to the mainstream media reports in national and transnational public spheres (Pelillo-Hestermeyer, 2018a).

Such an idea and practice of diversity should not be seen as necessarily linked to mixing two or more "languages". As the examples in this chapter show, promoting or hindering linguistic diversity is more about "doing diversity" vs. "doing otherness" by representing and performing language(s).

## 8.3 Concluding Remarks

At the beginning of this chapter, linguistic diversity was acknowledged to be one of the most common experiences in human life. This premise was aimed at emphasizing how, nevertheless, various ideologies at the core of mediatized language use lead either to representing diversity as something exceptional, or to standardizing and homogenizing hybrid language use. This is related, historically, to the institutionalization process of, respectively, national language(s) and media system(s), which has accompanied the formation of the nation state. After this discussion, I referred to the comments by Raymond Williams in 1961, who noticed that a new player, "the media", was starting to influence, de-centralize and pluralize the concept of "standard" codified and disseminated by institutions, such as schools and academies. Today, media can no longer be addressed as autonomous agents which directly influence the value of "languages", as they did when Williams' *The Long Revolution* was first published in the early 1960s. It appears rather to be more appropriate to look at practices of representing, disputing and standardizing diversity in the context of the overall transformation of public spheres, by referring to the four meta-processes indicated by Krotz (2009), namely globalization, mediatization, commercialization and individualization[150]. Bourdieu's concept of the "linguistic market" helps us to

---

149 For a more detailed analysis of interactional, discursive and journalistic practices, see Pelillo-Hestermeyer 2018a.

150 "Each of these meta-processes is an ordering principle, which helps us to think of specific events

understand the negotiations of power that are operative in this regard: Resistance towards the commercialization of culture, personified by the rise of global English (but also of Hinglish, even if in a minor tone), is expressed by various policies and politics that are aimed at safeguarding "heritage" languages, as exemplified by the examples in section 8.2. Practices of "parallel monolingualism" (Heller, 2006), or "pluralized monolingualism" (Makoni & Pennycook, 2007), follow a similar pattern by following the territorial principle in conceiving and promoting diversity by juxtaposing different "speech communities". The different examples illustrated demonstrate that, despite the different forms taken by standardization in different contexts, the homogenizing ideology at the core remains a constant. Questions of authenticity, which have emerged in all the discussed cases, demonstrate this. In *Tim's Pronunciation Workshop*, it is the territorial principle to be addressed as a guarantor of the "right" pronunciation ("let's meet the people of London"), a homologizing idealization which distorts the "superdiversity" which actually characterizes the English metropolis. In this case, the commercial pronunciation coaches point at accent reduction, which is in fact a way of standardizing diversity by deliberately selecting, case by case, which pronunciation traits can be preserved and which need to be erased. At the same time, the coaches emphasize how important it is "to be yourself" by altering one's native pronunciation. The principle of authenticity becomes individualized in this context: In a globalized "linguistic market" it is the "right" mix between specific linguistic resources to be of particular value. A personal coach should help, in this context, to skilfully select and erase only the "bad" phonological traits. This recalls what Blommaert (2010, p. 47) writes regarding linguistic inequality in the context of globalization:

> The crux of the matter is that we need to think of issues such as linguistic inequality as being organized around concrete resources, not around languages in general but specific registers, varieties, genres. And such concrete resources follow the predicament of their users: when the latter are socially mobile, their resources will follow this trajectory; when they are socially marginal, their resources will also be disqualified. In both cases, the challenge is to think of language as a mobile complex of concrete resources.

As a matter of fact, one of the pronunciation coaches pinpoints her mobile lifestyle and her passion for travelling as one of the major sources of her knowledge and ability. The dispute surrounding the rise of Hinglish confirms a similar polarization between, on the one hand, speakers who advocate the territorial principle as a guarantor of authenticity, and on the other hand, those who see it as a "new lifestyle mantra", regardless of how "correctly" one can use it. Those who advocate the territorial principle perceive as authentic only the use of Hinglish by speakers who know the

---

and developments as belonging together, as each one takes place in specific fields of culture and society and then affects many other fields" (Krotz, 2009, pp. 24–25).

original (that is, territorialized) meanings and contexts of use of both the languages in question, namely Hindi and English. They perceive as exoticizing the use of Hinglish by people who might not have the same "competence" in both languages, and in particular display a lesser "competence" of Hindi than their competence in English. On the other side, those who see Hinglish as a means of "being local and global" display multiple appropriations and re-signifying practices of Hinglish, as it typically occurs with global resources. Hinglish is perceived by some Indian observers as a symbol that unifies nation and diaspora, the (post)colonial experience and the global future of India. In England, however, young learners of Hinglish are not aware of this "trajectory" (Blommaert, 2010, p. 47, quoted above), and only perceive it as a way of "going global" by looking outside of England. This happens while learners of English try to get rid of their linguistic "otherness" by attending pronunciation coaches who assist with British English, the global language. In both cases, issues of authenticity and class permeate standardization practices. However, while defining a specific prestige language according to the territorial principle, continues a tradition originated within the consolidation of the nation state, relating prestige and class to a specific lifestyle is a more recent phenomenon, inserted into the overall "meta-process" (Krotz 2009) of commercialization of culture. In this context, while Hinglish displays the "right mix" to be considered "local and global", other "languages" do not. Worries concerning the "loss of competence" in both English and Hindi, originate, among others, from looking at other hybrid "languages" which, both within and outside India, have become marginalized.

At the same time technologies such as the Internet and digitalization more broadly have also opened up new opportunities for linguistic diversity in less institutionalized and mediatized public spheres. The radio magazine *Mediterradio* represents a symptomatic example of a new mode of "doing diversity" by opposing vernacular sensitivities to, respectively, the monolingualism of national mainstream media and the "parallel monolingualism" of transnational mainstream media. In this case, centres and peripheries become re-negotiated in a transnational and "fluid" public sphere. Certainly, this sort of "translingua" (Pelillo-Hestermeyer 2018a) represents a niche phenomenon. Research on mediated multilingualism (Kelly-Holmes & Milani, 2011b) highlights in this regard that most of the deconstructionist critique, as is expressed by post-structuralist sociolinguistics, of the hegemonic practices of mediatized multilingualism (e.g. the hegemonic idea of speech community as a homogeneous group, the tabooification of hybrid speech, or the need to categorize languages), has not yet reached the media-makers. They notice in this regard that media-makers are not essentially pitted against linguistic diversity but are rather used to adopting conceptual frameworks that, we have seen, are so ideologically marked. Kelly-Holmes and Milani go so far as to look at this gap as "one of the key challenges for scholarship on multilingualism and/in the media in the near future" (Kelly-Holmes & Milani, 2011b, p. 475).

Against this background, this chapter aims at raising awareness, also outside of academia, about ideological frames at work by "doing diversity" or "doing otherness" in mediatized public spheres and in everyday life in general. Mixing "languages" might appear, in this context, to be the ordinary and future default aspect of this subject area.

# References

Androutsopoulos, J. (Ed.). (2014). Mediatization and sociolinguistic change. De Gruyter.

American Pronunciation Coach. (n.d.). Retrieved March 2, 2020 from https://americanpronunciationcoach.com/welcome/aboutyourcoach

Appadurai, A. (1996). Modernity at Large: Cultural Dimensions of Globalization. Univ. of Minnesota Press.

ARTE. (n.d.). What we do. Retrieved March 24, 2020, from https://www.arte.tv/sites/en/corporate/what-we-do

Bailey, B. (2012). Heteroglossia. In M. Martin-Jones, A. Blackledge, & A. Creese (Eds.), The Routledge Handbook of Multilingualism (pp. 499–520). Routledge.

BBC (n.d.). Tim's Pronunciation Workshop. Retrieved March 2, 2020, from http://www.bbc.co.uk/learningenglish/english/features/pronunciation/tims-pronunciation-workshop-ep-30

BBC News (n.d.). Hinglish taught in UK 'for first time'. You Tube. Retrieved March 24, 2020, from https://www.youtube.com/watch?v=GTqvzmlfFqw&feature=youtu.be

Blommaert, J. (2010). The Sociolinguistics of Globalization. Cambridge University Press.

Blommaert, J. (2013). Ethnography, superdiversity and linguistic landscapes: chronicles of complexity. Multilingual Matters.

Blommaert, J., Collins, J., & Slembrouck, S. (2005). Spaces of multilingualism. Language and Communication, 25, 197–216.

Blommaert, J., Kelly-Holmes, H., Lane, P., Leppänen, S., Moriarty, M., Pietikäinen, S., & Piirainen-Marsh, A. (2009). Media, Multilingualism and Language Policing: an Introduction. Language Policy, 8(3), 203–207.

Blommaert, J., Rampton, B., & Spotti, M. (Eds.). (2011). Language and Superdiversities (Vol. 13 (2)): UNESCO.

Bourdieu, P. (with Thompson, J. B.) (1991). Language and symbolic power. Polity (Original work published 1982. Ce que parler veux dire.)

Busch, B. (2012). Das sprachliche Repertoire oder Niemand ist einsprachig. Drava.

Butler, J. (2006). Haß spricht: zur Politik des Performativen. Suhrkamp.

Canadian Pronunciation Coach (n.d.) Retrieved March 2, 2020, from http://www.canadianpronunciationcoach.com

Canadian Pronunciation Coach/ Training (n.d.). Retrieved March 2, 2020, from http://www.canadian-pronunciationcoach.com/training/method

Chow, R. (2014). Not like a Native Speaker. On Languaging as a Postcolonial Experience". Columbia University Press.

De Mauro, T. (2017). Storia linguistica dell'Italia unita. GLF editori Laterza. (Original work published 1963).

Derrida, J. (1996). Le monolinguisme de l'autre. Éditions Gallilée.

Euronews (n.d.). About Euronews. Retrieved March 24, 2020, from https://www.euronews.com/about

Foucault, M. (1972). The archaeology of knowledge and the discourse on language. Pantheon Books.

García, O., & Wei, L. (2014). Translanguaging: language, bilingualism and education. Palgrave Macmillan.

General Assembly Resolution 67/292, Multilingualism, A/RES/67/292. Retrieved April 3, 2020 from https://treaties.un.org/doc/source/a_res_67_292-Eng.pdf

Heller, M. (2006). Linguistic Minorities and Modernity: a Sociolinguistic Ethnography. Continuum.

Hepp, A. (2009). Differentiation: Mediatization and Cultural Change. In K. Lundby (Ed.), Mediatization: Concepts, Changes, Consequences (pp. 139–157). New York: Peter Lang.

Hepp, A. (2014). Mediatization. A Panorama of Media and Communication Research. In J. Androutsopoulos (Ed.), Mediatization and Sociolinguistic Change (pp. 49–66). De Gruyter.

Jacquemet, M. (2005). Transidiomatic practices: Language and power in the age of globalization. Language and Communication, 25, 257–277.

Kahane, H. (1982). American English: From a Colonial Substandard to a Prestige Language. In B. B. Kachru (Ed.), The other tongue: English across cultures (pp. 229–236). University of Illinois Press.

Kelly-Holmes, H., & Milani, T. M. (Eds.). (2011a). Thematising Multilingualism in the Media. Journal of Language and Politics. Special issue, 10(4), Benjamins.

Kelly-Holmes, H., & Milani, T. M. (2011b). Thematising Multilingualism in the Media. In H. Kelly-Holmes & T. M. Milani (Eds.), Introduction: Thematising Multilingualism in the Media. Journal of Language and Politics. Special issue, 10(4), 467–489. Benjamins.

Kothari, R. (2011). English AAJKAL: Hinglish in Hindi cinema. In R. Kothari & R. Snell (Eds.), Chutnefying English: The phenomenon of Hinglish (pp. 112–127). Penguin Books India.

Kothari, R., & Snell, R. (Eds.). (2011). Chutnefying English: the phenomenon of Hinglish. Penguin Books India.

Krotz, F. (2009). Mediatization: A Concept with which to grasp Media and societal Change. In K. Lundby (Ed.), Mediatization: Concept, Changes, Consequences (pp. 21–40). Peter Lang.

Lin, A. Y. M., & Li, D. C. S. (2012). Codeswitching. In M. Martin-Jones, A. Blackledge, & A. Creese (Eds.), The Routledge Handbook of Multilingualism (pp. 470–481). Routledge.

Livingstone, S. (2009). On the mediation of everything. Journal of Communication, 59(1), 1–18.

Lundby, K. (Ed.) (2009). Mediatization: Concept, Changes, Consequences. New York: Peter Lang.

Makoni, S., & Pennycook, A. (2007). Disinventing and Reconstituting Languages. In S. Makoni & A. Pennycook (Eds.), Disinventing and Reconstituting Languages (pp. 1–41). Multilingual Matters.

Martin-Jones, M., Blackledge, A., & Creese, A. (Eds.). (2012). The Routledge Handbook of Multilingualism. Routledge.

Mehta, S. (2020). Localization, diversification and heterogeneity: Understanding the linguistic and cultural logics of Indian new media. International Journal of Cultural Studies, 23(1), 102–120.

Official Journal 2012 C. Retrieved April 3, 2020, from https://eur-lex.europa.eu/LexUriServ/LexUriServ.do?uri=OJ:C:2012:326:FULL:EN:PDF

Orsini, F. (2002). The Hindi public sphere 1920–1940: language and literature in the age of nationalism. Oxford Univ. Press.

Pal, S., & Mishra, S. (2011). Hinglish and Youth: A campus perspective. In R. Kohari & R. Snell (Eds.), Chutnefying English: The phenomenon of Hinglish (pp. 161–175). Penguin Books India.

Pelillo-Hestermeyer, G. (2015). Mehrsprachiger und lokaler Radiojournalismus: ein interdisziplinärer Ansatz zur Förderung von Medien- und Sprachkompetenzen. In S. Witzigmann & J. Rymarczyk (Eds.), Mehrsprachigkeit als Chance: Herausforderungen und Potentiale individueller und gesellschaftlicher Mehrsprachigkeit (pp. 273–285). Peter Lang.

Pelillo-Hestermeyer, G. (2018a). Language diversity in a Mediterranean mediascape. Discourse, Context & Media, 24, 109–116. https://doi.org/10.1016/j.dcm.2018.02.006

Pelillo-Hestermeyer, G. (2018b). Transkulturelle Philologie: Über das Potential eines Überdenkens fachlicher und nationaler Grenzen. In J. Ettrich & M. L. Mäder (Eds.), Dialogpotentiale kulturwissenschaftlicher Forschung in den Fremdsprachenphilologien (pp. 157–172). Lang.

Ramesh, R. (2008, October 24). English is recast in Indian films. The Guardian. Retrieved April 4, 2020, from https://www.theguardian.com/education/2008/oct/17/bollywood-english

Sarwal, P., & Sarwal, A. (2014). Hinglish cinema: The confluence of East and West. In V. Kishore, A. Sarwal, & P. Patra (Eds.), Bollywood and its Other(s) (pp. 161–173). Palgrave MacMillan.

Snell, R. (2011). Hindi: Its threatened ecology and natural genius. In R. Kothari & R. Snell (Eds.), Chutnefying English: The phenomenon of Hinglish (pp. 22–36). Penguin Books India.

Thussu, D. K. (2011). Towards a political economy of Hinglish TV. In R. Kothari & R. Snell (Eds.), Chutnefying English: The phenomenon of Hinglish (pp. 98–111). Penguin Books India.

Times of India. (2018, March 10). UK college to expand Hinglish course offering. Retrieved April 4, 2020, from https://timesofindia.indiatimes.com/uk/uk-college-to-expand-hinglish-course-offering/articleshow/63244821.cms

Trivedi, H. (2011). Forward. In R. Kothari & R. Snell (Eds.), Chutnefying English. The Phenomenon of Hinglish (pp. VII–XXVI). Penguin Books India.

Vertovec, S. (2007). Super-diversity and its implications. Ethnic and Racial Studies, 29(6), 1024–1054.

Vertovec, S. (Ed.). (2010). Anthropology of migration and multiculturalism: new directions. Routledge.

Williams, R. (2011). The Long Revolution. Parthian. (Original Work published 1961).

Dagmar Reichardt

# 9 Style, Sense and Senses: The Iconic and Transcultural Language of Italian Fashion

*A dress tells more than a thousand words.*

## 9.1 Centre versus Periphery

If we start—as the title of this book *Diversity and Otherness: Transcultural Insights into Norms, Practices, Negotiations* suggests—from the axiom that *Diversity* and *Otherness* have become more and more visible in our life-worlds around the globe nowadays and that—in reaction to this—societies tend to control (by *Norms*), regulate (by *Practices*) and find their cultural identity (by *Negotiations*) within this multitude of otherness in order to express their rootedness as well as their transculturality, then the iconic language of Italian fashion seems to combine exactly these parameters. Converting it into an object of research, the topic of the Italian fashion system and history has, indeed, the potential to essentially show that the (philosophical and spiritual) sense and the (physical and body-related) senses of fashion (in the plural) mark a most appropriate, suitable and practical approach for looking at socio-political and artistic ways of negotiating between individuals and their society as well as of promoting emancipatory social discourses worldwide.

In this first section "Centre versus Periphery" (9.1), I will try to introduce to this topic, by taking a look at the borders that contour the world of fashion in the broader sense. In the section "Transcultural Theory and the Italian Habitus" (9.2), we will examine more closely the Italian blueprint of the history of fashion, before giving proof of our thesis with the help of a concrete case-study in section 9.3 "Karl Lagerfeld: 90 Years of Fendi—90 Years of Fairy Tales (2016)". To conclude, the section "Transmedia Content and Our Nomadic Lifestyle in Postmodern Times" (9.4) will fine-tune the transmedia and nomadic factors that generate transculturality in the fashion system, before the section "Fashion as an Aesthetic and Didactic Tool" (9.5) wraps up our reflections, focusing on the practical use of why fashion matters both, in the arts and in culture, as well as in the classroom.

Now, as far as methodological approaches are concerned, in the following I will mainly contextualize my source material with theoretical reflections connected to the *Iconic Turn* (Maar & Burda, 2004) and the notion of *transculturality,* as coined by Wolfgang Welsch (cf. Welsch, 1999). As far as the research within the field of Fashion Studies itself is concerned, I am interested in further developing the application of transcultural parameters to discourses of clothing and apparel that are visible in our daily life practices, after having noticed during the making of a book about Italian fashion released in 2016 (Reichardt & D'Angelo, 2016) that the—for me, most obvious—relation between fashion and transculturality had yet to be analysed systematically. With increasing industrial relevance since the turn of the century, the power of fashion has, however, not gone completely unnoticed on the level of research. Innovative fashion theorists range from the German cultural philosopher Georg Simmel (1858–1918) and his classic title *Philosophie der Mode* (Simmel, 1905), which was originally written in German and which defines fashion as a form of social relationship, to the French sociologist Frédéric Godart, who first published his study *Sociologie de la mode* (Godart, 2012) in French and in 2012 also in English, analysing fashion as an ever-changing but principally structured entity throughout history, focusing mainly on its European, i.e. French and Italian, roots although within a global context. Yet, among many others, it was Roland Barthes's *Système de la mode* that in 1967 influenced fashion theory most widely by pinpointing the semiotic power of clothing, the cultural importance of Coco Chanel, and the Hippy style in Morocco, while enhancing also the figure of the dandy or the language of colours and jewellery, among others. Immediately, already in the very year of its first publication (in 1967), Barthes's key work was translated into English under the title *The Fashion System* (Barthes, 1967). His main socio-aesthetic ideas are highlighted further by the American philosopher Nelson Goodman (1906–1998) who, only one year later, in the revolutionary year of 1968, published a volume entitled *Languages of Art: An Approach to a Theory of Symbols*, which was followed in 1978 by his *Ways of World Making*. Through Goodman's theoretical lens, we understand that what Barthes identified as a *Fashion System* was not only a "language" but also a way of creating new realities, or, as Goodman puts it, a—transcultural, transmediatic and so, nomadic—*World Making* of its own. It was only in 2019, though, that two university scholars working in Austria edited an anthology in German dealing expressively with fashion as a transcultural phenomenon between globalization and regionalism, offering case studies taken from Austrian, Romanian, Turkish, Iranian and African fashion, among other approaches (Schrödl & Allerstorfer, 2019). This edition certainly helps to fill the aforementioned research gap and to balance the pair of opposites "centre" versus "periphery" within the debates of Border Region Studies or Transcultural and Global Studies.

In this essay, I myself intend to investigate the modes of cultural transfer within the world of contemporary fashion by focusing on the presumably minority case study of Italy (whilst also paying close regard to France). Often, Italian fashion, in fact, appears to be second-ranked in regard to France even after WW II—a standard categorization that Carlo Maria Belfanti openly criticizes and rebuts in his cultural outline of the image historically associated with the label Made in Italy (Belfanti, 2019, pp. 198–199). By using the term *fashion*, I intend to include all aspects of how we dress, cover and expose nudity, and/or use cloth to protect it, in order to express ourselves physically, to reflect our inner attitudes and mind-sets, and, finally, to create our surroundings, in real life as well as in the fictitious sphere of literature and the arts. As I have tried to stress in my book *Moda Made in Italy* about Italian fashion (Reichardt & D'Angelo, 2016), which focusses on the transcultural significance of fashion's semiotic language and its connection to social habits in Italophone areas, following Roland Barthes's crucial analysis in his *Système de la mode*, this definition applies to all individuals and citizens of contemporary societies beyond all distinctions of race, class and gender. Fashion per se, thus, constitutes a category which has been transculturally coded throughout history (Reichardt & D'Angelo, 2016, pp. 20, 29–30). "Fashion", in this sense, is far from being applicable only to a presumable élite or upper class, but embraces both *haute couture* (i.e. handcraft and true art parameters), as presented by stylized models during a fashion show (and which is fabricated for a very restricted group of buyers and customers), and *prêt-à-porter*, as is offered by fashion chain stores or as is designed for special needs (e.g. sportswear, kids and baby-clothing, business looks, etc.). Fashion actually concerns, in a transversal way, everyone, even if this might be quite invisible, unconscious, perceived as remote controlled or not be obvious on first sight. As Italy's most prominent and acknowledged contemporary female writer, Dacia Maraini (b. 1936), metaphorically states in an interview: "Fashion is the foam of the wave" (Reichardt & D'Angelo, 2016, pp. 209–211),[151] meaning that fashion shows unconscious or subcultural currents of humankind as well as paradigmatic underground flows within specific sectors of any society. Fashion includes not only "superficial and ephemeral" flows and trends, but also more "profound" mainstreams that build up connections either with particular areas (thus being more "local"), or with general socio-cultural tendencies (thus being more "universal and globalized"), to quote Maraini (Reichardt & D'Angelo, 2016, p. 210–211). It is exactly between the poles of a "universal and globalized" fashion, on the one hand, and a more "locally rooted" tradition of how to dress, on the other hand (Reichardt & D'Angelo, 2016, p. 211),[152] that spatial concepts and expressive meanings are generated in fashion norms, practices and negotiations. In its continuously swinging back and forth between central and peripheral profoundness, Maraini finally concludes that in the long run "it's the universal fashion that wins and prevails" (Reichardt & D'Angelo, 2016, p. 211).[153]

Within this framework, the aim of my discussion is to give evidence of the *glocal* (according to the sociologist Roland Robertson (1992), as cited in Kumaravadivelu, 2008, p. 45) and transcultural lifestyle that fashion implies. In this context, it is suitable to pinpoint at first the history of how body language has been translated into postmodern and global public life (cf. section 9.2 "Transcultural Theory and the Italian Habitus")—i.e. from street-wear to high fashion, and from past to

---

151 "La moda è la schiuma dell'onda" (Reichardt & D'Angelo, 2016, pp. 209–210; the translation in English is mine). N.B.: All English translations of the quotations that were taken from this source are mine.

152 Maraini uses, in Italian, the terms of "una moda ... universale e globalizzata" versus "una moda legata al territorio" (Reichardt & D'Angelo, 2016, p. 211).

153 "... la moda universale è quella che vince e prevale" (Reichardt & D'Angelo, 2016, p. 211).

present—throughout Italian, European, and "western" history worldwide, thus creating significant communication tools, a multitude of styles, and empirically evident, nonverbal languages (in the plural) from today's perspective. I will mainly argue that fashion is—and potentially, always has been—heterogenous, i.e. fashion has always been based on openness, on a multitude of looks and a variety of styles, even if it is only in the third millennium that this might have become completely clear and undeniable. In fact, fashion has always been able to deconstruct and make uniform individuals and societies at the same time. Just think of the self-mocking, subversive, transgressive and polyphonic, and yet coherent, implications of the Sicilian brand Dolce & Gabbana, which even if pinpointing the most banal Italian stereotypes, paradoxically aims at a *Transcultural Turn* (cf. Bond & Rapson, 2014). Seen from the side of a critical perceiver, this target, for instance, clearly appears in the trailer for the Dolce & Gabbana collection, which carries the hybrid and bilingual title *Italia is Love* (Meet the style Hello, 2018), and which was designed for the 2016 summer season, introducing, among other motifs, seductive young women, well-dressed gentlemen and stylish ladies of all skin colours, tough Latin lovers, policemen, a priest, normal people and two nuns on the set. It uses shrill colours, cliché-ridden symbols and requisites, launching tourist souvenirs, pizza and coffee, all with the intention of creating a supposed "typical" Italian ambience, architecture, and location on the level of marketing—only to be stripped down, in the end, by its own hyperbolic manner. Many capabilities and examples of this overloaded, pseudo-aggressive marketing strategy may be found, not only in the case of this exemplary clip by Dolce & Gabbana, but also on many advertisements in print media, on huge posters (e.g. at the airport of Linate in Milan) or on photographs combined with the trailers of a brand-new fashion collection, posted on YouTube, social media or the company's website. In the case of Dolce & Gabbana, single icons and symbols of these campaigns—be it a kiss-mouth, a handbag, a red rose or just a coffee maker—are directly woven into the tissue or printed on the cloth, thus dominating also the fashion looks themselves.

So, through the veil of irony, a complex and interdisciplinary field of collective memory of the past (here, taken from the traditional Sicilian realm of the imagination) connects itself with representations of a present located between and beyond borders, that deal with global connections in a late capitalist, postmodern and neoliberal world order (and a world order which challenges and questions, indirectly, consumerism, sheer entertainment, or dystopian attitudes). Therefore, often the advertising techniques of Dolce & Gabbana try to generate a decentralized meta-level of a desirable, dynamic, carefree Mediterranean lifestyle in a real-life, cross-media 3D-format. They serialize and set in parallel promotion trailers of specific collections with the help of live fashion shows in Europe and overseas, they perform in television, print media and social media, all at the same time, while—as it happened in the case of *Italia is Love*—even the models are told to take selfies on the runway or behind the scenes, sending Tweets to themselves from the catwalk or from backstage to the audience, their communities and friends, releasing interviews to journalists, bloggers and influencers, etc. At the same time, though, this playful, kaleidoscopic and picaresque surface-experience is put into question, as if the viewer of this variegated, supercharged multichannel show is forced to look for deeper and more profound meanings himself, after having experienced the designer's joyful creativity or having attended a live fashion performance.

Thus, the Dolce & Gabbana trailer, semi-seriously entitled *Italia is Love*, perfectly demonstrates how to bombard the audience with rapid sound effects, quickly changing and vivid colours, and amusing short comedy sketches all shuffled together, while at the same time the presentation of dresses, clothes and accessories are, again, excessively associated with stereotypes and local symbols, in order to deconstruct the geopolitical and ethnic order of cultural areas through irony, hyperboles and transcultural twists. While the latter are presented in such an exaggerated way that the patience and perception of the watching audience are put to the test, the individual observer will ask himself why the video has been cut in such rapidity and why it is showing such an abundance of apparently stylistic perfection in this relatively short clip. In the end, there remain only two options: simply to reject the video, by classifying it as ethno-kitsch or similar, or, for the more self-reflective viewer, to question the essence of its making by deconstructing its strong but superficial visual impact, by spotting the Sicilian roots of the designer-duo in the negation of silence and isolation (which might be regarded as characteristic for certain Sicilian traits), and by identifying the viewer's own clichés and stereotypes that appear through the colourful vividness in his mind. The critical spectator, thus, unmasks the supposed "Mediterranean" style of the trailer as a provocative projection of his (or her) own prejudices and is at least amused—or, in the best case, constructively encouraged—by his own sweeping judgements, compounds and/or ways of thinking. Using this technique, this clip succeeds in completely puzzling the self and, at the same time, recomposing the brand's storytelling with the goal of landing an effect on every spectator, wherever on this planet a potential customer might be, and independently of any specific cultural sphere with which one might identify.

On the other hand, instead of deconstructing, reconciling might also represent a technique by which to act out otherness or, respectively, hybridity. By bridging fashion and literature, the Italo-American writer of Bengali origin, Jhumpa Lahiri—Pulitzer Prize Winner 2000 (*Interpreter of Maladies*, 1999) and holder of the 2014 National Humanities Medal received from President Barack Obama in 2015—starts her critical, though heartfelt, reflections about the art of designing book jackets by recalling "The Charm of the Uniform" (Lahiri 2016a, pp. 3–11). She writes that her Indian cousins were allowed to wear impressive uniforms when going to school in Kolkata (Calcutta), while the female first-person narrator (i.e. Jhumpa Lahiri's *alter ego*) was educated to freely wear what she liked when she went to school in the US as a child herself. Quite differently from Italy's most famous feminist voice, Dacia Maraini, who takes her distances from this kind of standardization by stating that "I am not in favour of impositions of any kind. I like everyone dressing how they feel. I wouldn't venture to impose a fashion on anybody. Only dictatorships love uniforms" (Reichardt & D'Angelo, 2016, p. 215),[154] Lahiri frankly admits that "I would have liked a uniform myself" (Lahiri, 2016a, p. 5). In *The Clothing of Books*—a multi-layered postcolonial essay about the editing of her books, which Lahiri programmatically first wrote in 2015, not in what was (for her) the hegemonic language of American English but in the secondary and European, if not third-rated, language, Italian, with which she had just fallen "in love" (Lahiri, 2016a, p. 17)—she further explains her inner reasons:

> I learned the hard way that how we dress, like the language we speak and the food we eat, expresses our identity, our culture, our sense of belonging. From childhood, I understood that the clothes I wore, wherever I was, rendered me an "other". ... When my books were first published, when I was thirty-two years old, I discovered that another part of me had to be dressed and presented to the world. ... I am forced, at times, to accept book jackets that I dislike, ... I sometimes think, as a writer too, that a uniform would be the answer. (Lahiri, 2016a, pp. 9–11)

Both these examples—the fashion duo Dolce & Gabbana, on one side, and the author Lahiri, on the other—represent different responses of how to cope with the transcultural challenge of combining different cultural spaces by letting "cultures ... interpenetrate or emerge from one another", thus articulating "the concept of transculturality" as an "altered cultural constitution" (Welsch, 1999, p. 197). This concept, actually, tries to propose an alternative to the dogma of letting cultures merely co-exist "as closed spheres or autonomous islands" (p. 195), as in Johann Gottfried Herder's (1744–1803) 18th century concept of "cultural racism"—as Wolfgang Welsch puts it critically (p. 195). Examined with the help of Welsch's concept of transculturality, Dolce & Gabbana as well as Lahiri both revert to fashion (or cloth) in order to accept the challenges and trends that are constantly moving and changing in postmodern and postcolonial times (cf. Schrödl & Allerstorfer, 2019, pp. 7–13) in a playful, unconventional and outcome-oriented, imaginative way. Both parties start from a subaltern position: Dolce & Gabbana originating from the extremely poor Italian south, and Lahiri from the minority position of a presumed-to-be-inferior hyphenated Indo-American female identity in the US (at least in terms of race and gender). Both try to invert the power relations that exist between periphery and centre by referring either to a fashion collection (Dolce & Gabbana) that recodes *italianità* (i.e. a typical, easily recognizable "Italian style" or "Italianness"), or to a school uniform that inspires the writer to invent the metaphor of how to *clothe* books (Lahiri) in order to trigger or, respectively, reflect transculturality. Floating between processes of interconnectedness and dichotomized concepts like "the feminine" vs. "the masculine", proceedings like these might fuse into one style or even just in a single outfit within the fashion

---

154 Maraini's original words in Italian read: "Non sono per le imposizioni di nessun genere. Mi piace che ciascuno si vesta come si sente. Non mi azzarderei a imporre una moda. Solo le dittature amano le divise" (Reichardt & D'Angelo, 2016, p. 215; the translation in English is mine).

system: just think of Yves Saint Laurent's (1936–2008) revolutionary women's suits, which are inspired by men's tuxedos but which are transformed into a completely feminine line, or of Giorgio Armani's spectacular triangle silhouette for his women collections in the 1980s.

After spotlighting the theory, history and mechanisms of the Italian fashion system in the next section 9.2 ("Transcultural Theory and the Italian Habitus"), in the subsequent section 9.3 ("Karl Lagerfeld: 90 Years of Fendi—90 Years of Fairy Tales (2016)") of this essay, I will come back to the postmodern nature of further fashion concepts by analysing extensively a specific fashion show that Karl Lagerfeld designed for the Italian fashion label Fendi and that he presented in 2016 in the picturesque old town of Rome. But already at this point, we may observe that in today's world, the tension between homogeneity and heterogeneity in the context of fashion discourses is manifestly inclined to dissolve the first (homogeneity) into the second (heterogeneity), thus enhancing diversification. In our introductory examples, this act of heterogenization operates by either exaggerating the *italianità*, in order to de-nationalize, de-territorialize and universalize the promoted fashion style (Dolce & Gabbana), or by turning the conventional association of a uniform either into a desirable and iconic outfit, or, on the contrary, into a consumer-friendly but shallow straightjacket—which might be, metaphorically speaking, advantageous or disadvantageous when also functioning as a book cover (Lahiri).

## 9.2 Transcultural Theory and the Italian Habitus

The mediatic and aesthetic circumstances that characterize the economic and cultural aspects of these first two cases—whether regarding Lahiri's books or Dolce & Gabbana's summer collection of 2016—merge into a transcultural wrapping, which is not only a sign of their postmodernity or diversification, but also turns our attention to the very origins of Transcultural Studies. In fact, it is due to the work of German philosopher Wolfgang Welsch (b. 1946) that we realize the modalities in which the centre and the periphery today overlap more and more, transgressing their (fictitious) former borders. In his view, our (post-) modern life-worlds are primarily the result of a horizontal, liquid hybridity, promoted and reinforced by new media and by virtual, i.e. digital, forms of communication:

> ... cultures today are in general characterized by *hybridization*. For *every* culture, all *other* cultures have tendentially come to be inner-content or satellites. This applies on the levels of population, merchandise and information. Worldwide, in most countries, live members of all other countries of this planet; and more and more, the same articles—as exotic as they may once have been—are becoming available the world over; finally the global networking of communications technology makes all kinds of information identically available from every point in space. (Welsch, 1999, p. 198)

The importance and influence of socio-economic parameters is even more pronounced by the Cuban sociologist, influential public intellectual, and prolific author, Fernando Ortiz (1881–1969), who coined the Spanish term *transculturación* as a neologism in his essay *Contrapunteo Cubano del tabaco y el azúcar* (1940), and which was translated into English by Harriet de Onís in 1947 as *transculturation* in the English translation of the book entitled *Cuban Counterpoint: Tobacco and Sugar*:

> With the reader's permission, especially if he happens to be interested in ethnographic and sociological questions, I am going to take the liberty of employing for the first time the term *transculturation*, fully aware of the fact that it is a neologism. And I venture to suggest that it might be adopted in sociological terminology, to a great extent at least, as a substitute for the term *acculturation*, whose use is now spreading. (Ortiz, 1995, p. 97)

Keeping in mind that Welsch—writing in the 1990s—manifestly connects his essay with Ortiz—dating back to the 1940s—and that, in my paper, I am interested in applying both of these approaches, which have merged to form specific aspects of today's Transcultural Theory, in the Italian case, as an instrumental value, we might add to our methodology the concept of *habitus*. This notion was first introduced by French sociologist Marcel Mauss (*Les techniques du corps*, 1934) and picked up shortly after by the German sociologist Norbert Elias in *The Civilizing Process* (1939), before it was further used also in the work of Max Weber, Gilles Deleuze and Edmund Husserl. However, it is the French philosopher Pierre Bourdieu (1930–2002) who is responsible for revitalizing and rendering the analytic utility of this notion by remarking that *habitus* is a system of durable dispositions or principles which organize practices and representations functioning as "structuring structures" (cf. Bourdieu, 1980a, p. 88; the translation in English is mine). More than Mauss's "body techniques", Bourdieu discovers *habitus* to be an agency within social *fields* which generates an infinity of possible practices, and which therefore stands at the beginning of what Bourdieu calls a "practical sense": in French, *Le sens pratique* (1980).

While Aristotle (384–322 B.C.) had already used the expression *habitus* as a synonym for "inner attitude", Bourdieu defines it as a describable social impact and a personal attitude, thus implicating the history of the body as well as the individual appearance, the language that somebody speaks or in which the person writes, together with his or her taste, style and way of dressing (cf. Bourdieu, 1980b). *Habitus* may therefore implicate a concept that is more precise and appropriate for academic reflections about fashion-related issues than the common term "style" (from the Latin *stilus*, meaning "stylus", "slate pencil", "spelling style" or "way of writing"), and derivative terms like "styling" or a "stylish" appearance. By connecting Bourdieu's sociological concept of *habitus* with Welsch's idea of a transcultural "way of life" (Reichardt, 2017, p. 49)—or even with transcultural "ways of thinking" (p. 51) in the plural—and, in a third step, with the methodological approach of Transcultural Studies that we are referring to here, following Welsch's crucial essay about *Transculturality: The Puzzling Form of Cultures Today* (1999), we notice that transculturality may in fact be applied to almost all academic subjects and domains. Seen against this backdrop, it seems obvious that this method is certainly also—and particularly—fruitful and illuminative when applied to the fashion system, since, for practical reasons, all people, ethnic groups and human beings around the globe have to cover their nakedness, to dress themselves, and therefore to choose a style, thus automatically producing their own habits, expressions and traditions as to their apparel throughout the centuries.

The Italian *habitus*—a term that I use as a homophonic pun in connection with the ambivalent Italian term *abito* (meaning "garment", as well as "habit"), in my introduction to *Moda Made in Italy* (2016)—might be considered as the result of a long and heterogenous history of foreign rule in Italy, of single city states, provinces and regions which became fragmented for centuries all over the country after the Roman Empire had collapsed. The Italophone culture, therefore, formed a prismatic patchwork of dialects, local customs, and politics from the Middle Ages until the 19th century, when the state of Italy was officially founded in 1860/1861. If we now ask ourselves what kind of model a transcultural Italy implies or represents today, we might either answer with Lüderssen and Sanna that the Italian lifestyle equals a de-centralized country—an *Italia de-centrata* (1995), i.e. a nation state (as well as a cultural sphere) that is not centralized like France, which historically has concentrated all political, creative and innovative powers in the capital city, Paris—or, alternatively, we might think about a "syncretic" *Italofonia* grown on a Foucauldian heterotopic basis. Without disesteeming the very helpful idea of Italy's decentralized structure, but, on the contrary, in order to emphasize even more the Italian case, I have extensively highlighted the latter, i.e. the option of a transcultural vision of an "Italophony" (or: "Italophonie"), in my book about *Italia transculturale* (2018), focusing on Italophone syncretism as a heterotopic model (cf. Reichardt & Moll, 2018, pp. 16–17). It is important to recognize this Italian *habitus* for its sociological and didactical potential, seen that it holds—particularly in relation to Italian fashion—a remarkable relevance also in relation to didactical purposes, as well as for Cultural and/or Literary Studies. Thus, with a view to make up the leeway that exists in Italian Studies so far, the third of five main theses, which I formulated in the introduction to the book *Moda Made in Italy* and which may be formulated in the context of the current state of research, states that "*The question of Italian fashion* has not even been opened yet" (Reichardt & D'Angelo, 2016, p. 20; the translation in English is mine; italics in the original).[155]

So, what is so remarkable about this Italian *habitus*? The remaining four theses illustrate its transcultural characteristics by enhancing the specific connection that the Italian fashion history generally holds with:
1. art ("Fashion is art"),
2. European (i.e. "occidental") culture,

---

155 "*La questione della moda italiana* non è stata ancora aperta" (Reichardt & D'Angelo, 2016, p. 20).

3. Italian history and literature, both of which are liberally influenced by fashion as a "language" *sui generis;* and, finally,
4. language teaching methodologies and sociolinguistics (cf. Reichardt and D'Angelo, 2016, pp. 13, 15, 27, 30).

All in all, it must be said that, even if Italy's fashion history features at some crucial turning points in western cultural history, it often risks disappearing in the shadow of the French fashion system. Therefore, it would seem useful to recall a few milestones that affected Italy's role in cultural fashion history worldwide, before evaluating the case study of Karl Lagerfeld's fashion design for the Italian label Fendi in a more thoroughgoing way in the following section 9.3 ("Karl Lagerfeld: 90 Years of Fendi—90 Years of Fairy Tales (2016)") and drawing further conclusions from it in the sections 9.4 ("Transmedia Content and Our Nomadic Lifestyle in Postmodern Times") and 9.5 ("Fashion as an Aesthetic and Didactic Tool").

Indeed, since the beginnings of the so-called "occident", Italian fashion has played a crucial role in the European history of culture and made a significant impact in international politics and economy, in continental literature, design, architecture, figurative arts, film, music and theatre. One of its main characteristics consists in the fact that we may talk about "Italian fashion" still today, because almost all successful fashion brands in Italy are managed and owned by Italian designers and Italian family dynasties, as the late director of *Vogue Italia*, Franca Sozzani (1950–2016), noted in 2010 (p. 117; cf. also Grünwald, 2009, pp. 75–76). Moreover, in the third millennium, Italian fashion boutiques are to be found all over the world in quite a high density, thus representing a clear economic USP and proving, at the same time, that today's Italy has adapted itself from the Middle Ages to the Modern Era by opening up to global transculturality (if we agree to follow Welsch's theoretical approach), on the levels of both marketing and lifestyle-trends beyond geographical borders (cf. Grünwald, 2009, p. 45). Therefore, Italian fashion might be understood, with Roland Barthes, as a semiotic, *ergo* a systemic, aesthetic language that constantly transfers and directly propagates an Italian way of life around the world. This corresponds with Welsch's thesis that "transculturality is in no way completely new historically", but "breaks through the fiction of homogeneity", since "styles [have] developed across the countries and nations" (Welsch, 1999, pp. 199–200). In fact, cultural trends have long shaped a network linking together states, people and spaces for extended periods on the European continent, thus transforming Europe into an exemplary showcase or, respectively, a "transcultural laboratory" par excellence (cf. Reichardt, 2006, p. 93; the translation in English is mine).

As is well known, the clothing in classical Greek and Roman antiquity imitated the Egyptian dress-code and formed the foundations of classical aesthetics, when it was rediscovered by the Italian designer Valentino Garavani (called Valentino, b. 1932) in its timeless elegance to become his evening robes in the 1960s. This itself also followed Anne Hollander's theory of apparel as expressed in her book *Seeing*

*Through Clothes* (1978), in which she states, in a nutshell, that a contemporary robe may be read just as a historical revelation, since it reveals its historical roots only if the wearer knows how to "see through clothes", i.e. how to explain their composition against a historical backdrop. Valentino deconstructed the somewhat hieratic, inflexible and static connotations of this historical background by recoding it symbolically with the help of his own shade of dynamic, lively, and bright red: the iconic *Rosso Valentino*. As the major book on the ideal of an early modern *Corteggiano* (1528), by Baldassare Castiglione, shows, in the aftermath of the classical era, the Italian noble court culture and its way of *Composing Ourselves in Style* (cf. Graham, 1990) again do make a remarkable appearance in Renaissance times (cf. Burke, 1995). The etiquette promulgated by *The Book of the Courtier* (as its English title reads) explains precisely the dress-code for courtiers and court ladies, and also demonstrates the relaxed principle of an omnipresent sense of style, nonchalance or casualness—or *sprezzatura*, as it was called at that time (cf. D'Epiro & Desmond Pinkowish, 2001; cf. also Paulicelli, 2014a). Although, at the end of the 16th century, in around 1600, it was the Italian-born Maria de' Medici who introduced the habit of wearing underpants at the French court (previously this was not very common in France), but already during the baroque, in Italy, we find a sumptuary law that follows the French example, befitting the image of aristocrats, monarchs and the bourgeoisie, and not anymore the other way round (i.e. the Frenchmen picking up fashion habits from the Italians).

Indeed, Italian culture starts to disengage from Paris only in the mid-19th century, slowly showing again a more and more autonomous and independent fashion style, until coining the fashion sector by means of the label *Made in Italy* after World War II (cf. Belfanti, 2019, pp. 198–240). This progression culminates in the *italianità* of the Fascist regime, that tried to promote Italian fashion and textiles by inaugurating (in 1933) the first national fashion exhibition in Turin, which had been the first Italian capital in 1861 and was then declared as the first fashion capital (*capitale della moda*) of Italy by Queen Elena of Italy (also: Elena of Montenegro, 1873–1952). After the Second World War (1939–1945), a new era began which marks the 1950s and 1960s as the *Golden Years* of Italian fashion. The fashion hotspot shifts from Turin to Florence, where in 1951 the wealthy Florentine aristocrat and businessman Giovanni Battista Giorgini (1898–1971) initiates in his Villa Torrigiani the first Italian fashion show ever in the context of a newly arising, international fashion system. Due to its immense economic and media success, in Italy as well as overseas and since 1954 until today, the Palazzo Pitti (the palace in which Maria de' Medici was actually born, back in 1575) now hosts transcultural fashion events, even if they all follow their own economic interests—a fact that raises the question to what extent it is reasonable or impossible to link together cultural and economic interests.

Back in those days, at the time of the Italian economic miracle (ca. 1950–1973), the land "where lemon trees do bloom" benefited highly from its historical past. As the single case studies collected in the anthology about *Moda Made in Italy* (cf. Reichardt & D'Angelo, 2016) illustrate in detail, since the Middle Ages, the Italophone area had been traditionally famous for its slowly expanding companies specialized in hand-craft, run by families, and for producing or elaborating leather, wool and fabrics like silk, linen, cotton and—from the 1970s onwards—also synthetically blended fibres. On top of that, since Renaissance times Italy enjoyed the highest prestige from the best trade connections via the former Sea Republics of Venice and Genoa, thus clearly mapping the advantages offered by the entangled history of the autonomous Italian city states, the international circulation of wares, and the cultural transfer that also shaped political power relations in the Far East (and the Silk Road) and Africa or India (with their cotton fields). During the *Golden Years* of fashion, i.e. during the late 1950s and 1960s, Florence and Rome were struggling for the title of the Italian capital for film and fashion, even if, in the end, Milan would win the race. The reason of this outcome was the promotion of the *Pronto Moda* (or *Alta Moda Pronta*), i.e. the Italian adaptation of Ready-to-wear-fashion, or, respectively, *Prêt-à-porter* that emerged in the 1970s.

Even if Milan would benefit enormously from its industrial and infrastructural location, back in the 1950s many Hollywood celebrities and world-famous stars came for their movies and shooting programmes to Italy's capital, Rome. Attracted by the booming business in the Roman film studios at Cinecittà and their low production costs, many international and US films were produced in Italy, and these productions were followed by the press, journalists, and media. In this field, the idea was born to use the red carpet that was habitually placed on the streets upon the arrival of well-known Hollywood stars, serving as a catwalk or runway (a so-called *passerella*), in order to present themselves as well as the newest fashion highlights. It was in the film *La dolce vita* (1960), directed by Federico Fellini (1920–1993), in which the script-writer Ennio Flaiano (1910–1972), historically inspired by the most famous Italian *paparazzo*, journalist and photographer at the time, Tazio Secchiaroli (1925–1998; cf. Mormorio, 1999, p. 30), created the figure of an intrusive photographer with the surname Paparazzo. This denomination quickly advanced to become the equivalent of a scandal or boulevard-photographer who tries to sell to people—backed by the stars' and starlets' glamour as well as by the red-carpet-effect invented in Italy—as many newspaper copies and, as a social outcome and unintentional collateral effect, also as many new dressess as possible, advertised by means of articles and circulating pictures, which addressed not only the local jet-set but also a global clientele.

## 9.3 Karl Lagerfeld: 90 Years of Fendi—90 Years of Fairy Tales (2016)

It is surely the spectacular architectural and historical background of the Fontana di Trevi—a world-renowned white marble and travertine fountain designed by Nicola Salvi, completed in 1762 and located in the heart of Rome—, but also exactly that stylish *habitus* of an internationally intermingled high society, together with the glamour of a media publicity, from which not only Federico Fellini drew inspiration. In early spring 1959, it is on this location, that he decided to film the famous fountain scene with young Italian actor Marcello Mastroianni (1924–1996) and the Swedish shooting star and "queen of the Roman night scene in 1958" (Gundle, 2011, p. XI), Anita Ekberg (1931–2015), for *La dolce vita*, released in 1960. Fifty-six years later, rather, in 2016, the German fashion designer Karl Lagerfeld (1933–2019), born and raised in Hamburg, comes back to this legendary setting, that was coined, cinematographically speaking, by Fellini and immortalized precisely by this film director and screenwriter originally from Rimini as *the* place of seduction. The plot of the film went down in movie history, and its Fontana di Trevi-scene offers unforgettable impressions, stimulating for sure also Lagerfeld's phantasy. One of the most powerful images is the moment when, in the early morning hours, and after a long and adventurous night in the Eternal City of Rome, Ekberg—cast as Sylvia—steps into the water of the fountain in a black, floating, full-length strapless gown to lure the epitome of a Latin lover—embodied by Mastroianni—to join her under the waterfall with the soft words: "Marcello! Come here!" (Pazyluz, 2016, 00:01:20).

On July 7th 2016, on the occasion of the 90th anniversary of Fendi, Lagerfeld realized—in a congenially subversive and, yet, crystal clear and transparent mode, working almost imperceptibly against the cliché-related *dolce-vita* myth—his grand and truly transcultural (by combining a multitude of various ways of life, as per Welsch) Fendi-show *Fendi Legends and Fairy Tales: 90 Years of Fendi.*[156] It opposed to any Fellini reminiscence an alternative world of myths—not a complex, interwoven Mediterranean stratification (as Chambers & Cariello illustrate; cf. Chambers & Cariello, 2019, p. 50), but a presumably unobtrusive, precise and "pure" Scandinavian line. Lagerfeld had been officiating, already then, as the Artistic Director of the Roman brand for over 50 years: when he passed away in 2019, this almost lifelong collaboration had reached a total time span of 53 years. In retrospect, transferring the human body (represented by the actors Ekberg and Mastroianni in Fellini's film) from the water of the fountain, above the water's surface in Lagerfeld's project, the light and bright colours of this fall/winter-collection 2016/2017, and the soft, meditative soundtrack and the light-flooded, yet nocturnal ambience, that underlines the show, evoke almost heavenly, otherworldly, yet secular, associations, while the models seem to hover above the fluid element like angels or, precisely, "fairies". This was rendered possible by constructing a special catwalk over the water, made out of a transparent plexiglass floor, running on the fountain across the large, fully illuminated, water basin, with the waterfall in full action behind it. By choosing this location, Lagerfeld added—in the imagination of the spectator—to his fashion show not only a flair of Hollywood, Cinecittà and the world of movie stars and visual arts, but

---

156 The official video showing the preview of the Fendi fall/winter fashion collection 2016/2017 in full length has been published by the Fendi company on YouTube (FF Channel, 2016).

also a northerly understatement, a tender fragility of contrasting images, and some literature, by referring explicitly in the show's title to the literary genre of *fairy tales*.

Despite the show's message that, according to Welsch's transcultural credo, nowadays "[t]ransculturality is gaining ground ... not only on the macro-cultural level, but also on the individual's micro-level" and that, because of our "multiple cultural connexions", we all might be defined as "cultural hybrids" (Welsch, 1999, p. 198), Lagerfeld's strong and deep connection to the Fendi label is generally not really out in the open. As a matter of fact, it is common knowledge that Hamburg-born Lagerfeld acted as chief designer for the French fashion house Chanel, whose history started with the first Chanel boutique opened in Paris in 1913 by Gabrielle "Coco" Chanel (1883–1971) herself, for some 30 years. Of course, his activities in France are quite evident not only because Lagerfeld spent his whole adult life in the French capital Paris, where he succeeded in saving the label Chanel from business failure, restructuring it continuously from 1982 onwards for success, before he passed away in Paris in 2019. But before, originally, Lagerfeld had started to work for the Italian trademark Fendi—whose logo with the two complementary, variegated "F"s were sketched by him as a young man—already at a much earlier stage of his career, precisely in 1964/1965. Historically speaking, at the same time when Karl Lagerfeld left Hamburg with his mother and came to Paris at the age of twenty in 1953 (cf. Kmieciak, 2019, p. 21), in Italy there were various single fashion designers, who were effectively busy in the Italian fashion world, namely Germana Marucelli (1905–1983), Emilio Pucci (1914–1992), the sisters Fontana, Valentino and also the Fendi family. They were all producing their outlines, models and items in a restricted number of pieces in small Italian factories, before selling them in their boutiques. Notably, in this very first post-war period of the 1950s, the master saddler Guccio Gucci (1881–1953) played a key role in Italo-American relationships and generally in the global fashion business, his successful economic rise being as exemplary for the victory of the *Alta Moda* in 20th century Italy as the brand's history of Fendi (cf. Paulicelli, 2001, p. 288).

Indeed, Lagerfeld himself was significantly involved in building up the most discussed *Alta Moda* fur-fashion that pushed Fendi to the top of a highly exclusive and solvent costumer base world-wide. When he began to work for the five Fendi sisters (Paola, Anna, Franca, Carla and Alda) in 1964/1965, their parents, Adele (née Casagrande) and Edoardo Fendi, had been running a small boutique in Rome's via del Plebiscito (Palazzo Fendi) since 1926, bringing all five of them within the company in the 1950s. While Lagerfeld very successfully launched both—the French (Chanel) and the Italian (Fendi) fashion house—over the years, guiding them to an exceptional economic height, later he actually began to strive towards reaching other classes too, including those with a lower income. Thus, in 1984, a year after his start at Chanel, he opened a competitive store for his brand *Karl*, targeting "everybody", before he created a reasonably prized *prêt-à-porter* collection to be sold in all European and US chainstores of the Swedish multinational clothing-retail company Hennes & Mauritz (H&M) in 2004. Finally, in 2012, he launched his label *Karl* (or: *Karl Lagerfeld*) online, serving not highly exclusive fashion but also offering "accessible price points" (LeWeb, 2013, 0:27:00) for women's fashion, accessories and products, available within an average price range.

Finally, after having organized for the first time in the history of fashion a show on the Great Wall of China in Beijing on 19th October 2007, presenting the Fendi spring/summer-collection 2008 not only outside of Europe, but also in a most spectacular open-air location,[157] in 2016, for the very first time a high fashion event-show took place at Rome's Fontana di Trevi. Since Fellini's film crew came here to shoot *La dolce vita* in 1960, no other red-carpet event had ever taken place on this site before, as the piazza in front of the fountain, built by the Italian architect Salvi in the 18th century in a late baroque, almost neoclassic style, has a minimal surface. The small-sized square is composed only of a few stone-steps in front of the water basin, a narrow passage-way arranged in a semicircle around it, and the pedestrian alley behind it, offering a very restricted space to the (limited, and therefore selected) international audience, that was able to assist the spectacular show and that mainly consisted of media and only several dozens of the most important fashion representatives, buyers and customers. Almost simultaneously, the video-taped show itself was published on the internet—featuring an almost analog-to-digital congruity—and presented live on the runway installed above the water-level of the fountain.

After having renovated the Fontana di Trevi for 2,13 million Euros as a part of the project *Fendi for Fountains* in 2015, the luxury fashion house, multinational brand, and, since 2001, member of the LVMH Group Fendi, invested apparently not only in the protection of Italy's historical heritage, but also in cultural industries, in order to promote its ninetieth anniversary on July 7th, 2016. Initially, the brand presented this show of *1001 nights* using the programmatically bilingual and "fabulous" motto *Fendi: 90 Years of Fairy Tale—Fendi: 90 anni da fiaba* (the online sources were not available any longer when this book went to press) for the purpose of a prestige advertising strategy. Consequentially, the event was recorded on video and firstly spread on YouTube under the title *Haute Fourrure 2016-17 Fashion Show: Legends and Fairy Tales*, featuring "romantic colors and ethereal materials such as organza, silk, and tulle", according to the advertising text of a former YouTube-video (under the entry "show more") which was removed from the internet later on, though. In a mode of production that took place in a "typical Italian atmosphere of family", in fact, Lagerfeld worked for Fendi in the last "several years" before he passed away in 2019 primary with Silvia Venturini Fendi—née Fendi, daughter of Anna Fendi—(Fendi, 2008, 0:00:18–0:00:30), always trying to illuminate Fendi's craftsmanship with printed and hand painted fabrics, embroidered lace or rich velvet jacquards. In light of this event, the multi-media embedding was particularly sophisticated on the occasion of the *90 Years*-show (that today circulates mainly under the short show title

---

**157** Cf. the full show on YouTube (FTV HOT, 2016).

*Legends and Fairy Tales*) in July 2016 at Fontana di Trevi, for which the most expensive and requested international female top-models were engaged and a video specially dedicated to the making of the collection and the collection's concept was produced (cf. Fendi, 2016). The whole choreography was enhanced by a background music mix that also performed the original soundtrack of *La dolce vita* at the end of the show, as it was originally composed by Nino Rota (1911–1979) for Fellini's movie, giving a slightly ironic touch to the fashion parade. Also, at the end of the show, Karl Lagerfeld walked over the transparent plexiglass runway "over water", together with Silvia Venturini Fendi, thanking the audience for their attention as if they were not in an open-air space but on an ordinary catwalk during a regular indoors fashion show. Standing side by side with her in the middle of the catwalk, face to face with his audience he threw, according to tradition, a coin into the fountain's water, thus transmitting a sign of eternity or symbolical farewell to the viewers (or later online users).

The chief attraction of this fall/winter collection 2016/2017 presented by Lagerfeld was, however, that he included the history and architecture of Fontana di Trevi into his concept, with which he was familiar having spent quite an amount of time living in Rome himself (as well as in various apartments, houses and villas that he temporarily owned in Paris, New York, Vermont, Monte Carlo, Hamburg, the Provence, and Biarritz). He also added a brilliant transcultural nuance of ostentatious, yet gentle and unexpectedly "quiet" hybridization to the setting. Accordingly, the garments of this special fashion collection are not inspired by typical Mediterranean traditions and costumes—in contrast to the "loud" and colourful example of the Dolce & Gabbana video-display that I quoted at the beginning of this essay, and, as memory of the scenery of *La dolce vita* could perhaps have suggested—but surprisingly by Nordic fairy-tales. Thanks to this artifice, the German designer, who spent his life abroad, thus feeling at home in the most variable places, succeeds in recoding the whole Roman ambience by means of patterns, cloths, webbing, applications, cuts, textiles, veils, decorations, combinations of accessories, hairstyles, lady's bags, shoes, furs and embroideries not by a typically southern esprit—as, again, the intense, vivacious and sanguine Dolce & Gabbana collection does—but by a Scandinavian, i.e. a much cooler, low-key, discreet and delicate flair. The latter does not create a clash, though, with the expectations of the viewer, but exceeds them, topping all stereotypes by smoothly fitting the illustrations, symbols and motives that Lagerfeld choose for the cloths and dresses in a harmonic but completely new and congenial, complementary relation between fashion style, live performance and the architectural masterpiece of the Trevi Fountain.

The filigree flowers, delicate fairies, sophisticated silhouettes of castles, enchanted skylines and landscapes, pastel shades and colours, and the long, drawn-out characters and animals that the garments were adorned with, have all been taken from drawings that Lagerfeld discovered by chance when he came across the work of Danish illustrator Kay Nielsen (1886–1957). Parallel to the Fendi show, not only was an exhibition with some of Nielsen's works shown in Palazzo Fendi, entitling the 2016 event in Rome also with the Italian motto *90 anni da fiaba* (in English literally: *90 Years of Fairy Tales*), but the German art-book publishing house Taschen Verlag, whose headquarters are in Cologne, also edited a special edition of Nielsen's illustrations in a beautiful coffee table book, poetically titled *East of the Sun and West of the Moon* (cf. Nielsen, 2015). So, Lagerfeld's transcultural synthesis produced this creative, intercultural German-Italian encounter at Fontana di Trevi, enriching it with a *tertium quid*, i.e. a third, intersecting cultural sphere, in which the German designer combined elements that are commonly associated with Italian, German, French or Danish culture. With his *Gesamtkunstwerk* on the Roman fountain, the stylist generated a unique, customized, new formula that was in perfect harmony with the architectural peculiarity of piazza di Trevi, the specific style of his collection, and the historic significance of the company anniversary.

Following Nielsen's exceptional, yet neither generally popular nor particularly Italy-oriented Nordic Art Nouveau aesthetics, first published in a book-format in 1914 and lavishly reissued by Taschen in three languages (English, Italian and German), Lagerfeld escapes the banality of historically idealizing "the 'Sweet Life'" (Gundle, 2011, p. 379) of the Rome of the 1950s. Instead, Lagerfeld avoids falling under Fellini's spell by neither seeing it as "one of the most powerful marketing tools of Italian products abroad" (p. 352) at the one extreme, nor by regarding past and present Rome exclusively through a socio-critical lens, at the opposite extreme. With the distance of half a century, in 2016, one could have been also tempted, actually, to rebel against the quite negatively connotated, never-ending story of Rome as a decadent, corrupt "bustling, class-divided city of the post-war years" (p. 344), when "the drugs traffic boomed in Italy" (p. 337) and social injustice oscillated between the "ecstasy of fame" represented by Anita Ekberg as "film goddess from the land of dreams" and "the tragedy of broken dreams" of ordinary people (p. 352). It is rather from a balanced, mediatorial point of view in-between these two perspectives that Lagerfeld's Fendi show exhibits itself as an aesthetic fashion highlight that transmits also didactically a multi-ethnic, collaborative and pacifistic message, which might be seen—if not, quite simply, as a total work of art—then surely as a transcultural language at its best.

The semiotic language and transcultural dynamics that support and sustain Lagerfeld's representation of *Fendi Legends and Fairy Tales*, though, do not address only a social elite but indeed manifest themselves everywhere, such as on the street and in street fashion, as is true to the definition of fashion that Lagerfeld gave himself in 2011 on the occasion of a podium event in Paris, that aimed to discuss the digital culture: "Fashion is what people wear, it's not only what you see on the runway" (LeWeb, 2013, 0:34:02). To this he adds, in fact, that "fashion is a nice way to escape banality" (LeWeb, 2013, 0:37:07), and finally concludes—picking up an idea that Anne Hollander expressed already in *Sex and Suits* (cf. Hollander, 1994, p. 11)—that fashion is unavoidable and is therefore a basic cultural need of humankind: "Everybody is interested in fashion. ... And when people say that they don't like fashion and that they don't care for it, they [still] cannot escape it ... because they have to dress"

(LeWeb, 2013, 0:39:25–0:39:31). In this Lagerfeld, who was renowned for his speedy answers and witticisms, shows himself to be fully aware of the civilizing power of fashion, remarking that, slightly smirking, "I know there are more important things in life than fashion, but as we don't run around naked, maybe we need fashion" (LeWeb, 2013, 0:43:08–0:43:14).

By combining and reuniting harmoniously his Nordic roots as well as his passion for the Mediterranean lifestyle, Lagerfeld's final, widely publicized performance for Fendi clearly demonstrates how his fashion thematizes the self-reflection of fashion shows in Italy on the one hand, and, on the other hand, how—through its local focus on the ground in Rome—his work opens up by drawing on other cultures: among others, on the German popular tradition (with its faeries collected by the Brothers Grimm in the early 19th century, its storybooks and closeness to the protection of nature, but also the somewhat supposed "Prussian" appearance of Lagerfeld himself), the Scandinavian fairy-tale world (with its legends, trolls, nordic spirits and elves but also strong Art Nouveau tradition and minimalistic design history), and on French *chic*, subtlety or savoir-vivre, which for centuries was so close to the Italian history of style, and in fashion. On the basis of these—both global and local, *ergo glocal*—considerations, Lagerfeld finds a transcultural synthesis beyond geopolitical spheres and social restrictions, which relate, most notably, to the categories of *Race, Class and Gender* (as Patricia Hill Collins and Margaret Andersen conceptualized in their homonymous anthology in 1992). This approach suits him not only because in the fashion business he encounters neither racism nor homophobia, and he is free to live his progressive and liberal convictions, but because it represents a cultural habitat that matches exactly his needs. Being an unconventional thinker, Lagerfeld found in the fashion world the freedom to act as one of the first true freelancers on the European market, working—in the beginning of his career—for some ten to twenty different brands, as a young German man living and working in Italy and France, at the same time, thus embodying a prototypical European citizen.

His *90 Years of Fairy Tales*-show of 2016 reflects to the spectator not only that fashion is a communication tool, but also that it may lead, by bridging one's own cultural identity and personal self-positioning, to even more transculturality and—hopefully—new representations of gender in future times, to still more individuality, to even more freedom of personal expression, styles of travelling, circulation or residency, and to greater age diversity and tolerance of corporality, physical shape and bodily *habitus*. The accuracy and entertainment that inhere in the 2016 Fendi show, hence, point in a promising direction and mark a seminal moment in transcultural history, without hiding its postmodern dislocation, gender issues or social gaps, but by acclaiming artistic visions, that invite the audience to critically decode complex cultural synergies and facets of nonverbal communication.

## 9.4 Transmedia Content and Our Nomadic Lifestyle in Postmodern Times

Before we may come to our conclusions (leading in section 9.5 to the synthetical idea of "Fashion as an Aesthetic and Didactic Tool"), reconsidering the application spectrum of fashion discourses in general, and of Italian fashion, in particular, we must first fill the missing link between transculturality, on one side, and transmediality and the idea of nomadism, on the other. As the case study of Lagerfeld shows, in postmodern times, the circulation and exchange of (luxury) goods, ideas and manners among cultures, individuals and places could, of course, be seen critically in various aspects. But so far I have intended to point out in this essay that, in terms of transculturality, transmediality and "nomadology"—the sociological notion introduced by Deleuze and Guattari in order to explore the sphere of interest *in-between* of consumerism and anthropology (cf. Deleuze & Guattari, 1986)—they may also have innovative, surprising, entertaining, enriching and liberating effects. From this point of view, we can say that the past seventy years, in a period spanning from 1950 until 2020, have revolutionized world fashion, that, since then, circulates literally *in-between* of countries, borders and cultures as an individual and social means of expression.

If we consider, furthermore, the increasing power that the media play in our globalized communities, we could think of fashion as a 3D-compound or simply as a "world language" *sui generis* that operates on various parallel levels in series, just like interconnected trends which appear in Italian food, music, architecture, design, visual arts or sports. Within the fashion business world, this transnational, yet uniquely human and ever-changing language enhances the visibility of all sorts of fashion collections, series or trends by transmitting a fashion hype—simultaneously to its material exposure in the analogue world (e.g. during a fashion week in New York)—also via social media on the Internet, via trailers on YouTube, print media, TV-spots, advertisements in journals and/or cinema, reports and articles on paper or online, thus truly manifesting the impact of the *iconic turn* in postmodern times (cf. Maar & Burda, 2004, p. 15–17). On a historical level, however, fashion has always acted as a bonding force between individuals and society, between social groups, multitudes and distinctive cultures creating continuously a plurality of human *in-between* or *third spaces* (cf. Bhabha, 1994, pp. 36–37), thus being originally more detached from technical media. Fashion melds and combines not only humanism with technology, but also various different aspects such as economic parameters, values of nation-branding and personal identity, the representations of race, class and gender, power discourses or a metaphorically decodable zeitgeist. Its complex polyphony and subversive transmedia structure show the transgressive, as well as the didactic potential of fashion discourses.

For centuries the centres of Europe, such as the courts in London or Paris, dictated the most treasured habits of dressing by means of the role-models represented by their kings and aristocrats. But, in the hidden shadow of power, also folk-tradition, subversive social discourses and popular customs were acted out by the people on the streets, in the suburbs, and in the peripheries of Europe, demonstrating themselves to be present, inventive and influential. Still today, they very often give proof of extremely original interpretations, opinion forming critique and even carnivalesque versions of higher standard looks, thus capturing their proud, even supercilious essences, making them theirs, recoding or reverting them, sometimes turning them into their opposite, sometimes adapting them by just making them their own or trend-setting new apparels among their peers. Furthermore, this phenomenon is reflected in the fanciful and creative crossover-looks exposed in popular surroundings, for instance, in Africa, if we think for instance of the so-called *sapeurs* in the capital of the Democratic Republic of the Congo, Kinshasa. Their characterization originates from the French word *sape*—meaning "stuff" or "gear", "duds"—and today defines itself through the acronym *S*ocieté des *A*mbianceurs et des *P*ersonnes *É*légantes (English: "Society of Entertainer and Elegant People"), whose distinguishing mark consists of a lifestyle targeted at fashionable and individualistic elegance, and orientated at the features of classic dandies and gentlemen. At the same time, due to their skin colour, their body language and their environment, the sapeurs transmit also a rebellious fun-factor and slight ironic appeal to the viewer.

In fact, the sapeurs developed from a subculture into a social movement, which has its roots in the 1920s (while in Europe we experienced the Art Nouveau, first, and, then, Art Deco period as the case of Kay Nielsen shows), having been originally founded by the Congolese freedom fighter André Matsoua (1899–1942), who had lived for several years in Europe before introducing into his home country an elegant "western" dress style when he came back. The members of this social group called sapeurs reached international visibility in the middle of the 1960s, when they protested against the politics of the military dictator and President of the Democratic Republic of the Congo (1965–1997) Mobutu in Brazzaville, Congo. These sapeurs—who phonetically almost match with the lexeme "saveurs" in French (i.e. in English: "savours", "tastes", or "flavours")—seem to live out, freely and peacefully, their postcolonial resistance against suppression and economic exploitation by means of clothes and personal performance in the public space. Since their historical beginnings, these people have been mostly neglected and discriminated against, and have never been taken seriously by the French high-brow fashion scene. Only recently, in 2012, two photographers Francesco Giusti and Mathilde Lloret finally curated an art exhibition with the title *Dressing Up*, which showed pictures of various sapeurs, their life-worlds and their mode of "dressing up" in Mulhouse, France (Atelier Photographique Hors Champs). In this sense, sapeurs not only give their fellow citizens a good example of how to stand up for one's own rights, but this exhibition is also an example of how to influence main-stream and public opinion in an illuminating way, taking over a visible, even prominent, social role, thus gaining visibility.

The outfit and overall social concepts of the sapeurs can both be "read" as a potpourri of characteristic traits, the most crucial and paradigmatic skill being the one to combine fashion with an ethical code, thus pioneering in real life Roland Barthes's semiotic theorem of transformation activities or so-called "Shifters" (cf. Barthes, 1967, pp. 5–6). According to Barthes, every dress or outfit that is being worn can be decoded and explained either as if it was a poem—i.e. by words—or as if it would mirror a social reality in its pure, direct and physical form, as an iconic language, that means, by images. Coming back from the political sapeurs-movement to the transmediality of Italian fashion, this is, actually, exactly how we could further analyse some dresses of the Dolce & Gabbana collection *Italia is Love* of 2016, which showed the title of the collection printed, stitched or reproduced on the textile itself by featuring the literal words *Italia is Love* sometimes in an overt and playful, and sometimes in a veiled or hidden way. There can be no doubt that the designer's approach to the wearer (first demonstrated by the model on the catwalk), as well as to a potential spectator (i.e. the ideal consumer), is a powerful technique in order to start a communication among the two of them, representing a clear attempt to come into contact together, or, indeed, a way of manifesting a semiotic language, whether on a provocative or on an entertaining or unifying level.

A similar unique, iconic example of the transcultural language of fashion, that combines words with images in order to launch also a political appeal, materializes in the famous women's *Pace*-dress—the so-called *vestito Pace*, in Italian—designed by Valentino Garavani in 1993. The pattern showed in various lengths, from a mini to a full-length dress, the word "peace" (Italian: "pace") on the dress, translated in up to fourteen different languages and/or alphabets, and stitched with a decorative silver thread on a white underground, the white colour obviously symbolizing peace or a plea for the absence of war activity. The writing of the Italian word *pace* in foreign languages echoed a multicultural, united "one-world-mentality" beyond ethnic and geographical borders, as it strikingly transmits, still today, not only a symbolic but also a political message. This dress programmatically relates to the time when it was designed in 1993, representing a clear reaction to the First Gulf-War (1980–1988) and the Second Gulf War (1990/1991) by literally "speaking up" for peace and for an end to the warfare. The many variations of this lettering were publicised, back in 1993, not only on the fashion items themselves but also in the show windows of Valentino's boutiques, where the polyglot word-series were used for decoration on their doors and windows, and as a strapline for the whole collection. Because of its historical textile story-telling, the *vestito Pace* was presented solemnly again in the Ara Pacis in Rome, on the occasion of Valentino's retrospective exhibition, with the bilingual (Italo-American) title *Valentino a Roma: 45 Years of Style* in 2009. The Lombard designer chose the congenial, strategic and symbolic frame of a museum after that the Ara Pacis Augustae (short: "Ara Pacis", from Latin: "Altar of Augustan Peace"—Valentino plays also in this architectural context on the word "peace" applying a transcultural tonality) had been restructured by the American architect Richard Meier from 1995 to

2006, in order to bundle his demands within the realms of arts, transmediality, publicity and classiness. Created in 1993, the message of the iconic Valentino *Pace*-dress also anticipated the popular *Pace da tutti i balconi*-movement in Italy against the war in Afghanistan and Iraq in 2002.[158]

Spanning from the dress-code of the African sapeurs, to the Dolce & Gabbana collections and to Valentino's *Peace*-dress, we might ask ourselves what these outfits "tell" us. Which stereotypes do they play with? What kind of motifs are used? Which stylistic devices dominate the seasons and campaigns, and why? What is global and what is local in these show-cases? Searching for answers to these questions that respect both the aesthetic-mediatic and the didactic-political parameters of fashion, we could certainly pinpoint its cross-media effect in a useful way by referring to Marshall McLuhan (*Understanding Media*; 1964), or by establishing a connection on the meta-level of communication by combining fashion with migration issues. Through migration and mobility, cultures meet, change and move, both physically and mentally, thus producing *Nomadic Subjects* (1994) as Rosi Braidotti puts it. These modern "nomads" follow Wolfgang Welsch's *ubi bene, ibi patria* principle (cf. Welsch, 2003, p. 40): your home is not necessarily where you come from or where you are meant to stay, but where you may freely choose to live—just as Lahiri did when moving from New York to Rome, or as Lagerfeld did when moving from Hamburg to Paris and Rome.

Through "migration processes" and "worldwide ... communications systems", on the basis of interweaving cultures, fashion also becomes hybrid, not only because, as Welsch states, "We are cultural hybrids" (Welsch, 1999, p. 198), but because fashion is hybridization *per se* (cf. Grünwald, 2009, p. 7), and has always been. It combines different styles, mixes materials, cuts and colours, overwrites gender roles, and is always intended to make transculturality visible. This technique could be illustrated by acting as a mosaic, a puzzle, a patchwork, a salad bowl, rainbow or melting pot, which are all different metaphors that may didactically be used to better describe what transculturality stands for, in order to bridge cultures, focus border-regions and create a *third space* (cf. Bhabha, 1994, pp. 36–37). Within these intersectional spaces, fashion also transcends media by addressing itself equally to literature, as well as to architecture, the figurative and performative arts, to film, music or to show business.

We could easily find plenty of evidence for the basic transmedia principle of transculturality, if we define transmediality as a term applicable to non-media specific phenomena, that various media produce together using their specific means,

---

**158** The *Pace da tutti i balconi*-movement was a social campaign in Italy, that started in 2002 as a demonstration against Italian participation in the Iraq war (2003–2011). During the protest, over one million rainbow-coloured textile banners showing the Italian word "pace" (for "peace") in white were put up on balconies, doors and windows all over the country, thus drawing a high degree of media attention. The *pace*-flag worked for almost a decade as a postmodern cult object and communicative tool "beyond horizons".

and that in the end are not clearly connected to one original source medium anymore (cf. Rajewsky, 2002, p. 13). For literature—to begin with—it is, indeed, obvious that no character and almost no interior space can be realistically described without mentioning dress-codes, textiles or any material made of cloth or cloth-like structures on the level of narration. In this sense, "fashion" is as unavoidable as Hollander and Lagerfeld put it. Just think, for instance, of the final key-moment in *The Leopard*—both, in the novel[159] and in the movie by Luchino Visconti from 1963—which deals with the "Death of a Prince" (Tomasi di Lampedusa, 2007, pp. 239–254) under the entry "July, 1888" (p. 241). In this scene, a sophisticated way of dressing and a pronounced and "exquisite sensation of one or two fine silk cravats" (p. 252) play a crucial role in the memories of the Prince (called Don Fabrizio) who, regarding "himself in the wardrobe mirror", recognizes himself merely with the help of "his own suit" (p. 246). At the moment of his passing away, death appears to him in the silhouette of a young woman, wearing an elegant brown travelling dress, who comes to pick him up for a (last) train-ride, as it seems, at the main train station of Catania, and who unveils her face in the very last moment before he dies:

> Suddenly amid the group appeared a young woman, slim, in brown traveling dress and wide bustle, with a straw hat trimmed by a speckled veil which could not hide the sly charm of her face. She slid a little suède-gloved hand between one elbow and another of the weeping kneelers, apologized, drew closer. It was she, the creature forever yearned for, coming to fetch him; strange that one so young should yield to him; the time for the train's departure must be very close. When she was face to face with him she raised her veil, and there, modest, but ready to be possessed, she looked lovelier than she ever had when glimpsed in stellar space. (Tomasi di Lampedusa, 2007, pp. 253–254)

In canonical Italian literature, the association between fashion and death is frequently to be found—for instance, in Giacomo Leopardi's (1798–1837) dialogue between the allegories of Death and Fashion in *Operette morali* (1827; cf. Reichardt & D'Angelo, 2016, p. 39) or in Gabriele D'Annunzio's (1863–1938) concise statement "Modernize or perish" ("O rinnovarsi, o morire", cf. Reichardt & D'Angelo, 2016, p. 11; the translation in English is mine). The film adaptation of Tomasi di Lampedusa's novel *Il Gattopardo* by Visconti who, back in 1963, employed the already then renowned costume-designer Piero Tosi (1927–2019) for the costumes (cf. Reichardt & D'Angelo, 2016, pp. 61–73) and used the music of Nino Rota, brings us not only back to Lagerfeld's reminiscence of Rota in his Fendi-show in 2016, but also reminds us of the transmedia content and the hybrid character of fashion. The latter becomes manifest in different forms of narration when combining fashion, dress-codes and textiles not only with literature but also with arts and film.

---

**159** *Il Gattopardo* by Tomasi di Lampedusa (2007) was first published in 1958 in Italian, while the first English translation, by Archibald Colquhoun, was published under the title *The Leopard* in 1960.

As for the figurative (and performative) arts, the connection to fashion, again, appears evident, since an oil painting starts with a canvas and many artists also use textiles for sculptures or installations, as shown by the work of the German conceptual, installation and process artist Franz Erhard Walther (b. 1939) or the US-artist-duo Christo (b. 1935) and Jeanne-Claude (1935–2009) when wrapping several monuments and landmarks in France, the US, Germany, Italy, Great Britain or Japan with cloth. For example, when building the *Floating Piers* on Lago d'Iseo in Northern Italy from June 18th to July 3rd 2016 as a work of art in a public space, installing over 100,000 square meters (cf. Christo & Jeanne-Claude, 2016, p. 46) of dahlia-yellow fabric over the piers in the water and the streets of Sulzano, Christo's textile art was used by the visitors of the exhibition *Walking on Water*—as the film of the making of the *Floating Piers* project was entitled, which Christo launched in 2019.[160] Thus, Christo transformed the piers into what locals called a catwalk—i.e. a true "passerella" (Christo & Jeanne-Claude, 2016, p. 4)—on water and turning the visitors of the exhibition into unusual "models" against the natural backdrop of the gentle highlands, that surrounded the open-air event. The spectators of this art performance—who came from all over the world to meet on Christo's piers of the Lago d'Iseo—within the art project, figured as active participants, temporarily filling it with life, different languages, voices, behaviour, manners and guise, forming a random, ephemeral melting-pot on this especially constructed "runway". The erratic composition of international culture travellers formed, thus, an intrinsic part of the *Floating Piers*-experiment, giving it (as all works of Christo and Jeanne-Claude do) a nomadic shade while being creatively enhanced, on an aesthetical level of art, as an unparalleled community of *Nomadic Subjects*, even if only for a restricted, actually short time (in this case, only for the duration of 15 days). Christo's land-art event was almost alike to how Lagerfeld staged his Fendi show at Fontana di Trevi that took place almost simultaneously on July 7th 2016: was this coincidence, inspiration, mimicry or just due to the spirit of the time in that very period? Probably both artists began to plan their events around 2014 and it is to be assumed that it was a zeitgeist-driven amalgam of the above, or a trendy way of thinking for both artists, who developed their projects independently, but in correspondence with the artistic *status quo*. Regardless, the analogy shows, again, how a cultural discourse might spontaneously emerge and disseminate (combining an art event with the element of water by mastering the latter), and how quick fashion picks up artistic, social and style-related movements or developments (gathering people "on" the water with a socializing and aesthetic transmedia effect).

---

160 The cinematic release *Walking on Water* (2019) was directed by the Bulgarian writer-director Andrey M. Paounov (b. 1974) (cf. MIFF, 2019, 0:02:28), while the official catalogue for *The Floating Piers* printed in 2016 still names only Antonio Ferrera as "the project's filmmaker" (Christo & Jeanne-Claude, 2016, p. 62). The trailer of Paounov's film *Walking on Water* can be found online (MIFF, 2019).

Finally, the transmedia fusion of fashion with film is certainly not restricted to modern art, but also happens in literature, as in Tomasi di Lampedusa's case and as many films that are based on books, like Brian De Palma's satire of the fashion world in his *The Bonfire of the Vanities* (1990), based on the book by Tom Wolfe from 1987. Other Hollywood productions may come to our minds: e.g. Baz Luhrman's *The Great Gatsby*, in which Leonardo Di Caprio features as the main character in 2013, after Jack Clayton directed this film in 1974 with Robert Redford and with costumes designed by Ralph Lauren, both of which are based on the novel with the same title, written by Francis Scott Fitzgerald (1925) that visualizes trendsetting discourses of fashion in cinema. Another US-American film production connected to fashion brands, that we could mention, is David Frankel's *The Devil Wears Prada* (2006) with Anne Hathaway and Meryl Streep based on the book by Lauren Weisberger (2003). In Italian cinema, though, the historical and handcrafts aspects of costuming often seem to prevail. This is, for example, the case in Roberto Faenza's film version of Dacia Maraini's novel *La lunga vita di Marianna Ucrìa* (1990). It was released in 1997 under the short title *Marianna Ucrìa* and presented costumes (created by Danilo Donati [1926–2001]) and a soundtrack composed by Ennio Morricone (1928–2020). On the other hand, on the level of social discourse, we can certainly define a distinguished *Italian Style* (Paulicelli, 2016)—and *Made in Italy* itself (cf. Belfanti, 2019)—in the transmedia representation of suits, dresses, costumes and outfits throughout the full history of Italian (and also international) cinema and visual media when revisiting it systematically and selectively from the angle of (Italian) fashion (cf. also Reichardt & D'Angelo, 2016, pp. 14–15).

As a matter of fact, it is Hollywood that dictates fashion rules in postmodern cinema, often with a blatant economic effect. This is shown by the case of *American Gigolo* (1980), written and directed by Paul Schrader, and which stars Lauren Hutton and Richard Gere, who wore only Armani suites in the film. It was revealed as a big unpaid advertising campaign, causing an Armani hype and big run for Armani-outfits in the US of the 1980s. After a first documentary exhibition of Yves Saint-Laurent's work as a fashion designer in the Metropolitan Museum of Art in New York in 1983, the programmatic exhibition *Art in Fashion* by Giorgio Armani followed in the Guggenheim Museum of New York in 2000. This was the first of various museum shows worldwide (e.g. Capucci, Schiaparelli, Prada) that focused on the role of Italian fashion in the international art system. This trend was flanked by openings of fashion museums, which were located mainly in Italy and which showed the work of Italian designers, culminating—abroad—in the London exhibition *The Glamour of Italian Fashion 1945-2014* at the Victoria and Albert Museum in in 2014. These Italy-related sociocultural activities and innovative initiatives are, again, all based on a public sensitisation, strongly promoted by a series of intermeshed—specific Italo-American—cinematic discourses. As a matter of fact, in postmodern times, the fashion affinity in cinema and movies primarily shows luxury as a global lust for life—the *dolce vita* or *savoir vivre*—which is historically rooted in the time of the *telefoni-bianchi* films ("white telephones" that were shown in Italian movies as a US-coined, iconic code for luxury and the privileges of the upper class). These films were produced in the post-war period in the studios of Cinecittà, when Alfred Hitchcock, Liz Taylor, Audrey Hepburn or Ava Gardner worked in Rome, the city which was then often dubbed *Hollywood sul Tevere* (Engl.: "Hollywood on the Tiber").

The step from *Marriage Italian Style* (*Matrimonio all'italiana*, 1964), directed by Vittorio De Sica with Sophia Loren, in which close-up views accentuate the female bosom, to postmodernity with *American Gigolo* in 1980, that zoomed in on men's wear, highlight the ongoing transformations of the predominant values in "western" societies. Furthermore, public behaviour of this time disclosed the affinities that connect the fashion system with a neoliberal spirit and popular culture. This mix exploded in Italy, on a political level, during the Berlusconi-era in the 1990s, revealing all its weaknesses and decadence but also demonstrating incontestably the new power of both, the *iconic turn* and media or transmedia effects. The same can be said of architecture, as the setting of the Fontana di Trevi illustrates, both in Fellini's film *La dolce vita* and in Lagerfeld's fashion show for Fendi. It is not just by chance that the term *supermodel* became prominent in the show-business of the 1980s and 1990s, combining pop culture with a postmodern taste, launching different ethnic groups, nationalities and *habiti*, spanning from neo-baroque and rather exhibitionist brands (such as Versace in the 1980s) to sober and minimalist labels (such as Jil Sander in the 1990s). In the TV documentary *Made in Italy 1951–2015* by Jean Lauritano (broadcast in 2015 on the German-French tv-channel *Arte*), it is said that Donatella Versace, the sister of Italian fashion designer Gianni Versace (1946–1997), was first Gianni Versace's scout who had the job to find out in clubs, discotheques and pubs what women liked to wear, and later on was the one to propose some models to him, who were not only handsome, tall and slim, but had also particular pretty faces. Finally, they all walked for him, including Linda Evangelista, Naomi Campbell, Cindy Crawford, Claudia Schiffer, and Nadja Auermann. In the 1980s, these supermodels worked all over the world on a transmedia level. They were portrayed on the most popular fashion magazine covers, preferably all at once, branded themselves as household names in order to have a worldwide presence, reputation, remuneration and high value to the market. They embraced old-style glamour, showed a professional working attitude, and availed themselves of the latest fashion in public and jewellery on the red carpet and at jet-set-events, thus slowly replacing film stars or at least extending the definition of their role and status in society, and, finally, becoming style-icons of luxury and wealth themselves. The circle that paradigmatically connects fashion with other ethnicities and life-practices (like the *sapeurs* in Africa, the attitudes in Italian culture towards the Gulf-War in the Mideast, various music genres, etc.), with literature (e.g. *The Leopard*), arts (e.g. Christo and Jeanne-Claude), film (from *La Dolce Vita* to *The Devil Wears Prada*, etc.), museum shows, the model business, etc., can't be closed without at least mentioning a last parameter that is crucial for any professional fashion concept: architecture.

In fact, apart from all the links that connect fashion to the industrial sectors and sociocultural *fields* (or *champs*, as Bourdieu originally calls them in *Les règles de l'art*, 1992) of entertainment, film, media, music, arts, photography, theatre, dance, food, design, sports, subculture or pop-culture, the closeness of fashion to architecture—at the end—becomes most evident when architecture is used as a catwalk or scenery for fashion shows. An architecturally sophisticated surrounding, a stunning, expressive landscape or a theatrical, even dramatic, building all enhance the impact and the message of any fashion performance, both on the analogue and the digital levels. When located in Italy, they often take place in open-air spaces, as in Rome on the Spanish Steps, in the Ara Pacis (Valentino, 2009) or at Fontana di Trevi (Fendi by Karl Lagerfeld, 2016), or even—for the first time in fashion history—abroad, on the Chinese Wall (Fendi by Karl Lagerfeld, 2007). Anyway, if in Italy or around the world, picturesque monuments, romantic ruins or iconic places function as settings for a suggestive photo-session or fashion event they do so not only in order to generate new transmedia synergies. They rather emphasize the essential nomadic baseline of fashion itself and serve as orientation devices or landmarks for the nomadic lifestyle that globetrotters, migrants, tourists, self-proclaimed world-citizens, jetsetters or frequent travellers perceive as most attractive and compatible with the plurality of their multi-faceted life-worlds in postmodern times.

## 9.5 Fashion as an Aesthetic and Didactic Tool

To complete this study about *The Iconic and Transcultural Language of Italian Fashion*, let's see, now, in this last chapter, how we can make use of it on a practical level. We have seen that in Italian fashion, local parameters merge with the "universal" language of fashion—to come back to Dacia Maraini's words that I quoted at the beginning of this essay—, if we agree that fashion implies not only the expression of a certain spirit of the time, but also mobility, individuality and style as the expression of one's personality (instead of blindly following mainstream trends). On the economic level, fashion represents "an aesthetic and symbolic choice that ... builds upon a technical dimension, ... a symbolic dimension and [finally] ... a trade-off between distinction and belongingness" (Grünwald, 2009, p. 6). In this dynamic sense, permanent change becomes a constant figure, just as D'Annunzio intended ("O rinnovarsi, o morire"), he himself also being an *arbiter elegantiae*—i.e. an arbiter of good taste, behaviour and refinement—who designed fashion for his female lovers using the label *Gabriel-Nuntius Vestiarius-Fecit* (cf. Sorge, 2015). Besides fashion studies that deal with Roman Antiquity (cf. Hollander, 1978) and the Renaissance (cf. Birbari, 1975), and generally semiotic interpretations as a crucial research approach to fashion, as proposed by Roland Barthes (cf. Barthes, 1967), theoretical theses concerning the paradox (cf. Esposito, 2004) and the unavoidability of fashion (cf. Hollander, 1994) have also tried to explain its extrovert charm and underground potential. The vital, historic, symbolic, subversive, sociopolitical and artistic-aesthetical impacts of fashion have always reflected, in praxis, the differences between north and south, orient and occident, and were, at the same time, merged in the way people dressed or in the way that textile elements were either combined in daily life or used and mentioned in Italian literature, cinema, arts, theatre and language.

Although designers like "Lagerfeld, Miuccia Prada and Rei Kawakubo say that fashion is not art, [and] it is difficult to disagree" (Barnard, 2014, p. 27), we may agree, on the contrary, also with their colleague Roberto Cavalli (b. 1940) who, as an artist, writes, on the contrary, that his "creations are meant to be worn and not attached to the wall" (cf. Reichardt & D'Angelo 2016, p. 17; the translation in English is mine). In other words, in the third millennium, the semiotic language of fashion openly illustrates: *First*, its synergetic aspects, not only in artistic but—according to the French poststructuralist Michel Foucault (1926–1984)—also, and even primarily, in its social *discourses* (cf. Foucault, 1971). They particularly focus on solidarity, subalternity and minority aspects that follow the advice of taking care of oneself by reverting to "techniques of self" (cf. Foucault, 1984). *Second*, the semiotic aspects of the fashion system reveal its iconic parameters, fully unfolding the *iconic turn* and most clearly appearing on the Internet, visual and digital media, and, finally, *third*, the semiotic power of fashion consists of its transcultural facets. In fact, the transculturality of fashion expresses itself through its ubiquity, mobility and social hybridity, stressing, according to Welsch, the fact that cultures are incommensurable and that they melt, meet and communicate everywhere by inspiring themselves and by being aesthetically interwoven and compared with one another. These circumstances are based not just on present-day globalization and on a way-of-life that approximates nomadism or the nomad as a theoretical figure—a key concept already envisioned by Gilles Deleuze and Félix Guattari in their 1986 essay about *Nomadology* (cf. Deleuze & Guattari, 1986). Moreover, they also refer to communication, synthesizing aesthetics, and functional optimization (cf. Grünwald, 2009, p. 8). In the light of their social role, garments express and represent emotions, cultural membership and uniqueness—in short: "fashion translates that sense of self into style" (Barnard, 2014, p. 26). In the end, outfits "are tools and ultimately prosthetic devices that make possible the representation or translation of an idea or an experience of the self and of ourselves, and thereby communicate it to other people" (p. 27), irrespective of whether their transcultural outlook is related, for example, with Italian fashion, and whether it is launched in Europe, Japan, the US, or in emerging markets such as China, India (cf. Grünwald, 2009, p. 45), or elsewhere.

Even if the phenomenology of fashion, sociological fashion studies and the aesthetic issues of fashion might all seem hybrid, superficial or hard to categorize, we may deduce from Zangemeister's and Stark's neurological study about *The Artistic Brain Beyond The Eye* (2007) that any image must be developed first in the brain of a designer before he sketches it as an empirical, two-dimensioned image. Later on, such a drawing will then be transformed into a look that is worn and presented on a catwalk by a model. Finally, his creation may be received through the eyes of a spectator in a real life, three-dimensional version. It is this inner image itself, again, that will be remembered by the receiver organically, with the help of the human brain, as if it came from an abstract sphere, before vanishing back into it, and, in the end, being tentatively adopted by cultural tradition—just as those immaterial units, with which we pass on our cultural heritage from generation to generation, called *memes*, as Richard Dawkins teaches (*The Selfish Gene*, 1976).[161]

On a didactical level, we can deduce that connecting fashion discourses to several theoretical approaches (Bourdieu, Welsch, Barthes) helps to illustrate the complexity of *style, sense and senses* and why fashion actually matters—both in our real lives and in academic discussion. Focusing on the specific (peripheral) case of Italy according to the current state of research in Cultural Studies, we have been able to recognize not only how fashion discourses (in a Foucauldian sense) clearly mark, constitute and visualize cultural identities throughout history, but also how closely Italian fashion discourses have influenced, among others, French culture. In fact, the typically "French" *Haute Couture* and the characteristic "Italian" *Alta Moda* were originally intertwined through iconic figures such as Maria de' Medici, who emblematically introduced Italian habits at the French court at Renaissance times. In (post-) modern times, this role is played for example by "the architect of fashion", Gianfranco Ferré (1944–2007), an Italian designer working as Stylistic Director for the French fashion brand Christian Dior and commuting between Milan and Paris, or Emanuel Ungaro (1933–2019), who was a French designer descending from an Apulian family that had emigrated to France with various economic and administrative ties to Italy. Karl Lagerfeld, added a transcultural stylistic element to the international fashion scene, working as a German for the Italian label Fendi and the French signature Chanel for decades, whilst at the same time spending most of his lifetime in France.

As a consequence, because fashion mirrors history and society so clearly, the Italian case might be used didactically to approach young students in order to make them familiar with the complexity of globally entangled history, focusing on the past centenary, and introducing fashion to gender studies, minority issues and transcultural approaches. How could then such a teaching unit be structured?—Well, starting with Coco Chanel's revolutionary capture of leg wear, "translating" trousers and

---

161 "Meme" is a neologism coined by Dawkins in 1976 in order to contrast the notion of a "gene" with a "meme", that he defines as an envisioned entity, idea, behaviour or style that humans inherit socio-culturally (in analogy to the biophysical heredity transmitted by a gene) on an individual as well as on a generational level from one mind to another. On this base, new collective (e.g. European) as well as national (e.g. Italian, British, etc.) identities and transcultural parameters arise (e.g. in the fashion system). Dawkins's fundamental concept of a meme in *The Selfish Gene* (1976) was picked up shortly by the English neuropsychologist Nicholas Keynes Humphrey, who defined memes as living structures, and later developed further by other European cultural scholars like Jan Assmann (*Das kulturelle Gedächtnis*, 1992) or Susan Blackmore (*The Meme Machine*, 1999).

pants from the man's world to the everyday life of women during the 1920s and 1930s, and ladies smoking proposed by Yves Saint Laurent in the 1960s, after World War II, the dynamic of "western" world fashion gives way to the Golden Era of Italian fashion. As we know, this lasted from the 1950s to date, in the third millennium, launching the Italian designers Valentino Garavani, Gianni Versace and Giorgio Armani particularly in the US. If we agree that the aesthetic highlights of these fashion trends have introduced transcultural parameters to global culture throughout the decades, we may consider that they pinpoint two peaks of modern culture in Europe: the first lasting from 1920 to 1935, distinguished by Italy's emancipation from the French fashion model, and the second from 1950 up to the present, which is characteristic in Italy's solidarity with the USA and its interest in transatlantic cultural impact. Indeed, on the political level we may realize that the Italian rise in contemporary fashion history is strongly linked to the increasing power of US-culture in the 20th century. The cachet of *Made in Italy*, actually, goes back to post-war Italy, when, after the end of the Second World War, people in Italy—as all over Europe—were faced with poverty, devastation and lack of resources. Like France, also in Italy many cities had been destroyed. While there was the necessity to start up the economy again everywhere on the so-called Old Continent, within the fashion business sector, Italy was well known to have always had a good quality of textiles and a prolific commercial experience, and it quickly showed itself able to modernize by new means of technology.

This historical overview could serve as a good starting point to delve into Italo-American relationships as a passport to fame for fashion products originating from Italy. In fact, as the USA had been Italy's principal economic and political ally at the end of World War II, America's political interest was directed on preventing Italy from falling into the clutches of communist Russia, once the war was over. Simultaneously, the Italian inventions in fashion in this very period were a perfect match with the Americans, who really liked the extroverted glamour that the Italians spread with their love for life on the red carpet on the one hand, and, on the other hand, the easy-going pace of the Italian *dolce vita*. They appreciated the Italian designs as being full of fantasy and peachiness, the vivid and bold colours of their textiles, the way they wore them stylishly in public, and, later on, the accessible, wearable Italian fashion of the *Pronto Moda*, while Italian aristocrats continued to invite the Americans in their *palazzi* to "society events [that] greatly contributed to making Italian fashion known internationally" (Paulicelli, 2001, p. 288; cf. also Belfanti, 2019, pp. 233–234). Historically, this American enthusiasm also openly reflects in the above-mentioned first fashion show organized by Giorgini in 1951 at his home, where he presented some young Italian fashion designers and their products initially to only four or five American critics and buyers, whom he had persuaded to come over to Florence to meet him during their stay in Paris in that year. As history shows,[162] they were so taken with the presentation that Giorgini repeated the event a year later in 1952, which paid off materially when all of a sudden three hundred US-Americans experts and clients showed up in Florence (cf. Belfanti, 2019, pp. 225–226). There were so many more than he had expected that he had to hire Palazzo Pitti in order to receive them all—and this was only the beginning of a long and stable transatlantic fashion friendship.

In this perspective, fashion offers a perfect entry to Italian culture, mentality, modern history and to the contemporary way of life, in general, both on the aesthetic and the didactic level. Throughout the centuries, the Italian casualness started blurring *From Sprezzatura to Satire* (Paulicelli, 2014a), until nowadays, in the late capitalist phase, it seems to converge in a transnational nomadic lifestyle as propagated by Wolfgang Welsch (cf. Welsch, 2017), especially when analysed from a cross-cultural perspective within a global framework, focusing the interdisciplinary fields of fashion, identity and globalization (cf. Paulicelli, 2008). Summarizing the key role of fashion *Made in Italy* today, if it is seen as a historical result of foreign and self-related interactions as well as a significant didactic vehicle, we may conclude that—speaking with Pierre Bourdieu—the *habitus* (i.e. the individual appearance and performance in public and private) in the cultural sphere of Italian fashion, opens out into a "nomadic" way of life in postmodern and globalized times. Thus, Italian fashion embodies in various empirical manifestations the phenomenon of *Nomadology* that Deleuze and Guattari spotted within the conflicting domains of capitalism, globalization and postmodernity (cf. Deleuze & Guattari, 1986), on the threshold of a transcultural anthropology that was about to be critically introduced by Wolfgang Welsch only a few years later.

To summarize, it seems that the success of modern Italian fashion is based on three historical promoting factors. Firstly, there was the role played by the landing of the US-American allies in Italy in 1943: due to their presence in the country until the end of World War II, a "reciprocal attraction" (Paulicelli, 2001, p. 288) built up between Italy and the US. Based on the two big historic emigration waves of the Italians to North America in the 19th (between the 1870s and 1930s) and 20th century (since the 1950s) and the newly formed Italophone diasporas in the USA, the Italo-American ties were socially reinforced and, at the same time, essentially renewed. Secondly, the rise of Cinecittà amidst the international film-industry, which was explicitly promoted by Mussolini, represents—not least also due to the active cooperation of Hollywood in the post-World-War-II period—the historic starting point of the success of Italian fashion trends in the 1950s, which still manifests its iconographic and media power until the present day. Thirdly, the advantages that the Italians gained, in terms of experience, in running handcraft-manufactures and traditional family-businesses

---

162 Cf. the website of the fashion center in Florence CFMI (Il Centro di Firenze per la Moda Italiana), "La storia", online (CFMI, 2015).

in the textile sector since Medieval times, deeply rooted in the European collective cultural memory, highly qualified them in modern times.

From the long-term-relation between Italian and French fashion throughout European history to the modernization and the final awakening of a genuine Italian style oriented towards the New World and the US-market in the post-war period, we can still identify various references to the exchange between the French and the Italian fashion systems from the beginning of the 20th century until today. But when they actually are assessed at the same time, one observes that they have become more and more hybrid and transcultural according to the progressive process of globalization. The interlaced, complex origins and European roots of these performative manifestations highlight, indeed, how the semiotic language (Barthes) and *habitus* (Bourdieu) of fashion have strongly co-influenced social and cultural attitudes, the economy, history, visual arts, literature, music and dance, industrial design, architecture, the film sector, transcultural ways of life and tastes, gastronomy, tourism, migration, sports, and even politics in the "western" world. It thus results that fashion is a historical non-verbal language, that has always reflected civilization and is multilaterally connected to the evolution of mankind on a cultural as well as a transcultural level. It depicts an endless field of experience between the poles of diversity and otherness, or—as Bhabha puts it—of identity and difference, opening a hybrid *third space*, in which entities of cultural difference meet without claiming any "assumed or imposed hierarchy" (Bhabha, 1994, p. 5).

In conclusion, in tracing transitions, contact zones, rivalries and creative competition as well as cultural shifts and cross-overs between styles, the controversies and mutual impact of French and Italian fashion designers, in an international context show that fashion discourses can be regarded as a form of symbolic capital—if not as an artistic subgenre or cultural activity *per se*—as well as a theoretical discourse (cf. Barthes, Foucault, Bourdieu). Nonetheless, in view of the fact that, even if theoretical approaches do exist, fashion still needs to be fully integrated into Cultural Studies, we have to reassess the binomial formula of *Diversity and Otherness*, as well as the formal and normative codes of fashion design throughout the centuries. Within this scope, the transcultural approach offers not only a multitude of case studies *in-between* of cultural spheres, academic disciplines and international market fields—or between *Style, Sense and Senses*—but also explains methodologically *The Iconic and Transcultural Language of Italian Fashion* as a 3D kaleidoscope or prism through which we can observe its diverse local (i.e. standard) bonds to a Mediterranean lifestyle, as well as its global attachment to the rest of other life-worlds. Therefore, as one of the most active international experts on Italian fashion studies, Eugenia Paulicelli, professor of Italian Studies at Queens College and the City University of New York, rightly considers that the label *"Made in Italy"* from the standpoint of its transnational underpinnings that are dialectically in conversation with ideas and ideals of national identity and character" opens up "the notion of *Made in Italy* to a larger transnational context", and thus continues to reinforce still today "the high levels of Italian craftsmanship, attention to detail, beauty and cultural heritage". These all count as values that Paulicelli stresses, given that they define "the Italian character and style at its best" (Paulicelli, 2014b, p. 169; italics by Paulicelli).

Precisely because fashion has always mirrored society, it seems difficult to understand why—since the academic boom of Cultural Studies, which slowly started in the 1980s—we have implemented and generally acknowledged in study programmes and syllabi film studies, gender studies or postcolonial studies, but academia has unaccountably neglected (Italian) Fashion Studies so far. While, up to now, the scientific *Otherness* of this domain might have restrained scholars of Italian and Transcultural Studies from including fashion discourses into canonical research fields, positive evidence is given, though—by political and artistic environments, as well as by daily life-experience—about how close societies across the world feel to the polymorphic languages of Italian fashion, which, *de facto*, stands as a paradigmatic case. Often overseen as positioned in the shadow of French *Haute Couture*, the presumably "simpler", more practical and, yet, variegated Italian way of life, *life-worlds* and skilful effortlessness (called *sprezzatura*) actually embrace a wide range of diverse cultures and layers of meaning.

In my contribution, I have tried to bridge this research gap and to illustrate the transcultural dynamics of Italian fashion by first pinpointing fashion as a semiotic language, indicating relations between fashion and traditional—even stereotyped— "Italian" habits, and second by discussing the transculturality of fashion *Made in Italy* as well as its subversive power, applying a range of theoretical and interdisciplinary approaches (Welsch, Deleuze, Barthes, Bhabha, Foucault, Goodman). For centuries experienced in handling foreign rules, the Italian mentality developed not only smart forms of entrepreneurship in order to survive and raise the economic status of their states, but also an inventive mind-set across the grain, which was distinct from their foreign rulers. Furthermore,—in spite of its Eurocentrism that can't be denied—the peculiarity of the topic concerning "Fashion made in Italy" consists in the circumstance that fashion from Italy is not as imperialistically self-centred as French or American fashion might appear. Instead of that, Italy-related fashion products and trends disperse themselves throughout the world in a subtle, almost imperceptible, heterotopic manner (cf. Reichardt & Moll, 2018, pp. 16–17). These two factors—Italian rebelliousness and heterotopic syncretism—catapulted the Italians in the second half of the 20th century to becoming the most requested and successful fashion designers in history. Like the US-Indian-Italian writer Lahiri or the postcolonial Franco-Congolese *sapeurs* in Africa, Italians keep on searching for their "decentralized", independent and deliberating own way, while constantly enriching and optimizing the transcultural spheres of fashion.

Always oscillating *between* centre and periphery, and in showing an open-minded *habitus* in the face of a US-writer originating from India who moved to Rome (like Jhumpa Lahiri) or a German designer living in France and also working in Italy (like Karl Lagerfeld), by focusing on iconic aspects of a language which is keen on using the media beyond borders in order to reach out to people all over the world, Italian fashion has developed its own aesthetics to reflect nomadic lifestyles in postmodern times. Symbolically, particularly in academic sciences, it takes on an assumed "peripheric" role within the global fashion system (mostly standing in the shadow of France, in the public perception) just like the European market does in the international context. In truth, though, Italian fashion is—at least historically speaking—of central standing and great importance because it represents a freely flowing font of traditional proposals, original inspiration and a permanent pool of creative and fresh ideas since WWII. Italian fashion, thus, offers—just like the transcultural practices that developed in Europe over the centuries—a lens of opportunity and an extremely broad choice of subjects which are still to be questioned and studied. For centuries, despite all Eurocentrism from which *world fashion* (in analogy to World Literature) suffers, Italian fashion has succeeded in showing how to express individualistic and ideological attitudes regarding style, gender and society with such a solid professionalism and—in the eye of an interested audience—unique *sprezzatura*, that make it worth including the Italian *habitus*—also as a didactic key-concept—in a much more visible way, if not in the curriculum of Cultural Studies in general, then at least in the standard reach, concern and research spectrum of Modern Italian Studies, today, both in Italy and abroad.

# References

Assmann, J. (1992). Das kulturelle Gedächtnis. Schrift, Erinnerungen und politische Identität in frühen Hochkulturen. C. H. Beck

Barnard, M. (2014). Fashion Theory. An Introduction. Routledge.

Barthes, R. (1967). The Fashion System. Translated from the French by Matthew Ward and Richard Howard. University of California Press.

Belfanti, C. M. (2019). Storia culturale del Made in Italy. Il Mulino.

Bhabha, H. K. (1994). The Location of Culture. Routledge.

Birbari, E. (1975). Dress in Italian painting 1460–1500. Murray.

Blackmore, S. (1999). The Meme Machine. Oxford University Press.

Bond, L., & Rapson, J. (Ed.). (2014). The Transcultural Turn: Interrogating Memory Between and Beyond Borders. De Gruyter.

Bourdieu, P. (1980a). Le sens pratique. Les Éditions de Minuit.

Bourdieu, P. (1980b). Questions de sociologie. Les Éditions de Minuit.

Bourdieu, P. (1992). Les règles de l'art. Éditions Seuil.

Burke, P. (1995). The Fortunes of the Courtier: The European Reception of Castiglione's Cortegiano. Penn State University Press.

CFMI [Il Centro di Firenze per la Moda Italiana]. (2015, December 5). Il centro di Firenze per la moda italiana [Center for Italian Fashion in Florence]—La storia. Retrieved December 22, 2019, from https://web.archive.org/web/20151205000734/http://www.cfmi.it/cfmi/hystory.html

Chambers, I. & Cariello, M. (2019). La questione mediterranea. Mondadori.

Christo & Jeanne-Claude. (2016). The Floating Piers. Lake Iseo, Italy, 2014–2016. Photographs by Wolfgang Volz. Edited by Simone Philippi. Taschen.

Dawkins, R. (1976). The Selfish Gene. Oxford University Press.

D'Epiro, P., & Desmond Pinkowish, M. (2001). Sprezzatura: 50 Ways Italian Genius Shaped the World. Anchor.

De Sica, V. (Director). (1964). Matrimonio all'italiana [Italian Wedding] [Film]. Compagnia Cinematografica Champion. Les Films Concordia.

Deleuze, G., & Guattari, F. (1986). Nomadology: The War Machine. Translated from the French by Brian Massumi, Semiotext(e). [Original work published in 1980]

Elias, N. (1939). The Civilizing Process. Blackwell.

Esposito, E. (2004). I paradossi della moda. Originalità e transitorietà nella società moderna. Baskerville.

Fellini, F. (Director). (1960). La dolce vita [Film]. Riama Film. Pathé Consortium Cinéma. Gray Films.

Fendi. (2016, July 8). Fendi Legends and Fairy Tales: Backstage [Video]. YouTube. https://www.youtube.com/watch?v=mp3Q2nvfWV4&ab_channel=Fendi

Fendi. (2018, September 22). Fendi Women's Spring/Summer 2019 Backstage [Video]. YouTube. https://www.youtube.com/watch?v=SUzkxNw86l0&ab_channel=Fendi

FF Channel. (2016, July 7). Fendi | Haute Couture Fall/Winter 2016/2017 Full Show | Exclusive [Video]. YouTube. https://www.youtube.com/watch?v=OfTa2UfatE0&t=5s&ab_channel=FFChannel

Foucault, M. (1971). L'ordre du discours. Gallimard.

Foucault, M. (1984). Histoire de la sexualité III. Le souci de soi. Gallimard.

FTV HOT. (2016, March 15). FENDI DONNA P/E-2008 GREAT WALL OF CHINA—FULL SHOW [Video]. YouTube. https://www.youtube.com/watch?v=tDKh4C-DJNo&t=1035s&ab_channel=FTVHOT

Godart, F. (2012). Sociologie de la mode. La Découverte. [First edition published 2010]

Goodman, N. (1968). Languages of Art: An Approach to a Theory of Symbols. The Bobbs-Merrill Company.

Goodman, N. (1978). Ways of World Making. Hackett Publishing.

Graham, R. J. (1990). Composing Ourselves in Style: The Aesthetics of Literacy in "The Courtier". Journal of Aesthetic Education. University of Illinois Press.

Grünwald, A. (2009). Mode Made in Italy—Kult oder Auslaufmodell? Die Bedeutung des Country-of-Origin Effektes für Marketing- und Positionierungsstrategien am Beispiel italienischer Modeunternehmen [Fashion Made in Italy—cult or obsolete? The importance of the Country-of-Origin effect for marketing and positioning strategies using the example of Italian fashion companies]. VDM Verlag Dr. Müller.

Gundle, S. (2011). Death and the Dolce Vita. The Dark Side of Rome in the 1950s. Canongate Books.

Hollander, A. (1978). Seeing Through Clothes. Viking. [First edition published 1975]

Hollander, A. (1994). Sex and Suits. Kodansha International.

Kmieciak, J. (2019, February 20). "Ich bin immer der gleiche Hamburger Jung". In Hamburger Abendblatt. Collector's Edition [n. 1, Karl Lagerfeld 1933–2019, special edition], 1(19), 60–63. Funke Zeitschriften.

Kumaravadivelu, B. (2008). Cultural Globalization and Language Education. Yale University Press.

Lahiri, J. (1999). Interpreter of Maladies. Flamingo.

Lahiri, J. (2016a). The Clothing of Books. Translated from the Italian by Alberto Vourvoulias-Bush. Vintage. [Original work published 2015]

Lahiri, J. (2016b). In Other Words. Translated from the Italian by Ann Goldstein. Bloomsbury. [Original work published 2015]

LeWeb. (2013, July 19). LeWeb 2011: Karl Lagerfeld, Natalie Massenet & Loic Le Meur [Video]. YouTube. https://www.youtube.com/watch?v=6Vq58Gkwpos

Lüderssen, C., & Sanna, S. A. (Ed.). (1995). Letteratura de-centrata. Italienische Autorinnen und Autoren in Deutschland. Diesterweg.

Maar, C., & Burda, H. (Ed.). (2004). Iconic Turn. Die neue Macht der Bilder. DuMont.

McLuhan, M. (1964). Understanding Media. McGraw-Hill.

Meet the style Hello. (2018, September 8). #ITALIAISLOVE Dolce&Gabbana [Video]. YouTube. https://www.youtube.com/watch?v=6LI1vgmgyus

MIFF. (2019, July 9). Walking On Water | Trailer [Video]. YouTube. https://www.youtube.com/watch?v=B2oTsdazcrU&ab_channel=kinolorber

Mormorio, D. (1999). Dolce Vita: Tazio Secchiaroli—Der Größte aller Paparazzi. Translated from Italian into German by Claudia Bostelmann, Te Neues. [Original work published 1998]

Nielsen, K. (2015). East of the Sun and West of the Moon. Taschen. [Original work published 1914]

Ortiz, F. (1995). Cuban Counterpoint: Tobacco and Sugar. Translated from the Spanish by Harriet de Onís. Duke University Press. [First edition published 1947]

Paounov, A. (2019). Walking on Water [Film]. Kotva Films.

Paulicelli, E. (2001). Fashion: Narration and nation. In Z. Baranski & R. West (Eds.), The Cambridge Companion to Modern Italian Culture (Cambridge Companions to Culture, pp. 283–292). Cambridge University Press. https://doi.org/10.1017/CCOL0521550343.015

Paulicelli, E., & Clark, H. (Ed.). (2008). The Fabric of Cultures: Fashion, Identity, Globalization. Routledge.

Paulicelli, E. (2014a). Writing Fashion in Early Modern Italy: From Sprezzatura to Satire. Ashgate.

Paulicelli, E. (2014b). Fashion: The Cultural Economy of Made in Italy. Fashion Practice, 6(2), 155–174.

Paulicelli, E. (2016). Italian Style: Fashion & Film from Early Cinema to the Digital Age. Bloomsbury Academic.

Pazyluz, A. (2016, May 23). La Dolce Vita - Anita Ekberg et Marcello Mastroianni La fontaine de Trevi (Rome) [Video]. YouTube. https://youtu.be/7_hfZoe9FHE

Rajewsky, I. (2002). Intermedialität. A. Francke UTB.

Reichardt, D. (2006). Paradigma mundi? Die Geschichte des postkolonialen Siziliendiskurses zwischen literarischer Alterität und Identität. In D. Reichardt (Ed.), L'Europa che comincia e finisce: la Sicilia. Approcci transculturali alla letteratura siciliana. Beiträge zur transkulturellen Annäherung an die sizilianische Literatur. Contributions to a Transcultural Approach to Sicilian Literature (pp. 87–107). Peter Lang.

Reichardt, D., & D'Angelo, C. (Ed.). (2016). Moda Made in Italy. Il linguaggio della moda e del costume italiano [With a preface by D. Reichardt & C. D'Angelo, presenting an interview with Dacia Maraini, Civiltà Italiana—Terza serie, n. 10]. Cesati.

Reichardt, D. (2017). On the Theory of a Transcultural Francophony. The Concept of Wolfgang Welsch and its Didactic Interest. In 900. Novecento transnazionale. Letterature, arti e culture/ Transnational 20th Century. Literatures, Arts and Cultures, 1(1), 40–56 [Open access article licensed under CC-BY]. University of Rome La Sapienza. http://doi.org/10.13133/2532-1994_1.4_2017

Reichardt, D., & Moll, N. (2018). Introduzione—Un'Italia transculturale: quale modello? In D. Reichardt & N. Moll (Eds.), Italia transculturale. Il sincretismo italofono come modello eterotopico [In collaboration with D. Brioschi] (Civiltà Italiana—Terza serie, n. 26, pp. 9–27). Cesati.

Schrader, P. (1980). American Gigolo [Film]. Paramount Pictures.

Schrödl, B., & Allerstorfer, J. (Ed.). (2019). Stoffwechsel. Mode zwischen Globalisierung und Transkulturalität [Mode global, n. 2]. Böhlau.

Simmel, G. (1995). Philosophie der Mode. Suhrkamp. [First edition published 1905]

Sorge, P. (2015). D'Annunzio e la magia della moda. Elliot.

Tomasi di Lampedusa, G. [= Giuseppe di Lampedusa]. (2007). The Leopard [Translated from the Italian by Archibald Colquhoun, foreword and appendix by Gioachino Lanza Tomasi, translated from the Italian by Guido Waldman]. Pantheon Books. [Original work published 1958]

Welsch, W. (1999). Transculturality: The Puzzling Form of Cultures Today. In M. Featherstone & S. Lash (Eds.), Spaces of culture: City, nation, world (Theory, Culture & Society, pp. 195–213). SAGE Publications Ltd. http://doi.org/10.4135/9781446218723.n11

Welsch, W. (2003). Rolle und Veränderungen der Religion im gegenwärtigen Übergang zu transkulturellen Gesellschaften. In D. C. Siedler (Ed.), Religionen in der Pluralität. Ihre Rolle in postmodernen Gesellschaften. Wolfgang Welschs Ansatz in christlicher und islamischer Perspektive (pp. 13–47). Alektor.

Zangemeister, W. H., & Stark, L. (2007). The Artistic Brain Beyond the Eye. Author House.

Marta Niccolai

# 10 Encounters with Alterity: Romani on the Contemporary Italian Stage

When the first written records about the Roma[163] by non-Roma started to appear in Western Europe in the fifteenth century, the use of derogatory language showed attempts by opponents to dominate a group with puzzling and unsettling ethno-cultural traits, primarily concerning their appearance and unconventional way of life (Toninato, 2014, p. 7). These narratives, according to Toninato, are "written ... with the aim of constructing the 'Gypsies' difference in negative terms ... deliberately marking out their behaviour as deviant and dangerous. Such narratives have played a fundamental role in defining the Gypsy as the 'ultimate alien' (Lucassen, Willems, & Cottaar, 1998, p. 61) in European society" (Toninato, 2014, pp. 7–8).

In Europe today, the portrayal of the Roma as thieves and beggars in local and national media is still highly commonplace. In Italy, where they are commonly known as "zingari" [gypsies], a pre-election campaign by the Centre-Right in 2018 proposed to dismantle Roma camps as a national priority, along with tackling the refugee crisis, in order to win people's consent and votes[164].

Contemporary theatre practitioners, however, have created counter-narratives, with the aim of telling different stories based on direct contact with members of Romani communities. The outcome, presented in the form of various stage productions, denotes a cultural interweaving that challenges popular views of Romani identity.

With this in mind, this chapter focuses on four contemporary Italian playwrights, namely Daniele Lamuraglia (Florence), Fiorenza Menni and Andrea Mochi Sismondi (Bologna), and Pino Petruzzelli (Genoa). Although their productions vary considerably, what these theatre practitioners have in common is an approach to 'the different other' based on their personal knowledge of the Roma, which communicates the need to give a voice to those excluded from society in theatrical discourse.

This chapter is divided into two parts. The first, theoretical section is centred on the transcultural concept theorized by the Cuban anthropologist Fernando Ortiz. According to Ortiz, the acceptance that cultures within a colonial environment influence one another through a process of losses and acquisitions helps to establish a greater balance in the relationship between the colonizer and the colonized. In this chapter I will explore how Ortiz's theory can be adopted in other contexts, within

---

163 I will employ the term "Roma" (pl. n.), "Rom" (m.s. n.), "Romni" (f.s. n.) "Romani" (adj.) throughout, while the term Gypsy will be employed when it is used by non-Roma or in citations.
164 Articles on the Italian press abound. See e.g. Matteo Salvini, leader of the North League party, promises to destroy all the Romani camps and to fly all the Romani people out of Italy (Rame, 2018).

this essay-collection's focus of transcultural life-worlds. In the first part I will also consider the dichotomy between centre and margin (or periphery), which plays an important role in both the research undertaken by theatre practitioners and the methodology concerning "difference", when they seek to put on stage Romani identity. In the second part of the chapter the theoretical concepts discussed will be applied to the following theatrical productions, Lamuraglia's *Cristo Gitano* (2003), *Telerom* and *Zingarità* (2004); *Comune spazio problematico* (2008) and *Open Option* by Menni and Mochi Sismondi; and, finally, *Non chiamarmi zingaro* (2008) by Petruzzelli. First, a discussion of the directors' approaches (or, in the case of Petruzzelli, the narrator) will provide an understanding of transcultural theory, as applied to what can be considered a preliminary phase of the theatrical production, during which the non-Roma and the Roma familiarize with each other through dialogue and extended periods of time spent together, primarily within a non-Roma family and/or community. This will be followed by an analysis of the performances themselves, primarily as cultural representations, which can shed light on the majority's perception of Romani people. These performances offer an opportunity to appreciate their mutual similarities and differences and reflect on how transcultural approaches attempt to change the centre/ periphery dichotomy in the relationship between non-Roma and Roma.

## 10.1 Transcultural Perspectives from the Periphery

"Transculturation" is a term coined in 1947 by the Cuban anthropologist Fernando Ortiz to indicate the transformative process undergone by a society in the acquisition of "foreign" cultural resources. More specifically, in Cuban society, it describes the interplay of influences between Africans and Latin Americans.

Transculturation was originally intended to replace various expressions in use such as "cultural exchange", "acculturation" "diffusion", "migration or osmosis of culture", and other terms that Ortiz considered inadequate (1947, p. ix). The term took into consideration the possibility that both foreign and indigenous peoples are modified by being in each other's presence. This means that change not only occurs as a process of acculturation undergone by foreigners settling in a different culture, but that cultural differences influence all the parties involved. This represents what Ortiz calls "… an exchange between two cultures, both of them active, both contributing their share, and both co-operating to bring about a new reality of civilization" (Ortiz, 1947, p. xi).

The concept of transculturation can be compared to the poetics of creolization, as theorized by the Caribbean philosopher from Martinique, Èdouard Glissant (1996), who saw the emergence of the Creole language as a fusion between French and Caribbean languages in a colonial context. The Creole language became, for Glissant, a metaphor for the emergence and transformation of cultures and identities.

When transferring Ortiz's concept of transculturation into a different socio-cultural context, one must take into consideration that it originated in a colonial milieu framed around the dominant and the dominated. Interestingly, although its transfer to "our" contemporary "Western" world requires us to consider the absence of a colonial relationship between foreign and indigenous parties, it has been observed that dominant attitudes towards "the other", whether immigrants, refugees, or Romani in the "Western" world, often perpetuate or recreate the binary opposition of dominant and dominated which was typical of colonial societies[165]. However, we should also highlight the differences with its colonial context, as in the case of creolization, which has been described as "a process of *contention* ... deeply embedded in the history of enslavement, racial terror and subaltern survival in the Caribbean, in conflict, trauma, rupture and the violence of uprooting" (Ahmed et al., 2003, p. 281).

In recent usage, Ortiz's transculturation has here become a term which can be adopted to indicate different forms of cultural mixing. As Diana Taylor says:

> The importance of stressing the liberating potential of the theory of transculturation is that it is one of the few theories that allows an opening to the impasse usually set up in relation to minority theories ... rather than being oppositional or strictly dialectical, it *circulates*. It is applicable to other dominated cultures and, unlike dominant theories, it highlights their vitality rather than their indebtedness to First World culture. Potentially, the hope might be that by engaging the many, previously marginalized *others*, these cultures may be able to decenter (not replace) the hegemonic. (Taylor, 1991, pp. 101–102)

The importance of this transcultural theory, therefore, lies in its potential to deconstruct the binary oppositions between centre and periphery and dominant and dominated, by including in society marginalized, peripheral voices that are usually unheard.

The outcome of transculturation is unpredictable; it is a process that touches the established and introduces new elements that can shape new realities (Glissant, 1996, p. xii).

Yet one wonders to what extent the unequal power relations in the "Western" world can ever lead to a cultural exchange where even the dominant agrees to undergo a partial disculturation, a process through which parts of the culture of origin are lost, and a process of partial acculturation, when elements of another culture are acquired, thus generating new cultural identities (Taylor, 1991, p. 93).

As in other contexts of unequal relationships, for example in the academic fields of postcolonial and gender studies, the question of "voice", and more specifically

---

**165** Postcolonial studies focus on the cultural legacy of colonialism and imperialism, for example Ania Loomba, Colonialism/Postcolonialism (2005); Robert J. C. Young, Postcolonialism: an historical introduction (2001) and Bill Ashcroft and Gareth Griffiths, Post-colonial studies, the key concepts (2007).

the suppression of ethnic minority voices in the public sphere, is of central concern to a theatre interested in differences. As De Martino writes, "[i]n a global world that is developing an ever more diverse fabric – both in linguistic and cultural terms – theatre cannot but acknowledge the presence of a multitude of voices that feel entitled to speak up"[166] (De Martino et al., 2013, p. 1).

In their still very relevant essay that maps out theatrical praxis in the presence of more than one culture, Jacqueline Lo and Helen Gilbert present a range of subdivisions to describe the different degrees of involvement with cultural differences on stage. Thus, "cross-cultural theatre" denotes the umbrella-term for the presence of and encounter with different "cultural fragments" that involve some form of negotiation. For Lo and Gilbert, the term "transcultural" has been seen as a sub-genre of "Intercultural theatre", a term which indicates "intentional encounters between cultures and performing traditions" (Lo & Gilbert, 2002, p. 37). Taking intentionality as a key component of the transcultural approach, a theatre director or practitioner will use cultures and traditions to identify similarities rather than differences (Pavis, 1996, p. 6). However, this does not mean that differences are erased. Theatre, based on a relationship between the director, actors, and audience, can present a particularly fertile soil for artistic métissage which is inclusive of multilingualism and multiculturalism. More specifically, within the context of this study, by placing Romani actors on stage, or by putting Romani issues at the centre of a performance, this type of theatre deliberately breaks away from majority representations, constructing emancipatory life-worlds of different experiences and new realities.

The dramatists discussed in this chapter approach "difference" in ways that can dismantle the static quality of the centre/periphery dichotomy. Their decision to meet the Roma in their communities allows them to learn from their ways of life and to reflect on themselves as members of a different community. This can be seen as akin to the work of the contemporary ethnographer, whose research requires reflection on the impact of one's own perspective on their work, and how in turn their perspectives will impact on others when they share their work. Like a contemporary ethnographer, these dramatists engage in conversation with the research-participants rather than interviewing them, and they partake in their life during the time they spend with them[167]. To a greater or lesser extent, the self-reflexive quality of these playwrights' works has influenced the staged works under analysis in this chapter,

---

166 On the question of 'giving a voice to disadvantaged people' it is worth mentioning Augusto Boal, a theatre practitioner from Brazil who, in the 1960s, founded the Theatre of the Oppressed. This was devised to educate people from poor communities and enable them to find a solution to their ongoing problems. In Italy, Annet Henneman, the director of Hidden Theatre (Teatro di Nascosto), based in Tuscany, has been putting refugees and the suffering of people in Middle Eastern conflict zones, at the center of her theatrical events.

167 On the subject of reflexive ethnography, see for example, Charlotte Aull Davies, *Reflexive Ethnography. A guide to researching Selves and Others* (2002).

which together present three different levels of representation of the Roma people. Lamuraglia places Romani culture, language and actors at centre stage, where they can present their own culture and voice their opinions of the way they are popularly represented in Italy. Menni and Mochi Sismondi, on the other hand, adopt a more anthropological approach, that aims to include Romani opinions in contemporary global, sociological and political issues, choosing to be a mouthpiece for the Romani and also working with them on stage. Finally, Petruzzelli in the role of narrator uses his voice to describe the racial discrimination and subsequent pain inflicted to the Roma in ordinary life, offering an emotive dimension which is largely absent from media coverage on the Romani.

## 10.2 The Roma Visible on Stage: Lamuraglia and the Rom Trilogy

The founder of 'Teatro del Legame' in Florence, Lamuraglia is the first playwright and theatre director to bring the Roma on stage with three plays: *Cristo Gitano*[168] (2003), *Telerom* and *Zingarità* (2004)[169]. His intention, in his own words, to "dare voce e portare alla luce quelle verità che sono oscurate e non possiedono altri spazi per mostrarsi"[170] (Teatro del Legame, n.d.) will be apparent from his theatrical choices.

The first play, *Cristo Gitano*, is the modern interpretation of an ancient myth which was previously mentioned by the Italian writer Antonio Tabucchi. It narrates the story of a Gypsy Christ born every three generations and crucified by his gypsy community[171]. In the story, a foreigner recruits the four Romani to act as disciples in a play about the passion of Christ. In exchange, they will receive a sum of money that will substantially improve their lives. The foreign man is named [the] Cristo Gitano and the four Romani are given the names of some of the biblical apostles: Giacomo, Giovanni, Giuda and Pietro. They all act for the director who wants to stage the Passion of the Christ. Soon, however, he will have to accept that the story will be told by his characters—four apostles instead of twelve, and a mysterious woman called Kundry—who will tell their own version of the Passion of the Christ. For nearly a year, Lamuraglia

---

**168** From now on the play will be cited as CG. Cristo Gitano was first performed at Teatro Rifredi in Florence on April 24, 2003.

**169** A third play, not included in this chapter, is *Zingarità* (2004).

**170** "to give voice and visibility to hidden truths that cannot be visible in another place" (Teatro del Legame, n.d.). Via this link it is also possible to watch a recording of the play: http://www.teatrodel-legame.it/cristo-gitano/.

**171** The legend is still narrated in some areas of Andalusia, where the statue of Cristo Gitano is carried during a procession (Lamuraglia, 2005, p. 11). Tabucchi wrote *Gli zingari e il Rinascimento: Vivere da Rom a Firenze* (Tabucchi, 1999), based on his personal experience of the area assigned to a Roma community on the outskirts of Florence. For Tabucchi the city is at once ancient and humanist, intolerant and politically uncompromising.

and his collaborators regularly visited Olmatello, the Romani community on the out-skirts of Florence, where they learned about their traditions and where Lamuraglia met the five Roma who became members of the cast for *Cristo Gitano*. One acted as Gypsy Christ and four others as characters named after four of the apostles: Giuda, Giacomo, Giovanni and Pietro. The other three characters—the director, his assistant, and Kundry, a female character from the legend—are Italians.

During the Theatre laboratories that ran for a year, they had to face challenges concerning theatrical concepts such as "character" and "theatrical fiction", which were not previously known by the Roma. In the end, it proved to be a very reward-ing experience for everyone involved: the director, his collaborators, the Town hall staff and the Romani community. The sheer fact that Romani and Italian families sat next to each other to watch the performance was a major achievement, that shows the revolutionary potential of theatre, as stressed by Lamuraglia: "non solo la sala è stracolma, ma vediamo anche intere famiglie di Rom, con padri, madri, figli, neonati, zii, nonni. Il primo miracolo di *Cristo Gitano* è già avvenuto. Fiorentini e Rom a sedere accanto, per vivere un'unica esperienza"[172] (Lamuraglia, 2005, p. 51).

As a theatre director, Lamuraglia is less interested in revealing the marginality of the Roma than he is in approaching them as a community living on the "border", as a space located furthest from the mainstream or centre. In his article "The Fascination of the Margins", Lamuraglia maintains that "the margins should not be marginal-ized; conversely, they hold a prominent position for the appreciation of the Centre in its spatial, existential and communal dimension ... the centre and the margin share a relationship of reciprocity in which the one continuously redefines itself starting from the other whose precious presence is guarded and protected" (2013, p. 131). Being fas-cinated by the marginal other implies a willingness to listen and find similarities even if what is immediately visible is difference. The Roma are regarded as "quintessen-tially" different because they choose to live according to their culture, even though this means being confined to the margins of Italian society. Lamuraglia says that a "traditional" mind finds it hard to understand Romani culture; for example, their rites are interpreted from the pagan, Jewish and Catholic traditions, on an individ-ual rather than a collective basis; they believe in destiny, they do not have a written history, and their preference for living in extended families has not changed, as it has in the mainstream Western world (Lamuraglia, 2005, p. 26).

The stage performs the important function of providing a space where "the margin" can become visible, being manifested through the voice of members of the Roma community. Theatre is a sacred space for Lamuraglia, the very space where the

---

172 "We have [a] full house, with Romani families coming into the theatre, mothers, fathers, child-ren, babies, uncles, grandparents. *Cristo Gitano* has performed its first miracle; Florentines and Ro-mani sit next to each other to share the same experience" (Lamuraglia, 2005, p. 51).

community and its "other", the "gipsies" meet and confront each other (Lamuraglia, 2013).

The play begins with four Roma praying in Romaní. From the outset, the Italian audience is placed in an alienating space since the language impedes their participation in the event on-stage. However, an attentive spectator can overcome the linguistic barriers by relating to whatever familiarity they can find, for instance, in the act of praying itself. From the beginning, Lamuraglia wants the audience to relate individually by looking for similarities rather than stopping at differences.

It is evident from the beginning that the five characters' versions of the Stations of the Cross will not be conventional. For the Italian spectators, the play becomes a liminal space where some familiarity with the story, and the unfamiliar, meet. At the first Station of the Cross, Jesus washes the feet of his disciples, whereas in the play, the disciples wash Jesus's feet with wine. At the second Station, Jesus shares bread and wine as symbols of his body and blood, but in *Cristo Gitano*, Jesus eats the bread and drinks the wine, leaving the disciples astonished. Unlike Jesus, Cristo Gitano does not wish to be known for his words, and he does not believe that his disciples are ready to receive his teachings. Furthermore, he does not want to fulfil his destiny; he would rather bribe Giuda to hide him, and thus avoid being sacrificed for the benefit of humanity. This is the exact opposite to what is narrated in the Bible; Jesus is betrayed by an apostle for thirty dinars, thus fulfilling his Father's will. It is evident that the gypsy Christ is an individual who will not keep his promise to be crucified, even though the four Romani want him to be sacrificed for the benefit of their people as a community. He is the reversal of the biblical Jesus: "Jesus Christ was God and became man"; "Cristo Gitano is a man who becomes God" (Lamuraglia, 2005, pp. 81–82). According to Lamuraglia, the performance had an enriching effect on the Romani actors, who were confronted with new insights to interpret and understand their own myth from a different perspective (Lamuraglia, 2005, p. 9).

Acknowledging that many aspects of Cristo Gitano are the reverse of Christian mythology does not destroy its meaning altogether; on the contrary, it generates new meaning. As an example of theatre at the margins, it does not hesitate to reveal strong differences because this is where similarities begin to be revealed, and this is the point when centre and margin can identify with each other and share the same space. Moreover, where the differences between Gağe (this is the term used by the Roma to define non-Roma) and Roma appear greater, a new awareness may appear, namely the recognition that, beyond different cultural veneers, expression of the sacred through ritual actions is found cross-culturally. As Lamuraglia outlines: "Cristo Gitano ... si è sacrificato, o è stato sacrificato, non sappiamo di chi sia la volontà. È il sacrificio per fondare il legame. Questo unisce il cristianesimo al paganesimo, e alla spiritualità dei Rom"[173] (2005, p. 45).

---

[173] "It is not known whether Cristo Gitano decided to sacrifice himself or [whether] he was sacrifi-

Lamuraglia's interpretation of Cristo Gitano also comprises a metatheatrical dimension. As director of the play he questions his choices, their impact on the story's denouement, and the effect on the Romani community in the theatre. This critical thinking is expressed through the character of the director. He has a central role because of his position of power, and when he makes his entrance before the crucifixion, he wants to have control of the play's development, as described by the stage-directions: "Al centro del palcoscenico, prende una sedia e si mette a sedere. I rom in terra sul proscenio"[174] (Lamuraglia, 2005, p. 68). When placed in the position to judge Cristo Gitano, he refuses, as Pilate refused to pronounce judgement on Jesus. As for the Romani characters, both the director and Cristo Gitano represent a means by which to strengthen the cultural bond with their community. However, the director is interested in acting and staging techniques, which are fictional, whereas the Roma want to perform a rite that for them is real and part of their culture. The director remains convinced of his approach to the play, but he decides to step back to allow the Roma to finish the play according to their own cultural knowledge of the myth (Lamuraglia, 2005, p. 43). It is arguable that the decision made by the director-as-character contains some autobiographical elements, because Lamuraglia was committed to the difficult task of mediating between cultural and religious traditions on the one hand, and making difference visible without distancing the audience too much or imposing his perspective on the Roma, on the other. His final choice was to provide guidance without imposing his own view excessively.

*Cristo Gitano* has succeeded in making a difference because the play has allowed the profane, at the margins, to share the centre with the sacred. In this union, theatre reveals its sacredness. The stage is the space where the margin can meet the centre, actors meet audience, reality meets fiction, and where, according to Lamuraglia: "It is now easier to see the sacred sense of the territory ... and the mental and material setting of a theatrical space. Two universes founded on a mutual agreement inspiring an order of distances, a dialectic between the inside and the outside, and the relationship between Centre and Margins" (Lamuraglia, 2013, p. 130).

The second play, *Telerom. La televisione degli zingari*[175] is a parody of well- known Italian television programmes, conducted by Roma from their own perspective. As in *Cristo Gitano*, adopting the technique of reversal adds another, different point of view that contrasts standard views marginalizing diversity.

---

ced. It is the notion of 'sacrifice' that provides the connection between Christianity and paganism, and the type of spirituality practised by [the] Romani people" (Lamuraglia, 2005, p. 45).

**174** "At the centre of the stage, he grabs a chair and sits down. The actors sit on the floor below him" (Lamuraglia, 2005, p. 68).

**175** First performed in April 27th, 2005, at Teatro Cantiere Florida in Florence. The play can be watched via this link: https://www.youtube.com/watch?v=yI8q2_Xfrp4.

Whilst the ironical news brings laughter, screen projections of Romani life elicit sadness for their living conditions. Whilst the part about television is dramatized, the drama of life is projected on the screen. The sketches in this play are performed by three Roma, whereas the assistants are Italians. Lamuraglia, as director, is an off-stage voice that provides guidance to the actors. In one instance, he includes a metatheatrical component when he openly says that he needs to copy well-known and appealing TV programmes because the Roma themselves do not attract spectators. Contrary to television studios, which are bright and stylish, the news programme *TGRom* is broadcast from a semi-dark space, with hardly any furniture. *TGRom* delivers ironical news based on common stereotypes about the Roma. So, for example, the news of a lorry from Eastern Europe carrying horses and a Romani family is read as an ordinary event rather than with the typical alarmism of the Italian newsreaders; the problem of Romani beggars at traffic lights is seen in reversal, since the replacement of lights with roundabouts creates unemployment among the Roma. Moreover, the "Lega Rom" (a parody of the nationalist Northern league party) wants all the inhabitants of the city of Bergamo to leave, because it has now been proved that the Roma inhabited the area long before them. Ironically, there are plans to build a "Bergarom" (a camp for the people of Bergamo) on the outskirts of the city. This use of irony serves to produce estrangement in the spectators; the truthfulness of the news is not challenged, but the altered tone reveals another side to conventional news broadcasts, which largely condemn the presence of Romani people in Italy.

The sketch *Il grande Olmatello – cinque anni chiusi in un container*[176] is a parody of the reality show *Il Grande Fratello (Big Brother)*. Parody, in Linda Hutcheson's definition, features a "repetition with critical distance that allows ironic signaling of difference at the very heart of similarity" (1988, p. x). The screening begins with footage of the Olmatello camp outside Florence, with the containers in full view. The camera looks inside a container where four Roma read on a sofa, whilst three children chase each other. The shot reveals the presence of a camera and the filmmaker, who is heard asking the children how long they have been living in the container. The camera zooms in with a close-up of the books, all classics of "Western" philosophy, such as Seneca and Plato. Through parody Lamuraglia raises questions as to what is taken for "natural". It is evident that the brief sketch is artificially constructed with the intention of inviting the spectator to reflect on Romani people reading classics, since the media representation of them has led to the assumption that the Roma cannot be literate, let alone educated. It is impossible to predict the outcome of this on the audience's consciousness and belief system, but the scene can bring to the surface ingrained prejudices and inherited stereotypes towards them.

Moreover, the sketch plays on the relationship between fiction and reality, since Roma actually do live in containers, but while the staging of the play is fictional, *Il*

---

176 "The great Olmatello – five years stuck in a container".

*grande Fratello* is a reality show which is taken to be real. Playing with the close association between reality and fiction is an invitation to consider that what is considered "real" about Roma can be "imagined" for one's own convenience.

The interplay between fiction and reality is repeated in the second part of the performance. Here an Italian man introduces himself as "the traveller". He makes his first, brief appearance at the beginning of the play, from a dark corner of the stage, where he introduces himself, saying he is there "to repair" by taking the Roma on a journey back home, where their journey began over a thousand years ago. With his second appearance towards the end of the play, he invites the three characters from *Telerom* to sit down and watch a screening. In the first part of the screening, the three characters are interviewed separately and are allowed to tell their story. The use of theatrical intermediality develops a dialectical relationship between the illusion of the stage and the realism of the filmic image, the fictional characters on-stage and their experience in life. This section is full of realism and offers material for reflection. Their stories tell of families, friends, work, and ordinary lives which were destroyed when the Balkan war broke out and the Romani people were forced to leave. The war forced them to leave and undertake a perilous journey, often as illegal immigrants in Europe, where they have been marginalized by the prejudice against them, denied work and forced to beg and steal to survive, thus reinforcing the negative stereotypes surrounding them.

The final part of the screening features a short film of an epic boat journey, with the five actors travelling from Italy to India. This is accompanied by a poetic commentary on life as a journey which starts with the first breath and ends with the last one. Interspersed with philosophical commentary, the end of the play aims to unite both actors and spectators to a common origin for a common future.

The third play of the trilogy, *Zingarità*[177] (2005), reinforces the poetics expressed in the two performances analysed thus far. *Zingarità* takes inspiration from two classic love stories with Romani characters: *Makar Ciudra* by Maxim Gorky and *Gli Zingari* by Alexander Pushkin. Aleko and Zemfira are the protagonists of the first story, Loiko and Radda those of the second. The four characters mirror each other, presenting their similarities to one another in reversal. Aleko has left everything to be with Zemfira, who prefers freedom to being possessed by one person. Loiko loves freedom, whereas Radda is possessive. Only a collective act of death can reconcile the disparity between possession and freedom. This version contrasts with the literary text, in which the death is inflicted by the male characters. The final scene is a tableau, with the four characters positioned to look as if they are all about to stab another and be stabbed in turn. The end is a paradox that does not offer a solution to the dramatic conflict between love and freedom, but gives the spectators the freedom

---

177 First performed on the 29th of April 2005 in Teatro cantiere Florida, Florence. The play can be watched via this link: https://www.youtube.com/watch?v=tIYei7hUdL0.

to draw their own conclusions. As stated by Lamuraglia in the introduction to the play, the conflict between possession and freedom is typical of the "Western" world, where individual freedom is practised to the detriment of long-lasting relationships, including the family (2011, pp. 105–106).

In the preface to the play, he says that Spanish and Russian literature, and Western literature in general, have fed our imagination with the description of the gypsy as a nomadic "free spirit", passionate musician and dancer (Lamuraglia, 2011). For this reason, Lamuraglia makes the choice to select only Italian actors, in order to establish the continuity of a Western point of view whilst at the same time being critical of this romanticized stereotype. However, the play resists reproducing and reinforcing the stereotype, by breaking the narrative to avoid the audience's identification with the theme of love. Classical literature constructs a romanticized version of the Roma, who are caught between destiny and the possession of a rebellious spirit.

Lamuraglia's thematization of love in the play is introduced in an epic form, with a group of musicians who also interact with the actors. The two actors, Roberto and Saverio, read out passages from Pushkin and Gorky, but they are unable to decide who should play Loiko and who should play Aleko. One of the musicians, Papini, who is aware that the spectators are waiting, takes the role of 'destiny' and makes the decision for the actors. The musicians interact with the actors on several occasions, making the play a work-in-progress before the spectators, a choice which shows that theatre is fiction. Yet in doing this, he shows that the stage is more real than fictional:

Radda: (*grida a Zemfira*) Zemfira! Io lo uccido . . .
Radda: (shouts to Zemfira) Zemfira! I will kill him . . .

Zemfira: (*grida a Radda*) Sì, Radda! Anch'io lo uccido . . .
Zemfira: (Shouts to Radda) Yes, Radda! I will kill him too. . .

*Musica*
*[music]*

*Papini: Stop! Fermi. . . (finisce la musica) Qui dicono "uccidere" e voi suonate. . . (ibid., p. 124)*
*Papini: Stop! Stop!. . . (music stops). They say "kill" and you play music (Lamuraglia, 2011, p. 124).*

Interruptions to the flow of the performance indicates a Brechtian technique of distancing, which is intended to discourage excessive involvement of the spectators in the love-story and the character development, and to encourage more intellectual participation, which is necessary in order to understand the relationship between reality and fiction and the illusion which it generates[178]. In doing so, Lamuraglia

---

**178** "Verfremdung" commonly translated as distancing, defamiliarisation and alienation, is an artistic strategy devised by Bertolt Brecht to distance the audience from emotional involvement in the play

brings together the timeless drama of love with the drama of being a Roma today. Thereby he makes the performance less about the novels and more about the process of staging the play, which incorporates popular contemporary views about gypsies. Anecdotes shared between the Romani and musicians mention "Western" attitudes towards the gypsies who become the scapegoat or locus of people's frustrations; blaming Romani is what the bank customer does who loses all his money through choosing the wrong investment plan. Outside the bank, he realizes that he has lost his wallet and blames a Roma who happens to be nearby: "Uno zingaro mi ha rubato il portafoglio"[179] (Lamuraglia, 2011, p. 125). The bank manager comes out and says: "Questi zingari andrebbero cacciati tutti dall'Italia"[180] (Lamuraglia, 2011, p. 125). They smile at each other, recognizing one another as members of the same community, and thereby excluding others. Their behavior is an example of ethnocentrism and xenophobia at the same time. Lamuraglia thereby connects classical literature with the Romani people through the use of contemporary anecdotes about the experience of being a Roma today. Loiko, being received by two musicians, tells the story of his family, who are nomads but not always by choice, since foreigners are more easily blamed and expelled from a community than a community's indigenous members. The family settled in Pristina, until they were forced out by the Balkan Wars. He tells that, before the Balkan Wars, his people could choose between travelling or staying at home, but after the war this was no longer possible. The question of nomadism indeed remains controversial. On the one hand, our globalized world has led to a sense of being uprooted, such that we speak occasionally of Neo-Nomadism. The October 2019 Condè Nast Traveller issue is entitled "The New Nomad Issue", showing glamorous pictures of Western families in idyllic places, with semi-naked children who can experience being 'wild', or adults free to journey inwardly and roam the planet, thanks to the digital age and a good internet connection which allows them to work anywhere. On the other hand, the movement of traditional travelers, such as the Roma, or migrants who leave their countries in search for better opportunities elsewhere, is opposed and persecuted. Therefore, more forcefully than the circulation of people, it seems that it is the circulation of capital that makes "nomadism" desirable in the first place.

---

through reminders to the artificiality of artistic performance. See Meg Mumford (2010).

**179** "That gypsy has stolen my wallet!".

**180** "These gypsies should be kicked out".

## 10.3 The Experience of Fiorenza Menni and Andrea Mochi Sismondi in a Romani Community in Macedonia: Whose Voices are on Stage?

Similarly to Lamuraglia, Menni, the founder of Teatrino Clandestino in Bologna, and Mochi Sismondi (then an actor in the same company) devised a performance after personally coming to know the members of a Roma community for an extended period of time. Unlike Lamuraglia, who met the Roma in Italy, Menni and Sismondi chose to travel to Shuto Orizari, a district of Skopje in Macedonia. This is indeed the only district in the world which is governed by Roma, who constitute the majority of the population. *Comune spazio problematico*[181] (2008) and *Open Option* (2009)[182] are the outcome of the playwrights' long stays in the community, written between 2007 and 2009. Their intention in these compositions was twofold: on the one hand, to explore their own engrained responses towards a people who are too often "translated" through stereotypes and prejudice, and, on the other hand, to explore the uneasiness felt by occupying a position which is socially unconventional, namely as foreigner and minority member, in a Roma community outside Italy. For Teatrino Clandestino the anthropological journey, which is experienced both inwardly and outwardly, is a fundamental component of being an actor. By choosing to work in Shuto Orizari, Menni and Mochi Sismondi became total strangers, an experience which they could not have had in a Roma camp in Italy, where their identities could perpetuate the dichotomy between locals and foreigners, with the locals in the privileged position of insiders looking at outsiders (Menni, personal communication, May 22, 2014).

Menni says that arriving in Shuto Orizari placed them in a position of alterity: "Siamo andati con nostro figlio ... e la sensazione è stata di essere lampeggianti"[183] (Lo Gatto, 2011). In other words, they felt like "outsiders" within a space possessed by "insiders". To be within a Roma borough as "Westerners" entailed being confronted in different ways by the challenges of being part of a community.

"Comune Spazio Problematico" and "Open Option" are the product of a close collaboration between Teatrino Clandestino and the Theatre Roma in Shuto, which is engaged in discussing and confronting various social and political subjects. Stereotypes and prejudice against the Romani, as well as more socio-philosophical topics such as freedom, equality and a better standard of life, were regular subjects of conversation. As Mochi Sismondi writes, "gli spettacoli sono stati messi in scena in Italia per sensibilizzare il pubblico sulla condizione dei Rom, e sulla possibilità di un

---

**181**  First performed June 6th 2008 at Città del Teatro, (Cascina, PI). A manuscript was made available but otherwise there is no written text, which explains the absence of page numbers when citing from the play. The play is also available on: https://vimeo.com/43252952.

**182**  Mochi Sismondi (2012) told the experience in his book, *Confini Diamanti. Viaggio ai margini d'Europa, ospiti dei rom*.

**183**  "We were with our son ... we felt as if the spotlight was shining on us" (Lo Gatto, 2011).

dialogo ... quella dei Rom è una questione emblematica che può aiutarci nell'analisi di alcuni punti critici della 'nostra' realtà, uno su tutti il rapporto che gli italiani stanno istituendo con gli stranieri ... il nostro scopo è quello di tessere un dialogo a sostegno di una visione diversa"[184] (Mochi Sismondi, 2012, p. 177). The intention of the performance was to share views to promote a better understanding of the Romani amongst the Italian community, and not to tell the story of the Romani themselves (Menni, personal communication, May 22, 2014).

*Comune spazio problematico* (Teatrino clandestino, 2012) takes inspiration from a conversation with Kadané, a Romani elder interviewed in Shuto Orizari about topics such as the meaning of life and capitalism. Menni acts as a young Kadané, whilst Mochi Sismondi adopts the role of an anthropologist who talks to her through an interpreter. According to Menni, the decision to keep Kadané out of the performance is motivated by the fact that her presence could be interpreted less as an attempt to dialogue with the Roma and more as a form of folkloristic attraction. This observation may seem controversial, however, Menni echoes Lamuraglia by raising awareness of the representation of gypsies as skilled musicians and dancers. This, undoubtedly, carries a stereotyping effect of gypsies and raises expectations about their role on a stage[185]. The set is minimalist: A gate divides Kadané from an interpreter and a "Westerner" anthopologist interested in her opinion on political and philosophical matters, rather than on their customs.

The language used is a key aspect of the performance. The questions addressed to Kadané are inspired by the German philosopher Matthias Kaufmann. The interviewer addresses Kadané using learned, academic language: "Il principale punto di avvio della mia ricerca è costituito dalla problematica della fondazione della miglior comunità politica possibile, quella che prevede la minor costrizione per l'individuo"[186] (Teatrino clandestino, 2012). The anthropologist uses typical academic jargon, which is unsuitable for a conversation with anyone without specialized knowledge, but he seems unable to find a different register that would bring him closer to the social background of the interlocutor. When asked "cosa vuol dire stare bene, essere felici?"[187] (Teatrino clandestino, 2012), Kadané replies by speaking about her experience of poverty. What she says is common to anyone in the same position: she describes the sense of being excluded from playing an active role in society, making decisions for herself, and expressing her opinions in her social context. Both Kadané and the

---

**184** "We staged the performances in Italy in order to make the spectators aware of Romani living conditions and to invite dialogue and give visibility to some deeply engrained issues in our society, for instance, our attitude towards 'foreigners' ... Our aim is to build a dialogue that can support an alternative vision" (Mochi Sismondi, 2012, p. 177).

**185** This point will be taken up again when mentioning the other performance "Open Option".

**186** "My research is centered around finding the best possible community, one that is the least limiting for the individual".

**187** "What does it mean for you to feel good and to be happy?".

anthropologist inhabit a "comune spazio problematico" [a shared, complex space]. In comparative philosophy, this definition refers to a space where different opinions are compared and contrasted, avoiding conflict in the attempt to integrate differences. In the process, those who pose the questions and collect data are also affected by the experience, and are also perhaps transformed[188]. It is very difficult to assess to what extent the subjects involved, both Romani and the two members of Teatrino Clandestino, were 'changed' by the experience. Undoubtedly, the work by Menni and Mochi Sismondi has generated great interest and opened a dialogue with the public and researchers by constrasting the negative stereotypes that feed the "antizingarismo" [anti-gypsy attitudes] in Italy (Mochi Sismondi, 2017).

Furthermore, Menni and Mochi Sismondi were able to make a theatrical version of "comune spazio problematico" only after having experienced it during their stay in Shuto Orizari. This explains why the role of Kadané has been taken by Menni and not by a Roma; Menni spent an extended period of time in close communication and physical proximity with Kadané, developing what can be described as "an experience" of her.

The staged dialogue between Kadané and the intellectually-minded character can be seen as a possible future community, where all citizens are visible and valuable members with equal rights. This ideal community is the common denominator between Kaufmann's philosophy, as expressed by the young intellectual, and Kadané. She cannot improve her living conditions because her people are not allowed to travel freely in the pursuit of better living conditions, thus forcing all future generations to experience the same poverty. Happiness as described by Kadané—"... avere soldi, una casa e un buon lavoro..." [to have money, a house, a good job] (Teatrino clandestino, 2012)—is the wish of people living in poverty everywhere.

Asking Kadané questions and listening to her point of view becomes, in other words, a political gesture. It shows how a fair society ought to behave and what the local government in Shuto Orizari fails to do. Kadané mentions a playground built by a well-meaning multinational company which failed to acknowledge that selling metal is one of the few ways which people can make some money and feed their children. Within a short time the playground was dismantled. This example shows an imbalance between the decision-making of local authority and its powerless inhabitants. However, even the dialogue between Kadané and the intellectual seems unequal from the point of view of Kadané herself, who is aware that the intellectual will be paid for his work, including the interview, whereas her contribution will not be acknowledged. The performance is not seeking a definite answer, or the perfect picture of the ideal society. It is a shared ground, a transcultural process where what truly counts is one's approach towards the other.

---

188  On Comparative Philosophy, see Maria Donzelli (2006).

Along with the jargon employed, language also plays an important role in *Comune spazio problematico*. Mochi Sismondi speaks Italian, but Menni speaks a made-up language, a choice which is motivated by the conscious desire to avoid imitating Romané. In this connection Menni says:

> When a stranger speaks, you listen to the music of his language, a music which does not lack emotional power. The meaning is not conveyed through words, but it passes through other ways. Only after comes, as a support, the translation, but first you have been able to sense the emotional quality of another animal that has expressed itself. When the words come to the spectator's ears, with his eyes he can recreate the link with the person who has spoken, he is freer to perceive the signs which originated the meanings that come to him through the translation. (Angelovska, 2012, p. 207)

Menni and the actress who plays the translator both know what concepts will be mentioned, but they choose not to pre-learn a text. In every performance the translator listens carefully to the answers given by Kadané, interpreting the sound and the feeling conveyed, which are based on pre-established concepts. This stage-technique avoids repetition of a text that can lose its vitality, whereas the change of sounds generates a fresh language each time instead of a script. The only critique of an otherwise wholly ethical and political approach is that, unless the public is told that the language heard is not Romaní, they may fail to realize it, believing that it is imitated, and thus miss the deeper philosophical and ethical meaning of using a made-up language.

## 10.4 Open Option (2009)

In "Open Option"[189] Menni and Mochi Sismondi continue to explore the philosophical theme of a better, more just community, which functions inclusively towards those members who stand at the periphery of it. In this performance the Romani play a central role, and perhaps in a more radical way than in the case of Lamuraglia. "Comune spazio problematico" seems to be an experiment before staging *Open Option*, an attempt through the use of a 'non-language' repeated with this second performance. The title of the performance reflects the content of such philosophical dialogues. During a laboratory with the Roma theatre group, mention was made of the experience of living in mobile homes; one of the Roma actors replied that no-one in the Suto community lived on camping sites, but the possibility was not excluded, further adding that it was an "open option", thus reflecting their openness and adaptability concerning the freedom to travel with no fixed territory and borders (Menni,

---

[189] First performed during the international Festival VIE for Contemporary scene, at Teatro Comunale in Carpi (Modena), 16 October 2009.

personal communication, May 22, 2014). The actors in "Open Options" were Italian and Roma. The Roma actors were members of the Theatre Roma in Suto Orizari who had been invited to Italy to be part of the performance. Menni requested and obtained a temporary visa for them, a process that was contested by the theatre group in a creative and theatrical manner. The programme for the performance was even printed on official documents to request a visa for 'family reunion' for those who are not part of the European community. The choice of a legal document is controversial, as it challenges the power of a nation to include or exclude those who live in their territory, whereas Menni and Sismondi think that it should be everyone's right to decide where to go to improve their living conditions. Thus, the programme displays a formal, bureaucratic language, which stands next to a statement spoken with confidence about the present time, such as in the words: "Siccome abbiamo fatto in modo di trovarci nella posizione di chi parla crediamo che sia necessario tentare di stimolare un pubblico che fa parte di una comunità molto danneggiata a livello di immaginario, quella italiana"[190] (Menni, personal communication, May 22, 2014).

The spectator is warned that the performance is the product of a community of Italian and Romani actors who disagree with the socio-political system, which keeps discriminating and marginalizing the Roma. Meanwhile, the Roma on-stage act as philosophers by raising questions based on facts; they question to what extent Italians are more literate than them, offering statistics which show that 20% of the Italian adult population is not entirely able to read. This reversal of roles, where the Romani ask questions and not the Italians, provides a silenced and marginalized community with the power to speak to a community that has always translated them, presenting knowledge and awareness that is normally unchallenged.

There are three languages on-stage at the same time: the Roma actors speak Romani, Menni speaks an invented language, Italian actors translate questions asked in Italian by the public into an invented language, and translate into Italian for them. The presence of Romani actors on-stage makes the issue of the invented language more poignant, as it seems to ask whether it is even possible at all to use the languages we know when we try to find new visions for a more inclusive society. Menni plays the character of Irina, a Romani living in the streets of Bologna, whom Menni and Mochi Sismondi came to know well and helped until she decided to go back to Romania. Irina did not want to be on-stage herself although she took part in the rehearsal. Could the use of the first person "I", used by Menni, be akin to putting oneself in the shoes of the other? I believe that theatre offers the opportunity of empathic embodiment by the actor, who acts as a bridge between the silent other and the citizens present in the theatre. Irina's story of being alone in Italy, dealing with homelessness and poverty, and having her visa denied because of her background,

---

190 "Since we are in a position to speak, we will do so trying to touch a community with a very damaged imagination, the Italian one".

raises serious questions about contemporary Italian and European society. Irina says: "La mia è una situazione senza sviluppo ed è per questo che voglio andare in Europa, ma non riesco ad avere il visto. In questo modo mi viene negato l'ingresso a quella società dei diritti a cui tutti i popoli europei aspirano"[191] (personal communication, May 22, 2014). The Roma philosophers share their point of view and remind the audience that they do not support or take part in any war. To have a nation, a national identity to defend, you need to go to have an army and go to war. The solution to the marginalization of the Roma is not building a state for them, as a state cannot guarantee the free movement of people, or inclusion of anyone in its territory. The "open option", is to leave in peace as a community that supports and includes its minorities. As noted by Angelovska: "[B]y critically pointing out to the Roma community's social exclusion in European nation-states, the play enacts a critique of nation-state as – by definition – supporting structural violence against minorities" (Angelovska, 2012, p. 211).

## 10.5 Fragments of Voices: Pino Petruzzelli

Petruzzelli is one of the most well-known and established narrators of Narrative theatre, a theatrical style developed in Italy in the later decades of the 20th century, in which there are no actors or actions, but only the narrator-performer. This means that the narrator, as author of the story, acts it out as well. The stories can be told verbatim from reality, or they can be invented around real events. Narrative theatre is also known as "civic theatre"; its content is rooted in society and the audience is conventionally acknowledged and addressed during the performance[192]. A story comes to life through the voice and body of the actor, usually without stage props to accompany the narration. It is performed both in a conventional theatre and in unconventional spaces, such as a public square or historical buildings, which can attract an audience that normally does not go to a traditional theatre.

Being sensitive to social injustice, Petruzzelli's staged works are centred on a knowledge of, and respect for, people from different backgrounds. Since the late 1980s, he has travelled to distant and disadvantaged areas, such as the Native American reservations in New Mexico, Palestine and Israel. On-stage he narrates what he

---

191 "In my home town there are no opportunities, this is why I want to come to Europe, but I don't qualify for a VISA. In this way I am denied access to a society that gives people their rights, which is aspired by all European countries". The text of the play has not been published. The quote refers to the version of the play which has been used by the actors to prepare the show and which has been sent via e-mail to the author of the chapter.

192 The books on this subject tend to focus on the works of individual narrator-actors. For an understanding of this theatrical field, see Daniele Biacchessi, *Teatro Civile* (2010).

has experienced, with the intention of giving a voice to those who are not heard. He says:

> Il teatro che amo è quello in cui il testo nasce da un viaggio fisico. Un viaggio in cui si è coinvolti totalmente e fisicamente ... dove è indispensabile vivere con e come le persone di cui si parlerà. Come li si potrebbe conoscere diversamente? Come si potrebbe rispettare il loro sudore? La mia è una scelta etica che prevede un approccio empatico. Sento forte la necessità di lasciar parlare quelli che, per la maggior parte di noi, non esistono. Quelli che la vita la trascorrono in silenzio.[193] (Petruzzelli, n.d.)

*Non chiamarmi zingaro* (2008) is a published collection of encounters with Romani people whom Petruzzelli met in Italy and other European countries.[194] It is the testimony of a journey undertaken to meet and get to know the 'gypsies' directly, rather than through the usual negative stereotypes about them. The homonymous, staged version is a selection of stories from different perspectives as to age, gender and place. Petruzzelli offers his conversations either in dialogue or as reported speech, weaving the voice of the Roma interlocutor together with his own voice. However, the narrator does not change clothes and speaks in a monotonous voice throughout. He intervenes personally in the narration by reporting factual details that expand on the context of the story. Empathy is felt through pauses or brief comments that punctuate heightened moments in the narrative, thus bringing it to the attention of the spectator.

Each story is narrated in the present, which makes it more vivid and direct before the spectators, implying that, apart from historical events, the experience of the Roma in Italy today follows similar patterns. The story happens in a specific location—Pisa, the German-speaking part of Switzerland, or Saintes Maries de la Mer in France—and the spectator is thereby placed within the frame of objective reality, a detail that adds a journalistic tone to the stories. The main theme of the stories is the "visibility" of the Roma people, which provokes aggressive reactions in the locals. These locals seek to confine the Romani to non-places with their gaze, such that they are removed from

---

**193** "A theatrical text for me is the outcome of a physical journey. I am wholly involved ... for me it is paramount to live with the people I meet and share their lives. How could it be otherwise? How else could I understand them? I make an ethical choice based on an empathic approach. I feel the urge to give a voice to those who are not seen and spend their lives in silence" (Petruzzelli, n.d.).

**194** "Non chiamarmi zingaro" was first performed in Teatro Stabile di Genova on July 20, 2009. The last chapter of the book was omitted from the performance and became another researched performance, *Zingari: l'olocausto dimenticato*, (Gypsies: the forgotten holocaust) to create a memory of the genocide of the Roma in concentration camps, since there has been little mention of them as victims of the Holocaust. It was first performed in Teatro Stabile, Genoa, January 24, 2004. Another version of the performance took the name ‚Porrajmos: l'olocausto dimenticato degli zingari' (Porrajmos: the forgotten holocaust of the gypsies) and took place in the Risiera di Sabba, a former concentration camp in Trieste, on January 27, 2009. The performance was shown on RAI 3 Friuli, the regional branch of the national broadcaster RAI.

any form of benefits or facilities that would make them part of a community. A non-place, as described by Augé, is one with no memories, more akin to a space that is not historical, relational and not concerned with identity (Augé, 1995, pp. 75–77). In a non-place, identity may suffer in isolation. Some Romani choose to become invisible. In one short story, an Italian woman that Petruzzelli met on a Greek island confesses to the narrator that she kept her "gypsy" origin a secret, even from her husband and children, for fear of being prejudiced: "Ho pensato a come sarebbe potuta essere la mia vita se queste origini fossero state visibili"[195] (Petruzzelli, 2008, p. 136) In another short story, Petruzzelli tells of Giuseppe Catter, named "Tarzan", a partisan who distinguished himself in the fight for the liberation of Italy in World War II, and who is remembered with great honour by General Alexander. In the collective memory, Catter is Italian, but he was a "gypsy". Petruzzelli expresses his comments in a sustained monotone to avoid any possible influence on the spectator, but at the same time inviting them to reflection. He ends Catter's story saying: "Peccato che nessuno lo sappia. Peccato che neanche molti Rom e sinti lo sappiano..."[196] (Petruzzelli, 2008, p. 222). By revealing Catter's identity, one may wonder whether the perception of him may change if he is found out not to be "Italian".

When he says that Catter's true identity is not even known by "his own" people, Petruzzelli muses in a long silence about the slow erosion of a people who choose to "die" as a group in order to survive as individuals. At the end of the story of the Italo-gypsy woman, Petruzzelli quotes from a book: "... Alcune isole sono gravate del pesante fardello del passato, che pesa sul loro equilibrio. Quelle che non riescono a iscriversi nel protocollo della costa restano per sempre dissidenti, orfane, solitarie, isolate"[197] (Petruzzelli, 2008, p. 137). The analogy between islands, as orphans of a "parent land", and the woman's identity, as an "orphan" of her "homeland", may be obvious, yet the metaphor gives the spectator the opportunity to look deeply into its implications. The Roma are not deprived of a homeland because they are nomadic; they still have a collective identity. But it is not the product of national borders; it is a group identity with shared history and traditions. Severing the origin, and thereby denying a belonging, brings on a form of death.

When the gagé—the Roma word for non-Romani—are involved in the narrative, they seem to be indirectly associated with the death of the Romani people. The death of two brothers and their little cousin in a sudden fire that broke out in a gypsy camp in Livorno can be seen as the outcome of a pursuit perpetrated by authorities and locals alike, until the families withdrew to a peripheral area, a non-place, retreating to precarious makeshift accommodation where the children met their death. In another

---

195  "I thought about how my life would be if my origins were known".
196  "Shame that nobody knows about it. Shame even the Roma and Sinti do not know".
197  "Some islands are burdened with a past that disturbs their equilibrium. Those islands that do not fit into 'parent land' remain orphaned and isolated".

story told by Doro, who formerly lived in a camp in Opera near Milan, we learn that his father died shortly after their camp was demolished and all their belongings were destroyed by order of the local authority. It was the outcome of months of attacks and illegal sit-ins by right-wing groups who shouted slogans against the Roma. "Non pensavo che qui in Italia saremmo stati trattati come bestie" [I would never have thought that we could be treated like animals in Italy], says Doro (Petruzzelli, 2008, p. 27).

The story of the Swiss writer Mariella Mehr and her people, which ends the performance, is also about death. Mehr is of Yenish origin. The Yenish, an itinerant group found primarily in some Northern European countries, are not Roma, although, like the Roma, they do not have a nationality, are itinerant and have long experienced persecution and social marginalization. It is because of these similarities that Petruzzelli decided to include Mehr's story in the performance. Although not specifically mentioned, the implementation of a project founded by Alfred Siegfried—to transform the Yenish People from nomadic to nationalized—with the permanent loss of a collective identity and with individual identities scarred and mutilated by losses and separation, can be equated with "death". The project involved eugenics and removing all the children from their families. Mehr is a victim of the project twice over; as a child she was taken away from her family and placed in an institution, while as a young woman she had her newborn baby taken away for adoption by a Swiss family. Just as the Italo-gypsy woman did, these children and adults have become islands without a homeland.

Petruzzelli's narration fulfils two important functions. On the one hand, it gives the stories a deeply human dimension, since news about the destruction of gypsy camps and evicted gypsies never portray the human aspect of these events. When Petruzzelli tells their stories, he mentions their feelings, their sense of loss and sadness, their pain of not being seen as other human beings. On the other hand, through mentioning events like the Swiss Project, which is perhaps still unknown by today's spectators, he preserves the memory of socio-historical persecution towards minority groups, and denounces the absence of a sense of humanity towards them.

In conclusion, the transcultural approach that features in this chapter consists primarily in the playwrights' intentions to get to know the Roma personally. This is the beginning of a mutual exchange of listening and speaking, in which even the voice from the margins can be heard. The significance of a physical journey undertaken to meet the Roma in their own environment "de-centers" them from a privileged "majority" position and symbolically challenges the binary opposition of centre/margin which remains alive in Italy today. The theatrical works adopt different approaches to place the voice of the Roma at centre stage for the attention of the spectators, with distinct, and sometimes similar, outcomes. Lamuraglia, Menni and Mochi Sismondi, and Petruzzelli, challenge traditional views on the use of a cultural space which is traditionally managed by norms that are apt to please the majority. Lamuraglia's use of irony, parody and the theatrical techniques of distancing to de-construct conventional views on the Roma reveal engrained habits of speaking of the Roma always in terms of how their presence negatively affects the majority. The use of irony allows the inverse result, with the Roma expressing their concerns at the way that the majority has negatively affected them. Lamuraglia also draws cultural similarities between Italians and the Romani thanks to his role as a cultural mediator. Staging religious beliefs means that differences are highlighted in the way that cultures conceptualize and regard the sacred, revealing that there are intrinsic similarities between the need of different peoples to ritualize and perform the sacred as a means of connecting community members together.

Similarities are also at the heart of the philosophical approach adopted by Menni and Mochi Sismondi, for whom the question of giving a voice to the Roma deeply shapes their theatrical approach. Giving a voice and revealing similarities go hand in hand. The Roma are not given an opportunity to express an opinion about living in the contemporary world. Therefore, Menni and Mochi Sismondi reveal that the issues the Roma have to face, such as poverty, being happy and having a job, and the feelings associated with them, are not dissimilar from the feelings of mainstream society. By adopting a transcultural approach based on equal sharing in dialogue, hearing multiple voices becomes a political act of social inclusion and emancipation. The new concept which Menni and Mochi Sismondi seem to suggest needs a different language to bring it to life. The process to carry out a performance is also a political act; inviting Romani actors to Italy is viewed as an opportunity to critically compare the Romanis' pacifist beliefs within a community without borders with a nation-based culture which is defended through conflict, such as is adopted across the "Western" world. Petruzzelli's gentle response contrasts with the aggressive responses manifested against gypsies. On-stage, he lends his voice to the Roma who told him their stories of painful exclusion, which forced them to live outside communities, or in some cases, to be completely removed and isolated from the family, as in Mehr's story. His narration reminds us that oppressive practices cause great pain. The Roma suffer greatly the effects of social exclusion, yet their pain is never considered when they are mentioned by media and authorities. Conventionally, loss is only mentioned when the majority complaints about the loss of safety and space when the Roma move in to their territories. The monologues show loss from the perspectives of the Roma, where it means the loss of lives, homes, communities, and both individual and communal identity. By speaking of their emotions, Petruzzelli gives them the humanity which is taken away by traditional attitudes towards them. It is a political act that denounces the dark side of civilized Italy and Europe at large.

The journey undertaken by the playwrights includes the "self", who have become "other", and the "minority", in order to hear voices which were previously unheard. By moving away from standard practices of the theatre, Lamuraglia, Menni and Mochi Sismondi and Petruzzelli all individually create a life-world that can open up other life-worlds, in the form of other new experiences that may generate new realities for both the Romani people and the spectators.

# References

Ahmed, S., Castaneda, C., Fortie, A.-M. (2003). Uprootings/Regroundings. Questions of Home and Migration. Berg Publishers.

Angelovska, D. (2012). Open Option: Roma, Discrimination and Peace Building in Macedonian Šuto Orizari. In O. Simić & Z. Volčić (Eds.), Peace, Psychology in the Balkans: Dealing with a Violent Past While Building Peace (pp. 199–214). Springer.

Ashcroft, B. & Griffiths, G. (Eds.). (2013). Postcolonial Studies: The Key Concepts. Routledge.

Augé, M. (1995). Non-Places. Introduction to an Anthropology of Supermodernity. Translated by John Howe. Verso.

Aull Davies, C. (2002). Reflexive Ethnograpgy. A guide to Researching Selves and Others. Routledge.

Biacchessi, D. (2010). Teatro Civile. Nei luoghi della narrazione e dell'inchiesta. Verdenero.

Condé Nast Traveller. October 2019. Retrieved April 4, 2020, from https://www.cntraveller.com/gallery/12-reasons to-buy-the-october-2019-issue-of-conde-nast-traveller

De Martino, A., Puppa, P., Toninato, P. (Eds.). (2013). Differences on Stage. Cambridge Scholars Publishings.

Donzelli, M. (Ed.). (2006). Comparatismi e filosofia, Quaderni del dip. di Filosofia politica. Università L'Orientale. Liguori editore.

Glissant, É. (1996). Introduction à une Poétique du Divers. Gallimard.

Hutcheson, L. (1988). A Poetics of Postmodernism. Routledge.

Lamuraglia, D (2005). Il Libro di Cristo Gitano. Pagnini Editore.

Lamuraglia, D. (2011). Opere Teatrali. A&B editrice.

Lamuraglia, D. (2013). The Fascination of the Margins. In Differences on Stage A. De Martino,, A., Puppa, P., Toninato, P. (Eds.), Differences on Stage (pp.128–144). Cambridge Scholars Publishing.

Lo, J. & Gilbert, H. (2002). Towards a Topography of Cross-cultural Theatre Praxis. Mit press, 46(3), 31–53.

Lo Gatto, S. (2011, May 18). Civile e problematico: è lo spazio di Teatrino Clandestino. Retrieved March 3, 2019, from http://www.klpteatro.it/teatrino-clandestino-civile-spazio-problematico

Loomba, A. (2005). Colonialism/Postcolonialism. Routledge.

Lucassen, L., Willems, W. H., & Cottaar, A. (1998). Gypsies And Other Itinerant Groups. A Socio-Historical Approach. Palgrave Macmillan.

Mochi Sismondi, A. (2012). Confini Diamanti. Viaggio ai margini d'Europa, ospiti dei rom. Ombre Corte.

Mochi Sismondi, A. (2017) "Linguaggio teatrale, dispositivi narrativi e anti-zingarismo" in Anuac, 6(1), 187–208.

Mumford, M. (2010). Bertolt Brecht. Routledge.

Ortiz, F. (1947). Cuban Counterpoint: Tobacco and Sugar. A. A. Knopf.

Pavis, P. (1996). The Intercultural Performance Reader. Routledge.

Petruzzelli, P. (2008). Non Chiamarmi Zingaro. Chiarelettere.

Petruzzelli, P. (n.d.). Viaggi. Retrieved October 25, 2019, from www.teatroipotesi.org/viaggi.html

Rame, S. (2018, January 11). Migranti, Salvini: "Se vinco riempio gli aerei e li riporto a casa". Il Giornale. http://www.ilgiornale.it/news/politica/migranti-salvini-se-vinco-riempio-aerei-e-li-riporto-casa-1482213.html

Tabucchi, A. (1999). Gli zingari e il Rinascimento. Vivere da Rom a Firenze. Feltrinelli.

Taylor, D. (1991). Transculturating Transculturation. Performing Arts Journal, 13(2), 90–104.

Teatrino clandestino. (2012, June 1). Comune Spazio Problematico [Video]. Vimeo. https://vimeo.com/43252952

Teatro del Legame. (2013, November 4). ZINGARITA' (del legame, dal legame) - testo e regia di Daniele Lamuraglia [Video]. YouTube. https://www.youtube.com/watch?v=tIYei7hUdL0

Teatro del Legame. (2014, December 31). TELEROM la televisione degli zingari - testo e regia di Daniele Lamuraglia [Video]. YouTube. https://www.youtube.com/watch?v=yl8q2_Xfrp4

Teatro del Legame. (n.d.). Teatro del Legame presenta CRISTO GITANO regia di Daniele Lamuraglia. Retrieved March 20, 2020, from http://www.teatrodellegame.it/cristo-gitano

Toninato, P. (2014). Romani Writing: Literary, Literature and Identity Politics. Routledge.

Young, J. C. R. (2001). Postcolonialism: An Historical Introduction. Wiley-Blackwell.

Marek Sancho Höhne

# 11 Negotiating Gender in Germany—Normalizing Trans*Imaginations. On Aspects of Belonging to and Resisting the Normative Binary Gender Order

Knowledge about someone's gender seems to be of central importance in classifying them. Gender in Germany is—as in many other places—registered in identity documents, birth certificates and/or is coded in an individual's social security number. Also in everyday encounters, people seem to have knowledge about how to classify people according to gender. I am not always able to guess one's gender, but I am surprised that most of the people assume to *know* the gender of people, and most of the time I do not know when, and do not understand how and based on what markers, people gender-classify me. Depending on my own behaviour, the way I dress, and the people with whom I move around, I am sometimes seen as female, sometimes as male and most of the time as confusing. There seems to be a discrepancy in knowledge between me and my observers, concerning questions of what *is* visible and how we are able to understand and classify what we *see*.

Since visibility has in modern times become an imperative—what is "seen" is what is believed, or what is acknowledged to be real and thus can be recognized (Schaffer, 2008, p. 13)—gendered realities are also believed to be real if they are visible, or if they are approved as real and thus can be seen and acknowledged in the normative binary gender order. What is implicit in this assumption is that visibility is not something that simply exists "but is always produced in the relation between knowledge and power and is in mutual proportion to invisibility"[198] (Schaffer, 2008, p. 13). Genders which are visible and thus are recognized do not denote a stable system but are rather embedded in the net of knowledge and power around gender. That the body is perceived as an important informant about one's gender in the "culture of dominance" (Rommelspacher, 1998) in Germany is part of this net of knowledge and power (Höhne, 2017, p. 25). This net is deeply embedded in questions of temporality and locality. Therefore, I do not argue simply for the greater visibility of trans* people in my paper, but rather for the need to question the possibilities of visibility and recognition of (different) genders (Schaffer, 2008, pp. 18–19).

In this chapter I will examine some features of mapping gender and belonging from the perspective of a culture of dominance by analysing some narrations about and by trans* people. How can we observe the negotiation of gender in the

---

198 This translation and the following translations show the original citation in German: "sondern immer in einem Zusammenhang aus Wissen und Macht produziert ist und in einem gegenseitigen Modulationsverhältnis zu Unsichtbarkeit steht" (Schaffer, 2008, p. 13).

imaginations of trans* individuals within the framework of a culture of dominance? In particular, I wish to question the ways that trans* people are imagined and rooted in ongoing German public discourse (e.g. in mainstream media) and medico-legal knowledge and how trans* lives are recognized in this setting: Are they seen and/or recognized and, if so, how and under what conditions? How does what Schaffer calls the "dehumanizing violence" by "non-status of the unreadable"[199] (Schaffer, 2008, p. 20) affect the lives of individuals who identify as trans*? How does stereotypical and pathologizing intelligibility form possibilities for trans*ness within a culture of gendered dominance? Conversely, if trans* people are only recognized in a pathologized intelligible form, it is still a form of visibility and does it thus gain political power in the frame of the culture of dominance (Schaffer, 2008, pp. 20–21)? How does this affect the lives of trans* people? I argue that by identifying certain trans* bodies as the only intelligible ones, which can enter into the normative binary gender-order, a process is thus initiated of normalizing certain imaginations of trans bodies. This signifies not only a negotiation of the boundaries of the binary gender order, but also the negotiation, taken in a broader sense, of belonging and the classification of "us" and "them". Furthermore, I will inquire into how simplification and attempts of separating intersectional, i.e. gendered, class-determined, and racialized realities (among others) fail to grasp trans* lives. This article hence also aims to illustrate how imaginations of trans* are connected to questions of (national) belonging.

I comprehend the different imaginations of passing trans* bodies into the normative binary gender order as negotiating precarious bodies and thus precarious lives (Butler, 2010, pp. 2-3). It is thus the negotiations of an individual's life that is produced according to certain deep-seated norms, through which we can observe how these norms of apprehending and recognizing a life are at stake while imagining trans identities. Imagining trans bodies that can pass in terms of the binary gender order I understand here as a b/ordering process of gendered normality at the intersection of gender with "race," ability, age, class, religion and ethnicity, and as thus entangled in the question of which "lives ... are not quite—or indeed, are never—recognized as lives" (Butler, 2010, p. 4). What life is to be recognized as a life? What body is to be constructed as a precarious body—a body whose life is always in danger of being denied? Moreover, how is the negotiation of trans entangled with negotiations of precarious bodies at its intersection with other power structures? Trans* realities are thus always part of negotiating the normative framework of the dominant binary gender-order and the circumstances through which bodies become recognizable or (more) precarious.

In my chapter I will first illustrate how trans* bodies are framed in the medico-legal system (section "Trans* Bodies From a Medico-Legal Perspective"). After this, I will analyse by means of two different examples—an attack against trans* women

---

[199] "entmenschlichende Gewalt" durch "Nicht-Status der Unlesbarkeit" (Schaffer, 2008, p. 20).

(section "First Insight: On the Racialization of Trans\* Discriminatory Violence"), and the election of a trans\* officer to the federal armed forces (section "Second Insight: Trans\* People and the Army–Trans\* Nationalism at Work")—how, with respect to trans lives, questions of gender and national belonging are discussed in Germany. I argue that the discussions do not actually care about the trans lives they are supposedly dealing with, but that they rather function as wildcards that argue for an assumed progressiveness of dominant society in Germany and thereby strengthen the distinction of the dominant society from the racialized other. In the last part of the article (section "Trans\* Life Stories–Self Narrations as Resistance"), I show how both medico-legal knowledge and the instrumentalization of trans\* themes in public discourse fail to grasp the challenges that concern the lives of trans people, by sharing some extracts of my ethnographic fieldwork on trans\* lives in contemporary Germany.

## 11.1 Trans\* Bodies From a Medico-Legal Perspective

Binary gendered attributions, as I argued above, are of importance for different aspects of life-worlds. Gender—in all its intersectional dimensions—is an important signifier in order to classify people. The culture of dominance in Germany is based on binary gendered norms that imply intersectional normative imaginations of the female and the male. Michel Foucault outlined how psychiatrists of the 19th century introduced "[t]he medicalization of the sexually peculiar" (Foucault, 1978, p. 44) and how the pathologization of diverse sexualities that diverge from the heterosexual, monogamous, reproductive couple was developed. By this dichotomy between girls and boys, the production of the "real sex" was manifested and sexual practices were regulated. The growing control of sexuality and the production of distance between, and shame towards, the female and male have exacted an enormous influence over the current normative binary gender order (Foucault, 1978, p. 46). Judith Butler (1991) similarly argues that the limits of the normative binary gender order also marks the boundaries of those genders which are acknowledged as "real," truthful, or authentic—or as Butler says—intelligible, and thus the imaginations of which "normal bodies" can pass (p. 38). Gendered bodies and/or identifications that differ from the normative imagination are in this pathologized system other-ed and labelled. Trans\* bodies are just one of them.

Using the term "trans\*" is already complicated, being embedded in medical classification and connected to colonial knowledge, since gendered practices of the normative binary are part of colonial knowledge (Aizura et al. 2014, p. 311). In colonial knowledge the assumption of a binary gender is naturalized and blended into the so-called modern sciences, as discussed by Lugones (2008, p. 84). In this context medico-legal knowledge becomes an important part of the modern sciences, since it reflects in a more detailed way on the question of gendered passing. As I (Höhne, 2017) have contended elsewhere, "ultimately medico-biological, violent dominant knowledge produces the *truth*, on which basis it is decided, which bodies fulfill the normalized categories and which don't"[200] (p. 33). Trans*-specific healthcare and the narrative of the "wrong body" that can be adjusted to the dominant imaginations of female and male is firmly embedded in the modern sciences. In this sense, as Thamar Klein and I (Höhne & Klein, 2019) have argued elsewhere, "it is important to question the alleged connection between trans* narratives of becoming and the naturalized assumption of the need for medical and surgical intervention to adjust the supposedly wrong body" (p. 10).

Medico-legal knowledge about trans* bodies is dominated by the (psycho)pathologization of trans* people. Transsexuality is listed in the "International Classification of Diseases" (ICD) in the chapter on "Classifications of Mental and Behavioural Disorder: Clinical Descriptions and Diagnostic Guidelines," the current ICD-10[201] as "gender identity disorders"[202] under the classification F64.0 and is defined as a cross-gender identification that is perceived as something curable, if the person can prove that they are suffering from it sufficiently (World Health Organization [WHO], 2016). This categorization differentiates between the "true transsexual" who suffers persistently and significantly owing to their gender assigned by birth and strives to change parts of their body with hormonal treatment and surgery, in order to be recognized—in normatively binary gendered orders—as the "opposite" gender and diagnosed with F64.0 and other gender-variant people (F64.1–9). The latter diagnosis does not allow people to obtain access to any gender reassignment procedure. In the classification of F64.0 the process, which is also described as transition, is connected to the idea of a journey and thus to the question of temporality and spatiality. Transition is understood, on the one hand, as a liminal time-frame at which end stands an assumed progress and arrival, whereupon the person arrives at their "desired gender"

---

200 "weil letzten Endes das medizinisch-biologische, gewaltvoll dominante Wissen die '*Wahrheit*' produziert, auf deren Grundlage darüber bestimmt wird, welche Körper den normierten Kategorien entsprechen und welche nicht" (Höhne, 2017, p. 33).

201 I refer to the ICD-10, even though the ICD-11 was adopted in May 2019. However, the ICD-10 will be still valid in Germany until 2022 and therefore will still structure the procedure in Germany for at least some more years.

202 I also refer here to a quote from another paper, which Thamar Klein and me (Höhne & Klein, 2019) wrote as it applies for this article in the same way: "While working on this paper, it has been announced that all trans*-related categories will be deleted from the ICD Chapter on Mental and Behavioural Disorders in the future ICD 11 (pending approval by the World Health Assembly in 2019) as a result of the tremendous effort by trans* activists from around the world. Instead, the new categories, 'Gender Incongruence of Adolescence and Adulthood' and 'Gender Incongruence of Childhood' have been placed in a new chapter, provisionally named 'Conditions Related to Sexual Health.' Thus, being trans* will no longer be regarded as an implication of a mental disorder. However, there is still a lot of work to be done, as othering and normative language has been preserved, and the dangerous GIC category aimed at eradicating gender diversity in childhood needs to be removed (for a more detailed critique, see [Asia Pacific Transgender Network] APTN 2017)" (p. 25).

in full (read: in a bodily sense). On the other hand, this phase is imagined as a space between female and male (Aizura, 2018, p. 2). Aren Aizura (2018) further argues that "[p]opular ideas about gender reassignment reflect the assumption that transness is the same for most people (we often assume that trans people desire hormones or surgery, for example)" (p. 3). On this understanding, all trans* people pass once through the liminal phase of transition, a phase where they move from the gender to which they were assigned by birth to the supposedly opposite one, which is made possible by modern medicine that offers gender reassignment treatment and surgery. Aizura (2018, p. 3) here argues

> that transsexuality, the normative Euro-American category of trans subjectivity, becomes intelligible as a modern concept through its staging as a journey through "elsewhere" spaces: spaces in which it is necessary, momentarily, to inhabit a gendered indeterminacy that is intolerable under the law of heteronormative binary gender but also necessary for narrating the seeming impossibility of gendered transformation.

This understanding does not just perpetuate the imperially-minded behaviour that assumes Euro-American colonial imaginations which are applicable to the whole world, but also makes any existence of trans*, inter*, non-binary, two-spirit or other gender-specific understandings beyond the normative binary impossible.

In Germany the *Medizinischer Dienst des Spitzenverbandes Bund der Krankenkasse e.V.* (MDS, 2009) [Medical Advisory Service of the German Social Health Insurance] publishes the "Begutachtungsanleitung Geschlechtsangleichender Maßnahmen bei Transsexualität" [guidelines for the examinations for gender reassignment treatment in case of Transsexuality]. In these guidelines trans* identities are treated—under the term *Transsexuality*—as a treatable condition that is classified and approved by healthcare professionals. These guidelines say that a medical authority needs to determine who and under what circumstances an individual is allowed access to hormonal treatment or surgeries. A person needs to undergo psychotherapy, a so-called "Alltagstest" [full-time real-life experience], according to which a person needs to live in the "opposite gender" and has "to be out" in the public and private sphere for one full year (MDS, 2009, p. 10). Co-morbidity should be precluded and one has to prove a "krankheitswertiger Leidensdruck" [pathologically significant degree of suffering] (MDS, 2009, p. 10). The guidelines justify the socio-medical assessment by the supposed complexity of the "disorder" that demands qualified experts. Their counseling and assessment serves—following these guidelines—as a protection of the insured person, in order to prevent "wrong-positive diagnosis" (MDS, 2009, p. 6). Neither are trans* people themselves considered experts nor is the assumed necessity of treatment—in the case that the "experts" diagnoses the person with F 64.0— questioned. Striking is also the significance of "normalization" in this context, that seems to be therapists' answer to pathologization (Nieder et al., 2012, p. 7). After the diagnosis has been given and the "suffering" has been acknowledged, therapists and doctors do their best in "normalizing" the life of the person, especially with regard to overcoming the ambiguity and mitigating the suffering of gender dysphoria. Just to make this point clear, suffering here is not meant as a suffering of the heteronormative binary gender order, but of one's individual (gendered) body. "Normalization" in this context is directly linked to the idea of making a person fit into the normative gender binary. I do not intend to convey any negative judgment about the individual decision of a person who chooses gender reassignment surgeries or hormonal treatment, as I myself have undergone hormonal treatment and body modifications in order to adjust my body to my own gender. Having access to gender reassignment surgeries or hormonal treatment (often people make use of only some of the available possibilities) can be, for some people, *the* access to survival and healing.

Problematic is the unquestioned link between medical treatment and trans* bodies. The dysphoria that may exist between one's own understanding of one's gender and possible gender identifications in the culture of dominance is treated as an individual problem that can be cured by medical treatment. This may be true in many cases, as it enables the recognition of a certain gender which one belongs to against the classification of a gender made by birth. However, this implies that being acknowledged as a trans* person (reads: true "transsexual" according to medical classification) in the culture of dominance requires access to the healthcare system. Further access to the German healthcare system requires a certain national belonging either by passport, residence status or by being granted permission to work there. All this already sets the condition for (national) belonging to those people that are entitled to have rights (Arendt, 2006, p. 614) and that have not been "illegalized" or are not forced into the abeyance of the "refugee status." Those whom Hannah Arendt (2016) names as suffering, especially from a fundamental lack of rights and who cannot claim their access because of having lost the right to have rights (p. 613), cannot even gain access to being acknowledged through the precarious status of pathologization. Moreover, the criteria of the healthcare system assumes able-bodied individuals, with the result that those bodies which are classified as "disabled," "mentally ill" or pathologized by a diagnosis such as "learning disabilities" are less frequently allowed access to trans* specific health care or are asked to perform further tests concerning their ability to make decisions about their own lives and bodies.

Knowledge of the normative binary gender order is more explicitly expected of gender-variant people and engages in very intimate spheres of their lives, and not just with respect to medico-knowledge. There is another aspect of trans* gender that seems to be highly important when looking at constructions of normatively binary gendered knowledge. To maintain the dominant knowledge (production), it is necessary to secure the legal aspects of gender markers in order to prevent the disturbance of the system itself. In Germany, gender is still registered in all legal documents, either by name, gender marker or number (e.g. for pension insurance). In order to change one's gender as registered in one's birth certificate and/or documentation as a trans* person, one needs to undergo a process which conforms with the "Transsexuellengesetz" [transsexual act] and be approved by two psychiatric/psychotherapist "experts," namely a diagnosis of F 64.0, after which a court makes a final decision about the change. However, if one changes one's gender marker from female to male and later gives birth (as lately confirmed by *Bundesgerichtshof* [Federal Constitutional Court]), the person needs to be registered as a mother with their name given by birth instead of being registered with their current gender marker and name.[203]

Both the medical and the legal complexities of this issue demand and reproduce a narrative of a linear development, where trans* people can be cured or saved by following a certain path of a logic of "from-to," which represents a journey through the liminal space and time, as discussed earlier. The problem of this path is its fixation on a linear movement, which fails to acknowledge the different decisions and life stories of trans* and other gender-variant people. On this logic there are persons who are denied access to treatment through the perception and classification of not being "trans* enough." What happens with trans* or other gender-variant people who resist or do not comply with the medico-legal knowledge? Do those resisting practices help to blur the boundaries of the normatively binary gender order, or do they unintentionally participate in strengthening them? And who is actually heard when reformulating classifications of trans*gender in Germany? What happens if medico-legal systems are changed almost entirely without the participation of gender-variant people? These questions cannot be answered thoroughly in all their aspects here. In this article, nevertheless, I raise these questions, as they are of great importance for the understanding of the different realities of trans* lives and they need to be discussed further.

## 11.2 Trans* People in Media Between Instrumentalization and Misrepresentation—Two Insights

A lot of media coverage in German popular newspapers and TV formats concerning trans* lives (see e.g., Reporter, 2018) focuses on medico-legal aspects of being trans*.

---

**203** In November 2017 the Federal Constitutional Court ruled about the question of registering Gender in official documents. The court gave two options: an abolition of gender markers in documents and birth certificates, or at least the introduction of a 3rd Gender—besides female and male—such as "diverse" or "inter*/ other". In November 2018 the Ministry for Internal Affairs published a draft law for a third positive gender marker "diverse". Instead of opening up the third positive gender marker for everybody without medical diagnosis, the third positive gender marker is linked to a medical certificate that proves the variance of sex-development ["Variante der Geschlechtsentwicklung"]. This new law neither pays tribute to the claims of inter* activists who demand a guarantee for no more unwilling surgeries on intersex children and access to a change of the gender marker without any medical certification, nor does it include the variety of trans* and non-binary people. The new regulation still demands a medical certificate and does not guarantee the prohibition of unwilling surgeries for inter* people.

This is presented as the real (read: scientific) dominant knowledge about trans* people, without, however, being presented by non-trans* people for other non-trans* people in order to prepare the dominant society for the gendered "Other". Trans* people are presented as a "Laune der Natur" [freak of nature], that seems to be different but is in fact part of the "norm_al," just in a different shape. As for the question of Othering processes, it is of interest that those reports, documentaries and articles that focus on the medico-legal complexities of trans* peoples issues are also the ones who allege to provide neutral reporting—as opposed to media that exoticize, fetishize or ridicule trans* people—and to present the "naked truth" about trans* people, by differentiating them from the norm_al and other "deviations" such as inter* people. "Us" is linked not only to questions of belonging, national identity, and self-identification but also the way one is read by Others. This becomes evident in two very illustrative examples which I will present in the following chapter. I choose these two examples because they display a certain kind of assumed normality concerning trans* people in Germany, while negotiating who counts as a trans* person by association with the individual's national belonging. In both cases the articles and documentaries try to show how a form of inclusion of trans* people, as something that belongs to Germany, makes Germany a part of the progressive "Western" world. In these articles it also becomes clear how this works in very different ways and how, still in this context, it is negotiated which trans* people are trans* enough within this frame of time and space.

### 11.2.1 First Insight: On the Racialization of Trans* Discriminatory Violence

Shortly after the events in Cologne at New Year's Eve in 2016, two trans* women were attacked in Dortmund. On New Year's Eve a chaotic situation in and around the main train station in Cologne arises. A big crowd of young men gathers, at the bridge next to the train-station a mass panic sets in, and in and around the train station several women were sexually harassed. Shortly after this night, this very unclear situation becomes a projection surface in the political debate on refugees. In the end, a racist atmosphere against refugees remains. The media coverage about an attack in Dortmund draws a parallel with New Year' Eve in Cologne and thus refers to anti-refugee sentiments. Discrimination and violence against trans* people happen in Germany on a regular basis, but is not part of the wider media coverage. The attacks in January 2016 were covered especially by private television broadcasters (Noislamisation, 2016), conservative and anti-feminist media such as the KOPP publisher (e.g., Jung, 2016) or in Catholic news [*Katholische Nachrichten*], via an online German Catholic newsportal (e.g., Katholische Nachrichten, 2016), the protest media *Telepolis* (e.g., Mühlbauer, 2016) and in papers with a wide circulation such as *BILD*, a popular German yellow press newspaper (e.g., Wegener & Engelberg, 2016), and *Focus*, a monthly popular political journal with an online format (e.g., Focus online regional, 2016). The story that is told is that the two "transsexuals" were first "verbally attacked in Arabic" and later suffered an attempt to stone them to death by three "North African men," but the two women were rescued by police who happened to be passing by (e.g. Noislamisation, 2016; Jung, 2016; Katholische Nachrichten, 2016; Mühlbauer, 2016; Wegener & Engelberg, 2016; Focus online regional, 2016). This reads as something planned and makes sure that the attacks are identified as something extraordinary connected to the origin and/or religion, age, and gender (male) of the potential attackers. Some of these articles identify the three men through such racial profiling as "North Africans," and all declare the attack as a threat to liberal society. It is not surprising that—apart from yellow press such as Bild or Sat. 1—it is mostly conservative and antifeminist media such as the Catholic news [*Katholische Nachrichten*], an online German Catholic newspage, the internet platform heise.de, or the media service Telepolis that covered the incident, all media of which are not known for their trans*-inclusiveness. On the contrary, all articles "other" the two women for being trans* women and reproduce highly trans*-discriminatory language, calling the two trans* women as "men, that dress as woman". Bild, for example, instead of writing about an attack against trans* woman, writes: "Because they were dressed in women's clothes two Transsexuals were stoned in Dortmund"[204] (Wegener & Engelberg, 2016). The Catholic News stated: "Three adolescents harassed the men that are living as women"[205] (Katholische Nachrichten, 2016). Focus feels the urge to clarify that the woman "who were born as men"[206] (Focus online regional, 2016) escaped the attack without any injuries and Kopp publisher states that "shortly after the ... North African man realized that they were actually dealing with transsexual men"[207] (Jung, 2016). In none of the articles or reports about the incident do the two women receive space to explain the situation in further detail. The internet platform heise.de, however, tries to give a more profound interpretation of the incident. They try to use female pronouns for the two trans* women and show that one of the attacked women also spoke Arabic. By giving a more detailed short history of stoning (which was focused on an Islamic context, but which also mentioned stoning in ancient Christian and Greek contexts), the report later connects this one incident to several others where people with a precarious legal status or racialized others are classified as perpetrators. The image of stoning somebody to death is in the German culture of dominance connected to a death penalty, which is practised mostly in contexts where Sharia is the basis for law. This is explained more explicitly in the article at the online

---

**204** "Weil sie in Frauenkleidern unterwegs waren, sind zwei Transsexuelle in Dortmund gesteinigt wurden" (Wegener & Engelberg, 2016).

**205** "Drei Jugendliche bedrängten Männer, die wie Frauen leben" (Katholische Nachrichten, 2016).

**206** "die als Männer geboren wurden" (Focus online regional, 2016).

**207** "Doch kaum hatten die ... Nordafrikaner erkannt, dass sie es mit transsexuellen Männern zu tun hatten" (Jung, 2016).

German Catholic news portal (Katholische Nachrichten, 2016), who refer to the press release of the media service Telepolis, who write: "According to the information of the media service Telepolis ... stoning to death is provided for a penalty for fornication in different Islamic countries such as Saudi-Arabia, United Arab Emirates, Brunei, Pakistan, Sudan, Iran and Northern Nigeria"[208] (Katholische Nachrichten, 2016).

Problematic is also the way that what is written about is not the condemnation of stoning or more generally the violence against trans* people, but that:

1. It is written just about this specific case, instead of writing in general about violence against trans* people, a case where the attackers are racialized.
2. By the wording of the attempt of stoning the two trans* women to death and the direct connection to Muslim countries per se, trans* discriminatory violence is racialized, while the victims are de-racialized. This suggests that, in the culture of dominance in Germany, trans* discriminatory violence does not happen (which is not true at all, as we can observe in the trans* discriminatory vocabulary of the articles for example).
3. Temporality is introduced by labelling "the others"—the attackers—as backward (because of their coming from North African ["Muslim"] countries, and producing an image of "us" as the progressive German dominant society. In this discourse the supposed trans*-inclusion is labeled as modern (read: "Western").
4. By racializing trans*-discriminatory violence the existence of trans* people of colour and Black trans* people is denied and the complex realities of trans* people and the actual violence and discrimination against trans* people, especially against trans* people of colour and Black trans* people, is silenced.
5. The violence and discrimination are classified into illegitimate (physical attack) and legitimate (structural discrimination, rejection of one's identity) forms of violence, by the wording in these different reports, in which structural violence and discriminatory language against trans* people is reproduced, while the physical attack is condemned.

All these processes and classifications that can be observed in the analysis of these articles are not new. Rather, they are connected to a complex power system along lines of "race," gender, class, age, and ability (among others) in a culture of dominance, which is spelled out in different ways in various spheres within which mass media discourses play an important role. In this complex power system (gender) identities are racialized by the supposed association of "gay- and trans*-friendliness" and non-sexism with white Germans, in opposition to homo-, trans*- and sexist discrimination, which is allegedly associated with traditional and non-white Germans. These

---

**208** "Nach Angaben des Mediendienstes Telepolis (Haar bei München) sehen mehrere islamische Länder die Steinigung als Strafe für Unzucht vor, beispielsweise in Saudi-Arabien, Vereinigte Arabische Emiraten, Brunei, Pakistan, Sudan, Iran, und Nordnigeria" (Katholische Nachrichten, 2016).

discourses are connected to the image of "homophobic Islam," and label imagined "Muslim communities" as "misogynist and brutal" (Çetin & Prasad, 2015, p. 108). In this context, white dominant society determines discourses about the acceptably sexualized, gendered, class-related, able-bodied and racialized subject. Acts of violence and hatred directed against trans* people are often imagined as springing from communities of colour (Haritaworn, 2012, p. 12). However, they also generate the new German core value of "women-and-gay" (and lately also "trans*") "friendliness" (Haritaworn, 2012, p. 14), that prevents narratives and embodiments beyond the dominant binary gendered discourses.

### 11.2.2 Second Insight: Trans* People and the Army—Trans*-Nationalism at Work

Another article was published almost one year later. This time a picture of a young Federal Armed Forces Officer is presented on the cover page of *Berliner Kurier* (a yellow local press newspaper) with the headline: "Lieutenant-colonel Anastasia from Berlin and her story, which gives courage. Ms. Officer was once a Man"[209] (Oberstleutnant Anastasia aus Berlin und ihre Geschichte, die Mut macht, 2017, p. 1). She looks straight into the camera and wears a chin-long blond layered modern haircut, has blue eyes and wears small studded earrings. Indeed, if she were being painted and not wearing a uniform, she could be the cover face for any article that focuses on middle-class women in Germany. In the short picture-descriptions (Ortmann, 2017, p. 29) the acceptance of the military towards trans* officers is celebrated. It is written that one day she decides to get her ears pierced—which is forbidden for men in the Federal Armed Forces—and that she has come out after 20 years of a double-life that gave her suffering, where she lived the life of a male officer at work and wore women clothing and a wig in the evening. "At work I tried to show off the man, I wanted to make a career and not confront myself all the time with my transsexuality"[210] (Ortmann, 2017, p. 29). She confesses—to put it in Foucauldian terms—that she suffered, reaffirming dominant imaginations in medico-legal knowledge of trans* gender, as described above, but also addressing the issue of the need to first make a career and just later being able to present herself at work. In the article, it is also described how step-by-step she reveals herself to different people at work and in private space, and the great acceptance she receives is emphasized. "Nobody abandoned me, I was supported at all levels. I am grateful for this"[211] (Ortmann, 2017, p. 29). It is written further that her wish to live

---

**209** "Oberstleutnant Anastasia aus Berlin und ihre Geschichte, die Mut macht. Frau Offizier war mal ein Mann" (Oberstleutnant Anastasia aus Berlin und ihre Geschichte, die Mut macht, 2017, p. 1).
**210** "Ich habe versucht im Dienst den Mann hervorzuheben, wollte Karriere machen und mich nicht ständig mit meiner Transsexualität auseinandersetzen" (Ortmann, 2017, p. 29).
**211** "Niemand hat sich abgewandt, ich hatte Unterstützung auf allen Ebenen. Dafür bin ich dank-

as a woman becomes stronger and that she was mentally in poor health, which is explained by the common narrative of "being trapped in the wrong body". Her coming-out as a trans*woman to her superiors is described as just one step in the path as a "Transsexual," as it is put in the article. Ortmann (2017) describes further: "But there is still a lot to be done. Therapeutic accompaniment, psychological testing, medical opinions, hormonal treatment, undergoing the every-day real-life experience." (p. 29) One important step she has already managed: the gender marker. The gender here named is officially changed in her new documents—even in the forces documents. At the end Anastasia is quoted: "Finally I am [a] woman—also in the Federal Armed Forces"[212] (Ortmann, 2017, p. 29). At the side of the article a small information box is placed under the title „Sex—Seminar at the Federal Armed Forces" (Ortmann, 2017, p. 29). The related seminar "Dealing with sexual Identity and Orientation" is part of the programme of the Ministry of Defence for welcoming diversity in the Federal Armed Forces. This article is not part of a serial of portraits of trans* people, nor is the issue of this specific day dedicated to gender or diversity and the newspaper is not known for its trans* respectful reporting.

The violence inherent in the described procedures or the discrimination she faces, for example by being addressed in the article as formerly being a man or by the prejudices she is confronted with, is not given. Neither does the article give any idea about her life and her personality. It is not the person Anastasia that is of interest here. It is the portrayed officer that fulfils stereotypical images of being German—blond, blue-eyed, white, able-bodied, serving the state—but particularly for the national body, which is represented here by the military itself. The article reads as if it would be a manual of how and under what circumstances a trans* person can gain access to belong to the national body, and as if it intends to prove the inclusiveness of the military by asserting that even (gender and sexual) minorities are (now) allowed access to this professional sector. Despite following the path of the medico-legal system, being German entails access to the military that completes the belonging. The figure of the portrayed officer is in this context pictured as a perfect (German) female person and thus as a certain norm of a trans* person who can gain access to the national body. By presenting the imagination of Anastasia and showing that even the Federal Armed Forces accepts trans* people, trans* people in the military become part of the imagined community of "us" (the German national body), while all violence against trans* people is silenced and thus all the ambiguities that are part of trans* realities in Germany are blanked out, even though they are also part of the article itself (such as calling Anastasia a former man). Here, we can observe a mechanism of trans*-nationalism[213] in power, which is derived and borrowed from

---

bar" (Ortmann, 2017, p. 29).

**212** "Ich bin endlich eine Frau—auch bei der Bundeswehr" (Ortmann, 2017, p. 29).

**213** I use the term *trans*-nationalism* as Jasbir Puar (2007) uses the concept of *Homonationalism*—

Puar's concept of Homonationalism (Puar, 2007). Homonationalism explains how the demands for gay and queer equality "are taken as an indicator of 'progress' in modern, Westernized societies, which at the same time racializes homophobia and risks perpetuating white-Western supremacy," a point that I have illustrated previously in an article with Dmitri Heerdegen (Heerdegen & Höhne, 2018, p. 240). This concept can be understood as an

> analytic to apprehend state formation and a structure of modernity: as an assemblage of geopolitical and historical forces, neoliberal interests in capitalist accumulation, both cultural and material, biopolitical state practices of population control, and affective investments in discourses of freedom, liberation and rights. (Puar, 2013, p. 337)

Homonationalism does not mean a substantial acceptance of homosexuality in Western societies, but rather a situational, instrumental and thus precarious use of Homosexuality as a wildcard. In this sense I translate the inclusion within homonationalism of trans*-nationalism. There is not a substantial acceptance of trans* people in Germany, but the article rather illustrates an instrumentalization of trans* lives for political goals without existing trans*-antidiscriminatory politics in the culture of dominance.

I argue that both cases analysed here are part of normalizing trans* representations as inherently German that proves German modernity and progress. Both are examples of a specific way of dealing and instrumentalizing trans* people in popular discourse. They are particular examples, since in both cases the trans* individual serves as a figure through which the connection of gender and belonging (to "us" or "them") in a German context is discussed. The life-worlds and experiences of trans* people do not lie at the centre of interest, but, on the contrary, trans* people are thereby instrumentalized to illustrate the understanding of belonging in the culture of dominance. All the contradictions inherent to these cases are hidden and the trans* discriminatory conditions under which trans* people survive the heteronormative binary gender order are blanked out. Even more starkly, in both cases such media coverage invokes trans* discriminatory topoi and reaffirms them.

## 11.3 Trans* Life Stories—Self Narrations as Resistance

The urge to change one's own body as a trans*person, as created in medico-legal knowledge, translates in popular as well as in scientific discourses into the suffering

---

which is explained later in this chapter—in order to describe the figuration of Western modern nationalism and Homosexuality. The term should not be confused with Steven Vertovec's (2009) concept of *transnationalism*. To make this clear I write trans*-nationalism.

of the wrong body. Jay Prosser (1998) calls this narrative a "transsexual leitmotif" (p. 69), which is not simply imposed on trans* people, but which is rather "material-ized as somatic feeling" in what transsexuality supposedly feels like (p. 70). Similarly, Josch Hoenes (2014) points to the ambivalence of the narrative of "being trapped in the wrong body," that may be an appropriate description of how some trans* people feel but is still a problematic normative view and limited in its description (pp. 102–103). I would add that it reaffirms the normative binary gender system and thus limits trans* narratives and life stories. No person is to blame for making the decision to take hormones or undergo gender reassignment surgery. No (gender-variant) person who decides for this reaffirms the normative gender binary more than dyadic-cis people do. I want to emphasize that this dominant narration brings up what I mentioned above: the very complex contradiction between deconstructing and questioning the binary gender order and its normalizing power on gender variant people on the one hand, and the materialized somatic feeling of the urge to adjust parts of one's body along imaginations implemented by the normative binary gender order, on the other hand. And this dilemma is big. Similarly, the decision "to resist" and not to adjust one's body also still remains in the same logic. In the somatic translation of trans* imaginations we can observe the strength of the normative binary gender order. Even though I would argue that any trans* body, as with all other gender variant bodies, is still an important disturbance of the normative binary gender order. Moreover, it is one thing to question and deconstruct normative binary gender orders and another to try to find solutions to survive all the violence directed against non-normative binary gendered bodies (among them trans* bodies) within the heteronormative binary gender system.

### 11.3.1 Healing and Reconciliation

One of my dialogue-partners, Tabea-Sophie, discovered at an early age that she[214] was somehow special. Tabea-Sophie describes having a searching perspective through all her life— a search for herself. This search however—once she realized her own wom-anhood—is not connected to the searching processes inscribed in dominant trans* narratives about how to make one's own body fit into a narrative of normatively binary gendered bodies. However, it is connected to the search for a place for her own existence in a normative order that was not expected of her. Her quest occurs in the search for the name that fits Tabea-Sophie's personality and her range of identifica-tions. Tabea-Sophie is sure about not wanting to fulfil expectations and not wanting to adapt either herself as a person or her body to dominant imaginations.

---

**214** Concerning pronouns I follow the wish of the respective person.

Well, I am who I am, and it's somehow enough all the inner struggles and problems I have, I needed to adjust myself my whole life somehow and disguise, and I do not want to do that any longer, now that I found out or while I am finding out who I am.[215] (Tabea-Sophie, personal communication, July 18, 2018)

Tabea-Sophie is highly concerned about the narratives that are offered about trans* issues—not just in media but also in activist contexts. She receives the documentation in television or on (autobiographical) books on trans*normativity, where she learns about the narrative of the wrong body and the medical adjustment or discriminatory procedure of changing documents after being approved by a court. However, she strongly feels that there has to be some other solution. She feels like, once she found herself, she does not want to reject herself and thus also parts of her body anymore. She wants reconciliation with herself and the opportunity to heal and love the body she has. She lacks spaces and imagination that help people to heal from the pressures of normativity of knowledge on gender, and criticizes that, even in trans* specific counselling, psychological support, and trans* support groups, she is always confronted with a focus on the medico-legal complex and on the need to change her body. Yet she wants to reach a conciliation with her body, about which she was told it was not what it should be throughout her whole life. And she is able to do so because of her belief which she separates from religion as an institution. She perceives the institution of religion as an element of the normatively binary gender order that did harm to her. Due to her faith, she accepts herself the way she is, and she believes she was made this way for some reason. She feels that following the medico-knowledge of changing her own body would harm her and would be against the perfection of herself by nature.

### 11.3.2 Heterogeneity of Trans* Embodiments

On the international day to end violence against sex workers in December 2016, a diverse group of people gathered in a neighbourhood project in the district where most of the trans* sex workers working on the street go to work. People attending the event differ in their age, origin, language, profession, gender, and in education. It feels like a meeting of different worlds—some queer and trans* activists from other quarters in Berlin mix with the sex workers from the neighbourhood. The sex workers from the neighbourhood all identify more or less as trans* people, but most of them would fail to be recognized of being trans* according to medico-legal knowledge as

---

**215** "Also ich bin ich und das, das reicht irgendwie, was ich für innere Kämpfe und Probleme habe und eh, ich hab, musste mich mein Leben irgendwie anpassen und verstellen und das will ich jetzt nicht mehr wenn ich jetzt raus gefunden habe, oder dabei bin raus zu finden wer ich bin" (Tabea-Sophie, personal communication, July 18, 2018).

well as in the dominant imagination of trans* people in Germany. Some of them are not 24/7 dressed as a woman, while others are; some of them switch names and when addressing each other they sometimes switch in gendering between female and male. Even though all of them identify as trans* sex workers the variety of this appearance is huge. Not all of them have access to the German health insurance system and just some of them decide for, or are interested in, taking hormones. Most of them migrated from Eastern-European countries to Germany and sex work was the option to earn money as an East-European migrant trans* person. Most of them do not have contact with trans* communities in Germany, as e.g. the survey of the peer-to-peer support structure and network *trans*sexworks* states (Transsexworks, n.d.).

In one instance Dunja enters the room wearing a black pullover and some jeans; her hair is cut medium-length. In everyday life she could pass for an intellectual guy, but in her self-perception she is no more or less a woman than later at night after dressing in a more female way and putting on make-up. After dressing up, just shortly before the event where she is asked to speak in public, she wears black stiletto boots, a short dark skirt and an elegant beige blouse with a scarf. She puts on some make-up and a blond wig. Even though I see the difference between her at the arrival and later speaking at stage, I cannot see any different gender than simply herself—Dunja. However, just an hour earlier, she would have been denied access to many women and/or women-lesbian-trans* only spaces, but not in this space during this day. Being in the room all together, it becomes obvious that the understanding of trans*ness differs deeply from dominant trans* discourses. All of them identify problems mostly because of the intersection of their profession, their migration, and the lack of opportunity to rent a flat (in some cases) which intersects with their being trans*sexworkers. However, they all work together on the same street and support each other (as long as they are able to in their current situation) based on their trans* identification and the intersection with their legal status, housing situation and profession.

Discourses of the culture of dominance on trans* people are rarely concerned with these individuals' precarious living conditions. They are more concentrated on treating trans* bodies themselves as precarious. In this frame of trans* activism, certain aspects of trans* lives are argued to be included into certain norms of recognition "to produce certain subjects as 'recognizable'" (Butler, 2010, p. 6). These norms concentrate on questions of depsychopathologization, self-informed consent for trans* specific health care, anti-discrimination legislation, and inclusion (Bundesvereinigung Trans*, 2018). However precarious the individual life may be, those that are in the frame of norms which are not recognizable are most likely found at the intersections of multiple power dimensions. The life-worlds of the trans* sex-workers are often not part of what is negotiated in dominant trans* activism, and aspects concerning trans* people that are negotiated by the trans* sex-workers sometimes differ quite a lot from those which are negotiated in established politics as well as in trans* activist spheres.

### 11.3.3 Invisible Gender

Another important moment concerning the perception of gender in general and of trans* gender more specifically occurred when I first met one of my interview partners, Florian with his partner Maja. Florian was wearing a blue shirt and blue trousers; his hair was cut short, and he had a beard. Maja was wearing a pale shirt with flowers and a half-length black skirt. Her hair was a dark brown wig, and she covered her five o'clock shadow with make-up. In this encounter it becomes obvious how gender is perceived, and so too trans* imaginations in the culture of dominance are based on visual aspects. Florian is blind and just heard my voice and knew that I am a trans* person with a name he reads as male. During this first encounter I was wearing make-up, big earrings, black trousers and a black summer blouse. Maja, a trans* woman that in the gaze of the culture of dominance sometimes had difficulties to pass as a female, asked me during our conversation "what I am". She wanted to know if I am a trans* woman or a trans* man or something in-between. She was even correcting Florian by using male pronouns addressing me, and instead used female pronouns. Florian was very embarrassed by this situation and said that one does not ask this question to trans* people, and she should know about the difficulty of the situation when people question your gender, as her womanhood was often questioned in public. In this situation I did not understand what actually was at stake. Later I realized that I forgot to pay attention to the difference of how both of them are gendering people. While the partner gendered myself, based on the supposed contradiction of my deep voice and my visual performance, visual aspects of gender were not accessible to Florian. The partner was confused, as I did not comply sufficiently with her visual expectations of trans*maleness or trans*femaleness. My deep voice and facial hair contradicted her expectations that a trans* woman would reach to dismiss any male associated aspects. My outfit instead contradicted her expectation of trans*maleness, as she categorized my clothes, make-up and jewellery to be female. In our second encounter I described to Florian what I was wearing and asked him if he wants to see me with his hands. He touched my hair, that was longer than he expected, and realized that I did not have a beard. I gave him my jewellery which I was wearing and suddenly the question of his partner made sense to him, because he could relate to the confusion of my deeper voice, my body, which both of them describe as male with a sportive back, and all the things I was wearing. These he could not see during our first encounter as I did not invite him to see me in a manner accessible to him. Both of them challenge and are challenged in their everyday life by the normatively binary gender order, yet they—as any other person—also reproduce the expectations of the order itself and are thus challenged if I do not fulfil their assumptions on how trans* individuals can survive in the assumptions of the culture of dominance concerning the binary gender order. I do not want to question their gendered self-perception or their strategies to survive the expectations of the normative binary gender order in the culture of dominance. Rather, I understand this brief side-comment as another important aspect of mapping the landscape of the normative binary gender order and imaginations of trans*lifes, that needs to be analysed further. What I observe in these encounters are of importance for questions of visibility and how different access to what is visible to whom stabilizes or destabilizes the normative binary gender order.

### 11.3.4 About Resistance and Adoption

Despite the negotiations of normative binary gender in the culture of dominance, trans* people do not simply adopt, accept or realize the conditions of the normative binary gender order. Rather, in life story narrations of trans* people, the complex mingling of normalizing narrations and the complexity and variety of gender in general, and of trans* gender specifically, becomes recognizable and accountable. It is not a one-way-street where the normative gender order narratives translate one-to-one into life stories of people of different genders, but rather an interaction and negotiation between different actors, aspects, narrations, and views. It is the interaction that spawns the different specific ways of trans* formations. These negotiations and impossibilities of belonging and gender can be observed specifically in the life stories of trans* people, as they are particularly often openly forced to navigate through the conditions spelled out in the dominant normative binary gender order. Furthermore, we can observe that trans* people are not passive victims but are engaged in the culture of dominance of the normative binary gender orders and adjust, influence and change dominant narrations. Zowie Davy argues in this context how:

> Transsexuals acknowledge that the medical discourses that are interpreted by the doctors and psychiatrists require perceptive manipulation. Thus, transsexuals' own discourses have both agentic and subjugating elements to them, which the participants utilise and/or rework at a discursive level as well as a phenomenological level. (Davy, 2010, p. 107)

By presenting glimpses of life stories of trans* people, I illustrate the everyday navigation through the normative binary gender order from the perspective of people who do not (fully) fit this normative order.

### 11.3.5 Reflections and Prospects

In my article I have shown how imaginations of trans*lives as they are present in the knowledge of the culture of dominance are imaginable against the backdrop of medico-legal knowledge and the normatively binary gender order. This knowledge is not just present in medico-legal contexts, but also resonates in popular media coverage as well as in activist discourses. However, I have shown that trans* people are not simply victims of oppression, but rather actors inside these negotiations. Current imaginations of trans* people are embedded in long, often painful stories on disbe-longing to certain gendered norms in the normative binary gender order. Following different sequences of current discourses on trans* gender, I have shown how the complex realities and ways of survival of trans* people are always entangled with various other aspects of their life-worlds. The realities of trans* people I outline as a puzzle with different pieces or a map with a different path. There is no single way of narrating and imagining trans* lives, but all different kinds of experiences are con-nected. They refer to each other, they deny each other, they connect to each other, they resist each other, they embrace each other. Taking a closer look on the current discourses concerning trans* issues in Germany, we can observe how deeply embed-ded they are in their intersections with questions of temporality and space, and thus of the discourse of gender in general. I have shown how, by taking up all these mul-tilayered fragments, we acquire not only a deeper understanding of the complexity of gendered existences, but also repudiate the power system of knowledge and (in) visibility has on gender and its impact on trans* realities. It is not possible to go one step back, to erase the imperial status of the normative binary gender order. Yet it is possible to question its privileged status and its fame, by showing its complexities and reinterpretations. This complexity is hard to grasp in a linear text and a text only gives us a very small extract. My text should be read as an invitation for readers to seek out deeper insights of the complex negotiations of gendered (national) belong-ing and how gendered belonging and national interests are often negotiated against each other—most often without, or just with little, attention for the lived realities of gender-variant people themselves.

# References

Aizura, A. Z., Cotton, T., Balzer, C./LaGata C., Ochoa, M., & Vidal-Ortiz, S. (2014). Introduction. Transgender Studies Quarterly, 1(3), 308–319.

Aizura, A. Z. (2018). Mobile Subjects. Transnational Imaginaries of Gender Reassignment. Duke University Press.

APTN [Asia Pacific Transgender Network]. (2017, October 8). The "Gender Incongruence of Childhood" Diagnosis Revisited: A Statement From Clinicians And Researchers [Open letter]. Retrieved February 2, 2019, from http://www.weareaptn.org/2017/10/08/the-gender-incongruence-of-childhood-diagnosis-revisited-a-statement-from-clinicians-and-researchers/

Arendt, H. (2006). Elemente und Ursprünge totalitärer Herrschaft [The Origins of Totalitarianism]. Piper.

Bundesgerichtshof. (2017, September 6). Beschluss - XII ZB 660/14 Frau-Zu-Mann- Transsexueller gilt rechtlich als Mutter eines von ihm geborenen Kindes. http://juris.bundesgerichtshof.de/cgi-bin/rechtsprechung/document.py?Gericht=bgh&Art=en&sid=fe10ed417991e6e6c0d229919616930f&anz=1&pos=0&nr=79597&linked=pm&Blank=1

Bundesverfassungsgericht. (2017, Oktober 10). Beschluss des Ersten Senats -1 BvR 2019/16 - Rn. (1–69). http://www.bverfg.de/e/rs20171010_1bvr201916.html

Butler, J. (1991). Das Unbehagen der Geschlechter [Gender Trouble]. Suhrkamp Verlag.

Butler, J. (2010). Frames of War. When Is Life Grievable? Verso.

Çetin, Z., & Prasad, N. (2015). Leerstellen im Diskurs um Frauenrechte ohne Rassismus und Klassismus. In Z. Çetin & S. Taş (Eds.), Gespräche über Rassismus. Perspektiven & Widerstände (pp. 107–116). Verlag Yılmaz-Günay.

Davy, Z. (2010) Transsexual Agents: Negotiating Authenticity and Embodiment within the UK's Medicolegal System. In: S. Hines and T. Sanger (Eds.), Transgender Identities: Towards a Social Analysis of Gender Diversity (pp. 106-126). Routledge.

Focus online regional. (2016, January 18). Angriff auf Frauen in Dortmund, Jugendliche wollten Transsexuellen-Paar steinigen: "Bin noch immer komplett fertig" [Attack on women. Adolecents wantet to stone a Transsexual couple to death: "I am still totally wasted"]. FOCUS online. Retrieved March 3, 2020, from https://www.focus.de/regional/dortmund/angriff-auf-frauen-in-dortmund-jugendliche-wollten-transsexuellen-paar-steinigen-bin-noch-immer-komplett-fertig_id_5218233.html

Foucault, M. (1978). History and Sexuality. Pantheon Books.

Gesetzesentwurf der Bundesregierung. (2018). Entwurf eines Gesetzes zur Änderung der in das Geburtenregister einzutragenden Angaben. https://www.bmi.bund.de/SharedDocs/downloads/DE/gesetzestexte/gesetzesentwuerfe/entwurf-aenderung-personenstandsgesetz.html

Haritaworn, J. (2012). Colorful Bodies in the Multikulti Metropolis. Vitality, Victimology and Transgressive Citizenship in Berlin. In T. T. Cotton (Ed.), Transgender Migrations. The Bodies, Borders, and Politics of Transition (pp. 11–31). Routledge.

Heerdegen, D., & Höhne, M. S. (2018). On Normativity and Absence: Representation of LGBTI* in Textbook Research. In A. Bock & E. Fuchs (Eds.), Handbook of Textbook Studies (pp. 239–249). Palgrave Macmillan.

Hoenes, J. (2014). Nicht Frosch—Nicht Laborratte: Transmännlichkeiten im Bild. Eine kunst- und kulturwissenschaftliche Analyse visueller Politiken [Not Frog—Not Laborartory Rat. Trans*masculinity in picture. An art- and cultural studies analysis of visual politics]. Transcript.

Höhne, M. (2017). Un_mögliches Passing? Das Nadelöhr der Norm [Im_possible Passing? The bottleneck of the Norm]. In I. Nagelschmidt, B. Borrego, D. Majewski & L. König (Eds.), Geschlechtersemantiken und Passing be- und hinterfragen (pp. 21–40). Peter Lang.

Höhne, M. S., & Klein, T. (2019). Disrupting Invisibility Fields—Provincializing 'Western Code' Trans* Narratives. Open Gender Journal. https://doi.org/10.17169/ogj.2019.24

Jung, C. (2016) Steinigung in Dortmund [stoning to death in Dortmund]. KOPP ONLINE. www.info.kopp-verlag.de/hintergruende/deutschland/christian-jung/steinigung-in-dortmund.html. Copy in possession of author.

Katholische Nachrichten. (2016, January 18). Dortmund: Nordafrikaner wollten Transsexuelle steinigen [Dortmund: North Africans wanted to stone transsexuals]. Katholische Nachrichten. Retrieved January 20, 2016, from http://www.kath.net/news/53639

LISTE mit empirischen MATERIAL Bundesvereinigung Trans*. (2018). Für geschlechtliche Selbst-bestimmung und Vielfalt! https://www.bv-trans.de/

Lugones, M. (2008). Colonialidad y género. Tabula Rasa 9, 73–101.

Medizinischer Dienst des Spitzenverbandendes Bund der Krankenkassen e.V. [MDS]. (2009). Richtlinie des GKV-Spitzenverbandes zur Sicherung einer einheitlichen Begutachtung nach §282 Absatz 2, Satz 3 SGB V. Begutachtungsanleitung Geschlechtsangleichende Maßnahmen bei Transsexualität.

Mühlbauer, P. (2016, January 17). Dortmund: Nordafrikaner wollten angeblich Transsexuelle steinigen [Dortmund: Northafricans allegedly tried to stone Transsexuals to death]. Telepolis. www.heise.de/tp/druck/ob/artikel/47/47138/1.html

Nieder, T. O., Briken, P., & Preuss, W. (2012). Schwerpunkte der Psychotherapie bei transsexuellen Entwicklungen. Der Neurologe und Psychiater, 13(10), 58–65.

Noislamisation. (2016, January 16). Steinigung in Dortmund [Video]. YouTube. https://www.youtube.com/watch?v=3GoubXlRsvs

Ortmann, J. (2017, January 31). Eine Frage des Outens. Die ungewöhnliche Karriere von Oberstleutnant Anastasia, die als Soldat begann [The unusual career of Lieutenant Anastasia, who began as a soldier] (p. 29). Berlin Kurier. Copy in possession of author.

Oberstleutnant Anastasia aus Berlin und ihre Geschichte, die Mut macht. Frau Offizier war mal ein Mann [Lieutenant Anastasia from Berlin and her story that gives courage] (2017, January 1). (p. 1). Berlin Kurier. Copy in possession of author.

Prosser, J. (1998). Second Skins. The Body Narratives of Transsexuality. Columbia University Press.

Puar, J. K. (2007). Terrorist Assemblages: Homonationalism in Queer Times. Duke University Press.

Puar, J. K. (2013). Rethinking Homonationalism. International Journal of Middle East Studies, 45(2), 336–339. https://doi.org/10.1017/S002074381300007X

Reporter. (2018, March 21). Transgender: Pattis geschlechtsangleichende Operation [Video]. YouTube. https://www.youtube.com/watch?v=ZnGdC4f_77E

Rommelspacher, B. (1998). Dominanzkultur. Texte zu Fremdheit und Macht. Orlando Frauenverlag.

Schaffer, J. (2008). Ambivalenzen der Sichtbarkeit. Über die visuellen Strukturen der Anerkennung. Transcript.

Transsexworks. (n.d.). Bedarfserhebung. Retrieved March, 2019, from http://transsexworks.com/?page_id=170&lang=de_DE

Vertovec, S. (2009). Transnationalism. Routledge.

Wegener, A., & Engelberg, M. (2016, January 16). Transsexuelle in Dortmund von drei Männern angegriffen—jetzt sprechen die Opfer: "Wir sollten auf offener Straße gesteinigt werden" [Transsexuals attacked in Dortmund by three men—now the victims are talking: "We were supposed to be stoned to death at the street"]. Bild-Zeitung online. Retrieved January 20, 2016, from https://www.bild.de/regional/ruhrgebiet/toetungsdelikt-steinigung/wir-sollten-auf-offener-strasse-gesteinigt-werden-44171194.bild.html#fromWall

World Health Organisation [WHO]. (2016). Classifications of Mental and Behavioural Disorder: Clinical Descriptions and Diagnostic Guidelines. International Classification of Diseases (ICD-10, 10th revision). Retrieved from https://www.icd10data.com/ICD10CM/Codes/F01-F99/F60-F69/F64-

Lisa Gaupp

# 12  How to Curate Diversity and Otherness in Global Performance Art

## (Essay Together with an Interview with Claude Jansen)

Global performance art worlds are often presented as borderless and international. Through internationally active curators, their festivals and other cultural organizations, a global art market has developed which adheres to the motto of "diversity" (Peres da Silva & Hondros, 2019) for increasing inclusivity. However, at the same time, global art worlds are criticized for being "too international" (Buț, 2017), and for standardizing an international canon which largely excludes, for example, "refugee" artists. So is diversity a "white word" (Cañas, 2017)?

The theoretical framework for this paper is formed by applying different postcolonial and transcultural perspectives to compare and criticize the application of different narratives of "diversity and otherness" in the field of global performance art.[216] This discussion will lead to an attempt to answer the research question of how diversity and otherness can be curated without labelling, paternalizing or exoticizing, i.e. by asking how curating can be decolonized, as structures and practices of neocolonialism, social inequality and exclusion persist on a global scale. This means that modes of transformation will be explored as forms of cultural expressions, which provide emancipatory views of cultural expression that are different from the hegemonic mainstream's entanglement with social inequalities.

The focus will lie on both the representation of diversity and otherness in the life-worlds of globally active performance art, music festivals and other cultural organizations, and the performativity of diversity and otherness in these fields of practice. While the former encompasses all structural conditions which influence how *intersectional diversity and otherness* are (re-)presented at festivals and other cultural organizations, the latter limits its attention to the practices and strategies of performing *cross-cultural diversity and otherness* as border-crossing. In other words, we shall take a look at how the concepts of intersectional and cross-cultural diversity and otherness are applied to the field of arts production, both in their symbolic uses in the

---

216 I have discussed the two narratives of diversity and otherness as intersectional and as cross-cultural in my other contribution in this volume as follows: Intersectional *diversity* encompasses intersecting social belongings which include, while intersectional *otherness* emphasizes these differences to exclude. Cross-cultural *diversity* describes ambiguous cultural symbols, cross-cultural *otherness* de-stabilizes differences.

politics of representation (such as striving for equal access) and with regard to how border-crossing concepts are performed, negotiated and mediated in these fields.

*Intersectional approaches to diversity and otherness* in global performance art typically focus on unequal economic and power relations on a global scale and on ways of how to overcome these inequalities. In this connection, I will discuss approaches for increasing inclusion through strategies of intersectional diversity, as well as how practices of intersectional otherness often increase exclusionary outcomes in the arts. The intersectional approach thereby refers to multiple intersecting types of identity, which mutually influence other markers of difference. *Cross-cultural notions of diversity and otherness* in global performance art, conversely, brings into focus how ambiguous cultural symbols of entanglement, interconnectedness and spaces in-between are negotiated, standardized and deconstructed in the field of practice.

Such an approach entails focusing on the practice of doing and undoing differences (Hirschauer in this volume), by providing a genuinely praxeological stance (Reckwitz, 2005; Schatzki, 1996; Bourdieu, 1978). Even though the part of this chapter dedicated to intersectional strategies of representation places more emphasis on structures, while cross-cultural practices of performativity rather emphasize the actions of individuals and how the un-doing of differences is performed, both approaches rely on the common assumption of performative approaches (Butler, 2013; Bharucha, 2001; Fischer-Lichte, 2004; Fischer-Lichte & Roselt, 2001; Goodman & DeGay, 2000; Bial, 2004). The acting-out of narratives cannot be analysed without reference to the structures of the surrounding conditions, such as policies, finances, economy, organizational structures, etc. The same entanglement applies to how to theorize these performative practices, which depend equally on the construction of certain symbolic meanings as well as on the structuring conditions that are involved. Narratives are performed under specific conditions (Austin, 2014). So it is not only structure and agency that need to be thought about together (Archer, 2005), but idealist and materialist stances cannot be separated (Zembylas & Niederauer, 2017).

This leads us to examine how curating is conceptualized in this chapter. Curating is a social practice embedded in a field of structures which enables as well as limits, and a social practice that combines the construction, performance and negotiation of situational meanings and their acting-out (Davida et al., 2019; Lind, 2012; Buden, 2012; Rugg & Sedgwick, 2012). So Buurman et al. write:

> To acknowledge both the structural constraints and the potentialities for agency, we suggest replacing theories of (fixed) identity with the notion of (changeable) positionality in relation to a number of intersecting and potentially shifting social affiliations (race, class, gender, age, location), ... to encourage casting aside the obsession with origins for one which is in favour of a perspective of practice and what one does, from being to doing, without forgetting that the options for agency are sometimes heavily confined and policed by outright violence, not to mention subtler mechanisms of discursive, social or biopolitical control. (2018, p. 20)

With regard to methodology, this chapter is based on literature reviews. These academic studies will be complemented with my own empirical data from the field, as well as with some additional "good or bad practice examples". Empirical results which are included in this chapter are deduced from the qualitative expert interviews which I have conducted with 26 curators, dramaturges, artists and representatives of cultural organizations in globally active festivals and organizations of performance art and music in the period of 2014–2018. This chapter is largely based on an interview with Claude Jansen, an independent scholar, performer, dramaturge and curator from Hamburg. This interview served as a debate about the possibilities of decolonizing "curating performance art" on a global scale. How can dualisms and dichotomies of diversity and otherness be overcome, and how can practices of representations be transformed and set in a more contextualized relationship?

## 12.1 Representation of Diversity and Otherness—An Intersectional Approach

Let us begin by taking a look at the fields of practice in global performance art and see how different academic studies look at social inequalities and multiple discriminations. It will also be necessary to exemplify notions of *intersectional otherness* and note how other approaches look at social inclusion from a perspective of *intersectional diversity* in these fields of cultural production. As stated in the introduction as well as in my other contribution to this volume, narratives that guide the area of *intersectional diversity and otherness* are mostly oriented towards the assumption that fields of global cultural production are interwoven with economical and power hierarchies. Social inequalities which result from processes of social determination are emphasized and intended to be overcome. Another important orientation is often the quest not only to unveil unequal power-relations but also to achieve greater equality and inclusivity within these cultural fields through, among other things, decolonization. Thus, differences between people or larger social groups are either emphasized in order to exclude outsiders from this group, or unity based on diversity is featured in order to include people with diverse and intersecting multiple identity-markers.

> This leads us to social inequality as a further central concept of diversity in diversity studies which refers to the systematic access (or lack of access) to socially validated assets and resources, based on belonging to a social group determined by categorisations of gender, class, ethnicity or race, sexuality, religion or disability. (Jungwirth, 2019, p. 11)

When we look at the representation of diversity and otherness in globally active performing arts and music festivals and other cultural organizations, by entangling the structural conditions that influence how diversity and otherness are staged in these fields, we must consider how the terms and narratives of *intersectional diversity and otherness* are applied. Sara Ahmed has described how in diversity-work in universities, terms stemming from earlier feminism such as "equal opportunities" or "anti-racism", which aspire to bear negative connotations by their confrontational and abundant use, have been replaced by the non-defined term of diversity "as a 'feel good' politics" (Ahmed, 2012, p. 69). "The shift from the language of equality to the language of diversity becomes linked to a shift from a confrontational to a collaborative working model, to sharing rather than enforcing values" (p. 64). For Ahmed, this use of the term has two sides. On the one hand, when diversity is used as such a "container term", the risk of obscuring inequalities (pp. 71–72) is apparent. On the other hand, the universal and plural possibilities of such a positive but non-defined term offers people the chance to fill it with their own content, and thereby "a community can take shape through the circulation of diversity. ... To speak the language of diversity is to participate in the creation of a world" (p. 81). In this light, is it possible to curate diversity and otherness in global performance art in an open-minded, non-hierarchical, postcolonial, anti-racist, transcultural and emancipated way? Even more importantly, how is this to be achieved? Is it possible to fill the concept of diversity in such a way? Does the term fulfil the promise of collaboration rather than confrontation?

The debate in global performance art is often concentrated on concepts such as participation, representation, access and inclusion (Gaupp, 2016). Questions that are raised in these contexts include, for example, how individuals can react to essentializing group identities and instead empower themselves, how cultural organizations can foster inclusivity without othering, and how institutionalized identity politics can avoid exclusion (Dobusch et al., 2020). For instance, suppose that one wants to create a more diverse audience for the audiences of art performances in Germany. The German debate particularly focuses on the participation of those citizens who have not so far been represented, especially young people and (young) immigrants, because the audience of tomorrow is not sufficiently reached by publicly funded culture. The established, publicly funded cultural institutions have therefore come under strong political pressure to prove their legitimacy. In particular after the so-called "refugee crisis" in 2015, these arguments can lead to the absurd situation, that, for example, in Berlin you can hardly find a refugee who has not been approached by at least three cultural institutions, asking if he or she wants to participate in a cultural project (Henze, 2017).

As I have shown in my PhD thesis (2016), the cultural policies concerning immigrant populations in Germany since the 1960s have mostly developed from the concepts of interculturalism, and multiculturalism. Intercultural or multicultural concepts of culture follow a traditional, nation-based concept of culture, and thereby foster differences between a homogenous "minority" and a homogenous "host society". Through this they construct and label their target group through markers of otherness, showing the mechanisms of "othering" or labelling (see also Köhl, 2001).

This is also the case in some approaches of so-called intercultural audience development (Haberkorn, 2010; Mandel, 2014). Suppose, here, that one wants to include people in art performances who have hitherto been under-represented, by designing and implementing an agenda of diversity affirmation. Even though data shows that under-representation is prevalent (Horz, 2014) and that established power hierarchies which are often dominated by male white individuals hardly change at all, such an approach for, e.g., the target group "immigrants" runs into the danger of essentializing certain identity traits over others. The target groups can, for instance, become further differentiated in an intersectional manner. It also emphasizes the divide between "us" and "them" and thus fosters exclusion rather than inclusion.

A solid body of literature analyses the underlying reasons for exclusionary practices and under-representation in the arts concerning a variety of artistic genres, such as visual arts (see below), film (Dovey, 2015) and theatre (Heeg & Hillmann, 2017). Scholarship has also previously focussed on the organizational side of implementing diversity in the arts, such as through cultural policies (Benzer, 2016; Sievers et al., 2018), audience research (Van Wel et al., 2006), community work (Pilić & Wiederhold, 2015) and education (Lutz-Sterzenbach et al., 2013; Keuchel & Kelb, 2015; Eremjan, 2016).

Many of these approaches apply postcolonial and/or poststructuralist theory to the field of interest, so again questions may be posed whether the outcome is really as it was theoretically intended—and in turn whether theory can learn from practice or is practice (Kolsteeg, 2019)—and how diversity and otherness can be curated without paternalizing and exoticizing. We will come back to these questions in the discussion.

Other examples do not obviously exhibit signs of exclusion, so the whole picture needs to be disentangled very carefully. An additional heuristic difficulty arises since diversity-sensitive and cross-cultural concepts, as well as transcultural and postcolonial theory, have become a major ingredient for many global arts organizations today (Do Mar Castro Varela & Haghighat, 2020). How, then, should we conduct theory when within a single cultural field the same concepts, such as academic postcolonial and poststructuralist critique, are being applied? Or to put the question differently: "What contribution can deconstructive readings and highly abstract conceptualizations make to the real liberation struggles from neo-colonial exploitation of the Global South?"[217] (Angermüller & Bellina, 2012, p. 34). For Johannes Angermüller and Leonie Bellina, this task can only be achieved by consequently bringing together theory and practice. Equally, Alexandra Karentzos suggests taking into account different levels that all need to be addressed simultaneously. Regarding the enforcement of a "postcolonial art history", it is not sufficient to apply postcolonial critiques to exclusionary

---

217 "Welchen Beitrag können dekonstruktive Lektüren und hochabstrakte Begriffsbildungen zu realen Befreiungskämpfen gegen neo-koloniale Ausbeutung des Globalen Südens leisten?" (Angermüller & Bellina, 2012, p. 34).

practices such as (re-)establishing hegemonies by curating certain objects as "other objects". An example of the latter is the exhibition *Primitivism in 20ᵗʰ Century Art* at the Museum of Modern Art in New York in 1984, which opposed European "masters of modernity" to the "traditional Other" (Karentzos, 2012, p. 250). Also, on an academic level, art history needs to be revised in order to deconstruct the established construction of "ethnic encoding of an artist" in academia. Thirdly, contemporary art practices which challenge these exclusionary practices of otherness in the museum, by offering a transdisciplinary view from combined art-historical, anthropological and artistic perspectives, in order to set a "transcultural polyphony" against those "linear master narratives" (p. 253), are in need of being critically re-considered. Such "postcolonial streams in contemporary art challenge art-scholars to rethink their own theory formation in a postcolonial manner"[218] (p. 249). Thus, this approach suggests simultaneously a decolonizing of practice and academia by including plural and transdisciplinary voices.

However, with such an approach, other difficulties can arise. The more people participate in, for example, curating processes, the more differentiated (political) agendas need to be negotiated in order to reach a common goal. These agendas can be more or less individual,[219] such as by adherence to a certain artistic understanding, or they can be related to group identity politics, such as wanting to increase the representation of a certain social group. For instance, in a transnational, collaborative project between German and "African" artists,

> you actually have two positions, on the one hand the diasporic, progressive one [in Germany] which wants to untangle that [Africa is not a country ... not the continent of illusions with all its fantasies] from a position that I find absolutely correct. ... But [on the other hand,] in African countries I know a lot of artists coming from a very strong political context, who speak more radically of the continent [in reference to the pan-African idea ... in order to not acknowledge the national, colonial borders].[220] (Jansen, personal communication, October 17, 2018)

---

218 "postkoloniale Strömungen zeitgenössischer Kunst [stellen auch] eine Herausforderung für die Kunstwissenschaft dar, die eigene Theoriebildung postkolonial weiterzudenken" (Jansen, personal communication, October 17, 2018).

219 However, the majority of the academic approaches in this area regard the cultural field (Bourdieu, 1993) or the art world (Becker, 2008) not as an individual task but rather as a social endevour. Thus, they can be related to the Sociology of Culture by also looking at the actions of individuals as stemming mainly from the social position of an individual and his or her relationships.

220 "in Referenz zur panafrikanistischen Idee, die ja vor 100 Jahren als erste, entsprechend der Verhandlungen mit den Partnerinnen und Partnern aus dem jeweiligen Land und es nach diesen Ideen gibt. Und das es eben viele meiner Co-Produktionspartnerinnen aus den Ländern sagen, dass sie die nationalen, kolonialen Grenzen nicht anerkennen und deswegen, eigentlich, aus ihrer Position, erneut von Afrika als einen Kontinent sprechen. Wobei und da haben wir schon den ersten Graben zu der Diaspora, die natürlich sehr stark auf ,Africa is not a country', eben sehr stark, in den Schulungsprozessen der EuropäerInnen darauf verweist, dass es eben viele Länder gibt und Afrika ist nicht der Illusionskontinent, mit all den Fantasien und so. Und da geht es eigentlich schon los:

In addition, both positions are situationally even more split up. The "German side" can be influenced heterogeneously by, among other factors, funding schemes and/ or postcolonial theory, which "want to dissolve the African cliché, in Germany" by including migrant Afro-Germans into the project, "whereas the African says, your clichés are of no interest to me"[221]. Furthermore, the "African" positions "already differ very vehemently among each other between Namibia and South Africa" (Jansen, personal communication, October 17, 2018). Likewise, "a great many positions come in"[222] (Jansen, personal communication, October 17, 2018). Thus, such an *intersectional diversity* of voices can both offer emancipatory views and foster *intersectional otherness*, by emphasizing the differences between all perspectives.

As stated above, there are numerous examples of academic studies which analyse the power-relations in different fields of global arts, which foster exclusion rather than inclusion. A large majority of these approaches to *intersectional otherness* in global cultural production is focused on the visual arts. In particular, the debates around the establishment of the Humboldt-Forum in the centre of Berlin, as a space for the display of "the cultures of the world" (Stiftung Humboldt Forum im Berliner Schloss, n.d.; Di Blasi, 2019), the decolonizing of more traditional anthropological museums, such as the former Museum für Völkerkunde Hamburg which has been transformed into the MARKK Hamburg (https://markk-hamburg.de; Kraus & Noack, 2015), post-colonially oriented biennales such as documenta XI[223] (2002 in Kassel) and the topic of colonial and Nazi-looted art and their restitution, have sparked considerable attention in several academic disciplines within art history (Rother, 2017; Macdonald, 1996). Other authors focus on "outsider art" (Zolberg & Cherbo, 1997) from under-represented visual artists, such as "primitive African art" (Zolberg, 1997), or on the power hierarchies in the visual arts (Below & von Bismarck, 2005; Behnke et al. 2015; Buchholz & Wuggenig, 2005[224]).

---

dann hast du eigentlich zwei Positionen, nämlich zum einen die diasporische, aufklärerische, die das aufdröseln möchte, aus einer Position, die ich absolut richtig finde, einerseits. Aber wie gesagt, in den afrikanischen Ländern kenne ich sehr viele Künstlerinnen und Künstler die aus einem sehr starken politischen Zusammenhang kommen, die viel radikaler wieder von Kontinent sprechen" (Jansen, personal communication, October 17, 2018).

221 "Wobei [diese Seite] ja das afrikanische Klischee auflösen will, in Deutschland. Während die Afrikanerin sagt, Was interessieren mich eure Klischees?" (Jansen, personal communication, October 17, 2018).

222 "Und da kommen dann noch einmal zig Positionen rein. ... Und die unterschieden sich ja schon vehement von Namibia zu Südafrika" (Jansen, personal communication, October 17, 2018).

223 This was curated by the first non-European curator Okwui Enwezor, who laid open the "asymmetry between curating and curated cultures" by citing Gerardo Mosquera in the documenta catalogue (Enwezor, 2002, p. 46; see Mosquera, 1994, as cited in Karentzos, 2012, p. 251).

224 The manifold relation between all kinds of art genres and power is the subject of another volume entitled "Arts and Power – Policies in and by the Arts", which I am editing, to be published in 2021 by Springer VS Gaupp et al., 2021).

Thanks to such critique, in the field of practice, new identity politics and interest groups, such as the Initiative Bündnis kritischer Kulturpraktiker_innen (https://mindthetrapberlin.wordpress.com) or the Diversity Arts Culture (http://www.diversity-arts-culture.berlin/en), have been developed. Both of these organizations host conferences and cultural events which are intended not to reproduce the mentioned exclusions. In order to protest against racist and extremist right-wing attacks on cultural organizations and artists in Germany, the association DIE VIELEN was founded in 2017 and published the declaration Wir sind Viele,[225] besides organizing a large array of events such as anti-racist lectures and discussions[226] (http://theaterder-welt2017.iti-germany.de). Elsewhere, others also criticize these exclusionary outcomes of such diversity-affirmative actions, but still see the need to follow such an agenda in the medium term, in order to change the hierarchical and neo-colonial structures of the cultural field in the long-run (https://www.kiwit.org/kultur-oeffnet-welten/kultur-oeffnet-welten.html).

One study by the global media company Pitchfork on diversity, which was concerned with the line-ups of major popular multi-genre music festivals in the US and Canada, shows that the same groups and artists tended to play at these festivals in 2017, and that these artists came mainly from European countries or at least were based in the so-called "West". (Pitchfork, n.d.) This study also showed that there is a homogeneity in the American and Canadian festival scene regarding gender balance and other diversity markers, "especially toward the top of the bill" (Bishop, 2018). These findings are no different if we take a look at the programmes of publicly funded festivals in Europe. The same groups and artists are playing at these festivals, and they are mainly artists from European countries or at least based in the so-called "West".

When it comes to these issues of representation, one also has to take into account structural conditions, such as the financing strategies of the festival producers themselves. For example, to keep costs down, festivals form networks to co-produce new productions. This practical strategy has consequences for diversity, as it contributes to having the same groups booked at a majority of these festivals in the "Western" world (Gaupp, 2020). Another very influential issue concerns visa permits, which sometimes prevent musicians from certain countries touring or travelling at all. Even if a record company manages to bring artists to Germany to record, other problems can arise when it comes to paying royalties to the musicians, since not every country has a royalty association, such as the GEMA in Germany (Record label representative, personal communication, May 3, 2018). For this reason, one could think that these networks, visa conditions and royalties would result in a closed circle of a kind of

---

225  We are Many.
226  At the end of 2019, nearly 3500 cultural organizations and persons working in the field, coming from 16 cities and regions and 15 German federal states, have signed the declaration and participated in the organization of such events.

"Western male white canon in global arts". However, in an interview I conducted with a curator, she stated that sometimes these networks are a very good way for unknown artists to become produced on an international level. After all, it only takes one of the curator gatekeepers to be convinced in order for a work to be produced. Moreover, once an artist is a part of the bigger and more established festivals, they will be more willing to feature the same artist (Gaupp, 2020).

But there is still a nationalistic focus in this process. One curator expresses this aptly when she states that—mainly due to the financial crisis—national funding bodies tend to focus on resident artists only (Kaup-Hasler, 2012). After all,

> in a field of cosmopolitan self-conception, territorial or rather national criteria still are meaningful regardless of their rejection. Artists without north-Western geographic origin are still underrepresented in the centre of the art field where actors with high field-specific symbolic recognition prevail. ... Field theory offers explanations for these facts by looking at the institutional structure of the art field, i.e. the distribution of relevant resources.[227] (Buchholz & Wuggenig, 2012, p. 179)

Fewer approaches appear to discuss how inclusion can be achieved in cultural organizations, which follow an approach of intersectional diversity and/or focus on other artistic genres besides the visual arts. For instance, Johan Kolsteeg has published some studies on the strategies of inclusivity in a Dutch theatre, and has shown that a complex process needs to take into account not only the structure of the organization itself (for instance, by implementing flexible management structures or rotating project leadership) and a carefully designed audience development strategy (by focussing on e.g. a "delta of niches"), but also to think of the cultural organization's stakeholders (by including plural collaborations with local and regional partners) as well as developing a talent development strategy (e.g. by connecting the local to the global) (Kolsteeg, 2019). Only by taking into account all of these levels (and probably more, in other contexts), by establishing Richard Sennetts' social triangle (2003) of authority, cooperation and trust, can social entrepreneurship in a cultural organization be achieved, which accounts for inclusivity as a starting point of cultural democracy (Kolsteeg, 2019).

For example, many performing art festivals organized by politically active or at least engaged organizations are trying to achieve a gender balance within their artists' roster. The Festival Theater der Welt at Kampnagel 2017 in Hamburg discussed these topics around discrimination processes (http://theaterderwelt2017.iti-germany.

---

227 "Territoriale bzw. nationale Kriterien haben ungeachtet ihrer Zurückweisung in einem Feld mit kosmopolitischem Selbstverständnis offenbar nach wie vor Bedeutung. Künstler/innen, die nicht auf eine nordwestliche geografische Herkunft zurückblicken, sind in jedem Zentrum des Kunstfeldes nach wie vor schwach vertreten, in dem sich die Akteure mit hoher feldspezifischer symbolischer Anerkennung konzentrieren. ... aus feldtheoretischer Perspektive [gibt es hierfür] Gründe ..., die nicht zuletzt in der institutionellen Struktur des sozialen Systems der Kunst zu suchen sind, d. h. in der Verteilung relevanter Ressourcen" (Buchholz & Wuggenig, 2012, p. 179).

de). Another example is taken from the music industry and is called the Keychange Initiative, which was granted 1.4 million Euro of the EU's Creative Europe funding scheme in October 2019 at the Reeperbahn festival in Hamburg. The initiative seeks to achieve a 50:50 gender balance in the industry by 2022, through activities such as supporting female artists and innovators with cross border collaborations and showcases, engaging more festivals in the 50:50 gender balance pledge, raising awareness and stimulating debate in events and panel discussions, and establishing female role models through Ambassadors and Inspiration Awards (https://keychange.eu).

Moreover, cultural policies are also seeking to increase intersectional diversity and thereby building a more inclusive society, by following the Creative Justice Model of access, diversity, inclusion, equity (Cuyler, 2019). In this regard, J. P. Singh distinguishes between four different international discourses in cultural policies, which operate in the grey area between consensus and conflict. Accordingly, consensus can be reached on a nation-state level either through hierarchical structuring or horizontally via different actors. More conflict-oriented discourses are rather found to stem from social pressures, either by mobilizing discourses of social movements or by counter-discourses of, for example, community projects (Singh, 2019). Can these examples show the way to support intersectional diversity in the global arts and decolonize unequal power structures? We will come back to these and other possibilities to decolonizing global curating and to curating diversity instead of otherness later in the discussion.

## 12.2 The Performativity of Diversity and Otherness—A Cross-Cultural Approach

Let us now turn to the concepts of *cross-cultural diversity and otherness* and examine how these concepts are applied in the field of practice of performance art. To this end, we will focus on the performativity of diversity and otherness, speaking of the practices and strategies of performing diversity and otherness in a cross-cultural way. While the previous section, which was devoted to the representation of intersectional diversity and otherness in the arts, focussed chiefly on individuals or groups, this section will concentrate on the aesthetic art forms, and especially on how artistic practices are performed. These practices are presented as border-crossing and cross-cultural, which means that they are either attributed to no pure genre or origin but are rather global and/or hybrid (Davida, 2011), or that they open up possibilities of in-between-spaces and re-readings of established (b-)ordering practices.

Likewise, these performativities of diversity and otherness can also be called diversity in the arts, aesthetic diversity, or the diversity of cultural expressions, as it has been defined in (e.g.) the 2005 UNESCO Convention on the Protection and Promotion of the Diversity of Cultural Expressions (UNESCO, 2013). According to this convention, the central goal is to increase the visibility of global artistic diversity. Cultural diversity, in the case of the UNESCO convention, strives for no less than worldwide peace, and in the convention one can read that: "Cultural diversity, flourishing within a framework of democracy, tolerance, social justice and mutual respect between peoples and cultures, is indispensable for peace and security at the local, national and international levels" (UNESCO, 2013, p. 3). As I will show, this remains one of the most challenging tasks in global art worlds. The UNESCO convention was founded to oppose the further liberalization of the global market for cultural goods and the market domination of the USA in the 1980s. Connected to these developments are discourses around the potential of cultural expressions for social transformation (Lettau & Knoblich, 2017; Kagan 2011), as well as peace-building activities through cultural policies (UNESCO, 2013; Schneider & Gad, 2014). However, for Singh, these cultural policies led by UNESCO should be criticized as protectionist, as they and further international regulations privilege national identity constructions, which are themselves used by post-colonial interest groups in their fight for indigenous rights (Singh, 2019; Pelillo-Hestermeyer in this volume).

Another example of the contradictory outcomes of cross-cultural agendas is the National Festival for Iranian Folk Music, which I was invited to attend for the purposes of field research in 2017. This festival takes place nationwide, and is organized by the government through the Iranian Music Council. It focuses exclusively on the genre of folk music, but in practice an enormous cross-cultural diversity of instruments, folk music styles, idioms, languages, dress, etc. is found there, which in turn supports national unity based on artistic diversity.

This artistic diversity not only means a variety of aesthetic styles, but can also include intermedial diversity (i.e. the use of different artistic media within one performance; Rajewsky, 2002) or inter-art diversity (i.e. the use of different art genres or the crossing of art genres boundaries within one performance; Bharucha, 2001). As this first kind of intermedial diversity is not the precise focus of this study, we can turn directly to look at inter-art diversity instead. The focus of the empirical study which I carried out lies on the "genre" performance art in general, and specifically on music understood as any kind of sound practice in the broadest sense (Small, 2010). In addition, considering my research focus on diversity, performance art offers a highly appropriate research field, as it includes a diversity of art genres and categories:

> Historically, performance art has been a medium that challenges and violates borders between disciplines and genders, between private and public, between everyday life and art, and that follows no rules. In process, it has energised and affected other disciplines–architecture as event, theatre as image, photography as performance. (Fischer-Lichte & Roselt, 2001, p. 241)

Another, but very similar, approach focuses on the arts in general or art festivals with specific regard to this organizational format. Many curators come to biennales such as the documenta, in order to find "new" artists who are able or willing to cross artistic genres, such as in the case of the visual video artist Wael Shawky, who produced a performance on the theatre stage at the festival Theater der Welt 2017 in Hamburg (http://theaterderwelt2017.iti-germany.de). His stage-setting is a visual piece of art in itself, which is surrounded by and embedded within music, drama and dance elements.

Nevertheless, music is still the focus of my research. For example, I have asked the curators why they would include music in their programme. There are many answers to this question. In most theatre and dance performances the musical layer is extremely prominent by default. This is why music is important to a curator I interviewed. For the purposes of staging pure music concerts, more specialized institutions in town are typically able to complete this task more successfully (Two festival curators, personal communication, May 26, 2015). Another performance art festival was founded as a music festival, and only later did it include more theatre and dance performances into its programme, still retaining a large music programme (Festival curator, personal communication, May 28, 2015). Yet another festival presents a large popular music programme at nights for "socializing" and the "enjoyment" of the audience (Festival curator, personal communication, June 17, 2015). Also in the same city, there is another performing art festival with a focus on contemporary music rather than theatre or dance performances, with the intention of not being a direct competitor of the other performance art festivals or dance festivals which are now established in town (Festival curator, personal communication, June 14, 2015).

As we can see, on the level of inter-art diversity, the practices in performance art seem to foster cross-cultural diversity, as genre barriers become dissolved, and a wide variety of artistic approaches are included in these festivals. However, when looking more closely at the differences between different kinds of genre in the eyes of curators, certain practices of cross-cultural otherness seem to be prevalent. For example, the genre of music[228] is slightly discriminated against when it is described as a "easy to consume" genre, in contrast to a "more intellectually challenging theatre performance". Of course there are many more reasons for such a curational approach, but in sum artistic genre boundaries are dissolved rather than enforced, given the cross-genre approach of performance art in general.

In performance studies a shift to "the global" can be detected, thus situating performance art within the "mobility, transnational and global turns" (see my other contribution in this volume). In other artistic genres, such a focus on "global arts" is also evident. Furthermore, there is an ongoing genre-crossing debate on translation (Apter, 2013), on migratory aesthetics (Durrant, 2007), on the (im-)possibility of defining "an African contemporary dance aesthetic" (Douglas et al., 2006) and on the

---

228 How musical genres are constructed in the first place and how genres serve to stabilise and destabilise communities is the subject of a wide corpus of sociological literature, that can be assigned mainly to the field of sociology of music. See, for example, Lena, 2019.

de-territorialisation of art (Dorn, 2004), which also belongs to the debate about cross-cultural diversity and otherness in the arts.

For instance, in literary studies, debate has recently focussed on the concept of "world literature" in light of globalization (Thomsen, 2008). Introduced by Johann Wolfgang Goethe in 1827, this term is as un-definable and contested as is, for example, "world music", which has been heavily criticized for its Eurocentric notions (Krüger, 2013; Peres da Silva, 2017). For Mads Rosendahl Thomsen, the more recent shift to the "global" highlights the point that it "will always be a world literature as seen from a particular place, even though some aspects are shared" (Rosendahl Thomsen, 2008, p. 1). He therefore looks at the processes of how certain kinds of literature become canonical on an international scale.[229] In this light, "world literature" can never be as universal as the term suggests.

It is with this in mind that Emily Apter and her colleagues focus on the "untranslatability of languages" (Cassin & Apter, 2014). Other scholars give attention to hybrid, transcultural and interweaving forms of literature (Hitzke, 2019) or seek to re-write "European Peripheries in the Postcolonial Literary Imagination" (Hauthal & Toivanen, 2021). Likewise, Ottmar Ette prefers the term "literatures of the world", which acknowledges the "vectorisation of all references"[230] (Ette, 2017, p. 59). One of the research foci of the renowned Leibniz-Zentrum für Literatur- und Kulturforschung in Berlin is also named "world literature", which demonstrates a similar critical approach that takes into account the fact that "world literature refers to the specific global conditions shaping the realm of literature and to the effects globalisation has had on literary production and its reception in a rapidly changing society" (https://www.zfl-berlin.org/world-literature.html). These approaches thus mirror the epistemological development of a cross-cultural view of the diversities and otherness of literature, by focussing on the entanglements of post-colonial writings.

Similarly, in the field of the visual arts, the notion of contemporaneity has been deconstructed (Osborne, 2013; Smith et al., 2009) and unmasked as deeply Eurocentric, on the grounds that it is often set in opposition to "non-Western" art forms, to which certain traits of traditionality are often ascribed (Dornhof et al., 2018; Horst & Schwartz, 2012). In fact, the two sides of cross-cultural diversity and cross-cultural otherness are often present in such approaches at the same time. When, for instance, the othering mechanisms which continue to prevail in art history are sought to be decolonized (Allerstorfer & Leisch-Kiesl, 2017), the movement of deconstructing hegemonic border demarcations shows the notion of cross-cultural otherness at play. When instead the focus lies more on how visual art forms and practices are themselves

---

229 This question is treated by, among others, Buţ (2017) in the field of visual arts, who shows that an international canon has developed which is "too international", excluding a wide variety of cultural expressions.
230 "Vektorisierung aller Bezüge" (Ette, 2017, p. 59).

presented as entangled and cross-cultural (Seliger, 2011), we can speak of strategies of cross-cultural diversity. This means "look[ing] at (global) art from a transcultural perspective that acknowledges the inherent transculturality of artistic practices and artefacts, [along with their] dynamic cross-cultural constellations, migrations and transformations, locations and dislocations" (Buurman et al., 2018, p. 17).

Thus, the focus of the cross-cultural entanglement is also present in visual art scholarship. However,

> in the methodical descriptions of entangled histories, what has remained unanswered is how this entanglement is constituted, who the actors are, on which levels societies, cultures etc. are entangled, and based on which subjects, objects and concepts these stories can be related. (Leeb, 2015, p. 211)

In this connection Susanne Leeb describes how "postcolonial narrations" have influenced art history. According to her, these "increasing approaches toward a transnational art historiography in the past years have made very little impact on the level of museum presentations" (Leeb, 2015, p. 214). What is at stake here is the strong connection of the concept of cross-cultural diversity with intersectional diversity, as discussed above. On the one hand, visual art forms that challenge the Eurocentric meta-narrative by including entangled, transcultural notions are increasingly presented as "entangled-global-but contextual". On the other hand, the quest to decolonize museums, to achieve a greater representation of those cross-cultural art forms and artists from the "Global South" within canonical museums, and to overcome the established divide between "fine arts" and "ethnic culture" is striven for. Museums are increasingly bound to curate "non-Western" artists and postcolonial topics, as well as to call established curatorial practices into question. For instance, the above-mentioned former Museum für Völkerkunde Hamburg (Ethnological museum) has been renamed the MARKK—Museum am Rothenbaum—Kulturen und Künste der Welt (Museum at Rothenbaum—Cultures and Arts of the World) in 2018, under the leadership of its new director, Barbara Plankensteiner, who has started an extensive reform on the aforementioned premises. Together with my co-authors I have shown in another empirical mixed-method study that, while the new self-image of the MARKK has already been implemented, the exhibitions still need further development to ensure that the content reaches visitors (Gaupp et al., 2020). We have also shown how, in the case of different museums and events, e.g. the Venice Biennale, the intended focus on postcolonial issues and the desire for greater representation of Artists of Colour for example, can indeed increase cross-cultural diversity in visual arts. However, the same intention can also lead to intersectional otherness, when only Artists of Colour are curated for those postcolonial topics, whereby they function as tokens without really challenging the structures of unequal representation and power relations.

Furthermore, in the field of music, similar approaches can be detected. The debate on deconstructing "world music" as Eurocentric (Guilbault, 1997), the quest to conceptualize music practices as inherently border-crossing (Peres da Silva & Hondros, 2019; Sardinha & Campos, 2016; Kim & Riva, 2014) and the bid to achieve greater visibility for globally underrepresented musical expressions (Beyer & Burkhalter, 2012; Beyer et al., 2015), by focusing on a "decolonial turn" in (ethno-) musicology[231],can be related to both the practices of cross-cultural diversity and cross-cultural otherness. Again, notions of intersectional diversity and otherness are interwoven with those same practices (Alisch et al., 2018). An example of this would be the web space NORIENT, which wants to act as "an advocate for music scenes from Bolivia to Ghana to Pakistan–and for a world beyond Eurocentrism, exoticism and discrimination" (https://www.startnext.com/en/norient).

Finally, focusing on the more conspicuously genre-crossing field of performance art, similar debates have influenced the theatre sector. The academic narrative has shifted from "intercultural theatre" (Shevtsova, 2009) to "transcultural theatre" (Heeg, 2017) on the level of the theatre texts and performances, i.e. artistic practices. Intersectional otherness in turn is present in many approaches to increase representation, for instance of "immigrant theatre" (Shevtsova, 2009) and the evolvement of the "postmigrant[232] theatre" movement in Berlin (Haakh, 2015; Sharifi, 2011). In 2008, Shermin Langhoff founded the theatre space Ballhaus Naunynstraße in Berlin-Kreuzberg as a "postmigrant theatre" with the intention to avoid focus on ethnic ascriptions and to increase participation of immigrants in the art scene (http://www.ballhausnaunynstrasse.de). Since then, the concept of postmigrant theatre and Langhoff herself has gained an enhanced reputation, for instance by receiving the most highly endowed Kairos Cultural Award in 2011 (Alfred Toepfer Stiftung, n.d.) or by her appointment as artistic director of the prestigious Maxim Gorki Theatre Berlin in 2013 (Maxim Gorki Theatre Berlin, n.d.).

Another prominent approach is the concept of "Interweaving Performance Cultures" (Fischer Lichte et al., 2014). As Fischer-Lichte writes, "[h]ere, moving within and between cultures is celebrated as a state of in-betweenness that will change

---

231 In the years 2019 and 2020, several musicological conferences focus on topics of decoloniality, for instance the research colloquium on "Sound / Music / Decoloniality" at Maynooth University in March 2020, the symposium on "Decolonising of Knowledges" at University of Music and Performing Arts Vienna in May 2019 and the symposium on "Decolonizing Europe through Music Scholarship?" at the International Congress of the German Musicological Society in September 2021 in Bonn.
232 The term "postmigrant" with regard to postmigrant society was coined by Naika Foroutan in 2012 and describes "not a finished process of migration but an analytical perspective that deals with the conflicts, processes of identity formation, and social and political transformation which have started after migration and after the recognition [of Germany] as a country of migration." "Postmigrantisch steht ... nicht für einen Prozess der beendeten Migration, sondern für eine Analyseperspektive, die sich mit den Konflikten, Identitätsbildungsprozessen, sozialen und politischen Transformationen auseinandersetzt, die nach erfolgter Migration und nach der Anerkennung, ein Migrationsland geworden zu sein, einsetzen" (Foroutan, 2016, p. 232).

spaces, disciplines, and the subject as well as her/his body in a way that exceeds what is currently imaginable" (Fischer-Lichte, 2014, p. 12). For this group of scholars, who have conceptualized performances as inherently interweaving, cross-cultural also describes a focus on the (historical) entanglements of drama. By going beyond postcolonial theory and employing concepts such as double criticism (Khatibi, 1985), Khālid Amīn and Mohammed Laamiri seek to find a different way, by asking: "Do we have to consider hybridity as the ultimate and inexorable condition of all postcolonial subjectivities? Or shall we think of it as a road map leading to alternative exchanges?" (Amīn & Laamiri, 2010, p. 7).

The utopian aspects, which are often connected with such a deconstructed meaning of diversity (or, in these cases, named interweaving cultures and hybridity) have to be critically approached. First, the critique towards concepts of cross-cultural diversity, which neglect existing social inequalities and unequal power relations by celebrating and consuming diversity, needs to be taken into account. Such inequalities will not become smaller purely through an increase in the number of interweaving performances. In addition, it needs to be clarified—especially in times when the US government, under the leadership of the President Donald Trump, presents lies as "alternative facts" (Moore, 2017) – what "alternative" means, i.e. alternative to what? (Bachmann-Medick, 2016) The positionality of all these concepts should be laid open in order not to present merely another dichotomy of "the West versus the rest" (Hall, 1994).

What can be summarized at this point is that, in all discussed artistic genres, similar debates have evolved which centre on practices which cross or are intended to cross (dichotomous) borders (genre, national/regional, ethnic, etc.) and foster spaces-in-between instead. Often these quests become entangled with notions of intersectional diversity and otherness, when not only the art practices but also the representation of artists, curators, audiences, etc. come into focus. Last but not least, such cross-cultural, border-crossing practices can at the same time construct new orders, which might be themselves declared as universal or result in other exclusionary practices again.

> Focusing on the transcultural topologies of global art thus permits the study of relational processes of circulation and exchange while also calling into question the idea of ethno-cultural locality as a nostalgic marker of authenticity as well as celebrations of multicultural plurality that disregard ongoing inequalities in capitalist and (neo-)colonial power relations. (Buurman et al., 2018, p. 18)

Thus, when we look at practices of cross-cultural diversity and otherness in the arts, the arts are either conceptualized as "global" and border-crossing or as situational, so as to require some kind of translation in order to foster inclusivity on a global scale (Apter, 2013; Dätsch, 2018; Charle et al., 2017; Klein, 2013). While the former approach relies on a concept of culture which is conceived as transcultural and dynamic per se, lacking in any pure origin (Stroh, 2005), the latter negates the fact that the arts can function as a "global language" (Binas-Preisendörfer, 2008), which is understandable globally, though differently appropriated. It rather follows a concept of culture which sets culture as socially transmitted, internalized, situationally performed (Dorn, 2004) and understandable only to members of a specific art world (Becker, 2008) or cultural field (Bourdieu, 1993).

These two opposing regimes have been pointedly summarized by Grace Brockington in relation to a dispute between Selwyn Image and Lewis F. Day at the beginning of the 20th century (Brockington, 2009). While for Image, art is locally or nationally embedded, it is "particular. Far from being a universal language, it is locally produced and historically conditioned, the individual expression of an artist, or ... of a nation" (Brockington, 2009, p. 1). It cannot fully be translated (Gaupp, 2018). However, Brockington states how Day takes the opposite view and rather tends towards the concept of cosmopolitan artists. "National traditions are innate but not homogeneous and do not need to be 'coddled.' The English are a 'mixed lot', a hybrid race, practicing a hybrid art" (Brockington, 2009, p. 2). In this dichotomy of conceptualizing cultural expressions, both cross-cultural diversity and otherness can be detected. While the particular, situational view on the diversity of artistic expressions can be related to the narrative of cross-cultural otherness, the latter concept, which portrays the arts as hybrid and cosmopolitan, can be described as an approach to cross-cultural diversity. Nevertheless, this debate is mainly situated on the level of narratives, while in this contribution we intend to look at how these concepts are applied in the field of practice.

Here, the picture becomes even more complicated and blurred. The majority of artists whom I spoke to conceptualize their artistic practices as transcultural rather than as connected to a certain geographic region (Two artists, personal communication, May 5, 2015). Art and diversity both appear to be a dynamic process that cannot be defined in any a priori sense. Their artistic practices are characterized by crossing borders, by connecting to many people with many world-views, thus producing seemingly perfect cross-cultural practices. For instance, the art space in Berlin and founded in 2009 by Bonaventure Soh Bejeng Ndikung "S A V V Y Contemporary, situates itself at the threshold of notions and constructs of the West and non-West, in order to understand and negotiate between, and thereby deconstruct, the ideologies and connotations eminent to such constructs" (SAVVY Contemporary, p. 1). Another example in performance art which seeks to decolonize the art field and thereby increase both intersectional and cross-cultural diversity is the Migrantpolitan at Kampnagel in Hamburg, which curated by among others Anas Aboura. Kampnagel describes this as:

> a campaigning space ... where diasporic and local artists enter into a process of exchange, develop joint transcultural strategies, and test out new forms of aesthetic praxis. This micro-cosmos is a laboratory for collaboration under conditions of solidarity, where new ideas can

be developed, where cultural self-determination has a home, and where a pinch of anarchy is always part of the mix. (Kampnagel, 2019)

For some artists themselves as well as audiences and curators, these and other practices of performing cross-cultural diversity are evident. Sociological research in the arts has shown extensively how interpretation is an individual and intrinsically social matter (Abbing, 2019). This means that the interpretation of symbolic meanings which are ascribed to certain artistic expressions by the artists themselves might not necessarily perceived in the same manner by the audiences. For instance, an artist whom I interviewed described himself as cosmopolitan (Artist, personal communication, January 9, 2015), while the same artist was labelled a "typically Middle-Eastern artist" by a curator (Curator, personal communication, January 22, 2015). Marketing experts, media representatives and audience members also have different approaches in how to present and perceive this artist(ic expression) (Festival curator, personal communication, May 28, 2015). As a result, transcultural or cross-cultural art forms do not exist per se—or, any artistic practice would need to be called cross-cultural, assuming the arts' dynamic and processual character. But certainly, an artist or art form can be constructed and perceived as cross-cultural. It may rather be only that this construction has less to do with the actual artistic content than with its situational use.

This situational semantics offers two different perspectives in how to curate diversity and otherness. The first is to acknowledge that labelling is a dynamic and thus influenceable, changeable process, and certain wording and concepts can be used strategically and/or negotiated every time anew. "Performance is … the joint execution in a (specific) situation. … It is not to be determined and not to be understood, (the execution is only) at the moment"[233] (Jansen, personal communication, October 17, 2018).

The second reading relates to an analysis of power inequalities in these negotiation processes. Those with more power have greater opportunities for defining the norm, and for standardizing certain interpretations over others. This leads us to the overarching question of how to decolonize the field of performance art without essentializing just another hegemonic norm. This will be discussed in the next section.

---

[233] "Performance ist … der gemeinsame Vollzug in der Situation. … Der ist nicht zu determinieren, und der ist nicht zu verstehen, der ist im Moment" (Jansen, personal communication, October 17, 2018).

## 12.3 How to Curate Diversity and Otherness—The Decolonization of Curating

As I have pointed out in my other chapter on epistemologies, the quest to decolonize is called for in several life-worlds and can be traced back to the political decolonization and liberation processes in the 1950s, which spurred the academic stream of postcolonial thinking. This stream of thinking called not only for political liberation from colonial structures but also wider cultural and epistemic decolonization. Transferred to the present day, this task continues to be relevant, as dichotomies in thinking persist. I have mentioned several de-constructivist, decolonial theoretical approaches in the study of culture, which seek to de-stabilise and re-think established ascriptions and borders. Also in today's fields of practice, decolonization appears not yet to be completely fulfilled. In this case, I have summarized as decolonization any fight for liberation from any unequal power structures, which need not necessarily be grounded in the colonial era. However, in general, unequal power structures on a global scale cannot be separated from their colonial legacies due to their entanglement with neoliberal capitalistic structures, which could only expand as such through colonialism (Dussel, 1998).

To achieve decolonization, I have also mentioned several theoretical approaches such as organizing networks (Mbembe, 2016, p. 37) or taking into account decolonial feminist-queer southern epistemologies and new subjectivities (Gutiérrez Rodriguez, 2016). In my chapter here, William Jamal Richardson's call for action, and for intervening in "physical spaces" (2018, p. 232) rather than only in debates, comes into focus. How should we decolonize the global arts in practise? While discussing this question, I also reflect upon my own positionality, as well as on what Eve Tuck and K. Wayne Yang call the risk of using the term decolonization as a mere metaphor (Tuck & Yang, 2012).

How can I write about issues of racism, inequality and decolonization as a White, heterosexual, privileged person from the "Global North"? Is this only appropriation, talking "about" and not "with" and/or the intention to white-wash myself from not really doing anything against inequalities and the collective guilt of colonialism? After all, knowledge production is always influenced by political interests (Richardson, 2018).

> What does it mean when the tools of a racist patriarchy are used to examine the fruits of that same patriarchy? It means that only the most narrow perimeters of change are possible and allowable. ... For the master's tool will never dismantle the master's house. (Lorde, 1984, pp. 110–114)

Audre Lorde criticizes how members of different minorities are merely used as tokens and reveals how White feminists are deeply racist.[234] She also suggests how to work against these mechanisms, by urging everyone to "reach down into that deep place of knowledge inside herself and touch that terror and loathing of any difference that lives there. See whose face it wears" (Lorde, 1984, p. 114). Lorde appears to call not only to a process of honest self-reflection, but she also incorporates another notion of diversity and otherness, one that could be called a combination of intersectional with cross-cultural otherness. For her, *differences* should be acknowledged, as by shedding difference, no real community can develop. "Difference must be not merely tolerated, but seen as a fund of necessary polarities between which our creativity can spark like a dialectic" (Lorde, 1984, p. 110). In most of the literature which is discussed in my two chapters in this book, diversity is framed positively and connected to inclusionary narratives, while otherness is rather related to processes of exclusion. Lorde, however, offers a perspective that turns these approaches around. It is exactly the intersectional difference that should be made productive for fostering inclusion, decolonizing the racist patriarchy, and recognizing "difference as a crucial strength" (Lorde, 1984, p. 111). Likewise, real cooperation can form that might meet up with the emancipatory quest that cross-cultural otherness seeks.

In other research, Rosalba Icaza and Rolando Vázquez have inquired into how the combination of intersectional with decolonial frameworks can offer an application of a perspective similar to Lorde's at the University of Amsterdam (Icaza & Vázquez, 2018). They show how positionality, relationality and transitionality can support decolonizing in the university. "Practices of positionality ..., even while teaching the canon, reveal the geopolitical location of knowledge. ... Relationality ... includes a transformation of the relationships established in the classroom and across the university" (p. 119–120), by rendering valuable differences. Last but not least, "the question of transition points towards the need for the university to actively address its own societal and ecological implications by enabling the students to bridge the epistemic border between the classroom and society" (p. 120). Thus, we see three levels of possible action for decolonizing knowledge. Always reflect upon the position of knowledge, come to view differences as strength, and not only theorize but also act. Let us see later whether this approach could help decolonize the global arts–which can be taken as forms of knowledge production (Hall, 1981).

Tuck and Yang also call for action rather than only speaking, writing and reflecting about inequalities. When decolonization is misused as no more than a metaphor, it is in danger of serving only the settlers, colonialists (and their ancestors today) as "moves to innocence" (Tuck & Yang, 2012, p. 3). Instead of using decolonization as a metaphor for any fight of social justice, for these scholars it should mean above all

---

234  bell hooks is another renowned scholar who addresses similar issues (hooks, 1995).

repatriating the land from the colonizers to the colonized. In this case, those involved are the settlers to the First Nation People in the USA.

> Decolonisation in the settler colonial context must involve the repatriation of land simultaneous to the recognition of how land and relations to land have always already been differently understood and enacted; that is, all of the land, and not just symbolically. This is precisely why decolonisation is necessarily unsettling, especially across lines of solidarity. (Tuck & Yang, 2012, p. 7)

Even though I would not agree to use the term exclusively with regard to the US American context, what is important in Tuck's and Yang's approach is not only their unveiling of colonial legacies and various strategies to innocence, but for them, the fact that "decolonization is not an 'and'. It is an elsewhere" (p. 36). "Opportunities for solidarity lie in what is incommensurable rather than what is common" (p. 28). Thus, first, we need a diversity of decolonization practices. Secondly, as Lorde has described it, solidary cooperation arises in the bridges which are forged between people and communities, not in the commonalities. As I have discussed in my other chapter, Bruno Latour writes to make traceable all dynamic associations (Latour, 2010). This again relates to the transcultural approach of this volume, which oscillates between the negotiations and standardizations of differences and their transcultural practices, which in turn go beyond these (b-)ordering differences.

Several authors also present suggestions of how to decolonize the arts through implementing anti-racist (Bayer & Terkessidis, 2017), decolonial (Caceres et al., 2017) or transcultural (Bhagwati, 2018; Lutz, 2018; von Osten, 2012) practices of curating. Besides the intersectional and cross-cultural strategies I have discussed for the avoidance of exclusion, fostering of representation and participation of underrepresented people and the increased visibility of minority perspectives within the arts sector, enabling reflection on hegemonic narratives and social inequalities, these curatorial approaches focus again on different aspects of joint cooperation (Sennett, 2012; Richter, 2012), polyphony (Bempeza et al., 2019), collectives (von Bismarck, 2012), social cohesion and conviviality (Heil, 2020; Espahangizi in this volume).

These partially activist debates and practical approaches emphasize both modes of solidarity and complicity as well as notions of conflict, complication and disruption (Dobusch et al., 2020). This means that any decolonial cooperation on a day-to-day level will inevitably involve conflict and disruption in order to foster new ways of doing things. "The moment of innovation is constituted here as conflictual permeation that initiates processes of hybridisation" (Büscher-Ulbrich et al., 2013, p. 17). This is what is meant by a transcultural way of inclusion, that involves critique and conflict as a major driving force.

A postcolonially oriented research agenda such as the one I propose seeks to dismantle all these different power-laden processes, by including many views through co-operation on an equal footing. This means that the terms and concepts with which we all operate in practice as well as in academia also need to be decolonized. I would instead suggest that we consider, research, teach and curate diversity as transcultural diversity. Lorenzo Ornaghi would probably speak of "glocal diversity", a "contamination" that exercises a genuinely "glocal power" beyond domestic and international politics (Ornaghi, 2017, p. 8). By transcultural diversity, I mean to underline that diversity cannot be fixed and defined. Instead, it is constructed and reconstructed or deconstructed every time by every curator, artist, cultural administrator or manager, student, audience, researcher, etc. Just as Ernesto Laclau and Chantal Mouffe have pled against apriorism (Laclau & Mouffe, 2012), in every situation it is possible to construct a new way of thinking and acting.

> The potential of the proposed transcultural perspective on global art that takes into account not only the global (and globalising) conditions of production but also specific localities is that it allows scholars to grasp cross-cultural connections, interactions as well as marginalised forms of knowledge and agency that are otherwise often overlooked or underestimated in their critical force. (Buurman et al., 2018, p. 18)

As the Cultural capabilities model–which is based on the capabilities approach of Martha Nussbaum and Amartya Sen–aims at fostering conditions of cultural opportunity in order to co-create versions of culture, in order to extend cultural democracy, this would mean including both top-down and bottom-up approaches as well as both global and local approaches. "It is only when 'substantive freedom' is realized in relation to culture–real, concrete freedoms to choose what culture to make, as well as what culture to appreciate–that people are genuinely empowered in their cultural lives" (Wilson et al., 2017, p. 5; Nussbaum, 2011; Sen, 2001).

By developing new approaches together with different partners, the study of culture can give valuable stimuli to discover new terms, concepts, cooperation forms, funding schemes, etc. for glocal spaces, without the claim of having either global or national effect. Nevertheless, it allows for more pluralistic voices and views to be taken into account, as J.P. Singh has suggested, and for the established thinking of a hierarchy of needs to transform into thinking about networks of possibilities (Singh, 2019).

Such transcultural insights into curating diversity and otherness also entails that we cannot answer the question of how to curate diversity and otherness, as the answer will always be bound to a radical diversity of possibilities and is never able to aim at universalism. However, we can instead learn from practice by looking at examples of how to decolonize the arts in general or the global performance arts more specifically. For this approach, we have learnt that it is important to expose unequal power structures as well as to overcome dichotomies in our own individual and collective thinking. However, this needs to go a lot farther still. In the arts, dichotomies in thinking are not only present regarding (e.g.) the border drawn between "Western" and "non-Western" art and artists. Dichotomies also target the way that things are expected to be done. For instance, in the German cultural sector, results are mainly measured through financial means, success, and evaluation. Artists and audiences are separated and performances are organized and scheduled. However, in different contexts, not even the division between different artistic genres necessarily exists. (Jansen, personal communication, October 17, 2018) What is needed then to overcome these and other dichotomies, is to "always stay in contact. First of all to ask the person, from which position are you speaking to me? What is my position? This negotiation has to start in the first second [of meeting each other]"[235] (Jansen, personal communication, October 17, 2018). Thus, cooperation on eye-level, decolonial curating and practices of transcultural diversity involve questioning all presuppositions and acknowledging other knowledge systems, concepts of art, practices of cultural expressions. But this must not necessarily lead to or hinder conflict. On the contrary, it is really a process of negotiations, of "situational practices, no determined categories"[236] (Jansen, personal communication, October 17, 2018).

Some Goethe Institutes in African countries now follow an approach of putting the power into the hands of local artists and not only collaborating with them, but letting them decide what and how to curate, and how to organize the cooperation by deciding on the use of these Goethe funds. An important factor for successful cooperation is transparency about decisions, finances, concepts, etc. Everyone involved should have the opportunity to partake in every process. But the desire to "always make everything right [leads to] forgetting to just talk with the people. ... One is permanently in discourse, but actually never really in contact"[237] (Jansen, personal communication, October 17, 2018). So the question remains, "[W]here can we meet?"[238] (Jansen, personal communication, October 17, 2018). This is again not to be answered generally, but needs to be negotiated every time anew. Curators understood in the etymological sense of the term as "carers" should "stop working with signs and stop representing, but should work rather with presence than with absence"[239] (Jansen, personal communication, October 17, 2018). Only in such situational practices of relations, can curating diversity and otherness as neo-colonial be overcome and can it transform practices of representation. "It is not about the structure, it is about the

---

235 "immer in Kontakt bleiben. Erst einmal die Person fragen, von welcher Position aus sprichst du mit mir? Was ist meine Position? Die Verhandlung muss in der ersten Sekunde anfangen" (Jansen, personal communication, October 17, 2018).

236 "situative Praktiken, keine festgelegten Kategorien" (Jansen, personal communication, October 17, 2018).

237 "immer alles richtig machen zu wollen – und dabei zu vergessen mit den Leuten eigentlich selbst zu reden. ... man ist die ganze Zeit, permanent im Diskurs und ist eigentlich nie in Kontakt" (Jansen, personal communication, October 17, 2018).

238 "Wo können wir uns treffen?" (Jansen, personal communication, October 17, 2018).

239 "aufhören, mit Zeichen zu arbeiten und zu repräsentieren, sondern mit der Anwesenheit, nicht in der Abwesenheit" (Jansen, personal communication, October 17, 2018).

relation. It is about the agency"[240] (Jansen, personal communication, October 17, 2018). Such an approach could be "the product of communication beyond space and time, beyond territorial boundaries. It questions out-dated ideas of culture, identity and community" (Burkhalter, 2012, p. 30), and can lead to a transcultural understanding of diversity and otherness as a way of decolonizing curating in global performance art.

# References

Abbing, H. (2019). The Changing Social Economy of Art: Are the Arts Becoming Less Exclusive? (1st ed. 2019). Palgrave Macmillan. https://doi.org/10.1007/978-3-030-21668-9

Ahmed, S. (2012). On Being Included: Racism and Diversity in Institutional Life. e-Duke books scholarly collection. Duke University Press. http://lib.myilibrary.com?id=366424

Alfred Toepfer Stiftung (n.d.). Kairos-Preis 2011: Shermin Langhoff. Retrieved November 24, 2019, from https://www.toepfer-stiftung.de/kairos-preis-2/kairos-preis-2011/

Alisch, S., Binas-Preisendörfer, S., & Jauk, W. (Eds.). (2018). Darüber hinaus … Populäre Musik und Überschreitung(en): 2. Iaspm D-A-CH Konferenz/Graz 2016. BIS-Verlag der Carl von Ossietzky Universität.

Allerstorfer, J., & Leisch-Kiesl, M. (Eds.). (2017). Linzer Beiträge zur Kunstwissenschaft und Philosophie: Band 8. "Global Art History": Transkulturelle Verortungen von Kunst und Kunstwissenschaft. transcript.

Amīn, K. (2014). Postcolonial Modernity: Theatre in Morocco and the Interweaving Loop. In E. Fischer-Lichte, T. Jost, & S. I. Jain (Eds.), Routledge Advances in Theatre and Performance Studies: Vol. 33. The politics of interweaving performance cultures: Beyond postcolonialism (pp. 25–41). Routledge.

Amīn, K., & Laamiri, M. (2010). Performing cultural diversity: Critiquing postcolonialism (1st ed). Series: Conderences and colloquia. Université Abdelmalek Essaâdi, Faculty of Letters and Humanities, Research Group of Performance Studies.

Angermüller, J., & Bellina, L. (2012). Poststrukturalismus und Postkolonialismus: Jacques Derridas "Grammatologie" sowie Gilles Deleuzes und Félix Guattaris "Tausend Plateaus". In J. Reuter & A. Karentzos (Eds.), Schlüsselwerke der Postcolonial Studies (Vol. 20, pp. 27–37). VS Verlag für Sozialwissenschaften. https://doi.org/10.1007/978-3-531-93453-2_2

Apter, E. S. (2013). Against world literature: On the politics of untranslatability. Verso.

Archer, M. S. (2005). Structure, Culture and Agency. In M. D. Jacobs & N. Weiss Hanrahan (Eds.), The Blackwell Companion to the Sociology of Culture (pp. 17–34). Blackwell Publ.

Austin, J. L. (2014). Zur Theorie der Sprechakte: = (How to do things with words) ([Nachdr.], bibliogr. erg. Ausg). Reclams Universal-Bibliothek: Nr. 9396. Reclam.

Bachmann-Medick, D. (Ed.). (2016). The trans/national study of culture: A translational perspective. De Gruyter.

Bayer, N., & Terkessidis, M. (2017). Über das Reparieren hinaus: Eine antirassistische Praxeologie des Kuratierens. In N. Bayer, B. Kazeem-Kamiński, & N. Sternfeld (Eds.), Edition Angewandte. Kuratieren als antirassistische Praxis (pp. 53–70). De Gruyter.

---

240 "Es geht nicht um die Struktur. Es geht um die Beziehung. Um die Handlungsmacht" (Jansen, personal communication, October 17, 2018).

Becker, H. S. (2008). Art worlds. University of California Press.

Behnke, C., Kastelan, C., Knoll, V., & Wuggenig, U. (Eds.). (2015). Art in the periphery of the center. Sternberg Press.

Below, I., & Bismarck, B. von (Eds.). (2005). Schriftenreihe des Ulmer Vereins, Verband für Kunst- und Kulturwissenschaften e.V: N.F., Bd. 1. Globalisierung, Hierarchisierung: Kulturelle Dominanzen in Kunst und Kunstgeschichte. Jonas-Verl.

Bempeza, S., Brunner, C., Hausladen, K., Kleesattel, I., & Sonderegger, R. (Eds.). (2019). Polyphone Ästhetik: Eine kritische Situierung. transversal texts.

Benzer, S. (Ed.). (2016). Kultur für alle: Gespräche über Verteilungsgerechtigkeit und Demokratie in Kunst und Kultur heute ([1. Auflage]). Folio Verlag.

Beyer, T., & Burkhalter, T. (Eds.). (2012). Out of the absurdity of life: Globale Musik (1. Aufl.). Traversion.

Beyer, T., Burkhalter, T., & Liechti, H. (Eds.). (2015). Seismographic sounds: Visions of a new world (1. edition). Norient.

Bhagwati, A. (2018). Of Maps, Nodes and Trajectories: Changing Topologies in Transcultural Curating. In S. Dornhof, N. Buurman, B. Hopfener, & B. Lutz (Eds.), Image: Vol. 89. Situating Global Art: Topologies - Temporalities - Trajectories (pp. 191–211). transcript.

Bhambra, G. K., Gebrial, D., & Nişancıoğlu, K. (Eds.). (2018). Decolonising the university. Pluto Press.

Bharucha, R. (2001). The politics of cultural practice: Thinking through theatre in an age of globalization. Oxford Univ. Press.

Bial, H. (Ed.). (2004). The performance studies reader. Routledge. http://catdir.loc.gov/catdir/enhancements/fy0650/2003005708-d.html

Binas-Preisendörfer, S. (2008). Musik – eine Weltsprache? Befunde und Vorschläge zur Dekonstruktion eines Mythos. In E. Schwind & O. Senn (Eds.), Musik - Wahrnehmung - Sprache: Eine Publikation der Musikhochschule Luzern (pp. 163–173). Chronos. https://uol.de/fileadmin/user_upload/musik-medien/Medien/Susanne-Binas-Preisendoerfer_Musik-eine-Weltsprache_2008.pdf

Bishop, S. (2018, May 23). With calls for more diversity in music festivals, is Forecastle doing enough? Leo Weekly Online. https://www.leoweekly.com/2018/05/forecastle-enough

Bismarck, B. v. (2012). The Exhibition as Collective. In B. v. Bismarck, J. Schafaff, & T. Weski (Eds.), Cultures of the curatorial: [... Based on the Conference "Cultures of the Curatorial" at the Hochschule für Grafik und Buchkunst Academy of Visual Arts Leipzig, January 22 - 24, 2010] (pp. 289–302). Sternberg Pr.

Bourdieu, P. (1978). Entwurf einer Theorie der Praxis auf der ethnologischen Grundlage der kabylischen Gesellschaft (1. Aufl.). Suhrkamp.

Bourdieu, P. (1993). The field of cultural production: Essays on art and literature. European perspectives. Columbia University Press.

Brockington, G. (2009). Introduction: Internationalism and the Arts. In G. Brockington (Ed.), Cultural interactions: vol. 4. Internationalism and the arts in Britain and Europe at the fin de siècle (pp. 1–24). P. Lang.

Buchholz, L., & Wuggenig, U. (2005). Cultural Globalization Between Myth and Reality: The Case of the Contemporary Visual Arts. ART-E-FACT Strategies of Resistance (4). http://artefact.mi2.hr/_a04/lang_en/theory_buchholz_en.htm

Buchholz, L., & Wuggenig, U. (2012). Kunst und Globalisierung. In H. Munder & U. Wuggenig (Eds.), Das Kunstfeld: Eine Studie über Akteure und Institutionen der zeitgenössischen Kunst am Beispiel von Zürich, Wien, Hamburg und Paris (pp. 163–188). JRP/Ringier.

Buden, B. (2012). Towards the Heterosphere: Curator as Translator. In M. Lind (Ed.), Performing the curatorial: Within and beyond art (pp. 23–46). Sternberg Press.

Burkhalter, T. (2012). Weltmusik 2.0: Musikalische Positionen zwischen Spass- und Protestkultur. In T. Beyer & T. Burkhalter (Eds.), Out of the absurdity of life: Globale Musik (1st ed., pp. 28–47). Traversion. https://norient-beta.com/academic/weltmusik2-0/

Büscher-Ulbrich, D., Kadenbach, S., & Kindermann, M. (2013). Einleitung: »The More Things Change«. In D. Büscher-Ulbrich, S. Kadenbach, & M. Kindermann (Eds.), Kultur- und Medientheorie. Innovation - Konvention: Transdisziplinäre Beiträge zu einem kulturellen Spannungsfeld (pp. 7–20). transcript.

Buț, G. (2017, August 31). Internationalisation as the (Invisible) Curated Object. European Sociological Association. 13th Conference of the European Sociological Association. (Un) Making Europe: Capitalism, Solidarities, Subjectivities, Athens.

Butler, J. (2013). Excitable Speech: A Politics of the Performative. Taylor and Francis.

Buurman, N., Dornhof, S., Hopfener, B., & Lutz, B. (2018). Situating Global Art: An Introduction. In S. Dornhof, N. Buurman, B. Hopfener, & B. Lutz (Eds.), Image: Vol. 89. Situating Global Art: Topologies - Temporalities - Trajectories (pp. 11–32). transcript.

Caceres, I., Mesquita, S., & Utikal, S. (2017). Anti*Colonial Fantasies/ Decolonial Strategies: A Conversation. In N. Bayer, B. Kazeem-Kamiński, & N. Sternfeld (Eds.), Edition Angewandte. Kuratieren als antirassistische Praxis (pp. 201–211). De Gruyter.

Cañas, T. (2017). Diversity is a white word: The superficial scramble for cultural diversity is not addressing the deep causes of exclusion and the power imbalance in the arts. https://www.artshub.com.au/education/news-article/opinions-and-analysis/professional-development/tania-canas/diversity-is-a-white-word-252910

Cassin, B., & Apter, E. S. (Eds.). (2014). Translation / transnation. Dictionary of untranslatables: A philosophical lexicon (S. Rendall, Trans.). Princeton University Press. https://www.jstor.org/stable/j.ctt5hhntn https://doi.org/10.2307/j.ctt5hhntn

Charle, C., Lüsebrink, H. J., & Mix, Y. G. (Eds.). (2017). Deutschland und Frankreich im wissenschaftlichen Dialog / Le dialogue scientifique franco-allemand: Volume 6. Transkulturalität nationaler Räume in Europa (18. bis 19. Jahrhundert): Übersetzungen, Kulturtransfer und Vermittlungsinstanzen = La transculturalité des espaces nationaux en Europe (XVIIIe-XIXe siècles); traductions, transferts culturels et instances de médiations (1. Auflage). V&R Unipress. https://www.vr-elibrary.de/isbn/9783847104797 https://doi.org/10.14220/9783737004794

Cuyler, A. (2019). The Role of Foundations in Achieving Creative Justice. GIA Reader, 30 (1), Article 6. https://www.giarts.org/role-foundations-achieving-creative-justice

Dätsch, C. (Ed.). (2018). Edition Kulturwissenschaft: Band 103. Kulturelle Übersetzer: Kunst und Kulturmanagement im transkulturellen Kontext. https://doi.org/10.14361/9783839434994

Davida, D. (Ed.). (2011). Fields in motion: Ethnography in the worlds of dance. Wilfrid Laurier University Press. http://lib.myilibrary.com/detail.asp?id=380988

Davida, D., Pronovost, M., Hudon, V., & Gabriels, J. (Eds.). (2019). Curating Live Arts: Global Perspectives on Theory and Practice. Berghahn Books Incorporated.

Di Blasi, J. (2019). Das Humboldt Lab: Museumsexperimente zwischen postkolonialer Revision und szenografischer Wende. transcript. https://doi.org/10.14361/9783839449202

Do Mar Castro Varela, María, & Haghighat, L. (Eds.). (2020). Double Bind postkolonial: Kritische Perspektiven auf Kunst und Kulturelle Bildung. Transcipt Verlag.

Dobusch, L., Kreissl, K., & Wacker, E. (Eds.). (2020). Diversitätsforschung: Von der Rekonstruktion zur Disruption [Special issue]. ZDfm – Zeitschrift für Diversitätsforschung und -Management, 5(1). Leverkusen-Opladen. Barbara Budrich.

Dorn, C. (2004). The Deterritorialization of Art. The Journal of Arts Management, Law, and Society, 34(2), 141–150. https://doi.org/10.3200/JAML.34.2.141-150

Dornhof, S., Buurman, N., Hopfener, B., & Lutz, B. (Eds.). (2018). Image: v.89. Situating Global Art: Topologies - Temporalities - Trajectories (1st ed.). transcript.

Douglas, G., Sichel, A., Liadi, A. M., Noël, K., Danster, R., Cuvilas, A., & Linyekula, F. (2006). Under Fire: Defining a contemporary African dance aesthetic - can it be done? Critical Arts, 20(2), 102–115. https://doi.org/10.1080/02560040608540458

Dovey, L. (2015). Curating Africa in the Age of Film Festivals. Framing Film Festivals. Palgrave Macmillan.

Durrant, S. (Ed.). (2007). Thamyris, intersecting: Vol. 17. Essays in migratory aesthetics: Cultural practices between migration and art-making. Rodopi.

Durrer, V., & Henze, R. (Eds.). (2020). Managing Culture: Reflecting on Exchange in Global Times. Sociology of the Arts. Palgrave Macmillan. https://doi.org/10.1007/978-3-030-24646-4

Dussel, E. (1998). Beyond eurocentrism: The world-system and the limits of modernity. In F. Jameson & M. Miyoshi (Eds.), The cultures of globalization (pp. 3–31). Duke Univ. Press.

Enwezor, O. (2002). Demokratie als unvollendeter Prozess: Documenta 11, Plattform 1; [dieser Band enthält alle Beiträge der Documenta 11 - Plattform 1 "Demokratie als Unvollendeter Prozess", einer Reihe von Konferenzen und Vorträgen in Wien, Akademie der Bildenden Künste, 15. März - 20. April 2001, und in Berlin, Haus der Kulturen der Welt, 9. - 30. Oktober 2001.] Hatje Cantz.

Eremjan, I. (2016). Transkulturelle Kunstvermittlung: Zum Bildungsgehalt ästhetisch-künstlerischer Praxen. Pädagogik. transcript.

Ette, O. (2017). WeltFraktale: Wege durch die Literaturen der Welt. J.B. Metzler.

Fischer-Lichte, E. (2004). Ästhetik des Performativen (Orig.-Ausg., 1. Aufl.). Edition suhrkamp: Vol. 2373. Suhrkamp.

Fischer-Lichte, E. (2014). Introduction: Interweaving performance cultures; rethinking "intercultural theatre"; toward an experience and theory of performance beyond postcolonialism. In E. Fischer-Lichte, T. Jost, & S. I. Jain (Eds.), Routledge Advances in Theatre and Performance Studies: Vol. 33. The politics of interweaving performance cultures: Beyond postcolonialism (pp. 1–21). Routledge.

Fischer-Lichte, E., & Roselt, J. (2001). Attraktion des Augenblicks: Aufführung, Performance, performativ und Performativität als theaterwissenschaftliche Begriffe. Theorien des Performativen, 237–253.

Fischer-Lichte, E., Jost, T., & Jain, S. I. (Eds.). (2014). Routledge Advances in Theatre and Performance Studies: Vol. 33. The politics of interweaving performance cultures: Beyond postcolonialism. Routledge.

Foroutan, N. (2012). Neue Deutsche, Postmigranten und Bindungs-Identitäten: Wer gehört zum neuen Deutschland? In J. Manemann & W. Schreer (Eds.), Quellen und Studien zur Geschichte und Kunst im Bistum Hildesheim: Vol. 6. Religion und Migration heute: Perspektiven - Positionen - Projekte; [Norbert Trelle, Bischof von Hildesheim, zum 70. Geburtstag] (1st ed., pp. 111–121). Schnell + Steiner.

Foroutan, N. (2016). Postmigrantische Gesellschaften. In H. U. Brinkmann & M. Sauer (Eds.), Einwanderungsgesellschaft Deutschland: Entwicklung und Stand der Integration (pp. 227–254). Springer VS.

Gaupp, L. (2016). Die exotisierte Stadt: Kulturpolitik und Musikvermittlung im postmigrantischen Prozess. Studies in Music: Vol. 1. Olms. https://hildok.bsz-bw.de/frontdoor/index/index/docId/547

Gaupp, L. (2018). Symbolische Räume kultureller Diversität: Verhandlungen, Grenzen und Überschreitungen in den performativen Künsten. In M. Nies (Ed.), Schriften zur Kultur- und Mediensemiotik Online: Vol. 4. Raumsemiotik: Räume – Grenzen – Identitäten (pp. 241–259). Virtuelles Zentrum für kultursemiotische Forschung.

Gaupp, L. (2020). The 'West' versus 'the Rest'? Festival Curators as Gatekeepers for Sociocultural Diversity. In V. Durrer & R. Henze (Eds.), Managing Culture: Reflecting on Exchange in Global Times. Sociology of the Arts. Palgrave Macmillan.

Gaupp, L., Abramjan, A., Akinay, F. M., Hilgert, K., Mulder, A. C., Schmidt, R., Schnitzler, V., Thurich, O., Tiemon, L., & Wurl, S. (2020). Curatorial practices of the "Global": Toward a Decolonial Turn in the Museum in Berlin and Hamburg? Journal of Cultural Management and Cultural Policy, Special Issue: Museum – Politics – Management. 2020(2), 107–138.

Gaupp, L., Barber-Kersovan, A., & Kirchberg, V. (Eds.). (2021). Arts and Power: Policies in and by the Arts. Serie Kunst und Gesellschaft. Springer VS.

Goodman, L., & DeGay, J. (Eds.). (2000). Performance Studies. The Routledge reader in politics and performance.

Guilbault, J. (1997). Interpreting World Music: A Challenge in Theory and Practice. Popular Music, 16(1), 31–44.

Gutiérrez Rodriguez, E. (2016). Decolonizing Postcolonial Rhetoric. In E. Gutiérrez Rodriguez, M. Boatcă, & S. Costa (Eds.), Global connections. Decolonizing European sociology: Transdisciplinary approaches (pp. 49–67). Routledge Taylor & Francis Group.

Haakh, N. (2015). Muslimisierte Körper auf der Bühne: Die Islamdebatte im postmigrantischen Theater. transcript.

Haberkorn, S. (2010). Neues Publikum für Kunst und Kultur gewinnen? Eine empirische Untersuchung zum Audience Development am Beispiel des Festivals der Kulturen MELEZ. VDM Verlag Dr. Müller.

Hall, S. (1981). The Whites of their Eyes: Racist Ideologies and the Media. In G. Bridges & R. Brunt (Eds.), Contributions to the Communist University of London. Silver Linings: Some strategies for the eighties (pp. 28–52). Lawrence & Wishart.

Hall, S. (1994). The West and the Rest: Discourse and Power. In S. Hall & B. Gieben (Eds.), The Formations of Modernity: (Introduction to Sociology) (pp. 275–331). Polity Press.

Hauthal, J., & Toivanen, A. L. (Eds.). (2021). European Peripheries in the Postcolonial Literary Imagination [Special issue]. Journal of Postcolonial Writing, 57. Routledge Taylor & Francis Group.

Heeg, G. (2017). Das transkulturelle Theater. Recherchen: Vol. 130. Theater der Zeit.

Heeg, G., & Hillmann, L. (Eds.). (2017). Recherchen: Vol. 134. Willkommen anderswo – sich spielend begegnen. Theater der Zeit.

Heil, T. (2020). Comparing Conviviality: Living with Difference in Casamance and Catalonia. Palgrave Macmillan.

Henze, R. (2017). Why we have to overcome paternalism in times of populism. In M. Dragićević Šešić, L. Rogač Mijatović, & N. Mihaljinac (Eds.), Cultural diplomacy: Arts, festivals and geopolitics (pp. 73–89). Culture Desk Serbia Creative Europe Desk Serbia; Faculty of Dramatic Arts in Belgrade Institute for Theatre Film Radio and Television.

Hitzke, D. (2019). Nach der Einsprachigkeit: Slavisch-deutsche Texte transkulturell. Postcolonial Perspectives on Eastern Europe: Vol. 6. Peter Lang GmbH, Internationaler Verlag der Wissenschaften.

hooks, b. (1995). Ain't I a woman: Black women and feminism (5. print). Pluto Press.

Horst, M. t., & Schwartz, G. (Eds.). (2012). Changing perspectives: Dealing with globalisation in the presentation and collection of contemporary art. KIT.

Horz, C. (2014). Medien - Migration - Partizipation: Eine Studie am Beispiel iranischer Fernsehproduktion im Offenen Kanal. transcript.

Icaza, R., & Vázquez, R. (2018). Diversity or Decolonisation? Researching Diversity at the University of Amsterdam. In G. K. Bhambra, D. Gebrial, & K. Nişancıoğlu (Eds.), Decolonising the university (pp. 108–128). Pluto Press.

Jungwirth, I. (2019). Introduction: Gender and Diversity Studies: European Perspectives. In I. Jungwirth & C. Bauschke-Urban (Eds.), Gender and Diversity Studies: European Perspectives (pp. 9–30). Verlag Barbara Budrich.

Kagan, S. (2011). Art and Sustainability: Connecting Patterns for a Culture of Complexity. transcript. http://www.transcript-verlag.de/ts1803/ts1803.php

Kampnagel (2019). Migrantpolitan: X-Mas Party. Retrieved December 18, 2019, from https://www.kampnagel.de/en/program/migrantpolitan-x-mas-party

Karentzos, A. (2012). Postkoloniale Kunstgeschichte. Revisionen von Musealisierungen, Kanonisierungen, Repräsentationen. In J. Reuter & A. Karentzos (Eds.), Schlüsselwerke der Postcolonial Studies (Vol. 2010, pp. 249–266). VS Verlag für Sozialwissenschaften. https://doi.org/10.1007/978-3-531-93453-2_19

Kaup-Hasler, V. (2012). In NXTSTP (Ed.), NXT.STP: Documentation 2007-2012. http://www.nxtstp.eu/files/NXTSTP_5_years.pdf

Keuchel, S., & Kelb, V. (Eds.). (2015). Perspektivwechsel Kulturelle Bildung: v.1. Diversität in der Kulturellen Bildung. transcript.

Khatibi, A. (1985). Double Criticism: The Decolonization of Arab Sociology. In H. I. Barakat (Ed.), Contemporary North Africa: Issues of development and integration (pp. 9–19). Croom Helm.

Kim, J. A., & Riva, N. (Eds.). (2014). Entgrenzte Welt? Musik und Kulturtransfer (1. Aufl.). Ries & Erler.

Klein, G. (2013). Übersetzen und Rahmen: Aufführungen in globalisierten Pop(ulär)kulturen. In D. Helms & T. Phleps (Eds.), Ware Inszenierungen: Performance, Vermarktung und Authentizität in der populären Musik (pp. 211–222). transcript.

Köhl, C. (2001). Strategien der interkulturellen Kulturarbeit. IKO - Verl. für Interkulturelle Kommunikation.

Kolsteeg, J. (2019). Inclusiviteit is de praktijk: Grand Theatre Groningen. Boekman Extra - Trends in Kunst En Cultuur (19), 1–10. https://www.boekman.nl/wp-content/uploads/2019/12/BmXtra_19_DEF-1.pdf

Kraus, M., & Noack, K. (Eds.). (2015). Edition Museum: v.16. Quo vadis, Völkerkundemuseum? Aktuelle Debatten zu ethnologischen Sammlungen in Museen und Universitäten. transcript.

Krüger, S. (2013). Undoing anthenticity as a discursive construct: A critical pedagogy of ethnomusicology and "world music". In B. Alge & O. Krämer (Eds.), Berliner Schriften: Band 116. Beyond borders: Welt – Musik – Pädagogik: Musikpädagogik und Ethnomusikologie im Diskurs (pp. 93–113). Wißner.

Laclau, E., & Mouffe, C. (2012). Hegemonie und radikale Demokratie: Zur Dekonstruktion des Marxismus (Dt. Erstausg., 4., durchges. Aufl.). Passagen Philosophie. Passagen Verlag.

Latour, B. (2010). Eine neue Soziologie für eine neue Gesellschaft: Einführung in die Akteur-Netzwerk-Theorie (1. Aufl.). Suhrkamp-Taschenbuch Wissenschaft: Vol. 1967. Suhrkamp.

Leeb, S. (2015). Entangled: But How? In C. Behnke, C. Kastelan, V. Knoll, & U. Wuggenig (Eds.), Art in the periphery of the center (pp. 210–219). Sternberg Press.

Lena, J. C. (2019). Entitled: Discriminating tastes and the expansion of the arts. Princeton University Press.

Lettau, M., & Knoblich, C. (2017). Foreign cultural policy in processes of transformation: Perceptions of German-Tunisian cultural exchange. ENCATC Journal of Cultural Management and Policy, 7(1). https://www.encatc.org/media/3725-7_encact-vol-7_meike-lettau-caroline-knoblich.pdf

Lind, M. (2012). Performing the Curatorial: An Introduction. In M. Lind (Ed.), Performing the curatorial: Within and beyond art (pp. 9–22). Sternberg Press.

Lorde, A. (1984). Sister outsider: Essays and speeches. The Crossing press feminist series. Crossing Press. https://collectiveliberation.org/wp-content/uploads/2013/01/Lorde_The_Masters_Tools.pdf

Lutz-Sterzenbach, B., Schnurr, A., & Wagner, E. (Eds.). (2013). Pädagogik. Bildwelten remixed: Transkultur, Globalität, Diversity in kunstpädagogischen Feldern. transcript.

Lutz, B. (2018). Curating as Transcultural Practice: Documenta 12 and the "Migration of Form". In S. Dornhof, N. Buurman, B. Hopfener, & B. Lutz (Eds.), Image: Vol. 89. Situating Global Art: Topologies - Temporalities - Trajectories (pp. 213–230). transcript.

Macdonald, S. (Ed.). (1996). Theorizing museums: Representing identity and diversity in a changing world. Blackwell.

Mandel, B. (2014). Interkulturelles Audience Development: Zukunftsstrategien für öffentlich geförderte Kultureinrichtungen. Schriften zum Kultur- und Museumsmanagement. transcript.

Maxim Gorki Theatre Berlin (n.d.). Shermin Langhoff. Retrieved November 24, 2019, from https://www.gorki.de/de/ensemble/shermin-langhoff

Mbembe, A. J. (2016). Decolonizing the university: New directions. Arts and Humanities in Higher Education, 15(1), 29–45. https://doi.org/10.1177/1474022215618513

Moore, M. (2017, January 22). Conway: Trump spokesman gave 'alternative facts'. New York Post. https://nypost.com/2017/01/22/conway-trump-spokesman-gave-alternative-facts-on-inauguration-crowd/

Mosquera, G. (1994). Some Problems in Transcultural Curating. In J. Fisher (Ed.), Global visions: Towards a new internationalism in the visual arts (1st ed., pp. 133–139). Kala Press in association with the Institute of International Visual Arts.

NORIENT (Ed.). (2020). Norient Space: The Now In Sound. https://www.startnext.com/en/norient

Nussbaum, M. C. (2011). Creating capabilities: The human development approach. Belknap Press of Harvard University Press. https://doi.org/10.4159/harvard.9780674061200

Ornaghi, L. (2017). Does Glocal Political Power Already Exist? Glocalism. Journal of Culture, Politics and Innovation (1), 1–11. https://glocalismjournal.org/does-glocal-political-power-already-exist/

Osborne, P. (2013). Global modernity and the contemporary: Two categories of the philosophy of historical time. In C. Lorenz & B. Bevernage (Eds.), Schriftenreihe der FRIAS School of History: Band 007. Breaking up Time: Negotiating the Borders between Present, Past and Future (1st ed., pp. 69–84). Vandenhoeck & Ruprecht.

Osten, M. von. (2012). Displaying the Absent: Exhibiting Transcultural Modernism. In B. v. Bismarck, J. Schafaff, & T. Weski (Eds.), Cultures of the curatorial: [... Based on the Conference "Cultures of the Curatorial" at the Hochschule für Grafik und Buchkunst - Academy of Visual Arts Leipzig, January 22 - 24, 2010] (pp. 189–212). Sternberg Pr.

Peres da Silva, G. (2017). Weltmusik: Ein politisch umstrittener Begriff. In C. Leggewie & E. Meyer (Eds.), Global Pop: Das Buch zur Weltmusik (1st ed., pp. 9–16). J.B. Metzler Verlag.

Peres da Silva, G., & Hondros, K. (Eds.). (2019). Music and sound culture: volume 35. Music practices across borders: (e)valuating space, diversity and exchange (1. Auflage). transcript.

Pilić, I., & Wiederhold, A. (2015). Kunstpraxis in der Migrationsgesellschaft: Transkulturelle Handlungsstrategien am Beispiel der Brunnenpassage Wien = Art practices in the migration society; transcultural strategies in action at Brunnenpassage in Vienna. Vol. 48. transcript; Brunnenpassage.

Pitchfork (n.d.). Are Music Festival Lineups Getting Worse? Retrieved June 18, 2018, from https://pitchfork.com/features/festival-report/10059-are-music-festival-lineups-getting-worse/

Rajewsky, I. O. (2002). Intermedialität. UTB für Wissenschaft Medien- und Kommunikationswissenschaft: Vol. 2261. Francke.

Reckwitz, A. (2005). Kulturelle Differenzen aus praxeologischer Perspektive: Kulturelle Globalisierung jenseits von Modernisierungstheorie und Kulturessentialismus. In I. Srubar (Ed.), Kulturen vergleichen: Sozial- und kulturwissenschaftliche Grundlagen und Kontroversen (1st ed., pp. 92–111). VS Verl. für Sozialwiss.

Richardson, W. J. (2018). Understanding Eurocentrism as a Structural Problem of Undone Science. In G. K. Bhambra, D. Gebrial, & K. Nişancıoğlu (Eds.), Decolonising the university (pp. 231–247). Pluto Press.

Richter, D. (2012). Artists and Curators as Authors: Competitors, Collaborators, or Teamworkers? In B. v. Bismarck, J. Schafaff, & T. Weski (Eds.), Cultures of the curatorial: [... Based on the

Conference "Cultures of the Curatorial" at the Hochschule für Grafik und Buchkunst - Academy of Visual Arts Leipzig, January 22 - 24, 2010] (pp. 229–248). Sternberg Pr.

Rosendahl Thomsen, M. (2008). Mapping World Literature: International Canonization and Transnational Literatures. Continuum Literary Studies. Bloomsbury Publishing.

Rother, L. (2017). Kunst durch Kredit: Die Berliner Museen und ihre Erwerbungen von der Dresdner Bank 1935. De Gruyter. https://doi.org/10.1515/9783110496093

Rugg, J., & Sedgwick, M. (Eds.). (2012). Issues in curating contemporary art and performance. Intellect.

Sardinha, J., & Campos, R. (Eds.). (2016). Transglobal sounds: Music, youth and migration. Bloomsbury Academic.

SAVVY Contemporary (Ed.). SAVVY Contemporary. The Laboratory of Form-Ideas: A CONCEPT reloaded. https://savvy-contemporary.com/site/assets/files/2811/savvy_concept_2017.pdf

Schatzki, T. R. (1996). Social practices: A Wittgensteinian approach to human activity and the social. Cambridge Univ. Press.

Schneider, W., & Gad, D. (Eds.). (2014). Studien zur Kulturpolitik. Cultural Policy: Vol. 16. Good Governance for Cultural Policy: An African-European Research about Arts and Development (1st, New ed.). Peter Lang GmbH Internationaler Verlag der Wissenschaften. https://doi.org/10.3726/978-3-653-03932-0

Seliger, I. (2011). The aesthetics of transcultural desire: Borderline interventions in Miao Xiaochun's The last judgment in cyberspace and The last judgment in cyberspace - where will I go? In H. Belting, J. Birken, A. Buddensieg, & P. Weibel (Eds.), Global studies: Mapping contemporary art and culture (pp. 174–193). Hatje Cantz.

Sen, A. (2001). Development as freedom. Oxford University Press paperback. Univ. Press.

Sennett, R. (2003). Respect in a world of inequality (1. ed.). W. W. Norton.

Sennett, R. (2012). Together: The rituals, pleasures, and politics of cooperation. Yale University Press. http://lib.myilibrary.com/detail.asp?ID=340905

Sharifi, A. (2011). Theater für Alle? Partizipation von Postmigranten am Beispiel der Bühnen der Stadt Köln. Zugl.: Hildesheim, Univ., Diss., 2011. Studien zur Kulturpolitik: Vol. 13. Peter Lang GmbH Internationaler Verlag der Wissenschaften.

Shevtsova, M. (2009). Sociology of theatre and performance. Sociology, communication and performing media. QuiEdit.

Sievers, N., Dengel, S., Blumenreich, U., & Hippe, W. (Eds.). (2018). Jahrbuch für Kulturpolitik: Vol. 16. Jahrbuch für Kulturpolitik 2017/18: Welt. Kultur. Politik. - Kulturpolitik in Zeiten der Global-isierung. transcript. https://doi.org/10.14361/9783839442524

Singh, J. P. (2019). Culture and International Development: Towards an Interdisciplinary Methodology [A study commissioned by the British Council]. https://www.britishcouncil.org/sites/default/files/final_manuscript_cultureintldev.pdf

Small, C. (2010). Musicking: The meanings of performing and listening. Music/culture. Wesleyan Univ. Press.

Smith, T., Enwezor, O., & Condee, N. (Eds.). (2009). Antinomies of art and culture: Modernity, postmodernity, contemporaneity. Duke University Press.

Stiftung Humboldt Forum im Berliner Schloss (n.d.). The Humboldt Forum im Berliner Schloss. Retrieved February 27, 2020, from https://www.humboldtforum.org/en/pages/hf-en

Stroh, W. M. (2005). Musik der einen Welt. In W. Jank (Ed.), Musik-Didaktik: Praxishandbuch für die Sekundarstufe I und II (1st ed., pp. 185–193). Cornelsen Scriptor.

Tuck, E., & Yang, K. W. (2012). Decolonization is not a Metaphor. Decolonization: Indigeneity, Education & Society, 1(1), 1–40. https://clas.osu.edu/sites/clas.osu.edu/files/Tuck%20and%20Yang%202012%20Decolonization%20is%20not%20a%20metaphor.pdf

UNESCO. (2013). Basic Texts of the 2005 Convention on the Protection and Promotion of the Diversity of Cultural Expressions. http://unesdoc.unesco.org/images/0022/002253/225383E.pdf

Van Wel, F., Couwenbergh-Soeterboek, N., Couwenbergh, C., ter Bogt, T., & Raaijmakers, Q. (2006). Ethnicity, youth cultural participation, and cultural reproduction in the Netherlands. Poetics, 34(1), 65–82. https://doi.org/10.1016/j.poetic.2005.06.001

Wilson, N., Gross, J., & Bull, A. (2017). Towards Cultural Democracy: Promoting Cultural Capabilities for Everyone. https://www.kcl.ac.uk/cultural/resources/reports/towards-cultural-democracy-2017-kcl.pdf

Zembylas, T., & Niederauer, M. (2017). Composing Processes and Artistic Agency: Tacit Knowledge in Composing (1st ed.). Routledge Advances in Sociology. Taylor and Francis.

Zolberg, V. L. (1997). African Legacies, American Realities: Art and Artists on the Edge. In V. L. Zolberg & J. M. Cherbo (Eds.), Cambridge cultural social studies. Outsider art: Contesting boundaries in contemporary culture (pp. 53–70). Cambridge Univ. Press.

Zolberg, V. L., & Cherbo, J. M. (Eds.). (1997). Cambridge cultural social studies. Outsider art: Contesting boundaries in contemporary culture. Cambridge Univ. Press.

Giulia Pelillo-Hestermeyer, Fabio Cismondi

# 13 Diversity in Scientific Communities: The Case of European-Japanese Cooperation at Fusion for Energy

Diversity enhances productivity. Since studies have shown this positive effect of diversity, plenty of manuals have been published which point to the allegedly "best" ways of managing cultural diversity in companies and public institutions (e.g. Konrad et al., 2006; Klarsfeld, 2010; Plummer, 2002). Despite the high number of publications on this topic, less attention has been devoted to the diversity which characterizes scientific and academic environments in particular. Although the development of science relies on mobility and exchange, the belief in the objectivity and impartiality of scientific results, the use of English as a professional *lingua franca*, and the convergence of resources (know-how, money, scientists) into big projects, might all distract from the specific differentiation which characterizes the scientific environment. In fact, scientists from different cultural and professional backgrounds develop their work by cooperating in a variety of laboratories and research centres spread throughout different countries. They share knowledge and techniques by negotiating concepts, norms and approaches developed in various contexts. The shared *lingua franca* consists more appropriately of a shared technical jargon, whereas the "global language", just like any other global resource, is appropriated and used very differently by the speakers (Blommaert, 2010). Science is affected by political, economic, social and environmental change, as well as by power (e.g. that of different interests competing in the development of specific scientific subjects), all fields of which are characterized by negotiations from the local to the national up to the transnational and global scale. In addition, science relies not only on scientific standards, but also on administrative and legal frameworks. As a result, scientific knowledge and what is generically addressed as "scientific culture" in the singular, reveal, after thoroughgoing analysis, a wide spectrum of diversities, all of which contribute, albeit in variable degrees, to the success of the whole scientific enterprise. Nevertheless, this has not been in the focus of the attention while looking at diversity in science, which is more commonly associated with the lack of representation of specific social groups (e.g. women, ethnic minorities, differently able people, etc.) and with the need of developing targeted strategies in order to increase their participation in the community. This is, of course, an important task in promoting access to educational and scientific institutions, which is a necessary prerequisite to address white male privilege in structures of power and in the production of knowledge.

This chapter, however, does not stake a claim to offer an exhaustive picture of this complex issue, which would deserve a far more extensive undertaking, but rather proposes to examine the phenomenon of (trans)cultural exchange in a particular scientific environment, which is that of the European-Japanese cooperation within Broader Fusion Development. With this purpose in mind, here are some initial observations about the impact of different scientific cultures on transnational cooperation that have been developed by integrating a cultural studies scholarly perspective on this topic, and the perspective of scientists experiencing it in everyday life. This chapter originates from a dialogical exchange which began with an interview with Dr. Pietro Barabaschi (P. Barabaschi, personal communication, January 15, 2018), who is Head of Department at Fusion for Energy and Director of the European-Japanese Broader Approach activities. These activities have been initiated in the context of negotiations related to the nuclear fusion research megaproject ITER (https://www.iter.org/). During the ITER negotiations, the decision to site ITER in Cadarache (in the south of France) was reached in 2005 through an agreement between Europe and Japan on a privileged partnership in the ITER project[241] and in a set of activities, to be performed jointly in Japan—the Broader Approach Activities (BA Activities) (BA, n.d.). The agreed joint programme consists of three projects, the Engineering Validation and Engineering Design Activities for the International Fusion Materials Irradiation Facility (IFMIF/EVEDA, n.d.), the International Fusion Energy Research Centre (IFERC, n.d.), and the Satellite Tokamak[242] Programme (STP) Project JT-60SA (n.d.), the last of which will be the particular object of analysis in this chapter.

The reason for choosing this project relies on the particularly successful cooperation between the partners, which has been understood, also in the context of evaluation processes, to relate to the ability of the work-team in constructively integrating differences in approaches and frameworks. The main challenge in managing multicultural teams effectively has been located in recognizing underlying cultural causes of conflict and intervening in ways that solve the current problem and empower the team members to deal with future challenges themselves (Brett et al., 2019). In the interview with Dr. Barabaschi, which we have jointly planned and conducted, we have focused on the construction of a shared project identity and (trans)culture as a fundamental goal of the JT-60SA project, beside the goal of the construction of the tokamak itself (P. Barabaschi, personal communication, January, 15, 2018). Thus, instead of adopting a normative concept of diversity (understood abstractly), as is frequently used in addressing diversity issues (see section on JT-60SA), we have adopted a constructivist approach by investigating the different scientific cultures within the European-Japanese community engaged in the construction of JT-60SA. Moreover, we highlight how diversity has influenced ways of working and negotiating norms and practices of the community, and how this has affected achieving the expected results by staying within the budget and respecting the deadlines.

---

**241** The intriguing story of the ITER negotiations is summarized at the Website (ITER, n.d.).

**242** A tokamak is a thermonuclear fusion device which uses a powerful magnetic field to confine a hot plasma in the shape of a torus. The tokamak is one of several types of magnetic confinement devices which are being developed to produce controlled fusion. ITER and JT-60SA are both tokamak and the tokamak configuration is, as of today, the leading candidate for a practical fusion reactor.

Before examining the case of JT-60SA in greater depth, we will first critically examine, in the next section, the most common representations of diversity in the field of science, with a particular focus on diversity management.

## 13.1 Diversity in the Scientific Community: A Critical Review

In the introduction to the volume "Diversity in the scientific community", the editors Nelson and Cheng start by quoting a Business Dictionary, which defines diversity as being a "feature of a mixed workforce that provides a wide range of abilities, experience, knowledge, and strengths due to its heterogeneity in age, background, ethnicity, physical abilities, political and religious beliefs, sex, and other attributes" (Business Dictionary, n.d., as cited in Nelson & Cheng, 2018a, p. 1). By illustrating the advantages of diversity at the workplace, they refer to the report "Diversity Matters" (Hunt et al., 2015), which summarizes the results of the work conducted by Mc Kinsey & Company on the impact of diversity on the financial performance of 366 public companies in Canada, Latin America, the United Kingdom and the United States, and which testify an overall positive impact of ethnic, racial and gender diversity. By extending the considerations of the report from business and industry to the academic and scientific contexts, with a particular focus upon Science, Technology, Engineering and Mathematics (STEM) organizations, Nelson and Cheng indicate a variety of advantages brought about by diversity, such as the availability of differentiated competences in teams, a higher degree of creativity in finding effective solutions for problems, and a network of global connections guaranteeing accessibility to various resources (2018a, p. 3). A particular emphasis is dedicated to the benefits of diversity with respect to impact factors and citations, as has been highlighted by a number of studies to which the authors refer. For example, Smith, Weinberger, Bruna, and Allesina point out that the papers with authors *from more countries* [emphasis added] fared better in journal placement and citation performance" (2014, as cited in Nelson & Cheng, 2018a, p. 3). In addition, statistics quoted by Freeman and Wei indicate that articles co-authored by *"scholars of similar ethnicity* [emphasis added]" tend to be published in lower-impact journals with fewer citations (2015, as cited in Nelson & Cheng, 2018a, p. 3). Thus, these studies indicate the ethnic identity of authors and their location in different countries as being responsible for a stronger impact of results on the scientific community. However, despite such positive results both in the scientific and business sectors, diversity is still considered to be a work in progress. One of the greatest challenges in this regard is seen in the "difficulty of managing diversity effectively" (Nelson & Cheng, 2018a, p. 3).

Page, who has researched issues of diversity in organizations by applying mathematical models (Page, 2007; 2011; 2017), speaks in one of his latest books of a "diversity bonus", which refers to the cognitive advantages that characterize heterogeneous teams working on high-dimensional, complex tasks, such as, for example, scientific research. Page's study contradicts one of the most common critiques of diversity politics, namely that they hinder meritocracy, for example by prioritizing, in hiring processes, candidates' gender, ethnicity or socioeconomic backgrounds over their ability[243]. He claims, on the contrary, that "a policy of hiring the best does not make sense on high-dimensional tasks", since the best team will not consist of the "best" individuals but rather of a range of diverse thinkers (Page, 2017, p. 13). However, he also warns against simplistic expectations:

> Diversity cannot be arbitrary. The space of possible diversities is enormous. We cannot convene a random collection of diverse people and expect diversity bonuses. We need theoretical understandings of whether and how diversity can produce benefit on particular tasks. We need to make reasoned judgements about what type of diversity might be germane to the task at hand. (Page, 2017, p. 2)

By referring to the enormous "space of possible diversities", Page's (2017) model is grounded on a plural conceptualization of diversity, in which diversity is not regarded as an absolute quality, that is definable once and for ever, but is rather considered with respect to the changeable contexts and to the respective tasks that need to be achieved. The potential of diverse teams relies, in his theory, on the variety of the *cognitive repertoires* available in the whole group. Cognitive repertoires consist of information, knowledge, heuristic tools, representations, mental models and frameworks (Page, 2017, pp. 52–67). In order to achieve complex tasks, a working group should be able to rely on the highest possible range of cognitive repertoires relevant for the goal which is being pursued. Differences in identity features, such as age, gender, religion, race, etc., are seen as contributing to, but are not themselves constitutive of, cognitive diversity. This approach allows Page to overcome a quite common, static conceptualization of diversity, whereby diversity is conceived as the sum of isolated features such as gender, ethnicity, race, age, etc. Promoting diversity is seen, from this perspective, as enhancing the participation of underrepresented minorities in the corresponding majority-dominated contexts. In the scientific context, this means, for instance, increasing the number of women and differently able people who are operative in the community. This is the aim, indeed, of numerous diversity programmes and working groups, a good number of which are examined in detail by Nelson and Cheng (2018b). One of the problems with such an understanding of promoting diversity is that conceptualizing diversity as a mere sum of single identity groups can generate controversies in developing and evaluating efficient strategies for promoting

---

**243** The widespread belief that ability or merit can be impartially defined would deserve a critical discussion of its own. Which abilities, or which candidates are considered to be "the best ones", always depends on the context and on the agency of specific traditions and power structures. For a critical discussion of meritocracy as a means of legitimation for neoliberal culture (e.g. white male privilege) s. Littler (2018).

it. This is the case, for instance, when a diversity programme that targets women is not considered to enhance diversity because it disadvantages people with disabilities or ethnic minorities. Similarly, statistics quoted by Dobbin and Kalev (2019) demonstrate that college recruitment programmes targeting women benefit Asian men more than Asian or Hispanic women; mentoring programmes do not benefit white women but instead Asian men. Even if the authors refer to such programmes as good practices, not everybody agrees. A reader's comment, for example, rightly points out: "It does seem that many of these purportedly successful diversity strategies simply expand the categories of men that men in power identify with" (O´Connor, as cited in Dobbin and Kalev, 2019)[244].

By considering such disputes from a transcultural perspective, it becomes evident that reasoning in terms of monolithic identities, and thereby conceiving diversity as the sum of single identity groups, can drive one's approaches to the absurd consequence that programmes intending to promote diversity end up being trapped in a quite homogeneous idea of it. Moreover, it has been demonstrated that conceptualizing diversity simply in terms of identity groups, and handling it accordingly, inhibits effectiveness in a wide range of organizations (Thomas & Ely, 2019). As a result, the need for a change of paradigm in addressing diversity has been voiced, by considering diversity with respect to the different perspectives and approaches to work brought by members of different identity groups. Such a proposed "integration paradigm" transcends both paradigms of assimilation ("we are all the same") and of differentiation ("we celebrate differences"), respectively, by connecting the role of real diversity to the "actual doing of work" (Thomas & Ely, 2019). Moreover, an intersectional-analytical approach, focused on "the intersections within and between the constructions of identity and commonality as well as the lines of difference and otherness", has been indicated as a possible way of escaping a normative approach to diversity, resulting as it does in unwanted hierarchizations of minorities (Kaufmann, 2016, pp. 121–143). Such a change of paradigm appears particularly significant in considering that research in managing diversity has been focused far more on *managing* rather than on *diversity*, insofar as it has investigated strategies for efficiently handling diversity but has not sufficiently questioned the concepts and practices on which it is ultimately based (cf. Ashcraft, 2011). It is not uncommon that reasoning about diversity starts with clarifications derived from dictionaries. Moreover, since dictionaries report the common meaning of terms, hegemonic ideas of diversity remain unquestioned and becomes recycled, facilitating, among other aspects, unintended consequences, such as a competition between the logic of enhancing productivity and the logic of increasing representativeness, a competition between single minorities, or controversies in evaluating programmes. The risk of perpetrating stereotypes and weakening the

---

244 Both the chapter and the respective, quoted comment on it are available online at the Harvard Business Review´s Website (Dobbin & Kalev, 2019).

action of valuable initiatives is not to be underestimated. Paradoxically, it has been noticed that the most successful strategies for enhancing the representativeness of minorities in companies are those which do not explicitly mention diversity, such as mentoring, cross-training and self-managed teams (Dobbin & Kalev, 2019, pp. 12–13, table).

Deeper inter- and transdisciplinary research is needed about diversity both as a concept and as a practice. Interrelating both perspectives of research in the social sciences and humanities, with a primary thematic focus upon diversity[245], and of research on managing diversity, which is primarily focused upon managing, can contribute to a better understanding of diversity in *specific contexts* and life-worlds, thus avoiding generalizing and essentializing socio-cultural categories. Research across the humanities and the social sciences has shown, indeed, that identity is a fluid category, which is constantly subjected to processes of negotiation. Halford and Leonard (2006) showed how social identities in the workplace are constructed not only by features such as class, gender and age, but also by contextual variables depending on space and place. Yet this is not to diminish the value of actions which are aimed at increasing the participation of underrepresented categories in the scientific environment. As pointed out by Gibbs (2014) in a blog post published on the Scientific American, diversity in science refers to "cultivating talent, and promoting the full inclusion of excellence across the social spectrum". ("What is diversity?" para. 4). In his view, "the large and persistent underrepresentation of certain social groups from the enterprise represents the loss of talent" (Gibbs, 2014, "Lack of diversity represents a loss of talent", para. 2). Yet increasing the pool of talent represents the prerequisite and not the outcome of the "full inclusion of excellence".

The creation of "inclusive cultures" is also considered by Page (2017) as the key aspect to making diversity succeed:

> Here, what I mean by an inclusive culture is one in which people have the ability to apply their full repertoires. A lack of inclusion means that someone feels that she has something to add and does not or cannot. (p. 221)

However, because of the changeable contexts and the wide range of possible tasks which require completion, there cannot be a "one-size-fits-all" solution.

---

245 Beside Page, other scholars like Hewlett, Marshall, and Sherbin (2013), Jehn, Northcroft, and Neale (1999) as well as Ross and Malveux (2013) have researched the nature of cognitive diversity and its impact on team performances, by distinguishing between *acquired* and *inherent* diversity, *identity* and *informational* diversity, *personality* and *behavioural* diversity (Hewlett et al., 2013 and Jehn et al., 1999, as cited in Page, 2017, pp. 53–54). Despite terminological asymmetries and respective differences in accentuating particular aspects of diversity over others, all these approaches share a dynamical conceptualization of diversity, which result from the interrelation between individuals and society.

Against this background, we will explore in the next section the case of the scientific community of Broader Fusion Development in the JT-60SA project, which is a part of Fusion for Energy. We will focus on the building process of a project-specific (trans) culture from the multiple diversities that characterize this scientific work, taking into account the input from recent advances in organizational studies, and intertwining them with the perspective of Transcultural Studies. Moreover, we will look into the dynamics of cooperation in JT-60SA by adopting the concept of "community of practice" (Lave & Wenger, 1991) and the corresponding framework of analysis developed by Wenger. A community of practice is defined as the result of a collective learning process developed by its members through both the pursuit of a common enterprise and its attendant social relations (Wenger, 1998, p. 45). Wenger's model stresses three main dimensions in which practice transforms a group of people into a community:

1. Mutual engagement;
2. A joint enterprise and
3. A shared repertoire.

Looking at JT-60SA as a "community of practice" hence allows us to highlight the social process of constructing a team by paying attention, simultaneously, to the personal and interpersonal engagements, the material-instrumental work carried on by the group, and the specific scientific context.

## 13.2 JT-60SA as a Transcultural "Community of Practice"

When we met Dr. Barabaschi for the interview, it became immediately clear to us that the JT-60SA project could not be described by only referring to the construction of the tokamak reactor in Japan. As a matter of fact, the story of the project can only be written by interweaving the progress which is attained in constructing the reactor with the development of a group project identity and culture. Without an *ad hoc* engagement in the development of such a (trans)culture, the construction of the reactor would not have advanced at such a quick pace. Working jointly on the construction of the reactor has represented the strongest glue for the scientific community cooperating in it, so that both of these processes have permeated and enriched each other. Therefore, both of them (constructing the reactor and constructing the team) shall be considered, by referring to Wenger's model, as a "joint enterprise" of the JT-60SA community.

As Wenger (1998) pointed out, a common goal is a fundamental glue of the community, but this "is not just a stated goal, but creates among participants relations of mutual accountability that become an integral part of the practice" (p. 78). In the following paragraphs, we will explain how both the "mutual engagement" of the community members and the development of a "shared repertoire" has contributed decisively to the scientific cooperation, and how diversity has influenced both processes.

Differences not only in attitudes towards hierarchies and authority, but also in communicating directly or indirectly (e.g. explicitly addressing problems or asking questions), as well as asymmetries in the use of the *lingua franca*, are considered to be among the most common challenges in managing multicultural teams (Brett et al., 2019). However, although cultural categories such as "European" vs. "Japanese", "Western" vs. "Easterners", "French" vs. "Italian" are most commonly addressed as responsible for cultural discrepancies, such categorizations might distract from other, more subtle, distinctions, which expand the range of diversities in the corresponding contexts. In the case of JT-60SA, Dr. Barabaschi (personal communication, January 15, 2018) mentioned at least 10 different "laboratory cultures" engaged in the project, of which 5 were particularly significant with respect to their impact on the project activities. These include: National Institutes for Quantum and Radiological Science and Technology (QST, Japan), National Institute for Fusion Science (NIFS, Japan), Commissariat à l'Energie Atomique et aux Energies Alternatives (CEA, France), Centro de Investigaciones Energéticas, Medioambientales y Tecnológicas (CIEMAT, Spain), Consorzio RFX, Padova (Italy), Agenzia nazionale per le nuove tecnologie, l'energia e lo sviluppo economico sostenibile (ENEA , Italy), Karlsruhe Institute of Technology (KIT, Germany), Studiecentrum voor Kernenergie - Centre d'Etude de l'Energie Nucléaire (SCK-CEN, Belgium), Joint European Torus (JET, UK), Max Planck Insitut für Plasmaphysik (IPP, Germany).

The diversity of such "laboratory cultures" manifests itself in practices which are fundamental to the development of the project, such as decision-making processes, ways of structuring meetings, and the criteria determining the order of mentioning co-authors in joint publications. Conflicting norms for decision-making can cause delays, thus slowing down the activity of the whole team. This is the case, for example, when a task which is commonly discussed and approved by community members in the context of a meeting is considered to have been definitively approved only by some of them, and put back to the final approval of absent supervisors by others. The reasons for such misunderstandings may rely in differences in handling hierarchies (e.g. prevalence of horizontal vs. vertical communication) or in a different use of English as the *lingua franca* (e.g. does "yes" signalize approval, agreement or only a willingness to further considering the issue?). Even if these differences might also be influenced by socio-cultural norms subsumable under categories such as "Japanese" or "Italian", such influences are only partial, and they intertwine with the "laboratory cultures". Particularly in scientific communities, whose members are used to moving among international centres and institutions spread all over the world, addressing the national or ethnic identity—even assuming that it would be clearly definable—as the only factor responsible for such misunderstandings would not only be mistaken, but would also strengthen stereotyping within the community, thus jeopardizing an efficient and collaborative cooperation.

The negotiation of norms regulating collective work processes has, therefore, been particularly important for the effective development of the project. This has resulted, among other aspects, in the creation of a shared documentation management system, which is accessible by all the partners and subjected to a set of agreed norms. Cooperating on it jointly has not only smoothened collective work processes, but has also contributed to strengthen the project identity, thus having positive effects in turn on both aspects of the "joint enterprise". The creation of a shared documentation management system can be seen as one of the most significant elements constituting the "shared repertoire" developed by the community. Wenger (1998) stresses that

> the elements of the repertoire can be very heterogeneous. They gain their coherence not in and of themselves as specific activities, symbols, or artefacts, but from the fact that they belong to the practice of a community pursuing an enterprise. The repertoire of a community of practice includes routines, words, tools, ways of doing things, stories, gestures, symbols, genres, actions, or concepts that the community has produced or adopted in the course of its existence, and which have become part of its practice. The repertoire combines both reificative and participative aspects. It includes the discourse by which members create meaningful statements about the world, as well as the styles by which they express their forms of membership and their identities as members. (pp. 82–83)[246]

Another significant element of the shared repertoire can be physically observed by accessing the entrance hall of the building in which the European Home Team of JT-60SA is located in Germany, at the Max-Planck-Institute for Plasma Physics in Garching. Here, a monitor—which can be considered a reification of the cooperation—shows in real time the advances in the construction of the actual research infrastructure in Japan, 100 km north from Tokyo. By "materializing" the intellectual work of the scientists into the very body of the reactor and making it visible for staff members, guests and visitors, the images not only motivate the team, but also connect, virtually, the community spread across different places and time zones, into a shared spatial-temporal simultaneity.[247] It would be valuable to explore in further depth the impact which this practice has on the life-world of the community, for example by collecting

---

246 Wenger (1998) refers to both reification and participation as the main aspects of negotiating meaning in a community (pp. 51–71). By participation, he stresses that the engagement in a community of practice implies more than mere doing. It transforms the individuals taking part in the "joint enterprise", who, in turn, transform the community. Participation does not mean in any case a collaborative relationship: "A community of practice is neither a haven of togetherness nor an island of intimacy insulated from political and social relations. Disagreement, challenges, and competition can all be forms of participation" (Wenger, 1998, p. 77). Reification, on the other hand, is understood as "the process of giving form to our experience by producing objects that congeal this experience into 'thingness'. In so doing we create points of focus around which the negotiation of meaning becomes organized" (Wenger, 1998, p. 58).

247 Sociological inquiry, such as research carried out in the context of actor-network-theory, has pointed out the agency of material objects (Latour, 2005). Gaupp's chapter on "Epistemologies of Diversity" in this volume considers this topic in further detail.

and analysing data about social routines and speeches that take place in front of and around the monitor.

Other examples of reification are gadgets, such as pens and tags, which display the name of the project, and the logo, which is shown in scientific presentations and events. These artefacts, employed in everyday practices, are not only a symbol of identity for the group members, but also construct a boundary between the JT-60SA community and other teams, such as those engaged in the other projects of the Broader Approach at Fusion for Energy. The logo and the gadgets contribute, in this context, to strengthening the feeling of belonging to the community, and to stimulate, at the same time, a process of "othering" towards out-groups, which might function as an additional competitive motivation in achieving results. A strategy of differentiation is thus a significant part of the development of the group identity. However, this does not mean that the cohesion of the community is linked to an idea of inner homogeneity. On the contrary, as stressed by Wenger (1998),

> [...] each participant in a community of practice finds a unique place and gains a unique identity, which is both further integrated and further defined in the course of engagement in practice. These identities become interlocked and articulated with one another through mutual engagement, but they do not fuse. Mutual relations of engagement are as likely to give rise to differentiation as to homogenization. Crucially, therefore, homogeneity is neither a requirement for, nor the result of, the development of a community of practice. (pp. 75–76)

Mutual engagement is also considered by Dr. Barabaschi (personal communication, January 15, 2018) to be a fundamental prerequisite for effective cooperation, because, among other aspects, it helps to reduce bureaucracy, thus speeding up work processes. In order to develop and strengthen mutual accountability and trust, the size of the team is of great importance. Big projects counting thousands of scientists are subjected to more complicated bureaucratic structures, which hinder scientific progress. In addition, in particularly politicized fields of research, such as the nuclear field, politics and change may dramatically influence the work progress of big projects.[248] Furthermore,

---

**248** The political influence on big scientific projects may take various shapes, as in the following examples:

1. Decision by specific governments to suspend funding for a project, as in the case of the retirement of the United States from the nuclear fusion research megaproject ITER in 1998, later reversed in 2005 when the US rejoined ITER;
2. Big projects might have a symbolic political meaning which is not directly linked to scientific issues (e.g. celebrating the cooperation between two or more countries which have recently settled terms of peace with one another). In these cases, scientists may encounter political resistance whenever they see a need for changing strategies or approaches. In other words, the scientific reasons might clash against political ones;
3. The leadership of big scientific projects may be set by following political, instead of scientific reasons, thus compromising the project performance;

proper team size allows members to get to know each other personally and to develop relationships of mutual accountability. In this regard, the JT-60SA community, which numbers around 400 members of which approximately half are based in Europe and half in Japan, is considered to have an adequate size. To what extent mutual trust and accountability have contributed to achieving the expected results by staying within the budget and respecting deadlines is shown in the following examples: since the technical planning, design and assembly of the reactor is split between Europe and Japan, regulation in contracting, and standards in designing may differ to some degree. Sometimes technical drawings realized in Europe are constructed by Japanese companies and in compliance with Japanese regulations. The Japanese contracting and procurement section of the project uses Japanese for important documents such as technical specifications of supply contracts. As a result, developing personal relations of trust with the Japanese colleagues who follow the contracts has allowed European partners to save much time in translating any details while concluding the contracts. Mutual trust is also important when something goes wrong. This has been the case, for instance, in the context of planning and constructing a connection of the cryogenic plant (which involves the providing of cryogenic Helium to the device superconducting magnet). Since the sight orientation in technical drawing differs between Japan and Europe, working jointly in designing and planning requires a process of "graphic translation", which specifies, for example, whether the section of an object follows the Japanese or the European orientation standard, so that the corresponding object can be constructed accordingly. This common proceeding is marked by a code, which, if omitted in the planning or overseen in the constructing process, prevents the "graphic translation". Because of such oversight, it happened that a component, which had been designed in Europe, did not match with the complementary part built in Japan. The costs deriving from this mistake were in the tens of thousands of euros. In such cases, relationships of mutual trust and accountability help colleagues to take collective responsibility instead of accusing each other, which would cost, according to a longer perspective, much more, since the weakening of mutual engagement would increase bureaucracy and slow down work progress. Moreover, the chance of community members to give and receive support is also fundamental with respect to scientific progress. The work of "community maintenance" is considered by Wenger (1998) as an intrinsic part of any practice (p. 74). As such, this aspect would be worth considered also as a part of the scientific work.

---

4. Political decisions may follow quick reactions to current events and produce sudden changes in specific scientific developments (Barabaschi, personal communication, January 15, 2018).

## 13.3 Concluding Remarks: Perspectives and Further Developments

The chapter has offered a concrete example of how transnational cooperation in scientific environments can be analysed with respect to the formation of transcultural communities rather than with respect to the sum of single identity groups. Although reasoning in terms of monolithic identities still remains dominant in common discourses and practices focused on diversity—including strategies aiming at promoting it—advances in organizational studies have pointed out the need for a change of paradigm, in which diversity is understood as a solution, instead of a problem, for approaching complex tasks and optimizing results (Page, 2017; Thomas & Ely, 2019). The case of scientific communities appears particularly interesting in this regard, because of the specific patterns of mobility that characterize scientific resources (human, economic, cultural), which generate a wide range of diversities influencing the development of science. The impact of diversity—in such a plural conceptualization—on work processes has been, so far, widely under-explored, especially if compared with the numerous studies focused on managing diversity in the business sector, which, in a neoliberal vein, focus exclusively on productivity.

This chapter has pinpointed this gap by stressing the potential of interweaving recent advances in management and organizational studies—proposing a more dynamical look at diversity than that based on single identity groups—with analytical frameworks of social and cultural studies. This would imply critically deconstructing static representations of diversity in society and at grasping the socio-cultural, political and economic dimensions of cooperation in a scientific environment. These first insights into the JT-60SA community have highlighted, indeed, the strong nexus between the socio-cultural dimension of scientific cooperation and its respective outcomes. Moreover, they have stressed the significance of considering such a nexus in managing and developing science, by showing the positive impact of specific strategies on the project's results.

Against this background, much work still has to be done in order to analyse in greater depth the influence of diversity on the development of science. In this regard, examining more elements of the shared repertoire of scientific communities and further investigating the forms of mutual engagement and their impact on pursuing the respective joint enterprise would both help to provide a more detailed picture. Moreover, analysing the dynamic of appropriating and negotiating technical and cultural resources (e.g. application of scientific skills, use of English as a *lingua franca*) by single scientists, and relating it to the development of the work within the community, would contribute to investigating the articulation between the local and the global, in doing science, at different scales (e.g. in a single laboratory, a big project, and in a global scientific community). In addition, analysing relationships of cooperation and competition between different teams would offer valuable examples for examining the process of "doing identity" (Hall, 1992) within a community, and the related process of "othering" with respect to other communities. With respect to the communication and the negotiation of differences, conflicts and misunderstandings are rich sources worthy of investigation. Moreover, collecting and comparing (auto)biographical narratives of scientists who have "migrated" through different laboratories and centres, would contribute to a better understanding of the multiple diversities within the so-called "scientific culture". All in all, further inter- and transdisciplinary research on diversity in scientific communities would contribute to expanding the concept of culture with respect to the scientific environment, linking socio-cultural realities to the practising of science and, consequently, developing a stronger awareness of culture in scientific management.

# References

Ashcraft, K. L. (2011). Gender and Diversity: Other Ways to "Make a Difference". In M. Alvesson, T. Bridgman, & H. Willmott (Eds.), The Oxford Handbook of Critical Management Studies (pp. 304–327). Oxford University Press.

Blommaert, J. (2010). The Sociolinguistics of Globalization. Cambridge University Press.

Brett, J., Behfar, K., & Kern, M. C. (2019). "Managing Multicultural Teams". In: Review, Harvard Business (Eds.) (2019), HBR's 10 Must Reads on Diversity. Harvard Business Review Press, Retrieved April 3, 2021, from https://hbr.org/2016/07/why-diversity-programs-fail

BA. (n.d.). What are the Broader Approach activities? Retrieved April 3, 2020, from https://fusion-forenergy.europa.eu/downloads/mediacorner/factsheets/Broader_Approach_poster.pdf

Dobbin, F. & Kalev, A. (2019). "Why Diversity Programs Fail". In: (2019), HBR's 10 Must Reads on Diversity. Harvard Business Review Press, Retrieved April 4, 2020, from https://hbr.org/2016/07/why-diversity-programs-fail

Freeman, R. B. & Wei, H. (2015). Collaborating with People Like Me: Ethnic Coauthorship within the United States". Journal of Labor Economics, 33, 289–318.

Gibbs, K., Jr. (2014). Diversity in STEM: What It Is and Why It Matters. Retrieved April 3, 2020, from https://blogs.scientificamerican.com/voices/diversity-in-stem-what-it-is-and-why-it-matters/

Halford, S. & Leonard, P. (2006). Place, Space and Time: Contextualizing Workplace Subjectivities. Organization Studies, 27(5), 657–676.

Hall, S. (1992). The Question of Cultural Identity. In: Hall, Stuart; Held, David & Mc Grew, Tony (Eds.) (1992), Modernity and its Futures (pp. 273–316). Cambridge Polity Press.

Hewlett, S. A., Marshall, M., & Sherbin, L. (December 2013). „How Diversity can Drive Innovation", Harvard Business Review.

Hunt, V., Layton, D., & Prince, S. (2015). Diversity Matters. Retrieved May 10, 2019, from https://assets.mckinsey.com/~/media/857F440109AA4D13A54D9C496D86ED58.ashx.

IFERC. (n.d.). International Fusion Energy Research Centre. Retrieved August 12, 2019, from http://www.iferc.org

IFMIF/EVEDA. (n.d.). The IFMIF/EVEDA phase. Retrieved August 12, 2019, from https://www.ifmif.org/?page_id=62

ITER; (n.d.). The ITER Story. Retrieved July 10, 2019, from https://www.iter.org/proj/iterhistory

Jehn, K. A., Northcraft, G. B., & Neale, M. A. (1999). "Why Differences make a Difference: A Field of Study of Diversity, Conflict, and Performance in Workgroups". Administrative Science Quarterly, 44, 741–763.

JT-60SA. (n.d.). JT-60SA. Retrieved August 12, 2019, from http://www.jt60sa.org

Kaufmann, M. E. (2016). Diversity is our Business: Research-based Diversity Concepts and Their Impact on the Public Use and the Organizational Implementation of Diversity. In: Richter,

Carola; Dupuis Indira & Averbeck-Lietz, Stefanie (Eds.) (2016), Diversity in Transcultural and International Communication (pp. 121–143). LIT

Klarsfeld, A. (Ed.). (2010). International Handbook of Diversity Management at Work. Elgar.

Konrad, A. M., Prasal, P. & Pringle, J. (Eds.). (2006). Handbook of Workplace Diversity. SAGE.

Latour, B. (2005). Reassembling the Social: an Introduction to actor-network-theory. Oxford University Press.

Lave, J. & Wenger, E. (1991). Situated Learning: Legitimate Peripheral Participation. Cambridge University Press.

Littler, J. (2018). Against Meritocracy. Culture, Power and Myths of Mobility. Routledge.

Nelson, D. J. & Cheng, H.N. (2018a). Diversity in Science: an Overview. In D. Nelson J. & H.N. Cheng (Eds.), Diversity in the Scientific Community (pp. 1–12). Oxford University Press.

Nelson, D. J. & Cheng, H. N. (Eds.). (2018b). Diversity in the Scientific Community (Vol. 1. Quantifying Diversity and Formulating Success). Oxford University Press.

Page, S. E. (2007). The Difference. How the Power of Diversity Creates Better Groups, Firms, Schools, and Societies. Princeton University Press.

Page, S. E. (2011). Diversity and Complexity. Princeton University Press.

Page, S. E. (2017). The Diversity Bonus. How Great Teams Pay Off in the Knowledge Economy. Princeton University Press.

Plummer, D. (Ed.). (2002). Handbook of Diversity Management. Beyond Awareness to Competency Based Learning. University Press of America.

Review, Harvard Business (Ed.). (2019). HBR's 10 Must Reads on Diversity. Harvard Business Review Press.

Ross, H. J. & Malveux, J. (2013). Reinventing Diversity: Transforming Organizational Community to Strenghten People, Purpose, and Performance. Rowman and Littlefield.

Smith, M. J., Weinberger, C., Bruna, E. M., & Allesina, S. (2014). The scientific impact of nations: journal placement and citation performance. PloS ONE, 9, 1–6.

Thomas, D. A. & Ely, R. J. (2019). Making Differences Matter: A New Paradigm for Managing Diversity. In: Review, Harvard Business (Ed.). (2019), HBR's 10 Must Reads on Diversity. Harvard Business Review Press. Retrieved April 4, 2020, from https://hbr.org/1996/09/making-differences-matter-a-new-paradigm-for-managing-diversity

Wenger, E. (1998). Communities of Practice: Learning, Meaning, and Identity. Cambridge University Press.

Lisa Gaupp

# 14 Decolonizing Otherness Through a Transcultural Lens: Conclusion

## 14.1 Norms of Otherness: Differences

The standardizations, practices and negotiations of diversity that have been discussed across different settings and disciplinary contexts throughout this book were mainly based on the common assumption that they go hand in hand with the doing and undoing of otherness in highly contingent and constructivist processes. While the introduction placed the different chapters of this book within the field of diversity and transcultural studies by discussing how diversity can be re-thought transculturally, this concluding chapter will close the topical bracket by specifically focusing on the study of otherness from a transcultural perspective. In other words, diversity is connected to otherness in so far as it can be understood as the multiplication of differences, which might at the same time be connected to a blurring of differences. Conversely, the common goal of such constructions and deconstructions of differences is to emphasize belonging and inclusivity to a group, network or similar associational constructs. In turn, otherness can equally encompass the destabilization of differences, but also place emphasis on such border-makings while enforcing exclusionary practices. On the whole, all these different concepts of diversity and otherness lay at the very core of cultural analysis, no matter how the differences are conceptualized, from which perspective this is conducted, or whether differences are thought to serve either normalizing or deconstructing processes. This perspective on differences can thus be called a difference-theoretical approach in the study of diversity and otherness, that runs throughout the entire book.

In sum, all chapters approach *culture* in a constructivist way while focussing on "not-so-clear" constructions by taking a deconstructivist stance. So, while keeping the different foci of the articles in mind, it is important to note that the topics of diversity are always connected to the processes of (de-)construction of otherness. Nevertheless, some contributions have placed greater emphasis on the standardization of diversity (Gaupp on Epistemologies, Pelillo-Hestermeyer on Linguistic Diversity, Espahangizi, Pelillo-Hestermeyer and Cismondi, Reichardt) whereas others have focussed more on processes of Othering (Hirschauer, Höhne, Ciaudo, Oettl, Marten-Finnis, Niccolai).

Looking at the basis of "differences" in the cultural analysis of diversity and otherness, what does "difference" mean in the first place? The etymological source of the term stems from the Latin *differentia*, which can both be translated into English as *diversity* or *difference* and *distinction* (Latin Dictionary, n.d.), which again stands as a synonym for *otherness* (Dictionary, n.d.). Hence, difference is about being different, being distinct, being non-identical. Philosophically speaking, difference can involve questions of identity. For instance, in the branch of the philosophy of language that focusses on semiotics, differences are conceptualized as necessary in order to be able to communicate at all. If one is not able to discriminate between any two issues, things, practices, etc., one would not be able to attach meaning to them and thus understand or act. Difference is thus needed for our perceptions and actions (Frege, 1990; Wittgenstein, 1977; Herder, 1772/1975; Cassirer, 1997).

In the social sciences[249] as well as in the humanities[250], the concept of differences can be traced back to the institutional foundation of these same disciplines at the end of the nineteenth century in Central Europe, as well as to other intellectual perspectives which have been developed long before this around the world, such as the thinking of Ibn Chaldūn (1332–1406) or the Vedas that were created in ancient India from 1700 B.C. The discipline of (cultural) sociology as it is nowadays institutionalized at universities and other organizations of higher education is mainly based on a founding legend that leaves out these earlier developments and, being almost exclusively Eurocentric, is traced back to the "founding fathers" of sociology, such as Émile Durkheim, Max Weber and Georg Simmel. Here, the term difference is put at the forefront, but mostly in this processual use as differentiation. Sociological differentiation theory describes mainly social change processes on different levels, which can

---

**249** Cultural social sciences encompass all (interdisciplinary) approaches in the study of culture that focus on how cultural constructions are practiced, and how they have an effect (or rather how they are made effective) in society. In other words, these approaches inquire into the nature, forms, causes, processes, purposes and effects of social life, i.e. any type and degree of human relations. In today's vast disciplinary system of academic life, these approaches bear the names of, among others, cultural sociology, sociology of culture, social anthropology, ethnomusicology, cultural politics, political studies of culture, cultural history, cultural economics, communication and media studies, as well as even more interdisciplinary fields such as area studies or gender and postcolonial studies. In this volume, especially (but not exclusively) the chapters by myself (Epistemologies and How to Curate), Hirschauer, Espahangizi, Höhne and Pelillo-Hestermeyer and Cismondi can be assigned to this line of thought in the study of culture, even though the overarching theme of the book intends to make the connections between more humanities-based approaches and more social science-oriented approaches fruitful, rather than emphasizing those "old disciplinary divides".

**250** Humanities-based studies of culture focus especially on how culture is transformed. Culture is thereby understood as the construction of meaning. Academic disciplines that traditionally belong to this critical perspective are e.g. linguistics and languages, literature, philosophy, visual and performing arts, cultural anthropology, and more recent fields within the scope of digital humanities. Given the disciplinary localization of the respective authors, especially the chapters by Ciaudo, Marten-Finnis, Oettl, Pelillo-Hestermeyer, Reichardt and Niccolai can be positioned in this line of thought. As I will further discuss in the last section of this conclusion however, we deeply believe in the need to overcome such disciplinary divides–which we regard as a mere matter of university policy–as most chapters in this book can be assigned both to the humanities-based as well as to the social sciences-approach. It is exactly this inter- and transdisciplinary diversity that the study of culture stands for.

be looked at by focusing on differentiations of, for example, social positions, professions, institutions etc. and the life-style changes involved. For instance, Simmel wrote at the end of the 19th century in "Über sociale Differenzierung" (1890/2016) about how every single person achieves greater individuality through the increase of social differentiations, as the individual is positioned at the crossing of a higher number of social circles through his or her development.[251] This point of view on social circles led, among others, to the development of current social network analysis (White, 2012). Durkheim also wrote, only three years after Simmel, in "Über soziale Arbeitsteilung" (1893/1996), about how the social differentiation of society goes hand in hand with economic specialization and corresponding differentiations of specialist knowledge.[252] Another prominent social theory which is based on differentiations or differences is Niklas Luhmann's system theory (Luhmann, 2018).[253]

More recent approaches in cultural social sciences often acknowledge processes of differentiations in human life too (such as "sociological difference", which describes the difference between theory and its object; Haker, 2020), as well as asking how these differentiations are constructed in the first place, how they are destabilized (see below for the section on deconstructions) and how they lead to unequal conditions (see below for the section on decolonizations, and compare e.g. Albrecht, 2020).

As we can see, processes of differentiation represent an interest for both humanities-based and social theory-based cultural analysis as well as in their interdisciplinary combinations. The differences that are thereby conceptualized are taken as constitutive and necessary for human life. In addition, it is not the fact of differences themselves that are problematized but rather the processes of normalizing certain differences and preferring them over others. This happens, for example, when the doing of otherness is given more attention than the undoing of otherness, which

---

251 A social circle means a random association of relations. A single person can be a member of different social groups and through this develops his*her personality. A society, for Simmel, then describes the social process of the crossing of social circles, i.e. individuals embedded in interactions and group relations. The number of social circles, in which an individual is embedded, also serves as an indicator for culture which is thought of as a system of coordinates. As stated, the more points of intersections exist, the higher one's individuality and personality is. Personality or subjectivity therefore describes the combination of elements of culture which becomes more specific, the more social circles lay next to each other. Individualization, for Simmel, is when an individual also occupies different relative positions within the social circles while based at a higher number of circles in the first place (Simmel, 1890/2016).

252 The division of labour thereby fulfils the function to bind people together by crystallizing social aggregates (socio-economic concentration-*Verdichtung*). This is why Durkheim's theory is also called functionalist differentiation theory (Durkheim, 1893/1996).

253 For Luhmann, difference is mainly conceptualized according to a constructivist perspective, which describes that something only becomes distinct or distinguishable when a difference is introduced in opposition to a sameness, an identity, for example when a system is differentiated from its environment (*Umwelt*) (Luhmann, 2018).

leads to homogenized conceptualizations of social groups and unequal living conditions. Hence, if the doing and undoing of diversity is always bound to the doing and undoing of otherness, it is not the *if* but the *how* this is done that is at stake.

The processual perspective is also adopted in this volume. We do not intend to define what diversity and otherness *are*, but rather to show different examples of how they are practised in a wide variety of situations and contexts, how they are done and undone. Diversity and otherness are not given facts but are normalized, practised and negotiated, which also implies following both a constructivist approach to culture and a situational perspective on different practices in different contexts. So, we shed light on all those different cultural processes of differentiations by examining a variety of normalizations, practices and negotiations of diversity and otherness.

In other words, the cultural study of diversity and otherness in this book looks at how, in different settings, times, and relations, the tension between constructing and stabilizing differences and the deconstruction as well as destabilization of differences is worked out. On the one hand, this entails a praxeological, processual focus which acknowledges the dynamics of any cultural forms (narratives, practices, negotiations, materializations, etc.). On the other hand, it is recognized that the construction of differences can both lead to standardization and even canonization of what diversity is supposed to be or how diversity should be practised, since the same norms and standardized practices can be challenged and undermined by deconstructivist and decolonizing practices, policies and agendas. The tension between these two "sides of the coin" does not necessarily have to be acted out between a somehow more powerful elite (who sets the norms) and a less powerful subaltern group (who has to bow to these rules or try to challenge them from a grassroot level), but both the construction (the doing) and deconstruction (the undoing; see Hirschauer in this volume) of differences can take place in practices at any micro-, meso- or macro-level of society. Moreover, as research in both Kulturwissenschaften and Cultural Studies has pointed out, power asymmetries and hegemony reveal themselves in society in much more subtle ways than the mere juxtaposition of single, clearly identifiable social groups. For example, the chapters by Pelillo-Hestermeyer (Linguistic Diversity), Höhne, Pelillo-Hestermeyer and Cismondi, Marten-Finnis, Espahangizi and myself (Epistemologies; How to Curate) all describe how various institutional players normalize the application of diversity policies as well as narratives and practices of diversity and otherness. Last but not least, Oettl, Ciaudo, Niccolai and Reichardt, while also referring to macro- and meso-levels, place an emphasis on individual settings in which diversity and otherness are performed. Again, these foci are interrelated and are treated in different specifications in all chapters of this book.

In places where these processes involve asymmetries in power and/or lead to a prioritization of certain identity traits over others, we sought to shed light not only on how such representations, homogenizations and canonizations take place, but also if and how they can eventually be better addressed if not overcome. I will come back to the transcultural approach of this book later by summarizing how the doing and undoing of otherness necessarily involves conflict and negotiations, rather than a supposedly tolerant celebration of diversity, as well as how the chapters of this volume discuss emancipatory approaches, among other ways by deconstructing dichotomous and static conceptualizations of culture and decolonizing, and thereby overcoming, inequalities and asymmetric power relations.

The first set of chapters takes a look at how, in the scholarly debate itself, the mentioned standardizations and canonizations of diversity and otherness take place and how these academic norms relate to social practices on different levels. As the transcultural approach of this book seeks to address critically the ways in which certain concepts of diversity and otherness are preferred and standardized over others, the first three chapters focused on academic terms and concepts in different settings which are connected to the field of the study of diversity and otherness and their applications and uses. In particular, my first chapter looked at the epistemologies of intersectional and cross-cultural diversity and otherness, Hirschauer approached the doing and undoing of social distinctions and Espahangizi analysed the historical contingency of different concepts of (multi)cultural diversity and social practices surrounding immigration processes in Switzerland.[254]

I showed how, in the study of culture in general, and in the sociological study of culture more specifically, two different basic narratives of diversity and otherness have been developed, normalized and canonized, which can be called first *intersectional* and second *cross-cultural* diversity and otherness. The majority of academic perspectives in the study of culture which I have discussed in this chapter approach *intersectional diversity* as intersecting social belongings, which tend to include socially, and *intersectional otherness* as emphasizing intersecting difference to fulfil exclusionary functions. Conversely, *cross-cultural diversity* is understood to assign meaning to ambiguous cultural symbols, whereas *cross-cultural otherness* is conceptualized as movements that de-stabilise differences and thus blur border-markings.

This summary of canonizing trends does not mean that it stands for any current academic debate in the study of culture whatsoever, nor that there are not many exceptions that were not mentioned at all. In addition, the analysis was itself conducted within the framework of a powerful epistemological setting (see also Brunner, 2020) in which I had to reflect on my own positionality. After all, academic approaches that seek to re-think normalizing tendencies and overcome unequal power relations in academia and beyond are also themselves part of those powerful epistemes they supposedly "fight against". As I have noted, not only are epistemes powerful in structuring symbolic orders (Foucault, 1974; Bourdieu, 1992), thereby exercising an

---

**254** Concepts such as cosmopolitanism (Marten-Finnis, Ciaudo), civilization (Marten-Finnis, Ciaudo), modernity (Ciaudo) or Westernism and Orientalism (Ciaudo, Marten-Finnis, Höhne) are equally challenged, but will not be highlighted separately in order to keep this conclusion focused on the main aspects of diversity and otherness in this volume.

"epistemic violence" (Spivak, 1988), but also we have to realize that knowledge production is always entangled with political interests (Richardson, 2018).

This book itself is no exception and can of course be critically placed in the row of both epistemological streams of *intersectional and cross-cultural diversity and otherness*. However, with our transcultural approach (which itself threatens to become another one of those standardized academic concepts), this volume has sought to open the debate to re-think not only unequal power relations that exist in academia, but also to point at emancipatory approaches in scholarly and non-academic social life. I will come back to this point in the last section of this conclusion. In my chapter on Epistemologies, I also concluded with the call to "transculturalize" the study of diversity and otherness by acknowledging the two main features of postcolonial critique in the analysis of diversity and otherness through decolonizing unequal (often Eurocentric) power structures, as well as through deconstructing dichotomies in our thinking. Also, by including as many perspectives and standpoints as possible, such a transcultural approach to the study of diversity and otherness could help to "rethink a Europe Otherwise" (Boatcă, 2010).

For Stefan Hirschauer any cultural phenomenon can be conceptualized as a meaningful distinction. He focussed on those meaningful differentiations that mark (multiple) social affiliations. All these processes are extremely heterogeneous and contingent with many possible grades of intensity. This is what Hirschauer described as the doing and undoing of differences, a processual model that takes into account the relativity and diversity of contingent processes of categorizations. The study of diversity and otherness should hence ask how individuals process differences and focus on the question of why, when and how a difference becomes (ir-)relevant as differences constantly are (re-)enforced, minimized or de-differentiated. In addition, the chapter outlined several theoretical concepts regarding social distinctions, such as hybridity, social circles and intersectionality, which show how the study of differences has been standardized within the study of culture. As such, Hirschauer's approach can be called a praxeological, constructivist perspective to the contingency of social distinctions, which also deconstructs standardized established theoretical models. This stands in line with the constructivist and deconstructivist, as well as with the processual and transcultural, approach of this book.

Likewise, Kijan Espahangizi conducted a constructivist analysis of how the "interpretative frameworks" on immigration and integration in public and scholarly debate in Switzerland changed throughout the 1980s, on what historicities they were based upon, and how they related to social processes of diversification following immigration. By looking at "micro-practices of postmigrant conviviality" and how they can be related to discourses that arise in the course of these practices at the same time, Espahangizi's approach not only emphasized the need in cultural analysis to acknowledge that any cultural practice, narrative, product, etc. is historically shaped and can hence only be understood as situational, dynamic and contingent. This approach also stands as a bridge in the above-mentioned disciplinary divide between humanities-based, interpretative approaches to culture, which consider the production of meaning, and social-theoretical ways of looking at social practices and uses of cultural "material". Here instead, the "mutually constitutive interaction between social and discursive change" was highlighted.

The chapter presented a parallel analysis of the "historical co-emergence of the concept and the object of (multi)cultural diversity" by comparing especially two projects in Swiss immigration policies and debates–the *Mitenand*-movement, a "coalition for solidarity with 'foreign workers'" and the Swiss refugee aid project–and related their histories to the public and academic discourse on diversity during the same time. The key question of the chapter, namely how "culture" could become the "key signifier with regard to immigration and integration", was answered by distinguishing the respective historicities of all practices and discourses that were analysed. In particular, two different notions of cultural diversity were detected: a traditional one that is based on regional multilingualism has served as an essential cornerstone for Swiss national identity for a long time, and a more recent one that is conceptualized around the "ethnic diversity" of immigrants in Switzerland in the course of the second half of the 20th century, which relies mostly on culturalist arguments. Again, both notions of diversity were repeatedly related to the social practices of postmigrant conviviality that took place in and around the analysed projects. Another project on the representations of diversity in Switzerland from 2015 showed that both notions of cultural diversity still have not been integrated with each other. However, Espahangizi did not conclude by highlighting only these standardizations of cultural diversity, but rather stressed their ambiguities, permanent transformations, controversies and contradictory histories, highlighting the permanent interplay of the contingent construction and deconstruction of diversity and otherness.

## 14.2 Transcultural Negotiations: Deconstructions

A focus on the processes of standardization as well as the destabilization of diversity and otherness is not only thoroughly assumed in these chapters, but many other cultural theories have also challenged dichotomous thinking beyond the scope of this book. Theories of modernity have been defied through these deconstructivist developments, as they are often based on dichotomous differentiations such as nature-culture, modernity-tradition, us-them etc. Following Gurminder Bhambra, theories of modernity assume that "Western" modernity developed through the Enlightenment, the French Revolution and processes of industrialization while distinguishing between stable differences. These differences are based on the assumptions of a temporal rupture between a traditional, agrarian past and a modern, industrial present, as well as on an imagined difference between Europe and the rest of the world, in which the "Western" side is put to be universal and superior (Bhambra, 2007, p. 1). Also, in more humanities-oriented fields in the study of culture, the logocentrism of

"Western" science has been criticized (Derrida, 2004), established notions of subjectivity have been questioned (Foucault, 1978) and possibilities of agency have been critically provoked (Spivak, 1988; Haraway, 2017). As I have stated in my chapter on the epistemologies of diversity and otherness, it was especially poststructuralism as well as postcolonial theory that developed different heuristic models to re-think, revise and read against the grain. Gender and queer studies and other theoretical strands, such as new materialism or ecofeminism, have complimented this vast array of approaches with other tools such as standpoint epistemologies, situated knowledges, psychoanalysis and queering perspectives.

To take the praxeological stance of this book as our departure point, the tension that arises between the above-mentioned standardizations of diversity and otherness and how, in practice, these and other norms become challenged, undermined and negotiated, is a further focal point that runs through many chapters of this book. However, these chapters put more emphasis on the tension between standardizations of diversity and otherness and various corresponding deconstructivist practices they have found in their respective fields of analysis. The chapters by Ciaudo, Marten-Finnis, Oettl, Pelillo-Hestermeyer (Linguistic Diversity), and Reichardt especially focus on how norms are established in the first place and on how irritations of the norm and challenging deconstructions sometimes blur the differences that have been constructed in different settings and intensities.

As such, a focus on these deconstructivist practices can lead to in-between spaces and ambiguous cultural symbols, and can therefore be called transcultural negotiations. As the transcultural approach of this book involves the constructions of (hegemonic) differences as well as their conflictual deconstructions at the same time, the tension between these two, which is in constant flux and is negotiated every time anew, is exactly what the transcultural practice stands for. The chapters by Niccolai, Höhne, myself (How to Curate) as well as Pelillo-Hestermeyer and Cismondi all make this tension into a subject of discussion. As they offer an analysis of unequal power relations and exemplify how the established norms are challenged in social life, they will be summarized in the next section on decolonizations. This does not entail that these latter chapters include a more detailed or even a more sophisticated transcultural approach than the former. The decision to summarize them in a section of their own was taken in order to highlight another focal point of this volume: decolonizations. Again, the constructivist and deconstructivist, processual and contingent focuses on norms, practices and negotiations of diversity and otherness from a transcultural perspective, which takes conflicts into account, are present in all chapters of this book, but only in different compositions.

Joseph Ciaudo in his chapter focused on how the rejection of "Western" clothes by a Chinese minister in the early 20th century offers insights into transcultural practices of negotiating the standardized meanings of the "West" and the "East". In this chapter, clothing is regarded not only as a tool in the fight between ruler (colonizer) and ruled (colonized), which serves as a standard to "justify European colonialism".

Clothing is also looked at concerning its social dimension, as a matter of defending and presenting one's identity, with the result that it serves perfectly as the basis for his analysis of the constructions and deconstructions of cultural differences. By looking at different texts written by the Chinese minister to the USA, Spain and Peru Wu Tinfang—a "central figure of Chinese political and intellectual life" during that time—, Ciaudo showed how Wu did not reject "Western" dress either in order to defend the "Chinese way" over the "American" one, or in order to negotiate between these two sides that are thought to oppose each other as clearly defined single cultures. Wu can rather be described as a "transculturalist", as he transcended "given cultures", explored "new horizons", navigated "through very blurry cultures" and thereby produced "a cohesive way of life that acted as a junction between different life-worlds". Ciaudo concluded that Wu's negotiation of a "transcultural modernity" with "hygiene" ("*weisheng*, living a civilized life in ethical and medical terms") as a salient aspect de-territorialises the "idea of civilization from the West", and can therefore be regarded as a transcultural negotiation which transcends static and dichotomous conceptualizations of culture in a contingent, deconstructivist and dynamic process which necessarily involves situational conflicts on individual, institutional and state-political levels.

Closely connected to the chapter by Ciaudo by its interest in the social practices surrounding (material) cultural productions, Susanne Marten-Finnis conducted an analysis of the performances of the *Ballets Russes* that took place in Paris, London and other European metropolis at the beginning of the 20th century. This analysis showed how these ballets led to the artistic upsurge called the "Russian Silver Age" at the turn of the century, which also influenced French couture and British domestic interiors through the adaptations of the Oriental themes displayed in set designs and costumes. These adaptations can therefore be seen as triggering rather than learning from integrated art forms that became popular in European Symbolism at that time. Similarly, Marten-Finnis described how the standardizations of the "Oriental Other" were constructed in the first place, and how, then, by drawing on other forms of Russian self-presentation that rely on associations beyond the established display of Russian folklore, a new Oriental theme that looked "East" and not "West" challenged and deconstructed those standardizations.

These standardizations of the "Oriental Other" were usually thought to reinforce stereotypes of outdated folklore associated with "familiar fairy-tale forests of Europe". Equally, in academic literature, the critique of Orientalism is most often linked to Edward Said's interpretation as an act of colonialism in which knowledge about the Orient serves "to subjugate the Other". Marten-Finnis questioned these standardized interpretations in her analysis of several performances of the *Ballets Russes,* as well as by linking their symbolic practices to other knowledge about the Orient that can be traced back to other practices of the ancient Silk Road, which Russian ethnographers had researched from a transcultural perspective at the end of the 19th century. These scholars and their influence on the displays in the *Ballets Russes* made it possible for

Marten-Finnis to analyse the ballets as *heterotopias* in Foucault's sense. Therefore, the performances understood as such "mythical and real counter-spaces" both provided the artists with a space to rehearse a "revamped identity" on European stages, and provoked a shift in imagining the "Oriental Other" as something familiar and desirable and no longer as unfamiliar and outdated for European audiences. Thus, the deconstructions of symbolic practices by dancers and decorateurs of the *Ballets Russes* are not only understood as PR acts to cater to the "Western" audiences, who enthusiastically perceived the performances as physical representations of an "Oriental Other", but also as negotiations of Otherness, which offer new insights in their corresponding counter-spaces when analysed from a transcultural point of view.

The chapter by Barbara Oettl approached negotiations of diversity and otherness in an even more deconstructivist way by making the performances and multi-media artworks of the artist ORLAN the subject of her discussion. ORLAN, born in 1947, not only questions standardized understandings of the body, identity, "Self" and "Other" with her radical artistic approaches from the 1960s onwards, but she also challenges the anthropocentric focus of most science on what it can mean to be human to the core. ORLAN literally changed, hybridized and multiplied her bodily identity and personality through live surgeries on her body, psychoanalysis and virtual self-hybridizations. Through intensive descriptions of many of ORLAN's "surgical performances", which took place especially at the beginning of the 1990s as well as corresponding and un-associated virtual 3D artworks, Oettl discussed how ORLAN critically examines legal and ethical issues on three distinct levels. On a juridical level, ORLAN lays open how a legal persona is normalized and expected to represent a stable identity. On a scientific transgenetic level, her "Carnal Art" shows how "we have all become cyborgs a long time ago". Finally, by breaching feminist and transgendered issues, ORLAN examined how standards of beauty are deconstructed. Instead, ORLAN depicts a transcultural, transnatural, technoscientific and posthuman condition by these crossings and transformations. Through Oettl's discussion, it became clear that standardizations of diversity and otherness, constructions of identities, the "Self" and "Other" can only be understood as interchanging, reproducing, multiplying and hybridizing, and hence as contingent processual and situational constructions. To become aware of this, Oettl concluded, is indispensable in "this world of growing inacceptance of the 'Other'". Thus, ORLAN's transcultural approach of deconstructing established self-understandings exposes how every presupposition of stable beings only rests on constructed shaky foundations.

In her chapter on linguistic diversity, Giulia Pelillo-Hestermeyer also discussed several examples of how linguistic practices are standardized as well as negotiated and deconstructed in "mediatized public spheres". Mediatized public spheres were understood in this context as spaces in which both these standardizations of "normative attitudes towards language(s)" and counter-hegemonic practices against these normalizations are practised. By focusing on this tension between construction and deconstruction, "doing diversity" and "doing otherness", and by highlighting the conflicts involved in these processes, the chapter outlined the transcultural approach of this volume in the field of linguistic diversity. The common static assumption of languages as "monolithic systems" was hence deconstructed by highlighting deconstructivist practices as well as the diversification processes of media and language(s) in relation to social changes, such as globalization and migration and the resulting transformation of public spheres. The chapter discussed these questions by focusing especially on two examples: first on the standardizations, institutionalizations and negotiations surrounding the discussion of English as a "global language"; and second, on how "language(s)" are represented and performed in institutional policies and politics on a European level. Pelillo-Hestermeyer concluded that, even while there are many deconstructivist practices of "multiple appropriations and re-signifying practices" that work against the "ideological frames" which are imposed, they have not yet arrived at European media-makers. However, given the ordinariness of mixing "languages" in mediatized public spheres as well as in every-day life, this might be acknowledged as the new standard in the future.

The chapter by Dagmar Reichardt took Italian fashion as another field of cultural analysis by highlighting the practices of standardizations and corresponding negotiations of diversity and otherness. Similarly to Ciaudo and Marten-Finnis, dress was understood in its material, social and discursive dimensions as a way of negotiating identities as well as promoting emancipatory transcultural approaches. By drawing equally from more humanities-based approaches in semiotics as well as from social theory, the case study of mainly Italian fashion was conducted to show fashion's potential to construct (standardize) and deconstruct at the same time. Through the examination of the fashion duo Dolce & Gabbana, Pulitzer Prize Winner Jhumpa Lahiri in her writings on fashion, the theory, history and mechanisms of the Italian fashion system in the last 70 years, and finally a specific fashion show by Karl Lagerfeld staged in 2016, Reichardt emphasized this tension between "dichotomized concepts" and "processes of interconnectedness", between homogeneity (standardization) and heterogeneity (diversification) that eventually lead to spaces that open "*in between* of countries, borders and cultures". She concluded by stressing how the inclusion of Fashion Studies within Cultural Studies and the topic of Italian fashion in Modern Italian Studies might more specifically meet the need to revert established power relations between centre and periphery. This quest to overcome unequal power relations also lies at the core of the decolonizing approach that runs through most chapters of this book in different specifications and which will be summarized more in detail in the following section.

## 14.3 Decolonizing Practices of Otherness

A further, but no less important, epistemological assumption regarding diversity and otherness in this book can be called equality-theoretical. Similarly to constructivist and/or deconstructivist epistemological assumptions, theoretical emphasis on differences and/or (in-)equalities is not a matter of "either/or", but is rather accentuated in all contributions in this book, only in different specifications. The underlying question is how the doing and undoing of diversity and otherness help to strengthen, challenge or even dissolve unequal conditions in both social realms and in discursive settings. This also encompasses the quest to overcome unequal power relations (decolonization) and deconstruct dichotomies in thinking, writing and speaking, as well as the attempt to offer emancipatory, transculturally sensitive ways in other domains.

Such decolonizing practices are mostly elaborated from multiple deconstructivist and postcolonial traditions of thought and activism. They lay open invisible power relations and how these impact different cultural constructions of differences. Equally, these approaches place an emphasis on how any construction and deconstruction of diversity and otherness can never be neutral, but are rather always biased and formed by standardizing norms, entangled with processes of inclusion and exclusion, in such a way as to contribute to hierarchical power relations.

The exercise of not only unveiling these power inequalities but also developing politics that help to subvert them can therefore be viewed as a central aspect of the concept of (transcultural) decolonization. As I have shown in both my chapters, this decolonial focus on political practice can be traced back to the political liberation struggles of former colonies in the 1950s. Hierarchical power relations persist up to this day and seem to even intensify. These inequalities do not necessarily have to relate (only) to colonial structures, even though, for example, the entanglement of today's neoliberal capitalist structures with social inequalities on a global scale remains obvious (Quijano, 2000). I have nevertheless argued that decolonization can be understood not only as political and epistemological liberation from (neo-)colonial structures in social life and thought, but also encompasses "any fight for liberation from any unequal power structures".

Yet, instead of merely opposing the more hegemonic side from below and thereby reproducing and strengthening the dichotomy that unequal power relations are based upon, decolonization means the permanent (conflictual) negotiation of diversity and otherness, while constantly acknowledging as many perspectives as possible in this process, in a corresponding way to the transcultural approach we have aimed at in this volume. For instance, Boatcă describes how the "double imperial difference in Europe"[255] leads to "two types of European subalterns to the hegemonic model of power" and "multiple Europes" (Boatcă, 2010, p. 4). Because of the countless

---

[255] This "double imperial difference in Europe" is understood as follows: "on the one hand, an external difference between the new capitalist core and the existing traditional empires of the Islamic and Eastern Christian faith–the Ottoman and the Tsarist one; on the other hand, an internal difference between the new and the old capitalist core, mainly England vs. Spain" (Boatcă, 2010, p. 4).

complexity of differences, it is required to highlight many different ways of decolonization (p. 5). This is again exactly what the transcultural focus of this volume entails.

As Homi K. Bhabha wrote, the complex and dynamic processes of the social articulation of differences is a constant contingent negotiation that questions normative traditions and expectations. Any political empowerment thereby relies on the possibility to pose questions from the perspective in-between. Likewise, negotiating the articulation of differences from such a transcultural perspective—by "dis-placing", "reading against the grain", "re-inscribing", "cultural border-work", "rebellious acts of cultural translation", "going beyond"[256]—can lead to "in-between (third) spaces" of "hybridity" that can serve as innovative spaces for both collaboration and antagonism (Bhabha, 1997, pp. 123–134). These hybrid cultural in-between spaces become spaces for interventions and political actions in the decolonial sense described, where it becomes possible to not only acknowledge (her*hi)stories of exploitation and inequality but also to develop strategies of resistance by creatively inventing new diversities and othernesses beyond mere dichotomies.

Thus, in close connection to the deconstructivist notion described above, and thereby blurring references and representations in or through these in-between counter-spaces, the last set of chapters by Niccolai, Höhne, Pelillo-Hestermeyer & Cismondi and myself (How to Curate) concentrate especially on how transculturally sensitive approaches to standardizations can be analysed as practices that, by manoeuvring differences, help to decolonize their respective life-worlds. The theoretical perspective on (in)equality, even when equally focusing on cultural differences as do the aforementioned chapters, implies describing a (political) tendency which seeks to overcome hegemonic normalizations of cultural differences in order to achieve, for instance, social equity in the form of fostering more inclusive theatrical practice (Niccolai), decolonizing the normative binary gender order (Höhne), curating diversity and otherness in performance arts without exoticizing or paternalizing (my chapter on How to Curate Diversity and Otherness) and establishing good practices in managing diversity in scientific environments (Pelillo-Hestermeyer and Cismondi).

In this light, Marta Niccolai's chapter on Romani on the contemporary Italian stage discussed how three Italian playwrights portrayed the discrimination of Roma people established in common stereotypes and prejudices as well as visible social injustices by offering new narratives in whose constructions Romani themselves were involved. An analysis of different plays by the playwrights Daniele Lamuraglia (Florence), Fiorenza Menni and Andrea Mochi Sismondi (Bologna), and Pino Petruzzelli (Genoa) as outcomes of personal encounters with Romani showed how such processes of interweaving challenge and deconstruct standardized views of "Romani identity".

---

**256** "Gegen-den-Strich-Lesen", "Neueinschreibung kultureller Zeichen", "kulturelle Grenz-Arbeit", "aufrührerischer Akt kultureller Übersetzung", "Darüberhinausgehen", "De-plazieren" (Bhabha, 1997, pp. 123–134).

As such, these plays can be read as transcultural emancipatory practices, that help to not only decolonize theatrical practice but also to serve as political acts to counter social injustice in general. In the context of unequal relationships such as the normalized one between Roma at the margins of society and non-Roma at the centre of society, the chapter shed light on how "the question of 'voice'" becomes important in the contingent process of construction and deconstruction of diversity and otherness.

While Niccolai focused on this processual tension between standardizing and negotiating cultural differences on stage through a transcultural lens, it became obvious how the plays analysed, by "break[ing] away from standard representations", can be understood not only as deconstructing but also as decolonizing practices that make visible new ways of creating "new realities". The first example regards a trilogy by Lamuraglia in which Roma are brought on stage, so "the margin becomes visible". Furthermore, new meanings are generated by different theatrical strategies such as the reversal of established symbols, parody narrated from a Roma perspective, and the re-reading of classics. In the second example, Menni and Sismondi not only play with a diversity of languages on stage, but have alienated themselves from their usual context by staying with Romani communities in Macedonia as part of the playwrighting process. These plays were interpreted as offering insights into a "transcultural process" such as an "anthropological journey", in which "what counts is one's approach toward the other". Finally, the third example of Narrative theatre by Petruzzeli also challenges the norm by de-centering it and giving the voice to the unprivileged. The chapter concluded that the transcultural approach of the three playwrights of personal exchange and deconstruction of the standard "becomes a political act of social inclusion and emancipation", and, as such, a decolonial act.

The next chapter by Marek Sancho Höhne can also be read as both focussing on standardizations and deconstructions of these, as well as providing insights into decolonial approaches to overcome social inequalities. Höhne discussed how the normative binary gender order relies on how gender is narrated and mapped and thereby standardized in public discourse and medico-legal knowledge. This "net of knowledge and power" is deeply entangled with both temporality (e.g. narrations of medical treatments for trans* people as a linear movement) and locality (e.g. "imaginations of trans* are connected to questions of national belonging"). The chapter analysed standardizations of trans lives with different examples. The first examples, which was taken from the medico-legal system in Germany, showed how trans* bodies are (psycho)pathologized and treated as "an individual problem", for whose "treatment" national belonging is required in order to have access to the healthcare system. The medico-legal system does not allow for negotiations of normative boundaries and does not take into account resisting practices that blur these norms. The second set of examples discussed different Othering processes regarding trans lives which were detectable in mainstream media contributions. Narratives on trans lives are thereby instrumentalized and serve to display an "assumed progressiveness" of Germany: such a trans* nationalism is at work, for instance, when seemingly inclusionary calls for more "gay and queer equality" at the same time produce exclusions through the embedded racialisations of trans\* discriminatory violence.

According to Höhne, in all these normalizations and negotiations of diversity and otherness regarding gender, contradictions are not spelled out nor are the realities of trans lives adequately grasped. Therefore, in the next step, different strategies of self-narrations for resisting these standardizations were highlighted, which can be called decolonial in the described sense. The life stories of several trans\* people can help to understand how the normative binary gender order can be not only deconstructed, but can also help to "try to find a solution to survive all the violence" directed against them. These life stories of "resistance and adoption", of "interaction and negotiation", the chapter concluded, show how trans\* people are "no[t] simple victims of oppression, but rather actors inside these negotiations". It is about the diversity of narrations and imaginations of trans lives that helps to decolonize the normative binary gender order, questions of belonging and classifications of "us" and "them".

In my chapter "How to Curate Diversity and Otherness in Gobal Performance Art", I similarly showed that such a diversity of narrations and imaginations is necessary to find different ways to decolonize the field of global performance art. In order to answer the question of how curating diversity and otherness in this field of practice could be possible without labelling or paternalizing and without essentializing "just another hegemonic norm", I discussed several approaches taken from both academic literature and interviews conducted in the field, that try to offer emancipatory views which go beyond the established "hegemonic mainstream's entanglement with social inequalities". In the main interview used, which was conducted with Claude Jansen, an independent scholar, performer, dramaturge and curator based in Hamburg, I considered the underlying question of how to decolonize the field of curating global performance art. Curating was hence understood as a social practice that is deeply embedded with structural conditions that mutually influence this practice in turn. Even though the main emphasis was put on the field of performance art, I nevertheless showed that these conditions and practices are similarly present in other art forms, such as literature, visual arts or music.

I first focused on structural conditions that enable and limit how diversity and otherness are represented in global performance art, for instance in politics, that strive for equal access. These representations of diversity and otherness focus largely on individuals and groups from an intersectional perspective and on how "unequal economic and power relations on a global scale" can be overcome. The examples I discussed show that these politics both foster "inclusionary and exclusionary outcomes in the arts" at the same time. I then discussed several cross-cultural artistic practices of performing diversity and otherness. This means that the focus was placed on how artistic practices are performed, which are conceptualized as hybrid, and which offer possibilities "for in-between spaces and re-readings of established (b-)ordering practices". I again showed how these cross-cultural agendas often have contradictory outcomes of both opening and closing in-between spaces, and of both standardizing and deconstructing norms of diversity and otherness. While referring to how decolonizing approaches in curating practice "emphasize both modes of solidarity and complicity as well as notions of conflict, complication and disruption", I concluded with the suggestion to understand diversity and otherness in a transcultural way, meaning that it is not understood as *a priori* but negotiated every time anew. Such a transcultural understanding of diversity and otherness could pose a way to decolonize curating global performance art by taking into account "a plurality of voices" in a communicative process of negotiations that also entails the negotiation of conflicts.

Last but not least, Giulia Pelillo-Hestermeyer and Fabio Cismondi focused on similar questions but in a seemingly completely distinct field: science. Regarding methodology, this chapter had further parallels to my earlier one, as it was also based mainly on academic literature reviews in the field of diversity management and organizational studies and on one interview which was conducted with Pietro Barabaschi, a scientist who is Head of Department at Fusion for Energy and Director of the European-Japanese Broader Approach activities. By deconstructing the established norm in diversity management that mainly looked at diversity as a "sum of single identity groups", the chapter examined from a constructivist perspective how the "doing" of diversity in scientific communities can rather be understood as a "fluid category", which involves permanent negotiations of (trans)cultural exchanges.

In taking one of the sub-projects of the nuclear fusion research megaproject ITER, the European-Japanese cooperation within Broader Fusion Development as an example, the authors showed how diversity, understood as a dynamic complex of negotiations and practices, influence both processes of constructing the reactor and of developing a group project identity, which in this case particularly contributed to the success of it. This "ability of the work-team in constructively integrating differences in approaches and frameworks", or the "diversity of laboratory cultures" of the cooperating research institutes, played a significantly greater role in the overall success than merely overcoming static stereotypes of e.g. national differences. The chapter concluded with an emphasis on this "strong nexus between the socio-cultural dimensions of scientific cooperation and its outcomes" that could help to decolonize diversity management (studies), by not only deconstructing certain norms and standardizations of diversity and otherness, but also highlighting the emancipatory approach followed in the discussed project of being aware of "culture" in scientific management. As such, this chapter closed the transcultural endeavour of this volume by bridging seemingly inter- and transdisciplinary divides in practices, norms and negotiations of diversity and otherness.

## 14.4 The Transcultural Study of Diversity and Otherness: An Overview

To sum up, the chapters of this book discussed different intertwined processes of doing diversity and otherness from a range of processual, praxeological and constructivist perspectives. The construction and standardization of differences are always connected to the deconstruction and negotiation of them in turn, resulting in both inclusionary and exclusionary outcomes. The situational approach of this volume entailed that a wide variety of these practices in tension between normalizations and negotiations were discussed from historical and contemporary perspectives, covering a wide range of different life-worlds and from different methodological and theoretical standpoints in the study of culture. One might be surprised not to find any explicit reference to a geographical diversity this book intended to cover. However, given the dynamic understanding of culture and thus of practices of diversity and otherness which is followed throughout the chapters, it should be obvious that any territorial or topographic representation can only be understood as another normed construction in itself. Hence, we wanted to pose the questions from the start as to how these unequal representations have been normalized, are negotiated and deconstructed and eventually can be overcome, i.e. decolonized instead. These questions were discussed in different settings and contexts, different cultural forms (narratives, politics, practices, negotiations, materializations, etc.) and at different micro-, meso- or macro-levels of society. The cultural practices conceived as life-worlds analysed in this volume range from the study of culture (myself on epistemologies), the contingency of human differentiations (Hirschauer), postmigrancy in Switzerland (Espahangizi), "Western" clothes in China (Ciaudo), *Ballet Russes* (Marten-Finnis), multi-media performance as well as bodily practices (Oettl), mediatized public spheres (Pelillo-Hestermeyer on linguistic diversity), "Italian" fashion (Reichardt), to Romani on stage in Italy (Niccolai), trans* gender narratives in Germany (Höhne), global performance art (myself on how to curate), and international scientific groups (Pelillo-Hestermeyer and Cismondi). While the majority of this book's articles took a look at contemporary life-worlds (Hirschauer, myself, Reichardt, Oettl, Pelillo-Hestermeyer, Niccolai, Höhne, Pelillo-Hestermeyer and Cismondi), Espahangizi, Marten-Finnis and Ciaudo applied a historical perspective on their respective research fields.

The wide variety of (inter- and trans-)disciplinary as well as "research field" approaches included, among others, concepts relating to cultural theory (myself on epistemologies, Hirschauer), mediatization (Pelillo-Hestermeyer on linguistic diversity), science and technology studies, feminist and cyborg studies (Oettl), gender and queer studies (Höhne, Oettl), neo-materialism (Ciaudo, Reichardt), entangled history (Espahangizi, Ciaudo, Marten-Finnis), artistic fields (myself on how to curate, Niccolai) and organizational studies (Pelillo-Hestermeyer and Cismondi).

This incomplete listing of positioning the chapters in inner-disciplinary fields within the study of culture highlighted two points in particular: firstly, the bridging of materialistic and idealistic perspectives along with the entanglement of more humanities-based approaches with more social theory-related ones; and secondly, that the cultural study of diversity and otherness needs a transcultural approach, which also takes into account its own conflicts, norms, and negotiations.

As stated above and as the contributions in this volume proved, both humanities-based and social theory-based approaches in the study of culture are no longer two opposing sides in academia, but their contextual entanglement is rather established in practice and proven fruitful without degenerating into mere theoretical eclecticism. Cultural scholars pose thematically framed questions and approach them from many points of view, in order to be able to grasp a tiny bit of cultural complexity from a constructivist stance. In this light, the old disciplinary divides should indeed be overcome, given this established constructivist and deconstructivist, i.e. transcultural practice in the study of culture. We at least deeply believe in the need to overcome such disciplinary divides, and thereby to deconstruct the field of the study of culture itself and negotiate new meanings within the field.

However, certain disciplinary norms and (b-)ordering standardizations persist in the field and remain powerful in structuring, especially in university policies and politics. Academic funding bodies such as the German DFG (*Deutsche Forschungsgemeinschaft*, German Research Foundation) do not have a department specialized in the study of culture in the way delineated in this volume.[257] Most professorships and associated positions attached to departments, faculties or institutes, that are called cultural studies or the like in Germany, are advertised for mono-disciplinary fields. Even if they are advertised rather openly and retain an interdisciplinary focus on thematic questions or, in very few cases, are entitled "cultural studies", in the selection processes those candidates are often preferred over cultural scholars who allow the most disciplinary connections to the established mono-disciplinary department members. Another example for the force of hegemonic norms is the establishment of "trend topics", such as globalization, digitization or social cohesion (including diversity), which function as "canonizers" in the study of culture (Heinze & Jappe, 2020). There are many more examples of such hierarchical power structures but also of subverting strategies. Certainly, selection processes, university and research politics are influenced by many more issues than just these. After all, powerful epistemes and their entanglement with political interests are at work anywhere, and they are difficult to decolonize. We nevertheless hope and believe that the study of culture could be decolonized by taking a transcultural approach not only in research practice but also with regard to policies and politics that structure the field. As this book has shown, such a transcultural approach reveals the construction processes of (hegemonic) differences as well as deconstructs them at the same time. The resultant tension is in constant flux and needs to be negotiated every time anew. This book

---

257 The "Review Board (*Fachkolleg*)" responsible for cultural studies (*Kulturwissenschaft*) of the DFG is called Literary Studies. "Cultural studies" is listed as a sub field of Literary Studies together with General and Comparative Literature. Even though there is the possibility to declare a research grant application as "interdisciplinary", practice shows how reviewers are still often drawn from mono-disciplinary fields (Folk, 2020).

has offered insights into emancipatory approaches in scholarly and non-academic social life by including a diversity of narrations, standardizations, imaginations, deconstructions and negotiations, which functioned as inter- and transdisciplinary bridges over established divides. All in all, it invites to re-think norms, practices and negotiations of diversity and otherness in further ways, in order to "transculturalize" the politics in the study of culture.

# References

Albrecht, M. (2020). Europas südliche Ränder: Interdisziplinäre Perspektiven auf Asymmetrien, Hierarchien und Postkolonialismus-Verlierer (1st ed.). Edition Kulturwissenschaft. transcript.

Bhabha, H. K. (1997). Verortungen der Kultur. In E. Bronfen, M. Benjamin & S. Therese (Eds.), Stauffenburg discussion: Vol. 4. Hybride Kulturen: Beiträge zur anglo-amerikanischen Multikulturalismusdebatte (pp. 123–148). Stauffenburg.

Bhambra, G. K. (2007). Rethinking modernity: Postcolonialism and the sociological imagination. Palgrave. https://doi.org/10.1057/9780230206410

Boatcă, M. (2010). Multiple Europes and the Politics of Difference Within. In H. Brunkhorst & G. Grözinger (Eds.), The Study of Europe (pp. 51–66). Nomos Verlagsgesellschaft mbH & Co KG. https://doi.org/10.5771/9783845225487-51

Bourdieu, P. (1992). Rede und Antwort (1st ed., Vol. 547). Edition Suhrkamp: 1547. Suhrkamp.

Brunner, C. (2020). Epistemische Gewalt: Wissen und Herrschaft in der kolonialen Moderne. Edition Politik. transcript.

Cassirer, E. (1997). Philosophie der symbolischen Formen (licensed edition). Primus-Verlag.

Derrida, J. (2004). Die différance: Ausgewählte Texte (P. Engelmann, Ed.). Universal-Bibliothek: Nr. 18338. Philipp Reclam jun.

Dictionary. (n.d.). Difference: Synonym. Retrieved February 25, 2020, from https://www.dictionary.com/browse/otherness?s=t

Durkheim, É. (1996). Über soziale Arbeitsteilung: Studie über die Organisation höherer Gesellschaften (2nd ed., Vol. 1005). Suhrkamp-Taschenbuch Wissenschaft. Suhrkamp. (Original work published 1893)

Folk, C. (2020). Kein Selbstzweck: Kreative Forschung und Drittmittelstrategien. Forschung & Lehre (3), 202–204.

Foucault, M. (1974). Die Ordnung der Dinge: Eine Archäologie der Humanwissenschaften (1st ed.). Suhrkamp-Taschenbuch Wissenschaft.

Foucault, M. (1978). Dispositive der Macht: Über Sexualität, Wissen und Wahrheit. IMD: Vol. 77. Merve.

Frege, G. (1990). Schriften zur Logik und Sprachphilosophie: Aus dem Nachlass (3rd ed.). Philosophische Bibliothek: Vol. 277. Meiner.

Haker, C. (2020). Immanente Kritik soziologischer Theorie: Auf dem Weg in ein pluralistisches Paradigma. Praktiken der Subjektivierung. transcript.

Haraway, D. (2017). A cyborg manifesto: Science, technology, and socialist-feminism in the late twentieth century. In R. Latham (Ed.), Science fiction criticism: an anthology of essential writings (pp. 306–329). Bloomsbury Academic.

Heinze, T., & Jappe, A. (2020). Fundamentales Spannungsfeld: Wissenschaftliche Relevanz und Originalität. Forschung & Lehre (3), 198–200.

Herder, J. G. v. (1975). Abhandlung über den Ursprung der Sprache. Universal-Bibliothek: 8729/30. Reclam. (Original work published Berlin 1772)

Latin Dictionary. (n.d.). Differentia. Retrieved February 25, 2020, from https://latin-dictionary.net/definition/17616/differentia-differentiae

Luhmann, N. (2018). Soziales System, Gesellschaft, Organisation (6th ed., Vol. 3). Soziologische Aufklärung. Springer VS.

Quijano, A. (2000). Coloniality of Power and Eurocentrism in Latin America. International Sociology, 15(2), 215–232. https://doi.org/10.1177/0268580900015002005

Richardson, W. J. (2018). Understanding Eurocentrism as a Structural Problem of Undone Science. In G. K. Bhambra, D. Gebrial & K. Nişancıoğlu (Eds.), Decolonising the university (pp. 231–247). Pluto Press.

Simmel, G. (2016). Über sociale Differenzierung: Soziologische und psychologische Untersuchungen (K.-M. Guth, Ed.) (1st ed.). Contumax; Hofenberg. (Original work published 1890)

Spivak, G. C. (1988). Can the subaltern speak? In C. Nelson & L. Grossberg (Eds.), Marxism and the interpretation of culture (pp. 66–111). University of Illinois Press.

White, H. C. (2012). Identity and Control: How Social Formations Emerge (2nd Edition). Princeton University Press. https://www.jstor.org/stable/j.ctt1r2fg1

Wittgenstein, L. (1977). Philosophische Untersuchungen (1st ed., Vol. 203). Suhrkamp-Taschenbuch Wissenschaft. Suhrkamp.

# Academic Biographies

**Joseph Ciaudo** is an Associate Professor at Orléans University, France, and has been a Postdoctoral research fellow at Ghent University, Belgium. His research delves into the history of concepts of culture and civilization at the end of the nineteenth and early twentieth centuries. He is mainly interested in how these concepts contributed in China to new apologetic narratives in favour of Confucianism, as seen from the perspectives of both conceptual and transcultural history.

**Fabio Cismondi** graduated as a nuclear engineer at the Polytechnic School or Torino (Italy) and obtained his doctoral degree at CEA (Commisariat a l'Energie Atomique) in Cadarache and University of Toulon and Var (France). He worked in CEA Cadarache (France) and the Karlsruhe Institute of Technology (KIT, Germany) in the Non-Destructive Examination and design of Plasma Facing Components for Nuclear Fusion devices, and in the design and analyses of Test Blanket Modules for ITER experimental reactor. Later, he worked in Fusion for Energy in Barcelona (Spain) as a responsible officer for the procurement of Electron Cyclotron Power Sources for ITER. He worked as part of the Programme Management Unit in Garching (Munich, Germany). He is currently working in F4E on the Linear Accelerator named LIPAC based in Rokkasho, Japan. Since 2010 he is a Member of the *Scientific Observatory of the written, oral and filmic memory and of the autobiographical patrimony (absl Mediapolis Europa, http://mediapoliseuropa.com/)* and part of its Scientific and Organizational Committee.

**Kijan Espahangizi** is a historian and presently works as scientific coordinator of the Center „History of Knowledge" (ETH & University of Zurich). He studied physics and history at the Universities of Cologne (Germany) and Seville (Spain). He received his PhD from the ETH Zurich in 2011. He teaches at the History Department of the University of Zurich. In his recent research, he works on the history of the concepts of migration and integration after World War II, with a focus on knowledge production. He has been a member of the German *Council on Migration* since 2015 and the *IMISCOE Standing Committee on Reflexivities in Migration Studies since 2019*. He is also co-founder of the independent postmigrant think & act tank *New Swiss Institute* INES (www.institutneueschweiz.ch).

**Lisa Gaupp** is an interim professor for cultural sociology at Leuphana University of Lüneburg. She studied cultural studies (*Kulturwissenschaften*) and intercultural & international studies at the Universities of Lüneburg and Barcelona and holds a PhD in ethnomusicology from Hanover University of Music, Drama and Media. Her scholarly work focuses on music, performance arts, migration, inequality, global interrelations, urban spaces, politics, diversity and decolonizations and has been supported by numerous grants, including from the German National Scholarship Foundation.

She received several awards for her publications, such as the Best Research Article Award 2020 (Journal of Cultural Management and Cultural Policy) for "Curatorial Practices of the 'Global'", the Best Early Career Research Paper Award in Sociology of Culture (ESA) for "Festival Curators as Gatekeepers for Sociocultural Diversity" and the SOPHIA Prize for University Graduates (Soroptomists International) for her dissertation. Lisa is also co-editor of "Arts and Power. Policies in and by the Arts" (Springer) and of a book series on "Urban Music Studies" (Intellect). Lisa is a board member of the research network Sociology of Culture of the European Sociological Association, a core member of the international research network "Brokering Intercultural Exchange" (https://managingculture.net), and a founding member of the Kulturwissenschaftliche Gesellschaft, Co-chair of its section "Transcultural Life-Worlds". She has lived in the USA, Haiti, Guatemala and Spain and was executive manager of the 2009 Hannover International Violin Competition (Stiftung Niedersachsen).

**Stefan Hirschauer** is a Professor of Sociological Theory and Gender Studies at the University of Mainz, Germany. He has been a Professor at the University of Munich (2002-06), a Visiting Professor at the Centre de Sociologie de l'Innovation, Paris (1999) and the University of Vienna (2000, 2015), and a Visiting Scholar at the Department for Science Studies, Cornell University (2001). His research includes work on theories of practices, ethnography, sociology of the body, Science- and Gender Studies; monograph-publications on the issues of transgenderism (1993), ethnography (1997, 2013), pregnancy (2014) and the theory of un/doing differences (2017); some English articles: On Doing Being a Stranger. (The Journal for the Theory of Social Behavior 35/2005). Putting Things into Words. Ethnographic Writing and the Silence of the Social (Human Studies 29/2006). Editorial Judgments (Social Studies of Science 40/2010). Gender (In)Difference in Gender (Un)Equal Couples. Intimate Dyads Between Gender Nostalgia and Post Genderism (Human Studies 40/2017).

**Marek Sancho Höhne** is a social anthropologist and cultural scientist. They studied cultural studies and socio-cultural studies with a focus on cultural and social anthropology, Central-Eastern Europe, migration and gender. Their research interests include gender, Passing and intersectionality, trans and queer studies, political activism, migration, belonging, normalization and stigmatization, pathologization, life story narrations, decolonization and knowledge production. Currently, they are working on their PhD project on the mapping of imaginations and narrations of trans* people in Germany, formerly with the support of a scholarship of the Graduate Center B/Orders in Motion. In 2020 they were engaged with contracted research for the Federal Anti-Discrimination Agency on genderdiverse people in professional life. They have worked as a project manager at Lola for Democracy in cooperation with the Amadeu-Antonio-Stiftung on local history, antidiscrimination and education from the perspective of LGBT people in Mecklenburg-Western Pommerania, as a research assistant at the Georg-Eckert-Institute for textbook research and the European University

Viadrina and for over ten years as an educator and trainer on recognition, antidiscrimination and inclusion. They have long been active in audio-journalism in free radio and in several feminist, antiracist, queer and trans* projects.

**Susanne Marten-Finnis** studied Russian language and literature, theoretical and applied linguistics, and translation and interpretation at the University of Leipzig. Following her PhD in applied linguistics at the University of Tübingen, she became interested in Jewish literary activities in Central and Eastern Europe, and in the Jewish contribution to modern journalism. Her more recent research interests include Russian cultural production in Western Europe during the period 1909-1929, Eurasianism, and urban heterotopias along the ancient Silk Road. These topics have remained the major research focus of her academic career, which includes ten years at Queen's University Belfast. In 2005, Susanne was appointed as a professor of applied linguistics at the University of Portsmouth (United Kingdom). Since 2017, she has held a joint appointment at the Universities of Portsmouth and Bremen (Germany) and is presently at work on a major research project on the historical German-Jewish press.

**Marta Niccolai** is a senior Teaching Fellow in the School of European Language, Culture and Society (SELCS) at UCL. She teaches European Theatre in Translation and Intercultural Communication, amongst other courses. She is the co-author of the book *Nuovo Scenario Italiano. Stranieri e Italiani nel teatro contemporaneo*, which concerns the presence of migrants and refugees in contemporary Italian plays. She has written numerous articles on the representation of migrants and refugees in Italian Literature and theatre. She is currently researching the performances of Hidden Theatre/Teatro di Nascosto, an Italian Theatre company working internationally in war zones, and she is part of the Refugee in a Moving World research network at UCL. Since 2018 she has been the director of the SELCS Theatre group, in which students adapt, rewrite and perform in plays for contemporary society.

**Barbara Ursula Oettl** studied Art History, American and Italian Linguistics and Literature, and Art at the University of Regensburg, Germany, and at the University of Urbana-Champaign, Illinois, USA. She obtained her PhD in Art History from the University of Jyväskyla, Finland and her habilitation-thesis with the title 'Existential Experiences: Breaking Taboos as a Strategy in Contemporary Art' from the University of Regensburg in 2018. She has published books on the colour white, transgressions of Art, and Richard Serra, as well as essays on historical and contemporary photography, color theory and color-painting, Gender and Body Art, BioArt, Land Art, Concept Art, art in the public space, the Material Turn, and Space Art. At present, she teaches variously at the Staatliche Kunstakademie Düsseldorf, the CICS (Cologne Institute of Conservation Sciences) at the Technical University of Cologne, and the University of Regensburg. For more information, please visit her website (http://barbara-oettl.de/).

**Giulia Pelillo-Hestermeyer** is a senior lecturer for Cultural Studies in the Department of Romance Studies of the University of Heidelberg (Germany). She studied Italian Studies and History in Rome and completed a PhD in Romance linguistics at the University of Heidelberg. Her current "habilitation" project, for which she has been awarded an Olympia-Morata-fellowship, examines linguistic and cultural diversity in the context of globalisation and mediatisation of communication. Giulia has published a book on the radio interview and numerous articles on media communication, linguistic and cultural diversity, transculturality, (auto)biography, and contemporary language development. She is a founding member of the Kulturwissenschaftliche Gesellschaft, Co-chair of the Section "Transcultural Life-Worlds" of the Society, and Co-editor of the book series *Studien der Kulturwissenschaftlichen Gesellschaft*. She is a former fellow of the Heidelberg Centre for Transcultural Studies (Cluster of Excellence "Asia and Europe in a Global Context") and has been awarded numerous grants for her research and activism in the field of media pedagogy and transculturality.

**Dagmar Reichardt** is a Professor of Cultural Industry and Head of the Graduate School (Doctoral Program of Cultural Studies) at the Department of International Culture and Media Management of The Latvian Academy of Culture LAC, Riga/Latvia, in cooperation with the Hamburg Media School in Hamburg/Germany, with a focus on Transcultural Studies and Cultural Industry. She has over 70 book publications edited with German publishers; over 200 further academic books and sociocultural essays on Contemporary Italian and European Studies, as well as Comparative Literary and Cultural Studies; various literary translations (Cesare Cases, Giuseppe Bonaviri, Pier Paolo Pasolini, Dacia Maraini, Igiaba Scego et al.). She has held visiting professorships in Urbino (1988), Innsbruck (2008), Macerata (2018), and Rome (2021). Her awards include the International Flaiano Prize (2007), Medal of Cicero (2009), External Fellow of the Royal Dutch Institute in Rome/Italy (2015). She initiated and co-directs the book series Transcultural Studies—Interdisciplinary Literature and Humanities for Sustainable Societies (TSIL) with Peter Lang Publisher (https://www.peterlang.com/view/serial/TSIL). Her latest book publication about Fashion Studies (with a programmatic introduction) is entitled *Moda Made in Italy* (2016).

# List of Figures

# Index